R

Internet Information Services 7.0 Resource Kit

Mike Volodarsky, Olga Londer, Brett Hill, Bernard Cheah, Steve Schofield, Carlos Aguilar Mares, and Kurt Meyer with the Microsoft IIS Team

Copyright © 2008 by Microsoft Corporation

Library of Congress Control Number: 2008920571

Printed and bound in the United States of America.

2 3 4 5 6 7 8 9   QWT   3 2 1 0 9 8

Distributed in Canada by H.B. Fenn and Company Ltd.

A CIP catalogue record for this book is available from the British Library.

Microsoft Press books are available through booksellers and distributors worldwide. For further information about international editions, contact your local Microsoft Corporation office or contact Microsoft Press International directly at fax (425) 936-7329. Visit our Web site at www.microsoft.com/mspress. Send comments to rkinput@microsoft.com.

Acquisitions Editor: Martin DelRe
Developmental Editor: Karen Szall
Project Editor: Victoria Thulman
Editorial Production: Custom Editorial Productions, Inc.
Technical Reviewers: Bob Dean, Bob Hogan; Technical Review services provided by Content Master, a member of CM Group, Ltd.
Cover: Tom Draper Design; illustration by Todd Daman

SubAssy Part No. X14-15138
Body Part No. X14-14918

Contents at a Glance

Table of Contents

What do you think of this book? We want to hear from you!

Microsoft is interested in hearing your feedback so we can continually improve our books and learning resources for you. To participate in a brief online survey, please visit:

www.microsoft.com/learning/booksurvey/

Part III   Administration

What do you think of this book? We want to hear from you!

Microsoft is interested in hearing your feedback so we can continually improve our books and learning resources for you. To participate in a brief online survey, please visit:

www.microsoft.com/learning/booksurvey/

Acknowledgments

The book that you now hold in your hands is the result of the collective effort of many people.

We'd like to start by thanking Bill Staples, Mai-Lan Tomsen Bukovec, and the whole IIS product team for their support. Several of us work in the IIS product team, and we know firsthand that we simply wouldn't be able to work on this book without the team's invaluable assistance.

Secondly, we are very grateful to Martin DelRe of Microsoft Press for his vision, his hard work in getting this project off the ground and ensuring its successful completion, and also for his never-ending support and encouragement.

It takes a lot of people and a lot of work to bring a book like this to life. There are several people in particular who we would like to acknowledge; the book would not be there without them. Brett Hill started this project and soldiered through till its completion. Special thanks to Mike Volodarsky, whose passion for quality and completeness resulted in him stepping up as the lead author. Kurt Meyer helped a lot as a project manager coordinating the writing and ensuring that the project milestones were not widely missed.

Many of our colleagues on the IIS product team had significant input into the book content. In fact, each chapter was reviewed by at least one member of the product team. Other product team members wrote the "Direct from the Source" sidebars that are peppered throughout the book, bringing you a unique insight into the design and development of IIS 7.0. We would like to express our sincere gratitude to the following members of the IIS product team who worked with us on this book, listed in alphabetical order by first name: Anil Ruia, Bill Staples, Edmund Chou, Eric Deily, Fabio Yeon, Jaroslav Dunajsky, Kanwaljeet Singla, Nazim Lala, Michael Brown, Thomas Marquardt, Tobin Titus, Ulad Malashanka, and Wade Hilmo.

We would also like to thank Tito Leverette for his guidance on and contributions to Chapter 17, "Performance and Tuning."

Many other teams in Microsoft provided technical reviews and shared their experience and insights. In particular, we are grateful to Tom Hawthorn of the Windows Performance team, as well as George Holman and the whole Microsoft.com Operations team. Nick McCollum of Quixtar Inc. also helped with technical reviews and suggestions in Chapters 5, 15, and 17.

Next, we would like to acknowledge our outstanding editorial team. In particular, we would like to thank the project editors, Karen Szall and Victoria Thulman of Microsoft Press, for their professionalism, mentoring, excellent editorial work, and, more than anything, their patience.

Bob Hogan and Bob Dean conducted the book technical reviews, ensuring the writing was consistent and easy to understand. Jean Findley of Custom Editorial Productions, Inc., did a great job managing the book production on a tight schedule.

In addition, we would like to thank Susan Chory and Isaac Roybal for helping us to get this project off the ground. We are also grateful to Simon Brown and Arvindra Sehmi for their encouragement for this work.

Thanks to everyone!

Sincerely,

The Author Team: Mike, Olga, Brett, Bernard, Steve, Carlos, and Kurt

Introduction

Welcome to the *Internet Information Services (IIS) 7.0 Resource Kit*! This book is a detailed technical resource for planning, deploying, and operating Microsoft Internet Information Services (IIS) 7.0, Microsoft's next generation Web server platform. Though this resource kit is intended primarily for IT professionals who have had experience with previous versions of IIS, anyone who is interested in learning about how to deploy and operate IIS 7.0 will find this resource kit extremely valuable.

Within this resource kit, you'll find in-depth information about the improvements introduced by IIS 7.0 and the underlying architectural concepts that will help you better understand the principles behind deploying and managing IIS 7.0 Web servers, and you'll discover techniques for taking advantage of new IIS 7.0 features and capabilities. You will also review detailed information and task-based guidance on managing all aspects of IIS 7.0, including deploying modular Web servers; configuring Web sites and applications; and improving Web server security, reliability, and performance. You'll also find numerous sidebars contributed by members of the IIS product team that provide deep insight into how IIS 7.0 works, best practices for managing the Web server platform, and invaluable troubleshooting tips. Finally, the companion media includes additional tools and documentation that you can use to manage and troubleshoot IIS 7.0 Web servers.

What's New in IIS 7.0

IIS 7.0 has been re-engineered at its core to deliver a modular and extensible Web server platform, forming the foundation for lean, low-footprint Web servers that power customized workloads and Web applications. The new extensible architecture enables the Web server to be completely customized; you can select only the required IIS features and add or replace them with new Web server features that leverage the new rich extensibility application programming interfaces (APIs). In addition, the Web server enables the use of a new distributed configuration system and management tools that simplify Web server deployment and management. The core feature set of IIS 7.0 continues to leverage the reliability and security-focused architecture established by its predecessor, IIS 6.0, and it adds additional improvements to enhance the reliability and security of the Web server platform. IIS 7.0 also includes extended support for application frameworks, including better integration with ASP.NET and built-in support for FastCGI-compliant application frameworks.

Among its many improvements, IIS 7.0 delivers the following:

- **Modular Web server architecture**   Unlike its monolithic predecessors, IIS 7.0 is a completely modular Web server, containing more than 40 components that the administrator can individually install to create low-footprint, reduced surface-area Web server deployments that play a specific role in the application topology. Furthermore, the new extensibility architecture enables any of the built-in modular features to be replaced with customized implementations that Microsoft and third parties provide.

- **.NET Extensibility through ASP.NET integration**   The new ASP.NET integration capabilities enable you to develop IIS 7.0 features with the power of ASP.NET and the .NET Framework, reducing development and maintenance costs for custom Web server solutions. You can use existing ASP.NET services in this mode to enhance any application technologies, even those that were not developed with ASP.NET in mind. These abilities enable Web applications using IIS 7.0 to further customize the Web server to their needs without incurring the higher development costs associated with the previously used Internet Server Application Programming Interface (ISAPI).

- **Enhanced application framework support**   In addition to improved ASP.NET integration for extending the Web server, IIS 7.0 provides more options for hosting other application frameworks. This includes the built-in support for the FastCGI protocol, a protocol used by many open source application frameworks such as PHP Hypertext Preprocessor (PHP) so that they can be reliably hosted in a Windows environment.

- **Distributed configuration system with delegation support**   IIS 7.0 replaces the centralized metabase configuration store with a new configuration system based on a distributed hierarchy of XML files, which enables applications to control their own configuration. The new configuration system enables simplified application deployment without the overhead of required administrative involvement and provides the foundation for more flexible Web server configuration management.

- **Improved management tools**   IIS 7.0 offers a host of management tools that leverage the new configuration system to provide more flexible and simpler configuration management for the Web server. This includes a brand new task-based IIS Manager tool, which offers remote delegated management; a new tool for command line management (Appcmd); and several APIs for managing Web server configuration from scripts, Windows Management Instrumentation (WMI), and .NET Framework programs.

- **Enhanced diagnostics and troubleshooting**   IIS 7.0 provides diagnostic features to help diagnose Web server errors and troubleshoot hard-to-reproduce conditions with a Failed Request Tracing infrastructure. The diagnostic tracing features are integrated with ASP.NET applications to facilitate end-to-end diagnostics of Web applications.

Overview of Book

The four parts of this book cover the following topics:

- **Part I: Foundation**   Provides an overview of IIS 7.0 features, describes the improvements introduced in IIS 7.0, and introduces the core architecture of the Web server

- **Part II: Deployment**   Explains the modular installation architecture for deploying IIS 7.0 and provides procedures for installing IIS 7.0 for common Web server workloads

- **Part III: Administration**   Describes the key concepts for managing IIS 7.0 and describes how to perform management tasks using the management tools that IIS 7.0 provides

- **Part IV: Troubleshooting and Performance**   Describes how to use the logging and tracing infrastructure to provide for smooth operation of the Web server and troubleshoot error conditions, as well as how to monitor and improve Web server performance

The book also includes several appendixes on various topics and a glossary for reference.

Document Conventions

The following conventions are used in this book to highlight special features or usage.

Reader Aids

The following reader aids are used throughout this book to point out useful details.

Reader Aid	Meaning
Note	Underscores the importance of a specific concept or highlights a special case that might not apply to every situation
Important	Calls attention to essential information that should not be disregarded
Caution	Warns you that failure to take or avoid a specified action can cause serious problems for users, systems, data integrity, and so on
On the CD	Calls attention to a related script, tool, template, or job aid on the companion CD that helps you perform a task described in the text

Sidebars

The following sidebars are used throughout this book to provide added insight, tips, and advice concerning different IIS 7.0 features.

Sidebar	Meaning
Direct from the Source	Contributed by experts at Microsoft to provide from-the-source insight into how IIS 7.0 works, best practices for managing IIS 7.0, and troubleshooting tips
How It Works	Provides unique glimpses of IIS 7.0 features and how they work

Command Line Examples

The following style conventions are used in documenting command line examples throughout this book.

Style	Meaning
Bold font	Used to indicate user input (characters that you type exactly as shown)
Italic font	Used to indicate variables for which you need to supply a specific value (for example, *file_name* can refer to any valid filename)
Monospace font	Used for code samples and command line output
%SystemRoot%	Used for environment variables

Companion Media

The companion media is a valuable addition to this book and includes the following:

- **Electronic book**   The complete text of the print book, in a searchable PDF eBook

- **Scripts**   Scripts to help you automate IIS tasks

- **Tools**   Links to tools for IIS, Windows® PowerShell, and more that you can put to use right away

- **Product information**   Links to information about the features and capabilities of IIA NS Windows Server® 2008 and other products to help you optimize Windows Server 2008 in your enterprise

- **Resources**   Links to guides, technical resources, webcasts, forums, and more to help you use and troubleshoot the features of IIS, Windows Server 2008, and other products

- **Sample Chapters**   Preview chapters from 15 Windows Server 2008 books, in PDF format

Find Additional Content Online

As new or updated material becomes available that complements your book, it will be posted online on the Microsoft Press Online Windows Server and Client Web site. Based on the final build of Windows Server 2008, the type of material you might find includes updates to book content, articles, links to companion content, errata, sample chapters, and more. This Web site will be available soon at: *http://www.microsoft.com/learning/books/online/serverclient* and will be updated periodically.

> **Digital Content for Digital Book Readers:** If you bought a digital-only edition of this book, you can enjoy select content from the print edition's companion CD.
> Visit **http://go.microsoft.com/fwlink/?LinkId=108439** to get your downloadable content. This content is always up-to-date and available to all readers.

Resource Kit Support Policy

We have made every effort to ensure the accuracy of this book and the content of the companion media. Microsoft Press provides corrections to this book through the Web at: *http://www.microsoft.com/learning/support/search.asp.*

If you have comments, questions, or ideas regarding the book or companion media content, or if you have questions that are not answered by querying the Knowledge Base, please send them to Microsoft Press by using either of the following methods:

E-mail:

rkinput@microsoft.com

Postal Mail:

Microsoft Press
Attn: *Microsoft Internet Information Services 7.0 Resource Kit,* Editor
One Microsoft Way
Redmond, WA 98052-6399

Please note that product support is not offered through the preceding mail addresses. For product support information, please visit the Microsoft Product Support Web site at: *http://support.microsoft.com.*

Part I
Foundation

Chapter 1

Introducing IIS 7.0

Microsoft Internet Information Services (IIS) 7.0 in Windows Server 2008 is a Web server that provides a secure, easy-to-manage platform for developing and reliably hosting Web applications and services. IIS 7.0 has been completely redesigned and offers major advantages over previous versions of IIS. With its new modular and extensible architecture, IIS 7.0 makes developing, deploying, and configuring and managing Web applications and infrastructure easier and more efficient than ever before.

To put it simply, IIS 7.0 is the most powerful Microsoft Web server platform ever released. It provides an array of new capabilities that improve the way Web applications and services are developed, deployed, and managed. The modular design of IIS 7.0 gives administrators full control over their Web servers' functionality, providing an extensible architecture that enables administrators and developers to build customized and specialized Web servers. New administration capabilities and the distributed XML-based configuration system make deploying and managing Web applications on IIS 7.0 more straightforward and efficient than on any other Web server. In addition, new diagnostic and troubleshooting capabilities of IIS 7.0 enable administrators and developers alike to minimize potential downtime.

In this chapter, we will focus on the major new features and functionality in IIS 7.0 and their advantages over previous versions of IIS. We will also look at basic administration tasks and discuss the differences in the availability of IIS 7.0 features in Windows Server 2008 and Windows Vista.

Overview of IIS 7.0

IIS 7.0 provides features and functionality that enable administrators to reliably and effectively manage Web infrastructures; developers to rapidly build Web applications and services; and hosters to provide a cost-effective, scalable, and reliable Web hosting to a broad set of customers.

For administrators, IIS 7.0 provides a secure, reliable, and easy-to-manage Web server platform. The customizable installation of IIS 7.0 ensures that they can minimize the attack surface, patching requirements, and the memory footprint of their Web infrastructure. The IIS 7.0 process model makes Web sites and applications more secure by automatically isolating them, providing sandboxed configuration and unique process identity by default.

IIS 7.0 reduces management complexity, providing a set of tools that make administration of Web infrastructures more efficient. IIS Manager has a new task-based, feature-focused management console, which provides an intuitive user interface for administrative tasks. In addition to IIS Manager, there is also a new command line administration tool, a Windows Management Instrumentation (WMI) provider, and a .NET application programming interface (API).

IIS 7.0 supports simplified management of Web farms where Web server configuration can be stored together with Web application code and content on a centralized file server and can be shared across front-end Web servers on a farm.

IIS 7.0 enables administrators to securely delegate site and application administrative control to developers and content owners without administrative privileges on the server, thus reducing the administrative burden and cost of ownership. Using IIS Manager from Windows Vista, Windows XP, Windows Server 2003, or Windows Server 2008, developers and content owners can manage their sites and applications remotely while connected to a server over HTTPS from any location.

In addition, new troubleshooting and diagnostics capabilities in IIS 7.0 enable administrators to reduce Web server downtime.

For developers, IIS 7.0 provides a flexible, more extensible Web server platform for developing and deploying Web applications on Windows Server 2008 and Windows Vista. Developers can build applications on IIS 7.0 using the Web framework of their choice, including ASP.NET, classic ASP, PHP, PERL, ColdFusion, Ruby, and many others.

IIS 7.0 provides unprecedented extensibility. It has a fully componentized architecture, with more than 40 pluggable modules built on top of public extensibility APIs. Developers can create new or replacement modules in native or managed code, extend IIS configuration, and build IIS Manager extensions that plug in seamlessly to the management console.

IIS 7.0 has a distributed file-based configuration system that enables IIS settings to be stored in web.config files along with the ASP.NET settings. This unified configuration system simplifies development and enables applications to be xcopy-deployed, preconfigured, to IIS 7.0 servers.

In addition, new diagnostic capabilities, including access to run-time information and automatically tracing failed requests, help developers to troubleshoot issues quicker and minimize Web site downtime.

For hosters, IIS 7.0 provides a cost-effective, more scalable Web server platform for delivering reliable Web hosting to a broad set of customers. IIS 7.0 lowers costs by providing a new, scalable shared hosting architecture that is capable of hosting thousands of Web sites on a single IIS 7.0 server without sacrificing isolation or reliability.

IIS 7.0 enables Web hosters to reach more customers by using a new FastCGI module that is capable of providing fast and reliable hosting for PHP and other Web frameworks.

In addition, IIS 7.0 provides a File Transfer Protocol (FTP) server that enables Web hosters to offer their customers a fully integrated Web/FTP platform with modern publishing capabilities, such as FTP over Secure Sockets Layer (SSL) and membership-based authentication.

What's New in IIS 7.0

IIS 7.0 has been completely redesigned and re-engineered from the ground up. The new features and functionality provide many new capabilities that enable administrators and developers to:

- Minimize patching and security risks with fine-grained control over the Web server footprint.

- Implement new Web solutions rapidly by using an extensibility framework.

- Go to market faster with simplified deployment and configuration of applications.

- Reduce administrative costs by managing Web infrastructures more efficiently.

- Reduce Web site downtime by quickly resolving faulty applications.

These advancements have been made possible because of major innovations in IIS 7.0, as follows:

- A modular, extensible core Web server

- A unified, distributed file-based configuration system

- Integrated health monitoring and diagnostics

- A set of new administration tools with delegation support

In addition, IIS 7.0 offers a new Windows Process Activation Service (WAS) that exposes IIS 7.0 processing model to both HTTP and non-HTTP based applications and services.

Let's look at these innovations and their advantages over previous versions of IIS in more detail.

Core Web Server

The IIS 7.0 core Web server has been completely redesigned and is very different from IIS 6.0. Its new, fully componentized architecture provides two fundamental enhancements that form a foundation for many advantages in security, performance, scalability, manageability, and flexibility. These two fundamental enhancements are modularity and extensibility.

Modularity

In previous versions of IIS, all functionality was built by default into a monolithic server. There was no easy way to extend or replace any of that functionality. In IIS 7.0, the core Web server has a completely modular architecture. All of the Web server features are now managed as stand-alone components. The IIS 7.0 Web core is divided into more than 40 separate components, each of which implements a particular feature or functionality. These components are referred to as modules. You can add, remove, and replace the modules depending on your needs.

In IIS 7.0, the ASP.NET run time is fully integrated with the core Web server, providing a unified request processing pipeline. Both native and managed code is processed through this single request pipeline. All notification events in the request pipeline are exposed to both native and managed modules. This integration enables existing ASP.NET features—including forms-based authentication, membership, session state, and many others—to be used for all types of content, providing a consistent experience across the entire Web application.

Figure 1-1 shows the unified request processing pipeline, with several stages shown at the beginning and at the end of request processing. At the Authenticate Request stage, Figure 1-1 shows authentication modules that are available for all requests. Basic Authentication, Windows Authentication, and Anonymous Authentication are native modules. Forms Authentication is a managed module. Both native and managed authentication modules provide services for any content type, including managed code, native code, and static files.

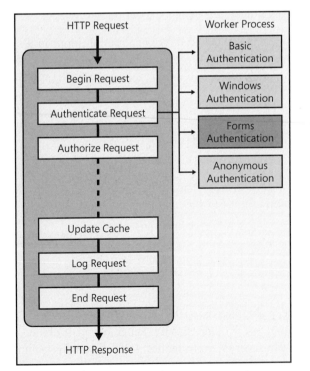

Figure 1-1   IIS 7.0 integrated request processing.

> **Note**   For more information on request processing, refer to Chapter 2, "Understanding IIS 7.0 Architecture."

IIS 7.0 modularity enables you to do the following:

- **Secure the server by reducing the attack surface area.**   Reducing an attack surface area is one of the major steps to a secure system. In IIS 7.0, Web server features that are not required can be safely removed without affecting the functionality of your applications, thus reducing the attack surface area.

- **Improve performance and reduce memory footprint.**   When you remove Web server features that are not required, the server's memory usage is reduced. In addition, the amount of code that executes on every request is reduced, leading to improved performance.

- **Build custom and specialized servers.**   Selecting a particular set of server features and removing the ones that are not required allows you to build custom servers that are optimized for performing a specific function, such as edge caching or load balancing.

> **Note**   For more information on server modularity, refer to Chapter 3, "Understanding the Modular Foundation."

Extensibility

The modular architecture of IIS 7.0 enables you to build server components that extend or replace any existing functionality and add value to Web applications hosted on IIS.

The core Web server includes a new Win32 API for building core server modules. You can add custom features to extend or replace the existing Web server features with your own or third-party core Web server extensions built using this new extensibility API.

The core Web server modules are new and more powerful replacements for Internet Server Application Programming Interface (ISAPI) filters and extensions, although these filters and extensions are still supported in IIS 7.0. The new C++ extensibility model in IIS 7.0 uses a simplified object-oriented API that promotes writing robust server code to alleviate problems that previously plagued ISAPI development.

Moreover, IIS 7.0 also includes support for development of core Web server extensions using the .NET Framework. IIS 7.0 has integrated the existing IHttpModule API for ASP.NET, enabling custom managed code modules to access all events in the request pipeline, for all requests.

ASP.NET integration in IIS 7.0 enables server modules to be rapidly developed using capabilities of ASP.NET and the .NET Framework, instead of using the lower-level IIS C++ API. ASP.NET managed modules are capable of fully extending the server and are able to service requests for all types of content including, for example, ASP, Common Gateway Interface (CGI), and static files.

Using ASP.NET or native C++ extensibility, developers can build solutions that add value for all application components, such as custom authentication schemes, monitoring and logging, security filtering, load balancing, content redirection, and state management.

Note   For more information on core Web server extensibility, refer to Chapter 12, "Managing Web Server Modules."

Configuration

The early versions of IIS had few configuration settings, and they were stored in the registry. IIS 5.0 introduced a binary store called the metabase for managing URL-based configuration. In IIS 6.0, the binary metabase was replaced with an XML-based metabase to store configuration data. IIS 7.0 introduces a distributed XML file–based configuration system that enables administrators to specify settings for IIS and its features in clear text XML files that are stored with the code and content. The XML files hold the configuration settings for the entire Web server platform, including IIS, ASP.NET, and other components. The files store settings on the server, site, and application levels, and they may optionally be set at the content directories level together with the Web content, enabling delegated management.

Because Web site and application settings are no longer tied to a centralized configuration store on the local machine—as in previous versions of IIS—this distributed file-based configuration system dramatically simplifies application deployment by providing xcopy deployment of configuration together with application code and content. In addition, this configuration system enables sharing configuration for a site or application across a Web farm.

IIS 7.0 configuration is based on the .NET Framework configuration store. This common format enables IIS configuration settings to be stored alongside an ASP.NET configuration in a web.config files hierarchy, providing one configuration store for all Web platform configuration settings that are accessible via a common set of APIs and stored in a consistent format.

The distributed configuration hierarchy includes the global, computer-wide, .NET Framework configuration files, machine.config and root web.config, the global IIS configuration file applicationHost.config, and distributed web.config configuration files located within the Web sites, applications, and directories, as shown in Figure 1-2.

The .NET Framework global settings for a server machine are stored in the machine.config file located in the *%SystemRoot%*\Microsoft .NET\Framework \<version>\config folder. Global ASP.NET settings for a Web server are stored in the root web.config file located in the same folder on the server machine.

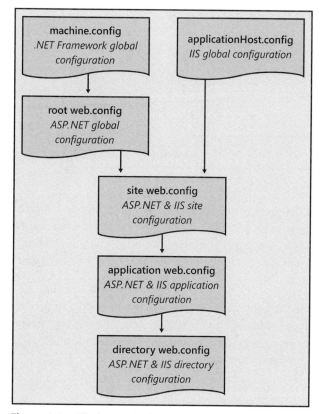

Figure 1-2   File-based distributed configuration store.

IIS 7.0 stores global configuration in the applicationHost.config file located in the *%SystemRoot%\System32\Inetsrv\Config* folder. ApplicationHost.config has two major configuration sections: *<system.applicationHost>* and *<system.webServer>*.

The *<system.applicationHost>* section contains settings for site, application, virtual directory, and application pools. The *<system.webServer>* section contains configuration for all other settings, including global Web defaults.

URL-specific configuration is stored in applicationHost.config via <location> tags. IIS 7.0 reads and writes URL-specific configuration in the web.config files hierarchy for sites, applications, and content directories on the server, along with ASP.NET configuration.

Figure 1-3 shows the structure of a site web.config file and its inheritance from global configuration files.

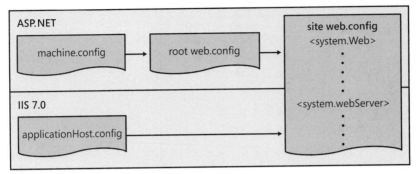

Figure 1-3   Site web.config file.

The server administrator may delegate different levels of the configuration hierarchy to other users, such as the site administrator or the application developer. By default, write access to configuration settings is limited to the server administrator only. The server administrator may delegate management of specific configuration settings to users without administrative privileges on the server machine.

The file-based configuration for a specific site or application can be copied from one computer to another, for example, when the application moves from development into test and then into production. Due to xcopy deployment of configuration beside code and content, it is significantly easier to deploy applications on IIS 7.0.

Distributed configuration system also enables configuration for a site or application to be shared across a Web server farm, where all servers retrieve configuration settings from a single server. After a Web site is in production, administrators can share configuration information across multiple front-end Web servers, avoiding costly and error-prone replication and manual synchronization issues.

The IIS 7.0 configuration system is fully extensible and allows you to extend the configuration store to include custom configuration. The system is backward compatible with previous versions of IIS at the API level, and with previous versions of the .NET Framework at the XML level.

 Note   For more information on IIS 7.0 distributed configuration system, refer to Chapter 4, "Understanding the Configuration System."

Administration Tools

IIS 7.0 administration tools have been completely rewritten. They provide different interfaces for reading from and writing to the hierarchy of configuration files on the server, including the applicationHost.config file, the .NET Framework root web.config file, and web.config files for sites, applications, and directories, as well as interfaces for working with run-time information and different providers on the server.

IIS 7.0 provides the following administration tools:

- IIS Manager is a new management console that offers an intuitive, feature-focused, task-oriented graphical user interface (GUI) for managing both IIS 7.0 and ASP.NET. IIS Manager in IIS 7.0 is implemented as a Windows Forms application that replaces the MMC snap-in used in previous versions of IIS.

- A command line tool, Appcmd.exe, replaces IIS 6.0 command line scripts. It provides command line access to configuration files hierarchy and other server settings.

- The Microsoft.Web.Administration interface provides a strongly typed managed API for managed code access to configuration and other server settings.

- A new WMI provider offers scripting access to all IIS and ASP.NET configuration. The legacy IIS 6.0 WMI provider is still available for backward compatibility with existing scripts.

You can also use Windows PowerShell for powerful scripting access to distributed configuration hierarchy.

Note   For more information on using PowerShell to manage IIS 7.0, refer to Chapter 7, "Using Command Line Tools."

In addition, the IIS 6.0 MMC snap-in is also provided with Windows Server 2008 to support remote administration and to administer FTP sites.

All new administration tools fully support the new IIS 7.0 distributed configuration, and all of them allow for delegation of access to configuration for individual sites and applications to users without administrative privileges on the server machine.

Note   You can install administration tools and Web server components separately.

Figure 1-4 shows the new IIS Manager user interface that has a browser-like feel with an address bar similar to Windows Explorer. The main body of the IIS Manager window is divided into three areas:

- The Connections pane on the left side of the IIS Manager window enables you to connect to servers, sites, and applications. The connections are displayed in a tree.

- A central area referred to as a workspace is located in the middle of IIS Manager window. The workspace has two views: Features View and Content View.
    - Features View enables you to view and configure features for the currently selected configuration path. Each IIS Manager feature typically maps to a configuration section that controls the corresponding Web server feature.

❑ Content View provides a read-only display of content corresponding to the currently selected configuration path. In Content View, when you select a node in the tree in the Connections pane tree, its content is listed in the workspace.

■ An Actions Pane is located on the right side of IIS Manager. Items in the Actions pane are task-based and context-specific.

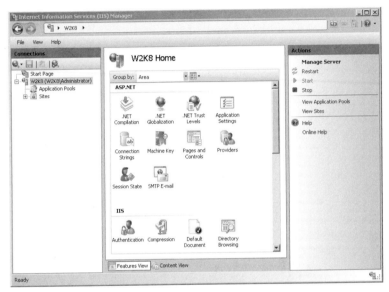

Figure 1-4   IIS Manager UI.

As with other administration tools, delegated management is one of the most important capabilities of IIS Manager. With this capability, users of hosted services can run IIS Manager on their desktops and connect remotely to manage their sites and applications on the server where they are hosted without having administrative access to the server machine. To identify users, IIS Manager can use Windows credentials and also alternative credentials stores. IIS Manager credentials are particularly useful in scenarios in which you don't want to create Windows accounts for all remote users, or when the credentials are already stored in a non-Windows authentication system and you want to keep them in a single store.

IIS Manager supports remote administration over a firewall-friendly HTTPS connection, allowing for seamless local and remote administration without requiring Distributed Component Object Model (DCOM) or other administrative ports to be opened on the firewall. In IIS 6.0, management console remoting was through the MMC and was always enabled. This is different in IIS 7.0, where remote management through IIS Manager is disabled by default and must be explicitly enabled. For remote administration of IIS 7.0, Web Management Service (WMSvc) must be installed on the server computer, and the remote connections to this service must be enabled. WMSvc is a Windows service that provides the ability to manage IIS 7.0 sites and applications remotely using IIS Manager. IIS Manager remoting architecture is shown in Figure 1-5.

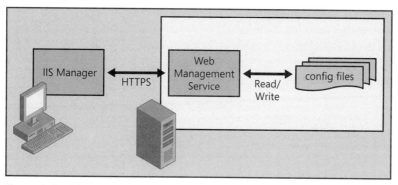

Figure 1-5   IIS Manager remoting.

IIS Manager in IIS 7.0 is customizable and extensible. It has its own configuration file, administration.config, that enables custom functionality to be added to the tool. Any added administration plug-ins are integrated into the tool and appear alongside IIS and ASP.NET features.

> **Note**   For more information on IIS Manager, refer to Chapter 6, "Using IIS Manager," and for more information on Appcmd.exe, WMI, and Microsoft.Web Administration API, refer to Chapter 7.

Diagnostics

IIS 7.0 introduces major improvements in diagnostics and troubleshooting of Web sites and applications. It enables you to troubleshoot issues quicker and minimize Web site downtime through powerful new diagnostic capabilities including access to run-time information and automatic tracing of failed requests. The diagnostics and troubleshooting changes in IIS 7.0 enable you to see, in real time, requests that are running on the server and to automatically trap errors with a detailed trace log.

Access to Run-Time Information

IIS 7.0 includes a new Runtime State and Control API (RSCA) that provides real-time state information about application pools, worker processes, sites, application domains, and running requests.

The RSCA is designed to give administrators an in-depth view into the current state of the run-time objects, including current worker processes and their currently executing requests, and also to enable administrators to use the same API to control those objects. RSCA allows administrators to get detailed run-time data that was not previously available.

This information is exposed through a native Component Object Model (COM) API. The API itself is wrapped and exposed through the new IIS 7.0 WMI provider, Microsoft.Web.Administration API, command line management tool Appcmd.exe, and IIS Manager.

For example, using IIS Manager, administrators can get run-time information on what requests are currently executing, how long they have been running, which URLs they are invoking, what client called them, and what their status is.

Failed Request Tracing

IIS 7.0 provides detailed trace events throughout the request and response path, enabling you to trace a request as it makes its way to IIS, through the IIS request processing pipeline, into any existing page-level code, and back out to the response. These detailed trace events enable you to understand not only the request path and any error information that was raised as a result of the request, but also elapsed time and other debugging information to assist in troubleshooting all types of errors and when a system stops responding.

Problems such as poor performance on some requests, authentication-related failures on other requests, or the server 500 error can often be difficult to troubleshoot unless you have captured the trace of the problem when it occurs. That's where failed request tracing can be helpful. It is designed to buffer the trace events for a request and then save them to disk into the trace log if the request fails. To enable the collection of trace events, you can configure IIS 7.0 to automatically capture full trace logs in XML format for any given request based on elapsed time or error response codes.

The diagnostic capabilities in IIS 7.0 are extensible, and new trace events can be inserted into custom modules.

Note   For more information on diagnostics and troubleshooting, refer to Chapter 16, "Tracing and Troubleshooting."

Windows Process Activation Service

IIS 7.0 provides a new protocol-independent Windows Process Activation Service (WAS) that is an extended and generalized successor to Windows Activation Service in IIS 6.0. The HTTP process activation model was introduced in IIS 6.0 with application pools. This service has been extended in IIS 7.0 to be available for more than just Web applications. It is capable of receiving requests or messages over any protocol and supports pluggable activation of arbitrary protocol listeners. In addition to being protocol-independent, WAS provides all types of message-activated applications with intelligent resource management, on-demand process activation, health monitoring, and automatic failure detection and recycling. The Windows Communication Foundation (WCF) ships with protocol adapters that can leverage the capabilities of WAS. Using these capabilities can dramatically improve the reliability and resource usage of WCF services.

Note   For more information on WAS and non-HTTP support in IIS 7.0, refer to Chapter 2.

Application Compatibility

IIS 7.0 is built to be compatible with previous releases of IIS. Most existing ASP, ASP.NET 1.1, and ASP.NET 2.0 applications are expected to run on IIS 7.0 without code changes, using the compatible ISAPI support.

All existing ISAPI extensions and most ISAPI filters also continue to work. However, ISAPI filters that use READ RAW DATA notification are not supported in IIS 7.0.

For existing Active Directory Service Interfaces (ADSI) and WMI scripts, IIS 7.0 provides feature parity with previous releases, enabling the scripts to use legacy configuration interfaces by using the Metabase Compatibility layer.

> **Note**   For more information on application compatibility, see Chapter 11, "Hosting Application Development Frameworks."

Basic Administration Tasks

For a Web server to start serving content, it must have a basic configuration: a site, an application, a virtual directory, and an application pool. IIS 7.0 provides a default configuration that includes the Default Web Site with a root application mapped to a physical directory *%SystemDrive%*\Inetpub\Wwwroot and a default application pool called DefaultAppPool that this application belongs to.

However, you may need to create your own site, add an application to the site, add a virtual directory to the application, create a new application pool, and assign an application to the application pool. The following sections describe how to perform these basic administration tasks by using IIS Manager.

> **Note**   For information on how to perform other common administrative tasks, refer to Appendix J, "Common Administrative Tasks Using IIS Manager."

To start IIS Manager, from the Administrative Tools program group, launch Internet Information Services (IIS) Manager.

Creating a Web Site

A site is a container for applications and virtual directories. Each site can be accessed through one or more unique bindings. The binding includes the binding protocol and the binding information. The binding protocol defines the protocol over which communication occurs between the IIS 7.0 server and a Web client such as a browser. The binding information defines the information that is used to access the site. For example, the binding protocol of a

Web site can be either HTTP or HTTPS, and the binding information is the combination of IP address, port, and optional host header.

To create a Web site using IIS Manager, perform the following steps:

1. In the Connections pane, expand the server node, right-click the Sites node, and then click Add Web Site. The Add Web Site dialog box appears.

2. In the Site Name box, type a name for your Web site, for example, **www.contoso.com.**

3. If you want to assign a different application pool than the one listed in the Application Pool box, click Select. Then in the Select Application Pool dialog box, choose an application pool from the Application Pool drop-down list and click OK.

4. In the Physical Path box, type the physical path of the Web site's folder or navigate to the folder by using the browse button (...).

    If the physical path that you entered points to a remote share, click Connect As and specify the required credentials. If no credentials are required to access the path, select the Application User (Pass-Thru Authentication) option in the Connect As dialog box.

5. Optional: Click Test Settings to verify the settings you specified.

6. Configure the desired bindings for your new site:

    ❑ If you are using HTTPS for the Web site access, in the Type drop-down list, change the protocol from HTTP to HTTPS.

    ❑ If you have a dedicated static IP address for the site, in the IP Address box, type that IP address. If you don't have a static IP address for the site, leave the default value of All Unassigned.

- ❑ If your site will use a different port number than the default port number of 80, in the Port box, type that port number.

- ❑ If your site will use a host header, in the Host Name box, type that host header name for your site. For example, type **www.contoso.com.**

7. If you want the Web site to be immediately available, select the Start Web Site Immediately check box.

8. Click OK. The new Web site has been created and appears in the Connections pane.

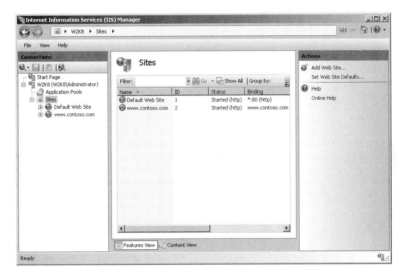

Creating an Application

An application is a group of files that delivers content or provides services over protocols, such as HTTP. When an application is created, the application's path becomes part of the URL.

A site can contain many applications including that site's default application, which is called the root application. In addition to belonging to a site, an application belongs to an application pool, which isolates the application from applications in other application pools on the server.

To create an application using IIS Manager, perform the following steps:

1. In the Connections pane, right-click the site where you want the new application to run. Then select Add Application. The Add Application dialog box appears.

2. In the Alias box, type a value for the application URL, such as **Ads**. This value is used to access the application in a URL.

3. If you want to assign a different application pool than the one listed in the Application Pool box, click Select. Then in the Select Application Pool dialog box, choose an application pool from the Application Pool drop-down list and click OK.

4. In the Physical Path box, type the physical path of the Web site's folder or navigate to the folder by using the browse button (...).

   If the physical path that you entered points to a remote share, click Connect As and specify the required credentials. If no credentials are required to access the path, select the Application User (Pass-Thru Authentication) option in the Connect As dialog box.

5. Optional: Click Test Settings to verify the settings you specified.

6. Click OK. The new application has been created and appears in the Connections pane.

Creating a Virtual Directory

A virtual directory is a directory name (also referred to as path) that is mapped to a physical directory on a local or remote server. That name becomes part of the URL, and a request to this URL from a browser accesses content in the physical directory, such as a Web page or a list of a directory's content.

An application can contain many virtual directories. Each application must have a root virtual directory that maps the application to the physical directory that contains the application's content.

To create a virtual directory using IIS Manager, perform the following steps:

1. In the Connections pane, right-click the site where you want the virtual directory to appear. Then select Add Virtual Directory. The Add Virtual Directory dialog box appears.

2. In the Alias box, type a value for the virtual directory URL, such as **Download**. This value is used to access the application in a URL.

3. In the Physical Path box, type the physical path of the Web site's folder or navigate to the folder by using the browse button (...).

    If the physical path that you entered points to a remote share, click Connect As and specify the required credentials. If no credentials are required to access the path, select the Application User (Pass-Thru Authentication) option in the Connect As dialog box.

4. Optional: Click Test Settings to verify the settings you specified.

5. Click OK. The new virtual directory has been created and appears in the Connections pane.

Creating an Application Pool

An application pool is a group of one or more applications that a worker process, or a set of worker processes, serves. Application pools set boundaries for the applications they contain, providing isolation between applications running in different application pools.

In IIS 7.0, ASP.NET requests within application pools can be executed in one of two managed pipeline modes: Integrated or Classic. In Integrated mode, the server uses the unified, or integrated, request processing pipeline to process the request. In Classic mode, the server processes ASP.NET requests using two different IIS and ASP.NET pipelines, in the same way as if the application were running in IIS 6.0.

To create an application pool using IIS Manager, perform the following steps:

1.   In the Connections pane, expand the server node and right-click the Application Pools node. Select Add Application Pool. The Add Application Pool dialog box appears.

2.   In the Name box, type a friendly name for the application pool, for example, **Advertising**.

3. From the .NET Framework Version drop-down list, select the version of the .NET Framework required by your managed applications, modules, and handlers. If the applications that you run in this application pool do not require the .NET Framework, select No Managed Code.

4. From the Managed Pipeline Mode drop-down list, select one of the following options:

    ❑ **Integrated**   Select this if you want to use the integrated IIS and ASP.NET request processing pipeline. This is the default mode.

    ❑ **Classic**   Select this if you want to use IIS and ASP.NET request-processing modes separately.

5. By default, the Start Application Pool Immediately check box is selected. If you do not want the application pool to start, clear the box.

6. Click OK. The new application pool has been created and appears in the Application Pools list.

Assigning an Application to an Application Pool

You can assign an application to its own application pool if you want to isolate this application from other applications running on the server. You can assign several applications to the same application pool if all the applications use the same run-time configuration settings, for example, worker process settings or ASP.NET version.

To assign an application to an application pool using IIS Manager, perform the following steps:

1. In the Connections pane, right-click an application you want to assign to a different application pool, select Manage Application, and then click Advanced Settings.

2. On the Advanced Settings page, select Application Pool and then click the browse button. The Select Application Pool dialog box appears.

```
Advanced Settings                                    ? X
┌─ (General)
│   Application Pool              DefaultAppPool
│   Physical Path                 C:\inetpub\contoso\ads
│   Physical Path Credentials
│   Physical Path Credentials Logon Type   ClearText
│   Virtual Path                  /Ads
└─ Behavior
    Enabled Protocols             http

        ┌─ Select Application Pool ──────────── ? X ─┐
        │   Application pool:                         │
        │   [Advertising                        ▼]    │
        │   Properties:                               │
        │   ┌─────────────────────────────────────┐  │
        │   │ .Net Framework Version: 2.0         │  │
        │   │ Pipeline mode: Integrated           │  │
        │   └─────────────────────────────────────┘  │
        │                                             │
        │            [   OK   ]    [  Cancel  ]       │
        └─────────────────────────────────────────────┘

  Application Pool
  [applicationPool] Configures this application to run in the specified application pool.

                                  [   OK   ]    [  Cancel  ]
```

3. Select the application pool you want the application to run in.

4. Click OK. The application has been assigned to the application pool.

IIS 7.0 Features in Windows Server 2008 and Windows Vista

IIS 7.0 is a part of Windows Server 2008 and Windows Vista. However, the availability of IIS 7.0 features varies between Windows Server 2008 and the editions of Windows Vista.

Windows Server 2008 includes all IIS 7.0 features. IIS 7.0 is available in all editions of Windows Server 2008. There is no difference in functionality among editions. IIS 7.0 is available on 32-bit and 64-bit platforms.

IIS 7.0 is supported in Server Core installations of Windows Server 2008. IIS 7.0 on Server Core provides you with a Web server on top of a minimal footprint server operating system, with a smaller disk space requirement, lower memory utilization, reduced attack surface, and lower servicing needs. IIS 7.0 installation on Windows Server 2008 Server Core is different from a regular Windows Server 2008 IIS 7.0 installation. On Server Core, there is no Windows shell and .no NET Framework. As a result, IIS Manager is not available, and you cannot run ASP.NET modules, handlers, and applications on Server Core. You can, however, run ASP, PHP, CGI, and other nonmanaged application code on Server Core installations of IIS 7.0.

> **Note**   For more information on installing IIS 7.0 on Server Core, refer to Chapter 5, "Installing IIS 7.0."

In Windows Vista editions, IIS 7.0 provides Web developers with a Web platform for building and testing Web applications for IIS 7.0 and also enables process activation and management infrastructure for Microsoft's Windows Communication Foundation (WCF) applications. This infrastructure is provided by Windows Process Activation Service.

The IIS 7.0 features available in a Windows Vista installations depend on the edition of Windows Vista, as follows:

- In Windows Vista Starter and Home editions, IIS 7.0 components only offer supporting infrastructure for WCF but do not provide a Web server that supports static content, Classic ASP, or ASP.NET.

- In Windows Vista Home Premium edition, most of the IIS 7.0 Web Server features required for Web site development are available. However, FTP server, advanced Web authentication and authorization, and remote administration are not available.

- In Windows Vista Business, Enterprise, and Ultimate editions, all of the IIS 7.0 features are available with exception of remote administration.

Table 1-1 lists availability of features in Windows Server 2008 and editions of Windows Vista. Within the table, the features are grouped into categories as follows:

- Common HTTP features
- Application development features
- Health and diagnostics features
- Security features
- Performance features
- Management tools
- Windows Process Activation Service
- File Transfer Protocol (FTP) publishing service features
- Simultaneous connection limits

Within each category, the feature availability is described as follows:

- **Default**   The feature is selected by default when you install IIS 7.0. You can decide not to install this feature if you do not need it.

- **Available**   The feature is available, but it is not selected by default when you install IIS 7.0. You can install this feature if you need it.

- **Unavailable**   The feature is unavailable and cannot be installed when you install IIS 7.0.

Table 1-1   IIS Features in Windows Server 2008 and Windows Vista

Feature Name	Windows Server 2008 Editions	Windows Vista Editions		
		Ultimate, Business, and Enterprise	Home Premium	Home Basic and Starter
Common HTTP Features				
Static Content	Default	Default	Default	Unavailable
Default Document	Default	Default	Default	Unavailable
Directory Browsing	Default	Default	Default	Unavailable
HTTP Errors	Default	Default	Default	Default
HTTP Redirection	Default	Default	Default	Default
Application Development Features				
ASP.NET	Available	Available	Available	Unavailable
.NET Extensibility	Default	Default	Default	Default
ASP	Available	Available	Available	Unavailable
CGI	Available	Available	Available	Unavailable
ISAPI Extensions	Available	Available	Available	Unavailable
ISAPI Filters	Available	Available	Available	Unavailable
Server-Side Includes	Available	Available	Available	Unavailable
Health and Diagnostics Features				
HTTP Logging	Default	Default	Default	Default
Logging Tools	Default	Default	Default	Default
Request Monitor	Default	Default	Default	Default
Tracing	Default	Default	Default	Default
Custom Logging	Available	Available	Available	Unavailable
ODBC Logging	Available	Available	Unavailable	Unavailable
Security Features				
Basic Authentication	Available	Available	Available	Unavailable
Windows Authentication	Available	Available	Unavailable	Unavailable
Digest Authentication	Available	Available	Unavailable	Unavailable
Client Certificate Mapping Authentication	Available	Available	Unavailable	Unavailable

Table 1-1   IIS Features in Windows Server 2008 and Windows Vista

Feature Name	Windows Server 2008 Editions	Windows Vista Editions		
		Ultimate, Business, and Enterprise	Home Premium	Home Basic and Starter
IIS Client Certificate Mapping Authentication	Available	Available	Unavailable	Unavailable
URL Authorization	Available	Available	Available	Available
Request Filtering	Available	Available	Available	Available
IP and Domain Restrictions	Available	Available	Available	Available
Performance Features				
Static Content Compression	Default	Default	Default	Default
Dynamic Content Compression	Available	Available	Available	Available
Management Tools				
IIS Management Console (IIS Manager)	Default	Default	Default	Unavailable
IIS Management Scripts and Tools	Available	Available	Available	Available
Management Service	Available	Available	Available	Unavailable
IIS 6.0 Management Compatibility	Available	Available	Available	Available
IIS Metabase Compatibility	Available	Available	Available	Available
IIS 6 WMI Compatibility	Available	Available	Available	Unavailable
IIS 6 Scripting Tools	Available	Available	Available	Unavailable
IIS 6 Management Console	Available	Available	Available	Unavailable
Windows Process Activation Service Features				
Process Model	Default	Default	Default	Default
.NET Environment	Available	Available	Available	Available
Configuration APIs	Available	Available	Available	Available
File Transfer Protocol (FTP) Publishing Service Features				
FTP Server	Available	Available	Unavailable	Unavailable
FTP Management Console	Available	Available	Unavailable	Unavailable
Simultaneous Connection Limits				
Simultaneous Connection Limits	Unlimited	10	3	3

Summary

IIS 7.0 has been completely redesigned and re-engineered from the ground up. IIS 7.0 offers major advantages over previous versions of IIS and makes developing, deploying, and configuring and managing Web applications and infrastructure easier and more efficient than ever before.

IIS 7.0 delivers many new powerful features and functionality based on the following key enhancements:

- **Modularity**   IIS 7.0 architecture is fully componentized. It enables administrators to customize which features are installed and running on the Web server. With more than 40 feature modules that can be independently installed, administrators can reduce the potential attack surface and lower the footprint requirements of the server.

- **Extensibility**   The core Web server features of IIS 7.0 have been built using a new set of comprehensive public APIs that developers can use to extend, replace, or add functionality to a Web server. These APIs are available as native Win32 APIs as well as managed .NET Framework APIs. Developers can also extend IIS configuration and build IIS Manager extensions that plug in seamlessly to the management console.

- **Unified distributed configuration system**   IIS 7.0 provides a unified distributed file-based configuration system for storing all IIS and ASP.NET settings in a single clear-text XML format in a configuration files hierarchy where configuration files are stored together with Web site and application content. This configuration system enables xcopy deployment of configuration alongside application code and content, and it also provides an easy way to share a configuration across a Web farm.

- **New administration tools**   IIS 7.0 offers a set of administration tools that simplify managing Web infrastructure and allow administrators to delegate administrative control for sites and applications to developers and content owners. IIS 7.0 includes a new GUI management console, IIS Manager; a new command line utility, Appcmd.exe; a new WMI provider for automating administration tasks; and a new managed API. All of these tools provide unified support for managing IIS and ASP.NET settings together. Administrators and developers can also use Windows PowerShell for scripting access to configuration information for the entire Web platform.

- **Integrated diagnostics**   IIS 7.0 enables administrators and developers to minimize downtime by using new diagnostics and troubleshooting capabilities. IIS 7.0 exposes run-time diagnostic information including currently executing requests. IIS 7.0 can also be configured to automatically log detailed trace events for failed requests for errant Web sites and applications.

Additional Resources

These resources contain additional information and tools related to this chapter:

- For more information on IIS 7.0 request processing, refer to Chapter 2, "Understanding IIS 7.0 Architecture."

- For more information about modularity, refer to Chapter 3, "Understanding the Modular Foundation."

- For more information on IIS 7.0 extensibility, refer to Chapter 12, "Managing Web Server Modules," and Chapter 13, "Managing Configuration and User Interface Extensions."

- For more information about the unified distributed configuration system, refer to Chapter 4, "Understanding the Configuration System."

- For more information about administration tools, refer to Chapter 6, "Using IIS Manager," and Chapter 7, "Using Command Line Tools."

- For more information about the troubleshooting capabilities of IIS 7.0 and how to use them, refer to Chapter 16, "Tracing and Troubleshooting," and Chapter 17, "Performance and Tuning."

Understanding IIS 7.0 Architecture

This chapter looks into the end-to-end request processing architecture in IIS 7.0. IIS 7.0 has been completely redesigned in comparison with the previous versions of IIS. As we have discussed in the previous chapter, the key architecture innovations are as follows:

- **Modularity**   IIS 7.0 core Web server functionality is implemented by more than 40 built-in native and managed modules. Because of IIS and ASP.NET run-time integration, both native and managed modules can serve requests for any content type. We will look into IIS 7.0 integrated request processing pipeline later in this chapter.

- **Extensibility**   IIS 7.0 is fully extensible and provides a set of public APIs to enable developers to extend its features and functionality. The core Web server modules in IIS 7.0 have been built using new public APIs that are available as native Win32 APIs as well as managed .NET APIs. In addition to extending Web server, developers can also extend IIS configuration and build extensions for the IIS Manager. The end-to-end IIS 7.0 extensibility is discussed in depth in Chapter 12, "Managing Web Server Modules" and Chapter 13, "Managing Configuration and User Interface Extensions."

- **Configuration system**   In IIS 7, IIS and ASP.NET configuration is unified. IIS 7.0 stores all IIS and ASP.NET settings together in clear-text XML-based files that form a distributed configuration hierarchy, also referred to as configuration store. This hierarchy replaces the legacy configuration store, the metabase. We will look into how configuration store is used in request processing later in this chapter. Further, the IIS 7.0 configuration hierarchy, schema, and settings are discussed in detail in Chapter 4, "Understanding the Configuration System."

- **Administration stack**   IIS 7.0 provides a set of administration tools that support managing IIS and ASP.NET settings together, and enable delegation of administrative control to users without administrative access to server machine. IIS 7.0 includes a new GUI management console, IIS Manager; a new command line utility, Appcmd.exe; a new WMI provider for automating administration tasks; and a new managed API. The administration tools are discussed in detail in Chapter 6, "Using IIS Manager," and Chapter 7, "Using Command Line Tools."

- **Diagnostics and troubleshooting**   Diagnostics and troubleshooting capabilities in IIS 7.0 enable administrators and developers to increase efficiency and minimize downtime. Moreover, because IIS 7.0 exposes its process model to non-HTTP applications and services, the diagnostic capabilities are also available to these applications and services. We will look into non-HTTP processing in IIS 7.0 later in this chapter. The diagnostic and troubleshooting of IIS 7.0 are discussed in depth in Chapter 16, "Tracing and Troubleshooting."

To fully understand the implications of these and other architectural changes, we need to look into how IIS 7.0 processes requests. The end-to-end request processing architecture in IIS 7.0 is the focus of this chapter. We will begin with the core IIS 7.0 components and their role in the processing of an HTTP request. We will then look at how a request is executed, focusing on the integrated request processing pipeline and core Web server modularity. Finally, we will discuss non-HTTP request processing in IIS 7.0.

Overview of IIS 7.0 Architecture

IIS 7.0 includes several core components that work together to process client HTTP requests. Each component has different responsibilities in the request processing, such as listening for requests made to the server, activating and managing processes, and executing requests. Figure 2-1 shows IIS 7.0 architecture and core components.

The core components shown in Figure 2-1 are as follows:

- **HTTP protocol stack (HTTP.sys)**   HTTP.sys is the kernel mode protocol listener that listens for HTTP and HTTPS requests.

- **World Wide Web Service Publishing Service (W3SVC)**   W3SVC is an HTTP listener adapter. It owns communication with HTTP.sys and Windows Process Activation Service and provides configuration information to HTTP.sys.

- **Windows Process Activation Service (WAS, also known as WPAS)**   WAS provides management of worker processes. It starts, stops, and recycles application pools and monitors the health of worker processes at run time. In addition, it obtains configuration information from the configuration store.

- **Configuration store**   Configuration store is a distributed XML-based file hierarchy that stores both IIS and ASP.NET settings. IIS server-wide configuration information is contained in the IIS global configuration file applicationHost.config located on the top of the hierarchy. The global.NET Framework configuration files, machine.config and root web.config, are also located on the top of the hierarchy.

■ **Worker process w3wp.exe**   W3wp.exe is a long-running process that processes requests and generates responses. The requests are executed within a worker process. Multiple worker processes can run concurrently. A worker process can execute requests in one of two ways: in .NET Integrated mode by using IIS and the ASP.NET integrated request processing pipeline, or in Classic mode where IIS and ASP.NET requests processing is not integrated, as in IIS 6.0. These modes are discussed in the section titled "Request Processing in Application Pool" later in this chapter.

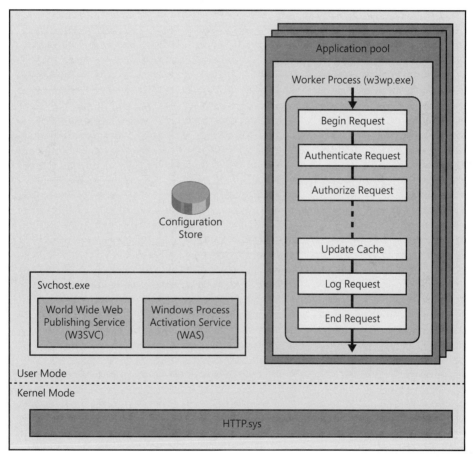

Figure 2-1   IIS 7.0 architecture.

IIS 7.0 core components perform key functions in the processing of an HTTP request. Before looking into the roles that IIS 7.0 core components play in request processing, we need to understand how the server determines which worker process should execute a particular request.

When an HTTP request arrives at the server from the client, the path in the request URL is parsed to determine which site and application the request is for. Each application runs within an application pool. One or more worker processes serve an application pool.

When IIS 7.0 receives a request for an application, IIS maps the request to a worker process for an application pool the application belongs to. If this is the first request for the application pool, the worker process is started, and the server functionality is loaded into the process. Then, the request is passed to the worker process. The worker process executes the request, and the resulting HTTP response is returned to the client.

Figure 2-2 shows the end-to-end HTTP request processing and the interaction between IIS 7.0 components.

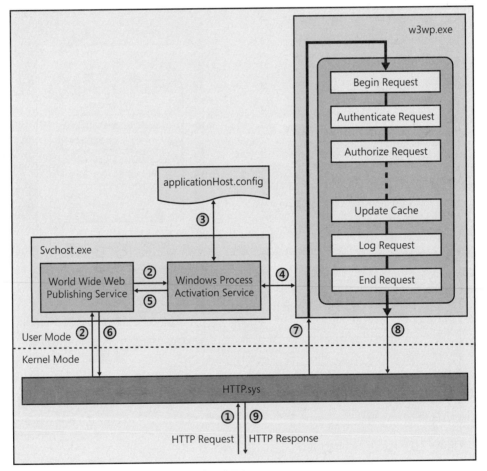

Figure 2-2   HTTP request processing in IIS 7.0.

In IIS 7.0, HTTP request processing consists of the following steps, as shown in Figure 2-2:

1. An HTTP request from a client browser arrives to the server. HTTP.sys intercepts the request.

2. HTTP.sys checks if it has the configuration information for an application the request is sent to.

   ❑ If HTTP.sys has the configuration information, it forwards the request to an appropriate worker process (see step 7).

   ❑ If HTTP.sys doesn't have the configuration information, it contacts W3SVC, which passes the request for information to WAS.

3. WAS obtains configuration information from the IIS global configuration file, applicationHost.config.

4. WAS checks the worker process in the application pool to which the request is made. If there is no worker process, WAS starts a worker process for that application pool.

5. WAS passes configuration, including as application pool and application configuration settings, to W3SVC.

6. W3SVC uses configuration received from WAS to configure and update HTTP.sys.

7. HTTP.sys forwards the request to the worker process.

8. The worker process begins a request processing pipeline to execute the request. A request processing pipeline is an ordered list consisting of components that perform specific tasks to process a request. At the end of this processing, a response is generated and returned to HTTP.sys. We will discuss the request processing pipeline in the section titled "Request Processing in Application Pool" later in this chapter.

9. HTTP.sys sends a response to the client.

IIS 7.0 Core Components

In this section, we will look at IIS 7.0 core components and their role in process activation and request processing.

HTTP.sys

HTTP.sys is the protocol listener that listens for HTTP and HTTPS requests. HTTP.sys was introduced in IIS 6.0 as an HTTP-specific protocol listener for HTTP requests. In IIS 7.0, HTTP.sys also includes support for Secure Sockets Layer (SSL), which Lsass.exe provided in IIS 6.0.

HTTP.sys is a kernel-mode device driver for HTTP protocol stack. It is part of the networking subsystem of the Windows operating systems. Beginning with IIS 6.0, this kernel-mode driver replaced Windows Sockets API (Winsock), which was a user-mode component that previous versions of IIS used to receive HTTP requests and send HTTP responses.

When a client browser requests a Web page from a site on the IIS 7.0 server, HTTP.sys picks up the request on the site binding on the server machine and then passes it to the worker process for processing. After the request has been processed, HTTP.sys returns a response to the client browser.

Apart from intercepting and returning HTTP requests, HTTP.sys also performs the following tasks:

■ Preprocessing and security filtering of the incoming HTTP requests

■ Queuing of HTTP requests for the application pools

■ Caching of the outgoing HTTP responses

Figure 2-3 shows HTTP.sys request queues and response cache.

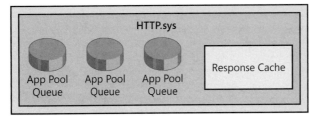

Figure 2-3   HTTP request queue and response cache.

Having a request queue and a response cache served by a kernel-based HTTP listener reduces overhead in context switching to user mode and results in performance enhancements, as follows:

■ **Kernel-mode request queuing**   Requests cause less overhead in context switching because the kernel forwards requests directly to the correct worker process. If no worker process is available to accept a request, the kernel-mode request queue holds the request until a worker process picks it up.

■ **Kernel-mode caching**   Requests for cached responses are served without switching to user mode.

HTTP.sys maintains a request queue for each worker process. It sends the HTTP requests it receives to the request queue for the worker process that serves the application pool where the requested application is located. For each application, HTTP.sys maintains the URI namespace routing table with one entry. The routing table data is used to determine which application pool responds to requests from what parts of the namespace. Each request queue corresponds to one application pool. An application pool corresponds to one request queue within HTTP.sys and one or more worker processes.

If a faulty application causes a worker process failure, service is not interrupted, and the failure is undetectable by an end user because the kernel queues the requests while the WAS service starts a new worker process for that application pool. When the WAS service identifies an unhealthy worker process, it starts a new worker process if outstanding requests are waiting to be serviced. Although a temporary disruption occurs in user-mode request processing, the user does not experience the failure, because TCP/IP connections are maintained, and requests continue to be queued and processed. Only those requests that are running in the worker process when it fails will result in users seeing an error status. The requests that haven't been processed yet will be redirected to the new worker process.

Other than retrieving a stored response from its internal cache, HTTP.sys does not process the requests that it receives. Therefore, no application-specific code is ever loaded into kernel mode but is processed inside the worker process that runs in the user mode. As a result, bugs in application-specific code cannot affect the kernel or lead to system failures.

World Wide Web Publishing Service

World Wide Web Publishing Service (W3SVC) changed significantly in IIS 7.0 in comparison with IIS 6.0.

In IIS 6.0, W3SVC was responsible for HTTP.sys management, configuration management, process management, and performance monitoring, as shown in Figure 2-4.

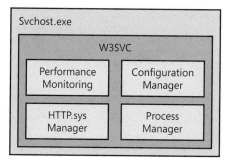

Figure 2-4   W3SVC in IIS 6.0.

In IIS 7.0, this functionality is split between two services: W3SVC and a service that is new to IIS 7.0, WAS. These two services run as LocalSystem in the same Svchost.exe process, and they share the same binaries. W3SVC and WAS in IIS 7.0 are shown in Figure 2-5.

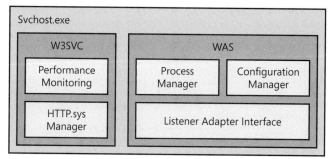

Figure 2-5   W3SVC and WAS in IIS 7.0.

In IIS 7.0, W3SVC acts as listener adapter for the HTTP listener, HTTP.sys. Listener adapters are components that establish communication between WAS and protocol listeners. WAS includes a listener adapter interface that provides communication with listener adapters.

W3SVC is responsible for configuring HTTP.sys, updating HTTP.sys when configuration changes, and notifying WAS when a request enters the request queue. Additionally, W3SVC continues to collect the counters for Web sites. However, it no longer reads configuration information from the configuration store or manages application pools and worker processes. Instead, responsibilities for reading configuration and process activation and management are factored into WAS.

The changes in W3SVC service functionality between IIS 7.0 and IIS 6.0 are summarized in the following list:

■ Configuration management

   ❑ In IIS 6.0, W3SVC reads configuration information from IIS 6.0 configuration store, the metabase.

   ❑ In IIS 7.0, W3SVC no longer reads configuration information from configuration store. Instead, WAS reads the configuration info from IIS 7.0 configuration store, applicationHost.config, and then passes it to W3SVC.

■ HTTP.sys management

   ❑ In IIS 6.0, W3SVC configures and updates HTTP.sys using configuration information it read from the metabase.

   ❑ In IIS 7.0, W3SVC configures and updates HTTP.sys by using configuration information received from WAS. As a listener adapter for HTTP protocol, W3SVC owns communication between WAS and HTTP.sys.

■ Process management

   ❑ In IIS 6.0, W3SVC manages application pools and worker processes, including starting, stopping, and recycling worker processes. Additionally, W3SVC monitors the health of the worker processes and invokes rapid fail detection to stop new processes from starting when several worker processes fail in a specified amount of time.

   ❑ In IIS 7.0, W3SVC no longer has any responsibilities for managing worker processes. These responsibilities have been passed to WAS.

■ Performance monitoring

   ❑ In IIS 6.0, W3SVC monitors performance and provides performance counters for Web sites and for IIS cache.

   ❑ In IIS 7.0, W3SVC continues to collect the counters for Web sites.

> **Note**   Because performance counters remain part of W3SVC, they are HTTP-specific and do not apply to WAS.

Windows Process Activation Service

The HTTP process activation model was introduced in IIS 6.0 with application pools. In IIS 7.0, this service has been extended and is called Windows Process Activation Service (WAS). It is capable of receiving requests or messages over any protocol and supports pluggable activation of arbitrary protocol listeners.

In IIS 7.0, WAS manages application pool configuration and worker processes. W3SVC performs this function in IIS 6.0. WAS includes the following components, as shown in Figure 2-5:

- Configuration manager, which reads application and application pool configuration from configuration store.

- Process manager, which maps application pools to existing worker processes and is responsible for starting new instances of W3wp.exe to host new application pools in response to activation requests.

- Listener adapter interface, which defines how external listeners communicate activation requests they receive to WAS. For example, the W3SVC service owns the communication with HTTP.sys and communicates HTTP activation requests to WAS across the listener adapter interface.

On startup, the configuration manager in WAS reads information from the configuration store and then passes that information to the HTTP listener adapter, W3SVC, which is responsible for communication with the HTTP listener, HTTP.sys. After W3SVC receives configuration information, it configures HTTP.sys and prepares it to listen for requests.

The configuration manager in WAS obtains the following information from configuration store:

- Global configuration information
- Protocol configuration information
- Application pool configuration, such as the process account information
- Site configuration, such as bindings and applications
- Application configuration, such as the enabled protocols and the application pools to which the application belongs

If configuration changes, the configuration manager in WAS receives a notification and subsequently updates W3SVC with the new information. After W3SVC receives the new configuration, it updates and configures HTTP.sys. For example, when you add or delete an application pool, the configuration manager processes the configuration changes and communicates them to W3SVC, which updates HTTP.sys to add or delete the application pool queue.

The process manager in WAS is responsible for managing the worker processes, which includes starting the worker processes and maintaining information about the running worker processes. It also determines when to start a worker process, when to recycle a worker process, and when to restart a worker process if it becomes blocked and is unable to process any more requests.

When HTTP.sys picks up a client request, the process manager in WAS determines if a worker process is already running. If an application pool already has a worker process servicing requests, then HTTP.sys passes the request to the worker process for processing. If there is no worker process in the application pool, the process manager starts a new worker process so that HTTP.sys can pass the request for processing to that worker process.

In addition to HTTP, WAS supports other protocols. The same configuration and process model used for HTTP are made available to non-HTTP applications and services. We will look into this capability in the section titled "Non-HTTP Request Processing" later in this chapter.

Configuration Store

In IIS 6.0, configuration data is stored in the XML-based metabase. IIS 7.0 no longer uses the metabase. Instead, configuration settings are stored in a distributed XML file–based configuration system that combines both IIS and ASP.NET settings.

The distributed configuration hierarchy includes the global, computer-wide, .NET Framework configuration files machine.config and root web.config; the global IIS configuration file applicationHost.config; and distributed web.config configuration files located within the Web sites, applications, and directories, as shown in Figure 2-6.

Because configuration files are stored together with Web site and application content, this configuration system enables xcopy deployment of configuration alongside application code and content, allows the server administrator to delegate administration of sites and applications to users without administrative privileges on the server computer, and also provides an easy way for sharing configuration across a Web farm.

IIS global server-wide configuration is stored in the applicationHost.config file located in the %SystemRoot%\system32\Inetsrv\Config folder. The WAS service obtains application pools and application configuration information from this file.

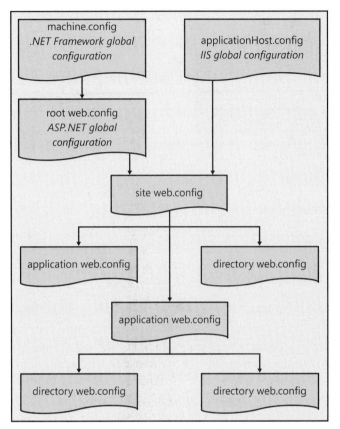

Figure 2-6   IIS 7.0 distributed configuration store.

IIS 7.0 provides several administration tools and application programming interfaces (APIs) that read and write configuration in the IIS 7.0 configuration system. The configuration files are clear text-based XML files, so you can use Notepad to work with IIS 7.0 configuration if you really wish. However, even for simple web.config files, this is very much prone to error and better to be avoided.

To simplify administration tasks, IIS 7.0 provides redesigned, task-based, feature-focused IIS Manager for graphical user interface (GUI)–based Web server management, and also offers a command line administration tool, Appcmd.exe. For programmatic access, there is a COM API for managing configuration programmatically from C++ programs, and a .NET API, Microsoft.Web.Administration, for .NET programs. Most of IIS Manager features are implemented using this new .NET API. An IIS 7.0 Windows Management Instrumentation (WMI) provider for scripting is provided as well, together with the legacy IIS 6.0 WMI provider that is available for backward compatibility with existing scripts.

Microsoft.Web.Administration API, Appcmd.exe, and the WMI provider are written on top of the COM API. This new administration stack is shown in Figure 2-7.

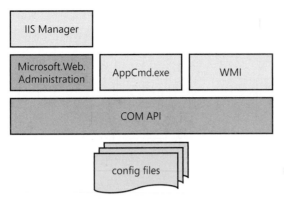

Figure 2-7   IIS 7.0 administration stack.

> **Note**   For more information on the IIS 7.0 configuration system and global applicationHost.config file, refer to Chapter 4, "Understanding the Configuration System."

The legacy configuration store, the metabase, is not a part of IIS 7.0. However, for backward compatibility, IIS 7.0 provides the optional Metabase Compatibility feature that installs the IIS Administration Service (IISADMIN), which reads and writes the metabase in IIS 6.0. The Metabase Compatibility feature also installs the Inetinfo.exe process, which hosts the IISADMIN service. These two components provide the translation layer called the Admin Base Objects (ABO) Mapper. The ABO Mapper supports the legacy ABO APIs for working with the metabase but stores configuration directly in the IIS 7.0 configuration files. If you do not install the Metabase Compatibility feature, IIS 7.0 does not use IISADMIN service or the Inetinfo.exe process.

Worker Process

The role of a worker process is to process requests. A worker process is a self-contained long-running user mode process that runs as an executable named w3wp.exe.

Each worker process provides the core Web server functionality. As a result of a request processing within the worker process, the response is generated and is subsequently returned to the client. Each worker process uses HTTP.sys to receive requests and to send responses.

One worker process serves one application pool. An application pool groups together one or more applications. Because of this, you can apply specific configuration settings to groups of applications and to the worker processes servicing those applications.

Each application runs within an application pool. An application pool can be served by a set of worker processes. A worker process can serve only one application pool. Multiple worker processes that serve different application pools can run concurrently, as shown in Figure 2-8.

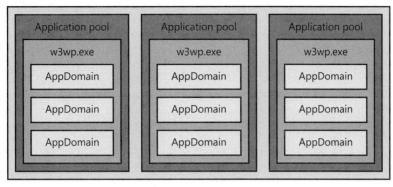

Figure 2-8   Process and application isolation.

The worker process boundaries separate application pools, which enables all application code to run in an isolated environment so that individual applications can execute within a self-contained worker process. The worker process isolation model was first introduced in IIS 6.0. This model prevents applications running within one application pool from affecting applications in a different application pool on the server, providing sandboxing of applications.

Within a worker process, application domains provide application boundaries for .NET applications. Each .NET application runs in its own application domain (AppDomain), as shown in Figure 2-8. An application domain loads the application's code when the application starts. Virtual directories within an application are served by the same AppDomain as the application to which they belong.

Direct from the Source: Application Pool Isolation in IIS 7.0

The application pool design introduced by IIS 6.0 has been the foundation of enabling greater security isolation of multiple applications and improving the fault-tolerance of the Web server. IIS 7.0 continues to leverage this concept, and it no longer provides support for the legacy IIS 5.0 Isolation Model. The majority of the features that made application pools successful with IIS 6.0 remain, including the ability to run each application pool with different credentials and configure intelligent health monitoring and recycling settings to maintain application reliability.

IIS 7.0 goes further, by providing automatic application pool isolation through automatically generated Security Identifiers (SIDs) for application pools, and automatically isolating server-level configuration such that it can only be read by the application pool it affects. This makes it easier than ever before to configure fully isolated Web applications by leveraging application pools.

In addition, IIS 7.0 in Windows Server 2008 delivers a number of performance improvements that significantly increase the number of application pools that can be configured and active on a single Web server, both through lower worker process footprint and intelligent worker process management features. These improvements make it easier for Web hosting providers to place each individual application into a separate application pool, in order to achieve the maximum security and fault isolation for those applications.

Be sure to fully utilize the capabilities afforded by application pool isolation when designing your Web application infrastructure.

Mike Volodarsky

IIS Core Server Program Manager

Requests within each worker process can be executed in one of two different ways: in .NET Integrated mode when both IIS and ASP.NET requests use the same integrated request processing pipeline, or in Classic mode when two separate pipelines are used for IIS and ASP.NET processing. You can configure an application pool to determine in which of the two modes to execute ASP.NET requests. In the next section, we will focus on the request processing architecture within worker processes serving the application pools.

Request Processing in Application Pool

In IIS 7.0, two modes are available for an application pool: Integrated mode and Classic mode. When you configure an application pool with Integrated mode, IIS 7.0 processes ASP.NET requests using the integrated IIS and ASP.NET request processing pipeline. When you configure an application pool with Classic mode, IIS 7.0 processes ASP.NET requests using the separate IIS and ASP.NET request processing pipelines, as in IIS 6.0.

Application pools configured with different modes can run on the same server machine. You can specify the mode for an application pool by configuring the Managed Pipeline Mode setting in IIS Manager.

To use IIS Manager to configure the ASP.NET processing mode for an application pool, perform the following steps:

1. In IIS Manager, expand the server node and select the Application Pools node in the Connections pane.

2. On the Application Pools page, select the application pool you'd like to configure.

3. In the Actions pane, under Edit Application Pool, select Basic Settings.

4. In the Edit Application Pool dialog box, in the Managed Pipeline Mode drop-down list, choose the desired mode (Integrated or Classic) and click OK.

Classic Mode

Classic mode in IIS 7.0 provides backward compatibility with IIS 6.0. When an application pool is in Classic mode, IIS 7.0 processes ASP.NET requests using two separate IIS and ASP.NET request processing pipelines, as in IIS 6.0. To understand Classic mode in IIS 7.0, let's first look into how ASP.NET requests are processed in IIS 6.0.

Figure 2-9 shows ASP.NET request processing in IIS 6.0. In IIS releases up to version 6.0, ASP.NET connects to the Web server as a stand-alone application framework. In these releases, ASP.NET is implemented as an IIS Internet Server Application Programming Interface (ISAPI) extension.

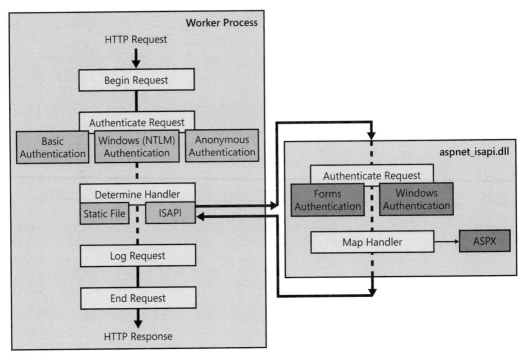

Figure 2-9 ASP.NET request processing in IIS 6.0.

In IIS 6.0, the ASP.NET ISAPI extension (aspnet_isapi.dll) is responsible for processing the content types that are registered to it, such as ASPX and ASMX. For those requests, it offers powerful features, for example, Forms Authentication and Response Output Caching. However, only content types registered to ASP.NET can benefit from these services. Other content types—including ASP pages, static files, images, and Common Gateway Interface (CGI) applications—have no access to these features at all.

A request to an ASP.NET content type is first processed by IIS and then forwarded to aspnet_isapi.dll that hosts the ASP.NET application and request processing model. This effectively exposes two separate server pipelines, one for native ISAPI filters and extension components, and another for managed application components. ASP.NET components execute entirely inside the ASP.NET ISAPI extension and only for requests mapped to ASP.NET in the IIS script map configuration. Requests to non-ASP.NET content, such as ASP pages or static files, are processed by IIS or other ISAPI extensions and are not visible to ASP.NET.

In addition, even for ASP.NET resources, certain functionalities are not available to ASP.NET because of run-time limitations. For example, it is not possible to modify the set of outgoing HTTP response headers before they are sent to the client because this occurs after the ASP.NET execution path.

In IIS 7.0 in Classic mode, ASP.NET requests are also processed using the ASP.NET ISAPI extension, as shown in Figure 2-10. The core Web server in IIS 7.0 is fully componentized, whereas in IIS 6.0, it is monolithic. However, the ASP.NET requests in Classic mode are processed by asnet_isapi.dll in the same way as in IIS 6.0. After the request has been processed by asnet_isapi.dll, it is routed back through IIS to send the response.

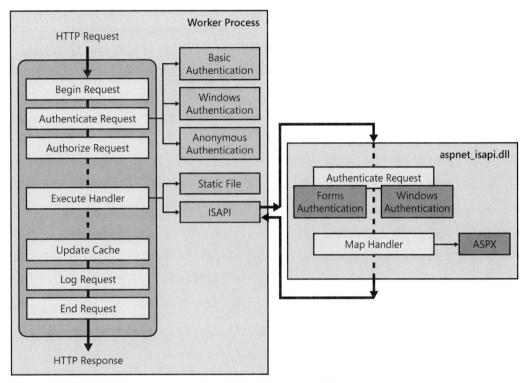

Figure 2-10   ASP.NET request processing in Classic mode in IIS 7.0.

Classic mode in IIS 7.0 has the same major limitations as ASP.NET processing in the IIS 6.0. In summary, these limitations are as follows:

- Services provided by ASP.NET modules are not available to non-ASP.NET requests.

- Some processing steps are duplicated, such as authentication.

- Some settings must be managed in two locations, such as authorization, tracing, and output caching.

- ASP.NET applications are unable to affect certain parts of IIS request processing that occur before and after the ASP.NET execution path due to the placement of the ASP.NET ISAPI extension in the server pipeline.

Classic mode is provided only for backward compatibility with IIS 6.0. Simply put, you should add an application to an application pool in Classic mode only if the application fails to work in Integrated mode.

> **Note**   For more information on application compatibility in IIS 7.0, see Chapter 11, "Hosting
> Application Development Frameworks."

.NET Integrated Mode

When an application pool is configured with .NET Integrated mode, you can take advantage of the integrated request processing architecture of IIS 7.0 and ASP.NET.

In IIS 7.0, ASP.NET run time is integrated with the core Web server. The IIS and ASP.NET request pipelines are combined, providing a unified (that is, integrated) request processing pipeline that is exposed to both native and managed modules.

The IIS 7.0 request processing pipeline is implemented by the core Web server engine. It enables multiple independent modules to provide services for the same request. All of the Web server features are implemented as stand-alone modules. There are over 40 separate native and managed modules. Each module implements a particular Web server feature or functionality, such as logging or output caching.

> **Note**   For the full list of IIS 7.0 built-in modules, both native and managed, refer to
> Appendix C, "IIS 7.0 Modules Listing."

Native modules are implemented as dynamic-link libraries (DLLs) based on public IIS 7.0 C++ extensibility APIs. Managed modules are implemented as managed .NET Framework classes based on the ASP.NET integration model in IIS 7.0. (IIS 7.0 has integrated the existing IHttpModule API for ASP.NET.) Both of these APIs enable modules to participate in the IIS 7.0 request processing pipeline and access all events for all requests.

An IIS 7.0 integrated request processing pipeline is shown in Figure 2-11. A pipeline is an ordered list consisting of native and managed modules that perform specific tasks in response to requests. When a worker process in an application pool receives a request from HTTP.sys, the request passes through an ordered list of stages. As a result of processing, the response is generated and sent back to HTTP.sys.

Each stage in the pipeline raises an event. Native and managed modules subscribe to events in the stages of the pipeline that are relevant to them. When the event is raised, the native and managed modules that subscribe to that event are notified and do their work to process the request. The pipeline event model enables multiple modules to execute during request processing.

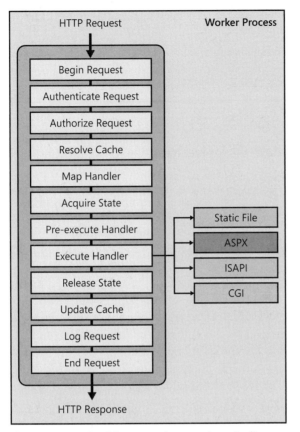

Figure 2-11 IIS 7.0 integrated processing pipeline.

Most of the pipeline events are intended for a specific type of task, such as authentication, authorization, caching, and logging. The following list describes stages and corresponding events in the request processing pipeline:

- **Begin Request stage**   This stage starts request processing. The *BeginRequest* event is raised.

- **Authenticate Request stage**   This stage authenticates the requesting user. The *AuthenticateRequest* event is raised.

- **Authorize Request stage**   At this stage, the *AuthorizeRequest* event is raised. This stage checks access to the requested resource for the authenticated user. If access is denied, the request is rejected.

- **Resolve Cache stage**   At this stage, *ResolveRequestCache* event is raised. This stage checks to see if the response to the request can be retrieved from a cache.

- **Map Handler stage**   At this stage, the *MapRequestHandler* event is raised. This stage determines the handler for the request.

- **Acquire State stage**   At this stage, the *AcquireRequestState* event is raised. This stage retrieves the required state for the request.

- **Pre-execute Handler stage**   At this stage, the *PreExecuteRequestHandler* event is raised. This stage signals that the handler is about to be executed and performs the preprocessing tasks if needed.

- **Execute Handler stage**   At this stage, the *ExecuteRequestHandler* event is raised. The handler executes and generates the response.

- **Release State stage**   At this stage, the *ReleaseRequestState* event is raised. This stage releases the request state.

- **Update Cache stage**   This stage updates the cache. The *UpdateRequestCache* event is raised.

- **Log Request stage**   At this stage, the request is logged. The *LogRequest* event is raised.

- **End Request stage**   At this stage, the *EndRequest* event is raised, which signals that the request processing is about to complete.

Modules that subscribe to an event provide specific services appropriate for the relevant stage in the pipeline. For example, Figure 2-12 shows several native and managed modules that subscribe to the *AuthenticateRequest* event at the Authenticate Request stage, such as the Basic Authentication module, the Windows Authentication module, the ASP.NET Forms Authentication module, and the Anonymous Authentication module. Basic, Windows, and Anonymous Authentication modules are native modules, whereas Forms Authentication is a managed module.

.NET integrated pipeline provides several key advantages over previous versions of IIS, as follows:

- Allowing services provided by both native and managed modules to apply to all requests.

  All file types can use features that in IIS 6.0 are available only to managed code. For example, you can now use ASP.NET Forms authentication and Uniform Resource Locator (URL) authorization for static files, ASP files, CGI, static files, and all other file types in your sites and applications.

- Eliminating the duplication of several features in IIS and ASP.NET.

  For example, when a client requests a managed file, the server calls the appropriate authentication module in the integrated pipeline to authenticate the client. In previous versions of IIS, this same request goes through an authentication process in both the IIS pipeline and the ASP.NET pipeline. Other unified IIS and ASP.NET functionality includes URL authorization, tracing, custom errors, and output caching.

- Managing all of the modules in one location, thus simplifying site and application administration on the server.

  Instead of managing some features in IIS and some in the ASP.NET configuration, there is a single place to implement, configure, monitor, and support server features. For example, because of the run-time integration, IIS and ASP.NET can use the same configuration for enabling and ordering server modules, as well as configuring handler mappings.

- Extending IIS with ASP.NET managed modules.

  IIS 7.0 enables ASP.NET modules to plug directly into the server pipeline, in the same way as modules developed with the native C++ IIS API. ASP.NET modules can execute in all run-time stages of the request processing pipeline and can be executed in any order with respect to native modules. The ASP.NET API has also been expanded to allow for more control over request processing than was previously possible.

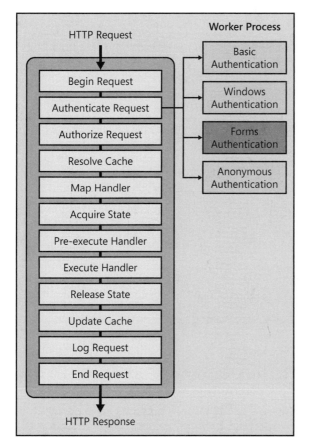

Figure 2-12   Native and managed modules in the integrated processing pipeline.

> **Note**   For more information on extending IIS 7.0, refer to Chapter 12, "Managing Web Server Modules."

How ASP.NET Integration Is Implemented

Though native and managed modules implement the same logical module concept, they use two different APIs. To enable an integrated pipeline model for both native and managed modules, IIS 7.0 provides a special native module called Managed Engine. The Managed Engine module in effect provides an integration wrapper for ASP.NET modules that enables these managed modules to act as if they were native IIS modules and handlers. It acts as a proxy for event notifications and propagates a required request state to the managed modules. Together with the ASP.NET engine, it sets up the integrated pipeline and is also responsible for reading the managed modules and handlers configuration.

When a request requires a managed module, the Managed Engine module creates an AppDomain where that managed module can perform the necessary processing, such as authenticating a user with Forms authentication. Figure 2-13 shows the Managed Engine module, with the managed Forms Authentication module executing within an AppDomain.

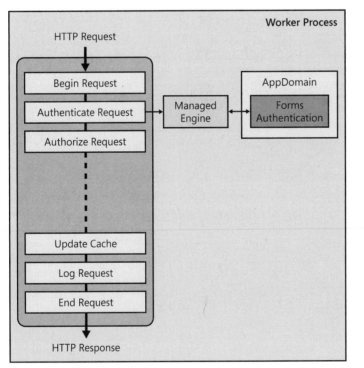

Figure 2-13   Managed Engine module.

All managed modules are dependent on the Managed Engine module, and they cannot execute without it. For the integrated pipeline and ASP.NET applications to work, the Managed Engine module must be installed and enabled in IIS 7.0.

In Windows Server 2008, the Managed Engine module is installed as a part of the Role Service component and .NET Extensibility Component. In Windows Vista, it is installed as a part of the .NET Extensibility component.

> **Note**   For more information on ASP.NET integration, refer to Chapter 12.

Module Scope

Modules can be installed and enabled on different levels. Modules that are enabled on the server level provide a default feature set for all applications on the server. The IIS global configuration store, applicationHost.config, provides the unified list of both native and managed modules. Each time WAS activates a worker process, it gets the configuration from the configuration store, and the worker process loads all globally listed modules.

Native modules can be installed only at the server level. They cannot be installed at the application level. At the application level, the global native modules that are enabled at the server level can be removed, or those that are installed but not enabled globally can be enabled for that application.

Managed modules can be added at the server, site, and application levels. Application-specific modules are loaded upon the first request to the application. Application managed modules can be xcopy-deployed together with other application files.

You can manage both native and managed modules using the Modules feature in IIS Manager.

> **Note**   For more information on managing modules, refer to Chapter 12.

Module Ordering

The pipeline model ensures that the typical Web server processing tasks are performed in the correct order. For example, authentication must happen before authorization: authenticating the user associated with a request at the Authenticate Request stage has to happen before checking that user's access to the requested resource at the Authorize Request stage.

The server uses the sequence of modules list in the <modules> configuration section to order module execution within each request processing stage. By executing during the relevant stage, the majority of modules automatically avoid ordering problems. However, multiple modules that execute within the same stage may have ordering dependencies. For example, the built-in authentication modules that run at the Authenticate Request stage should be executed in the strongest to weakest order so that the request is authenticated with the strongest credentials available.

To manage ordering dependencies, the administrator can control the ordering of modules by changing the order in which they are listed in the <modules> section. This can be done, for example, using the Modules feature in IIS Manager.

To view, and optionally change, the ordered list of modules for a server, perform the following steps:

1.   In IIS Manager, in the Connections pane, select the server node.

2.   In the server's home page, open the Modules feature.

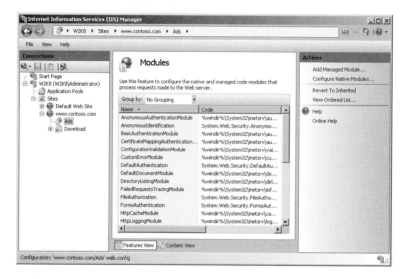

3.   In the Actions pane, click View Ordered List.

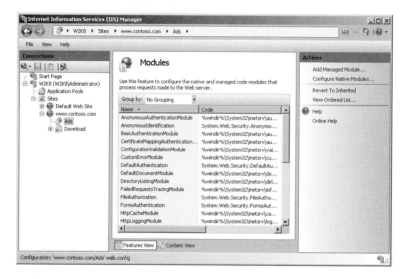

4.   You can change a position of a module in the processing sequence by selecting the module and then using Move Up and Move Down options in the Action pane to move it to the desired position in the list.

> **Note**   For information about the default order of built-in modules, refer to Appendix D, "Modules Sequence."

Non-HTTP Request Processing

In IIS 7.0, WAS supports non-HTTP protocols, enabling you to use IIS to host non-HTTP–based applications and services. The WAS process model generalizes the process model for the HTTP server by removing the dependency on HTTP. Because WAS manages application pool configuration and worker processes in IIS 7.0, the same configuration and process model that is used for HTTP can be used for non-HTTP applications. All IIS process management features, such as on-demand activation, process health monitoring, enterprise-class manageability, and rapid failure protection, are available to non-HTTP–based applications and services in IIS 7.0.

To support services and applications that use protocols other than HTTP and HTTPS, you can use technologies such as Windows Communication Foundation (WCF). The WAS process model enables WCF-based applications and services to use both HTTP and non-HTTP protocols in a hosting environment that supports message-based activation and offers the ability to host a large number of applications on a single machine. Windows Communication Foundation ships with protocol adapters that can leverage the capabilities of the WAS, improving the reliability and resource use of WCF services.

WAS is capable of receiving requests or messages over any protocol, and it supports pluggable activation of arbitrary protocol listeners. Protocol listeners receive protocol-specific requests, send them to IIS for processing, and then return responses to requestors. With WCF, a listener adapter includes the functionality of a protocol listener. Figure 2-14 shows WAS with listener adapters for non-HTTP protocols.

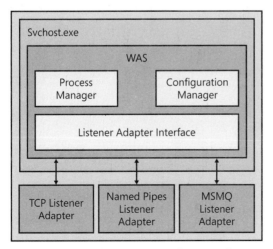

Figure 2-14   Non-HTTP protocol support in WAS.

Listener adapters are Windows services that receive messages on specific network protocols and communicate with WAS to route incoming requests to the correct worker process. The listener adapter interface is used to communicate activation requests that are received over the supported non-HTTP protocols. There are several non-HTTP listener adapters, as follows:

■   NetTcpActivator for TCP protocol

■   NetPipeActivator for Named Pipes

■   NetMsmqActivator for Message Queuing (also known as MSMQ)

If you do not need HTTP functionality, you can actually run WAS without W3SVC. For example, you can manage a Web service through a WCF listener adapter, such as NetTcp-Activator, without running W3SVC if you do not need to listen for HTTP requests in HTTP.sys.

The global IIS configuration store, applicationHost.config, can contain configuration for non-HTTP protocols. For example, a TCP listener adapter, NetTcpActivator, can be configured based on information that WAS reads from configuration store. After NetTcpActivator is configured, it listens for requests that use the TCP protocol. When a listener adapter receives a request, WAS starts a worker process so that the listener adapter can pass the request to it for processing. This architecture is shown in Figure 2-15.

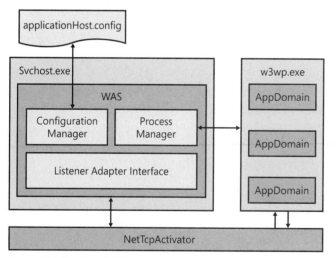

Figure 2-15   Non-HTTP processing in IIS 7.0.

Because WAS manages processes for both HTTP and non-HTTP protocols, you can run applications with different protocols in the same application pool. For example, you can host an application over both HTTP and TCP protocols.

In addition to being protocol independent, the WAS process model in IIS 7.0 provides all types of message-activated applications with intelligent resource management, on-demand process activation, health-monitoring, and automatic failure detection and recycling. It allows these applications to take advantage of the IIS process model without requiring the deployment footprint of a full IIS installation.

> **Note** For more information on listener adapters, see the article titled "WAS Activation Architecture" at *http://go.microsoft.com/fwlink/?LinkId=88413*.

Summary

In this chapter, we looked at the end-to-end request processing architecture of IIS 7.0. IIS 7.0 includes several core components that work together to execute the HTTP request. These components are as follows:

- HTTP.sys, the kernel-level HTTP protocol listener
- World Wide Web Publishing Service (W3SVC), the HTTP listener adapter
- Windows Process Activation Service (WAS), which provides process activation and management
- Configuration store, the distributed XML file–based configuration hierarchy that contains both IIS and ASP.NET settings
- Worker process, w3wp.exe, the self-contained user mode process that executes HTTP requests and generates responses

Each worker process serves one application pool. An application pool can be configured in one of two Managed Pipeline modes: Integrated mode and Classic mode. Depending on this configuration setting, an ASP.NET request can be executed in one of two ways within the worker process that serves the application pool:

- In the Integrated mode, IIS and ASP.NET processing is unified into an integrated processing pipeline.
- In the Classic mode, IIS and ASP.NET pipelines are separate, as in IIS 6.0.

The integrated processing pipeline provides the foundation for IIS 7.0 modular architecture. It exposes the request to more than 40 built-in, self-contained native and managed modules that implement the Web server functionality. The key benefits of the integrated processing pipeline are as follows:

- Enabling services provided by both native and managed modules to apply to all content types
- Eliminating duplication of features in IIS and ASP.NET

- Managing all of the modules in one location, thus simplifying site and application administration on the server

- Extending IIS with ASP.NET managed modules

In addition to executing HTTP requests, IIS 7.0 supports hosting of non-HTTP applications and services that can take advantage of its process model.

On the Disc   Browse the CD for additional tools and resources.

Additional Resources

These resources contain additional information and tools related to this chapter:

- For more information about IIS 7.0 configuration system, refer to Chapter 4, "Understanding the Configuration System."

- For more information about application compatibility, refer to Chapter 11, "Hosting Application Development Frameworks."

- For more information about integrated processing pipeline and managing Web server modules, refer to Chapter 12, "Managing Web Server Modules."

- For a full list of IIS 7.0 native and managed modules, refer to Appendix C, "IIS 7.0 Modules Listing."

- For the default sequence of IIS 7.0 built-in modules, refer to Appendix D, "Modules Sequence."

- For more information on listener adapters, see the article titled "WAS Activation Architecture" at *http://go.microsoft.com/fwlink/?LinkId=88413.*

Chapter 3
Understanding the Modular Foundation

What does *modular core* mean to Microsoft Internet Information Services (IIS) 7.0? How does it make IIS 7.0 the most powerful Microsoft Web server ever? And what are the built-in modules shipped with IIS 7.0? No worries—by the end of this chapter, you will be able to answer all these questions and have a clear understanding of the new design concept behind IIS 7.0. You will take a look at the idea of componentized design in IIS 7.0, the intentions behind the revamped architecture, and the advantages of the design. You'll also get detailed information about the built-in modules that ship with IIS 7.0.

Concepts

One of the core changes for IIS 7.0 is its component-based architecture, which incorporates lessons learned from IIS 6.0 and feedback from customers. IIS 7.0 debuts with a completely redesigned architecture; the Web server core is now broken down into discrete components called modules. For the first time, as a Web administrator, you have the power to custom build an IIS server according to your requirements. You can easily add built-in modules whenever they are needed or, even better, add or replace functionality with modules of your own design, produced commercially or provided by the developer community on IIS.net. In this way, the modular engine enables you to achieve exactly the functionality you want from the Web server and at the same time provides flexibility so that you can remove unwanted modules to better lock down the Web server.

Although the main modularity point in IIS 7.0 is the Web server itself, features throughout the entire platform are implemented as modules. The administration stack, for example, is modular. For detailed information about extensibility of the IIS 7.0 Web server and the administration stack, see Chapter 12, "Managing Web Server Modules," and Chapter 13, "Managing Configuration and User Interface Extensions."

The Ideas

A module resembles a brick in a child's LEGO toy set, which comes with bricks in many different colors and shapes. When combined with additional bricks from other sets, you can assemble many different structures in a variety of shapes. IIS 7.0 uses the same idea in the design of its framework foundation. By using modules as the building blocks, this pluggable architecture combined with the flexible configuration system and an extensible user interface (UI) make it possible to add or remove any capability to craft a server that fits the specific needs of your organization. This new and open design is revolutionary for Microsoft and opens new doors for the Web platform.

How It Works: The Modular Design

IIS 7.0 ships with many different modules. Each module is a component (but not in the Component Object Model [COM] sense) that provides services to the Web server's HTTP request processing pipeline. For example, StaticFileModule is the module that handles all static content such as HTML pages, image files, and so on. Other modules provide capabilities for dynamic compression, basic authentication, and the other features you typically associate with IIS. Modules are discretely managed in IIS 7.0. They can easily be added to or removed from the core engine via the new configuration system.

Internally, the IIS Web server core provides the request processing pipeline for modules to execute. It also provides request processing services, whereby modules registered in the processing pipeline are invoked for processing requests based on registered event notifications. As an administrator, you cannot control which events the modules are coded to use. This is done in the code within the module. However, you have the ability to control which modules are loaded globally, and you can even control which modules are loaded for a specific site or application. For details about how to control module loading, see Chapter 12.

Each time the IIS 7.0 worker process starts, it reads the server configuration file and loads all globally listed modules. Application modules are loaded at the time of the first request to the application. It is the modular design and configuration system that make it easy for you to plug in, remove, and replace modules in the request pipeline, offering full extensibility to the IIS 7.0 Web server.

Types of Modules

IIS 7.0 ships with approximately 40 modules, including security-related authentication modules and modules for content compression. Modules build up the feature sets of the Web server, and the Web application is made up of many modules servicing the requests. In terms of roles, modules can be categorized as providing either *request services* such as compression and authentication or *request handling* such as delivering static files, ASP.NET pages, and so on. Regardless of their roles, modules are the key ingredients to IIS 7.0. Developers can create two types of IIS modules:

■ **Managed modules** A managed module is a .NET Framework component based on the ASP.NET extensibility model. With the IIS 7.0 integrated processing architecture, ASP.NET application services are no longer restricted to requests for .ASPX pages or other content mapped to ASP.NET. The managed modules are plugged in directly to the Web server's request processing pipeline, making them as powerful as the modules built using the native extensibility layer in IIS 7.0. In order to use services provided by ASP.NET modules for all requests, your application must run in an application pool that uses Integrated mode. This integration is possible via the ManagedEngine module, which provides the .NET integration into the request processing pipeline. Managed modules are loaded globally only when the application pool is marked as integrated. For more information about the new integrated pipeline processing mode, see Chapter 12.

■ **Native modules** A native module is a Microsoft Windows dynamic-link library (DLL) typically written in C++ that provides request processing services. In IIS 7.0, a new set of native server (C++) application programming interfaces (APIs) have replaced the Internet Server API (ISAPI) filters and extension APIs provided by earlier versions of IIS. These new APIs are developed in an object-oriented model and are equipped with more powerful interfaces that give you more control when it comes to processing requests and handling responses. Developers familiar with ISAPI and the new native module APIs have been very positive about how much easier it is now to code using native code than in previous versions of IIS.

> **Note** For details on how to write native modules, see "How to Build a Native Code IIS7 Module Using C++" at *http://www.iis.net/go/938*.

Developers can manage and configure native and managed modules the same way in IIS 7.0, with the exception of how they deploy the modules. Native modules are installed globally on the server, and can be enabled or disabled for each application. Managed modules can be enabled globally or provided by each application. For more information about the deployment of modules, see Chapter 12.

Modules and Configuration

For modules to provide certain features or services to IIS 7.0, the modules must be registered in the configuration system. This section of the book looks at the relationship between modules and various sections in the configuration file, and it provides a high-level overview of the module settings in the configuration store. For more information about the IIS 7.0

configuration system, which is based on Extended Markup Language (XML), see Chapter 4, "Understanding the Configuration System."

Inside the `<system.webServer>` section of the ApplicationHost.config file (the main server configuration file), there are three different sections related to modules:

■ **`<globalModules>`** Configurable at the server level only, this section defines all native code modules that will provide services for requests. The module declaration in the configuration section also specifies the related DLL file that provides the module's features. All native modules must be defined or registered in this section before they can be turned on or enabled for application usage as defined in the `<modules>` section.

```
// Example of <globalModules> configuration section
<globalModules>
...
<add name="StaticCompressionModule" image="%windir%\...\compstat.dll" />
<add name="DefaultDocumentModule" image="%windir%\...\defdoc.dll" />
<add name="DirectoryListingModule" image="%windir%\...\dirlist.dll" />
...
</globalModules>
```

■ **`<modules>`** Configurable at the server level and the application level, this section defines modules enabled for the application. Although native modules are registered in the `<globalModules>` section, native modules must be enabled in the `<modules>` section before they can provide their services for requests to applications. Managed code modules, however, can be added directly to the `<modules>` section. For example, you can add a custom managed basic authentication module to an application's Web.config file or you can deploy the ApplicationHost.config file at the server level.

```
// Example of <modules> configuration section
<modules>
...
<add name="BasicAuthenticationModule" />
<add name="WindowsAuthenticationModule" />
<add name="OutputCache" type="System.Web.Caching.OutputCacheModule"
 preCondition="managedHandler" />
<add name="Session" type="System.Web.SessionState.SessionStateModule"
 preCondition="managedHandler" />
...
</modules>
```

■ **`<handlers>`** Configurable at the server level, the application level, and the Uniform Resource Locator (URL) level, this section defines how requests are handled. It also maps handlers based on the URL and HTTP verbs, specifying the appropriate module that supports the related handler. By parsing the handler mapping configuration, IIS 7.0 determines which modules to call when a specific request comes in.

```
// Example of <handlers> configuration section
<handlers accessPolicy="Script, Read">
...
```

```
<add name="ASPClassic" path="*.asp" verb="GET,HEAD,POST"
 modules="IsapiModule" scriptProcessor="...\asp.dll" resourceType="File" />
<add name="SecurityCertificate" path="*.cer" verb="GET,HEAD,POST"
 modules="IsapiModule" scriptProcessor="...\asp.dll" resourceType="File" />
<add name="SSINC-stm" path="*.stm" verb="GET,POST"
 modules="ServerSideIncludeModule" resourceType="File" />
...
</handlers>
```

Key Benefits

The modular architecture in IIS 7.0 offers many advantages compared with previous versions of IIS. This section outlines the benefits derived from this design. It also provides scenarios illustrating how a Web administrator can take advantage of these benefits while building a robust Web server.

Security

Security is of the utmost concern when it comes to today's Web applications. IIS 6.0 is not installed by default except in the Windows Server 2003 Web Server edition. The IIS 6.0 default installation serves static content only. All other functionality is disabled. IIS 7.0 reflects the Web server's modular nature, enabling the user to install only the modules that are required for the application. Binaries that comprise the other features are not installed, but instead are kept in a protected operating system installation cache. This means that you will not be prompted for a CD or asked to point to a source location when installing new updates or adding features. The binaries that you are not using are not loaded by the IIS worker processes; rather, they are quarantined so that they cannot be accessed. When security updates from Microsoft are applied, the features that have not been installed will be fully updated in the installation cache. This can eliminate the need to reapply service packs when you install new features later.

From the security perspective, the modular design brings several key advantages including:

- **Minimized attack surface**   By giving you the power to install only those components that are needed, IIS 7.0 directly minimizes the areas of possible attack. The attack points are limited to the installed components because the binaries exist only for the installed components. Because only the installed components can be subject to potential exploits, this is the best defense. For example, with the IIS 7.0 default installation, about 10 components are installed to support internal IIS logging and management as well as serving static content requests. Technically speaking, these are the only surfaces that are exposed for potential attack.

- **Reduced maintenance overhead**   Modular design not only provides new flexibility when adding, removing, and even replacing components, it also provides a new maintenance experience through opt-in patching. You need apply fixes or patches only to required or installed components. Unused components or modules that have not been installed do not require *immediate* attention, and no downtime is required when patching components that are not installed. It also means that fewer administrative tasks are needed for routine maintenance and upgrades. For example, if an IIS 7.0 server uses Windows authentication only for its applications, only Windows authentication module patches are applicable to the server. On the other hand, if Basic authentication module is subject to a known exploit, immediate patching is not required because the module is not in use. Note, however, that Microsoft recommends that you apply all patches to ensure that modules and features you are not using will be current in the event they are installed later.

> **Important**   Microsoft recommends that you apply all patches to the server. When patching components that aren't in use, the server doesn't have to experience any downtime. If the components are eventually installed, the latest versions of their binaries will be used automatically, and there is no need to reapply any patches.

- **Unified Security Model**   IIS 7.0 is now better integrated with ASP.NET. Having both IIS 7.0 native modules and ASP.NET managed modules running in the same request pipeline yields many benefits including unifying the configuration system and security models for both IIS and ASP.NET. From the security perspective, ASP.NET advanced security services can be plugged in directly to the IIS main request processing pipeline and used together with the security features that IIS offers. In short, with IIS 7.0, it is now possible to configure ASP.NET security services for non-ASP.NET requests. For example, with earlier versions of IIS, if an application consists of both PHP and ASP.NET resources, ASP.NET Forms authentication can be applied to only ASP.NET resources. With the IIS 7.0 integrated process model, it is now possible to have Forms authentication for PHP, ASP.NET, as well as other types of resources such as static content (HTML, Images) and ASP pages.

Direct from the Source: The Most Secure Web Server in the World

The first time we presented IIS 7.0 to a large audience was also my first TechEd breakout session, hosted at TechEd 2005. My first demo showcased the componentization capabilities of IIS 7.0 by showing off what we jokingly called "the most secure Web server in the world."

As part of the demo, I walked through how to edit the configuration in the Application-Host.config file, removing all of the modules and handler mappings. After saving the file, IIS automatically picked up the changes and restarted, loading absolutely no modules. After making a request to the default Web site, I would swiftly get back an `empty 200` response (this configuration currently returns a `401 Unauthorized` error because no authentication modules are present). The server had no modules loaded and therefore would perform virtually no processing of the request and return no content, thus truly becoming the most secure Web server in the world. After a pause, I commented that, though secure, this server was also fairly useless, and then I segued into adding back the functionality that I needed for my application.

I had done this demo earlier for internal audiences to much acclaim, but I will always remember the audience reaction during that TechEd session. The people in the audience went wild, some even breaking into a standing ovation. This was a resounding confirmation of our efforts to give administrators the ability to start from nothing, building up the server with an absolutely minimal set of features to produce a simple-to-manage Web server with the least possible surface area.

Mike Volodarsky

IIS7 Core Server Program Manager

Performance

With its componentized architecture, IIS 7.0 provides very granular control when it comes to the Web server memory footprint. Modules are loaded into memory only if they are installed and enabled. By removing unnecessary IIS 7.0 features, fewer components are loaded in the processing pipeline—in other words, fewer steps are needed to fulfill incoming requests and, therefore, overall server performance improves. At the same time, by reducing memory usage for the IIS 7.0 server, more free memory space is available for the Web application and operating system. For example, in IIS 6.0, all authentication providers (Anonymous, Windows, Digest, and so on) are loaded in the worker process. In IIS 7.0, only the necessary authentication modules are loaded and included in the request processing. For more details on removing modules you do not require, see Chapter 12.

Extensibility

In earlier versions of IIS, extending or adding IIS features is not easy, because it can be done only through ISAPI programming with limited API support and limited access to information in the request processing pipeline. With the new modular-based engine and the tight integration between ASP.NET and IIS, extending IIS 7.0 is much easier. IIS 7.0 modules can be developed with the new native Web Server C++ API or using the ASP.NET interfaces and the functionality of the .NET Framework. Not only are you able to decide which features to include in the Web server, but you can also extend your Web server by adding your own custom components to provide specific functionality.

For example, you can develop an ASP.NET basic authentication module that uses the Membership service and a SQL Server user database in place of the built-in IIS Basic authentication feature that works only with Windows accounts. In short, you can build your own custom server to deliver the feature sets your applications require. You might, for example, deploy a set of IIS 7.0 servers just for caching purposes, or you might deploy a custom module to perform a specific function in an application such as implementing your own ASP.NET application load balancing algorithm based on customer requirements. For more information on customizing modules in IIS 7.0, see Chapter 12.

Built-in Modules

Modules shipped with IIS 7.0 are grouped into different categories according to the roles of the services they provide. Table 3-1 highlights the different service categories and lists sample built-in modules within those categories. A complete list of modules is included in Appendix C, "Module Listing."

Table 3-1   Module Categories

Category	Module
Application Development	CgiModule (%windir%\system32\inetsrv\cgi.dll)
	Facilitates support for Common Gateway Interface (CGI) programs
	FastCgiModule (%windir%\system32\inetsrv\iisfcgi.dll)
	Supports FastCGI, which provides a high-performance alternative to old-fashioned CGI-based programs
	System.Web.SessionState.SessionStateModule (ManagedEngine)
	Provides session state management, which enables storage of data specific to a single client within an application on the server
Health and Diagnostics	FailedRequestsTracingModule (%windir%\system32\inetsrv\iisfreb.dll)
	More commonly known as Failed Request Event Buffering (FREB), this module supports tracing of failed requests; the definition and rules defining a failed request can be configured
	RequestMonitorModule (%windir%\system32\inetsrv\iisreqs.dll)
	Implements the Run-time State and Control API (RSCA), which enables its consumers to query run-time information such as currently executing requests, the start or stop state of a Web site, or currently executing application domains
HTTP Features	ProtocolSupportModule (%windir%\system32\inetsrv\protsup.dll)
	Implements custom and redirect response headers, handles HTTP TRACE and OPTIONS verbs, and supports keep-alive configuration
Performance	TokenCacheModule (%windir%\system32\inetsrv\cachtokn.dll)
	Caches windows security tokens for password-based authentication schemes (anonymous authentication, basic authentication, and IIS client certificate authentication).
	System.Web.Caching.OutputCacheModule (ManagedEngine)
	Defines the output caching policies of an ASP.NET page or a user control contained in a page

Table 3-1   Module Categories

Category	Module
Security	RequestFilteringModule (%windir%\system32\inetsrv\modrqflt.dll)
	Provides URLSCAN-like functionality in IIS 7.0 by implementing a powerful set of security rules to reject suspicious requests at a very early stage
	UrlAuthorizationModule (%windir%\system32\inetsrv\urlauthz.dll)
	Supports rules-based configurations for content authorization
	System.Web.Security.FormsAuthenticationModule (ManagedEngine)
	Implements ASP.NET Forms authentication against requested resources
Server Components	ConfigurationValidationModule (%windir%\system32\inetsrv\validcfg.dll)
	Responsible for verifying IIS 7.0 configuration, such as when an application is running in Integrated mode but has handlers or modules declared in the `<system.web>` section
	ManagedEngine/ManagedEngine64 (webengine.dll)
	Managed Engine has a special place within all the other modules because it is responsible for integrating IIS with the ASP.NET run time

For more information regarding the module configuration store, module dependencies, and potential issues when a module is removed, see Appendix C.

Summary

The key features delivered by IIS 7.0 come from its modular design. This is the first time Web administrators have full control over the IIS server. It is also the first version of IIS that is fully extensible. It provides a unified request processing model that integrates ASP.NET and IIS. Modules are fundamental building blocks in IIS 7.0 server. IIS 7.0 provides numerous ways to manage modules (the basic units of the IIS feature set) so that you can implement efficient low-footprint Web servers optimized for a specific task. By choosing the right set of modules, you can enable a rich set of functionality on your server, or you can remove features you do not need so as to reduce the security surface area and improve performance. In Chapter 12, you can learn more about the different types of modules IIS 7.0 supports, how they work, and how to properly deploy and manage them in the IIS environment.

Additional Resources

These resources contain additional information and tools related to this chapter:

- Chapter 4, "Understanding the Configuration System," for information about the new XML–based configuration system and important configuration files in IIS 7.0.

- Chapter 12, "Managing Web Server Modules," for information about modules loading and managing modules in IIS 7.0.

- Chapter 13, "Managing Configuration and User Interface Extensions," for information about extending the IIS 7.0 configuration system.

- Chapter 14, "Implementing Security Strategies," for information about security strategies.

- Appendix C, "Module Listing," for information about the complete detail of each built-in module that shipped in IIS 7.0.

- "Develop a Native C\C++ Modules for IIS 7.0" article on the Web Resource page at *http://www.iis.net/go/938.*

Chapter 4
Understanding the Configuration System

 On the Disc Browse the CD for additional tools and resources.

Many of the new features and capabilities of Internet Information Services (IIS) 7.0 can be attributed to its entirely new configuration system. The metabase of old has been transformed into a .NET configuration–inspired system that is much easier on many levels to support. The new design provides the basis for delegated configuration, centralized configuration, ASP.NET integration, xcopy deployment of configuration, and many other benefits.

In many cases, the IIS 7.0 configuration system will "just work," and you won't need to know what's going on behind the scenes. However, when you add flexibility to a system, you often introduce complexity, which is the case with the IIS 7.0 configuration system. This chapter details the configuration's operation so that you'll have a thorough understanding of what's going on.

As shown in Figure 4-1, the configuration of IIS 7.0 as a whole is composed of several systems that work both together and independently. For administrators with an understanding of the .NET configuration files and how they work, IIS 7.0 configuration is a quick study. If your only exposure to IIS configuration has been using a tool such as Metabase Explorer, then there's a bigger—but worthwhile—learning curve.

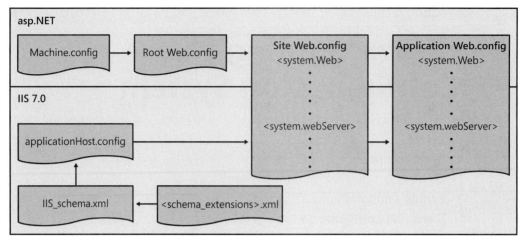

Figure 4-1   The IIS 7.0 configuration system.

Overview of the Configuration System

The IIS 7.0 configuration system is in many ways a complete departure from the metabase, the configuration model that previous IIS versions use. The new architecture reflects requirements that the IIS 7.0 configuration system be more manageable and flexible in supporting key deployment scenarios.

The IIS 7.0 configuration system is based on a hierarchy of XML configuration files, which contain structured XML data that describes the configuration information for IIS and its features. This hierarchy includes the .NET Framework configuration files, machine.config and root web.config; the main IIS configuration file called applicationHost.config; and distributed web.config configuration files located inside the Web site directory structure. One key benefit of this hierarchy is the ability to unify the location of IIS and ASP.NET configuration information. The other is the ability to include IIS configuration together with the Web site's content, which makes the Web site portable and alleviates the need to have administrative privileges to deploy the Web site.

The configuration files in the hierarchy contain configuration sections, which are structured XML elements that describe configuration settings for specific IIS features. Unlike the property/value model used by the metabase, the structured XML nature of the IIS 7.0 configuration sections helps the configuration become cleaner and easier to understand. This makes configuration self-explanatory, and you can easily edit it by hand. For example, the application developer can place the following configuration in a web.config file located in the root of the Web site to enable the IIS default document feature and configure a specific default document to be used.

```
<system.webServer>
  <defaultDocument enabled="true">
    <files>
      <add value="home.aspx" />
```

```
    </files>
   </defaultDocument>
 </system.webServer>
```

Because the IIS 7.0 configuration system uses the same web.config files as the ASP.NET configuration system, your application can provide both ASP.NET and IIS configuration settings side by side in the same file. Because this file travels with your application content, it enables the application to be deployed to an IIS server simply by copying its contents, without having to modify any central configuration.

At the same time, the server administrator can place server-level IIS configuration, such as the Web site and Application pool definitions, in the server-level applicationHost.config file. This file can also contain the default configuration for other IIS sections, which are by default inherited by all Web sites on the server. Unlike the Web site's web.config files, which may be accessible to the Web site or application administrator, applicationHost.config is accessible only to the server administrator. Using the configuration-locking mechanisms that the configuration system provides, the administrator can specify which configuration can be modified by applications through the use of distributed web.config files.

All in all, the new configuration file hierarchy offers a lot more flexibility than the IIS 6.0 metabase and enables key deployment and management scenarios. Next, we will look at how the configuration file hierarchy works and the syntax of configuration sections.

Configuration File Hierarchy

The metabase in previous versions of IIS was comprised of a single configuration file, Metabase.xml, that contained a URL-centric configuration tree. Nodes of that tree corresponded to URLs on the server, and each node contained a set of properties that specified the configuration for that URL along with properties inherited from parent nodes. If you are familiar with the IIS 6.0 metabase, you may remember that these nodes are addressed via paths that look something like "LM\W3SVC\1\ROOT", which translates to "the root of the Web site with ID of 1."

In IIS 7.0, configuration file hierarchy includes multiple configuration files. Instead of encoding the entire URL hierarchy in a single file, the configuration file hierarchy maps to the URL hierarchy. Each file defines configuration that is implicitly associated with a specific URL level based on the position of this file in the configuration hierarchy. For example, application-Host.config contains global settings applying to all sites on the server, and web.config, contained in the Web site root, is site-specific—and when contained in an application directory, it is directory-specific. Web.config typically maps to a URL such as *http://www.contoso.com/ appfolder*. Note that the use of web.config to contain distributed configuration information is optional (but enabled by default for certain settings). ApplicationHost.config can and often does contain site- and application-specific settings. There are other configuration files involved with IIS 7.0 that we will discuss later in the chapter, but for the sake of simplicity, we'll focus on the files used to configure sites and applications, as listed in Table 4-1.

Table 4-1   IIS 7.0 Configuration Files

File	Location	Configuration Path
machine.config	%windir%\Microsoft .NET\Framework \ <version>\config	MACHINE
root web.config	%windir%\Microsoft .NET\Framework \ <version>\config	MACHINE/WEBROOT
applicationHost.config	%windir%\system32\ inetsrv\config	MACHINE/WEBROOT/APPHOST
distributed web.config files	Web site directory structure	MACHINE/WEBROOT/APPHOST /<SiteName>/<VirtualPath>

Just like the metabase, the IIS 7.0 configuration system uses a *configuration path* to describe the level in the configuration hierarchy where a particular configuration setting is set. This level corresponds both to the URL namespace at which the configuration is effective and a configuration path used in commands (such as when using Appcmd) to reference the correct configuration store. In this way, the IIS 7.0 configuration file hierarchy maps to the URL namespace and can correspond to an actual configuration file where this configuration is set.

When the configuration system retrieves configuration for a specific configuration path, it merges the contents of each configuration file corresponding to each segment of the path, building an effective configuration set for that path. This works well with the ability to specify distributed web.config files inside the Web site's directory structure, which may enable any part of the Web site to set specific configuration for its URL namespace simply by including it in a web.config file in the corresponding directory.

In this system, the configuration path for a particular URL becomes MACHINE/WEBROOT/ APPHOST/<SiteName>/<VirtualPath>, where the <SiteName> is the name of the site and the <VirtualPath> is the URL's virtual path. When reading configuration for this path, the server will merge the configuration in machine.config, root web.config, applicationHost.config, and all distributed web.config files that exist in the physical directories corresponding to each segment of the virtual path, starting with the site's root.

> **Important**   The root web.config corresponding to WEBROOT in the configuration system is the one located in %windir%\Microsoft .NET\Framework \<version>\config. This is not the same as a web.config file that can placed in a Web site's home directory, which is often referred to as the *web root*. In the first case, we are talking about web.config used by .NET that is the parent, or root of all Web site web.config files. In the latter case, we're talking about the web.config found in a Web site's home folder. The web.config in the Web site's home folder will inherit configuration settings found in the .NET root web.config.

Server-level configuration for IIS features is stored in the applicationHost.config file. This file stores configuration for sections that only make sense globally on the server, as well as configuration defaults for other sections that are inherited by all URLs on the server unless another file lower in the configuration hierarchy overrides them.

For example, if you wanted to configure the server to disable directory browsing by default, you would put that configuration in the applicationHost.config file. Then, if you wanted to allow directory browsing for the /App1 application in the default Web site, you would place a web.config file containing configuration that enables directory browsing in the physical directory root of the /App1 application. When a request is made to the root of the default Web site, the server will read configuration for the "MACHINE/WEBROOT/APPHOST/ Default Web Site/" path and apply the inherited configuration from applicationHost.config that disables the directory browsing. However, when an HTTP request is made to the /App1 application, the server will read configuration for "MACHINE/WEBROOT/APPHOST/Default Web Site/App1/", which merges the configuration set by the application's web.config and enables directory browsing for that URL.

machine.config and root web.config

Even though machine.config and the root.web.config are .NET Framework configuration files, they are read and mapped in by the IIS configuration system. This allows IIS 7.0 to share its configuration with ASP.NET in site and application web.config files, consume .NET modules in the managed pipeline, and integrate .NET configuration that is enabled in the IIS Manager. As previously mentioned, machine.config contains machine-wide .NET Framework configuration settings loaded by all .NET applications on the machine, and root web.config contains ASP.NET-specific configuration settings loaded by all ASP.NET applications. These files are modifiable only by machine administrators.

These files are located in the %windir%\Microsoft .NET\.NET Framework \<version>\config, where the <version> is determined by the *managedRuntimeVersion* setting for the application pool within which the configuration is being read. This way, IIS application pools that are set to use different versions of the .NET Framework automatically include the configuration files for the right .NET Framework version. Note that as in IIS 6.0, an application pool cannot host more than one version of the .NET Framework.

applicationHost.config

The main IIS configuration file is applicationHost.config, which is located in the %windir%\ system32\ inetsrv\config directory. It is modifiable only by machine administrators.

ApplicationHost.config contains configuration sections and settings that only make sense globally on the server. For example, it contains site, application, and virtual directory definitions in the <sites> section and the application pool definitions for the <applicationPools> section. Other global sections include the <globalModules> configuration section, which contains a list of native modules that are loaded by all IIS worker processes, and the <httpCompression> section that lists enabled compression schemes and content types that can be compressed.

These sections cannot be overridden at lower levels, and the server only reads them at the MACHINE/WEBROOT/APPHOST level.

ApplicationHost.config also stores all of the default settings for IIS configuration sections, which are inherited by all other URLs unless another configuration file lower in the configuration hierarchy overrides them. In fact, if you examine the contents of applicationHost.config, you will see that it declares all IIS configuration sections.

```
<configSections>
    <sectionGroup name="system.applicationHost">
        <section name="applicationPools" allowDefinition="AppHostOnly"
overrideModeDefault="Deny" />
        <section name="sites" allowDefinition="AppHostOnly"
overrideModeDefault="Deny" />
        <section name="webLimits" allowDefinition="AppHostOnly"
overrideModeDefault="Deny" />
        …
    </sectionGroup>

    <sectionGroup name="system.webServer">
        <section name="asp" overrideModeDefault="Deny" />
        <section name="caching" overrideModeDefault="Allow" />
        <section name="cgi" overrideModeDefault="Deny" />
        <section name="defaultDocument" overrideModeDefault="Allow" />
        <section name="directoryBrowse" overrideModeDefault="Allow" />
        …
    </sectionGroup>
</configSections>
```

You may notice that these section definitions include an element named *allowDefinition* that is set in our example to "AppHostOnly". The *allowDefinition* settings assign a scope to the section that limits where the section can be used. In this case, the Sites section can only be used in applicationHost.config and is not legal in any other location. It is strongly recommended that you do not edit the *allowDefinition* settings from the defaults.

Finally, this file also contains information about which configuration sections are allowed to be overridden by lower configuration levels, and which are not. Child override is controlled by the *overrideModeDefault* attribute in the example just provided of the configuration sections declarations. The server administrator can use this attribute to control the delegation of IIS features to the site administrators. We will review controlling section delegation in the Delegating Configuration section of this chapter.

Distributed web.config Files

The IIS 7.0 configuration hierarchy enables the site directory structure to contain web.config configuration files. These files can specify new configuration settings or override configuration settings set at the server level for the URL namespace corresponding to the directory where they are located (assuming the configuration sections used are unlocked by the administrator).

This is the foundation for the delegated configuration scenario, which enables applications to specify required IIS settings together with their content, and which makes simple xcopy deployment possible.

Finally, because the ASP.NET configuration system also reads these files, they can contain both IIS and ASP.NET configuration settings.

redirection.config

You will also find redirection.config located in the %windir%\system32\ inetsrv\config directory, and it is used to store configuration settings for Shared Configuration. It is not part of the IIS 7.0 configuration hierarchy, but the configuration system uses it to set up redirection for the applicationHost.config file.

When in use, it specifies the location and access details required for IIS 7.0 to load application-Host.config from a remote network location, instead of the local inetsrv\config directory. This enables multiple IIS 7.0 servers to share a central configuration file for ease of management. You can learn more about shared configuration in the "Sharing Configuration Between Servers" section of this chapter.

administration.config

The IIS Manager tool uses administration.config (also not part of the IIS 7.0 configuration hierarchy) exclusively to specify its own configuration. It is also located in the %windir%\system32\ inetsrv\config directory.

Among other things, administration.config contains the list of IIS Manager extensions that the tool loads. These extensions provide the features you see in the IIS Manager. Like IIS, the IIS Manager is fully extensible. You can learn more about the extensibility model provided by IIS Manager and how its extensions are configured in Chapter 12, "Managing Web Server Modules."

Temporary Application Pool .config Files

One of the new IIS 7.0 features is enhanced Application Pool Isolation. At run time, IIS 7.0 reads applicationHost.config configuration and generates filtered copies of it for each application pool, writing them to:

```
%systemdrive%\inetpub\temp\appPools\<ApplicationPoolName>.config
```

The filtered configuration files contain only the application pool definitions for the current application pool (other application pool definitions that may contain custom application pool identities are filtered out). Also removed are all site definitions and site-specific configuration specified in location tags for sites that do not have applications in the current application pool.

The temporary configuration file created for each application pool is protected in such a way that only the application pool for which it is created can read the file. This ensures that no worker process (application pool) can read the configuration settings for any other worker process.

The application pool configuration files are not intended to be used for updates, and neither administrators nor developers should edit them directly or indirectly. Their use is completely transparent, but it is part of the configuration system, so we thought it should be called out here. For more details, see Chapter 14, "Implementing Security Strategies."

Configuration File Syntax

Each configuration file uses special XML elements called *configuration sections* to specify configuration information. A configuration section is the basic unit of configuration, typically defining the behavior of a specific part or feature in the Web server.

Here is an example of a configuration file that specifies multiple configuration sections:

```
<?xml version="1.0" encoding="UTF-8"?>
<configuration>

    <system.webServer>

        <asp>
            <cache diskTemplateCacheDirectory="%SystemDrive%\inetpub\temp\
ASP Compiled Templates" />
        </asp>
        <defaultDocument enabled="true">
            <files>
                <add value="index.html" />
                <add value="default.aspx" />
            </files>
        </defaultDocument>

        <directoryBrowse enabled="false" />

    </system.webServer>
<configuration>
```

As you can see, this is a well-formed XML file, with a mandatory root <configuration> element that contains multiple subelements. These subelements are either configuration section elements directly, or *section group* elements such as <system.webServer>. Section groups do not define any settings, they simply group related section elements together. For example, all of the IIS Web server features are under the <system.webServer> section group. Sections are the elements, shown in bold, that contain specific configuration settings.

The configuration section elements each follow a specific structure defined by their schema, which controls what attributes and child elements are allowed inside the section, the type of data they can contain, and various other configuration syntax restrictions. The schema information is provided inside configuration schema files registered with the IIS 7.0 configuration system. Unlike the ASP.NET configuration system, which uses code to define the structure of its configuration, the IIS 7.0 configuration system is based entirely on declarative schema information. We will examine this schema mechanism a little later in the chapter.

In addition to section groups and configuration sections themselves, configuration files can also contain *section declarations* and *location tags*. Section declarations are necessary to declare a particular section before it can be used, and they also indicate what section group the section belongs to. Location tags enable configuration to be scoped to a specific configuration path, rather than to the entire namespace to which the current configuration file corresponds.

Direct from the Source: Working Around Limits on web.config File Size

By default, the IIS 7.0 configuration system enforces a limit of 100 KB on the file size of web.config files. This is for security purposes, to avoid possible denial-of-service attacks on the server by providing very large configuration files.

In most cases, this size should be sufficient for most situations, but what if your configuration file is bigger than 100 KB? This can happen for applications that use web.config files extensively to store custom configuration. To allow these larger files, you can override the maximum limit by adding a registry key. Create the following key.

```
HKLM\Software\Microsoft\InetStp\Configuration
```

Then create a DWORD value.

```
MaxWebConfigFileSizeInKB
```

Set this value to the file size in kilobytes (make sure you select Decimal when entering the value) to set this as a new machine-wide limit on web.config file size.

Section Declarations

Each section that is used in a configuration file contains a *section declaration* in applicationHost.config. Section declarations are generally created during the installation of the feature and do not typically need to be added manually. For example, following is an excerpt from the applicationHost.config configuration file that declares all IIS configuration sections.

```
    <configSections>
        <sectionGroup name="system.applicationHost">
            <section name="applicationPools" allowDefinition="AppHostOnly"
overrideModeDefault="Deny" />
            <section name="sites" allowDefinition="AppHostOnly"
overrideModeDefault="Deny" />
        </sectionGroup>
        <sectionGroup name="system.webServer">
```

```
        <section name="asp" overrideModeDefault="Deny" />
        <section name="defaultDocument" overrideModeDefault="Allow" />
        <section name="directoryBrowse" overrideModeDefault="Allow" />
        <sectionGroup name="security">
            <sectionGroup name="authentication">
                <section name="anonymousAuthentication" overrideModeDefault="Deny" />
                <section name="basicAuthentication" overrideModeDefault="Deny" />
            </sectionGroup>
            <section name="authorization" overrideModeDefault="Allow" />
        </sectionGroup>
    </sectionGroup>
</configSections>
```

This fragment defines a number of IIS configuration sections, including the global <sites> and <applicationPools> sections read by WAS, and various sections for Web server features, including <asp> and <anonymousAuthentication>. You'll also notice that these sections are nested within the appropriate section groups. Section declarations can specify a number of properties that control where the section is available, including *allowDefinition,* which determines at which level in the configuration hierarchy the section can be used, and *overrideModeDefault,* which determines if lower configuration levels can use the section by default. After the section is declared, it can be used in the current configuration file or anywhere lower in the configuration file hierarchy, meaning it does not need to be re-declared in configuration files below (re-declaring this section will actually result in a configuration error). In fact, all IIS configuration sections are declared in applicationHost.config and therefore are available in any Web site web.config configuration file. The *allowDefinition* and *overrideModeDefault* attributes control the actual ability to use this configuration section in the lower levels.

Section Groups

You use *section group* elements to group related configuration sections together. When you declare each section, it specifies which section group it belongs to by placing its <section> element within the corresponding <sectionGroup> element. This implicitly declares the section group itself. Section groups cannot define any attributes and therefore do not carry any configuration information of their own. Section groups can be nested within one another, but sections cannot. Think of section groups as a namespace qualification for sections.

When specifying the configuration section, you must place it inside the section group element according to the declaration. For example, when providing configuration for the <authorization> section, which is declared in the <system.webServer>/<security> section group, the configuration section must be nested in the corresponding section group elements as follows.

```
<configuration>
    <system.webServer>
        <security>
            <authorization bypassLoginPages="true" />
        </security>
    </system.webServer>

</configuration>
```

Table 4-2 lists most of the section groups you will find in the IIS 7.0 configuration system by default, what configuration they contain, and where they are declared.

Table 4-2   Section Groups

Section Group	Description	Declared In
system.applicationHost	Contains global protocol-neutral IIS configuration used by the Windows Process Activation Service, including <sites>, <applicationPools>, <listenerAdapters>, and more	applicationHost.config
system.webServer	Contains all configuration for the IIS Web server engine and features, including <modules>, <handlers>, <serverRuntime>, <asp>, <defaultDocument>, and dozens more; also contains several child section groups	applicationHost.config
system.webServer /security	Contains security-related Web server configuration, including <authorization>, <isapiCgiRestriction>, <requestFiltering> and more	applicationHost.config
system.webServer /security /authentication	Contains configuration for all authentication Web server features, including <anonymousAuthentication>, <windowsAuthentication>, and more	applicationHost.config
system.webServer /tracing	Contains configuration for tracing Web server features, including <traceFailedRequests> and <traceProviderDefinitions>	applicationHost.config
system.web	Contains all ASP.NET configuration	Framework machine.config

Not listed in Table 4-2, for the sake of brevity, are section groups declared in .NET's machine.config. These sections control various aspects of the .NET Framework behavior, including system.net, system.xml.serialization, and others.

Sections

The *configuration section* is the focus of the IIS 7.0 configuration system, because it is the basic unit of configuration. Each configuration section has a specific structure defined by its schema, containing specific attributes, elements, and collections of elements necessary to express the required configuration for the corresponding IIS feature.

A configuration section may contain 0 or more of the elements (depending on the schema) shown in Table 4-3.

Table 4-3 Configuration Section Elements

Element	Description
Attributes	A named XML attribute, using a type specified in the schema. Supported types include int, string, timespan, enumerations, and others. Attributes may have associated validation rules, which restrict the allowed values. They may also have additional metadata such as default values, or they may specify whether or not the attribute must be specified when the section is used.
Child elements	Child XML elements, which in turn can contain attributes and other child elements.
Collections	A collection is a child element that can contain a list of other child elements (typically <add>, <remove>, and <clear>) that can be used to create lists of configuration items. Collection elements have metadata associated with them that define their behavior, including what attributes serve as collection item keys, the order in which collection items are added when collections are merged between configuration files, and more.

Most configuration sections specify default values for all of the attributes in their schema. This becomes the default configuration for that section if it's not defined in any configuration file (by default, collections are always empty). Each configuration file can specify the section element to explicitly set the value of one or more attributes, or modify the collections in the section. The section can be specified at multiple configuration files, in which case when the configuration system retrieves the contents of this section for a particular configuration path, it merges the contents of all instances of this section. Merging attributes overrides the values specified in the configuration levels above, and merging collections adds/removes/clears items in collections based on the usage of collection elements.

For example, here are the contents of a web.config file that you could place in the root of a PHP application. The contents contain the configuration for the <defaultDocument> section and enable the index.php page to serve as a default document.

```
<configuration>
  <system.webServer>
    <defaultDocument enabled="true">
      <files>
        <add value="index.php" />
      </files>
    </defaultDocument>
  </system.webServer>
</configuration>
```

This configuration overrides the global *enabled* attribute set in applicationHost.config or a higher order web.config, setting its value to "true". It also adds a new item to the *<files>* collection to enable "index.php" to serve as a default document. If configuration files earlier in the hierarchy defined other default document types in the *<files>* collection, then the effective collection for your application would contain those items plus the item we just added at our scope. Likewise, if the parent configuration files disabled the default document feature by setting its *enabled* attribute to "false", our configuration will override that value for the application.

The section titled "Editing Configuration" later in this chapter discusses setting configuration by specifying configuration sections.

Configuration Section Schema

All IIS configuration sections are defined in the IIS_Schema.xml file located in a schema file in the %windir%\system32\inetsrv\config\schema directory. To learn more about the syntax of each configuration section, you can review its schema. For example, here is an excerpt from the schema definition for the <defaultDocument> configuration section.

```
<sectionSchema name="system.webServer/defaultDocument">
  <attribute name="enabled" type="bool" defaultValue="true" />
  <element name="files">
    <collection addElement="add" clearElement="clear" removeElement="remove"
mergeAppend="false">
      <attribute name="value" type="string" isUniqueKey="true"/>
    </collection>
  </element>
</sectionSchema>
```

The schema contains the definitions for the "enabled" attribute and the <files> collection that we used earlier to set default document configuration. As you can see, the schema contains more information than just the structure of the configuration section—it also contains various metadata about the format and behavior of attributes and collections, including the types for attributes and which attributes serve as unique keys for collections. The <defaultDocument> section is a fairly simple section, so it doesn't fully illustrate the flexibility of section schema information, but it is a good example of how you can use the schema information to define configuration sections and control their behavior.

> **Note**   When working with IIS configuration, you will likely never have to work with section schema. However, it is useful to know where the schema information is located if you need a reference for the structure and semantics of IIS configuration sections. You should *never* attempt to modify the IIS schema files. However, if you are developing new IIS features, you can publish custom configuration schema files into the inetsrv\config\schema directory in order to use new configuration sections with the IIS configuration system.

In the schema directory, you will also find the FX_schema.xml and ASPNET_schema.xml files, which contain the schema definitions for .NET Framework and ASP.NET configuration sections respectively.

The IIS 7.0 configuration system is fully extensible. Custom configuration sections registered with the IIS 7.0 configuration schema will have their own schema files published in the schema directory.

Location Tags

By default, configuration specified in a particular configuration file applies to the entire URL namespace corresponding to that file. For example, configuration set in applicationHost.config applies to the entire server, and configuration set in the site's root web.config file applies to the entire site (unless overridden by more specific web.config files). This works most of the time. However, in some cases it is necessary to apply configuration to a specific subset of the URL namespace, or to a specific URL. *Location tags* are the mechanism that enables this by specifying a configuration path for which all configuration specified within a location tag applies.

Here is an example of using a location tag to scope configuration to a specific Web site.

```
<location path="Default Web Site">
    <system.webServer>
        <directoryBrowse enabled="true" />
    </system.webServer>
</location>
```

This location tag, when specified in applicationHost.config, applies the <directoryBrowse> configuration section to the "MACHINE/WEBHOST/APPHOST/Default Web Site/" configuration path.

You can find Location tags in use with three common scenarios in IIS 7.0:

1. Defining site-specific directory or file configuration in applicationHost.config. This is necessary to apply specific configuration for a content in a Web site without defining it in the site's web.config. For example, this is the technique commonly used by shared hosting servers to set site-specific configuration without giving the site administrators control over that configuration. When making changes to configuration in the IIS Manager or one of the programmatic interfaces, if a setting is not delegated, it is written to applicationHost.config by using location tags.

2. Locking or unlocking a specific configuration section for a particular configuration path. By placing a configuration section inside the location tag for a particular path, you can use the *overrideMode* attribute on the location tag to lock or unlock this configuration section for that path. For example, this is necessary for configuration sections declared with overrideModeDefault = Deny so that you can allow delegated configuration in web.config files.

3. Specifying configuration for a specific nonphysical URL. If you need to apply specific configuration to a URL that does not correspond to a physical directory (a file or a virtual URL), it's necessary to define it using a location tag inside a physical parent directory.

   You can use a location tag to keep all of the configuration for a site or application in a single web.config file, instead of placing pieces of it in many different web.config files in various subdirectories.

We will discuss using location tags in more detail later in this chapter.

The IIS 7.0 Configuration System and the IIS 6.0 Metabase

So far, we've been discussing in some detail the contents and mechanics of the configuration system, but we should back up a bit and discuss applicationHost.config itself rather than its contents.

Differences Between the IIS 7.0 Configuration System and the IIS 6.0 Metabase

The IIS 6.0 configuration store is Metabase.xml and is stored in %windir%\system32\inetsrv. For IIS 7.0, Metabase.xml is transformed into applicationHost.config located in %windir%\system32\inetsrv\config.

Why did the IIS team invest such time and effort in a wholesale change to the structure and mechanics of the configuration system? Primarily to make a quantum leap in performance, scale, and manageability. The IIS 6.0 configuration system is based on a system conceived and implemented with IIS 4.0 that was part of Windows NT. It was time to rebuild with a new set of design criteria.

The resulting system is quite a bit more complex because it is very ambitious. Yet at the same time, it is more manageable, scalable, and flexible. Table 4-4 compares some of the key differences between the IIS 6.0 metabase and the IIS 7.0 configuration files.

Table 4-4   Metabase.xml Comparison to IIS 7.0 Configuration System

Feature	IIS 6.0 Metabase.xml	IIS 7.0 Configuration System	Why This Matters
Delegated configuration	Not possible—all configuration is centrally stored and requires Administrative privileges to change	Enables both administrator-controlled configuration in applicationHost.config and delegated configuration in web.config files	Administrators can delegate configuration tasks to application owners; applications can be xcopy-deployed with all of their configuration
Structural organization	Properties are not grouped	Provides a hierarchy of section groups, sections, elements, and subelements	Easy to read, search, and manage; enables use of shorter element name because each item is logically grouped in a section rather than in a flat listing
Simplified description of properties with multiple values	Uses multi-sz key types and bit masks to handle multiple element values such as NT Authentication-Providers	Uses collections with simple add/remove/clear syntax based on .NET Framework configuration syntax and usage	Easier to read, edit, and query settings that can have multiple values

Table 4-4   Metabase.xml Comparison to IIS 7.0 Configuration System

Feature	IIS 6.0 Metabase.xml	IIS 7.0 Configuration System	Why This Matters
Memory vs. file-based configuration	Metabase is a memory construct that is written to Metabase.xml; synchronization issues can occur	Configuration is file-based; configuration writes are persisted directly to the configuration files	IIS configuration is always fully represented in .config files
Schema extensibilty	Difficult to extend for use with custom apps; inhibits innovation from the community	Based on IIS_Schema.xml; schema easily extended with XML snippets	Enables application developers to easily integrate application settings into IIS 7.0

IIS 6.0 Metabase Compatibility

Despite the complete overhaul of the configuration system, IIS 7.0 continues to maintain backward compatibility with existing configuration scripts and tools that target the metabase for configuring the server.

This is accomplished by providing a metabase emulation layer that enables the metabase APIs, exposed through the Active Base Objects (ABO) interfaces on which all other metabase tools and scripting APIs are based. The metabase emulation layer, called the ABO Mapper, provides immediate translation of the metabase configuration structure and actions triggered by callers to the new configuration system. This maps all writes and reads to the metabase to the corresponding IIS 7.0 configuration.

This service performance is transparent to the caller so that the existing installers, configuration scripts, and tools continue to work as if they were working on IIS 6.0. The ABO Mapper makes a best-effort attempt to map all IIS 6.0 metabase properties to the corresponding IIS 7.0 configuration properties that have a known mapping. In the end, virtually all metabase properties can be successfully mapped to the IIS 7.0 configuration, with rare exceptions.

Note   You can find documentation that describes how IIS 6.0 metabase properties map to the new IIS 7.0 configuration schema at *http://msdn2.microsoft.com/en-us/library/aa347565.aspx*.

Metabase compatibility is not enabled by default, and you don't need it if you are not running any legacy IIS 6.0 configuration scripts or using third-party installers that require ABO. If you are, though, you will need to install the IIS 6.0 Metabase Compatibility component from the IIS/Metabase Compatibility category in the Turn Windows Features On And Off page of Control Panel\Programs And Features on Windows Vista, or the IIS role in the Server Manager tool on Windows Server 2008, as shown in Figure 4-2.

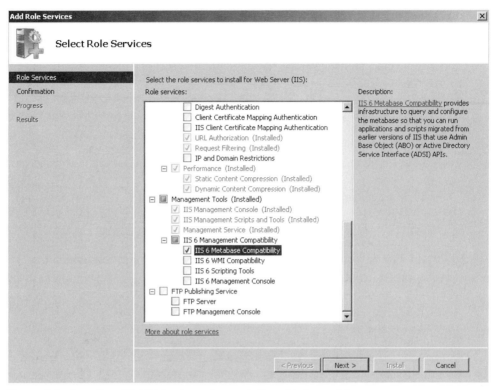

Figure 4-2   Installing IIS 6.0 Metabase Compatibility with Server Manager.

You can also chose to install the legacy IIS 6.0 configuration scripts from the IIS 6.0 Metabase Compatibility category, which provides scripts such as adsutil.vbs and iisweb.vbs. However, we recommend that for your configuration scripts and programs, you start to use the new configuration tools and APIs that the IIS 7.0 configuration system provides.

IIS 7.0 and the .NET Configuration Systems

The .NET configuration files on IIS 7.0 (machine.config, root web.config, and application web.config) behave exactly the same as they do on IIS 6.0. In fact, the .NET configuration system isn't really aware it's running on IIS 7.0 and does not read any of the IIS 7.0 configuration settings. However, IIS 7.0 is very aware of .NET. The IIS 7.0 configuration hierarchy includes the server-level .NET configuration files, machine.config and root web.config (in addition to applicationHost.config), but the .NET configuration system does not include IIS configuration stored in applicationHost.config.

One of the primary benefits of this design is that IIS 7.0 configuration settings can be stored in the same distributed web.config configuration files as the ASP.NET configuration settings. This enables applications to contain all of the configuration they need to run on the IIS platform in the web.config file, and it also enables simple xcopy deployment.

From a developer perspective, it also enables managed modules developed for IIS 7.0 to access .NET configuration by using IIS 7.0 Microsoft.Web.Administration and other .NET classes in the same way they can access IIS 7.0 configuration sections. Likewise, the IIS 7.0 configuration APIs can be used to manage the .NET configuration sections in automated deployment and management scenarios.

In addition, the IIS Manager tool exposes a number of ASP.NET configuration features. For example, you can configure database connection strings in the IIS Manager instead of having to open up the .config file. IIS Manager also enables you to manage users and roles by using the .NET role and membership providers. This is very useful for managing user information for features such as forms authentication and storing IIS Manager users. You can learn more about IIS Manager support for ASP.NET features in Chapter 6, "Using IIS Manager."

The unification of the .NET and IIS 7.0 configuration hierarchies does pose a few issues that stem from the fact that the two configuration systems have completely separate implementations, yet they work with the same configuration hierarchy and configuration sections. The fact that the ASP.NET configuration system does not read IIS 7.0 configuration sections eliminates a lot of potential problems with the differences in behavior. However, some problems do still exist.

One of the key limitations stems from the difference in encryption support between the two configuration systems. The .NET configuration files may contain user names and passwords that the developer can encrypt. This way, when you view the .config file, you see an encrypted secret rather than plain text. The problem arises because IIS 7.0 and the .NET configuration system use different methods for encrypting secrets. The .NET configuration system supports section-level encryption, which encrypts the entire contents of the configuration section. The IIS 7.0 configuration system supports only attribute-level encryption, which encrypts specific attributes. Because of this, if you attempt to read an encrypted ASP.NET configuration section through the IIS 7.0 configuration system or any of the APIs that use it, you will receive an error. For example, this will happen if you encrypt any of the configuration sections that the IIS Manager uses to administer ASP.NET functionality. Likewise, you cannot encrypt ASP.NET configuration sections with IIS 7.0 configuration encryption because ASP.NET will fail to read their contents. For more details on this issue and how to solve it, see Chapter 14. Another limitation stems from the lack of a versioning mechanism for the .NET configuration schema files provided by the IIS 7.0 configuration system. As of this writing, the IIS 7.0 configuration system provides schema files only for the .NET Framework 2.0 configuration, and therefore IIS 7.0 might experience problems when writing configuration to configuration files for .NET Framework 1.1 or future versions of the .NET Framework. Moreover, some of the tools in the IIS 7.0 configuration stack, including Appcmd.exe, can't write to .NET Framework configuration files for versions other then 2.0. Future versions of IIS may address this problem.

The use of IIS 7.0 configuration in ASP.NET web.config files may also create a problem for ASP.NET applications that are using .NET Framework 1.1. This is because the ASP.NET configuration system is not aware of the IIS 7.0 configuration sections located in the

<system.webServer> section group (or any custom configuration sections you create using the IIS 7.0 section extensibility mechanism), and the configuration system will generate an error when it encounters these sections in web.config files. ASP.NET 2.0 includes a special configuration declaration in machine.config that maps <system.webServer> to a special configuration section handler type that ignores the sections when they are found.

```
<section name="system.webServer" type="System.Configuration.IgnoreSection,
System.Configuration, Version=2.0.0.0, Culture=neutral, PublicKeyToken=b03f5f7f11d50a3a" />
```

However, ASP.NET 1.1 does not include this special configuration declaration because ASP.NET was released long before IIS 7.0 development began. Therefore, you may need to manually add this section declaration for <system.webServer> and other custom IIS 7.0 sections/section groups so that you can use them in web.config files.

Editing Configuration

The IIS 7.0 configuration system provides a lot of flexibility for editing server configuration. Because the configuration is stored in plain-text XML files and uses a well-structured, human-readable syntax, you can edit it manually using Notepad or your favorite text editor. In fact, many people prefer this approach when editing configuration for distributed web.config files located within the site's directory structure.

In addition to enabling configuration to be edited by hand, IIS 7.0 provides a complete administration stack that offers tools and APIs for editing configuration. This includes the IIS Manager, a completely redesigned GUI task-based experience for managing most of the IIS 7.0 configuration. It also includes the Appcmd command line tool, which you can use to edit configuration quickly from the command line. Finally, it includes several administrative scripts and APIs for editing configuration programmatically, including the IIS 7.0 configuration COM objects that can be accessed from native C++ programs (called the Application Host Administration objects or AHADMIN) and Windows scripts, a WMI provider, and new Microsoft.Web.Administration APIs for managing configuration from .NET programs.

> **Note**   Where possible, use tools to manipulate IIS 7.0 configuration instead of changing configuration by hand. This is much easier and provides protection against generating incorrect configuration.

In fact, you should choose to use tools to edit the configuration on the server, because doing so ensures that you are interacting correctly with the underlying complexity of the configuration system and guarantees that the configuration is written using the correct syntax. The IIS Manager is a great way to do this, because it provides a simplified task-based view of many IIS 7.0 features, so you don't need to understand their configuration structure. You can read about managing IIS 7.0 with the IIS Manager in Chapter 6.

However, there are times when you need to specify configuration by hand or use one of the lower-level tools like Appcmd or programmatic interfaces like the Microsoft.Web.Administration namespace provided in .NET. In this case, you do need to understand the structure of configuration sections and inheritance behavior of the configuration hierarchy in order to do this correctly. In the remainder of this section, we will discuss the basics of editing IIS 7.0 configuration that will help you to do it correctly.

> **Note**   Use Appcmd to edit configuration in situations in which IIS Manager does not expose the desired configuration functionality. Appcmd can perform most configuration tasks you can do by hand, and it offers the benefit of additional validation. It also allows you to perform configuration tasks in an automated fashion on other machines if needed. For more information on using Appcmd, see Chapter 7, "Using Command Line Tools."

> **Caution**   Before modifying configuration, always make sure you have a backup of the current state so you can come back to it if necessary. See the section titled "Backing Up Configuration" later in this chapter for more information on how to easily back up and restore IIS configuration.

Deciding Where to Place Configuration

Earlier in the chapter, I described the IIS 7.0 configuration hierarchy. This hierarchy contains multiple configuration files, comprising the .NET configuration files, applicationHost.config, and distributed web.config files in your site directory structure. This hierarchy allows you to map configuration to a URL namespace on your server by placing it in the right configuration file. When the server reads configuration for a particular Web site or URL, it merges all configuration files along the configuration path, merging the configuration specified in them to achieve the effective set of configuration for a given path.

Because of the configuration merging, configuration specified at a higher configuration path always inherits to all child paths, unless it is overridden lower down. For example, configuration specified in applicationHost.config is inherited by all sites and URLs on the server, unless it is overridden in their respective web.config files.

Table 4-5 indicates where you may chose to place configuration in order to apply it to the desired scope.

Table 4-5   Placement of Configuration

Configuration For	Place In
Entire server	applicationHost.config
A specific site	web.config in the site's physical root directory
A specific application	web.config in the application's physical root directory
A specific virtual directory	web.config in the virtual directory's physical root
A specific URL	If the URL corresponds to a physical directory, in web.config in that directory; otherwise, in any existing parent web.config file with a *location tag* for the specific URL

When specifying configuration at a specific site or URL, you always have a choice of specifying configuration in a distributed web.config file corresponding to the URL or placing it in a configuration file higher in the hierarchy (for example, applicationHost.config) and applying it to the specific URL by using location tags. Both have advantages and disadvantages you need to consider.

Using location tags can allow you to place all configuration in a single location, instead of multiple web.config configuration files which may be harder to discover and manage. Also, if configuration is locked at a particular configuration path (for example, configuration that should only be set by server administrators is typically locked in applicationHost.config), you are forced to use location tags at that path in order to apply configuration to child paths. However, placing configuration in distributed web.config files allows the site/application/ directory to become portable and xcopy-deployed to other servers or places in the site structure without having to set any configuration elsewhere or requiring administrative privileges on the server. This is a very powerful ability.

Finally, a note about configuration delegation—not all configuration sections are allowed to be specified in distributed web.config files by default. It is up to the server administrator to decide which configuration sections are delegated and to unlock them in application-Host.config. This may impact your ability to run applications that specify configuration in distributed web.config files, generating errors if locked configuration is specified. We will discuss managing configuration delegation in the section titled "Delegating Configuration" later in this chapter.

Setting Configuration

To set configuration, you need to know three things: the name of the section that contains the desired configuration settings, the desired property of that section, and the configuration path at which you want to set this setting to apply (as we discussed in the previous section). You will typically know the first two from the documentation of the feature you are attempting to configure. For more information about what configuration sections are available and their format, you can consult the schema files in the %windir%\system32\inetsrv\config\schema directory.

When you know this information, you can specify the corresponding section element in the configuration file.

```
<configuration>
  <system.webServer>
    <defaultDocument … />
  </system.webServer>
<configuration>
```

Note the <configuration> element—this must always be the root element of any configuration file. Also, notice the <system.webServer> element—this is the section group element for the <defaultDocument> section (and all other IIS 7.0 configuration settings) that is being configured.

Configuration sections contain the properties that you intend to configure, such as *default-Document*, but you need to do more than just provide a name. You turn the default document feature on and off and provide the list of default documents using attributes or collection elements contained inside the section.

Setting Section Attributes

The majority of configuration settings are expressed via attributes, which may either be exposed on the collection element itself or in one of the child elements of the collection.

To specify a value for the attribute, you simply need to set the value of that attribute. This effectively overrides any default value or value previously set to this attribute in earlier configuration paths. Following is an example of setting the *enabled* value on the <default-Document> section.

```
<defaultDocument enabled="true" />
```

Each attribute has a specific type and may have additional validation rules associated with it in the schema definition of the section. Likewise, attributes may be given default values that are taken on by them if they are not explicitly set in configuration. This will be documented for each section to assist you in setting their values.

Manipulating Configuration Collections

In addition to attributes, configuration sections can also contain collections. Collections allow lists of items to be represented in configuration, and they support additional behaviors such as adding or removing elements in multiple configuration levels and preventing duplicate items from being added.

Collections are typically configured through three different operations: adding collection elements, removing collection elements, and clearing the collection.

Adding Items to a Collection with <add />   To add items to a collection, you typically use the <add /> element and specify the desired attribute values inside of it. For example, following is an excerpt from the <files> collection of the <defaultDocument> section specified in applicationHost.config after installation.

```
<defaultDocument enabled="true">
    <files>
        <add value="Default.htm" />
        <add value="Default.asp" />
        ...
    </files>
</defaultDocument>
```

In this case, elements in the <files> collection only support a single attribute called "value". However, collection elements are not limited to a single attribute—they can define any number of attributes, child elements, or even subcollections. In fact, each collection element has the same schema flexibility as any other configuration element or the section itself. Following is an example from the <sites> section.

```
<sites>
    <site name="Default Web Site" id="1">
        <application path="/">
            <virtualDirectory path="/
" physicalPath="%SystemDrive%\inetpub\wwwroot" />
        </application>
        <bindings>
            <binding protocol="http" bindingInformation="*:80:" />
        </bindings>
        <traceFailedRequestsLogging enabled="true" />
    </site>
</sites>
```

The <sites> section is a collection of <site> elements (notice that it uses <site> as the name for its <add> element—this is a capability provided by the IIS configuration schema that some sections take advantage of for readability). Each <site> element in turn is a collection of <application> elements, which in turn contain a collection of <virtualDirectory> elements. Each <site> element also has a <bindings> child element, which itself is a collection of site bindings. You can find a detailed description of the new site, application, and virtual directory structure in Chapter 9, "Managing Web Sites."

Luckily, the <sites> section is the most complicated section on the entire IIS 7.0 configuration schema, and most other sections are a lot simpler.

Most collections enforce item uniqueness to prevent duplicate items from being added. This is done by marking one or more of the attributes allowed on the collection <add> elements as the collection key. If an item with a duplicate key is specified, the collection will trigger a configuration error when accessed.

When you add collection elements at a particular configuration level, they add to the existing elements that were inherited from a parent level. For example, the <defaultDocument> section can use this to specify a base set of default documents in applicationHost.config and then add specific default documents at the site or virtual directory levels.

The ordering of collection items inside a collection is determined by the order in which they are added. When collection items are inherited from the parent configuration levels, they are placed before the collection items specified at the current level. This is true for most collections, except for collections that elect to have a prepend order—these collections place the elements declared at the current level before elements inherited from parent levels. These include the IIS <handlers> and the ASP.NET <authorization> sections.

Removing Items from a Collection with <remove />   Because of the collection inheritance, it is sometimes necessary to remove elements that are declared at a higher configuration level. For example, you may want to remove a specific module from the <modules> configuration collection for a specific application if you do not need this module to run. For more about managing modules, see Chapter 12.

> **Note**   If you are removing a collection element that is added at the current configuration level, you can simply delete the corresponding <add> element. Use <remove> to remove the elements that are specified by parent configuration levels.

To do this, you can use the <remove> element. Each remove element specifies the attributes that together comprise the collection key to uniquely identify the element that is to be removed. For example, following is the configuration you can use to remove "Default.asp" from the <files> collection of the <defaultDocument> section.

```
<defaultDocument>
    <files>
        <remove value="Default.asp" />
    </files>
</defaultDocument>
```

Clearing the Collection with <clear />   Sometimes you may want to completely clear the collection items that are defined by the parent configuration levels and specify only the items that are required. This is often done whenever the current configuration level has to have complete control over the contents of the collection and cannot inherit parent items.

This is accomplished with the <clear/> element. The <clear/> element removes all of the inherited collection items, leaving only the items that are added at the current level after the <clear/> element. The following example clears the default document collection and adds back a single element to make sure that only Default.aspx is treated as a default document.

```
<defaultDocument>
    <files>
        <clear/>
        <add value="Default.aspx" />
    </files>
</defaultDocument>
```

> **Important**   Be careful when using the <clear/> element, however, because it completely stops the inheritance of parent collection items to the current configuration level or its children. This means that if the administrator adds new collection items at the server level, they will not be propagated to the current level. Therefore, use <clear/> only when you want to take complete control over the contents of the collection.

Understanding Configuration Errors

In contrast to IIS 6.0, when editing configuration with tools like the IIS Manager and Appcmd, or programmatically with APIs like Microsoft.Web.Administration, the underlying configuration system APIs will make sure that the resulting configuration is correct. This will catch most attempts to produce incorrect configuration, including using data of the wrong type for attribute values, attempting to set nonexisting attributes, or using data out of range of accepted values. It will even prevent you from adding a duplicate collection element or attempting to write configuration that has been locked at a parent configuration level. This is the reason why you should always prefer to use tools to write configuration, rather than doing it manually.

Note Use tools to set configuration—this will catch most mistakes and prevent you from generating incorrect configuration.

However, there are times when you may still run into a situation in which configuration is incorrect. This is most likely if you edit configuration by hand and make a mistake in the section syntax or set attributes to unsupported values. However, it may also happen in other cases—for example, if an application that defines configuration is deployed to a server where some of the sections are locked at the server level, resulting in a lock violation.

Because of this, it is important to be able to understand various configuration error conditions, and be able to use the resulting configuration error information to resolve them.

Caution Always back up configuration before making changes to it. You can learn more about backing up configuration in the section titled "Backing Up Configuration" later in this chapter.

There are several types of configuration errors that are handled differently by the configuration system and have varying degrees of impact on IIS. Table 4-6 summarizes some of the common error conditions and the impact they have on the server.

Table 4-6   Common Error Conditions

Error	Impact
Configuration file is not valid XML	■ If Framework machine.config, root web.config, or IIS 7.0's applicationHost.config: the entire server will be taken offline.
	■ Otherwise: All URLs corresponding to the configuration file and below will return configuration errors.
Configuration file cannot be accessed: The file is locked by another process, access denied, no network connectivity for UNC paths.	■ If Framework machine.config, root web.config, or applicationHost.config: the entire server will be taken offline.
	■ Otherwise: All URLs corresponding to the configuration file and below will return configuration errors.

Table 4-6   **Common Error Conditions**

Error	Impact
Configuration section syntax error: The configuration section has unexpected elements or attributes, or it is missing required attributes.	■ If the error is in one of the system. applicationHost configuration sections that are read by WPAS, the server may be taken offline. ■ If the error is in one of the core Web server sections, all requests to the URLs affected by the errors will return configuration errors. ■ Otherwise, requests that use features that read the configuration section will return configuration errors.
Attribute validation error: There is an invalid data type; value fails attribute validation rules.	Same as above.
Collection validation error: There are duplicate collection elements.	Same as above.
Lock violation: Specifying configuration for the section or attribute that is locked at a parent level.	Same as above.

The key to understanding these error conditions is to understand how the configuration system handles errors. Errors that cause the entire configuration file to become unavailable, because it cannot be read or because it contains invalid XML (as shown in Figure 4-3), cause all attempts to read configuration from that file to fail. Because of this, all operations that require reading this file will fail—if this file is applicationHost.config, which is read by the Windows Process Activation Service component of IIS that is responsible for managing IIS worker processes, the entire server will be taken offline. In this case, you will not be able to get a detailed request error describing the error condition, because the server will not be able to start any IIS worker processes to serve the request. In this case, the error information will be logged by WPAS to the System EventLog.

If the file is a distributed web.config file that corresponds to a particular URL namespace, that namespace will not be available. However, IIS worker processes will still be able to start and generate a detailed configuration request error that will describe the reason, and sometimes even the position in the file, where the error has occurred.

Finally, for all other errors in configuration sections that are not invalid XML, only accesses to the affected section will fail. If the error is in one of the system.applicationHost sections that are read by WPAS, including <sites> and <applicationPools>, WPAS may again fail to start IIS worker processes, resulting in the entire server being offline and errors being logged to the System EventLog. If the error is in one of the core IIS configuration sections that are read on every request, which include <serverRuntime>, <modules>, and <handlers>, all requests to the URL namespace corresponding to the invalid configuration will return configuration errors.

These errors will contain the exact reason why the configuration access failed, including details such as the line number and the element or attribute in question that has incorrect configuration, as shown in Figure 4-4. You can use this information to quickly pinpoint the location of configuration syntax error and resolve it.

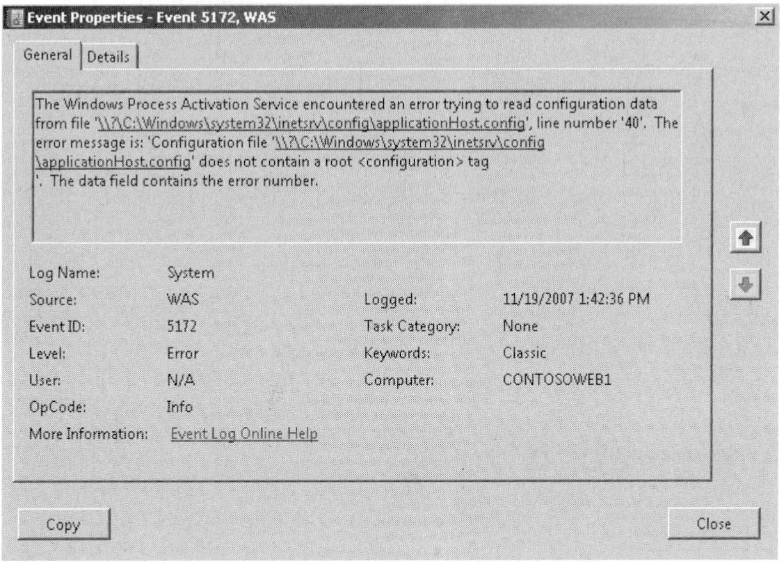

Figure 4-3   EventLog error from malformed XML in applicationHost.config.

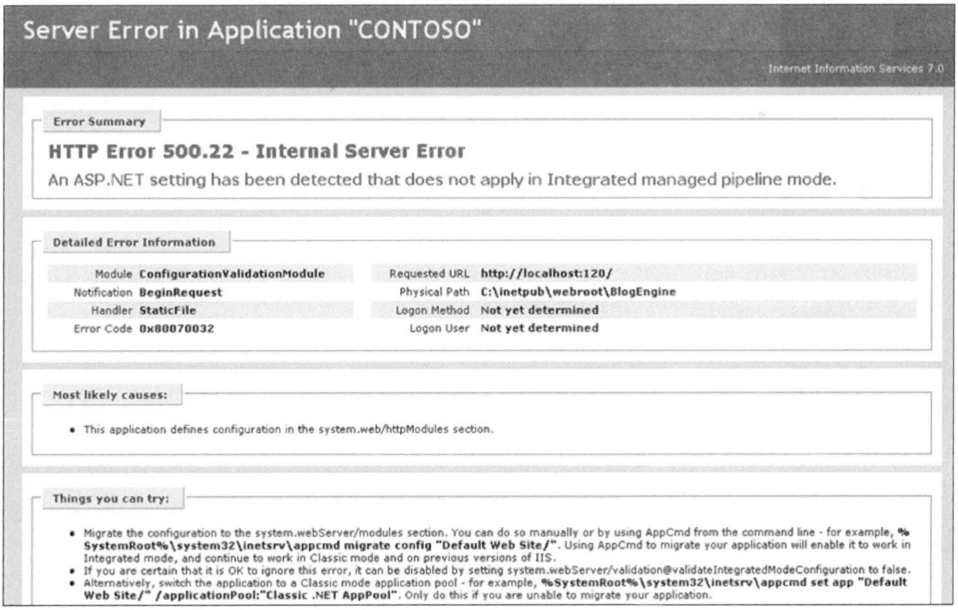

Figure 4-4   IIS 7.0 configuration error message.

> **Note**   To see the detailed configuration error, you will need to either make a request locally on the server or enable detailed errors.

For all other sections, only requests that use features whose configuration has the error will trigger request errors. This also means that if you make a mistake in configuration for a feature that is not being used (for example, the module is disabled), no error will be given and invalid configuration will remain ignored.

Finally, if the error is in an ASP.NET configuration section, which is read by the ASP.NET using the .NET configuration system, you may get an ASP.NET exception error page containing the configuration error details.

> **Note**   To see the detailed ASP.NET configuration exception, you will need to either make a request locally on the server or enable ASP.NET detailed errors.

Managing Configuration

In the course of working with IIS configuration, you will need to perform a variety of management tasks in addition to editing the configuration itself. Notably, you will need to back up and restore configuration, in order to revert from unintended changes or recover from corrupted configuration files. This is especially critical because the ease of editing IIS XML configuration files also makes it easy to make undesired changes.

In fact, when working with IIS configuration, you should always insure that you make a backup that can be used to go back to the state before the changes. Luckily, IIS makes it very easy to do this.

In this section, we will review the management tasks around backing up and restoring IIS configuration. We will also discuss setting up shared configuration between multiple servers and setting up configuration delegation that enables some configuration to be set in distributed web.config configuration files.

Backing Up Configuration

Before making changes to IIS configuration files, you should back them up so that you can restore them later if your changes corrupt configuration or result in incorrect server operation. The latter is a critical reason—the server may look like its working properly initially until a future time when problems are detected, at which point you may want to come back to the previous configuration state.

Typically, it is not necessary to make special arrangements to back up delegated configuration located in web.config inside your Web site structure, because those files are backed up together with your site content (of course, you need to maintain backups of your site content for this to work).

However, if you make changes to the server-level configuration files, you should make a backup of server configuration. Thankfully, IIS 7.0 makes it easy to do that via the Appcmd command line tool.

From an administrative command prompt, type

%windir%\system32\inetsrv\ AppCmd Add Backup MyBackup

This creates a backup of IIS configuration files, including applicationHost.config, redirection.config, and administration.config, and custom schema files if there are any. The backup is created as a named directory under the %windir%\system32\inetsrv\backup directory, using the name you specified to the "Add Backup" command. This directory will contain the backed-up files.

> **Note**   If you do not specify a backup name, Appcmd will automatically create a name using the current date and time.

You can list the backups made on your system by using the List Backups command.

`%windir%\system32\inetsrv\AppCmd List Backups`

Then, you can restore any of the listed backups by using the Restore Backup command.

`%windir%\system32\inetsrv\AppCmd Restore Backup "MyBackup"`

The restore command will restore all of the files in the backup folder, overwriting the current server configuration with those files. No confirmation prompt is given, so always consider backing up the current configuration first before restoring another set.

A note about configuration file security and encryption: the backup process simply copies the server configuration files to the inetsrv\backup directory, which by default is secured with the same NTFS permissions as the inetsrv\config directory, which contains the original files. If the files contain encrypted configuration, those details will stay encrypted in the backed-up copies. No additional encryption is performed as part of the backup mechanism. Therefore, the files are only protected when they are in the backup directory and are not safe to place in an offline location without additional protection.

Using Configuration History

By default, IIS 7.0 via the AppHostSvc will check every two minutes to see if applicationHost.config has changed, and if so will make a backup of the file. You'll find the backed-up configuration files in the Inetpub\history folder by default. You can change both the location of the backups as well as several other configurable parameters in the <configHistory> configuration section, as shown in Table 4-7.

Table 4-7   <configHistory> Attributes

Attribute	Default Setting	Definition
Enabled	True	This value indicates whether configuration history is enabled or disabled
Path	%systemdrive%\ inetpub\history	The path where history directories will be created and stored
maxHistories	10	The maximum number of directories retained by IIS 7.0
Period	00:02:00	The time between each check made for changes by IIS 7.0

If you do nothing at all, the values listed in Table 4-7 are preconfigured for you. To modify these values, you need to enter them into applicationHost.config, because the IIS Manager does not have a UI for configuring this section of applicationHost.config. You can use Appcmd for this. For example, the following command will change the path for storing backups to %systemdrive%\MyWebHistory. Note that the path must exist first or the service will not work.

```
%windir%\system32\inetsrv\Appcmd set config /section:configHistory
"/path:%systemdrive%\MyWebHistory"
```

You can use the **Appcmd Restore Backup** command to restore any of the configuration history backups the same way you restore manual backups performed by the **Appcmd Add Backup** command. You can list all of the available backups, including both manual and configuration history backups, by doing the following.

```
%windir%\system32\inetsrv\AppCmd List Backups
```

For more information about configHistory, see the article "Using IIS7 Configuration History" at *http://www.iis.net/articles/view.aspx/IIS7/Managing-IIS7/Configuring-the-IIS7-Runtime/ Understanding-AppHost-Service/Using-IIS7-Configuration-History?Page=1*.

Exporting and Importing Configuration

By default, IIS 7.0 configuration stores no secrets and therefore is not tied to a specific server as it was in previous versions. The reason for the IIS 6.0 metabase to be tied to a local server and protected is that by default it contains the passwords for the anonymous user and IWAM user. If these passwords were discovered, it is feasible they could be used to log on to the server. They were random and complex, which provided a high very high degree of security.

In IIS 7.0, the anonymous user (IUSR) is a "built-in" account rather than a local account, so it does not require a password. Don't worry, even though there is no password, you can't use this built-in account to log on to the server. There is no possibility that the IUSR account can be used to log on locally or remotely except through IIS. In addition, there is no IWAM account, since IIS5 application isolation mode is not part of IIS 7.0. Since there are no secrets by default in applicationHost.config, there is no need to key it to an individual server.

This means that you can take applicationHost.config from one server and copy it to another server provided you also synchronize the server encryption keys, presuming the target server has the same content and directory structure. This provides a simple mechanism for exporting and importing configuration between servers.

> **Note**   To use the applicationHost.config file from one server on another server, you do
> need to make sure the servers use the same configuration encryption keys. This is because
> applicationHost.config contains encryption session keys that are themselves encrypted using
> the server's RSA configuration key. You can learn more about exporting and importing server
> encryption keys in the section titled "Sharing Configuration Between Servers" later in this
> chapter.

In the case in which your configuration files do contain encrypted information, such as application pool identities, the configuration files are tied to the specific server on which the encryption information is generated. You can, however, export and import the configuration keys in order to allow multiple servers to share the same encrypted configuration—in fact, this is one of the requirements for the shared configuration feature supported by IIS 7.0. You can learn more about setting up shared configuration later in this chapter. You can also find an in-depth discussion of configuration encryption in Chapter 14.

Unlike IIS 6.0, IIS 7.0 does not provide a built-in mechanism to export configuration for a particular site, as opposed to exporting the entire server's configuration. In a lot of cases, this can be accomplished by manually re-creating the site definition on the target server and then simply copying the site content, which can now define its configuration in the web.config files contained within the site's directory structure.

However, if the site configuration is located inside location tags in applicationHost.config, there is no automated mechanism to export it. You can, of course, simply copy the contents contained in the location tag (including the location tags) and add it to the bottom of another applicationHost.config. An automated mechanism may become available in the future.

Delegating Configuration

The new configuration system in IIS 7.0 was designed to provide rich support for feature delegation. This term has a special meaning in IIS 7.0—the ability to designate features that Web site administrators or application managers can control at the site or application level—without making them administrators on the server. As you will see, feature delegation works hand in hand with remote administration and is built into the IIS Manager, which allows you to configure delegation and at the same time respects delegation settings, limiting access to locked or limited features.

Feature delegation is implemented in two ways. First, the configuration hierarchy itself allows configuration to be specified in distributed web.config files, which are typically under control of the site administrator or application developer who do not have to be server administrators to set or change configuration therein. The server administrator has control over what configuration can be set in the delegated manner in web.config files, versus what configuration can only be set by a server administrator in applicationHost.config. This control is accomplished through configuration locking, which can be done at the section level by locking the section in applicationHost.config or at the granular level by locking specific configuration settings in a particular configuration section. Granular configuration locking is described in more detail in this chapter in the section titled "Granular Configuration Locking."

The second way is implemented by IIS Manager, which subsumes the configuration section locking mechanism and provides a way to manage the delegation of the underlying configuration and the corresponding IIS Manager UI features for seamless integration with remote administration through the tool. Managing feature delegation through the IIS Manager has the advantage of ensuring correctly configured delegation. The IIS Manager will respect delegation settings so that a remote user cannot see features that are hidden (marked as Not Delegated in the IIS Manager), and cannot make changes to features that are marked as Read Only in the IIS Manager.

> **Important**   Any user that can upload a web.config can overwrite IIS 7.0 and ASP.NET settings in web.config. If you use the IIS Manager to write configuration, these settings will be properly maintained and users will only be allowed to change configuration for which they have access. If a web.config file is created outside of using the IIS Manager and then uploaded to the site, it may contain configuration settings that are not permitted by the delegation settings. In this event, IIS 7.0 will present a configuration locking error, and the previous, correct, web.config details may be lost, since the original web.config has been overwritten.

When you delegate control to others, there will be a strong incentive for them to control their site or application configuration using the IIS Manager, as it will show only features that the user has the right to see or control.

In general, features in IIS 7.0 are related to configuration "sections" in applicationHost.config. We've already described this in the discussion earlier in this chapter on section definitions and the value for "overrideModeDefault" associated with each section. The IIS Manager, of course, is the main tool for controlling configuration of these sections, and it's much easier to understand and manage delegation using the IIS Manager than any other way.

Delegation Settings in the IIS Manager

Let's examine the various settings in the IIS Manager related to delegation. Figure 4-5 shows the results you'll see if you select the server node in the tree view and then Feature Delegation from the features pane.

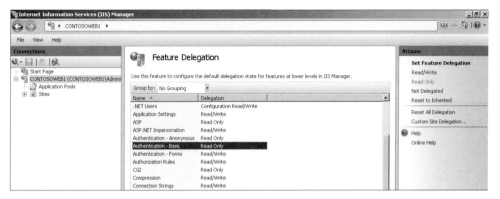

Figure 4-5   Feature Delegation in the IIS Manager.

The Delegation column lists the current delegation setting for each feature. The names for these various states for delegation may not be as clear as they might be to describe what's going on, so you should not try to infer a great deal from the terms:

- **Not Delegated**   When a feature is marked as Not Delegated, the corresponding configuration section will be locked in applicationHost.config by placing it inside a <location> tag with the **overrideMode** value set to Deny. When a feature is marked as Not Delegated, any changes you make to this feature at server level (that is, with the server icon selected in the tree view) will be recorded in applicationHost.config. Changes at the site or application level can only be made by the server administrator and will be recorded in applicationHost.config using <location> tags to apply them to the required path. When using the IIS Manager to connect to the site or application, remote users will not be able to see the corresponding feature icon or change its settings. If a web.config file is uploaded that contains settings for a Not Delegated feature, a configuration error occurs.

- **Read Only**   This is the same as Not Delegated, except that remote users will be able to see this feature; however, they cannot change any values. This is a useful setting when you want users to know, for example, what authentication methods are available to them, but you don't want them to be able to turn them on or off.

- **Read/Write**   When a feature is marked as Read/Write, the configuration section will be unlocked for distributed web.config files. This is accomplished by placing the configuration section in a <location> tag with the overrideMode value set to Allow. Any changes you make to this at feature at server level will be recorded in application-Host.config. Changes to this feature at the site or application level will be recorded in the appropriate web.config. (A reference to site level designates the web.config in the site root. The application level refers to the web.config file that resides in a folder within the site that has been designated as an application.) When using the IIS Manager to connect to the site or application, remote users will be able to see and change the settings.

Additional delegation values may be provided by third-party extensions to the tool that have extension-specific meaning.

You can learn more about configuring IIS Manager feature delegation and determining which users have the right to manage the Web server configuration remotely in Chapter 8, "Remote Administration."

Default Settings for Delegated Configuration

As mentioned, certain settings in IIS 7.0 are delegated by default, whereas others are specifically locked down. Table 4-8 is from a prerelease version of the *IIS 7.0 Hosting Deployment Guide*, which can be located on IIS.net. The information in the table details which features are delegated and why. You may want to make different decisions than the IIS team regarding these default settings, but a great deal of thought has gone into these settings, so we would advise not making changes to the global settings without good reason.

Table 4-8   Features and Delegated Settings

Feature	Delegated Setting	Reason
.NET Compilation	Read Only (changed from Read/Write)	Specifies settings for ASP.NET compilation processing directives like the temporary compilation directory.
		Prevents users from setting the temporary compilation directory manually.
.NET Globalization	Read/Write	Specifies settings for default culture and globalization properties for Web requests.
.NET Profile	Read/Write	Specifies settings for user-selected options in ASP.NET applications.
.NET Roles	Read/Write	Specifies settings for groups for use with .NET users and forms authentication.
.NET Trust Levels	Read Only (changed from Read/Write)	Specifies the trust level. By locking down the trust level when you follow the ASP.NET guidance in this document, you will be setting this to Read Only and locking it for the server.
		Prevents Web site owners from setting the trust level to a higher level than set by the server administrator. For example, if a custom trust level is set by the administrator, this setting should be set to Read Only so it cannot be overridden.
.Net Users	Configuration Read/Write	Specifies settings for management of users who belong to roles and use forms authentication.
Application Settings	Read/Write	Specifies settings for storing data (name and value pairs) that managed code applications can use at run time.
ASP	Read Only	Specifies Classic ASP settings.
ASP.NET Impersonation	Read/Write	Specifies impersonation settings. Site owners can use this to run their site under a different security context.

Table 4-8   Features and Delegated Settings

Feature	Delegated Setting	Reason
Authentication—Anonymous	Read Only	Specifies anonymous authentication settings.
Authentication—Forms	Read/Write	Specifies forms authentication settings.
Authentication—Windows	Read Only	Specifies Windows authentication settings.
Authorization Rules	Read/Write	Specifies the list of Allow or Deny rules that control access to content.
CGI	Read Only	Specifies properties for CGI applications.
		Should be left set to Read Only to prevent users from changing settings.
Compression	Read/Write	Specifies settings to configure compression.
Connection Strings	Read/Write	Specifies connection strings that applications can use.
Default Document	Read/Write	Specifies default documents for the Web site.
		By leaving this Read/Write, users will be able to specify a custom default document for their site without contacting the server administrator.
Directory Browsing	Read/Write	Specifies directory browsing settings.
Error Pages	Read Only	Specifies what HTTP error responses are returned.
Failed Request Tracing Rules	Read/Write	Specifies settings for failed request tracing rules. Enables users to create rules for tracing requests based on parameters like time taken or status code and to diagnose problems with their site.
Feature Delegation	Remove Delegation (changed from Read/Write)	Specifies settings for delegating features to applications.
		It can be turned off unless server administrators want to enable this feature for site owners.
Handler Mappings	Read/Write	
HTTP Response Headers	Read/Write	Specifies HTTP headers that are added to responses from the Web server.
ISAPI Filters	Read Only	Specifies ISAPI filters that process requests made to the site or server, such as ASP.NET.
Logging	Remove Delegation	
Machine Key	Read/Write	Specifies hashing and encryption settings for applications services, such as view state, forms authentication, and membership and roles.
MIME Types	Read Only	Specifies what file types can be served as static files.

Table 4-8   Features and Delegated Settings

Feature	Delegated Setting	Reason
Modules	Read/Write	Specifies native and managed code modules that process requests made to the site or server.
Output Caching	Read/Write	Specifies rules for caching output.
Pages and Controls	Read/Write	Specifies page and control settings for applications.
Redirect Rules	Read/Write	Specifies settings for redirecting requests to another file or URL.
Session State	Read/Write	Specifies session state and forms authentication cookie settings.
SMTP E-mail	Read/Write	Specifies e-mail address and delivery options for e-mail sent from the site.
SSL Settings	Read Only	Specifies settings for SSL.

Directly Configuring Delegation

Although you can manage the delegation of many IIS features in the IIS Manager, it only allows you to manage the underlying configuration delegation for features that have corresponding UI pages in the IIS Manager. For those features, selecting the IIS Manager delegation state also generates the required configuration delegation settings to control whether the corresponding configuration sections can be used at the site or application level.

However, there are times when you will need to manage configuration delegation directly. One such case is when the configuration section does not have a corresponding IIS Manager feature. For example, IIS 7.0's URL Filtering feature does not, at the time of this writing, have a UI component. In these cases, you can work with the configuration system directly or the Appcmd command line tool to configure the desired configuration delegation.

The initial ability to delegate a specific configuration section is controlled by the **override-ModeDefault** attribute on its declaration (see the "Section Declarations" section earlier in this chapter). Some of the built-in IIS 7.0 configuration sections like <defaultDocument> allow delegation by default by specifying Allow for this attribute in their declarations, and others like <serverRuntime> do not by specifying Deny. This decision is typically made by the developer of the feature that reads this configuration section, based on whether or not the feature configuration should be by default delegated to users who are not server administrators.

Caution   Do *not* change the **overrideModeDefault** setting on section declarations to unlock them. The IIS team recommendations for default delegation settings are well reasoned. If you need to override the default setting globally, use Location tags referencing the "*" path (or a null path, "").

The overrideModeDefault setting on the section declarations in applicationHost.config sets the default value for delegation. You can modify the delegation status of each configuration section by locking or unlocking it. Unlocking sections is often needed in order to be able to specify configuration for certain sections in web.config files of your Web site. Likewise, you may want to lock certain other sections if you do not want the Web sites on your server to be able to override the settings set in applicationHost.config.

To unlock a section, you can use the Appcmd.exe command line tool as follows.

```
%windir%\system32\inetsrv\AppCmd Unlock Config /section:<SectionName>
```

Where <SectionName> is the name of the section, for example, "system.webServer/serverRuntime".

To lock a section that is currently unlocked, you can use the following command.

```
%windir%\system32\inetsrv\AppCmd Lock Config /section:<SectionName>
```

Locking or unlocking a section produces a location tag in applicationHost.config that sets the delegation state of the configuration section by setting the **overrideMode** attribute to Allow or Deny. For example, if we use the unlock command shown previously to unlock the <serverRuntime> section, we will generate the following in applicationHost.config.

```
<location path="" overrideMode="Allow">
    <system.webServer>
        <serverRuntime />
    </system.webServer>
</location>
```

Likewise, you can lock or unlock configuration sections for a particular configuration path only, by specifying this path in the command. This can allow you, for example, to keep the configuration section locked for the entire server but allow a specific site to override its settings.

```
%windir%\system32\inetsrv\AppCmd Unlock Config "Default Web Site/"
/section:system.webServer/serverRuntime /commit:apphost
```

In this example, we unlock the <serverRuntime> section for the "Default Web Site" only and commit these changes to applicationHost.config (this is required). This produces a location tag in applicationHost.config that uses the *path* attribute to apply itself only to "Default Web Site/".

This enables you to quickly manage the configuration delegation on a section level. However, sometimes it is necessary to allow the delegation of the section but keep control over a specific setting inside that section. This can be accomplished using granular configuration locking, which we'll discuss in the section titled "Granular Configuration Locking" later in this chapter.

Additional Configuration for Remote Administration

For a user to manage a site or application remotely using the IIS Manager, it is necessary to assign specific permissions to the content. The service account for the Web Management Service (WMSvc) must have read and write permissions to web.config in order to successfully connect remotely. Please refer to Chapter 8 for these and other details.

Granular Configuration Locking

You have explored the configuration's ability to lock and unlock sections for delegation and used the location tag for creating settings for a site or directory that override the inherited defaults. Feature delegation controls whether or not the entire section can be used in a configuration file at a certain level. However, there are some cases in which the configuration section contains some configuration that should be delegated and some configuration that should be locked.

To support these scenarios, the configuration system allows you to exercise more fine-grained control over what specific configuration settings should be delegated through granular locking. Granular locking is achieved through the use of special locking directives supported by the configuration system.

To use granular configuration locking, you have to edit the configuration through some means other than the IIS Manager. At this time, the IIS Manager does not support configuring granular locking.

Note   The semantics for granular locking are based on the configuration system for ASP.NET, so if you are familiar with that, you will be ahead of the game.

Granular configuration locking is accomplished by using one of the special attributes listed in Table 4-9.

Table 4-9   Granular Configuration Locking

Locking Directive	Used To
lockAttributes	Lock specific attributes to prevent them from being specified.
lockAllAttributesExcept	Lock all attributes on the element other than the specified attributes.
lockElements	Lock the specified elements to prevent them from being specified (and therefore lock all other attributes and child elements of the specified elements)
lockAllElementsExcept	Lock all elements on the current element except the specified elements.
lockItem	Lock the current collection element to prevent it from being removed.

lockAttributes, lockAllAttributesExcept   The *lockAttributes* configuration directive can be specified on a configuration element in order to lock specific attributes on the element and prevent them from being specified at lower configuration levels. The *lockAttributes* directive specifies a comma-separated list of attribute names that are valid for the current element.

For example, in order to allow the <defaultDocument> section to be delegated but make sure that the feature itself cannot be disabled, we can set the *enabled* attribute to "true" and then lock it using the *lockAttributes* directive as follows:

```
<defaultDocument enabled="true" lockAttributes="enabled">
  <files>
    <add value="Default.htm" />
    <add value="Default.asp" />
    <add value="index.htm" />
    <add value="index.html" />
    <add value="iisstart.htm" />
    <add value="default.aspx" />
  </files>
</defaultDocument>
```

In this example, *lockAttributes* instructs IIS 7.0 to disallow any change to the *enabled* attribute. As a result, if the Web administrator attempts to turn off the default document feature (enabled="false") the error message shown in Figure 4-6 occurs.

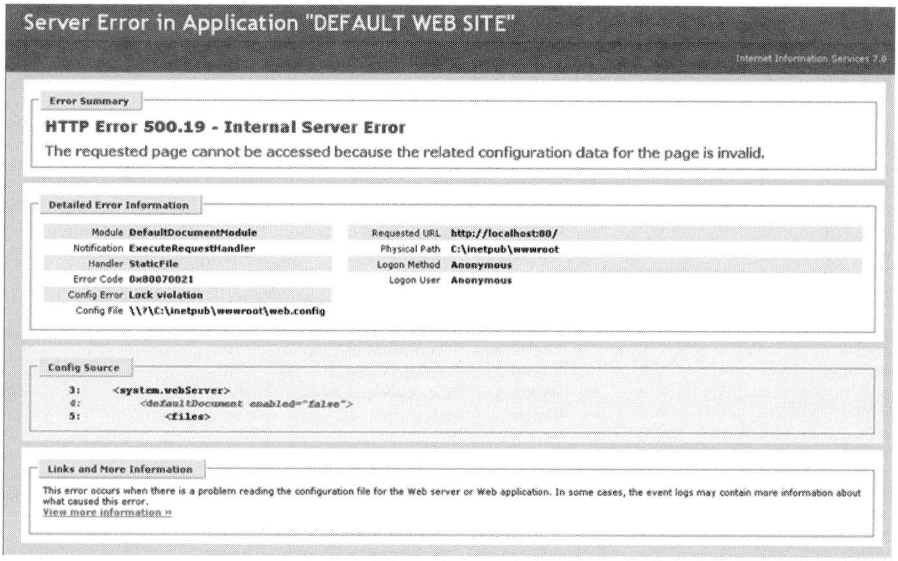

Figure 4-6   Error message due to configuration locking.

As you can see in Figure 4-6, the lock violation is called out and the offending line in web.config is clearly displayed. Removing this line, in this case, clears the error.

The *lockAllAttributesExcept* form of the attribute lock provides a convenient mechanism for cases in which you want to lock all attributes on the element except for one or two attributes that should be unlocked. In that case, you can use it instead of the *lockAttributes* element and specify the attributes that you want to keep unlocked.

lockElements, lockAllElementsExcept   The *lockElements* locking directive allows you to lock a particular child element of the current element (as opposed to an attribute). This prevents this element from being specified at lower configuration levels. The *lockElements* directive specifies a comma-separated list of element names to lock.

For example, we can use the *lockElements* directive to prevent the <files> collection of the <defaultDocument> section from being specified, therefore effectively preventing lower configuration levels from changing the contents of the default document list.

```
<defaultDocument enabled="true" lockElements="files" >
  <files>
    <add value="Default.htm" />
    <add value="Default.asp" />
    <add value="index.htm" />
    <add value="index.html" />
    <add value="iisstart.htm" />
    <add value="default.aspx" />
  </files>
</defaultDocument>
```

This setup prevents a Web administrator from changing the files in the default document list, but it does permit turning the feature on and off (via the enabled attribute).

The *lockElements* directive can also be used to do collection locking. By locking the ability to use certain collection elements (such as <add>, <remove>, and <clear>) it is possible to prevent the collection from being changed or prevent elements from being removed while still allowing new elements to be added.

For example, if you lock the <add> element (or the corresponding element that acts as the <add> element for the collection), lower configuration levels will not be able to add new elements to the collection. Likewise, if you lock the <remove> and <clear> elements, lower levels will not be able to remove elements from the collection but will be able to add new ones.

The *lockAllElementsExcept* directive can be used with configuration elements that have multiple subelements, when you want to lock all of them but one. In practice, we don't expect that this will be widely used, but it is a possibility to keep in mind should you encounter a situation in which it is applicable.

lockItem   The *lockItem* directive can be used to lock specific collection elements from being removed or modified, as opposed to preventing all elements in the collection from being removed by locking the <remove> element using *lockElements*. The *lockItem* directive is specified on each collection element that is to be locked and accepts Boolean values.

Returning to our example, we want to allow a Web site administrator to be able to add new entries to the list of default pages but not remove Default.aspx from the list. In application-Host.config, you can lock in the Default.aspx page by finding the configuration section in applicationHost.config as follows.

```
<defaultDocument>
    <files>
        <add value="Default.htm" />
        <add value="Default.asp" />
        <add value="index.htm" />
        <add value="index.html" />
        <add value="iisstart.htm" />
        <add value="default.aspx" lockItem="true" />
    </files>
</defaultDocument>
```

This will prevent lower configuration levels from being able to explicitly remove the Default.aspx entry, as well as using <clear/> to remove all items from the collection. They will still be able to add new entries to the collection.

An important use of *lockItem* is implemented in applicationHost.config. If you examine the <modules> section, you'll notice that modules are added with *lockItem* set to "true." This means that if IIS 7.0 encounters a <clear> or <remove> in a web.config or location tag that references the locked module, you will get a locking error. These locks are enabled by default since delegation is enabled for modules in order to permit .NET applications to add modules, a feature that is quite common. However, by delegating the modules section, it is also possible to remove modules in web.config. This could allow a user to inadvertently create an insecure or nonfunctional configuration. To prevent this from occurring, while at the same time ensuring maximum compatibility with .NET, modules are declared with *lockItem* specified as true.

Sharing Configuration Between Servers

An entirely new feature in IIS 7.0 is the ability to have multiple Web servers share a single configuration file. This feature was designed with load-balanced Web farms in mind in order to eliminate the need to keep multiple server configuration in sync. Toward this end, shared configuration is an excellent feature that will be useful in many Web farm situations.

 Note   Shared configuration is not a complete Web farm solution in itself, because it does not eliminate the need to synchronize application content and local components like SSL certificates or .NET assemblies registered in the GAC.

Enabling Shared Configuration

You can enable shared configuration using the IIS Manager. You'll find the IIS Manager Shared Configuration icon in the features pane when the Server node is selected in the tree view. Look for it at the bottom in the Management section, as shown in Figure 4-7.

Note   It is possible to enable shared configuration without using IIS Manager by modifying IIS configuration manually and performing all the necessary import steps. However, IIS Manager is recommended because it automates a lot of these steps and makes setting up shared configuration a lot easier than it otherwise would be.

Figure 4-7   The Shared Configuration icon in IIS Manager.

How Shared Configuration Works

The basic notion behind shared configuration is to place the main configuration files for IIS 7.0 on a shared UNC path and have all the servers in the farm use the remote configuration store as if it were local. In addition, if you direct command line administration tools to modify settings on a server that uses the shared configuration, those instructions are redirected to the shared store. The net result is that if you have 10 servers sharing configuration, and you add an application pool, all 10 servers will have that pool immediately.

Setting up shared configuration involves three main actions: First, you have to create a location with the proper permissions and a user identity that will be used to access the content. Second, you must export the configuration files to a centralized location. Third, you have to set up the servers to use the shared configuration files instead of the local configuration files. At that point, they are all functionally identical.

Step 1: Preparing for Shared Configuration   The IIS Manager has to write to the remote configuration as a user of some kind, so it must be provided with the credentials of a local or domain user that has the correct permissions. So the first task is to create a user that has the correct permissions and then assign NTFS permissions for that user to the shared location.

1. Create a user that you will use to provide read and write access to the shared configuration files. This can be a local user that has the same credentials on each server, or a domain user presuming all the servers are joined to a domain.

   ```
   net user ConfigAccess HighSecurePasswordhere /add
   ```

2. Create a folder that will contain the shared configuration files. This can be on one of the Web servers or the file server. The only real requirement is that it be accessible via a standard UNC share from all the servers.

3. Configure the folder for sharing with the appropriate share permissions. We'll use the SharedConfig folder in this example.

   ```
   Net share sharedconfig$=%SystemDrive%\sharedconfig /grant:ConfigUser,Read
   /grant:Administrators,Full /grant:System,Full
   ```

4. Carefully inspect the configuration of the server you plan to use as the source for the shared configuration. The IIS 7.0 configuration you export will be shared by all the other servers, so take some time to make sure it is correct. You can, of course, change it after you've enabled shared configuration, but the changes will affect multiple servers at that time.

5. Back up the existing configuration files with the following commands from an administrative command prompt.

   ```
   windir%\system32\inetsrv appcmd add backup SharedConfigBackup
   ```

Step 2: Export the Configuration Files

1. In the IIS Manager, click the server node and then double-click the Shared Configuration icon.

2. In the Actions pane, click Export Configuration to open the Export Configuration dialog box, as shown in Figure 4-8.

3. Under Configuration Location in the Physical Path text box, enter the UNC path to shared configuration.

> **Note**   You can export the configuration files to a local, nonshared path if you prefer and then manually copy the files to the shared location.

Figure 4-8   The Export Configuration dialog box.

4.   Click Connect As and enter the credentials that have write access to the share. You could also enter administrative credentials here. These credentials are just used to write the configuration file in this export step and are not used for regular access to the shared configuration settings.

> **Caution**   Do not use the ConfigAccess credentials you created for accessing the configuration from the Web server. These credentials should not have write access to the share.

5.   Under Encryption Keys, enter a password that will be required to protect the exported encryption keys when transported off the server. You will need to provide this password on any server that will use the shared configuration files so that it can import the exported encryption keys. Note that the password must be at least eight characters, have a symbol, mixed case, and a number before it will be accepted. At this time, creating the encryption key cannot be automated.

6.   Press OK. You will see a message that says the export was successful.

At this point you have not yet enabled shared configuration, just created a set of files that could be used for shared configuration. Before you proceed, you might want to see what was (and was not) copied. See the sidebar titled "Inspecting the Exported Configuration Files" for more information.

Inspecting the Exported Configuration Files

Open the location where you exported the files and examine the contents. You'll find a copy of applicationHost.config, administration.config, and an encrypted file named ConfigEncryptedKey.key. The .key file is used to decrypt any secrets stored in the .config files. For this to work, all the servers in the farm have to know a shared secret, and that's the reason for a strong key to be entered when you export these configuration settings. By default, there are no secrets in the config files, because the anonymous user is now a built-in account and no longer requires a password since it cannot be used to log on to the server. In addition, the IWAM account found on IIS 4.0, IIS 5.0, and IIS 6.0 is deprecated. However, many companies use unique identities as principals for application pools and the IIS anonymous user in order to increase security and provide more granular details in audit logs.

Passwords created in the IIS manager associated with UNC paths, applications pool principals, and custom anonymous users are encrypted and stored in the configuration files. These encrypted items cannot be deciphered by default on other IIS 7.0 servers. Shared configuration, however, makes this possible by allowing you to export the encryption keys from the server whose configuration is being exported and reimport them to all other machines using the shared configuration.

You should note that you will not see any web.config, custom modules, Web site content, certificates, or other files that are related to the server configuration. Centralized configuration enables sharing of applicationHost.config and administration.config files only. All other items needed to keep the servers functionally identical need to be managed by processes you institute outside of IIS 7.0.

Note that you can expect to see tools or updates to this feature from the IIS team after Windows Server 2008 is released that will help with replication and synchronization tasks.

Step 3: Enable Shared Configuration   You're now ready to enable shared configuration. Typically, you'll start with the server used for the shared configuration export. Exporting the configuration does not automatically cause the server to start using the exported settings. In fact, if you make any changes at this point to the IIS 7.0 configuration, you will see them on the local server, but unless you re-export the configuration, the shared configuration will not have the most recent changes.

The procedure is simple and is the same for each server:

 1.   In the Shared Configuration feature, select the Enable Shared Configuration check box.

2. Enter the Physical Path, User Name, and Password you used to create the share and user for the share. In our example, this would be:

   Path: **\\Contoso\SharedConfig**
   User: **ConfigAccess**
   Password: **HighSecurePasswordHere**

3. At the prompt, enter the password you used to export the settings. You will see the message shown in Figure 4-9.

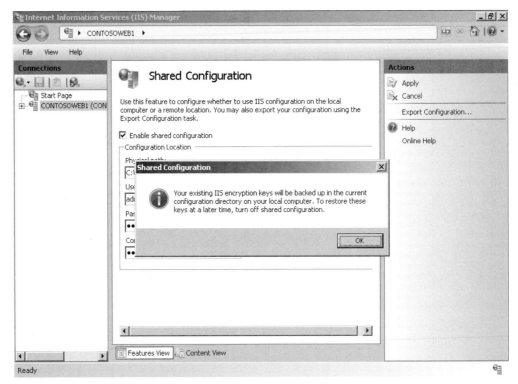

Figure 4-9   Backing up encryption keys.

This message informs you that if you decided to revert back to your local settings, the IIS Manager will fix your encryption keys so they will work on your local configuration files. Otherwise, any passwords you entered in the configuration system for UNC paths, custom anonymous users, or application pool identities could not be deciphered by IIS.

4. Click OK to close the message box. You will see another message that says you need to close and reopen the IIS Manager and reset (stop and start) the Web Management Service for changes to take effect. When you close and reopen the IIS Manager, you will load the redirected configuration files instead of the local files. Restarting the Management Service will cause remote administration requests to be redirected.

You will need to repeat this procedure on each server.

Shared Configuration Considerations

Shared configuration will help to reduce the administrative burden of configuration replication between servers in a Web farm. It is not, however, a Web farm management tool. You will still need to manage replication of any content or configuration item that is local to a server in the farm. This typically involves such items as content replication, directory structure maintenance, SSL certificates, recycling of services, operating system updates, registering COM objects, placing new content in the .NET global assembly cache, network configuration, and other settings that are stored locally.

Consider the scenario in which you want to change the type of application pool from Classic to Integrated. This is one of the few settings that will cause an application pool to recycle. Making changes that affect the application pool environment, such as the application pool type or pool identity, will cause all of your application pools to recycle across all the shared servers, potentially resulting in your Web application becoming unavailable for a short period of time. As a result of this and other scenarios such as content updates, you will want to devise a method for rolling in updates so that you can more precisely control the settings.

For example, if you need to make a configuration change that would result in a recycle, you should export the settings from a second server to a new shared location. This server will be the only one using that location while the other servers in the farm continue to deliver requests. You then make the updates you want to this server and test the results. When you are satisfied, you move the other shared servers to the new shared location in series. If at any time you don't like what's going on, you can roll back to the prior configuration. If things proceed well, you will continue moving each server over until all the servers are using the new configuration.

Summary

The IIS 7.0 configuration system is the foundation for many key deployment and management capabilities of the server. For the first time, it enables scenarios including delegated management of configuration, true xcopy deployment of IIS applications, and sharing configuration between multiple servers.

In this chapter, you reviewed the basics of editing Web server configuration, and performing key configuration management tasks such as backing up configuration and setting up shared configuration for multiple servers on a Web farm.

The configuration system is the core of the IIS 7.0 Administration stack, which offers a full set of options for managing the server. To learn how to manage IIS using GUI, see Chapter 6. You can also learn about managing IIS 7.0 configuration from the command line in Chapter 7.

In the spirit of IIS 7.0 end-to-end extensibility, the IIS 7.0 configuration system is also completely extensible, allowing third-party Web server modules to store their configuration in the IIS 7.0 configuration system. This extensibility allows developers to make use of the same configuration capabilities and management tools used by IIS 7.0. For example, an administrator could configure the custom feature using Appcmd or a developer could use .NET to manage the feature state and configuration.

For more information about protecting configuration on your server, including using configuration encryption and properly taking advantage of configuration isolation, see Chapter 14.

Additional Resources

These resources contain additional information and tools related to this chapter:

- The IIS 7.0 Web Reference can be found at *http://msdn2.microsoft.com/en-us/library/ ms691259.aspx*.

- You can search for configuration information on the IIS Web site at *http://www.iis.net* and in the IIS 7.0 online help files.

- You'll find information about how IIS 6.0 metabase properties map to IIS 7.0 configuration schema at *http://msdn2.microsoft.com/en-us/library/aa347565.aspx*.

- For more information about configHistory, see the article "Using IIS7 Configuration History" at *http://www.iis.net/articles/view.aspx/IIS7/Managing-IIS7/Configuring-the-IIS7-Runtime/Understanding-AppHost-Service/Using-IIS7-Configuration-History?Page=1*.

Part II
Deployment

Chapter 5

Installing IIS 7.0

On the Disc   Browse the CD for additional tools and resources.

Windows Server 2008 has a great story when it comes to installing and configuring your Web server. Internet Information Services (IIS) 7.0 has a modular setup design that gives you complete control when you set up your Web server.

Windows Server 2008 introduces new tools to install IIS 7.0. You can use Server Manager, a graphical user interface (GUI)-based tool, or two command line tools called Package Manager (Pkgmgr.exe) and ServerManagerCMD. Along with the new tools, IIS 7.0 supports legacy scripts that use Active Directory Service Interfaces (ADSI) or Windows Management Instrumentation (WMI).

In addition to the various ways to install IIS 7.0, the new XML-based configuration system introduced in Windows Server 2008 allows you to copy your base build files to other machines. After you have created your master image, you can copy the IIS 7.0 configuration files to another IIS 7.0 server. The new modular architecture enables you to design and implement a server that meets your needs.

But before you start to install IIS 7.0, you should do a little planning.

Planning the Installation

IIS 7.0 has a modular architecture that enables you to customize exactly which features are installed and run on the Web server. The Web server features are now separated into more than 40 modules that can be independently installed, enabling you to greatly reduce the potential attack surface. (See Chapter 3, "Understanding the Modular Foundation," for more

117

details.) A smaller installation footprint also minimizes your patching requirements. If you implement a default installation, IIS 7.0 installs with 10 modules and will deliver only static content as an anonymous user. However, you will likely want to do more than this.

To take full advantage of the modular architecture, you should plan your IIS 7.0 installation to match the requirements of the applications you plan to deploy. This chapter provides specific information about what modules you'll need to handle various workloads. Reducing the number of installed modules makes it easier to support, monitor, and troubleshoot your applications once they are deployed in a production environment.

When you plan your installation, think about which installation tool you want to use. Server Manager (which first launches when you log into Windows Server 2008) provides an intuitive UI that gives you complete control over which roles and features are installed. Server Manager automatically takes care of any dependencies necessary to support the various modules. You can use Server Manager to determine which modules are required for a particular workload and then use this information to automate your installation with command line tools. The Server Manager UI is not available on Server Core installations of Windows Server 2008.

ServerManagerCMD is a command line version of Server Manager. It is a managed code executable that offers more flexibility when automating your server installation. ServerManagerCMD is easy to use as a command line installation tool because it has knowledge of server roles, role services, and their dependencies. For example, with a single command, you can install all the components necessary to run a static Web server. Other roles and features such as Message Queuing can be installed in a similar way. ServerManagerCMD is intended to be a global tool used at a server level. ServerManagerCMD is not available on Server Core installations.

Package Manager is a command line tool that provides for custom and automatic installations of IIS 7.0. Package Manager offers the most flexibility and the most granularity for your IIS 7.0 installations. Unlike with Server Manager, you have to be aware of the modules and their dependencies. If you do not install the appropriate modules and the associated dependencies, your server won't work as expected. Package Manager is available on all versions of Windows Server 2008.

Which of these tools you use depends on your environment. If you do not need to automate the installation process, Server Manager will fill your needs. If you are designing the rollout of servers for an enterprise or hosting company, you'll want to look at Package Manager or ServerManagerCMD. But you'll probably want to choose only one of these rather than learn and maintain two tools. If you plan to have Server Core machines, Package Manager is your only option, and it will do the job well. If you do not plan to deploy Server Core machines, ServerManagerCMD becomes an option. Whatever tool you use, IIS 7.0 provides multiple tools to help automate your server installs. You'll find a discussion of ServerManagerCMD and Package Manager in the "Using ServerManagerCMD" and "Using Package Manager" sections in this chapter.

Installation Scenarios for IIS 7.0

One concept introduced in Windows Server 2008 is workload-specific setups. Some common workload scenarios that can be used in Windows Server 2008 are

- Static Content Web Server (Default installation)
- ASP.NET
- Classic ASP
- FastCGI-based applications
- IIS Managed Modules and .NET Extensibility
- IIS Full Install
- Server Core Web Edition

Static Content Web Server (Default Installation)

Web Server with the Static Content role service is the default installation and one of the most commonly used installation workload types. Other workloads and product installations use it. The preselected setup defaults of IIS 7.0 provide all the IIS modules required to support this configuration. This includes the ability to serve static HTML files, documents, and images. Additionally, it provides support for default documents, directory browsing, logging, and anonymous authentication. The IIS Manager Console is also installed.

Table 5-1 lists all the components that are selected by default when you install IIS 7.0. The table includes the appropriate update names. Update names are the names used to perform Package Manager installations.

Table 5-1   Default Server Install Components

Server Manager	Update Name
Static Content	IIS-StaticContent
Default Document	IIS-DefaultDocument
Directory Browsing	IIS-DirectoryBrowsing
HTTP Errors	IIS-HttpErrors
HTTP Logging	IIS-HttpLogging
Logging Tools	IIS-LoggingLibraries
Request Monitor	IIS-RequestMonitor
Request Filtering	IIS-RequestFiltering
Static Content Compression	IIS-HttpCompressionStatic
IIS Management Console	IIS-ManagementConsole

To install IIS features for a Static Content Web server via Package Manager, use the following command from a command prompt. (The command has been formatted to fit on the printed page.)

```
start /w pkgmgr.exe /iu:IIS-WebServerRole;IIS-WebServer;IIS-CommonHttpFeatures;
  IIS-StaticContent;IIS-DefaultDocument;IIS-DirectoryBrowsing;
  IIS-HttpErrors;IIS-HealthAndDiagnostics;IIS-HttpLogging;
  IIS-LoggingLibraries;IIS-RequestMonitor;IIS-Security;
  IIS-RequestFiltering;IIS-HttpCompressionStatic;
  IIS-WebServerManagementTools;IIS-ManagementConsole;
  WAS-WindowsActivationService;WAS-ProcessModel;
  WAS-NetFxEnvironment;WAS-ConfigurationAPI
```

To install IIS features for Static Content Web Server via ServerManagerCMD, use the following command from a command prompt:

```
ServerManagerCMD.exe -install Web-Server
```

ASP.NET

The Microsoft ASP.NET Web server is probably the most commonly used server workload type. ASP.NET has proven to be very popular among developers. IIS 7.0 and ASP.NET are designed to work closely together, and ASP.NET is a first-class citizen in IIS 7.0. Developers can deploy managed code at the same level as native modules. The integrated pipeline option provides this functionality. The Static Content Web Server modules, along with specific ASP.NET options, make up the ASP.NET workload server.

Table 5-2 lists all components that are installed when you configure your server to use the ASP.NET workload server. The table includes the appropriate update names.

Table 5-2   ASP.NET Workload Server Options

Server Manager	Update Name
Static Content	IIS-StaticContent
Default Document	IIS-DefaultDocument
Directory Browsing	IIS-DirectoryBrowsing
HTTP Errors	IIS-HttpErrors
HTTP Logging	IIS-HttpLogging
Logging Tools	IIS-LoggingLibraries
Request Monitor	IIS-RequestMonitor
Request Filtering	IIS-RequestFiltering
Static Content Compression	IIS-HttpCompressionStatic
IIS Management Console	IIS-ManagementConsole
ASP.NET	IIS-ASPNET
.NET Extensibility	IIS-NetFxExtensibility
ISAPI	IIS-ISAPIFilter
ISAPI Extensions	IIS-ISAPIExtensions

To install IIS features for the ASP.NET server workload via Package Manager, use the following command from a command prompt:

```
start /w pkgmgr.exe /iu:IIS-WebServerRole;IIS-WebServer;
  IIS-CommonHttpFeatures;IIS-StaticContent;IIS-DefaultDocument;
  IIS-DirectoryBrowsing;IIS-HttpErrors;IIS-ApplicationDevelopment;
  IIS-ASPNET;IIS-NetFxExtensibility;IIS-ISAPIExtensions;
  IIS-ISAPIFilter;IIS-HealthAndDiagnostics;IIS-HttpLogging;
  IIS-LoggingLibraries;IIS-RequestMonitor;IIS-Security;
  IIS-RequestFiltering;IIS-HttpCompressionStatic;
  IIS-WebServerManagementTools;IIS-ManagementConsole;
  WAS-WindowsActivationService;WAS-ProcessModel;
  WAS-NetFxEnvironment;WAS-ConfigurationAPI
```

To install IIS features for the ASP.NET server workload via ServerManagerCMD, use the following command from a command prompt:

```
ServerManagerCmd.exe -install Web-Server
ServerManagerCmd.exe -install Web-ASP-NET
ServerManagerCmd.exe -install Web-NET-Ext
ServerManagerCmd.exe -install Web-Filtering
ServerManagerCmd.exe -install Web-ISAPI-Filter
ServerManagerCmd.exe -install Web-ISAPI-Ext
```

Classic ASP

Before Microsoft released ASP.NET, classic ASP was used as the main programming language on IIS. Many Web sites still use classic ASP today, and IIS 7.0 supports classic ASP. Your classic ASP applications will easily port to IIS 7.0. You can take advantage of the new benefits such as diagnostics, logging, and troubleshooting, while at the same time maintaining your existing applications, enabling you to have the best of both worlds. You will be able to keep your classic ASP around and have the benefits of IIS 7.0. The static file modules, along with specific classic ASP options, make up the ASP workload server.

Table 5-3 lists all components that are installed when you configure your server to use the classic ASP workload server. The table includes the appropriate update names.

Table 5-3   Classic ASP Workload Server Options

Server Manager	Update Name
Static Content	IIS-StaticContent
Default Document	IIS-DefaultDocument
Directory Browsing	IIS-DirectoryBrowsing
HTTP Errors	IIS-HttpErrors
HTTP Logging	IIS-HttpLogging
Logging Tools	IIS-LoggingLibraries
Request Monitor	IIS-RequestMonitor
Request Filtering	IIS-RequestFiltering

Table 5-3   Classic ASP Workload Server Options

Server Manager	Update Name
Static Content Compression	IIS-HttpCompressionStatic
IIS Management Console	IIS-ManagementConsole
ASP	IIS-ASP
ISAPI Extensions	IIS-ISAPI-Extensions

To install IIS features for the classic ASP server workload via Package Manager, use the following command from a command prompt:

```
start /w pkgmgr.exe /iu:IIS-WebServerRole;IIS-WebServer;
  IIS-CommonHttpFeatures;IIS-StaticContent;IIS-DefaultDocument;
  IIS-DirectoryBrowsing;IIS-HttpErrors;IIS-ApplicationDevelopment;
  IIS-ASP;IIS-ISAPIExtensions;IIS-HealthAndDiagnostics;
  IIS-HttpLogging;IIS-LoggingLibraries;IIS-RequestMonitor;
  IIS-Security;IIS-RequestFiltering;IIS-HttpCompressionStatic;
  IIS-WebServerManagementTools;IIS-ManagementConsole;
  WAS-WindowsActivationService;WAS-ProcessModel;
  WAS-NetFxEnvironment;WAS-ConfigurationAPI
```

To install IIS features for the classic ASP Web server workload via ServerManagerCMD, use the following command from a command prompt:

```
ServerManagerCmd.exe -install Web-Server
ServerManagerCmd.exe -install Web-ASP
ServerManagerCmd.exe -install Web-Filtering
ServerManagerCmd.exe -install Web-ISAPI-Ext
```

FastCGI Server Workload

FastCGI is an alternative to CGI (Common Gateway Interface). This is a language-independent extension to CGI that provides high performance without being tied to a specific server platform.

> **Note**   For more information on the FastCGI module for IIS, please read Bill Staples's blog at *http://blogs.iis.net/bills/archive/2006/10/31/PHP-on-IIS.aspx*. The blog discusses how to enhance your PHP applications with IIS 7.0 and FastCGI modules.

One of the design goals of Windows Server 2008 is to provide a common Web server platform for all types of applications. This includes applications based on Microsoft technology such as ASP.NET and classic ASP, as well as non-Microsoft technology such as PHP.

Table 5-4 lists all components that are installed when you configure your server to use the FastCGI workload server. The table includes the appropriate update names.

Table 5-4   FastCGI Workload Server Options

Server Manager	Update Name
Static Content	IIS-StaticContent
Default Document	IIS-DefaultDocument
Directory Browsing	IIS-DirectoryBrowsing
HTTP Errors	IIS-HttpErrors
HTTP Logging	IIS-HttpLogging
Logging Tools	IIS-LoggingLibraries
Request Monitor	IIS-RequestMonitor
Request Filtering	IIS-RequestFiltering
Static Content Compression	IIS-HttpCompressionStatic
IIS Management Console	IIS-ManagementConsole
CGI	IIS-CGI

To install IIS features for the FastCGI server workload via Package Manager, use the following command from a command prompt:

```
start /w pkgmgr.exe /iu:IIS-WebServerRole;IIS-WebServer;
  IIS-CommonHttpFeatures;IIS-StaticContent;IIS-DefaultDocument;
  IIS-DirectoryBrowsing;IIS-HttpErrors;IIS-ApplicationDevelopment;
  IIS-CGI;IIS-HealthAndDiagnostics;IIS-HttpLogging;
  IIS-LoggingLibraries;IIS-RequestMonitor;IIS-Security;
  IIS-RequestFiltering;IIS-HttpCompressionStatic;
  IIS-WebServerManagementTools;IIS-ManagementConsole;
  WAS-WindowsActivationService;WAS-ProcessModel;
  WAS-NetFxEnvironment;WAS-ConfigurationAPI
```

To install IIS features for the FastCGI server workload via ServerManagerCMD, use the following command line:

```
ServerManagerCmd.exe -install Web-Server
ServerManagerCmd.exe -install Web-CGI
```

IIS Managed Modules and .NET Extensibility Server Workload

It is possible to take advantage of .NET without installing ASP.NET. You probably wonder when this type of server workload would be appropriate. Imagine you have developed your own custom HTTP modules specific to your environment. (This could include various content handling, redirection, session management, logging, or other custom application components.) This type of server workload would enable you to deploy servers with only the necessary modules to support your applications. You would have the power of IIS 7.0 and a small secure Web server footprint to meet your needs. The static file modules, along with the IIS Managed Modules and .NET Extensibility, make up this workload type.

Table 5-5 lists all components that are installed when you configure your server to use the IIS Managed Modules and .NET Extensibility workload server. The table includes the appropriate update names.

Table 5-5   IIS Managed Modules and .NET Extensibility Server Options

Server Manager	Update Name
Static Content	IIS-StaticContent
Default Document	IIS-DefaultDocument
Directory Browsing	IIS-DirectoryBrowsing
HTTP Errors	IIS-HttpErrors
HTTP Logging	IIS-HttpLogging
Logging Tools	IIS-LoggingLibraries
Request Monitor	IIS-RequestMonitor
Request Filtering	IIS-RequestFiltering
Static Content Compression	IIS-HttpCompressionStatic
IIS Management Console	IIS-ManagementConsole
.NET Extensibility	IIS-NetFxExtensibility

To install IIS features for the IIS Managed Modules and .NET Extensibility server workload via Package Manager, use the following command from a command prompt:

```
start /w pkgmgr.exe /iu:IIS-WebServerRole;IIS-WebServer;
  IIS-CommonHttpFeatures;IIS-StaticContent;IIS-DefaultDocument;
  IIS-DirectoryBrowsing;IIS-HttpErrors;IIS-ApplicationDevelopment;
  IIS-NetFxExtensibility;IIS-ISAPIExtensions;IIS-ISAPIFilter;
  IIS-HealthAndDiagnostics;IIS-HttpLogging;IIS-LoggingLibraries;
  IIS-RequestMonitor;IIS-Security;IIS-RequestFiltering;
  IIS-HttpCompressionStatic;IIS-WebServerManagementTools;
  IIS-ManagementConsole;WAS-WindowsActivationService;
  WAS-ProcessModel;WAS-NetFxEnvironment;WAS-ConfigurationAPI
```

To install IIS features for the IIS Managed Modules and .NET Extensibility server workload via ServerManagerCMD, use the following command from a command prompt:

```
ServerManagerCmd.exe -install Web-Server
ServerManagerCmd.exe -install Web-Net-Ext
```

IIS Full Install

You might want to do a complete IIS 7.0 installation in a test environment to evaluate everything IIS 7.0 has to offer. When you install all 40-plus modules, you are guaranteed that everything you need is available. In a true development scenario, however, it is probably not a good idea to do a full installation, because you could run into issues when you migrate your applications to a production environment that contains only a subset of modules. If you install only the minimum number of modules and features in your development environment, you will gain a complete understanding of what modules are needed and why. This will help keep your production server installation footprint smaller and more secure. The fewer modules deployed, the better your application performance will be. The more you do to match your development environment to your production servers, the more likely it is that you'll have a smooth transition from development to production.

Table 5-6 lists all the components installed when you do a full installation of IIS 7.0. The table includes the appropriate update names.

Table 5-6   Full Server Install Components

Server Manager	Update Name
Internet Information Services	IIS-WebServerRole
World Wide Web Services	IIS-WebServer
Common HTTP Features	IIS-CommonHttpFeatures
Static Content	IIS-StaticContent
Default Document	IIS-DefaultDocument
Directory Browsing	IIS-DirectoryBrowsing
HTTP Errors	IIS-HttpErrors
HTTP Redirection	IIS-HttpRedirect
Application Development	IIS-ApplicationDevelopment
ASP.NET	IIS-ASPNET
.NET Extensibility	IIS-NetFxExtensibility
ASP	IIS-ASP
CGI	IIS-CGI
ISAPI Extensions	IIS-ISAPIExtensions
ISAPI Filters	IIS-ISAPIFilter
Server-Side Includes	IIS-ServerSideInclude
Health and Diagnostics	IIS-HealthAndDiagnostics
HTTP Logging	IIS-HTTPLogging
Logging Tools	IIS-LoggingLibraries
Request Monitor	IIS-RequestMonitor
Tracing	IIS-HttpTracing
Custom Logging	IIS-CustomLogging
ODBC Logging	IIS-ODBCLogging
Security	IIS-Security
Basic Authentication	IIS-BasicAuthentication
Windows Authentication	IIS-WindowsAuthentication
Digest Authentication	IIS-DigestAuthentication
Client Certificate Mapping Authentication	IIS-ClientCertificateMappingAuthentication
IIS Client Certificate Mapping Authentication	IIS-IISCertificateMappingAuthentication
URL Authorization	IIS-URLAuthorization
Request Filtering	IIS-RequestFiltering

Table 5-6   Full Server Install Components

Server Manager	Update Name
IP and Domain Restrictions	IIS-IPSecurity
Performance	IIS-Performance
Static Content Compression	IIS-HttpCompressionStatic
Dynamic Content Compression	IIS-HttpCompressionDynamic
Management Tools	IIS-WebServerManagementTools
IIS Management Console	IIS-ManagementConsole
IIS Management Scripts and Tools	IIS-ManagementScriptingTools
Management Service	IIS-ManagementService
IIS 6 Management Compatibility	IIS-IIS6ManagementCompatibility
IIS Metabase Compatibility	IIS-Metabase
IIS 6 WMI Compatibility	IIS-WMICompatibility
IIS 6 Scripting Tools	IIS-LegacyScripts
IIS 6 Management Console	IIS-LegacySnapIn
FTP Publishing Service	IIS-FTPPublishingService
FTP Server	IIS-FTPServer
FTP Management Console	IIS-FTPManagement
Windows Process Activation Service	WAS-WindowsActivationService
Process Model	WAS-ProcessModel
.NET Environment	WAS-NetFxEnvironment
Configuration APIs	WAS-ConfigurationAPI

To install IIS features for a full server install via Package Manager, use the following command from a command prompt:

```
start /w pkgmgr.exe /iu:IIS-WebServerRole;IIS-WebServer;
  IIS-CommonHttpFeatures;IIS-StaticContent;IIS-DefaultDocument;
  IIS-DirectoryBrowsing;IIS-HttpErrors;IIS-HttpRedirect;
  IIS-ApplicationDevelopment;IIS-ASPNET;IIS-NetFxExtensibility;
  IIS-ASP;IIS-CGI;IIS-ISAPIExtensions;IIS-ISAPIFilter;
  IIS-ServerSideIncludes;IIS-HealthAndDiagnostics;IIS-HttpLogging;
  IIS-LoggingLibraries;IIS-RequestMonitor;IIS-HttpTracing;
  IIS-CustomLogging;IIS-ODBCLogging;IIS-Security;
  IIS-BasicAuthentication;IIS-WindowsAuthentication;
  IIS-DigestAuthentication;IIS-ClientCertificateMappingAuthentication;
  IIS-IISCertificateMappingAuthentication;IIS-URLAuthorization;
  IIS-RequestFiltering;IIS-IPSecurity;IIS-Performance;
  IIS-HttpCompressionStatic;IIS-HttpCompressionDynamic;
  IIS-WebServerManagementTools;IIS-WebServerManagementTools;
  IIS-ManagementConsole;IIS-ManagementScriptingTools;
  IIS-ManagementService;IIS-IIS6ManagementCompatibility;
  IIS-Metabase;IIS-WMICompatibility;IIS-LegacyScripts;
  IIS-LegacySnapIn;IIS-FTPPublishingService;IIS-FTPServer;
  IIS-FTPManagement;WAS-WindowsActivationService;WAS-ProcessModel;
  WAS-NetFxEnvironment;WAS-ConfigurationAPI
```

To perform a full server install via ServerManagerCMD, use the following command from a command prompt:

```
ServerManagerCMD.exe –install Web-Server –allSubFeatures
```

Table 5-7 lists all ServerManagerCMD update names. Note that to perform a full installation using ServerManagerCMD, you can simply specify the –a switch. Refer to Table 5-7 when you need to install specific modules.

Table 5-7   Complete List of ServerManagerCMD Update Names

Server Manager	Update Name
Common HTTP Features	Web-Common-Http
Static Content	Web-Static-Content
Default Document	Web-Default-Doc
Directory Browsing	Web-Dir-Browsing
HTTP Errors	Web-Http-Errors
HTTP Redirection	Web-Http-Redirect
Application Development	Web-App-Dev
ASP.NET	Web-Asp-Net
.NET Extensibility	Web-Net-Ext
ASP	Web-ASP
CGI	Web-CGI
ISAPI Extensions	Web-ISAPI-Ext
ISAPI Filters	Web-ISAPI-Filter
Server Side Includes	Web-Includes
Health and Diagnostics	Web-Health
HTTP Logging	Web-Http-Logging
Logging Tools	Web-Log-Libraries
Request Monitor	Web-Request-Monitor
Tracing	Web-Http-Tracing
Custom Logging	Web-Custom-Logging
ODBC Logging	Web-ODBC-Logging
Security	Web-Security
Basic Authentication	Web-Basic-Auth
Windows Authentication	Web-Windows-Auth
Digest Authentication	Web-Digest-Auth
Client Certificate Mapping Authentication	Web-Client-Auth
IIS Client Certificate Mapping Authentication	Web-Cert-Auth
URL Authorization	Web-Url-Auth
Request Filtering	Web-Filtering
IP and Domain Restrictions	Web-IP-Security

Table 5-7   Complete List of ServerManagerCMD Update Names

Server Manager	Update Name
Performance	Web-Performance
Static Content Compression	Web-Stat-Compression
Dynamic Content Compression	Web-Dyn-Compression
Management Tools	Web-Mgmt-Tools
IIS Management Console	Web-Mgmt-Console
IIS Management Scripts and Tools	Web-Scripting-Tools
Management Service	Web-Mgmt-Service
IIS 6 Management Compatibility	Web-Mgmt-Compat
IIS 6 Metabase Compatibility	Web-Metabase
IIS 6 WMI Compatibility	Web-WMI
IIS 6 Scripting Tools	Web-Lgcy-Scripting
IIS 6 Management Console	Web-Lgcy-Mgmt-Console
FTP Publishing Service	Web-Ftp-Publishing
FTP Server	Web-Ftp-Server
FTP Management Console	Web-Ftp-Mgmt-Console
Windows Process Activation Service	WAS
Process Model	WAS-Process-Model
.NET Environment	WAS-NET-Environment
Configuration APIs	WAS-Config-APIs

Server Core Web Edition Server Workload

Windows Server 2008 introduces Server Core, which is a complete command line shell operating system.

> **Note**   A good introduction to IIS 7.0 Server Core is available at *http://www.iis.net/articles/ view.aspx/IIS7/Explore-IIS7/Getting-Started/IIS7-on-Server-Core.*

Server Core provides an installation option that produces a server that can be treated as an appliance. Traditional UI components such as Microsoft Internet Explorer and Windows Media Player are not installed. Server Core Web Edition is perfect for hosting IIS 7.0 when you want to support classic ASP; static, PHP-based; Internet Server Application Programming Interface (ISAPI); and other Web applications that do not require .NET. Server Core does not include ASP.NET and .NET functionality. Even without ASP.NET, you can use Server Core Web Edition for various workloads. For example, you can use Server Core to serve images. Only two modules are required for this server workload: the StaticFileModule and AnonymousAuthenticationModule. The following example shows the power and flexibility of the IIS 7.0 modular architecture.

Installing IIS 7.0 on Server Core Web Edition

To install IIS 7.0 on Server Core Web Edition, follow these steps:

1. Install Server Core Web Edition and configure the Server Core instance with an IP address. You'll need two commands to configure your server with an IP address. Enter the following command at a command prompt:

   ```
   netsh interface ipv4 show interfaces
   ```

   The output is similar to the following:

   ```
   Idx  Met   MTU     State         Name
   ---  ---   -----   -----------   -------------------
     2   10    1500   connected     Local Area Connection
     1   50 4294967295 connected    Loopback Pseudo-Interface
   ```

   Next, enter the following command at the command prompt (replace the IP information with appropriate values for your environment):

   ```
   netsh interface ipv4 set address name="2" source=static
     address=192.168.0.10 mask=255.255.255.0 gateway=192.168.0.1
   ```

2. Now, to perform a default installation of IIS 7.0, run the following command at the command prompt:

   ```
   start /w pkgmgr /iu:IIS-WebServerRole;WAS-WindowsActivationService;
     WAS-ProcessModel
   ```

3. Back up the current ApplicationHost.config file by running the following command at the command prompt:

   ```
   %windir%\System32\Inetsrv\appcmd add backup "ContosoComConfig"
   ```

4. Open the file *%windir%*\System32\Inetsrv\Config\ApplicationHost.config in Notepad. To do this, you can type the following from the command line:

   ```
   Notepad %windir%\system32\inetsrv\config\applicationHost.config
   ```

5. Locate the Global Modules section and change it as follows:

   ```
   <globalModules>
       <add name="StaticFileModule"
           image="%windir%\system32\inetsrv\static.dll" />
       <add name="AnonymousAuthenticationModule"
           image="%windir%\system32\inetsrv\authanon.dll" />
       <add name="HttpLoggingModule"
           image="%windir%\system32\inetsrv\loghttp.dll" />
   </globalModules>
   ```

6. Locate the Modules section in ApplicationHost.config and change it to match the following:

```
<modules>
    <add name="StaticFileModule" lockItem="true" />
    <add name="AnonymousAuthenticationModule" lockItem="true" />
    <add name="HttpLoggingModule" lockItem="true" />
</modules>
```

7. Open a browser from a remote machine and visit *http://<IPAddressOfServerCore>/welcome.png*.

This should display the Welcome message.

From a command prompt on the Server Core, you can verify that just three modules related to IIS 7.0 are loaded. To do so, run the following command from the command prompt:

```
tasklist /m /fi "Imagename eq w3wp.exe"
```

The resulting output should look like this:

```
Image Name                  PID Modules
========================= ======== ===========================================
w3wp.exe                   1108 ntdll.dll, kernel32.dll, ADVAPI32.dll,
                                 RPCRT4.dll, msvcrt.dll, USER32.dll,
                                 GDI32.dll, ole32.dll, IISUTIL.dll,
                                 CRYPT32.dll, MSASN1.dll, USERENV.dll,
                                 Secur32.dll, WS2_32.dll, NSI.dll,
                                 IMM32.DLL, MSCTF.dll, LPK.DLL, USP10.dll,
                                 NTMARTA.DLL, WLDAP32.dll, PSAPI.DLL,
                                 SAMLIB.dll, w3wphost.dll, OLEAUT32.dll,
                                 nativerd.dll, XmlLite.dll, IISRES.DLL,
                                 rsaenh.dll, CLBCatQ.DLL, mlang.dll,
                                 comctl32.dll, SHLWAPI.dll, iiscore.dll,
                                 W3TP.dll, w3dt.dll, HTTPAPI.dll, slc.dll,
                                 faultrep.dll, VERSION.dll, mswsock.dll,
                                 DNSAPI.dll, NLAapi.dll, IPHLPAPI.DLL,
                                 dhcpcsvc.DLL, WINNSI.DLL, dhcpcsvc6.DLL,
                                 wshtcpip.dll, wship6.dll, static.dll,
                                 authanon.dll, loghttp.dll
```

Notice the last three dynamic-link libraries (DLLs) are static.dll, authanon.dll, and loghttp.dll. The DLLs are loaded in the same order as they are listed in the ApplicationHost.config file. The other modules are related to the operating system.

This example demonstrates a lightweight yet flexible server that can serve images and log the hits in standard IIS logs. You can use your normal Web reporting tools to track the images being served.

> **Caution**   Back up your ApplicationHost.config file whenever you manually edit the file. Doing so allows you to restore your server to its original state if a problem should occur. You would not make it a regular task to restore your ApplicationHost.config file, however; you would only run the restore command if there was an issue, or for this example, to restore your server to its original state.

Windows Server 2008 modular architecture provides the ability to customize your server setup. Except for the Server Core workload example, the examples presented in this chapter are common workload scenarios that show how to customize IIS 7.0 to fit your everyday application needs.

> **Note**   For more information about administering IIS 7.0 on Server Core installations of Windows Server 2008, go to *http://blogs.iis.net/metegokt/archive/2007/06/26/administering-iis7-on-server-core-installations-of-windows-server-2008.aspx.*

Ways to Install IIS 7.0

Server Manager, Package Manager (Pkgmgr.exe), and ServerManagerCMD are the basic tools you use to install IIS 7.0. In addition, when you are deploying IIS 7.0 throughout an enterprise, you should know about some alternative techniques. The following sections offer some basic pointers and tips that you should keep in mind when using each tool and option for installing IIS 7.0.

Using Server Manager

Before you install IIS 7.0, you need to be aware of least-privileged user accounts (LUA). The goal of Windows User Account Control is to reduce the exposure and attack surface. It requires that all users run in standard user mode. If you are logged onto an account other than the built-in local administrator account, you might see the security alert dialog box shown in Figure 5-1.

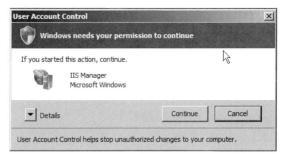

Figure 5-1   Windows security (User Account Control).

Preparing Local User Administrator Security

Make sure to either log on using the built-in Administrator account or else to explicitly start your applications by using the built-in Administrator account credentials. You can use the **runas** command line tool. For example, to launch Notepad, you could run the following command:

```
runas /user:Administrator Notepad.exe
```

You will then be prompted for the password of the Administrator account.

> **Note**   It's useful to have a command prompt shell that already has elevated credentials. You can start such a shell with the following command:
>
> ```
> runas /user:administrator cmd.exe
> ```
>
> Every application you run from the resulting command prompt will use elevated credentials as well, and you will not need to use the **runas** command line tool from that command prompt.

Installing IIS 7.0 Using Server Manager

Server Manager provides a single console to perform all administrative functions on Windows Server 2008. When you first log into Windows Server 2008, Server Manager should automatically launch. To manually launch Server Manager, from the Start menu, click All Programs, Administrative Tools, and then Server Manager.

Follow these steps to install the Web Server (IIS) Server Role using Server Manager:

1. Start Server Manager.

2. Select Roles and then click Add Roles.

3. Follow the Add Roles Wizard prompts and select the IIS features you want to install.

> **Note**   The following article walks you through an installation of IIS 7.0 using Server Manager: *http://www.iis.net/articles/view.aspx/IIS7/Deploy-an-IIS7-Server/Installing-IIS7/Install-IIS7-on-Longhorn-Server?Page=2.*

Using Package Manager

Windows optional features in both Windows Vista and Windows Server 2008 can be installed using Package Manager (pkgmgr). The command line syntax using Package Manager is as follows:

```
start /w pkgmgr.exe /iu:update1:update2...
```

Note If you run Package Manager without the `start  /w` prefix, the `pkgmgr` command will return immediately, and you will not know when the installation has completed.

See the following list for the most common Package Manager commands. For a complete list of available commands, run the following command:

```
Pkgmgr.exe /?
```

- **/iu:{update name};** Specifies updates to install by update name. You can specify multiple updates to install by separating each update with a semicolon.

- **/uu:{update name};** Specifies updates to uninstall. You can specify multiple updates to uninstall by separating each update with a semicolon. At least one update name must be specified.

- **/n:{unattend XML}** Specifies an XML file that provides information for an unattended installation. (For information about performing an unattended installation, see the section titled "Unattended Answer Files" later in this chapter.)

Note For more information about IIS.NET and Package Manager, see *http://www.iis.net// articles/view.aspx/IIS7/Deploy-an-IIS7-Server/Installing-IIS7/Install-IIS7-from-the- Command-Line.*

Using ServerManagerCMD

ServerManagerCMD, along with the GUI version of Server Manager, enables you to query, install, and remove roles and features from the server. ServerManagerCMD also displays all roles, role services, and available features, and it shows which are installed on the computer. You can run the following command from the command prompt:

```
ServerManagerCMD.exe -query
```

Figure 5-2 shows an example of the resulting output.

If you want to install the Web Server role, for example, you could use the following command:

```
ServerManagerCmd -install Web-Server
```

You can also place the installation actions in an XML document like this (the `xmlns` string has been formatted on multiple lines to fit on the printed page):

```
<ServerManagerConfiguration Action="Install"
    xmlns="http://schemas.microsoft.com/sdm/Windows/ServerManager
           /Configuration/2007/1">
   <Role Id="Web-Server"/>
</ServerManagerConfiguration>
```

```
Administrator: C:\Windows\system32\cmd.exe
[X] Web Server (IIS)  [Web-Server]
    [X] Web Server  [Web-WebServer]
        [X] Common HTTP Features  [Web-Common-Http]
            [X] Static Content  [Web-Static-Content]
            [X] Default Document  [Web-Default-Doc]
            [X] Directory Browsing  [Web-Dir-Browsing]
            [X] HTTP Errors  [Web-Http-Errors]
            [X] HTTP Redirection  [Web-Http-Redirect]
        [X] Application Development  [Web-App-Dev]
            [X] ASP.NET  [Web-Asp-Net]
            [X] .NET Extensibility  [Web-Net-Ext]
            [X] ASP  [Web-ASP]
            [X] CGI  [Web-CGI]
            [X] ISAPI Extensions  [Web-ISAPI-Ext]
            [X] ISAPI Filters  [Web-ISAPI-Filter]
            [X] Server Side Includes  [Web-Includes]
        [X] Health and Diagnostics  [Web-Health]
            [X] HTTP Logging  [Web-Http-Logging]
            [X] Logging Tools  [Web-Log-Libraries]
            [X] Request Monitor  [Web-Request-Monitor]
            [X] Tracing  [Web-Http-Tracing]
            [X] Custom Logging  [Web-Custom-Logging]
            [X] ODBC Logging  [Web-ODBC-Logging]
        [X] Security  [Web-Security]
            [X] Basic Authentication  [Web-Basic-Auth]
            [X] Windows Authentication  [Web-Windows-Auth]
            [X] Digest Authentication  [Web-Digest-Auth]
            [X] Client Certificate Mapping Authentication  [Web-Client-Auth]
            [X] IIS Client Certificate Mapping Authentication  [Web-Cert-Auth]
            [X] URL Authorization  [Web-Url-Auth]
            [X] Request Filtering  [Web-Filtering]
            [X] IP and Domain Restrictions  [Web-IP-Security]
        [X] Performance  [Web-Performance]
            [X] Static Content Compression  [Web-Stat-Compression]
            [X] Dynamic Content Compression  [Web-Dyn-Compression]
    [X] Management Tools  [Web-Mgmt-Tools]
        [X] IIS Management Console  [Web-Mgmt-Console]
        [X] IIS Management Scripts and Tools  [Web-Scripting-Tools]
        [X] Management Service  [Web-Mgmt-Service]
        [X] IIS 6 Management Compatibility  [Web-Mgmt-Compat]
            [X] IIS 6 Metabase Compatibility  [Web-Metabase]
            [X] IIS 6 WMI Compatibility  [Web-WMI]
            [X] IIS 6 Scripting Tools  [Web-Lgcy-Scripting]
            [X] IIS 6 Management Console  [Web-Lgcy-Mgmt-Console]
    [X] FTP Publishing Service  [Web-Ftp-Publishing]
        [X] FTP Server  [Web-Ftp-Server]
        [X] FTP Management Console  [Web-Ftp-Mgmt-Console]
[ ] Windows Deployment Services  [WDS]
```

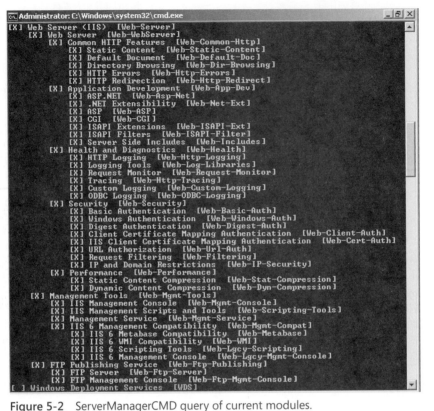

Figure 5-2 ServerManagerCMD query of current modules.

If the XML were saved in a file named WebServerInstall.xml, you could then use the following -whatIf switch from a command prompt to determine what would be installed based on the input file.

```
ServerManagerCmd.exe -inputPath WebServerInstall.xml -whatIf
```

The resulting output is shown in Figure 5-3.

```
Administrator: Command Prompt

C:\Users\Administrator>ServerManagerCmd -inputPath WebServerInstall.xml -whatIf
...
Note: Running in 'WhatIf' Mode.
Specified for installation: [Web Server (IIS)] Management Tools
Specified for installation: [Web Server (IIS)] Web Server
Specified for installation: [Web Server (IIS)] Security
Specified for installation: [Web Server (IIS)] Health and Diagnostics
Specified for installation: [Web Server (IIS)] IIS Management Console
Specified for installation: [Web Server (IIS)] Performance
Specified for installation: [Web Server (IIS)] Common HTTP Features
Specified for installation: [Web Server (IIS)] Static Content Compression
Specified for installation: [Web Server (IIS)] Default Document
Specified for installation: [Web Server (IIS)] HTTP Errors
Specified for installation: [Web Server (IIS)] Static Content
Specified for installation: [Web Server (IIS)] Request Monitor
Specified for installation: [Web Server (IIS)] HTTP Logging
Specified for installation: [Web Server (IIS)] Request Filtering
Specified for installation: [Web Server (IIS)] Directory Browsing

This server may need to be restarted after the installation completes.

C:\Users\Administrator>_
```

Figure 5-3 ServerManagerCMD output from the -whatIf switch.

To actually perform the Web Server installation, run this command:

```
ServerManagerCmd –inputPath WebServerInstall.xml
```

Recall that if you want to find out what roles and features are installed, you can use the following query:

```
ServerManagerCmd -query
```

To save the list of installed roles and features to an XML file, use the following command:

```
ServerManagerCmd -query currentConfig.xml
```

Viewing the Currentconfig.xml file gives you all the information you need to figure out which roles and features are installed on a server.

Here is the complete syntax for ServerManagerCMD:

```
        -query [<query.xml>] [-logPath <log.txt>]
        -install <name>
            [-setting <setting name>=<setting value>]* [-allSubFeatures]
            [-resultPath <result.xml> [-restart] | -whatIf] [-logPath
            <log.txt>]
        -remove <name>
            [-resultPath <result.xml> [-restart] | -whatIf] [-logPath
            <log.txt>]
        -inputPath <answer.xml>
            [-resultPath <result.xml> [-restart] | -whatIf] [-logPath
    <log.txt>]
        -help | -?
        -version
Switch Parameters:
  -query [<query.xml>]
        Display a list of all roles, role services, and features available,
        and shows which are installed on this computer. (Short form: -q)
        If <query.xml> is specified, the information is also saved to a
        query.xml file, in XML format.
  -inputPath <answer.xml>
        Installs or removes the roles, role services, and features
        specified in an XML answer file, the path and name of which
        is represent by <answer.xml>. (ShortForm: -ip)
  -install <name>
        Install the role, role service, or feature on the computer that is
        specified by the <name> parameter. (Short form: -i)
  -setting <setting name>=<setting value>
        Used with the -install parameter to specify required settings for
        the installation. (Short form: -s)
  -allSubFeatures
        Used with the -install parameter to install all subordinate
        role services and features along with the role, role service, or
        feature named with the -install parameter. (Short form: -a)
  -remove <name>
        Removes the role, role service, or feature from the computer that
        is specified by the <name> parameter. (Short form: -r)
```

```
-resultPath <result.xml>
      Saves the result of the ServerManagerCmd.exe operation to a
      <result.xml> file, in XML format. (Short form: -rp)
-restart
      Restarts the computer automatically, if restarting is necessary to
      complete the operation.
-whatIf
      Display the operations to be performed on the current computer
      that are specified in the answer.xml file. (Short form: -w)
-logPath <log.txt>
      Specify the non-default location for the log file. (Short form: -l)
-help
      Display help information. (Short form: -?)
-version
      Display the version of the Server Manager command that is running,
      Microsoft trademark information, and the operating system.
      (Short form: -v)
Examples:
   ServerManagerCmd.exe -query
   ServerManagerCmd.exe -install Web-Server -resultPath installResult.xml
   ServerManagerCmd.exe -inputPath install.xml -whatIf
```

Unattended Answer Files

Windows Server 2008 unattended answer files, including IIS 7.0, are now formatted as XML, unlike in previous versions of Windows. An answer file can provide a consistent, repeatable approach when you need to install IIS 7.0 on many servers. You can use an answer file with Package Manager and ServerManagerCMD. Each tool requires a slightly different format when using an answer file. This section examines a sample answer file for each tool.

Package Manager is a Windows Server 2008 native tool provided to install IIS 7.0. To experiment with an unattended installation, use Notepad to create the sample answer file on the next page and then save it as Unattend.xml.

You'll need to determine the *version* and *processorArchitecture* settings for your environment and appropriately change the bold type lines shown in the code before proceeding with an unattended install using Package Manager.

> **Note**   To obtain the version number, open Windows Explorer, navigate to
> *%windir%*\System32, right-click Regedt32.exe, and select Properties. Select the Details tab,
> locate the File Version property (as shown in Figure 5-4), and use this value for the *version*
> setting in your Unattend.xml file. To obtain the architecture, run Set from a command prompt
> and look for the *processor_architecture* variable.

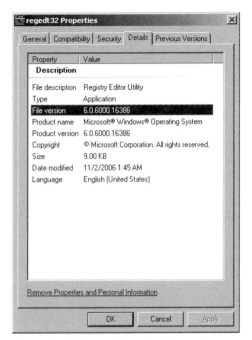

Figure 5-4   Determining the file version.

```xml
<?xml version="1.0" ?>
<unattend xmlns="urn:schemas-microsoft-com:unattend"
          xmlns:wcm="http://schemas.microsoft.com/WMIConfig/2002/State">
<servicing>
   <!-- Install a selectable update in a package that is in the Windows
        Foundation namespace -->
   <package action="configure">
      <assemblyIdentity
         name="Microsoft-Windows-Foundation-Package"
         version="6.0.XXXX.XXXXX"
         language="neutral"
         processorArchitecture="x86"
         publicKeyToken="31bf3856ad364e35"
         versionScope="nonSxS"
      />
<selection name="IIS-WebServerRole" state="true"/>
<selection name="WAS-WindowsActivationService" state="true"/>
<selection name="WAS-ProcessModel" state="true"/>
<selection name="WAS-NetFxEnvironment" state="true"/>
<selection name="WAS-ConfigurationAPI" state="true"/>
  </package>
 </servicing>
 </unattend>
```

To run the installation process, enter the following command at the command prompt:

```
pkgmgr /n:unattend.xml
```

You can save your XML unattended answer file on a network share and point Package Manager to this file. Maintaining a single installation file helps streamline administration of your installation processes.

ServerManagerCMD is the command line version of Server Manager. The syntax for the unattended answer file is slightly different than the Package Manager syntax. You can use ServerManagerCMD on all versions of Windows Server 2008 except Server Core.

Here is a sample file you can use with ServerManagerCMD. This example shows installing a Static Content Web Server. Save the following content as Default.xml in your local disk (again, the *xmlns* string has been split to fit on the printed page).

```
<ServerManagerConfiguration Action="Install"
    xmlns="http://schemas.microsoft.com/sdm/Windows/ServerManager
        /Configuration/2007/1">
        <Role Id="Web-Server" />
</ServerManagerConfiguration>
```

To use this answer file with ServerManagerCMD, open a command prompt and type the following:

```
ServerManagerCMD.exe -inputPath Default.xml
```

> **Note**   For more information about ServerManagerCMD and various workloads, see *http://blogs.iis.net/metegokt/archive/2007/04/13/installing-iis-7-0-using-servermanagercmd-exe.aspx.*

Sysprep/New Setup System

Sysprep has been used for years to prepare standard image files as part of a server deployment process. Windows Server 2008 and IIS 7.0 support Sysprep-based deployments. As an alternative approach to running an unattended install every time you deploy a new server, you can build a single server and install and configure IIS 7.0 on the server to fit your environment. Once you run Sysprep, you can use an image capture program such as ImageX, which is included in the Windows Automated Installation Kit (WAIK). You could then use Windows Deployment Services (WDS) to deploy the image to servers in your environment.

One limitation to be aware of when using Sysprep with an IIS 7.0 installation is that the original machine key values are encrypted and stored in the ApplicationHost.config file. When the image is rolled out to a new machine, you'll need to correct the machine key value as part of your post-build process that occurs as part of the first logon procedure. The first logon procedure can vary, depending on which tools you use to deploy images in your environment.

Auto-Installs

Microsoft introduced Windows Deployment Services (WDS) in Windows Server 2003 Service Pack 2 (SP2).

Windows Server 2008 includes Windows Deployment Services (WDS), which is the successor to Remote Installation Services (RIS). WDS uses Pre-boot Execution Environment (PXE) to deploy a Sysprep image or a scripted installation.

Whatever tools you decide to use, Windows Server 2008 and IIS 7.0 provide a variety of options to help streamline your server deployment.

Note   For more information about WDS, see *http://technet2.microsoft.com/WindowsVista/en/library/9e197135-6711-4c20-bfad-fc80fc2151301033.mspx?mfr=true*.

For more information about the WDS role that is included in Windows Server 2008, see *http://technet2.microsoft.com/windowsserver2008/en/library/b279dfef-892e-4b12-bb6b-c250cf8c95f41033.mspx?mfr=true*.

Windows Server 2008 Setup for Optional Features

The tools introduced in Windows Server 2008 completely replace previous installation tools such as Sysocmgr.exe and Setup.exe. A common install base provides many benefits. Windows Server 2008 offers a componentized install architecture.

Note   For more information about installing optional features, see *http://www.iis.net/articles/view.aspx/IIS7/Deploy-an-IIS7-Server/Installing-IIS7/Understanding-Setup-in-IIS7*.

Direct from the Source: Debating Which Features to Include in IIS 7.0

During the design of Windows Vista, the IIS team started to consider how to integrate the new modular design of IIS 7.0 with the new installation technologies of Windows Vista. (Windows Vista and Windows Server 2008 are based on the same code base, so the many technologies that appear in Windows Server 2008 first appeared in Windows Vista.) Although there were numerous technical issues to resolve, of course, the philosophical debate about what to install with IIS 7.0 by default was one of the hot topics.

When IIS 6.0 is installed, it has a lot of capabilities such as digest authentication, compression, default document handling, and other features that are more or less taken for granted, because they are always there. With IIS 7.0, these and other features are individual .dll files that can be installed or removed using the various operating system installation technologies (Server Manager, ServerManagerCMD, or Package Manager). The question facing the IIS team was whether IIS 7.0 should be installed by default with features equivalent to those in the default installation of IIS 6.0, or—since the new architecture is modular—whether only a minimal set of features should be installed.

The argument for IIS 6.0 equivalency is that this is what customers are expecting, and IIS 6.0 was considered secure out of the box. The argument for a reduced feature set is that it follows best practices to install only the minimal set required and have customers opt-in for features explicitly.

In the end, the minimal feature set was the choice, and I think it is the right choice. If you decide to install the Web Server (IIS) role and no other options, the only capability IIS 7.0 will have is to deliver static, anonymous content. You need to explicitly select additional capabilities.

The nice thing is that Server Manager and ServerManagerCMD will respect dependencies that are fully described in the underlying packages that make up the installation components for the various subsystems. So, if a customer wants to install ASP.NET, they just need to select that option, and the installation system will automatically install ISAPI capabilities and any other features that may be required to support the requested feature. In this way, the customer gets enhanced security out of the box, and an easy way to add functionality to the server.

Brett Hill, Technical Evangelist

Post Installation

After your installation is complete, one of the first things you need to do is back up your ApplicationHost.config, Administration.config, and Redirection.config files. These are stored in the *%windir%*\System32\Inetsrv\Config folder. You can either make copies of these files manually or use the Appcmd.exe Backup feature to make copies as follows:

```
//How to make a backup using Appcmd
%windir%\system32\inetsrv\appcmd.exe add backup "MyBackup"
```

This process will place critical files in the *%windir%*\System32\Inetsrv\Backup\MyBackup folder. The Administration.config, ApplicationHost.config, Mbschema.xml, Metabase.xml, and Redirection.config files are stored in this location.

After you back up your configuration, use the Web Server (IIS) Role Page to view the status of IIS. Use the IIS Manager Console to configure the IIS features you installed.

Folders and Content

Use the following list to validate your installation. These key files and folders store the critical content and binaries for your IIS 7.0 installation.

- **%windir%\system32\inetsrv**   Root install folder of all IIS processes.

- **%windir%\system32\inetsrv\config**   Contains all configuration files related to IIS including the ApplicationHost.config, Administration.config, and Redirection.config files. These configuration files store all critical configuration information and data related to IIS.

- **%windir%\system32\inetsrv\config\schema**   Stores all XML schema definition files used by configuration files.

- **%SystemDrive%\inetpub**   Default root folder for IIS content. Note that it is suggested you place your Web sites on a drive other than *%SystemDrive%*.

- **%SystemDrive%\inetpub\AdminScripts**   Contains scripts used for administering IIS and related services. This folder is not installed by default. This folder is only installed when compatibility components are installed.

- **%SystemDrive%\inetpub\custerr**   Location for all IIS custom error Web pages. This is a new location in IIS 7.0.

- **%SystemDrive%\inetpub\history**   Contains the automatic backups of the configuration made by the ConfigHistory features in IIS 7.0. See Chapter 4, "Understanding the Configuration System," for details.

- **%SystemDrive%\inetpub\ftproot**   Default FTP root folder for the built-in FTP Publishing Service.

- **%SystemDrive%\inetpub\logs\failedreqlogfiles**   Location for all IIS Failed Request Event Tracing. This is a new location in IIS 7.0.

> **Note**   The built-in FTP Publishing Service and SMTP Service logs are stored by default in *%windir%*\System32\LogFiles.

- **%SystemDrive%\inetpub\mailroot**   Root folder for all SMTP Service–related processes. This is not installed by default.

- **%SystemDrive%\inetpub\temp**   Used by ASP.NET and IIS to store ASP compiled templates and IIS temporary compressed files.

- **%SystemDrive%\inetpub\wwwroot**   Root Folder for Default Web Site. Note that it is suggested you place your Websites on a drive other than *%SystemDrive%*.

- **%windir%\IIS7.log**   Setup Log file used to record the installation.

- **%windir%\system32\inetsrv\config\applicationHost.config**   Core configuration file used by IIS. This is the main file that replaces the metabase in previous IIS versions.

Registry

The IIS 7.0 installation also records information about what is installed in the registry key.

HKEY_LOCAL_MACHINE\Software\Microsoft\InetStp\Components\.

This registry key contains only items that are currently installed. Modules that have never been installed or that have been uninstalled are not listed.

 Note   For more information about this topic, including a reference table with each registry key value, see *http://www.iis.net/articles/view.aspx/IIS7/Deploy-an-IIS7-Server/Installing-IIS7/Discover-Installed-Components*.

Services

Table 5-8 is a list of the system services that get installed during a Web server role installation, when all role services are selected.

Table 5-8   List of System Services Installed with the Web Server Role

Service Name	Description
ASP.NET State Service	Provides support for out-of-process session states for ASP.NET. If this service is stopped, out-of-process requests will not be processed.
IIS Admin Service	Enables this server to administer metabase FTP services. If this service is stopped, the server will be unable to run metabase or FTP sites.
Web Management Service	Enables remote and delegated management capabilities so that administrators can manage the Web server, sites, and applications present on the machine.
Windows Process Activation Service (WAS)	Provides process activation, resource management, and health management services for message-activated applications.
World Wide Publishing Service	Provides Web connectivity and administration through the IIS Manager.
FTP Publishing Service (Built-in)	Enables this server to be a File Transfer Protocol (FTP) server.

Validation

To validate the Web Server (IIS) Server Role, you can open Server Manager and select Web Server (IIS) Server Role. This provides a central console to view event logs, services related to IIS, and other related services. You can also open the IIS Manager Console directly from the Administrative Tools program group. One of the features in the IIS Manager Console you can use to verify your installation is Modules. Double-click Modules to see if the appropriate modules are listed as installed.

WebUI

IIS 7.0 introduces an entirely new IIS Manager. This application provides a single interface to manage all IIS 7.0 Web sites and ASP.NET settings. Windows Server 2008 also provides the Internet Information Services (IIS) 6.0 Manager to manage the built-in FTP Publishing and SMTP Services. Chapter 6, "Using IIS Manager," provides in-depth information about using IIS Manager.

Users and Groups Provided in Windows Server 2008

New accounts and groups have been added in Windows Server 2008 for IIS 7.0. The IUSR account replaces the IUSR_*MachineName* account. This is the default identity used when anonymous authentication is enabled. The IUSR_*MachineName* account is still created and used only when the FTP server is installed. If FTP is not installed, this account is not created.

The IIS_IUSRS group replaces the IIS_WPG group. This built-in IIS_IUSRS group has been granted access to all the necessary file and system resources so that an account, when added to this group, can act as an application pool identity.

Both the IUSR account and IIS_IUSRS group are built into Windows Server 2008. The IUSR account is a limited account and does not need a password. This enables you to use Xcopy.exe /o to seamlessly copy files along with their ownership and access control list (ACL) information to different machines. (Note that these user accounts will not be localized. Regardless of the language of Windows you install, the IIS account name is always IUSR, and the group name is IIS_IUSRS.) The IUSR account is the same type of account as the NETWORK SERVICE or LOCAL SERVICE accounts. It has the same Security Identifier (SID) across all machines.

Troubleshooting Installation

The new XML declarative installation process provides rich and detailed log information. This can be helpful when you want to determine if the installation was successful. You can use several areas to determine how the installation completed. You can use the traditional Windows Event Logs, the IIS7.log file, and the ServerManagerCMD log file that was created if you specified the appropriate ServerManagerCMD switch (see the section titled "Other Related Logging Options" below).

Event Logs

You can use the built-in Application, Security, and System event logs to help troubleshoot and determine if your installation was successful. These are important sources of information that are maintained by the operating system. The event logs catalog all kinds of events including errors that happen during a failed installation. This can help you track down specific errors.

IIS 7.0 Log

The new componentized installation provides rich and detailed logging of information to help troubleshoot installation issues. The most common errors are related to not being logged in as Administrator or not having administrative privileges. IIS provides a detailed log located in the file *%windir%*\IIS7.log. This log contains easy-to-read and descriptive text for each component's installation. This information can be used to troubleshoot your entire IIS installation or to troubleshoot a specific component. The following is an example of the IIS log:

```
[05/09/2007 00:43:31] [ ***** IIS 7.0 Component Based Setup ***** ]
[05/09/2007 00:43:31] "C:\Windows\System32\inetsrv\iissetup.exe"
    /install SharedLibraries
[05/09/2007 00:43:31] Created NetFrameworkConfigurationKey
[05/09/2007 00:43:32] Set ACLs on NetFrameworkConfigurationKey
[05/09/2007 00:43:32] Created iisWasKey
[05/09/2007 00:43:32] Created iisWasKey user key
[05/09/2007 00:43:32] Created iisConfigurationKey
[05/09/2007 00:43:33] Created iisConfigurationKey user key
[05/09/2007 00:43:33] Set ACLs on iisConfigurationKey
[05/09/2007 00:43:33] iisConfigurationKey already exists
[05/09/2007 00:43:33] Created AesProvider
[05/09/2007 00:43:33] Created IISWASOnlyAesProvider
[05/09/2007 00:43:33] Install of component SharedLibraries succeeded!
[05/09/2007 00:43:33] Success!
[05/09/2007 00:43:33] [ End of IIS 7.0 Component Based Setup ]
```

Whenever you need to troubleshoot installation issues, the IIS7.log should be the first place you look for errors.

Other Related Logging Options

The ServerManagerCMD tool provides extensive logging capabilities. This section describes how to invoke the logging option when you use ServerManagerCMD.

To capture output of your installation results, use the following command:

```
ServerManagerCMD.exe –install Web-Server –resultPath InstallResults.xml
    –logPath InstallResults.txt
```

To capture output of your uninstall results, use the following command:

```
ServerManagerCMD.exe -remove Web-Server -resultPath UnInstallResults.xml
    -logPath UnInstallResults.txt
```

Each of these result logs contains detailed information that can help you troubleshoot issues or determine your installation status. You can use a text editor such as Notepad to view the results. If you are experiencing an error, you can locate the error by using the Find command inside your text editor.

Package Manager (pkgmgr.exe) also provides logging to help troubleshoot deployments. The location of the log file and folder is *%windir%*\Logs\CBS\CBS.log. Here is an excerpt showing a command executed. The following example shows the command issued to install the Default Web-Server role:

```
2007-11-20 05:27:44, Info                CBS    Pkgmgr: called with:
"pkgmgr.exe  /iu:IIS-WebServerRole;IIS-WebServer;IIS-
ommonHttpFeatures;IIS-StaticContent;IIS-DefaultDocument;IIS-
irectoryBrowsing;IIS-HttpErrors;IIS-HealthAndDiagnostics;IIS-
ttpLogging;IIS-LoggingLibraries;IIS-RequestMonitor;IIS-Security;IIS-
equestFiltering;IIS-HttpCompressionStatic;IIS-WebServerManagementTools;
IS-ManagementConsole;WAS-WindowsActivationService;WAS-ProcessModel;WAS-
etFxEnvironment;WAS-ConfigurationAPI"
2007-11-20 05:27:44, Info                CSI
0000001@2007/11/20:13:27:44.373 WcpInitialize (wcp.dll version 0.0.0.5)
called (stack @0x700e7ee9 @0xca1672 @0xc9b8fa @0xc9c378 @0x77cb1cc2
@0x77d88785)
```

Removing IIS 7.0

As easy as it is to install IIS 7.0 using Server Manager, ServerManagerCMD, or Package Manager, these tools allow for similarly efficient and straightforward techniques to remove specific features or to remove the entire Web Server (IIS) Server Role.

The User Interface in Windows Server 2008 and Windows Vista

To uninstall IIS or the Web Server Role by using ServerManager, complete the following steps:

1. Start Server Manager by clicking Start Menu, All Programs, Administrative Tools, Server Manager. The Server Manager window is displayed.

2. In the Server Manager, select Roles.

3. The Roles Summary view is displayed, as shown in Figure 5-5.

4. Click the Remove Roles link to display the Remove Roles Wizard.

5. Click Next to display the Remove Server Roles page.

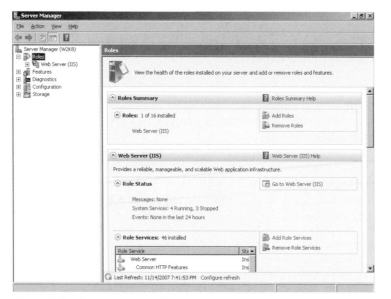

Figure 5-5   Server Manager, Roles Summary view.

6. Clear the Web Server (IIS) check box to uninstall the Web Server Role, as shown in Figure 5-6.

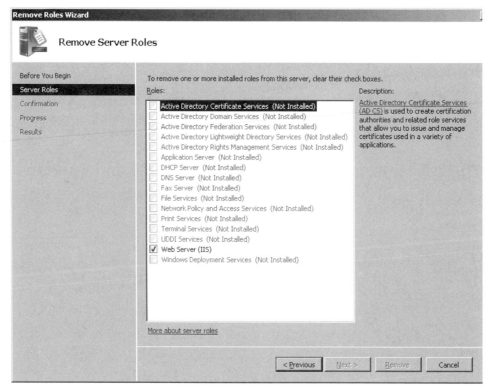

Figure 5-6   Clear the Web Server (IIS) check box to uninstall the Web Server Role.

7. Click Next to display the Confirm Removal Selections page, as shown in Figure 5-7.

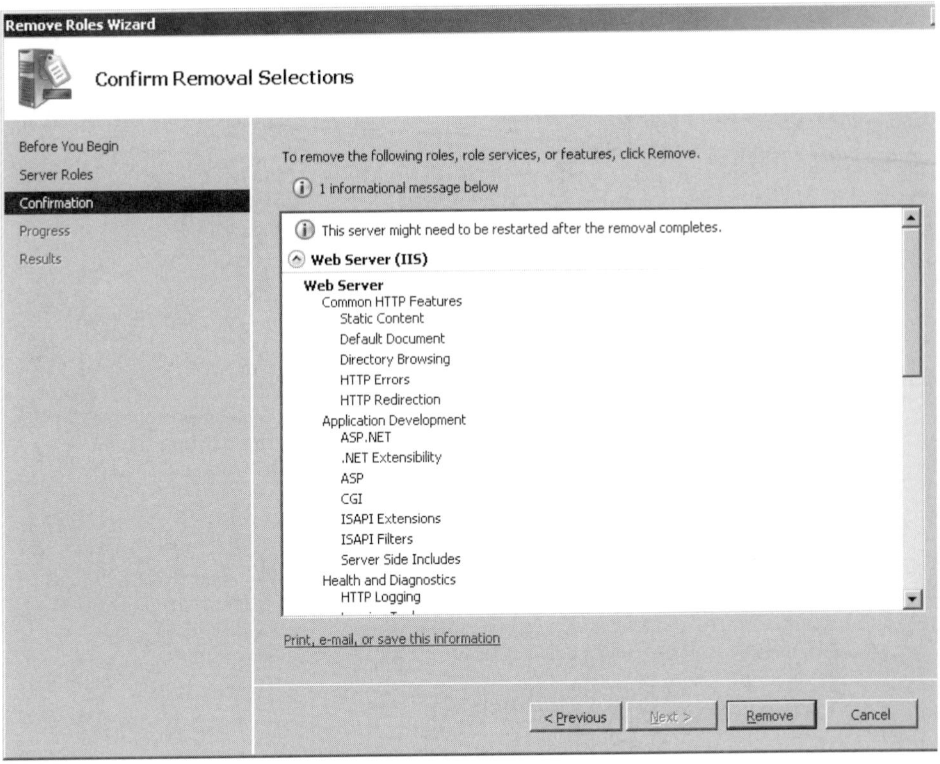

Figure 5-7   Remove Roles Wizard confirmation page.

8. Click Remove.

9. Click Close to return to Server Manager. You might be prompted to restart your computer depending on the roles that were uninstalled. When you return to Server Manager, the Web Server Role will have been removed.

Command Line Method

You can use either Package Manager or ServerManagerCMD to uninstall the Web Server Role.

Using Package Manager

This section contains the process for using Package Manager to uninstall IIS. This example assumes that all components were installed. Here is the syntax used:

```
start /w pkgmgr.exe /uu:{<update name>}
```

The parameter /uu:{<update name>} specifies the updates to uninstall. You can list multiple updates by separating them with a semicolon. At least one update name must be specified.

> **Note** /*uu* indicates uninstall and is then followed by the selected update names.

The following command uninstalls everything related to the Web Server (IIS) Server Role using Package Manager:

```
start /w pkgmgr.exe /uu:IIS-WebServerRole;IIS-WebServer;
  IIS-CommonHttpFeatures;IIS-StaticContent;IIS-DefaultDocument;
  IIS-DirectoryBrowsing;IIS-HttpErrors;IIS-HttpRedirect;
  IIS-ApplicationDevelopment;IIS-ASPNET;IIS-NetFxExtensibility;
  IIS-ASP;IIS-CGI;IIS-ISAPIExtensions;IIS-ISAPIFilter;
  IIS-ServerSideIncludes;IIS-HealthAndDiagnostics;IIS-HttpLogging;
  IIS-LoggingLibraries;IIS-RequestMonitor;IIS-HttpTracing;
  IIS-CustomLogging;IIS-ODBCLogging;IIS-Security;
  IIS-BasicAuthentication;IIS-WindowsAuthentication;
  IIS-DigestAuthentication;IIS-ClientCertificateMappingAuthentication;
  IIS-IISCertificateMappingAuthentication;IIS-URLAuthorization;
  IIS-RequestFiltering;IIS-IPSecurity;IIS-Performance;
  IIS-HttpCompressionStatic;IIS-HttpCompressionDynamic;
  IIS-WebServerManagementTools;IIS-ManagementConsole;
  IIS-ManagementScriptingTools;IIS-ManagementService;
  IIS-IIS6ManagementCompatibility;IIS-Metabase;IIS-WMICompatibility;
  IIS-LegacyScripts;IIS-LegacySnapIn;IIS-FTPPublishingService;
  IIS-FTPServer;IIS-FTPManagement;WAS-WindowsActivationService;
  WAS-ProcessModel;WAS-NetFxEnvironment;WAS-ConfigurationAPI
```

Using ServerManagerCMD

You can also use ServerManagerCMD to uninstall the Web Server Role. To uninstall, use the following syntax:

```
ServerManagerCMD.exe -remove Web-Server
```

To generate a detailed log of the uninstall process, you can pipe the results and command line syntax to a log file called ServerManagerCMD_Uninstall.txt, as shown here:

```
ServerManagerCMD.exe -remove Web-Server -resultPath results.xml
  -logPath ServerManagerCMD_Uninstall.txt
```

Summary

We have covered the various ways you will be able to install the Web Server Role, specific role services, and IIS 7.0 features. Windows Server 2008 offers a variety of ways to install, configure, and remove IIS 7.0. The additional logging features can help you troubleshoot installation problems. The information in this chapter should help make IIS 7.0 easier to install and faster to configure, and the information can guide you in creating a cookie-cutter approach to rolling out IIS 7.0 throughout your enterprise.

Additional Resources

These resources contain additional information and tools related to this chapter:

- Go to "Setup and Migration" in the TechCENTER on IIS.net at *http://www.iis.net/ default.aspx?CategoryID=13&tabid=2.*

- View the "IIS7–Setup and Migration" forums at *http://forums.iis.net/1047.aspx.*

- For more information about the FastCGI module for IIS, read Bill Staples's blog at *http://blogs.iis.net/bills/archive/2006/10/31/PHP-on-IIS.aspx.*

- A good introduction to IIS 7.0 Server Core is available at *http://www.iis.net/articles/ view.aspx/IIS7/Explore-IIS7/Getting-Started/IIS7-on-Server-Core.*

- For more information about administering IIS 7.0 on Server Core installations of Windows Server 2008, see *http://blogs.iis.net/metegokt/archive/2007/06/26/administering-iis7-on- server-core-installations-of-windows-server-2008.aspx.*

- The following article will walk you through an IIS installation using Server Manager: *http://www.iis.net/articles/view.aspx/IIS7/Deploy-an-IIS7-Server/Installing-IIS7/ Install-IIS7-on-Longhorn-Server?Page=2.*

Part III
Administration

Chapter 6
Using IIS Manager

IIS Manager is a graphical user interface (GUI) administration tool for Internet Information Services (IIS) 7.0. It provides an intuitive, feature-focused, task-oriented management console for working with both IIS 7.0 and ASP.NET settings. The user interface (UI) has fine granularity and enables you to configure IIS 7.0 server and ASP.NET applications from within one console. With IIS Manager, you can set up delegated management to allow application owners to manage their applications remotely without having administrative access to the server. IIS Manager is highly customizable and provides an extensible platform that you can use to plug in your own features to manage custom settings and applications.

In this chapter, we will focus on the IIS Manager interface, discuss feature and configuration mapping, and talk about IIS Manager customization and extensibility. We will also look at configuring IIS Manager for remote administration.

Note For a more detailed remote administration discussion, please refer to Chapter 8, "Remote Administration," and for instructions on how to use IIS Manager to perform common administration tasks, see Appendix J, "Common Administration Tasks Using IIS Manager."

Overview of IIS Manager

IIS Manager is a server administration tool that enables you to configure IIS 7.0 and ASP.NET features from one fully integrated interface. You can get health and diagnostic information and monitor a server's operation including currently running requests, and you can also administer membership. With its task-based intuitive GUI interface, the tool is aimed at simplifying the administration tasks and reducing management complexity.

153

IIS Manager in IIS 7.0 is much easier to use in comparison with the previous versions of the IIS management console. In previous versions of IIS, the server management console was implemented as a Microsoft Management Console (MMC) snap-in called Inetmgr.exe. The MMC snap-in interface consisted of tabs with configuration settings. IIS 7.0 exposes many more settings, and exposing more settings in the old management console would require additional tabs in the snap-in. Having many tabs would make it difficult to locate a setting and perform the administration tasks.

In IIS 7.0, the server administration tool has been completely rearchitectured and rewritten from the ground up. Instead of an MMC snap-in, the management console for IIS 7.0 is implemented as a user-friendly Windows Forms application that provides an easy-to-use, feature-focused, task-based interface for configuring both IIS and ASP.NET features. As in previous versions of IIS, the IIS 7.0 Manager application is also named Inetmgr.exe and is located in the *%SystemRoot%*\System32\Inetsrv folder. But make no mistake—despite the same name and location, it is a completely different IIS Manager!

One of the most important capabilities of IIS Manager is delegated management. IIS Manager enables delegated management, letting application owners manage their applications remotely without having administrative access to the server. With this capability, users of hosted services can run IIS Manager on their desktop and remotely manage their sites and applications on the server where they are hosted. Securely delegating administrative responsibilities can save a significant amount of time for a server administrator and can help to eliminate the Web administration bottleneck. The server administrator, of course, has complete control over what features are delegated to site and application owners.

IIS Manager supports remote administration over a firewall-friendly HTTPS connection, with an option to support both Windows-based and other credentials for authentication. In addition to Windows credentials, IIS Manager can also use alternative credentials stores to identify users. IIS Manager credentials are particularly useful in scenarios in which you don't want to create Windows accounts for all remote users, or when the credentials are already stored in a non-Windows authentication system and you want to keep them in a single store.

To connect to the server, IIS Manager uses HTTPS to establish a connection with the Web Management Service (WMSvc). WMSvc is a Windows service that provides the ability to manage IIS 7.0 sites and applications remotely using IIS Manager. By default, WMSvc listens for requests on port 8172 on all unassigned IP addresses, but an alternate port and an IP address can be configured if necessary. After the connection is established, based on user actions in the UI, IIS Manager sends Management Service requests, for example, requesting a change to a configuration setting in a web.config file. When the Web Management Service gets a request from IIS Manager, it performs the requested action and returns a response. All interactions between IIS Manager on the remote machine and WMSvc on the server computer are over HTTPS. This architecture is shown in Figure 6-1.

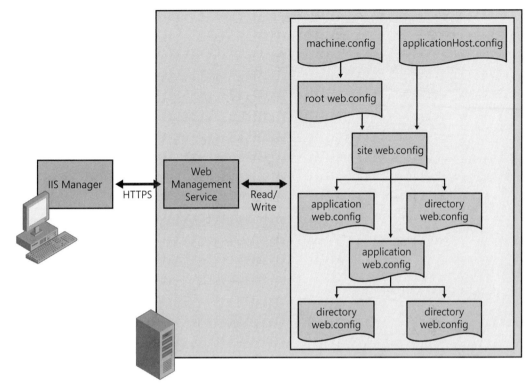

Figure 6-1   IIS Manager and the Web Management Service.

Most requests from IIS Manager to the Web Management Service are to read from, and write to, the hierarchy of configuration files on the server, including applicationHost.config file, .NET Framework root web.config, and web.config files for sites, applications, and directories. Other IIS Manager requests include requests to read the run-time state and work with providers on the server.

What's more, IIS Manager is extensible. It has its own configuration file, administration.config, that enables custom functionality to be added. Any added administration plug-ins are integrated into IIS Manager and appear alongside IIS and ASP.NET features. From this perspective, IIS Manager is not just an application, but rather an extensible platform that developers can use to plug in their own features to manage custom settings.

Starting IIS Manager

You can start IIS Manager from the Administrative Tools program group, or you can run *%SystemRoot%*\System32\Inetsrv\Inetmgr.exe from the command line or from Windows Explorer. The IIS Manager Start page is shown in Figure 6-2.

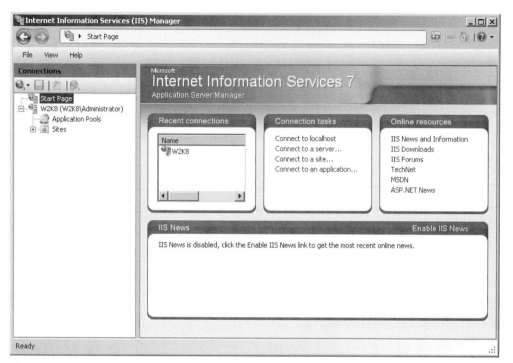

Figure 6-2 IIS Manager Start page.

> **Note** To run IIS Manager with administrative privileges on the server machine, instead of logging on as an administrator, it is recommended you use the **runas** command in the non-administrative user context, for example: **runas /user:<*AdministratorAccount*>** **"%SystemRoot%\system32\inetsrv\inetmgr.exe"**.

The Start page enables you to open recent connections by double-clicking them in the Recent Connections list. You can create new ones by selecting a task from the Connection Tasks list. You may need to provide account credentials to create a new connection.

The Start page also provides links to online IIS resources and enables you to obtain recent online news. The news is disabled by default. To enable news, click Enable IIS News in the upper-right corner of the IIS News pane.

IIS Manager User Interface

IIS Manager has been completely redesigned in IIS 7.0. The look and feel differs from the previous versions of IIS. IIS Manager navigation has a more browser-like feel with an address bar similar to Windows Explorer. When you select a server, site, or application, the list of their features in the central area somewhat resembles the Control Panel. Though some interface elements are consistent with the previous versions of IIS, most of the interface is different. Figure 6-3 shows the typical view of the IIS Manager user interface, with a server home page in the central area.

Figure 6-3   IIS Manager: server home page.

IIS Manager window is divided into several sections. In the top section of IIS Manager window, there are two bars:

- The Navigation toolbar, which provides buttons and an address bar for easy navigation within the UI.

- The Menu toolbar, which provides three menus: File, View, and Help.

The main body of IIS Manager window is divided into three areas:

- The Connections pane and toolbar enable you to connect to servers, sites, and applications. The connections are displayed in a tree.

- The central pane, referred to as a workspace, displays pages that list information and enable you to change settings. The workspace has two views: Features View and Content View.

  - Features View enables you to view and configure features for the currently selected configuration path. Each IIS feature typically maps to a configuration section that controls the corresponding Web server feature.

  - Content View provides a read-only display of content corresponding to the currently selected configuration path. In Content View, when you select a node in the Connections pane tree, its content is listed in the workspace.

- The Actions pane is task-based. The list of displayed tasks is context-specific and reflects the currently selected node and feature.

Let's look into these interface sections in more detail.

Direct from the Source: Content View and Features View . . . Why?

At the early stages when we were building IIS Manager, it had a very different look and feel. It was a radical change from what we had in IIS 6.0 and earlier versions. For example, it didn't have a tree view to navigate the objects; it would open multiple tabs, similar to Web browsers today, for managing different objects; the home page had only links and images in a complex layout; and there were many more ways in which it differed from the final IIS 7.0 version. At the time, all of the differences made sense to us—we always thought that earlier versions of IIS Manager gave too much relevance to content. The UI was displaying the files and folders of your site, but when you needed to change a setting, you ended up with a small modal dialog box with lots of tabs that only had a small UI area left to list a few settings and was extremely limited in functionality (for example, no sorting, grouping, filtering, etc.). Our idea for IIS 7.0 was to allow the UI space for what the tool is intended to do—managing configuration—and enhance the experience while doing so.

Then we started doing some usability studies, and it turned out that we were not entirely right. The people in the studies raised a lot of concerns, and they told us that many features we thought were useful were not so useful, and many features we thought were not needed actually were important to users. The most remarkable thing we learned was about the tree view: it turned out to be a critical feature for almost every user, as it helped people to understand the hierarchy of the system as well as which configuration is being changed. So of course that was one of the first features we brought back!

Next, users really wanted to see a similar view of what earlier versions offered—essentially, the list of folders and files, and to have the "right-click properties" experience. That's when we decided that we needed something that could yield a similar paradigm but without the problems of small modal dialogs and lots of tabs.

Content View was the answer to this issue. When you use Content View, you get almost the same look and feel that older versions of IIS Manager had, allowing you to drill down to any object, right-click it, and choose properties to change any of its settings. However, in this case, rather than selecting the properties context menu item, it shows a switch to Features View that has the same effect.

In the end, we were happy to be able to offer both views. Immediately, the results of usability studies increased, and users really liked what IIS Manager became. It was an amazing experience to really use customer feedback directly in every decision we made and to take the time to validate again and again most of the design decisions.

Carlos Aguilar Mares

Senior Development Lead, IIS

Navigation Toolbar

The top bar in IIS Manager is the navigation toolbar, from which you can navigate the UI. The navigation toolbar contains:

- The Address bar, which shows a breadcrumb path to your location within the UI
- Navigation buttons that may be available or may appear dimmed, depending on your location or selection within the UI; they provide the familiar functionality:
  - ❏ Back button goes back one page view
  - ❏ Forward button goes forward one page view
  - ❏ Refresh Page button updates the view of the currently selected object in the UI
  - ❏ Stop button stops the current action in the UI from completing
  - ❏ Home button navigates to the home page of the current selection
  - ❏ Help button opens a list of links to Help documentation

Connections Pane

On top of the Connections pane, there is a toolbar from which you can connect to Web servers, sites, and applications.

When you connect to a Web server, site, or application from the Connections pane, the connection is loaded into the pane as a tree hierarchy that displays the children of the parent connection, as follows:

- When you connect to a server, the tree displays the server connection with the application pools and the sites on that server.
- When you connect to a site, the tree displays the site connection with the applications within that site.
- When you connect to an application, the tree displays the application connection with the physical and virtual directories within that application.

> **Note**   You can also display a file node in a tree hierarchy, within a connection the file belongs to. To add a file node, switch to Content View, select the file, and then switch to Features View from the Actions pane or from the shortcut menu.

The Connections toolbar contains the following buttons:

- **Create New Connection**   Opens a menu with three options: connect to a server, a site, or an application. Selecting an option starts the appropriate connection wizard so that you can connect to a Web server, a site, or an application.

> **Note** The same options are available from the Start Page (Connection Tasks list) and from the File menu.

- **Save Current Connections** Saves the connection information for the current connections in the tree.
- **Up** Moves the current selection up one level in the tree hierarchy.
- **Delete Connection** Removes the selected connection from the tree. If the currently selected node is not the connection node, the parent connection is removed from the tree. For example, if a virtual or physical directory is selected when the user clicks this button, the parent application will be removed.

Creating New Connections

To create a new connection, click the Create New Connection button on the Connections toolbar and select the desired action. You can also select these actions from the File menu or from the Start page. Selecting an action from any of these locations opens the same wizard.

To connect to a server, the wizard prompts you for the server name, as shown in Figure 6-4. If WMSvc on the server is listening on a port that is different from 8172 (the default port number), you'll need to provide the port number preceded by a colon, for example, www.contoso.com:8080. If you connect to the local computer, type **localhost** instead of a server name. Then, the wizard prompts you for the user credentials for the connection. Only server administrators can connect to a server. Finally, you can specify a friendly name for this connection. This name will appear as that server connection node name in the Connection pane tree.

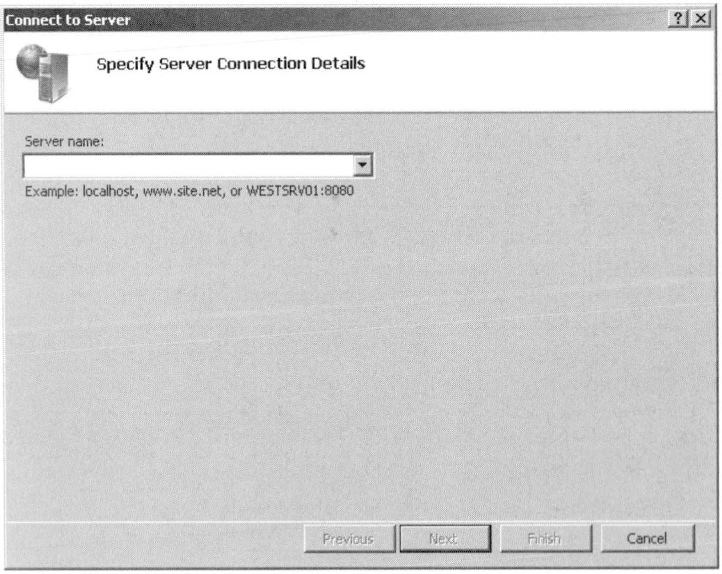

Connect to Server

Specify Server Connection Details

Server name:

Example: localhost, www.site.net, or WESTSRV01:8080

Previous   Next   Finish   Cancel

Figure 6-4 Connect To Server Wizard.

To connect to a site, the wizard prompts you for the name of the server where the site is hosted, as well as that site name, as shown in Figure 6-5. If WMSvc on the server is using a port that is different from 8172, then you'll need to provide the port number. Then, the wizard prompts you for the user credentials for the connection. Server administrators and designated site administrators can connect to Web sites. Finally, the wizard enables you to specify a friendly name for this connection. This name will appear as that site connection node name in the tree.

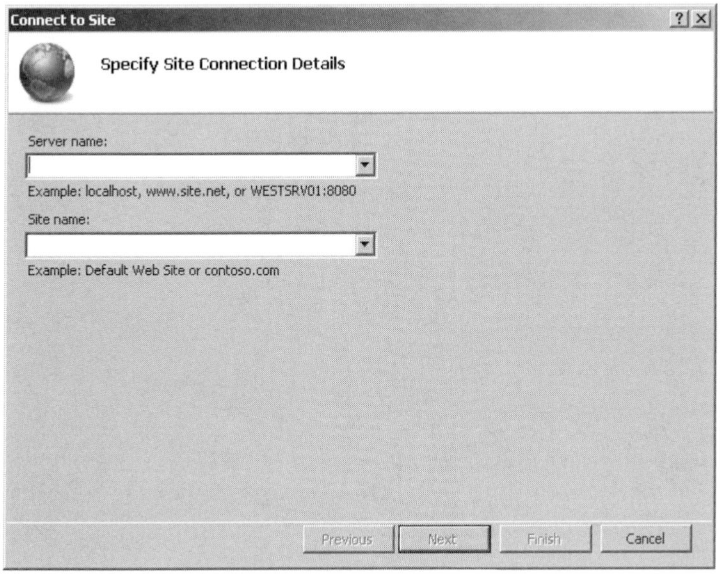

Figure 6-5   Connect To Site Wizard.

To connect to an application, the wizard prompts you for the name of the server where the application is hosted, the name of the site the application belongs to, and then the full name of the application including the path within the site, as shown in Figure 6-6. If WMSvc on the server is using a port that is different from 8172, you'll need to provide the port number. Then, the wizard prompts you for the user credentials for the connection. Server administrators, site administrators for the application's parent site, and designated application administrators can connect to an application. Finally, the wizard enables you to specify a friendly name for this connection. This name will appear as that application connection node name in the tree.

 Note   For more information about troubleshooting remote connections, refer to Chapter 8.

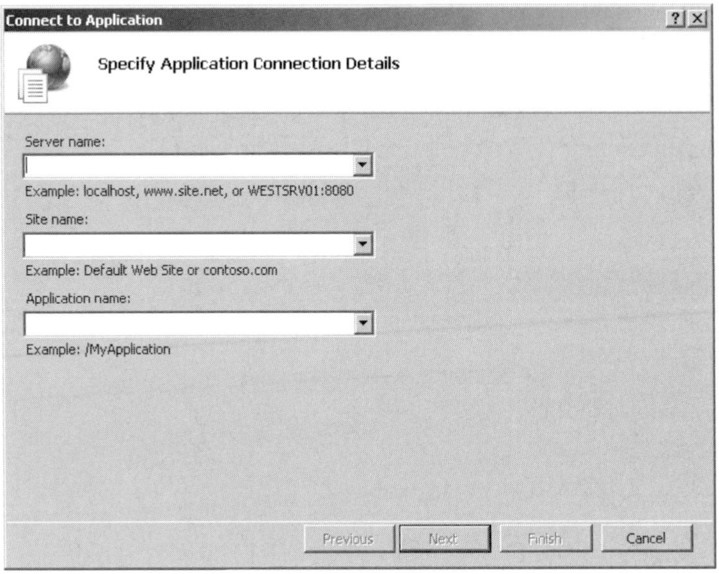

Figure 6-6   Connect To Application Wizard.

Workspace

The workspace is the central area of IIS Manager, located between the Connections pane and the Actions pane. The workspace displays pages that list features, provide other information, and enable you to change settings.

The workspace has two views: Features View and Content View. You can switch between these views by using the buttons at the bottom of the workspace, as shown in Figure 6-7.

Figure 6-7   Features View and Content View buttons.

Features View

When you select Features View, a list of features for a currently selected object in the Connections pane—such as a server, a site, an application, a virtual directory, a folder, or a file—is displayed. For example, Figure 6-3 shows the list of features displayed when the user selects a server connection in the Connections pane.

Each feature reads from and writes to configuration section(s) in a .config file hierarchy. Features View enables you to view and change configuration settings for features.

Home Page   When you select a server, a site, an application, a virtual directory, a folder, or a file node in the tree, a corresponding home page for that object is displayed. The home page displays a feature list for that node.

For example, when you select a site node in the tree, the home page for that site is displayed, as shown in Figure 6-8 for site www.contoso.com.

Figure 6-8   Site home page grouped by area.

The feature list on a home page can be grouped by area or category, viewed in different layouts, and sorted by feature name or description.

The IIS Manager features are listed in Table 6-1. For each feature, the table provides a brief description, an area and category the feature belongs to, and a feature scope (tree levels and corresponding home pages where this feature appears).

Table 6-1   IIS Manager Features

Feature	Description	Area	Category	Scope
.NET Compilation	Configure properties for compiling managed code	ASP.NET	Application Development	Server, site, application, virtual directory, folder, file
.NET Globalization	Configure globalization properties for managed code	ASP.NET	Application Development	Server, site, application, virtual directory, folder, file
.NET Profile	Configure options for the ASP.NET Profile feature, which tracks user information in ASP.NET applications	ASP.NET	Application Development	Site, application, virtual directory, folder, file

Table 6-1   IIS Manager Features

Feature	Description	Area	Category	Scope
.NET Roles	Configure roles for the ASP.NET Roles feature, for use with .NET Users and Forms authentication	ASP.NET	Security	Site, application, virtual directory, folder, file
.NET Trust Levels	Configure trust levels for managed modules, handlers, and applications	ASP.NET	Security	Server, site, application, virtual directory, folder, file
.NET Users	Manage users for the ASP.NET Membership feature	ASP.NET	Security	Site, application, virtual directory, folder, file
Application Settings	Configure name/value pairs that managed code applications can use at run time	ASP.NET	Application Development	Server, site, application, virtual directory, folder, file
Authentication	Configure authentication settings for sites and applications	IIS	Security	Server, site, application, virtual directory, folder, file
				Note: Some options within the Authentication feature are only available at the server level.
Compression	Configure settings to compress responses	IIS	Performance	Server, site, application, virtual directory, folder, file
Connection Strings	Configure strings that ASP.NET applications can use to connect to data sources	ASP.NET	Application Development	Server, site, application, virtual directory, folder, file
Default Document	Configure default files to return when clients request the root of a directory	IIS	HTTP Features	Server, site, application, virtual directory, folder, file
Directory Browsing	Configure whether or not IIS displays a directory listing when clients request the root of a directory	IIS	HTTP Features	Server, site, application, virtual directory, folder, file
Error Pages	Configure pages to return when HTTP errors occur	IIS	HTTP Features	Server, site, application, virtual directory, folder, file

Table 6-1   IIS Manager Features

Feature	Description	Area	Category	Scope
Failed Request Tracing Rules	Configure logging of failed request traces	IIS	Health and Diagnostics	Server, site, application, virtual directory, folder, file
Feature Delegation	Configure the default delegation state for features at lower levels in IIS Manager	Management	Security	Root node of the connection (server, site, application)
Handler Mappings	Specify handlers that handle responses for specific request types	IIS	Server Components	Server, site, application, virtual directory, folder, file
HTTP Redirect	Specify rules for redirecting incoming requests to another file or URL	IIS	HTTP Features	Server, site, application, virtual directory, folder, file
HTTP Response Headers	Configure HTTP headers that are added to responses from the Web server	IIS	HTTP Features	Server, site, application, virtual directory, folder, file
IIS Manager Permissions	Configure users who can set up delegated features in sites or applications for which they are granted permissions	Management	Security	Server
IIS Manager Users	Manage IIS Manager users	Management	Security	Server
ISAPI and CGI Restrictions	Restrict or enable specific Internet Server Application Programming Interface (ISAPI) extensions and Common Gateway Interface (CGI) programs on the Web server	IIS	Security	Server
ISAPI Filters	Specify ISAPI filters that modify IIS functionality	IIS	Server Components	Server, site
Logging	Configure how IIS logs requests on the Web server	IIS	Health and Diagnostics	Server, site, application, virtual directory, folder, file
Machine Key	Configure hashing and encryption settings for ASP.NET application services such as view state, Forms authentication, membership and roles, and anonymous authentication	ASP.NET	Application Development	Server, site, application, virtual directory, folder, file

Table 6-1   IIS Manager Features

Feature	Description	Area	Category	Scope
MIME Types	Configure file extensions and associated content types that are served as static files	IIS	HTTP Features	Server, site, application, virtual directory, folder, file
Modules	Configure native and managed code modules that process requests on the Web server	IIS	Server Components	Server, site, application, virtual directory, folder, file
Output Caching	Specify rules for caching response content in the output cache	IIS	Performance	Server, site, application, virtual directory, folder, file
Pages and Controls	Configure settings for ASP.NET pages and controls	ASP.NET	Application Development	Server, site, application, virtual directory, folder, file
Providers	Configure providers for provider-based application services	ASP.NET	Application Development	Server, site, application, virtual directory, folder, file
Server Certificates	Request and manage certificates for Web sites that use Secure Sockets Layer (SSL)	IIS	Security	Server
Session State	Configure session state settings and Forms authentication cookie settings	ASP.NET	Application Development	Server, site, application, virtual directory, folder
Shared Configuration	Configure shared configuration	Management	Other	Server
SMTP E-mail	Configure e-mail address and delivery options to send e-mail from Web applications	ASP.NET	Application Development	Server, site, application, virtual directory, folder, file
SSL Settings	Specify requirements for SSL and client certificates	IIS	Security	Site, application, virtual directory, folder, file
Worker Processes	View information about worker processes and about currently executing requests running inside those worker processes	IIS	Health and Diagnostics	Server

Features on the home page can be displayed in groups. Using the Group By drop-down list on the home page toolbar or the Group By option on the View menu, you can set up how features are organized in groups, as follows:

■ Selecting the Area option displays ASP.NET features and IIS features separately in two groups (for the server node on a local machine, an additional Management group is displayed):

- ❏ ASP.NET

- ❏ IIS

> **Note**   Additional groups may appear when default IIS installation is extended. For example, adding the Media pack adds the Media group.

An example of Area grouping is shown in Figure 6-8. Table 6-1 shows which area each IIS Manager feature belongs to.

■ Selecting the Category option displays the features for both ASP.NET and IIS in six categories (for the server node on a local machine, there may be an additional category called Other):

- ❏ Application Development

- ❏ Health and Diagnostics

- ❏ HTTP Features

- ❏ Performance

- ❏ Security

- ❏ Server Components

An example of category grouping is shown in Figure 6-9. Table 6-1 shows which category each IIS Manager feature belongs to.

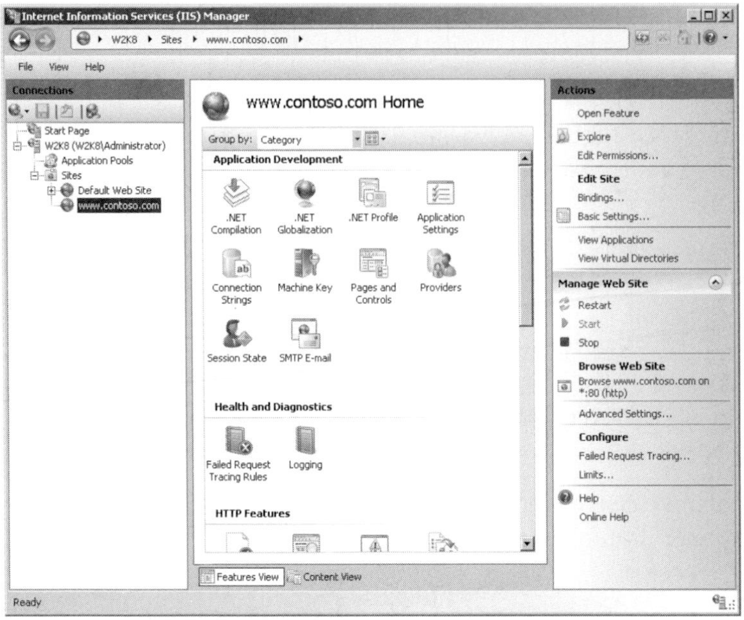

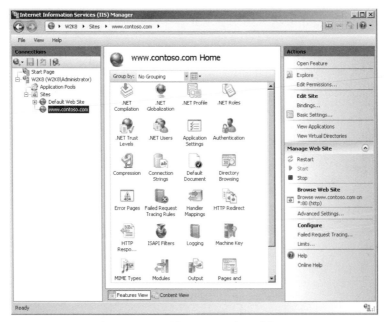

Figure 6-9   Site home page grouped by category.

■   Selecting the No Grouping option lists all features in alphabetical order, as shown in Figure 6-10.

Figure 6-10   Site home page without grouping of features.

Using the View button on the home page toolbar or the View option from the View menu, you can view the list of features in different layouts:

- *Details* view displays the list of features in a table. For each feature, the first column contains a small icon and a name, and the second column contains a brief description. In this view, you can sort the features in ascending or descending order by feature name or description by clicking the column header. The sorting is applied within feature groups. For example, Figure 6-11 shows Details view for the site home page, with both ASP.NET and IIS groups sorted by feature name.

Figure 6-11   Site home page Details view.

- *Icons* view displays the list of icons. This view has a feel that is similar to Control Panel. This is the default view.

- *Tiles* view displays the list of tiles (smaller icons with the feature name).

- *List* view shows a list of feature names.

Features are used to view and change configurations. For example, if you need to configure the default file(s) for a site, double-click the Default Document feature on that site's home page to display the Default Document page (shown in Figure 6-12) and make the changes.

Note the Configuration line on the left of the status bar at the bottom of IIS Manager in Figure 6-12. The line points to the web.config file for that site. When the feature settings are displayed, the status bar shows the configuration file where the configuration settings for that feature would be written to. In this example, it is web.config for the site www.contoso.com.

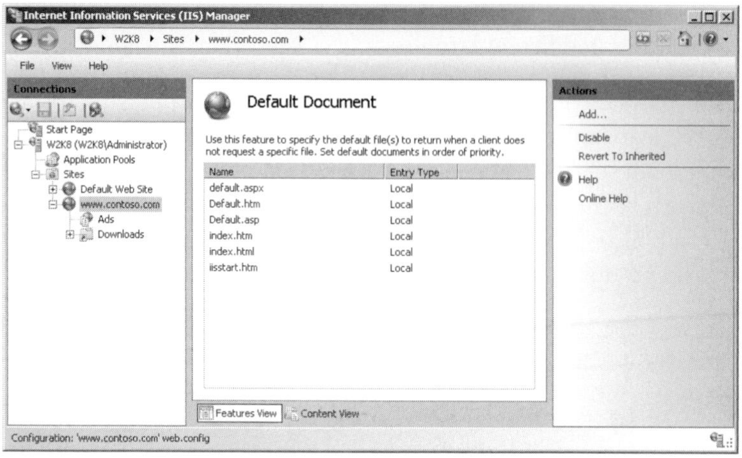

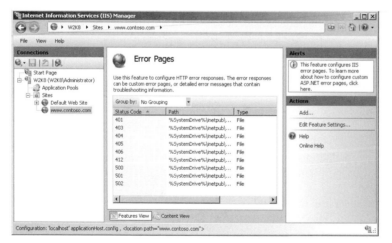

Figure 6-12   Default Document feature.

Page Layouts   Information and configuration settings on feature pages can be presented in different layouts. Depending on the page layout, there are three types of feature pages:

- List pages
- Property pages
- Dialog pages

The most frequently used layout of a page is a list page. A list page contains a list displayed in a table. By using the Group By drop-down list, you can group the list by values in one or more columns. In addition, you can sort the data by value in a column by clicking on the column header. An example of a list page is shown in Figure 6-13. It is an Error Pages feature page.

Figure 6-13   Error Pages page: an example of a list page layout.

Sites and application pools pages are list pages that let you filter the list entries by searching in a column for entries that match a search string. Specify the search string in the Filter drop-down list and then select the column from the Go drop-down list. Figure 6-14 shows a Sites page with available column filters.

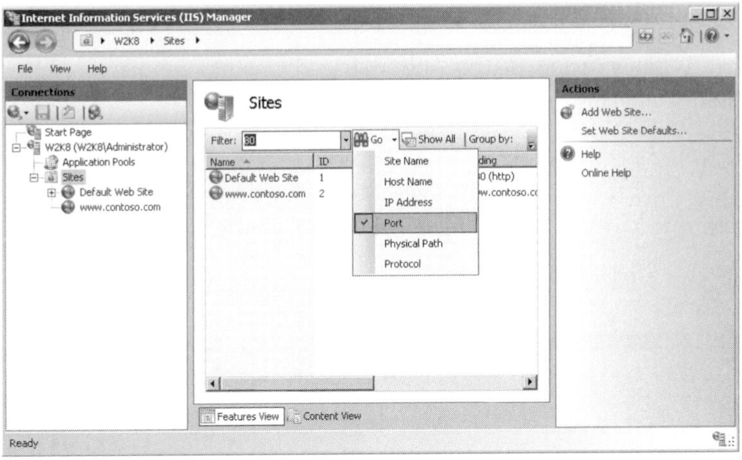

Figure 6-14   Filtering the Sites page.

On the Sites page, you can search in the following columns:

- Site Name
- Host Name
- IP Address
- Port
- Physical Path
- Protocol

On the Application Pools page, you can search in the following columns:

- Name
- .NET Framework Version
- Identity
- Managed Pipeline Mode

Filtering functionality is particularly useful for list pages with a large number of entries when you need to quickly locate the entry, for example, for servers that host a large number of sites.

A property page layout is also frequently used. A property page shows a property grid with a look and feel that is similar to a Microsoft Visual Studio property grid. When you select a property in the grid, a description of that property appears at the bottom of the grid. The Display drop-down list at the top of the property grid lets you choose how you would like the property names to be displayed:

- **Friendly Names**   (default setting)

- **Configuration Names**

- **Both Names**   When you choose this option, friendly names are displayed followed by configuration names in square brackets.

After you've made your selection in a grid, click Apply in the Actions pane to save the changes. If you navigate away from the property grid without clicking Apply to save changes, IIS Manager will prompt you to save the changes; otherwise, your changes will be lost.

Figure 6-15 shows the .NET Compilation property grid with friendly names displayed.

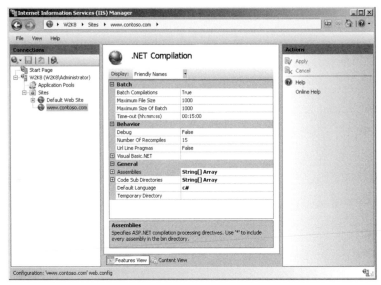

Figure 6-15   .NET Compilation page: an example of a property grid page layout.

The third type of page layout is a dialog page. Dialog pages display check boxes, text boxes, and radio buttons. After you've made your selection in a dialog page, click Apply in the Actions pane to save the changes. If you navigate away from the dialog page without clicking Apply to save changes, IIS Manager will prompt you to save the changes; otherwise, your changes will be lost.

Figure 6-16 shows a Session State feature page that is a good example of a dialog page. You can see the radio buttons for the Session State Mode Settings, the text boxes for Connection String and Time-Out, and a check box for Enable Custom Database.

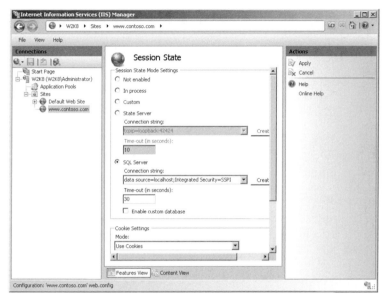

Figure 6-16 Session State page: an example of a dialog page layout.

Content View

When you select Content View, the actual content of the currently selected object in the Connections pane is displayed. For example, when you select a site node from the tree, the contents of that site are displayed, including virtual directories, folders, and files. Figure 6-17 shows Content View for the site www.contoso.com, which contains a default document default.aspx, a site configuration file web.config, an application, and a virtual directory.

Figure 6-17 Content View.

Content View is a read-only display. You cannot create, copy, move, or delete files or folders in this view. You can browse to selected content by selecting Browse either from the Actions pane or by right-clicking the object in Content View.

You can navigate within the Content View by double-clicking an object to see its contents. For example, double-clicking a directory in Content View displays the content of that directory in the workspace, and the node of this directory becomes selected in the tree in the Connections pane.

You can access Content View by clicking Content View at the bottom of IIS Manager or by right-clicking a tree node and selecting Switch To Content View.

Content View has the list layout. You can filter content by searching in the Name and Type columns for a search string specified in the Filter drop-down list, sort content by name and type by clicking a column header, and group content by type by using the Group By drop-down list.

If you select an object in Content View, such as a directory or a file, you can configure the features for that object by switching to Features View. You can switch to Features View at the bottom of IIS Manager by selecting Switch To Features View in the Actions pane or by right-clicking an object in the Content View and selecting Switch To Features View.

> **Note**   The only way to set configuration for a file is to switch to Content View, select the file, and then switch to Features View from the Actions pane or right-click the menu.

When you are in Content View, you can view the Windows properties of a selected object, such as a file or directory. To view the Windows properties for a selected object in Content View, select Edit Permissions either from the Actions pane or by right-clicking the object.

Actions Pane

The Actions pane is used to configure IIS, ASP.NET, and IIS Manager settings. You can use the Actions pane to open dialog boxes and wizards that let you complete tasks in IIS Manager, such as creating a site, configuring authentication, or adding a connection string for an application.

Items in the Actions pane are task-based. The list of displayed tasks is context-specific and depends on the currently selected object, such as a selected node in the tree in the Connections pane, and the selected feature or content in the workspace.

For example, Figure 6-3 shows that when a server node is selected in the tree, the Actions pane displays tasks that are specific to the server connection level, such as starting and stopping the Web server or delegating a feature. Figure 6-8 shows that when a site node is selected in the Connections pane, the Actions pane displays tasks that are specific to the site connection level, including starting and stopping that Web site or editing bindings for that Web site.

Items in the Actions pane are also available from the context menu when you right-click an object in IIS Manager.

Understanding Features

IIS Manager features read from and write to corresponding configuration section(s) in the .config files hierarchy. For example, the Application Settings feature corresponds to the *<appSettings>* section in the web.config files, whereas the Directory Browsing feature corresponds to the *<directoryBrowse>* element in the *<system.webServer>* section.

Few exceptions read and write configuration into other locations outside of IIS that are different from the configuration files hierarchy. For example, the Server Certificates feature gets its settings from the certificate store on the local server, and the Management Service feature gets its settings from the registry on the local server.

Feature to Module Mapping

IIS Manager features and the corresponding configuration section(s) in the .config files are listed in Table 6-2.

In addition, the table shows the server modules that consume the configuration sections. For each server module, both the module name and the type or dll name are listed, with the type or dll name in parentheses.

In some cases, a configuration section can be consumed directly by the IIS core Web server, IIS Manager, .NET Framework, or ASP.NET run time, which are shown in square brackets.

Table 6-2   IIS Manager Features Mapping to Configuration and Modules

Feature Name	Configuration Section	Consumed By
.NET Compilation	system.web/compilation	[ASP.NET compilation system]
.NET Globalization	system.web/globalization	[ASP.NET runtime]
.NET Profile	system.web/profile	Profile (System.Web.Profile. ProfileModule)
.NET Roles	system.web/roleManager	Roles service, RoleManager (System.Web.Security.Role-ManagerModule), and the configured default Roles provider
.NET Trust Levels	system.web/trust	[ASP.NET run time]
.NET Users	system.web/membership	[Membership service, the configured default Membership provider]

Table 6-2   IIS Manager Features Mapping to Configuration and Modules

Feature Name	Configuration Section	Consumed By
[Authentication] Anonymous	system.webServer/security/ anonymousAuthentication	AnonymousAuthentication-Module (authanon.dll)
[Authentication] Basic	system.webServer/security/ basicAuthentication	BasicAuthenticationModule (authbas.dll)
[Authentication] Digest	system.webServer/security/ digestAuthentication	DigestAuthenticationModule (authmd5.dll)
[Authentication] Forms	system.web/authentication	FormsAuthentication (System.Web.Security. FormsAuthenticationModule)
[Authentication] Windows	system.webServer/security/ windowsAuthentication	WindowsAuthenticationModule (authsspi.dll)
Application Settings	appSettings	[ASP.NET application code]
ASP	system.webServer/asp (indirect)	IsapiModule (isapi.dll)
Authorization Rules	system.webServer/security/ authorization	UrlAuthorizationModule (urlauthz.dll)
CGI	system.webServer/cgi	CgiModule (cgi.dll)
Compression	system.webServer/httpCompression system.webServer/urlCompression	DynamicCompressionModule (compdyn.dll) StaticCompressionModule (compstat.dll)
Connection Strings	connectionStrings	[ASP.NET features and application code]
Default Document	system.webServer/ defaultDocument	DefaultDocumentModule (defdoc.dll)
Directory Browsing	system.webServer/directoryBrowse	DirectoryListingModule (dirlist.dll)
Error Pages	system.webServer/httpErrors	CustomErrorModule (custerr.dll)
Failed Request Tracing Rules	system.webServer/tracing/ traceFailedRequests system.webServer/tracing/ traceProviderDefinitions	FailedRequestsTracingModule (iisfreb.dll)
Handler Mappings	system.webServer/handlers	[IIS Server Core]
HTTP Redirect	system.webServer/httpRedirect	HttpRedirectionModule (redirect.dll)
HTTP Response Headers	system.webServer/httpProtocol	ProtocolSupportModule (protsup.dll)
IIS Manager Permissions	administration.config: system.webServer/management	[IIS Manager, Web Management Service (WMSvc)]
IIS Manager Users	administration.config: system.webServer/management	[IIS Manager, Web Management Service (WMSvc)]

Table 6-2   **IIS Manager Features Mapping to Configuration and Modules**

Feature Name	Configuration Section	Consumed By
IPv4 Address and Domain Restrictions	system.webServer/ipSecurity	IpRestrictionModule (iprestr.dll)
ISAPI and CGI Restrictions	system.webServer/security/ isapiCgiRestriction	CgiModule (cgi.dll) IsapiModule (isapi.dll)
ISAPI Filters	system.webServer/isapiFilters	IsapiFilterModule (filter.dll)
Logging	system.applicationHost/log	[IIS Server Core]
	system.webServer/httpLogging	HttpLoggingModule (loghttp.dll)
Machine Key	system.web/machineKey	[ASP.NET run time and features that use cryptography]
Management Service	Registry: HKLM\SOFTWARE\Microsoft\ WebManagement\Server	[Web Management Service (WMSvc)]
MIME Types	system.webServer/staticContent	StaticFileModule (static.dll)
Modules	system.webServer/globalModules	[IIS Server Core]
	system.webServer/modules	
Output Caching	system.webServer/caching	HttpCacheModule (cachhttp.dll)
Pages and Controls	system.web/pages	[ASP.NET]
Providers	system.web/membership	[ASP.NET Roles, Membership, and Profile features]
	system.web/roleManager	
	system.web/profile	
Server Certificates	[Local Machine Certificate Store]	[Operating System, HTTP.SYS, Windows applications]
Server Side Includes	system.webServer/ serverSideInclude	ServerSideIncludeModule (iis_ssi.dll)
Session State	system.web/sessionState	Session (System.Web. SessionState.SessionStateModule)
	system.web/sessionPageState	
Shared Configuration	redirection.config: configurationRedirection	[IIS configuration system]
SMTP E-mail	system.net/mailSettings/smtp	[.NET Framework]
SSL Settings	system.webServer/access	[IIS Server Core]
Worker Processes	applicationHost.config: system. applicationHost/applicationPools	[Windows Process Activation Service]

Where the Configuration Is Written

When the feature configuration settings are changed, IIS Manager writes those settings to a configuration file. Depending on the connection level (server, site, or application) and the locking in the configuration files hierarchy, the IIS Manager feature settings appear as Read/Write or Read-Only.

Server connections can write to server-level configuration files, applicationHost.config and root web.config, and all distributed web.config files on that server. Only a server machine administrator can connect to a server. Features on the server level can both read from and write to configuration files. Even if a configuration section is locked in applicationHost.config, the corresponding feature will be Read/Write in a server connection. The configuration changes will be written to applicationHost.config in a <location> tag.

Site connections can write only to web.config files in or below the site's root folder. Server administrators and designated site administrators can connect to Web sites. If a configuration section is locked in applicationHost.config, the corresponding feature will appear Read-Only in that site connection, because site connections cannot write to applicationHost.config (even in a <location> tag).

Application connections can only write to web.config files in or below the application's root folder. Server administrators, site administrators for the application's parent site, and designated application administrators can connect to an application. If a configuration section is locked in applicationHost.config or the site's web.config file, the corresponding feature will appear Read-Only in that application connection.

Provided that a feature is not Read-Only and enables the settings to be saved, two rules define what files the configuration settings for that feature are written to:

- applicationHost.config vs. root web.config for server level configuration:
  - ❑ If the feature is listed under the ASP.NET area in IIS Manager, server-level configuration will be written to the root web.config file for .NET Framework.
  - ❑ If the feature is listed under the IIS area in IIS Manager, server-level configuration will be written to applicationHost.config.
  - ❑ The only exception is Forms Authentication, which is in the Authentication feature under the IIS area. The Forms Authentication configuration will be written to the root web.config file.

> **Note**   IIS Manager makes a choice between saving server-level configuration for a feature to applicationHost.config or root web.config, depending on where a corresponding configuration section is defined. If the section is defined in applicationHost.config, the configuration will be saved there; otherwise, it will be saved to root web.config.

- Locked versus unlocked configuration for site level and application level configuration:
  - ❑ All ASP.NET configuration sections, and a few IIS configuration sections, are unlocked by default. For unlocked sections, IIS Manager will write to the site's web.config if the configuration is changed for the site or to an application's web.config if the configuration is changed for an application.

❑   Most IIS configuration sections are locked by default. For locked sections, IIS Manager will always write to applicationHost.config, even when modifying configuration for sites and applications.

IIS Manager determines where to save configuration using the following logic: it always tries to save the configuration to the configuration file that is the closest in the hierarchy to the object being configured. For example, for directory configuration, IIS Manager will try to save settings in that directory's web.config; for application configuration, it will try to save to that application's web.config; and so on. However, if the corresponding section is locked in the closest file, then it moves to the closest parent and tries saving it there using a location tag. If the section is locked in the parent configuration file, IIS Manager continues this process until it reaches the top configuration file for the connection. If the section is still locked, then configuration is considered Read-Only.

When you select feature configuration settings, IIS Manager shows you the location of the file where those settings are stored. The configuration file location is shown on the lower-left side of IIS Manager and is identified by the Configuration prefix. The format is as follows.

```
Configuration: 'config_file_object_path' config_file_name
```

The *config_file_object_path* is the path to the configuration file object. Let's look at a couple of examples:

■   **'localhost'**   Appears for the server-level configuration on the local machine. For IIS features, it is followed by applicationHost.config. For ASP.NET features, it is followed by root web.config. Figure 6-15 shows the .NET Compilation feature page as an example of the latter.

■   **www.contoso.com**   Appears as the path to the web.config file in the www.contoso.com physical folder (www.contoso.com is followed by web.config).

The *config_file_name* is the name of the target configuration file. Let's look at several examples:

■   **applicationHost.config for IIS features**   For example, for Directory Browsing for the server connection, the status bar will display the following text.

```
Configuration: 'localhost' applicationHost.config
```

■   **root.web.config for ASP.NET features**   For example, for the .NET Trust Levels feature for the server connection, the status bar will display the following text.

```
Configuration: 'localhost' root web.config
```

■   **web.config, a target web.config file**   For example, as Figure 6-16 shows, for the Session State feature in the site www.contoso.com, the status bar will display the following text.

```
Configuration: 'www.contoso.com' web.config
```

The *location_path* is the location path to the object being configured (for more information on location paths, see Chapter 4, "Understanding the Configuration System"). This portion of the text appears only if the feature's corresponding configuration section is locked at a higher level. For example, as Figure 6-13 shows, for the Error Pages feature for the site www.contoso.com, the status bar will display the following text.

```
Configuration: 'localhost' applicationHost.config , <location path="www.contoso.com">
```

Feature Scope

Home pages for nodes in different levels in the tree may display different features. Table 6-1 shows where each feature appears by default.

A feature appearance in a home page for a selected object is defined by three factors:

- **Object level**   Some features are applicable only to certain levels.

- **Delegation**   If feature delegation is specifically set to Not Delegated, that feature will not appear on a home page.

- **Local Connection or Remote Connection**   Some features only appear in Local Connection.

Most IIS Manager features are applicable to all nodes in the tree: server, site, application, virtual directory, folder, and file. These features appear on home pages for all levels. However, there are exceptions for a server level. Some features are applicable only to the server level. They configure server-wide configuration, data, or information. These features appear only on a server home page:

- IIS Manager Users
- IIS Manager Permissions
- ISAPI and CGI Restrictions
- Server Certificates (this feature doesn't appear in remote connections)
- Management Service (this feature doesn't appear in remote connections)
- Worker Processes
- Active Directory and Client Certificates options that are within the Authentication feature

In addition, some features appear on all home pages except the server home page. These are the features that refer to application configuration and therefore make more sense on levels other than server. Other features, such as SSL, work better that way. These features are:

- .NET Users
- .NET Roles
- .NET Profile
- SSL Settings

Another exception is the Feature Delegation feature that appears only for the root node of a connection, such as server, site, or application. This feature is not available for virtual directories and folders.

In addition, feature delegation settings change the way that a feature appears in IIS Manager. For details on feature delegation, refer to Chapter 8.

IIS 7.0 Manager Customization and Extensibility

IIS Manager is not just an application, but rather an extensible platform that developers can use to plug in their own features to manage custom settings and applications. Developers can change the UI, remove existing features, and add new administration features.

Direct from the Source: IIS Manager—Built on Top of Public Extensibility API

During the design phase of the new IIS Manager, we decided to make extensibility a core feature and to build IIS Manager as a real platform so that not only could we extend and enhance its functionality, but third-party developers could as well. To make sure we were designing a flexible API, we decided to implement all the features using this API so that none of our features would be a special case inside the product. That's why there are several dlls in the IIS installation, such as Microsoft.Web.Management.Iis.dll and Microsoft.Web.Management.Aspnet.dll. By following these strict guidelines of building the API outside the core framework, we've made sure that anything that we built others could enhance or even replace with their own implementation. This of course was a challenging process, but at the same time, it made our platform flexible enough to ensure that additional IIS features such as FTP, WebDAV, and others will have a place inside the new IIS Manager.

Carlos Aguilar Mares

Senior Development Lead, IIS

IIS 7.0 ships with an application programming interface (API) that enables developers to change the IIS Manager UI and to manage custom settings and applications on the server. For example, this API provides the extensibility mechanism to develop UI features represented as list pages, property grids, and dialog pages; a custom-designed Actions pane; wizards and dialog boxes; and the ability to add custom nodes to the Connections pane.

IIS Manager is designed to have distributed client-server architecture. In addition, IIS Manager has a modular infrastructure in which every UI feature is its own entity. Each feature follows the client-server paradigm. This architecture of IIS Manager separates the logic that manipulates server settings from the presentation code, which displays these settings in a user-friendly manner for each of the UI features.

IIS 7.0 Management and Administration API

The API is located within two assemblies that provide a framework for modifying IIS Manager UI and developing new features to manage custom applications on the server. These assemblies are as follows:

- **Microsoft.Web.Management.dll**   This assembly provides the framework that enables developers to create new UI features and make modifications to IIS Manager. It provides the base classes and other functionality that enables the newly developed extensions to appear with a look and feel identical to the built-in IIS and ASP.NET features. It does not support changing the settings on the server.

- **Microsoft.Web.Administration.dll**   This assembly provides the framework for developers to change settings on the server. It gives developers a programmatic way to access and update the Web server configuration and administration information. It does not support adding any UI extensibility or functionality. In fact, most features in IIS Manager use this API to manage configuration settings on the server.

Each IIS Manager feature has two components:

- A client-side module that provides UI experience
- A server-side module service that manipulates the settings on the server

This architecture is illustrated in Figure 6-18. IIS Manager extensions must follow this architecture that is enforced by the base classes provided within the API.

The first step to deploy the new IIS extension is to install its client and server components in the global assembly cache (GAC) on the server. The second step is to register the new extension with IIS Manager. Each extension has to be individually registered with IIS Manager. IIS Manager is built on top of configuration system extensibility that enables custom functionality to be easily added.

IIS Manager uses a special file called administration.config that defines IIS Manager configuration. The administration.config file is located on the server in the folder *%SystemRoot%* System32\Inetsrv\Config. Administration.config is an XML configuration file that includes a list of IIS Manager built-in features and extensions. On IIS Manager startup, this file is checked to determine what features should be displayed in IIS Manager. If IIS Manager is connecting remotely, then the Web Management Service compares the module providers available on the server with the module providers available on the client. If a new extension is available on the server, the client is prompted to download and install that extension.

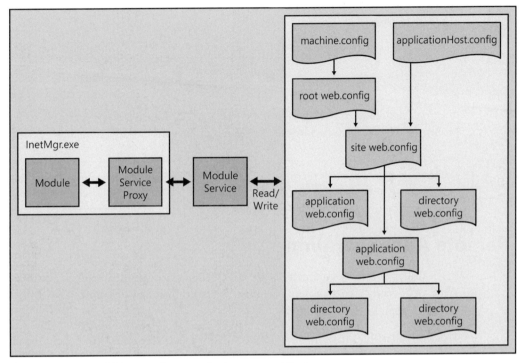

Figure 6-18   An IIS Manager feature client server architecture.

The *<moduleProviders>* section in the administration.config file defines all IIS Manager extensions that are registered on the system. To register an extension, you need to add the fully qualified type name of that extension module provider to the *<moduleProviders>* section and add the module name to the *<modules>* section. Depending on the desired extension scope, you may need to add the corresponding module name to the appropriate *<location path>* section that will define the sites and applications where this extension will appear in IIS Manager. The following excerpt from the administration.config file shows a built-in module provider for the DefaultDocument module in the *<moduleProviders>* section and the module DefaultDocument in the *<modules>* section with the root location path of "." that makes it available to all sites and applications on the server.

```
<moduleProviders>
    <!-- Server Modules-->
    <add name="DefaultDocument"
type="Microsoft.Web.Management.Iis.DefaultDocument
DefaultDocumentModuleProvider, Microsoft.Web.Management.Iis,
Version=7.0.0.0, Culture=neutral, PublicKeyToken=31bf3856ad364e35" />

</moduleProviders>
```

```
<!-- For all Sites -->
<location path=".">
    <modules>
        <add name="DefaultDocument" />
        ...
    </modules>
</location>
```

After you've registered the extension, on the next IIS Manager startup, the client will be prompted to download and install the client component of that extension.

> **Note**   For more details on extending IIS Manager and also creating custom configuration sections in .config files, see Chapter 13, "Managing Configuration and User Interface Extensions."

Remote Administration

In IIS Manager, remote connections are not available by default. To manage IIS 7.0 running on Windows Server 2008 remotely, you need to set up the client machines and configure the server for remote administration.

To administer IIS 7.0 running on Windows Server 2008 remotely from client machines running Windows Vista Service Pack 1 (SP1), Windows Server 2003 SP1, and Windows XP SP2, you need to install IIS Manager on these client machines and then connect to sites and applications on the server you need to manage. You can download IIS Manager for these operating systems from *http://iis.net/downloads*.

On the server, you must explicitly enable remote management of IIS 7.0 through IIS Manager. This is different than IIS 6.0, where management console remoting was through the MMC and was always enabled. For remote administration of IIS 7.0, Web Management Service (WMSvc) must be installed and running on the server, and remote connections to the service must be enabled.

Web Management Service is not installed by default—you need to install Web Management Service manually. During installation, you can specify the IP address and port number the service will listen on or accept the defaults: All Unassigned for the IP address, and 8172 for the port number. For detailed WMSvc installation instructions, refer to Chapter 8.

After you have installed Web Management Service, the Management Service Feature appears on the home page for the server in IIS Manager, and you can configure this feature to enable remote connections to service.

To enable remote connections, perform the following steps in IIS:

1. Select the server node in the Connections pane. The server home page is displayed.

2. Double-click the Management Service feature to open the Management Service feature page.

3. In the Management Service feature page, in the Actions pane, click Stop to stop the service.

![Internet Information Services (IIS) Manager window showing the Management Service feature page with options for Enable remote connections, Identity Credentials, Connections, SSL certificate, and Log requests settings.]

4. Check the Enable Remote Connections check box. Doing so enables server administrators to connect remotely to the server, as well as to sites and applications.

> **Note**   The setting that enables remoting is stored in the dword registry value *EnableRemoteManagement* under the registry key HKLM\SOFTWARE\Microsoft\ WebManagement\Server.

5. If you would like users without administrative privileges to manage sites and applications on this server, choose the type of identity credentials for these users. Configure other settings if needed, such as connections and logging options and IPv4 and domain restrictions. Click Apply in the Actions pane to save the changes and then click Start to start the service.

> **Note**   For a detailed discussion of remote administration, including the Web Management Service settings, refer to Chapter 8.

Summary

IIS Manager has been completely redesigned and rearchitectured from the ground up in IIS 7.0, and it differs significantly from the MMC snap-in used in previous versions of IIS. IIS Manager in IIS 7.0 is a client application with an intuitive, feature-focused, task-oriented, granular interface that significantly reduces management complexity.

IIS Manager provides integrated management of IIS and ASP.NET features within one tool. Features in IIS Manager map to configuration sections in the .config files and provide an easy-to-use interface for working with complex settings in the hierarchy of .config files.

IIS Manager is fully customizable and provides an extensible platform that developers can use to plug in their own administration features for managing custom settings and applications.

IIS Manager supports remote administration and feature delegation, enabling users without administrative privileges on the server to manage sites and applications remotely from their client computers.

Additional Resources

- For information on command line tool Appcmd.exe, WMI management provider, and PowerShell, refer to Chapter 7, "Using Command Line Tools."

- For information on using IIS Manager remotely, refer to Chapter 8, "Remote Administration."

- For information on extending IIS Manager, refer to Chapter 13, "Managing Configuration and User Interface Extensions."

- For a list of common administration tasks performed using IIS Manager, refer to Appendix J, "Common Administrative Tasks Using IIS Manager."

- For getting started with IIS 7.0 Manager, refer to *http://www.iis.net//articles/view.aspx/ IIS7/Use-IIS7-Administration-Tools/IIS-Manager-Administration-Tool/Getting-Started-with-IIS-Manager*.

Chapter 7
Using Command Line Tools

 On the Disc   Browse the CD for additional tools and resources.

Using Command Line Management Tools

It isn't always possible or practical to use IIS Manager to perform administration tasks. Quite often, Microsoft Internet Information Services (IIS) administrators need to use command line tools for on-demand or automated tasks. Common administration tasks such as creating and configuring sites, application pools, and virtual directories can be performed more efficiently through command line tools and programming interfaces.

This chapter focuses on command line management of IIS 7.0 by using Appcmd.exe, a single command line tool that replaces multiple scripts and tools provided by previous versions of IIS. Appcmd is installed by default and is immediately available for managing IIS from the command line. It can be used to manually perform almost any management task in IIS 7.0

quickly from the command line and to efficiently perform large numbers of configuration operations in an automated fashion.

In addition to Appcmd, IIS 7.0 provides a number of other automation options that require the development of custom script code. These options may be appropriate for more complex automation tasks or tasks that must be executed in the context of another program. These options are not covered in depth in this chapter, but resources are given at the end of the chapter so that you can learn more about them.

These options include:

- **Microsoft.Web.Administration**   Use the Microsoft.Web.Administration (MWA) namespace to perform common administration tasks from an .NET Framework based application.

- **Windows PowerShell**   Install this Windows Server 2008 feature to configure and manage IIS in a command line environment. (Windows PowerShell is also a free download for computers running Windows Vista, Windows Server 2003, and Windows XP.)

- **WMI Provider**   The new Windows Management Instrumentation (WMI) provider exposes the ability to manage IIS 7.0 configuration by using the WMI object model from scripts.

- **IIS 7.0 Configuration COM objects**   You can use the IIS 7.0 Configuration Component Object Model (COM) objects directly from C++ programs, script, or managed code to access the IIS 7.0 configuration system directly.

When you select the option for command line or programmatic administration of IIS 7.0, your choice is frequently guided by preferences for the programming model and the environment within which the management functionality needs to exist. Additionally, you should also consider the benefits and limitations of the available options, described in Table 7-1.

Table 7-1   Benefits and Limitations of Command Line Administration Options

Option	Pros	Cons
Appcmd	■ Quick management with no code required ■ Works on Windows full and Server Core installations ■ Provides best performance for many operations next to configuration COM objects	■ No remote management support ■ Requires Administrative privileges ■ Command line may be limited for complex management tasks

Table 7-1 **Benefits and Limitations of Command Line Administration Options**

Option	Pros	Cons
Microsoft.Web.Administration	■ Best option for .NET Framework programs ■ Supports remote management	■ Code required ■ Is not available on Server Core but can be used to manage Server Core servers remotely
Configuration COM objects	■ Best option for native C++ programs and scripts ■ Works on Windows full and Server Core installations ■ Supports remote management ■ Provides best performance	■ Code required
WMI	■ Supports remote management ■ Works on Windows full and Server Core installations ■ Allows remote management from down-level Windows operating systems	■ Code required ■ Introduces WMI overhead ■ Requires administrative privileges
PowerShell	■ Provides the flexibility of the Windows PowerShell command line environment	■ Does not support remote management directly in Windows Server 2008 ■ Is not available on Server Core but can be used to manage Server Core servers remotely ■ Requires the development of custom cmdlets

Appcmd.exe

Appcmd.exe is a new command line tool included with IIS 7.0. It exposes most of the Web server management tasks through a single intuitive command line interface. This tool replaces a host of command line tools and scripts provided in IIS 6.0 to perform key management scenarios.

Appcmd enables a Web server administrator to do the following from the command line:

- Add and configure Web sites, applications, virtual directories, and application pools
- Install, enable, and configure Web server modules
- Start and stop sites and recycle application pools
- View currently running worker processes and list requests that are currently executing
- Search, list, and manipulate IIS and ASP.NET configuration
- Configure Failed Request Tracing (FRT) settings

Most notable is the ability to list and edit IIS configuration, which enables administrators to quickly perform or automate any configuration task regardless of the feature they are trying to configure. The other functionality exposes some of the common configuration and management tasks for convenience.

Appcmd.exe is intended for local management of the Web server (it does not support remoting in IIS 7.0) and requires the user to have administrative privileges when using it. If you require remote management or the ability to configure the Web server without being an administrator on the server, you need to use the remote delegation support that IIS Manager provides. For more information, see Chapter 8, "Remote Administration."

Getting Started with Appcmd

Appcmd.exe is located in the *%SystemRoot%*\System32\Inetsrv directory. Because this directory is not part of the PATH environment variable by default, you will need to either add it to the PATH or always use the full path to the command to be able to run Appcmd commands. For example, when using the latter, you can always run Appcmd as follows.

```
%systemroot%\system32\inetsrv\Appcmd list sites
```

In the commands in the rest of this chapter, we will omit the full path when showing Appcmd commands, assuming that you have either added the Inetsrv directory to the PATH environment variable or will manually add the full path to each command.

> **Note**   To run Appcmd.exe, you will need to either add the Inetsrv directory to the PATH environment variable or use a full path to Appcmd.exe to run Appcmd commands.

To run Appcmd, you must be logged in as a member of the Administrators group on the local computer. Additionally, when using Appcmd on Windows Vista, you will need to run the tool as Administrator to make sure that the User Account Control does not prevent the tool from executing correctly. To do this, you should launch Appcmd commands from an elevated command prompt by launching the command prompt with the Run As Administrator option.

To do this, open the Start menu, click All Programs, select Accessories, right-click Command Prompt, and choose Run As Administrator.

> **Note**   To use Appcmd, you must be logged in as a member of the Administrators group. On Windows Vista, you will need to launch Appcmd commands from a command prompt started with the Run As Administrator option.

Appcmd commands use a natural language syntax of *verb object*, instead of the *object verb* syntax that some other Windows tools use to support commands on multiple object contexts (for example, *netsh*). For example, to list the Web sites on the server that are using the *Site* object, you would use the following command.

```
Appcmd list sites
```

Each command outputs one or more object instances or messages generated during the command execution. For example, the previous command may have the following output.

```
SITE "Default Web Site" (id:1,bindings:http/*:80:,state:Started)
SITE "TestSite" (id:2,bindings:http/*:80:testsite,state:Started)
```

The output is a list of *Site* objects, including their identifiers (*Default Web Site, TestSite*, and some of the key attributes of the object [*id, bindings, state*]).

Appcmd supports a number of objects, and most of the objects support a standard set of verbs such as *List, Add, Set,* and *Delete*. Some objects have additional verbs specific to the object. All verbs accept one or more parameters that you can use to customize the behavior of each command. Finally, some verbs accept a special parameter called the *identifier*, which uniquely identifies an instance of an object on which the verb should operate using an object-specific naming convention.

For example, you can use the *Delete Site* command with the site name as the identifier to delete a Web site, as in the following example.

```
Appcmd Delete Site "TestSite"
```

This has the following output.

```
SITE object "TestSite" deleted
```

The Appcmd syntax and the list of supported objects are explained further in the following section titled "Appcmd Syntax."

Appcmd Syntax

Appcmd uses the following syntax.

```
Appcmd <verb> <object> [identifier] [/parameter:value]
```

This syntax includes the following parts:

- **Verb**   The verb is the action to be performed on the specified object. Each object supports a fixed set of verbs, and each verb may support using the identifier and one or more parameters, some of which may be required. Most objects support basic commands such as *List*, *Add*, *Set*, and *Delete*, and some objects support additional commands. The verb must always be specified. It is not case-sensitive.

- **Object**   The object is the name of the management object on which the specified verb is being invoked. Together with the verb, it determines the actual command that will be executed. The supported objects are listed in Table 7-2. The object must always be specified. It is not case-sensitive.

- **Identifier**   The identifier is an optional argument that follows the object, which you can use to uniquely identify the specific instance of the object that the command is being performed on. It is required by most commands that perform actions on a specific instance of the object, such as the *Set* and *Delete* commands. The identifier has an object-specific format used to identify instances of that object, and it may or may not be case-sensitive. For information about the identifier format, refer to the section in this chapter that corresponds to each object.

- **Parameter**   Each verb supports zero or more parameters, which are in the */name:value* format, to control the execution of the command. The parameter names are not case-sensitive, but the values may be. For information about the supported parameters, refer to the section in this chapter that corresponds to each object. In addition, the tool itself supports a set of general parameters that affect the execution of every command. For more information on these parameters, see the section titled "General Parameters" later in this chapter.

Each Appcmd command must at minimum specify the object and verb. For example, to use the *List* verb on the *Site* object to list Web sites on the server, you can use the following command.

```
Appcmd List Site
```

The *List* verb of the *Site* object can accept an optional identifier to uniquely specify the Web site you are interested in listing. The *Site* object uses the Web site name as the unique identifier (not the Web site id). Therefore, to find a specific Web site named Default Web Site, we can use the following syntax.

```
Appcmd List Site "Default Web Site"
```

Alternatively, we can use optional parameters instead of the identifier to search for all Web site instances that have certain attributes. In fact, you can specify any of the configuration attributes in the Web site definition as parameters to the *List Site* command, to find all sites that have those configuration parameters set to the provided values. For example, to find all

Web sites that have the *serverAutoStart* configuration attribute set to false, you can use the following syntax.

```
Appcmd List Site /serverAutoStart:false
```

For the list of supported objects and verbs, see the following section titled "Supported Objects."

Supported Objects

Appcmd supports the objects and corresponding commands listed in Table 7-2.

Table 7-2   Appcmd-Supported Objects

Object	Description	Commands
Site (Sites)	Manage Web sites	*List, Set, Add, Delete, Start, Stop*
App (Apps)	Manage applications	*List, Set, Add, Delete*
Vdir (Vdirs)	Manage virtual directories	*List, Set, Add, Delete*
Apppool (Apppools)	Manage application pools	*List, Set, Add, Delete, Start, Stop, Recycle*
Config (Configs)	Manage IIS configuration sections	*List, Set, Search, Lock, Unlock, Clear, Reset, Migrate*
Wp (Wps)	List currently executing worker processes	*List*
Request (Requests)	List currently executing HTTP requests	*List*
Module (Modules)	Manage Web server modules	*List, Set, Add, Delete, Install, Uninstall*
Backup (Backups)	Manage configuration backups	*List, Add, Delete, Restore*
Trace (Traces)	Manage Failed Request Tracing (FRT) configuration and trace logs	*List, Configure, Inspect*

Note   Note that in the Object column, the plural form of each object name is also listed. This is because Appcmd supports an alias for each object and uses this to enable the plural form of the object to also be used to refer to it. Because of this, you can use the *List Sites* (plural) command to list Web sites while using *Set Site* (singular) to set a configuration attribute on the Web site.

Each of the objects and supported commands is described in more detail later in this chapter. You can also get information about the supported objects, verbs, and the syntax for each verb by using the built-in Appcmd command line help. Find out more about this in the following section titled "Getting Help."

Getting Help

Because Appcmd supports such a variety of objects and verbs, and each has a different set of parameters, it provides a fairly extensive help system to aid you as you navigate the usage of the tool.

You can get three levels of help from Appcmd:

1. **Top-level help.** Provides a list of objects supported by Appcmd, as well as the general tool parameters that you can use with any command. To obtain this help, simply run Appcmd with no parameters or use the */?* parameter, for example, *Appcmd /?.*

2. **Object help.** Provides a list of verbs supported on a specific object. To obtain this help, use the */?* parameter following the object name, for example, *Appcmd Site /?.*

3. **Verb help.** Provides a list of supported parameters and examples for a specific verb of a specific object. To obtain this help, use the */?* parameter following the verb and object names, for example, *Appcmd List Site /?.*

These three levels represent the typical ways people use the Appcmd help system to learn how to perform a particular command. First, you can display the list of the supported objects by using the top-level help. The resulting output will include the list of supported objects, as shown here.

```
General purpose IIS command line administration tool.
APPCMD (command) (object-type) <identifier> </parameter1:value1 ...>
Supported object types:

  SITE      Administration of virtual sites
  APP       Administration of applications
  VDIR      Administration of virtual directories
  …


(To list commands supported by each object use /?,
e.g. 'appcmd.exe site /?')

General parameters:
/?              Display context-sensitive help message.

/text<:value>   Generate output in text format (default).
                /text:* shows all object properties in detail view.
                /text:<attribute> shows the value of the specified
                attribute for each object.
/xml            Generate output in XML format.
                Use this to produce output that can be sent to another
                command running in /in mode.

Use "!" to escape parameters that have same names as the general
parameters, like "/!debug:value" to set a config property named "debug".
```

In addition, the top-level help shows the list of general tool parameters that control the operation of the tool regardless of the command. For more information on these parameters, see the section titled "General Parameters" later in this chapter.

At this point, you can get more information about a specific object type by using the *Appcmd Object* /? syntax to display the list of supported verbs. For example, to get the list of supported verbs on the *Site* object, use the following.

```
Appcmd Site /?
```

The output will contain the following.

```
Administration of virtual sites
APPCMD (command) SITE <identifier> <-parameter1:value1 ...>

Supported commands:
  list      List virtual sites
  set       Configure virtual site
  add       Add new virtual site
  delete    Delete virtual site
  start     Start virtual site
  stop      Stop virtual site

(To get help for each command use /?, e.g. 'appcmd.exe add site /?'.)
```

At this point, the final step is to obtain the specific syntax of the required verb by using the Appcmd *Verb Object* /? syntax. For example, to get the specific syntax for the *List Site* command, use the following.

```
Appcmd List Site /?
```

This will have the following output.

```
List virtual sites
APPCMD list SITE <identifier> <-parameter1:value1 ...>
Lists the virtual sites on the machine.  This command can be used to find a
specific site by using its identifier or url, or match zero or more sites
based on the specified site attributes.

Supported parameters:
 identifier
    Site name or url of the site to find

 /site.name
    Site name or url of the site to find (same as identifier)

 /?
    Display the dynamic site properties that can be used to find one
    or more site objects

Examples:
 appcmd list sites
    List all sites on the machine.
```

```
appcmd list site "Default Web Site"
   Find the site "Default Web Site".

appcmd list site http://localhost/app1
   Find the site associated with the specified url.

appcmd list site /serverAutoStart:false
   Find all sites that have the "serverAutoStart" configuration
   property set to "false".
```

Note that the help output contains the list of supported parameters, including the identifier. The /? parameter listed here indicates that you can also use dynamic parameters exposed by each instance of the object. With the *List Site* command, you can specify any of the configuration attributes in the Web site definition as parameters to find all Web site instances that have the specified values.

> **Note**   To get the list of dynamic parameters, you can use the *Set* verb with an instance of the object specified with the identifier and then use the /? parameter to list the supported attributes. For example: *Appcmd Set Site "Default Web Site" /?*. This is not ideal, but it does provide a quick way to look up dynamic parameters you can use for each command that supports dynamic object parameters.

The list of examples for each command is valuable, because it showcases the common ways for using each command. For example, for the Web site object, it shows how to list all sites, list sites using their identifier (name), list sites that serve a particular URL, or list sites by searching for a specific configuration parameter value.

> **Note**   Be sure to review examples in the verb help to get a quick feel for different ways of using the command.

Understanding Appcmd Output

The output of Appcmd typically contains a list of items. For commands that retrieve lists of object instances, such as the *List* command, it is the list of object instances. For commands that perform actions on object instances, it is a list of messages that indicate the action that was performed.

For instance, for the *List Site* command, the output contains a list of Web site object instances. Here is an example.

```
SITE "Default Web Site" (id:1,bindings:http/*:80:,state:Started)
SITE "TestSite" (id:2,bindings:http/*:80:testsite,state:Started)
```

By default, Appcmd uses a friendly list view that lists the object type, the identifier that can be used to identify each of the instances in subsequent commands, and several common attributes of each object instance. For the *Site* object, it is the Web site id, a list of configured bindings, and the state of the Web site (indicating whether it is started or stopped).

In fact, each *Site* object instance contains more attributes than are shown in the friendly list view. To display those parameters, you have several options:

- **Text view**   In this view, all of the attributes of each object instance are displayed in a hierarchical text property/value tree.

- **Single parameter view**   In this view, you can display the value of a particular attribute of each object instance.

- **Configuration view**   In this view, the underlying configuration element for each object instance is shown as a configuration fragment.

> **Note**   For the list of general parameters, see the section titled "General Parameters" later in this chapter.

The text view can be a quick way to show all of the attributes of each object instance. To use the text view, you need to use the */text:** general parameter. For example, following is a fragment of the output for the *List Sites* command when using the */text:** parameter.

```
SITE
  SITE.NAME:"Default Web Site"
  SITE.ID:"1"
  bindings:"http/*:80:,https/*:443:
  state:"Started"
  [site]
    name:"Default Web Site"
    id:"1"
    serverAutoStart:"true"
    [bindings]
      [binding]
        protocol:"http"
        bindingInformation:"*:80:"
      [binding]
        protocol:"https"
        bindingInformation:"*:443:"
    [limits]
      maxBandwidth:"4294967295"
      maxConnections:"4294967295"
      connectionTimeout:"00:02:00"
```

As you can see, this output contains more information about each Web site instance than the default output.

Alternatively, if you are interested in just the specific attribute of each object instance, you can use the single parameter view by using the */text:ParameterName* general parameter, where

ParameterName is the attribute whose value you want to display. Here is the output of the *List Sites* command when using the */text:name* parameter to show just the site names.

```
Default Web Site
TestSite
```

Finally, you can use the configuration view to display the configuration element associated with each object instance as a configuration fragment. You can do this by using the */config* general parameter to display all explicitly set configuration or by using */config:** to display all configuration. The *Config* object uses this format by default. Here is the output of the *List Sites* commands with the */config* switch.

```
<site name="Default Web Site" id="1">
  <bindings>
    <binding protocol="http" bindingInformation="*:80:" />
    <binding protocol="https" bindingInformation="*:443:" />
  </bindings>
  <limits />
  <logFile />
  <traceFailedRequestsLogging enabled="true" />
  <applicationDefaults />
  <virtualDirectoryDefaults />
  <application path="/">
    <virtualDirectoryDefaults />
    <virtualDirectory path="/" physicalPath="C:\inetpub\wwwroot" />
  </application>
</site>
```

You can also use the */xml* switch to output the results of Appcmd commands in XML. This switch can be used to pipe the results from one Appcmd command to chain multiple related commands together when using command pipelining.

> **Note**   For more information about command pipelining, see *http://mvolo.com/blogs/serverside/archive/2007/06/19/Do-complex-IIS-management-tasks-easily-with-appcmd-command-piping.aspx.*

The XML output mode can also be used to export results of Appcmd commands to other software programs and perform bulk operations.

> **Note**   For more information on bulk operations, see *http://mvolo.com/blogs/serverside/archive/2007/10/06/Create-IIS7-websites-and-application-pools-fast-with-appcmd.aspx.*

General Parameters

In addition to verb-specific parameters, Appcmd also supports general parameters that affect the execution of all Appcmd commands. These parameters are listed in Table 7-3.

Table 7-3   Appcmd General Parameters

Parameter	Description
/?	Display context-sensitive help message. For more information, see the section titled "Getting Help" earlier in this chapter.
/text	Generate the output in text format. This is the default. You can also specify /text:* to show a detailed text view containing all attributes of each object being displayed. Alternatively, you can also specify /text: *attribute* to display only the value of the specific attribute for each object. For more information, see the section titled "Understanding Appcmd Output" earlier in this chapter.
/xml	Generate the output in XML format. You can use this format to store or transport the output of the tool to another program, and it is the basis for the command pipelining support.
- or /in	Perform the command on the dataset provided from the standard input. Use this parameter to execute Appcmd commands on sets of objects provided by the output of another command.
/config	Show the configuration associated with each displayed object. You can also use /config:* to display all configuration, including values that are inherited from the schema defaults.
/metadata	Show the configuration metadata when displaying configuration objects and using /text:*. This includes information about the type of each configuration attribute.
/commit	Controls for which the command commits configuration. By default, the configuration is written to the same configuration path where it applies, which by default favors delegated configuration when setting configuration at the Web site, application, or URL levels. However, using this parameter allows you to control this independent of the configuration path to which the configuration is being applied. You can specify a fixed configuration path, or *apphost*, *machine*, and *webroot* for the corresponding server-level configuration files. Alternatively, you can use the *Site*, *App*, and *Parent* values to commit to a segment of the current configuration path. For more information, see the sidebar titled "Understanding Where Configuration Is Saved" later in this chapter.
/debug	Display debug information about the execution of each command, including the time taken to execute, the parameters passed in, how many objects were returned, and any errors. You can use this to debug or optimize Appcmd commands.

If you need to pass a parameter to a command that has the same name as a general parameter, you can escape it with a *!* sign. For example, if you need to set the *commit* configuration attribute on the fictional *mysection* configuration section, you can use the following syntax.

```
appcmd set config /section:mysection /!commit:somevalue
```

Using Range Operators

When using the *List* verb on any Appcmd object, you can include parameters to filter the returned results by the values of the specified attributes. For example, if you are looking for all sites that have the *serverAutoStart* attribute set to false, you can use the following syntax.

```
appcmd list sites /serverAutoStart:false
```

> **Note**   For more information on using the *List* command to list objects, see the section titled "Using the *List* Command to List and Find Objects" later in this chapter.

However, filtering by exact values of object attributes may be limiting in some scenarios. Often, you need the ability to search for objects that fall into a range of possible values. To support this, Appcmd enables the use of range operators to filter for objects that satisfy an expression on each attribute, rather then a fixed value.

For example, if we wanted to find all Web sites that have ids larger than 300, we could use the >= operator as follows.

```
appcmd list sites "/id:$>=300"
```

> **Note**   Because the > and < characters have special handling at the command line, be sure to enclose the entire parameter by placing the ranged operator in quotation marks.

You can specify the range operators for any supported attribute by using the *$OPVAL* syntax, where *OP* corresponds to the ranged operator, and *VAL* corresponds to the value for the operator. Table 7-4 shows the supported operators.

Table 7-4   Appcmd-Supported Operators

Operator	Description
>	Greater than operator, for numeric attributes. Matches all values of the attribute that are greater than the value specified. For example, */id:$>10* matches 11 but not 9.
>=	Greater than or equal to operator, for numeric attributes. Matches all values of the attribute that are greater than or equal to the value specified. For example, */id:$>=10* matches 10 but not 9.
<	Less than operator, for numeric attributes. Matches all values of the attribute that are less than the value specified. For example, */id:$<10* matches 9 but not 10.
<=	Less than or equal to operator, for numeric attributes. Matches all values of the attribute that are less than or equal to the value specified. For example, */id:$<=10* matches 10 but not 11.

Table 7-4   **Appcmd-Supported Operators**

Operator	Description
=	Wildcard match expression for string attributes. The wildcard expression can contain * and ? characters. For example, /name:$=*Site matches *MySite* and *Default Web Site* but not *Site 1*.
< >	The not operator. Matches all of the objects that do not have the exact specified value for the attribute. For example, /name:$<>MySite matches everything but *MySite*. This operator does not support wildcards.

You can use the ranged operators to find objects that satisfy one or more ranged conditions on their attributes. For example, to find all sites that are stopped and have the name *Site N* where *N* is a one-digit number, you can use the following syntax.

```
appcmd list sites /state:stopped "/name:$=Site ?"
```

Avoiding Common Appcmd Pitfalls

When using Appcmd, you should keep in mind a few particulars of the command line to avoid unexpected behavior. Use the following techniques to keep out of trouble:

- Surround the identifier and command parameters with quotation mark (") characters to make sure that the command line correctly keeps all of the parameter content together, especially if it contains spaces or special characters such as > or <. You should always do this when you are writing scripts or batch files that call Appcmd commands. For example: *appcmd list sites "/id:$>10"*. This is a command line shell limitation, not a limitation of Appcmd.

- Be sure to use the standard ASCII characters for - and / parameter delimiters, and the double quotation mark (") and single quotation mark (') characters, instead of the extended characters such as (") and ('). When commands are sent in e-mail or pasted into Microsoft Office programs, these characters may change to their extended versions, which are actually different characters and may not be processed correctly by the command line shell or Appcmd. For this reason, err on the side of using / to begin parameter names instead of the - character. For example, use */parameter*, not *-parameter*.

- Watch out for parameters ending with the \" characters, because the \"combination escapes the "character instead of using it to end the parameter. To avoid this, use a double \\. For example, "/physicalPath:c:\test\\".

Using Basic Verbs: *List, Add, Set, Delete*

Most Appcmd objects support the basic set of verbs: *List, Add, Set,* and *Delete.* These verbs operate in a fairly consistent way across objects, which makes Appcmd easy to use after you get a feel for how these verbs work.

Using the *List* Command to List and Find Objects

The *List* verb is one of the most useful verbs, and Appcmd provides it for all of its object types. It is responsible for listing all of the available instances of each object type, optionally enabling you to find a specific instance of the object, and for searching for one or more instances of the object by issuing queries involving one or more attributes.

You can use the *List* verb to list all object instances of a specific object type by using the following Appcmd syntax:

```
appcmd list Object
```

where Object is the object whose instances you wish to list. For example, to list all of the Web sites configured on your server, use this.

```
appcmd list sites
```

You can also specify one or more parameters so that you can restrict the list to only the Web sites that have the specified attributes. The list of attributes available for this operation is based on the Web site's configuration definition and also includes any of the attributes Appcmd generated for each *Site* object (such as the *State* attribute).

For example, if you want to look for any sites that have been stopped, type the following command.

```
appcmd list sites /state:Stopped
```

This command output will only return the sites that are in a stopped state. You can specify as many parameters as you want in the command. For instance, if you want to query sites that do not automatically start when the server starts but are currently running, you can issue the following command.

```
appcmd list sites /serverAutoStart:false /state:Started
```

In addition to specifying exact values for attributes when querying for objects, you can use expressions to broaden your query by using the Appcmd range operators. For example, you can find all Web sites with ids larger than 300 by doing the following.

```
appcmd list sites "/id:$>300"
```

The range operator support includes not equal to, greater than, greater than or equal to, less than, less than or equal to, and a wildcard matching expression for string value types. For more information on using ranged operators, see the section titled "Using Range Operators" earlier in this chapter.

Finally, you can always find a unique Web site instance by using its unique identifier, which is the site name for Web sites. When listing objects, the identifier is displayed for each object instance to make it easier to use later for referencing this object. For example, to locate the Web site with the name Default Web Site, you can use the following syntax.

```
appcmd list site "Default Web Site"
```

Additionally, the *Site* object supports the use of a URL as the identifier, in which case the tool will automatically resolve the URL to the Web site by using the binding information for each Web site. This also works when listing the *App* and *Vdir* objects. For example, to list the Web site configured to serve the *http://localhost/test.html* URL, you can use the following syntax.

```
appcmd list site "http://localhost/test.html"
```

Keep in mind that the *List* verb works for all object types. In addition to displaying Web sites, you can list application pools, applications, virtual directories, worker processes, and active HTTP requests. Try the *List* verb against all the supported object types. Refer to the supported object table in Table 7-2 or issue an *Appcmd.exe /?* command if you need help remembering what object types are supported.

Using the *Add* Verb to Create Objects

Many of the Appcmd objects support the ability to create new object instances. For example, you can create new Web sites, applications, virtual directories, and application pools. As you might guess, you'll use the *Add* verb to perform this task. The *Add* verb typically has the following syntax:

```
appcmd add Object [/parameter:value]*
```

Where Object is the object whose instance you are creating. The *Add* verb for each object requires a certain set of parameters to be specified to be used during the creation of the object instance. In addition, you can typically specify any additional parameters that are available for the *Set* verb when using the *Add* verb to have those attributes set immediately after object creation. You can get the list of required parameters that must be specified in the verb help for the *Add* command. For example, to learn how to add a site, you can issue the following command.

```
appcmd add site /?
```

The output of our command line help request shows that you can add a site by providing the *name*, *bindings*, and *physicalPath* parameters. Here is an example of adding a Web site by using the *Add Site* command.

```
appcmd add site /name:MyWebSite /bindings:"http/*:81:"
/physicalPath:"c:\inetpub\wwwroot"
```

> **Note**   For more information about using Appcmd to create Web sites, see Chapter 9, "Managing Web Sites."

The *Add* command output typically shows the objects the command created. In the previous example, the *Add Site* command creates a new Web site, root application, and root virtual directory.

> **Note**   Unlike the *Set* and *Delete* commands, the *Add* command does not accept an identifier.
> This is because the *Add* command doesn't use the identifier to look up an existing object—it
> creates a new object and requires the underlying parameters that may comprise the identifier
> for later lookups to be provided to create the object. For example, when using the *Add Site*
> command, you must provide the */name* parameter instead of specifying the name as the
> identifier.

Using the *Set* Verb to Change Existing Objects

In addition to creating new objects by using the *Add* verb, you can also set configuration
attributes on existing objects with the *Set* verb by using the following syntax:

```
appcmd set Object identifier [/parameter:value ...]
```

Where Object is the object whose instances you would like to modify The *Set* verb requires the
identifier to uniquely identify the object instance being modified. To ensure correctness, the
exact identifier must be used, for example, use the site name instead of a URL for the *Site* object.

> **Note**   Unlike the *Add* verb, you do not identify the desired object instance by specifying
> object-specific parameters, such as */name* for the *Site* object. Instead, you must use the
> identifier to uniquely identify the object instance.

To find out what attributes you can set by specifying them as parameters for the *Set* verb, you
can use the verb help. For example, to find out which parameters you can use with the *Set
Site* command, use the following.

```
appcmd set site /?
```

If the displayed parameter list includes "/?", this means that you can set configuration
parameters that are not listed in the help screen. This is the case for virtually all objects
Appcmd provides, because most have associated configuration information that you can
modify. To find out which configuration attributes you can use with the *Set* verb, you have
to inspect an existing object's attributes using the *List* verb with a detailed text view or by
using the /? switch with the *Set* verb. For example, to see the object properties you can set
for each *Site* object, you can use the following syntax.

```
appcmd set site "Default Web Site" /?
```

> **Note**   You need to specify an existing object instance with the *Set* verb when using the /?
> switch to list the supported parameters. Otherwise, you will get the default verb help screen.

The output of this command is a message that lists all parameters that can be used with the *Set* verb (as well as the *List* verb when querying) for the object. For example, here is a fragment of the output of the previous command.

```
-name
-id
-serverAutoStart
-bindings.[protocol='string',bindingInformation='string'].protocol
-bindings.[protocol='string',bindingInformation='string'].bindingInformation
-limits.maxBandwidth
-limits.maxConnections
...
```

> **Note**   For more information on addressing and setting configuration attributes, as well as modifying configuration collections, see the section titled "Working with Configuration" later in this chapter.

Using the *Delete* Verb to Remove Objects

No configuration utility would be complete without providing you with the ability to remove data. Appcmd provides an obvious syntax for removing configuration by deleting objects with the *Delete* verb.

```
appcmd delete Object identifier
```

Similar to the *Set* verb, the *Delete* verb requires the identifier to uniquely identify the object instance being modified. To ensure correctness, the exact identifier must be used, for example, use the site name instead of a URL for the *Site* object.

> **Note**   Unlike the *Add* verb, you do not identify the desired object instance by specifying object-specific parameters, such as */name* for the *Site* object. Instead, you must use the identifier to uniquely identify the object instance.

For example, you can delete a Web site by using the *Delete Site* command as follows.

```
appcmd delete site "MyNewWebSite"
```

> **Caution**   Deleting a Web site deletes all of the contained application and virtual directory definitions. It does not delete the content.

Working with Configuration

Editing IIS 7.0 configuration is a key task for Appcmd. Appcmd commands are a great way to encapsulate configuration changes such that you can show them to other users, save them for future use, or use them to quickly automate management tasks. This is why, when showing how to perform them using IIS Manager is too time-consuming, the IIS 7.0 online help documentation uses Appcmd to show how to perform most configuration tasks, as does this book itself.

Though you can manage the configuration for key Web server objects—such as the Web site, application, virtual directory, and application pools—through the corresponding Appcmd-friendly objects, the majority of configuration sections are not exposed through friendly objects. Instead, you use the *Config* object to manipulate configuration settings. By using the *Config* object, you can edit any configuration section exposed through the IIS 7.0 configuration stack (built-in or third-party).

The *Config* object supports the verbs listed in Table 7-5.

Table 7-5   Supported Verbs for the *Config* Object

Verb	Description
List	Show the configuration for any specific configuration section, for any URL or configuration path
Set	Set the configuration for any specific configuration section, for any URL or configuration path
Search	Find where the configuration is defined
Lock	Lock a specific configuration section to prevent it from being delegated to child configuration levels
Unlock	Unlock a specific configuration section to prevent it from being delegated to child configuration levels
Clear	Clear a particular configuration section, collection, or attribute
Reset	Used by Window Setup to restore each built-in configuration section to setup default; do not use this command
Migrate	Migrate ASP.NET configuration sections to an IIS configuration for running in Integrated pipeline; see Chapter 11, "Hosting Application Development Frameworks," for more information

You can use the *List Config* command to display the effective configuration for a specific URL or configuration path, either in its entirety or for a specific configuration section. You can use the *Set Config* command to set the configuration for a specific URL or configuration path for a specific configuration section. Finally, you can use the *Clear Config* command to clear the configuration for a specific section, at the specified URL or configuration path. You can also manage the delegation state of configuration sections by using the *Lock Config* and *Unlock Config* commands. For more information about managing delegation for configuration sections, see Chapter 4, "Understanding the Configuration System."

Most of the configuration commands enable the use of the identifier, which for the *Config* object represents the configuration path for which you are performing the command. By default, if the identifier is not specified, it defaults to MACHINE/WEBROOT/APPHOST, which targets the configuration to the Web server level in the applicationHost.config file. You can specify the identifier as both a configuration path in the format of *SiteName/UrlPath* (for example, "Default Web Site/myapp") or as a normal URL (for example, *http://localhost/myapp*). If you are using the former, Appcmd will automatically append the "MACHINE/WEBROOT/APPHPOST" prefix to form the configuration path. If you are using the latter, Appcmd will resolve the URL to a configuration path by using the Web site bindings.

For example, to display the effective settings for the *system.webServer/asp* section at *http://localhost/myapp*, you can use the following command.

```
appcmd list config "Default Web Site/myapp"
```

Or you can use this command.

```
appcmd list config "http://localhost/myapp"
```

For more information about forming configuration paths, see Chapter 4.

Viewing Configuration with the *List Config* Command

To view a configuration, you can use the *List Config* command. This command has the following syntax.

```
appcmd list config ConfigurationPath [/section:SectionName]
```

ConfigurationPath is the configuration path or URL at which Appcmd will read configuration. If you omit it, Appcmd will read configuration at the Web server level, using the "MACHINE/WEBROOT/APPHOST" configuration path. Keep in mind that Appcmd reads the effective configuration at the specified path, which is a product of merging all configuration paths in the hierarchy corresponding to the provided configuration path. Therefore, it is not the same as just opening a configuration file at the specified path in Notepad.

If the */section* parameter is not provided, Appcmd will list the configuration for *all* configuration sections. This is a lot to process, so most of the time you will want to specify the name of the section you'd like to view. If you are not sure what the section name is, you can list all registered sections by using the following trick.

```
appcmd list config /section:?
```

This will list all of the sections. You can use wildcards after the *?* to search for sections with a specific name. For example, *"?*security*"* shows all sections that have the string security in their names.

The output of the *List Config* command uses the configuration view by default. For more information on selecting an output view, see the section titled "Understanding Appcmd Output" earlier in this chapter.

Setting Configuration with the *Set Config* Command

The *Set Config* command is a versatile command that enables you to set or edit any configuration properties. This command uses the following syntax.

```
appcmd list config ConfigurationPath [/section:SectionName] [/attribute:value]
[/+attribute] [/-attribute]
```

As with the *List Config* command, *ConfigurationPath* is the configuration path or URL at which Appcmd will apply configuration changes. If you omit it, Appcmd will apply configuration to the Web server level, using the "MACHINE/WEBROOT/APPHOST" configuration path. By default, Appcmd will write the configuration to the file corresponding to the configuration path. This facilitates the creation of delegated configuration.

However, you can choose to persist the configuration setting to a higher location in the configuration hierarchy, using a location tag to apply it to the specified configuration path. You may want to do this for cases in which the configuration section being edited is locked and does not enable configuration settings to be set at the configuration path for which is it being applied. To do this, you can use the */commit* parameter. For more information, see the section titled "General Parameters" earlier in this chapter and also see Chapter 4.

Direct from the Source: Understanding Where Configuration Is Saved

It is important to understand the difference between the configuration path for which the configuration is applied and the configuration path where it is persisted. The two are the same by default, but you may want to decouple them by writing the configuration changes to a higher configuration path by using a location tag to apply the settings to the configuration path specified for the command. To do this, you can use the */commit* parameter provided by Appcmd.

When using this parameter, you can explicitly specify a configuration path where the settings should be saved. You can specify *machine*, *webroot*, or *apphost* for specific server-level configuration files, to keep all configuration in administrator-controlled configuration files. This is a good option when the configuration sections are locked and are not allowed to be specified in the distributed web.config files.

Alternatively, you can specify *site* or *app* to save the changes in a web.config file corresponding to the Web site root or application root for the provided configuration path. Finally, you can use the *parent* value to specify the parent path segment of the provided URL.

You should use the *site, app,* or *parent* values when applying a configuration to a specific URL that does not correspond to a directory, because Appcmd will otherwise fail to generate the web.config file. Additionally, you can use these values to place a configuration for multiple URLs in a single distributed web.config file in the root of the Web site or application, maintaining the benefit of distributed configuration and avoiding too many disparate web.config files.

The right choice depends on your configuration delegation strategy and your requirements for producing portable configuration.

Mike Volodarsky

IIS Core Server Program Manager

The */section* parameter is required for the *Set Config* command, and it must specify a valid configuration section for which you want to set the configuration.

Note   You may want to use the *List Config* command to find the configuration section you are interested in.

Use additional parameters to actually make the changes to the configuration, including setting attribute values and adding, removing, or editing collection elements. These topics are explained in more detail in the following section titled "Setting Configuration Attributes" and in the section titled "Managing Configuration Collections" later in this chapter.

Setting Configuration Attributes

To set configuration attributes on a specific section by using the *Set Config* command, you specify each attribute you'd like to set as a parameter and provide its value as a parameter value. For example, to set the *allowDoubleEscaping* attribute of the *system.webServer/security/ requestFiltering* section, you can use the following syntax.

```
appcmd set config /section:system.webServer/security/requestFiltering
/allowDoubleEscaping:true
```

Some configuration sections contain subelements. To address attributes in those sections, you can use the "." notation to specify the full element path to the attribute. The element path is relative to the section, so it is not used for top-level attributes on the section element. For example, to set *allowUnlisted* in the *fileExtensions* element of the section we just edited, you can use the following syntax.

```
appcmd set config /section:system.webServer/security/requestFiltering
/fileExtensions.allowUnlisted:false
```

> **Note**   You can specify multiple parameters to set multiple configuration attributes of a section in a single command. You cannot specify each parameter more than once, however. Due to a bug, if you specify the same attribute more than once, the last value takes effect.

You can also use the "/-*Attribute*" syntax to delete values set for the *attribute* in a configuration, to return the configuration to the value inherited from the parent configuration level or configuration default from the schema definition of the configuration section. For example, to delete the explicitly set value for the *allowDoubleEscaping* attribute we set earlier, you can use the following syntax.

```
appcmd set config /section:system.webServer/security/requestFiltering
/-allowDoubleEscaping
```

Direct from the Source: Case Sensitivity in Appcmd

Appcmd treats parameter names in a case-insensitive manner, which means you do not have to worry about the correct case of each configuration attribute you are setting. However, the underlying configuration system is case-sensitive with respect to attribute names. Therefore, in the highly unlikely event that a configuration element has two attributes that differ only in case, you will not be able to address the second attribute, because Appcmd will always target the first one. This decision was the result of a heated discussion about correctness versus the usability of the tool and is a case (pun intended) of optimizing for the common experience. In general, the ability to use case-sensitive names for attributes should never be taken advantage of, because it produces a very confusing user experience and is so error-prone. So, think twice before designing configuration sections that have multiple attributes that differ only in case.

Likewise, the names of the configuration sections specified in the /*section* parameter for configuration commands are also case-insensitive, even though it is technically possible to have multiple sections that differ only by case.

In the end, the case-insensitive nature of attribute names and section names makes it significantly easier to use the tool for configuration tasks. However, keep in mind that configuration attribute values themselves can be, and often are, case-sensitive due to how the Web server features interpret the values.

Mike Volodarsky

IIS Core Server Program Manager

Managing Configuration Collections

For configuration sections that contain collections, you can use the *Set Config* command to add new collection elements, remove existing elements, or edit the configuration contained by each existing element.

To add a collection element, you can use the "/+*elementpath*.[*attribute*='*value*',...]" syntax, where *elementpath* is the path to the collection element using the "." notation, and each *attribute /value* pair represents each attribute on the collection element. You must specify the values for all required attributes to create a new collection element, and you can optionally specify other attributes supported by the collection element. For example, to add a new entry to the collection in the *fileExtensions* element of the *system.webServer/security/requestFiltering* section, you can use the following command.

```
appcmd set config /section:system.webServer/security/requestFiltering
/+fileExtensions.[fileExtension='.test',allowed='true']
```

> **Note**   If you do not specify all of the required attributes for the new collection element, the *Set Config* command will fail with the "Element is missing required attributes" error message.

The preceding command will create a child element in the collection with the *fileExtension* and *allowed* attributes set to the specified values. Note that if the section itself is a collection, you simply specify the bracket expression and don't need an element path.

You can control where in the collection you add the new element. By default, the element is added at the end of the collection for collections configured to use the merge append mode in the configuration schema, and at the beginning of the collection if the collection is configured to use the merge prepend mode. You can override this default position by using the position qualifier, which can have the values of *@start*, *@end*, and *@Position* where *Position* is the 0-indexed position in the collection. The position qualifier should be the first item in the bracketed list. For example, to insert the element we added in the preceding command at the start of the collection, you could use the following syntax.

```
appcmd set config /section:system.webServer/security/requestFiltering
/+fileExtensions.[@start,fileExtension='.test',allowed='true']
```

> **Note**   If the collection already has an element that contains the same values for the key attributes as the one being added, the *Set Config* command will fail with a "Cannot add duplicate collection entry" error message.

To remove a collection element, use the "/-*elementpath*.[*attribute*='*value*',...]" syntax, which must specify *attribute / value* for all attributes that comprise a collection key to uniquely identify the collection element to be removed. For example, to remove the collection element added in the previous example, use the following syntax.

```
appcmd set config /section:system.webServer/security/requestFiltering
/-fileExtensions.[fileExtension='.test']
```

Because the *fileExtension* attribute is the single unique key of the collection, it is sufficient to remove the desired element.

Instead of specifying the key attributes, you can remove collection elements by using the position qualifier we discussed earlier. For example, to remove the first element in the collection, use the following syntax.

```
appcmd set config /section:system.webServer/security/requestFiltering
/-fileExtensions.[@start]
```

Finally, to set attributes for a specific collection element, you can use the standard element path notation for setting configuration attributes but also use the bracketed collection indexer expression to select the required collection element. For example, to set the *allowed* attribute on the collection entry we added earlier, you can use the following syntax.

```
appcmd set config /section:system.webServer/security/requestFiltering
/fileExtensions.[fileExtension='.test'].allowed:true
```

Note that we had to identify the element by using the unique key of the collection, much as we do for the deletion of collection elements. However, also note that the attribute we are setting is specified outside of the bracketed expression—the attributes in the bracketed expression serve to uniquely identify the element you are modifying. Because of this, you need to use the full element path notation to set each attribute on a collection element. As before, instead of using the key attributes to identify the collection element, we can also use the position qualifier.

Managing Configuration Delegation

You can also use the *Config* object to manage configuration delegation; to determine which configuration sections are allowed in distributed web.config configuration files; and to configure fine-grained configuration locking for specific elements, attributes, and collections. Appcmd provides the following support for this:

- *Lock Config* **command**   Lock a configuration section to prevent it from being delegated at a specific configuration level and below.

- *Unlock Config* **command**   Unlock a configuration section to allow it to be delegated at a specific configuration level and below.

- *Set Config* **command**   Set the special configuration attributes including *lockAttributes*, *lockElements*, and *lockItem*, to configure fine-grained configuration locking.

To learn more about using Appcmd to lock and unlock sections, see Chapter 4. To learn about using fine-grained configuration locking, see the section titled "Granular Configuration Locking" in Chapter 4.

Managing Configuration Backups

Appcmd provides a *Backup* object that you can use to create backups of global configuration files and to restore them. Creating a backup can be as simple as using the *Add* verb on the *Backup* object as shown here.

```
appcmd add backup
```

Issuing this command creates a new backup with a name based on the current date and time. The format is as follows: *YYYYMMDDThhmmss* (where *YYYY* is the four-digit year, *MM* is the two-digit month, *DD* is the two-digit day, *T* is a delimiter between the date and time, *hh* is the two-digit hour, *mm* is the two-digit minute, and *ss* is the two-digit second). If you prefer to provide your own name for the backup, you can simply add it to the end of your Appcmd request.

```
appcmd add backup "MyServerBackup"
```

By issuing the *List* verb against the *Backup* object, you can see your newly created backup.

```
appcmd list backup
```

To restore a configuration backup, use the *Restore* verb and the name of the backup you want to restore. For instance, to restore a backup named "MyServerBackup", type the following.

```
appcmd restore backup "MyServerBackup"
```

> **Note** The backup files are stored as subdirectories of the *%SystemRoot%*\System32\ Inetsrv\Backup folder with the name given to the backup instance. When you create a new backup, administration.config and applicationHost.config are among the files that are stored.

You can learn more about managing IIS 7.0 configuration backups in the section titled "Backing Up Configuration" in Chapter 4.

Working with Applications, Virtual Directories, and Application Pools

Appcmd can be an effective way to create and configure many of the key Web server objects, including Web sites, applications, virtual directories, and application pools. The *Appcmd Site, App, Vdir,* and *Apppool* objects provide a convenient mechanism for managing these objects, even though you can perform most of the tasks that these objects expose by using the *Config* object to directly edit configuration files.

The *Site* object provides a convenient way to enumerate Web sites, as well as to create new Web sites and set configurations on existing Web site definitions. For example, you create a Web site in a single step by using the *Add Site* command.

```
ppcmd add site /name:MySite /bindings:http/*:81: /physicalPath:c:\mysite
```

This command creates a new Web site, listening on port 81, and automatically creates a root application and a root virtual directory pointing to C:\mysite. You can also create the Web site separately by omitting the *physicalPath* parameter and then create applications and virtual directories for the Web site by using the *Add App* and *Add Vdir* commands respectively.

You can use the *List Sites* object to list the Web sites on the server or find specific Web sites by attributes or URL. For example, to determine which Web site is configured to serve requests to *http://localhost:83*, you can use the following syntax.

```
appcmd list sites http://localhost:83
```

To find all sites that are currently stopped, you can use the following syntax.

```
appcmd list sites /state:Stopped
```

You can also manually start and stop Web sites by using the *Start Site* and *Stop Site* commands. Find more details on how to use Appcmd to list, create, and configure Web sites and virtual directories in Chapter 9.

Similar to Web sites, you can also create, list, and manipulate applications, virtual directories, and application pools. Find more information about how to create and configure applications and application pools in Chapter 10, "Managing Applications and Application Pools."

Working with Web Server Modules

The *Module* object in Appcmd provides convenient methods for installing, enabling, and managing Web server modules. Again, you can perform the majority of these tasks by using the *Config* object to directly edit configuration files.

For example, you can install native modules by using the *Install Module* command.

```
appcmd install module /name:MyNativeModule /image:c:\mymodule.dll
```

You can use the same command to add new managed modules.

```
appcmd add module /name:MyManagedModules /type:MyModules.MyManagedModule
```

You can also manage which modules are enabled on your Web server or application by adding or deleting modules.

Find details about how to use Appcmd to install, enable, and configure Web server modules in Chapter 12, "Managing Web Server Modules."

Inspecting Running Worker Processes and Requests

Viewing and changing configuration data is not the only thing that you can do with Appcmd. You can also inspect the run-time state of the Web server by listing the currently executing worker processes and even requests.

Listing Running IIS Worker Processes

You can use the *List Wp* command to list all currently running IIS worker processes. This command uses the following syntax.

```
appcmd list wp [pid] [/apppool.name:string] [/wp.name:string]
```

The *List Wp* command supports the use of the Process ID (PID) as an identifier to locate the specified IIS worker process. Additionally, you can specify the application pool name by using the */apppool.name* parameter to list IIS worker processes belonging to a specific application pool.

For example, to list all IIS worker processes that are currently running, you can use the following syntax.

```
appcmd list wp
```

The output of this command includes the PID of each IIS worker process, as well as the application pool to which it belongs.

```
WP "3284" (applicationPool:DefaultAppPool)
```

Listing Currently Executing Requests

In addition to viewing the currently running worker processes, you can also look deeper into the Web server operation by listing currently executing requests. This can give you a snapshot of current system activity, as well as show which requests have been executing for a long time (thus possibly indicating a problem).

You can list the currently executing requests by using the *List Request* command. For example, to list all currently executing requests on the server, you can use the following syntax.

```
appcmd list requests
```

The output contains all requests that were executing in all IIS worker processes at the moment of query.

```
REQUEST "fd00000180000004" (url:GET /wait.aspx?sleep=10000, time:4072 msec,
client:localhost, stage:ExecuteRequestHandler,
module:ManagedPipelineHandler)
```

As you can tell, each displayed request object contains quite a bit of information about the currently executing request, including:

- The request URL and verb.

- The time that the request has spent executing.

- The client issuing the request.

- The pipeline stage that the request is currently in, and the module that is currently executing.

You can use the time information—as well as the current pipeline stage and module data—to effectively troubleshoot request hangs and performance degradation problems, by pinpointing the exact URL and in some cases even the module that is causing the slowdown.

In addition to listing all requests on the server, which can be an expensive operation and may give too much information to be useful in a lot of scenarios, you can use a variety of filters to list only the relevant requests. To see how to do this, let's look at the detailed syntax of the *List Requests* command.

```
appcmd list requests [identifier] [/site.name:string] [/wp.name:string]
[/apppool.name:string] [/elapsed:uint] [/url:string] [/verb:string]
[ClientIp:string] [/stage:string] [/module:string]
```

This command supports the parameters listed in Table 7-6.

Table 7-6   Parameters for the *List Requests* Command

Parameter	Description
identifier	The request identifier to look up a specific request multiple times. The request identifier is a randomly generated string similar to "fd00000180000004" that is shown when requests are displayed in Appcmd.
site.name	The site name for which to display currently running requests.
wp.name	The IIS worker process PID for which to display currently running requests. This improves the efficiency of the query because only the specified IIS worker process is polled.
apppool.name	The application pool name for which to display currently running requests. This improves the efficiency of the query because only the IIS worker processes for the specified application pool are polled.
elapsed	The minimum elapsed time in milliseconds for requests to show. Requests that have taken less time to execute are not returned. This may increase the efficiency of the query by returning fewer requests. Using the *elapsed* attribute is an effective way to determine hung requests.

Table 7-6 Parameters for the *List Requests* Command

Parameter	Description
url	The URL of the request. You can specify the exact URL or wildcard expressions on URLs to show requests only to specific URLs (note that the URL may contain the query string as well).
clientip	The IP of the requesting client. This can be in both IPv4 and IPv6 format depending on the client's connection.
stage	The request processing stage. Use to show only requests that are currently executing in the specified request processing stage. For a list of valid request processing stages, see the section titled "The Request Processing Pipeline" in Chapter 12.
module	The name of the module. Use to show only the requests that are being processed by the specified module.

Working with Failed Request Tracing

The *Trace* object in Appcmd provides a convenient way to enable and use the Failed Request Tracing (FRT) feature in IIS 7.0 to diagnose server problems.

> **Note** For more information about using Failed Request Tracing, see Chapter 16, "Tracing and Troubleshooting."

You can use the *Trace* object to do the following:

- Turn FRT on and off for each Web site
- Manage FRT tracing rules for any URL
- Search for and inspect FRT log files

Turning on Failed Request Tracing

To turn on FRT for a particular URL, you must first enable the feature for the Web site. You can do this with Appcmd by using the *Configure Trace* command.

```
appcmd configure trace SiteName /enablesite
```

The */enablesite* parameter enables the use of FRT for the site specified by the *SiteName* identifier (this identifier can also be a URL, in which case Appcmd will turn on tracing for the corresponding site). For example, to enable FRT for the "Default Web Site" site, use the following syntax.

```
appcmd configure trace "Default Web Site" /enablesite
```

> **Note**   Be sure to disable FRT when not using it with the */disablesite* parameter.

You can also use the */disablesite* parameter to turn off FRT for the Web site when you are not using it. Doing so allows you to leave the Failed Request Tracing rules configured for URLs on the site and simply toggle tracing on or off at the Web site level.

Creating Failed Request Tracing Rules

To produce FRT trace logs, you need to create rules that indicate the failure conditions that trigger the trace to be logged, as well as which trace events should be captured. To do this, you use the */enable* parameter of the *Configure Trace* command. This has the following syntax.

```
appcmd Configure Trace <URL> /enable [/path:string] [/areas:string]
[/verbosity:level] [/timetaken:timespan] [/statuscodes:string]
```

This command supports the parameters listed in Table 7-7.

Table 7-7   Parameters of the *Configure Trace* Command

Parameter	Description
path	The URL path for which the rule is enabled. This can be an extension in the form of *"*.extension"* or *"*"* to indicate all requests. If not specified, defaults to *"*"*.
areas	The list of providers and their areas to trace. This is in the form of *"provider/area1,area2:verbosity,..."*, where the area list and verbosity are optional for each provider entry. If not specified, this uses all registered providers and their subareas at *"Verbose"* verbosity level.
verbosity	The verbosity level of an event that causes the request to meet the failure definition and generate the trace log. You can use this to generate trace logs if an event of Warning or Error verbosity is encountered. Allowed values are *Ignore, CriticalError, Error,* and *Warning*. If not specified, the default is *Warning*.
timetaken	The execution time (in time span format) that causes the request to meet the failure definition and generate the trace log. You can use this parameter to generate trace logs only if the request exceeds the specified execution time, to capture slow or hung requests. If not specified, defaults to one minute.
statuscodes	Response status codes that cause the request to meet the failure definition and generate the trace log. This is in the form of *"status.substatus,..."*, where *substatus* is optional. You can use this to generate the trace log for requests that fail with specific error response codes. If not specified, defaults to *"500,400,401,403"*.

When you use the */enable* command without specifying the */path* parameter, it creates an entry that matches all requests to the URL with *path* set to "*". For example, we can use the following syntax to quickly enable FRT tracing using all default configurations.

```
appcmd configure trace "Default Web Site/" /enable
```

This generates the following configuration for the *system.webServer/tracing/traceFailedRequests* configuration section.

```
<tracing>
    <traceFailedRequests>
        <add path="*.aspx">
            <traceAreas>
                <add provider="ASPNET"
areas="Infrastructure,Module,Page,AppServices" />
            </traceAreas>
            <failureDefinitions statusCodes="404" />
        </add>
        <add path="*">
            <traceAreas>
                <add provider="WWW Server"
areas="Authentication,Security,Filter,StaticFile,CGI,Compression,Cache,RequestNotifications,
Module" verbosity="Verbose" />
                <add provider="ASP" areas="" verbosity="Verbose" />
                <add provider="ISAPI Extension" areas=""
verbosity="Verbose" />
                <add provider="ASPNET"
areas="Infrastructure,Module,Page,AppServices" verbosity="Verbose" />
            </traceAreas>
            <failureDefinitions timeTaken="00:01:00"
statusCodes="500,400,401,403" verbosity="Warning" />
        </add>
    </traceFailedRequests>
</tracing>
```

Note that the rule uses a path of "*" to apply to all requests at or below the URL at which the configuration is set, specifies all the registered trace providers and areas with the Verbose verbosity level, and specifies the default failure definition triggers.

You can specify the */path* parameter to create additional rules for specific extensions, for example, to enable tracing for ASPX pages only.

```
appcmd configure trace "Default Web Site/" /enable /path:*.aspx
```

You can use the */disable* parameter instead of */enable* to remove the rules, specifying the */path* parameter to indicate which rule you'd like to remove. If you omit the */path* parameter, the tool will attempt to remove the rule with a path of "*".

Additionally, you can override both the list of trace providers and areas that are being captured by each rule—as well as the failure definition for the rule—by using the optional parameters listed in Table 7-7. For example, to configure an FRT trace rule that intercepts only the events from the ASP.NET provider and only generates log files for the 404 status code, you can use the following syntax.

```
appcmd configure trace "Default Web Site/" /enable /path:*.aspx
/areas:ASPNET/Infrastructure,Module,Page,AppServices /statuscodes:404
```

Searching Failed Request Tracing logs

Besides enabling and configuring Failed Request Tracing rules, Appcmd also provides a convenient ability to search the trace log files. You can use this to quickly find the trace log, and even the event inside of the log, to help you with diagnosing a particular problem.

You can search the existing trace log files by using the *List Trace* command. This command has the following syntax.

```
appcmd list traces [identifier] [/url:string] [/site.name:string] [apppool.name:string]
[/statuscode:string] …
```

This command accepts the parameters listed in Table 7-8.

Table 7-8   Parameters of the *List Trace* Command

Parameter	Description
identifier	The unique identifier of each trace log, which is in the form of *"SiteName/logfilename.xml"*. You can use this to look up a specific trace log.
url	The URL of the request. Appcmd supports partial URLs by default, doing a prefix match on a normalized version of the URL.
site.name	The name of the Web site for which to show the request logs. Using this can improve the efficiency of the command because only the logs for the specified Web site are retrieved.
apppool.name	The name of the application pool for which to show the request logs.
statuscode	The status code for the request.

In addition, you can specify other attributes of the trace object to filter the results on. To see the available attributes, list the trace logs with a *"/text:*"* parameter. For example, to list all trace logs for a particular Web site, use the following syntax.

```
appcmd list traces /site.name:"Default Web Site"
```

To list all trace logs for a particular URL, use the following syntax.

```
appcmd list traces /site.name:"Default Web Site"
/url:http://localhost/myapp/test.html
```

The output of the command contains the trace log objects, as in the following example, and includes the trace log identifier, the URL of the request, the status code, and the worker process.

```
TRACE "Default Web Site/fr000021.xml"
(url:http://localhost:80/myapp/test.html,statuscode:200,wp:3284)
TRACE "Default Web Site/fr000022.xml"
(url:http://localhost:80/,statuscode:200,wp:3284)
```

When displayed in the "/text:*" mode, each trace log also has many additional attributes (which you can also use to filter the resulting output when you use the *List Traces* command).

```
TRACELOG
  TRACE.NAME:"Default Web Site/fr000022.xml"
  PATH:"C:\inetpub\logs\FailedReqLogFiles\W3SVC1\fr000022.xml"
  URL:"http://localhost:80/myapp/test.html"
  STATUSCODE:"200"
  SITE.ID:"1"
  SITE.NAME:"Default Web Site"
  WP.NAME:"3284"
  APPPOOL.NAME:"DefaultAppPool"
  verb:"GET"
  remoteUserName:"Administrator"
  userName:"Administrator"
  tokenUserName:"contoso\Administrator"
  authenticationType:"Basic"
  activityId:"{00000000-0000-0000-0300-0080010000FD}"
  failureReason:"STATUS_CODE"
  triggerStatusCode:"200"
```

Note that the log provides additional information about the request, including the authentication type and the reason the request failed. It also includes the physical path to the log file so that you can open the associated log file in a browser, using the FRT style sheet for more in-depth diagnostics.

Finally, you can inspect the trace log file to peer into actual events, to quickly locate the events that caused a particular request to fail. To do this, you can use the *Inspect Trace* command. This command has the following syntax.

```
appcmd inspect trace <identifier> [/event.name:string]
[/name:string] [/level:int] [/providerid:string]
```

This command supports the parameters in Table 7-9.

Table 7-9   Parameters for the *Inspect Trace* Command

Parameter	Description
identifier	The trace log identifier. This is required.
event.name	The unique identifier of the event in this trace log. This is in the form of *tracelogidentifier#index*, as in "*Default Web Site/ fr000001.xml#174*". You can use this identifier id to look up a specific event in the trace log.
name	The friendly name of the event. Use this to filter for specific events.
level	The numeric verbosity level of each event. Use this to filter for events with specific verbosity, such as Warning, Error, or CriticalError.
providerid	The globally unique identifier (GUID) of the provider that generated this event.

In addition, you can specify other trace object attributes to filter the results on. To see the available attributes, inspect a trace log with a "*/text:*" parameter.

You can use the *Inspect Trace* command to quickly find the event that indicates the desired error condition. For example, to show all events in the trace log that have a Warning or above verbosity level, use the following syntax.

```
appcmd list traces "Default Web Site/fr000001.xml" "/level:$>4"
```

To look for a specific event, use the following syntax.

```
appcmd list traces "Default Web Site/fr000001.xml"
"/name:WARNING_ _SEND_CUSTOM_ERROR"
```

You can combine these simple techniques with command pipelining to quickly analyze multiple trace log files. See the blog post at *http://mvolo.com/blogs/serverside/archive/2007/06/19/Do-complex-IIS-management-tasks-easily-with-AppCmd-command-piping.aspx* for more information.

Microsoft.Web.Administration

Another way to access configuration data is through the managed application programming interface (API) found in the Microsoft.Web.Administration (MWA) assembly. The MWA assembly enables you to access or change a configuration and access some server object's properties and state data through top-level administration objects such as sites, application pools, and worker processes.

The following sections describe how to use MWA for common administration tasks. These sections assume you have some familiarity with managed code and the C# programming language. Because this book is not targeted at developers, these sections will not be an exhaustive discussion of how to use MWA in all scenarios.

Creating Sites with MWA

The following example uses MWA to create a new site called Fabrikam Site that listens on port 8080 and uses C:\inetpub\wwwroot\fabrikam as the root directory for content.

```
using System;
using Microsoft.Web.Administration;
namespace Example {
    class Program {
        static void Main(string[] args) {
            ServerManager mgr = new ServerManager();
            Site site = mgr.Sites.Add("Fabrikam",
            @"C:\inetpub\wwwroot\fabrikam", 8080);
            site.ServerAutoStart = true;
            mgr.CommitChanges();
        }
    }
}
```

In the example, note the use of the *ServerManager* object. It is the entry point for all actions using the MWA APIs. The *ServerManager* object provides access to properties, methods, and collections that provide access to the other classes in the assembly. Though it is possible to manage server data directly through XML or state APIs, MWA provides easy access to the data through these APIs.

The next thing to look at is the use of the *Sites* collection accessed through the *Sites* property of the *ServerManager* object instance. The *Sites* collection provides access to all of the sites currently configured on the system. You can add or remove sites as well as change existing sites.

As you'll notice, you can access the properties of individual sites as well. In this example, you set the automatic start option of the site to true. You can modify many site properties directly through the *Site* class. You can also access the sites collection by accessing it by name, as seen here.

```
mgr.Sites["Fabrikam"].ServerAutoStart = true;
```

The last line to note is the call to the *CommitChanges* method. Up until that line is called, all changes are done in memory only and are not committed to the configuration system.

```
mgr.CommitChanges();
```

It is necessary to call *CommitChanges* whenever you want to update a configuration. If your program does not call *CommitChanges,* the configuration changes made in your application will be lost.

After the changes are committed, you should be able to see your site configuration in the applicationHost.config file. Your configuration should contain a section that looks something like this.

```
<site name="Fabrikam" id="1000" serverAutoStart="true">
    <application path="/">
        <virtualDirectory path="/"
            physicalPath="c:\inetpub\wwwroot\fabrikam" />
    </application>
    <bindings>
        <binding protocol="http" bindingInformation=":8080:" />
    </bindings>
</site>
```

Creating Application Pools with MWA

You can also use the MWA APIs to create application pools and assign them to a site. The following example shows how to do this.

```
using System;
using Microsoft.Web.Administration;
namespace Example {
    class Program  {
```

```
        static void Main(string[] args) {
            ServerManager mgr = new ServerManager();
            ApplicationPool pool =
                mgr.ApplicationPools.Add("FabrikamPool");
            pool.ManagedPipelineMode
                = ManagedPipelineMode.Classic;
            Site = mgr.Sites["Fabrikam"];
            site.Applications[0].ApplicationPoolName =
                @"FabrikamPool";
            mgr.CommitChanges();
        }
    }
}
```

The first line of this sample should look familiar. You use the *ServerManager* object to get a reference to the Fabrikam site. In the next line, you add an application pool by using the *Add* method of *ApplicationPoolsCollection*, which is returned from the *ApplicationPools* property.

```
ApplicationPool pool =
            mgr.ApplicationPools.Add("FabrikamPool");
```

You want to set your application pool's pipeline mode to Classic. You do this with the next line by using the *ManagedPipelineMode* property of the *ApplicationPool* class.

```
pool.ManagedPipelineMode
                = ManagedPipelineMode.Classic;
```

Next, you access the root application of the Fabrikam site and set the application's pool to your newly created "FabrikamPool".

```
Site = mgr.Sites["Fabrikam"];
    site.Applications[0].ApplicationPoolName =
                @"FabrikamPool";
```

Finally, you want to commit the changes.

```
mgr.CommitChanges();
```

Setting Configuration

The following code demonstrates how to use Microsoft.Web.Administration APIs to enable the default document of the "Default Web Site".

```
using System;
using Microsoft.Web.Administration;
namespace Example {
    class Program    {
        static void Main(string[] args)  {
            ServerManager mgr = new ServerManager();
            Configuration config =
                mgr.GetWebConfiguration(
```

```
                "Default Web Site");
ConfigurationSection section =
    config.GetSection(
    "system.webServer/defaultDocument");
ConfigurationAttribute enabled =
    section.GetAttribute("enabled");
            enabled.Value = true;
                mgr.CommitChanges();
        }
    }
}
```

In this section, you used the *Configuration* class to directly access a configuration section and set a node's value. To do this, you first have to access the root web configuration file by using the *GetWebConfiguration* method of the server manager.

```
ServerManager mgr = new ServerManager();
Configuration config =
    mgr.GetWebConfiguration(
    "Default Web Site");
```

This returns an instance of a *Configuration* class to the application. Use that object instance to access a configuration section directly and then request the attribute you want to change.

```
ConfigurationSection section =
    config.GetSection(
    "system.webServer/defaultDocument");
ConfigurationAttribute enabled =
    section.GetAttribute("enabled");
```

Last, make a change to the attribute and follow that change up with a call to CommitChanges to update the configuration system.

```
enabled.Value = true;
    mgr.CommitChanges();
```

You can use Microsoft.Web.Administration to perform many more tasks. Familiarize yourself with some of the properties and methods of the assembly through MSDN reference documentation. You will find that most tasks are made available through the API and are much easier to perform than editing a configuration directly.

Windows PowerShell and IIS 7.0

Windows PowerShell provides a full-featured command shell. Taking advantage of the Microsoft C# scripting language and using an object model based on the .NET Framework, Windows PowerShell provides powerful capabilities for redirecting objects and dynamic manipulation of a result set. You can run commands directly from the command line, and you can run them from within scripts.

When working with Windows PowerShell, you use built-in commands called *cmdlets* as you would use a command or utility at the command line. Cmdlets are both simple and powerful. They are named using an easy-to-understand word pairing:

- **New-**   Creates a new instance of an item or object
- **Remove-**   Removes an instance of an item or object
- **Set-**   Modifies specific settings of an object
- **Get-**   Queries a specific object or a subset of a type of object

For example, the *Get-Credential* cmdlet gets a credential object based on a password. You can get a list of all cmdlets by typing **help** * at the Windows PowerShell prompt.

As new cmdlets that are specific to managing IIS servers become available, you can install them through server updates or by downloading and installing an installation package.

The following books are excellent resources for learning more about using Windows PowerShell in IIS 7.0:

- *Internet Information Services (IIS) 7.0 Administrator's Pocket Consultant* by William R. Stanek (Microsoft Press, 2007)
- *Microsoft Windows PowerShell Step by Step* by Ed Wilson (Microsoft Press, 2007)
- *Windows PowerShell Scripting Guide* by Ed Wilson (Microsoft Press, 2007)

WMI Provider

IIS 7.0 continues to support the legacy WMI provider used in IIS 6.0 to manage the Web server. This WMI provider works via the IIS 6.0 Metabase Compatibility role service that translates the IIS 6.0 configuration settings and actions into the IIS 7.0 configuration structure. To use existing scripts that use the IIS 6.0 WMI object model, you need to install the IIS 6.0 WMI Compatibility role service (from the Management Tools\IIS 6 Management Compatibility category) when managing the Web Server (IIS) role in Server Manager on Windows Server 2008. Alternatively, use the Turn Windows Components On And Off page in Windows Vista. To learn more about the IIS 6.0 Metabase Compatibility layer, see Chapter 4.

> **Note**   To use configuration scripts that call into the legacy IIS 6.0 WMI object model, you need to install the IIS 6 WMI Compatibility role service.

The translation layer between the WMI script, the metabase format, and the new configuration system may introduce slight deviations in the configuration mapping when using legacy IIS 6.0 configuration scripts and APIs, so it is recommended that you migrate your existing scripts to use the new configuration APIs. You may choose to use the new WMI provider, which exposes the new configuration system directly and has a different object model from the IIS 6.0 WMI provider.

> **Note**   To use the new WMI provider in IIS 7.0, you need to install the IIS Management Scripts And Tools role service. Do not install the IIS 6 WMI Compatibility role service to use the new WMI provider.

To learn about the new WMI provider object model, see the online documentation available at *http://msdn2.microsoft.com/en-us/library/aa347459.aspx*.

IIS 7.0 Configuration COM Objects

You can also use the IIS 7.0 configuration COM objects directly to manage IIS configuration and access the administration functionality in IIS 7.0. You can access these COM objects from native C++ programs, .NET applications, or script environments. For the latter, the configuration COM objects may provide a more straightforward alternative to using the WMI provider both because of simpler syntax and because the overhead of the WMI infrastructure has been removed.

These COM objects are also always available when IIS 7.0 is installed, and they do not depend on any externals components. They do not require .NET Framework to be installed.

To learn more about using the IIS 7.0 configuration COM objects, see the online documentation for the *Microsoft.ApplicationHost.WritableAdminManager* and *Microsoft. ApplicationHost.AdminManager* classes.

Summary

In this chapter, you learned about the options available for managing IIS 7.0 from the command line. Specifically, we focused on using Appcmd—the unified command line tool for IIS 7.0 management—to perform most basic IIS 7.0 management tasks.

You can use Appcmd to quickly manage basic IIS 7.0 objects, including Web sites, applications, virtual directories, and application pools. You can also use it to generically edit Web server configuration to perform any other required configuration tasks. In addition, Appcmd provides a convenient path to certain other key tasks, such as managing Web server modules, configuring Failed Request Tracing, and backing up and restoring configuration.

Appcmd has the benefit of not requiring any programming to effectively manage the Web server. However, if you are required to perform management tasks from a programming environment, you have multiple options for developing more comprehensive management automation, including the Microsoft.Web.Adminstration API for .NET Framework applications and the new WMI provider. You can also develop custom Windows PowerShell scripts.

You can learn more about using these options in the MSDN online documentation and articles on *http://www.iis.net*.

On the Disc   Browse the CD for additional tools and resources.

Additional Resources

These resources contain additional information and tools related to this chapter:

■ For articles on managing IIS from command line, go to *http://www.iis.net*, and look at the MSDN documentation for Appcmd, Microsoft.Web.Administration, and WMI reference.

■ Chapter 4, "Understanding the Configuration System," provides more information about the IIS 7.0 configuration system.

■ Chapter 6, "Using IIS Manager," offers more information about managing IIS 7.0 using IIS Manager.

Chapter 8
Remote Administration

 On the Disc Browse the CD for additional tools and resources.

The ability to successfully manage the server remotely is a critical requirement for server administrators. Administrators often have to perform global administrative tasks on the server, such as changing the settings for an application pool or configuring default logging rules, as well as perform granular tasks such as enabling tracing for a particular application. However, server administrators are not the only ones who need to configure settings on a server. For example, in a hosted environment, users should be able to edit the settings of their sites remotely. Or, in an enterprise environment, developers might need to change application settings even if they're not administrators on the machine. Generally, these tasks also need to be performed without physical access to the server. With the release of version 7.0, for the first time, Internet Information Services (IIS) provides you with all the configuration tools that you need, whether you are a server administrator or a hoster providing remote access to your users.

IIS 7.0 offers several tools that will help you manage it from a remote machine. Some of them include the following:

- The Internet Information Services (IIS) 7.0 Manager UI–based administration tool over HTTPS

- The Application Host Administration API (AHADMIN) COM library, which scripts and applications can use

- The Microsoft.Web.Administration managed code library, which can be used from managed code applications

- The new Windows Management Instrumentation (WMI) provider, which uses scripts or managed code to manage configuration

This chapter will discuss how to set up and use the remote platform offered by the IIS Manager. This remoting platform provides a new infrastructure for managing Web sites remotely and introduces several enhancements such as delegation support, remoting over HTTPS, and many new features and configuration options that give you the flexibility you need to manage IIS 7.0, including the ability to administer it using nonadministrator Windows accounts.

The IIS Manager

The IIS Manager is the redesigned user interface (UI) that provides access to the configuration settings of IIS 7.0 and ASP.NET via an integrated tool. It was designed from the ground up to be an easily extensible platform for exposing all the Web platform settings in a unified way. Part of this platform design includes providing a remoting infrastructure for built-in features as well as third-party features. For more information about IIS Manager, see Chapter 6, "Using IIS Manager."

To remotely manage a server, the IIS Manager needs to work in conjunction with a separate IIS 7.0 service called the Web Management Service (WMSvc), which is installed as part of the IIS Management Scripts And Tools role service.

> **Note** To remotely manage IIS 7.0 running on Windows Server 2008, IIS Manager is required on the client machine. Out of the box, only Windows 2008 has the ability to do that. However, you can download support for this for Windows XP Service Pack 2 (SP2), Windows 2003 SP1, and Windows Vista SP1 at *http://iis.net/downloads* for both x86 and x64 versions of these operating systems.

Web Management Service

The Web Management Service is a service from IIS 7.0 that runs on the IIS server—that is, the server that is going to be managed remotely. It provides two important features:

- It handles remote administration for the IIS Manager by listening for incoming HTTPS requests from remote users running IIS Manager. It then executes the request operations locally.

- It provides access for Windows users without administrative privileges and non-Windows users, whether they are using IIS Manager from local or remote machines.

> **Note** This service is not functional in Windows Vista. This means that IIS running under Windows Vista cannot be managed remotely using IIS Manager.
>
> Windows Server 2008 Server Core does not include managed code support, which means the Web Management Service is not installable on that configuration.

Installation

Because it is not part of the default IIS 7.0 install, the Web Management Service is an optional role service that needs to be installed and its startup type configured. To install it, you can use Server Manager or the ServerManagerCMD command line tool. To install using Server Manager, follow this procedure:

1. Start Server Manager.

2. In Server Manager, select Roles.

3. In the Web Server (IIS) role group, click the Add Role Services.

4. Under Management Tools, select Management Service and then click Next.

5. Click Install.

Figure 8-1 shows the Select Role Services window.

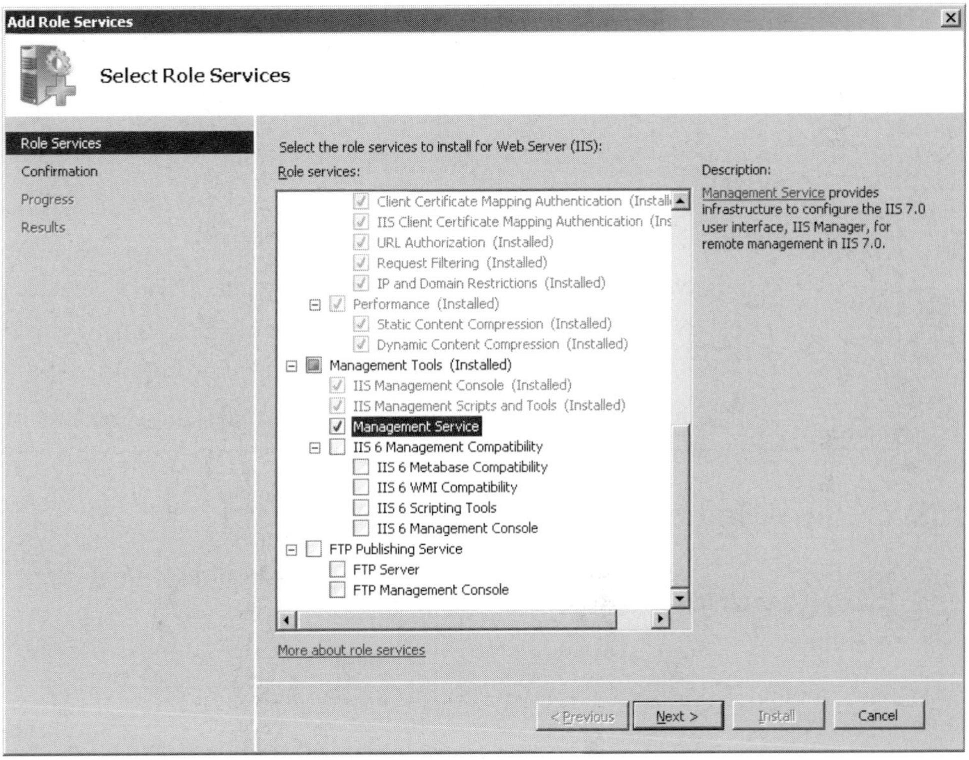

Figure 8-1   Server Manager Role Services.

To install the Web Management Service by using ServerManagerCMD, run the following command line.

```
ServerManagerCMD -install Web-Mgmt-Service
```

For more information on how to install features, see Chapter 5, "Installing IIS 7.0."

Web Management Service Setup

Installing the Web Management Service makes the following changes to your server:

■ The service is configured to run as Local Service. However, thanks to the new service isolation feature in Windows Server 2008 and Windows Vista, all the resources required for the service are protected via the WMSvc service–specific security identifier (SID) called NT Service\WMSvc.

■ The folder *%SystemDrive%*\Inetpub\Logs\Wmsvc is created and "NT Service\ WMSvc" is granted Modify permissions to it.

■ A new inbound firewall rule called Web Management Service (HTTP) for TCP port 8172 is created and enabled.

■ A new self-signed secure sockets layer (SSL) certificate is created for the machine by using a name in the form of WMSvc-*machinename*.

■ SSL configuration for the service is set up within HTTP.sys to use the self-signed certificate, and port 8172 is reserved for it.

■ The configuration is written to the registry key HKLM\Software\Microsoft\ WebManagement\Server.

■ Permissions are granted to the ASP.NET infrastructure:

❑ Add and Modify permissions for the .NET Framework v2.0 Temporary ASP.NET Files directory

❑ Read permissions for the *%SystemRoot%*\System32\Inetsrv\config directory

❑ Modify permissions for the ASP.NET CompilationMutexName registry key

---

WMSvc Configuration

After the Web Management Service is installed, you need to make some configuration changes to optimize the service for your environment. Some of the tasks that are important to set up include:

■ Configuring the service to start automatically

■ Enabling Remote connections, SSL certificate, and IP configuration

■ IPv4 address restrictions

■ Connection authentication options

Configuring the Service Startup Type to Automatic

When installed, the Web Management Service is configured to start manually, which means that it will not start automatically when the service is stopped, for example, when the machine is restarted. This also means that to enable remote management again, someone has to manually start the Web Management Service whenever the service is stopped. For this reason, it is important to set up the service to start automatically, which ensures that remote management is enabled at all times. To do this, you can use the Services console or the Sc.exe command line tool.

To configure the service to start automatically using the Services console, perform the following steps:

1. From the Administrative Tools program group, launch Services.

2. Double-click Web Management Service.

3. In the Startup Type drop-down list, select Automatic and then click OK.

Figure 8-2 shows the Web Management Service Properties dialog box.

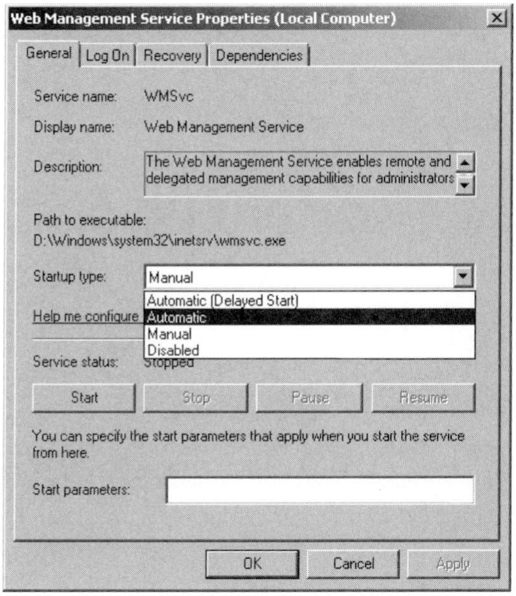

Figure 8-2   Web Management Service properties dialog box.

To configure the service to run automatically using the Services Configuration (Sc.exe) command line tool, run the following command from an elevated command prompt.

```
sc config WMSvc start= auto
```

> **Note**   WMSvc is the name of the service in the services configuration database. Make sure to use a white space after the = sign in the preceding command line. Otherwise, the command will not execute correctly.

Enable Remote Connections, SSL Certificate, and IP Configuration

By default, the Web Management Service is configured to allow only local connections to connect to the service to perform administration tasks. This enables delegated users (non-administrators) to connect to and manage their sites and applications on the local machine. However, it will not let users connect from a remote machine. To allow that, you need to specify that remote connections are enabled by using the IIS Manager Management Service feature.

Also, during setup, a self-signed certificate is created that is used for SSL registration on port 8172 with HTTP.sys. This certificate provides a simple way to set up a test configuration. However, it is strongly recommended that you get a valid certificate issued by a trusted certificate authority (CA) for use by the users that will connect to this machine. With a built-in self-signed certificate, any remote machine that connects to the server gets a warning asking if the certificate is trusted and if the connection to the server should go ahead, giving the user the ability to view the certificate details. Figure 8-3 shows the Server Certificate Alert that users see when they use a self-signed certificate.

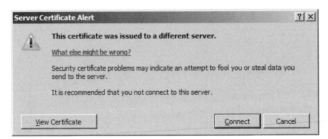

Figure 8-3   Server Certificate Alert.

To avoid this warning, you need to acquire and configure a valid certificate for server authentication from your own trusted certificate authority or from a known certificate authority. Such a certificate can be installed on the server by using different tools, including the Certificates console and the IIS Manager Server Certificates feature. After the certificate is installed on the machine, you can configure the Web Management Service to use the certificate via the IIS Manager Management Service feature. To do this, follow these steps:

1.   From the Administrative Tools program group, launch the Internet Information Services (IIS) Manager.

2.   In the Connections pane, select the IIS computer node and then double-click the Management Service in the Features View pane. To make changes, you need to first stop the Web Management Service.

3. At the top of the page, you can enable remote connections by checking the Enable Remote Connections check box.

4. In the Connections section, you can set the IP address and the port that you want the service to bind to. You can set the SSL certificate by using the SSL Certificate drop-down list that includes all the available certificates for server authentication.

5. After making any necessary changes, click Apply to start the service.

Figure 8-4 shows the Management Service configuration settings.

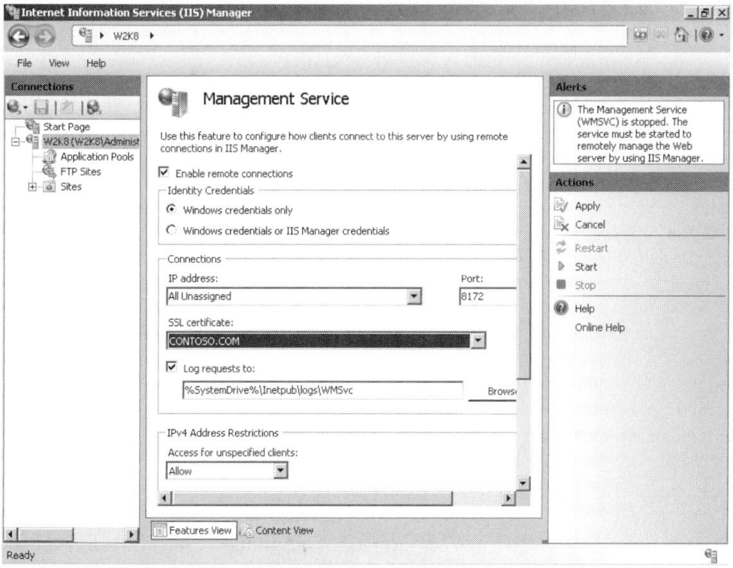

Figure 8-4 Management Service feature.

Note If the Web Management Service is running, the Management Service options will be disabled. To change the configuration, you need to click Stop in the Actions pane.

Note If you change the port the service uses and if you want to allow remote connections, you need to create a firewall exception rule for the port; otherwise, it will fail to connect. By default, during setup, a firewall exception rule called Web Management Service (HTTP) is added and enabled for port 8172. Also, when remote users enter the server name in the Connect To Server dialog box, they need to type the port in the Server Name text box (for example, MyServerMachine:8173). For more information on the Connect To Server dialog box, refer to the section titled "Using Remote Administration" later in this chapter.

All the settings configured by the Management Service feature are stored in the registry under the following key.

```
HKLM\SOFTWARE\Microsoft\WebManagement\Server
```

Table 8-1 shows the Web Management Service registry entries.

Table 8-1 Web Management Service Registry Entries

Value	Description
EnableLogging	Specifies if logging should be enabled. The default value is 1 (enabled).
EnableRemoteManagement	Specifies if the service should enable remote connections or if only local delegated connections should be enabled. The default value is 0 (not allowed). Set this to 1 to allow remote connections.
IPAddress	Specifies the IP address that the service is bound to. The default is All Unassigned. *Note:* Changing this value in the registry has no effect, because IIS Manager performs the SSL configuration and the URL reservation with HTTP.sys. (This is discussed in more detail later in this chapter.)
LoggingDirectory	Specifies the directory where the log files should be generated. The default value for this is *%SystemDrive%*\Inetpub\logs\Wmsvc.
Port	Specifies the port that the service should use. The default is 8172. *Note:* Changing this value in the registry has no effect, because IIS Manager performs the SSL configuration and the URL reservation with HTTP.sys. (This is discussed in more detail later in the chapter.)
RemoteRestrictions	Provides a serialized value of the list of IP address restrictions that are configured. This value should not be edited directly.
RequiresWindowsCredentials	Specifies if only Windows credentials are allowed when connecting remotely or if the IIS Manager credentials are supported. The default value is 1, which specifies that only Windows credentials are allowed. Set this to 0 to allow both credentials. (For more information on this topic, refer to the section titled "Connection Authentication Options" later in this chapter.)
SelfSignedSslCertificateHash	Contains the certificate hash of the self-signed certificate generated during setup.
SslCertificateHash	Specifies the certificate hash to use for SSL. *Note:* Changing this value in the registry has no effect, because IIS Manager performs the SSL configuration and the URL reservation with HTTP.sys. (This is discussed in more detail later in the chapter.)

As mentioned previously, changing some of the values such as *IPAddress*, *Port*, or *SslCertificateHash* directly in the registry does not cause the service to use them automatically, because they are set only by the UI in the HTTP.sys URL registration and SSL configuration. Therefore, if you want to automatically configure those settings, you need to update the registry as well as perform the registration with HTTP.sys manually using the network configuration command line tool Netsh.exe. Then restart Web Management Service.

IPv4 Address Restrictions

When the Web Management Service is running and remote connections are enabled, all IP addresses can connect. The Management Service enables you to enhance security by configuring a specific IP address or a range of IP addresses that you want to either allow or deny access to. You can also specify the access that is granted for any client that is not listed in the list. The configuration for this is better understood through examples:

■ Allow a specific set of clients. To configure this, you need to set the Access For Unspecified Clients drop-down list to Deny so that only the clients listed in the restriction list are allowed. You also need to add each of the clients or IP ranges by using the Allow button. Figure 8-5 shows an example of this configuration.

IPv4 Address Restrictions

Access for unspecified clients:

Deny

Mode	Requestor	
Allow	172.30.189.13(255.255.255.255)	Allow...
Allow	172.30.188.0(255.255.255.0)	Deny...
		Delete

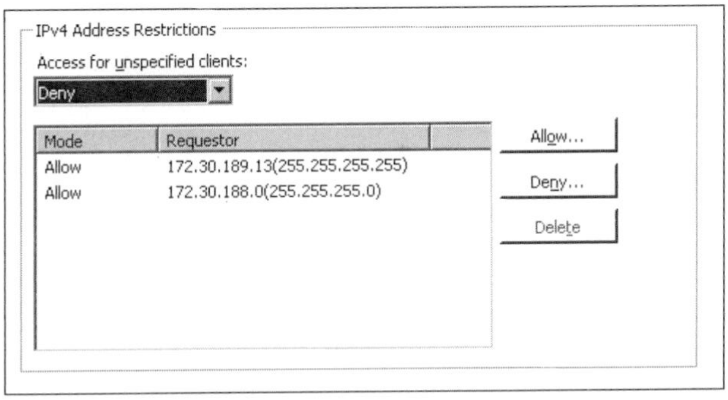

Figure 8-5   IPv4 Address Restriction that allows only a specific set of clients.

■ Deny access to a specific set of clients. To configure this, you need to choose Allow from the Access For Unspecified Clients drop-down list. By selecting Allow, everyone is allowed, and only the clients listed in the restriction list are denied access. Next, you need to use the Deny button to add each of the clients or IP ranges you want to deny. Figure 8-6 shows an example of this configuration.

Note   These settings apply only to IPv4 addresses. To change them, remote connections must be enabled.

Note   The IPv4 restriction list that Web Management Service uses is different from the IPv4 Address and Domain Restrictions configured in IIS for the Web Server. In addition, each of them applies only to the correspondent service independently.

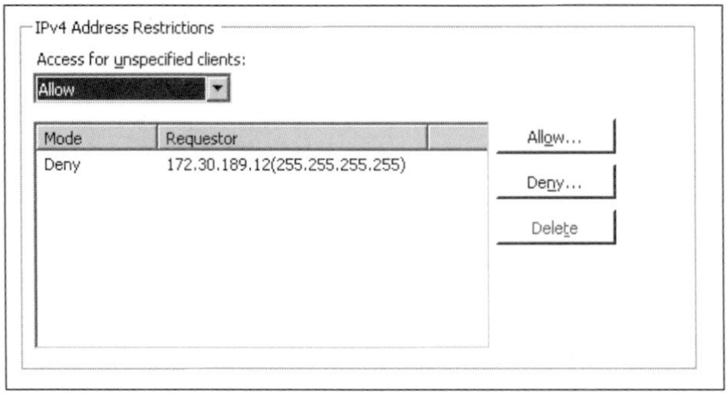

Figure 8-6 IPv4 Address Restriction that denies access to a specific set of clients.

Connection Authentication Options

One of the most powerful features of the delegated configuration support in IIS 7.0 is that it enables users without administrative privileges to configure their site and application settings in their own Web.config files. The Web Management Service takes it to the next level by not only providing them the UI for doing that, but also enabling users to change settings in their own Web.config files even without having a Windows user account. These users are called IIS Manager users and can be configured using IIS Manager. Having a clear understanding of the differences between these authentication models can help you choose the best strategy for your environment.

Windows Credentials   Using Windows credentials is the recommended setting for enabling remote management, because Windows provides you with a robust solution for managing users and groups and establishing policies such as password account policies. In addition, Windows provides several tools to simplify management of these tools. When using Windows credentials, every action the remote user performs is performed via their identity on the server. This means you can use the security mechanisms in Windows, such as access control lists (ACLs), to offer increased protection of the resources on the server. You also gain more granular control over them. This, of course, means that you need to specifically grant the user access to all the resources that he will manage. In particular, you will need to grant write access for at least Web.config files that the user manages.

Windows administrators are the only users that can connect to a server and manage it entirely, and they are always allowed to connect to the server in addition to any site or application. Windows users that do not have administrative privileges will be allowed to connect only to their own sites and applications, and only when the administrator has granted them access.

IIS Manager Credentials   IIS Manager credentials provide an alternative for scenarios in which creating Windows accounts for all the remote users is not an option, or when the users that are allowed to connect are already stored in a different authentication system, such as a customer database, and you want to keep them in a single store. IIS Manager users use a combination of user name and password only, and they do not have any correspondence with Windows principals. As such, their requests always run as the process identity, which is configured in the Log On setting of the Web Management Service. By default, the Web Management Service is configured to use Local Service, but thanks to the Service Isolation feature in Windows Server 2008, you can use the service-specific SID NT Service\WMSvc to protect access to content and resources.

One drawback of using IIS Manager credentials is that, for every resource that needs to be used, you need to grant access to it by using the same identity (NT Service\WMSvc), independent of the site, application, or user that will be connecting. This provides no isolation at the operating system level. The IIS Manager built-in features are designed to carefully protect against enabling users to perform actions outside their scope, which means this shouldn't be a concern. However, IIS Manager functionality is extensible, and it is important that you install IIS Manager administration features only from trusted sources because they run inside WMSvc.

One interesting characteristic of using IIS Manager users is that this functionality is built using an extensible architecture that you can replace. This gives you the ability to authenticate and authorize against your own Users store, whether it is an existing database, an LDAP provider, or anything else. For more information, see *http://msdn2.microsoft.com/Microsoft.Web. Management.Server.ManagementAuthenticationProvider.aspx.*

The built-in implementation of the authentication provider uses our configuration APIs to store the user's credentials in a file called Administration.config located in the *%SystemRoot%* System32\Inetsrv\Config directory. Credentials are stored inside that file, including the user name and the SHA256 hash of the password on it. This proves to be really useful when enabling the IIS Shared Configuration feature and provides a simple, convenient way to have a centralized list of users for a set of machines.

Another consideration when using IIS Manager credentials is to consider if the content of your sites or applications is stored in a universal naming convention (UNC) path on a remote machine. Given that the operations performed by IIS Manager Users are executed as the process identity, and that by default the Web Management Service runs as Local Service, IIS Manager users will not be able to manage any resources outside the local machine unless you change the service logon identity of the Web Management Service.

Table 8-2 summarizes the types of users and their characteristics.

Table 8-2 User Types and Their Characteristics

Type of User	Connection Scope	Execution Identity
Windows Administrators	Windows administrators are always allowed to connect to the server or to any site or application in the machine.	Every action in the server is performed as the Windows administrator caller identity.
Windows Users	Windows users are allowed to connect only to sites or applications if they have been granted access to them via IIS Manager Permissions. In other words, regular Windows users are never allowed to connect to manage the entire server, only sites or applications.	Every action in the server is performed as the Windows user caller identity.
IIS Manager Users	IIS Manager users are allowed to connect to sites or applications only if IIS Manager users are allowed in the Management Service feature and only if they have been granted access to them via the IIS Manager Permissions feature. They are never allowed to connect to manage the entire server, only sites or applications.	Every action in the server is performed as the process identity, which is configured in the service logon identity. For simplicity, you can always assume NT Service\WMSvc.

Managing Remote Administration

The previous section focused on tasks to enable the service and get you started. This section covers the set of tasks you need to perform regularly for remote administration, for example, adding new users, granting permissions, and customizing delegation for them.

Managing Users and Permissions

The procedures to manage users and permissions vary depending the type of authentication option you choose. The following are not detailed provisioning guidelines, but instead are some of the steps required to provision a simple site. For more information on provisioning guidelines, search for Secure Hosting on *http://iis.net*.

Windows Credentials   With Windows users, you can use any of the native Windows tools to create and manage users. Windows users that will manage only sites or applications do not need to belong to the administrators group or any other group. One easy way to add users is using the command line tool Net.exe. For example, to add a new local Windows user, DelegatedUser1, you can just run the following command line.

```
net user /add DelegatedUser1 Str0ngP@ssw0rd!
```

Now, you can create a site called DelegatedUser1Site and protect the content and configuration for this user so they can edit the settings. The following command lines create a directory, grant modified permissions for the user to that folder, and finally register the folder as a site in IIS 7.0 via Appcmd.

```
Mkdir c:\Sites\DelegatedUser1Site
icacls c:\Sites\DelegatedUser1Site /grant DelegatedUser1:(OI)(CI)(M)
%windir%\system32\inetsrv\appcmd.exe add site /name:"DelegatedUser1Site"/
physicalPath:c:\Sites\DelegatedUser1Site /bindings:http/*:8080:
```

Note   Long commands are sometimes shown formatted on multiple lines to fit on the printed page.

Finally, with the user and the site created and configured, you can go to the IIS Manager Permissions feature and grant access to this newly created user to manage its own site. This task can also be automated by using Managed Code and calling the Microsoft.Web.Management API, which will be described later in this chapter using Windows PowerShell.

The following steps will grant permissions to connect to the site DelegatedUser1Site for the user DelegatedUser1:

1. From the Administrative Tools program group, launch Internet Information Services (IIS) Manager.

2. In the Connections pane, expand the IIS computer node and then expand the Sites node and click DelegatedUser1Site in the tree view.

3. Double-click the IIS Manager Permissions feature.

4. In the Actions pane, click Allow User, type **DelegatedUser1** in the Windows text box, and then click OK. Note that in this text box, you can also specify the name of a group to allow entire Windows groups at once.

Figure 8-7 shows the Allow User dialog box. Notice that if only Windows credentials are enabled in the Management Service page, an informational alert is displayed at the top of the Actions pane and the IIS Manager option will be disabled in the Allow User dialog box. You can also use the Select button to search for existing Windows users and groups.

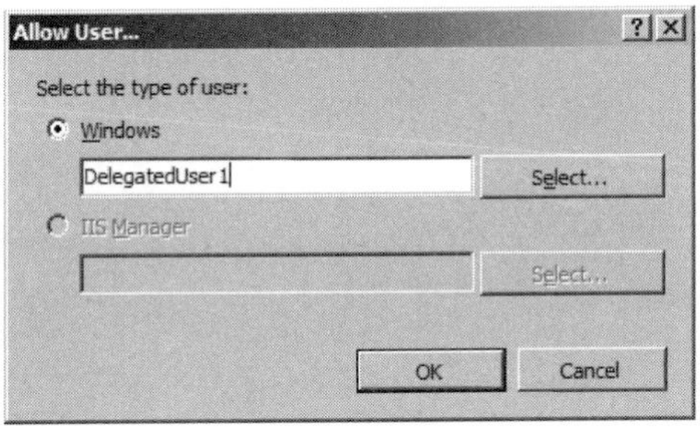

Figure 8-7   Allow User dialog box for Windows users.

After following the preceding steps, the user DelegatedUser1 will be able to use IIS Manager remotely or locally to connect to this site and manage it successfully.

IIS Manager Credentials   With IIS Manager credentials, you can use IIS Manager to manage the users. As specified earlier in this chapter, this functionality is built using an extensible architecture through a provider-based model. The built-in functionality uses Administration.config to store the user name and the SHA256 hash of the password, so it is not as straightforward as using Notepad to edit Administration.config and add users. We recommended two ways of adding users: use IIS Manager or use the underlying managed code API (Microsoft.Web.Management). Luckily, calling managed code objects is easy using Windows PowerShell, and we will see how you can use it to manage the IIS Users without having to use IIS Manager. Following is an example similar to the one we looked at before, in which we create a new IISUser1 and provision a new site for it. This way, IISUser1 can manage the site successfully.

First, we create a site called IisUser1Site and protect the content and configuration for NT Service\WMSvc to be able to edit the settings. The following command lines create the directory, grant modify permissions for the service to that folder, and finally register the folder as a site in IIS 7.0 using Appcmd.

```
Mkdir c:\Sites\IISUser1Site
icacls c:\Sites\IISUser1Site /grant "NT Service\WMSvc":(OI)(CI)(M)
%windir%\system32\inetsrv\appcmd.exe add site /name:"IISUser1Site"
/physicalPath:c:\Sites\IISUser1Site /bindings:http/*:8081:
```

Finally, using the IIS Manager Users and IIS Manager Permissions features, we create the user and assign permissions for it.

1.   From the Administrative Tools program group, launch Internet Information Services (IIS) Manager.

2.   In the Connections pane, select the IIS computer node and double-click the IIS Manager Users feature.

3.   Click Add User from the Actions pane, type **IISUser1** in the User Name text box, provide and confirm a strong password, and then click OK.

Figure 8-8 shows the Add User dialog box.

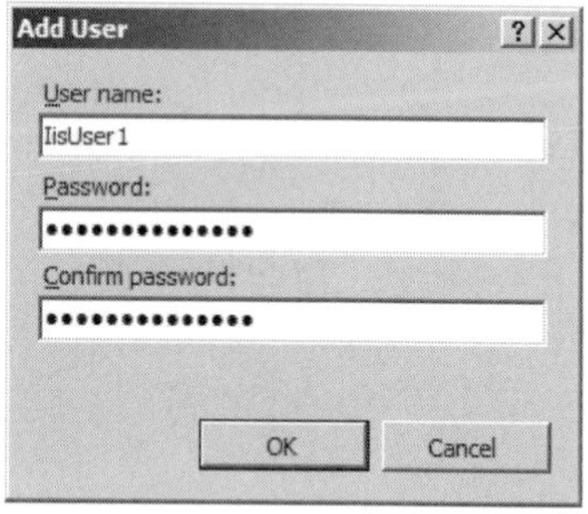

Figure 8-8   Add User dialog box.

After creating the user, you can go to the site and use the IIS Manager Permissions just as with Windows users to grant access to it.

The following steps will grant permission to connect to the site IISUser1Site for the user IISUser1:

1. From the Administrative Tools program group, launch Internet Information Services (IIS) Manager.

2. In the Connections pane, expand the IIS computer node. Then expand the Sites Node and click IISUser1Site in the tree view.

3. Double-click the IIS Manager Permissions feature.

4. Click Allow User from the Actions pane and select the IIS Manager option. Then type **IISUser1** in the text box and click OK.

Figure 8-9 shows the Allow User dialog box with the IIS Manager option selected. Note that you can click the Select button to get a list of the existing IIS Manager users.

> **Note**   When using the IIS Manager Permissions page to grant access for IIS Manager Users, you need to make sure that the Management Service has been configured to enable Windows credentials and IIS Manager credentials. Otherwise, the IIS Manager option is disabled in the Allow User dialog box.

Figure 8-9   Allow User dialog box for IIS Manager users.

After following the preceding steps, the user IISUser1 is granted access to its site, and because we are using the built-in authentication, it is stored in *%SystemRoot%*\System32\Inetsrv\ Config\Administration.config by using syntax similar to that shown here.

```
<system.webServer>
    <management>
        <authentication
            defaultProvider="ConfigurationAuthenticationProvider">
            <providers>
                <add name="ConfigurationAuthenticationProvider" type="Microsoft.Web.Management.
Server.ConfigurationAuthenticationProvider,
..." />
```

```
            </providers>
            <credentials>
                <add name="IISUser1" password="DE499719..." />
            </credentials>
        </authentication>

        <authorization
            defaultProvider="ConfigurationAuthorizationProvider">
            <providers>
                <add name="ConfigurationAuthorizationProvider" type="Microsoft.Web.Management.
Server.ConfigurationAuthorizationProvider,
... " />
            </providers>
            <authorizationRules>
                <scope path="/DelegatedUser1Site">
                    <add name="CONTOSO\DelegatedUser1" />
                </scope>
                <scope path="/IISUser1Site">
                    <add name="IISUser1" />
                </scope>
            </authorizationRules>
        </authorization>
    ...
```

Using Windows PowerShell to Manage IIS Users and Permissions   The best way to automate the creation of IIS users or to assign IIS Manager permissions to either Windows users or IIS users is to use the underlying API that is exposed by the IIS Manager extensibility model in Microsoft.Web.Management. In this case, there are two static classes you can call to manage the authentication and authorization for IIS users. Luckily, Windows PowerShell makes this really simple.

To create a new IIS User, IisUser2, and grant permissions for it to connect to the site, IisUser1Site, you can execute the following commands inside a Windows PowerShell console.

> **Note**   Windows PowerShell is included as an installable feature of Windows Server 2008, and you can install it using Server Manager.

```
# First Load the Microsoft.Web.Management Assembly
[System.Reflection.Assembly]::LoadWithPartialName("Microsoft.Web.Management")
# Create another IIS User
[Microsoft.Web.Management.Server.ManagementAuthentication]::CreateUser("Iis
User2", "Str0ngP@ssw0rd!")
# Assign Permissions for it to connect to the IisUser1Site Web Site
[Microsoft.Web.Management.Server.ManagementAuthorization]::Grant("IisUser2",
"IisUser1Site", 0)
```

Because this API internally uses the configured provider in Administration.config to process the calls, it will correctly store the settings regardless of the provider store. Therefore, it will work correctly independent of the fact that it should be stored in Administration.config or the password should be stored in SHA256. If a developer creates his own authentication or authorization provider, the preceding code will work correctly against their users' stores, whether it is a database or something else.

Feature Delegation

The previous section discussed how to create users and grant them the ability to connect remotely so that they can manage their sites and applications. However, nothing has been discussed about what settings they should be able to see and configure after they are connected, and how you can customize that. It is now that feature delegation comes into play.

Feature delegation gives you the ability to configure what options the users should not be able to see when they connect, which features should be read-only, and which features they should be able to change. For example, you could specify that all the sites should be able to modify the Directory Browsing settings and have only read access to the CGI settings. But at the same time, you might want to specify that users of a particular site or application can change the CGI settings and that other applications should not be able to see the CGI settings (and thus you should entirely remove it from their view).

Figure 8-10 shows the Feature Delegation page with the default settings for all the sites on the server.

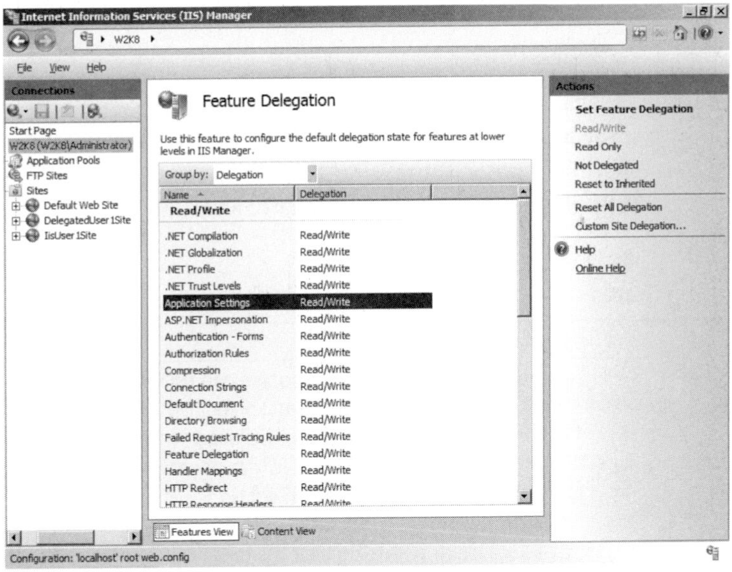

Figure 8-10   Feature Delegation page.

This page has two modes of operation. The first is the Default Delegation mode, which is shown when you first access the page, and which enables you to specify the delegation state for all the children of the current selected object. For example, Figure 8-10 shows the default settings for all the sites in the server. The second mode of operation is called Custom Site

Delegation, and it enables you to choose the specific site or application on which you want to configure the delegation state. Figure 8-11 shows the Custom Site view. Notice the Site drop-down list, which enables you to select the site that you want to customize. Any changes will impact only the selected site or application and its children.

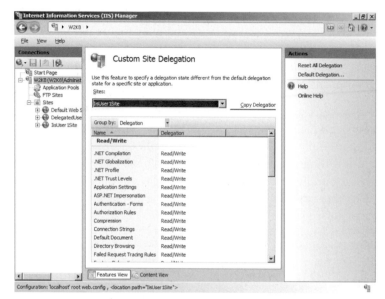

Figure 8-11   Custom Site Delegation page.

Delegation States   The Delegation column in the Feature Delegation page specifies the delegation state for each of the features. It can contain values that enable you to specify various items, including whether or not a feature should be visible to its child sites or applications. Table 8-3 shows the possible values and the behavior of all of the built-in features in IIS Manager.

Table 8-3   Delegation States

Delegation	Description
Read/Write	Completely delegated, and users can modify the feature settings. If the feature uses configuration sections, these sections will be unlocked so that they can be used within the Web.config files in the sites, applications, or folders below the current object. Unlocking the configuration sections will also cause IIS Manager to store all the settings in the deepest configuration path possible, saving settings for a site or applications in their Web.config files.

Table 8-3   **Delegation States**

Delegation	Description
Read-Only	Read-only so that delegated users can only look at the feature settings but not change them. If the feature uses configuration sections, they will be locked so that they cannot be used in the Web.config files below the current object. Locking their configuration sections will cause IIS Manager to store all the settings for child objects in the current configuration path and use location paths within that configuration file for the objects. For example, marking a feature as Read-Only at the server level will cause all the settings for the sites and applications to be stored in ApplicationHost.config using the location paths instead of saving them in their Web.config files.
Not Delegated	Not shown to delegated users. If the feature uses configuration sections, they will be locked just as for Read-Only. In addition, the feature will be removed in Administration.config so that it is not shown to the user.
Configuration Read/Write	Same as Read/Write except it is used for features that also have settings or data that is stored and managed outside IIS. It is used for features such as ASP.NET Roles and ASP.NET Users that specify some of these features' settings, such as the provider to be used in the configuration system. However, the specific provider handles the actual data, and IIS Manager cannot protect the data. In this case, Configuration Read/Write means that changing the configuration aspect of the feature will be enabled for delegated users, and its configuration sections will be unlocked so that they can be set in their Web.config files.
Configuration Read-Only	Same as Read-Only, except it is a special delegation state used for ASP.NET features that have some of their settings in configuration and some of them on a different store, for example, databases. In this case, Configuration Read-Only means that the configuration aspect of the feature will not be allowed for delegated users, and its configuration sections will be locked. However, the data that the provider manages might still be modifiable by the user.

 Note   The list of delegation states varies depending on the feature being managed, because each feature individually provides the delegation states and their settings, and—when using third-party features—their values and their behavior could be implemented differently from the ones specified previously.

As mentioned in Table 8-3, feature delegation is built on top of the locking capabilities of the configuration system discussed in Chapter 4, "Understanding the Configuration System," as well as the extensibility of IIS Manager in Administration.config. It is important to emphasize that IIS Manager uses the configuration settings to determine where to save configuration settings for each of the features. To help figure out where the settings are being saved, IIS

Manager will show in the status bar a textual indication of the configuration file that will be modified when changes are performed.

Figure 8-12 shows how the status bar is displayed when you're managing a feature for an application called BlogApp under Default Web Site, which is delegated. In this case, the settings will be stored in the Web.config of the application.

Figure 8-12   Status bar indicating changes stored in Web.config.

Figure 8-13 shows how the status bar is displayed when you're managing a feature for an application called BlogApp under Default Web Site, which is not delegated. In this case, the settings will be stored in applicationHost.config, and a location path Default Web Site/BlogApp will be used.

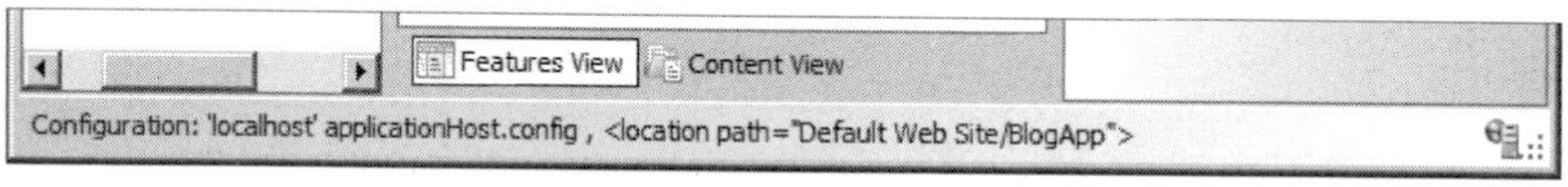

Figure 8-13   Status bar indicating changes stored in applicationHost.config.

When managing the server, you see the feature delegation page only at the server level, and it enables you to customize the delegation settings only for the sites. To customize the delegation settings for applications, you need to connect directly to the site that you want to manage by using the IIS Manager Connect To A Site option. After it's connected, you see the Feature Delegation page at the site level, and it lets you change the settings for all the site's applications. Alternatively, you can use Custom Application Delegation to change settings for a specific application. To understand more about the types of connections, see the section titled "Using Remote Administration" later in this chapter.

The Custom Site Delegation page also enables you to copy settings from one site to another. (This functionality is also available in the Custom Application Delegation page.) This is a convenient way of easily ensuring the same level of delegation is used among two sites without altering the default settings for the rest of your sites. Figure 8-14 shows the Copy Delegation dialog box. In this case, the Delegation settings of the site IisUser1Site will be copied to the site DelegatedUser1Site.

> **Note**   The delegation configuration is stored in both Administration.config and application-Host.config. This means that when Shared Configuration is enabled, the delegation configuration is automatically shared by all the servers configured to use Shared Configuration because they all share both files.

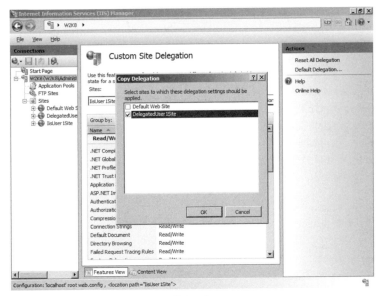

Figure 8-14 Copy Delegation dialog box.

Using Remote Administration

To use remote administration in IIS Manager, you need to establish a connection to a remote machine that is running the Web Management Service. To provide more flexibility, IIS Manager introduces three types of connections that provide different granularity and different scopes and capabilities for management: Connect To A Server, Connect To A Site, and Connect To An Application. Figure 8-15 shows the three options in the File menu of IIS Manager. You can also find these options on the Start page and the Connections pane context menu.

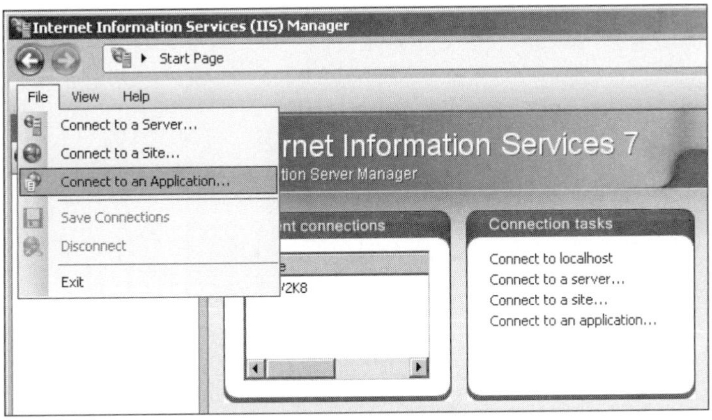

Figure 8-15 IIS Manager connection options.

Server connections let the server administrator manage the entire server. The administrator will have full control over every setting and every feature on the machine. Only Windows users with administrative privileges are allowed to make this type of connection. For these users, configuration locking alters only where the configuration settings are saved, and these users are the only ones who can make modifications in applicationHost.config and the root Web.config.

Site connections enable both server administrators and site administrators (delegated users that have been granted permissions to connect to the site) to manage the entire site, including any of its applications. Their scope is limited to the site, and they will never be able to modify any of the server-level configuration files such as applicationHost.config or the root Web.config. If configuration is locked at the server level for any configuration section, the related feature will automatically become Read-Only, and no changes will be allowed.

Application connections enable server administrators, site administrators, and application administrators (delegated users that have been granted permissions to connect to the application) to manage the entire application including folders and virtual directories, but not applications underneath the particular application. Their scope is limited to the application, and they will never be allowed to change either server-level configuration files or site-level configuration files. If configuration is locked at the site level or at any parent folder, the feature will automatically become Read-Only, and no changes will be allowed.

Figure 8-16 shows the Connect To Application dialog box.

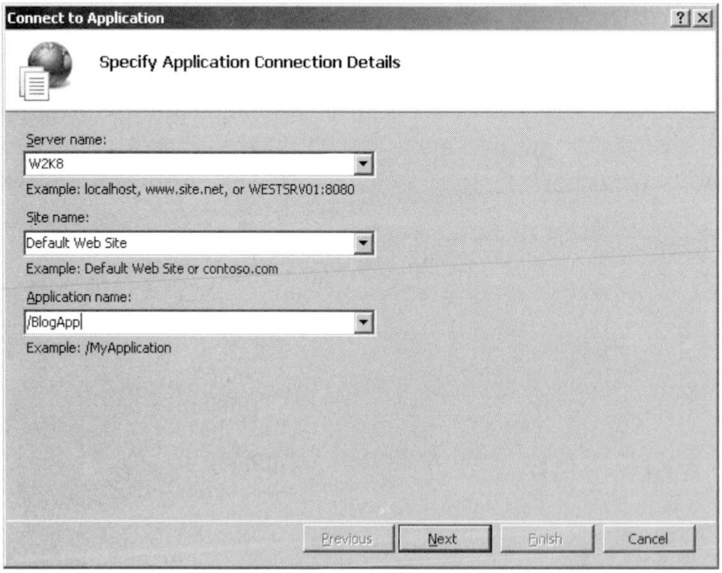

Figure 8-16   Application connection details in the Connect To Application dialog box.

After clicking Next, you will be prompted for credentials in the dialog box shown in Figure 8-17. As mentioned before, these can be Windows user or IIS Manager users credentials.

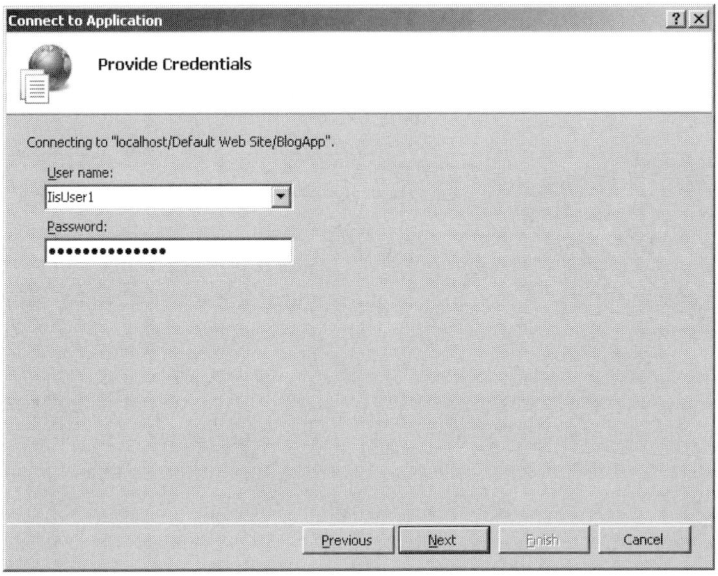

Figure 8-17   User credentials in the Connect To Application dialog box.

After the connection is established you will see a new entry in the Connections pane, indicating the type of connection as well as the user name supplied to make the connection. Similarly, at the lower-right corner of the status bar, you will see the server name, the port, and the user name used for the connection. On the Home page, only the features that have been delegated (either Read-Only or Read/Write) will be shown. Figure 8-18 shows how the ASP feature setting is shown as read-only for an application connection because its configuration is locked by default.

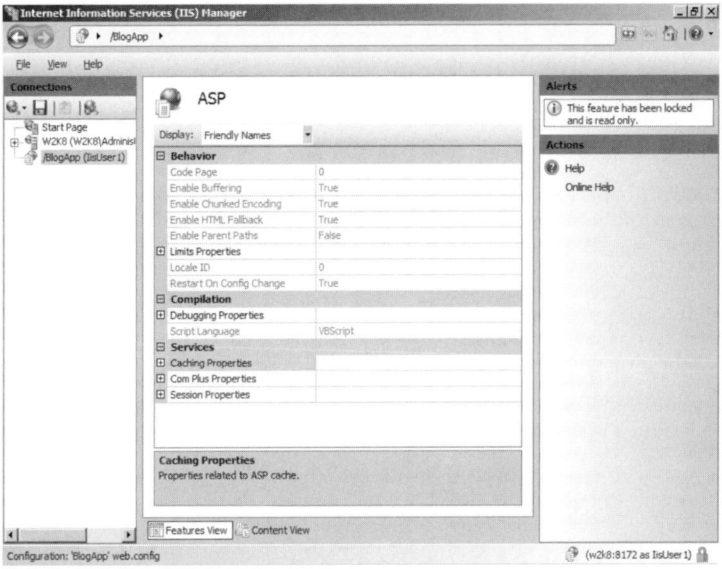

Figure 8-18   ASP feature shown as read-only in an application connection.

> **Note**   When using a different port than the default 8172, you will need to enter it in the server name text box when making the connection, for example, *MyMachine:8173*.

Administration.config and Feature Delegation

Administration.config is the file that contains all the settings for IIS Manager and remote administration. Just as the IIS configuration system does, it uses configuration sections to organize the settings into logical units. The most important are *<moduleProviders>* and *<modules>*. The *<moduleProviders>* section contains the centralized list of features that a server administrator will get when using IIS Manager. In other words, it includes the list of features that will be used when a server connection is activated. The *<modules>* section contains the list of modules that will be enabled for delegated connections (site and application connections). If a feature is listed only in the *<moduleProviders>* section, only server connections will show that feature. To make that feature available for all the sites, you can add it in the <modules> list inside a location tag by using the special path "." that denotes it should be available for everyone. Alternatively, you can add it in the name of the site if it should be available only for that site. The Feature Delegation page modifies the <modules> list when you change the delegation state. One thing to mention is that the delegation for applications is stored in another Administration.config file in the parent site physical path.

Troubleshooting

The most common source of problems with remote administration can be categorized by two error messages: "Unable to connect to the remote server" and "(401) Unauthorized."

Unable to Connect to the Remote Server

When you try to connect remotely and don't receive a response from the remote server, you will get an error message such as "Unable to connect to the remote server." You can get this error message for several reasons, including:

- The Web Management Service has not been started on the remote machine. As mentioned earlier in this chapter, the Web Management Service is responsible for listening for remote requests, and it must be running.

- A firewall is blocking the client requests. Make sure that a firewall is not blocking the port that Web Management Service uses. By default, the service uses port 8172 and includes a Windows Firewall exception for it. However, if you change the port, you will need to create a firewall exception for it.

- The client and the server are using different configurations. If you are using a port other than the default 8172, specify it in the Server Name text box in the Connect To Server dialog box.

- The configuration settings in HTTP.sys are not set correctly. This configuration is set when you are using the Management Service feature in IIS Manager. In this case, you need to make sure that the URL reservation and the SSL configuration are registered correctly. To do so, you can use the Netsh.exe command line tool. The output of a machine configured correctly is shown in the following code. Note that some of the fields might be different, specifically the port and the certificate hash.

```
netsh http show urlacl
URL Reservations:
-----------------
    Reserved URL            : https://*:8172/
        User: NT SERVICE\WMSVC
            Listen: Yes
            Delegate: No
            SDDL: D:(A;;GX;;;S-1-5-80-257763619-...)


netsh http show sslcert

SSL Certificate bindings:
-------------------------

    IP:port                 : 0.0.0.0:8172
    Certificate Hash        : 2e302fb76cbb0ff0cec2b759820fec5cd1f7a0cd
    Application ID          : {00000000-0000-0000-0000-000000000000}
    Certificate Store Name  : MY
    Verify Client Certificate Revocation    : Enabled
    Verify Revocation Using Cached Client Certificate Only    : Disabled
    Usage Check     : Enabled
    Revocation Freshness Time : 0
    URL Retrieval Timeout    : 0
    Ctl Identifier          : (null)
    Ctl Store Name          : (null)
    DS Mapper Usage     : Disabled
    Negotiate Client Certificate     : Disabled
```

If the HTTP.sys configuration is not set correctly, you can try to use the Management Service feature in IIS Manager to set it correctly. Another advanced option is to manually use Netsh.exe to configure the values.

(401) Unauthorized

You might get this error for several reasons, including:

- The user or password is invalid. Whenever an invalid user or password is used to try to access the Web Management Service, an entry will be logged in the Windows Event Viewer in the Security Log. This will include all the details, as shown here.

```
An account failed to log on.

Subject:
    Security ID:        LOCAL SERVICE
    Account Name:       LOCAL SERVICE
    Account Domain:     NT AUTHORITY
    Logon ID:           0x3e5
```

```
Logon Type:                   8

Account For Which Logon Failed:
    Account Name:             Administrator
    Account Domain:           CARLOSAG1-IIS

Failure Information:
    Failure Reason:           Unknown user name or bad password.
    Status:                   0xc000006d
    Sub Status:               0xc0000064

Process Information:
    Caller Process ID:        0x8d8
    Caller Process Name:      D:\Windows\System32\inetsrv\WMSvc.exe
```

- The delegated user, either Windows or IIS Manager User, is not allowed to connect to the site or application. In this case, an entry with Source: IIS-IISManager and an Event ID:1105 will be logged in the Windows Application Event Log. It will look similar to the following code.

```
IISWMSVC_AUTHORIZATION_FAILED

The user 'IisUser1' is not authorized for the path '/Default Web Site'

Process:WMSvc
User=NT AUTHORITY\LOCAL SERVICE
```

To correct this, you can go to the specific site or application level inside IIS Manager and use the IIS Manager Permissions feature to grant the delegated user permissions to log on.

- A delegated user is trying to establish a server connection. As mentioned previously, only Windows users with administrative privileges are allowed to connect to the server. If a delegated user tries to connect to the server, the attempt will be denied. An entry with Source: IIS-IISManager and an Event ID:1104 will be logged in the Application Event Log. It will look similar to the following.

```
IISWMSVC_AUTHORIZATION_SERVER_NOT_ALLOWED

Only Windows Administrators are allowed to connect using a server
connection. Other users should use the 'Connect To Site or Application'
task to be able to connect.

Process:WMSvc
User=IisUser1
```

Logging

You'll find it useful to understand the activity of the Web Management Service's logging functionality. By default, the log files are stored in the *%SystemDrive%*\Inetpub\Logs\ Wmsvc\ folder. Below this, you will find a folder named W3SVC1 that contains all the log files detailing the activity of the Web Management Service. The log file uses the World Wide

Web Consortium (W3C) log file format to log information about all the activity on the server. This format is handled by HTTP.sys and is an ASCII text-based format that is easy to read and understand. Fields are separated by spaces, and time is recorded in Universal Coordinated Time (UTC). For more information on this format, see Chapter 15, "Logging." Table 8-4 shows the list of fields that are available in the log file for each of the requests the service processes.

Table 8-4   Fields Included in the Log File

Field	Description
date, time	The date and time of the activity, in UTC format
s-ip	The IP address of the server
cs-method	The HTTP method used, for example, *GET* or *POST*
cs-uri-stem	The target of the action; most remote client requests will use /service.axd as the target
cs-uri-query	The query information for the target; for /service.axd, it will include the module used, the method invoked, and the site and application path if you are using delegated connections
s-port	The server port used
cs-username	The user that generated the request
c-ip	The client IP address
cs(User-Agent)	The type of client used for this call, including its name and the version information
sc-status	The HTTP status code
sc-substatus	The HTTP substatus code
sc-win32-status	The Windows status code
time-taken	The time it took to execute the request

The best way to analyze the log file is to use an existing tool called Log Parser that lets you easily issue queries by using a SQL-based syntax. The following section shows how to do this.

> **Note**   Log Parser is a tool that provides query access to text-based log files, XML files, and CSV files. You can download Log Parser by going to *http://www.microsoft.com/downloads* and searching for Log Parser. You must execute queries from within the context of the Log Parser command prompt. To open the command prompt, launch Log Parser from the Log Parser program group.

Analyzing Remote Administration Logs by Using Log Parser

Log Parser is a powerful tool that provides access to several different file formats and that offers simple universal query syntax to exploit them. This section of the chapter provides some useful queries that show how to use Log Parser against the Web Management Service log. All of the following queries can be executed using the LogParser.exe command line tool included with Log Parser. Use the following syntax to do so.

```
LogParser.exe "<QUERY>" -i W3C
```

The argument −i specifies that the input format of the logs uses W3C.

Summary of Status Codes   The following query displays a table showing all the different status codes that have been generated as well as the number of times each has been hit.

```
SELECT TOP 25
    STRCAT(TO_STRING(sc-status), STRCAT('.', TO_STRING(sc-substatus))) As
Status,
    COUNT(*) AS Hits
FROM c:\inetpub\logs\wmsvc\w3svc1\*.log
WHERE cs-uri-stem='/Service.axd'
GROUP BY Status ORDER BY Status ASC
Status Hits
------ ----
200.0  264
401.1  7
401.2  89
403.6  2
```

Number of Requests per User   The following query shows the number of request issued per user.

```
SELECT TOP 25
    cs-username As User,
    COUNT(*) as Hits
FROM c:\inetpub\logs\wmsvc\w3svc1\*.log
WHERE User Is Not Null
GROUP BY User ORDER BY Hits DESC
User          Hits
------------- ----
administrator  219
DelegatedUser1 75
IisUser1       19
```

Number of Times a Module Has Been Used   The following query uses the information in the request to determine how many times a module has been used.

```
SELECT TOP 25
    EXTRACT_VALUE(cs-uri-query,'Module') as Module,
    COUNT(*) As Hits
FROM d:\inetpub\logs\wmsvc\w3svc1\*.log
WHERE Module IS NOT NULL
GROUP BY Module
ORDER By Hits DESC
Module           Hits
---------------- ----
Framework         138
WebObjects         90
```

```
AppSettings        51
ConnectionStrings  16
ClassicAsp          7
```

List the Number of Delegated Calls for Each Site   The following query lists the number of calls that delegated connections, either site or application connections grouped by site.

```
SELECT TOP 25
    TO_LOWERCASE(EXTRACT_VALUE(cs-uri-query,'Site')) as Site,
    COUNT(*) As Hits
FROM c:\inetpub\logs\wmsvc\w3svc1\*.log
WHERE Site IS NOT NULL
GROUP BY Site ORDER By Hits DESC
Site               Hits
------------------ ----
default%20web%20site 305
delegateduser1site   8
```

Summary

IIS 7.0 introduces a new remote administration architecture that enables users without administrative privileges to connect remotely and manage IIS 7.0 running in Windows Server 2008. This remote administration is done over HTTPS that enables its use both over the Internet as well as on an intranet, offering the flexibility to use Windows users or IIS Manager users for managing IIS 7.0 and allowing the server administrator to customize the feature set that should be exposed to the delegated users.

Additional Resources

These resources contain additional information and tools related to this chapter:

- You can find information on using Microsoft.Web.Administration.ServerManager remotely at *http://msdn2.microsoft.com/en-us/library/Microsoft.Web.Administration. Servermanager.OpenRemote.aspx*.

- Find more information about IIS 7.0 WMI Provider at *http://msdn2.microsoft.com/ en-us/library/aa347459.aspx*.

Chapter 9

Managing Web Sites

The Web site is the basic unit of functionality on the Internet Information Services (IIS) server, defining the set of content and services the server provides and specifying how they are available to requesting clients. IIS 7.0 provides a set of tools for creating and managing Web sites, including IIS Manager and the Appcmd command line tool, in addition to the ability to edit server configuration directly or through programmatic application programming interfaces (APIs). Although in many ways administering IIS 7.0 Web sites is similar to doing so in previous versions of IIS, the IIS Manager UI has significant differences. In addition, when managing IIS 7.0 Web sites, it is important to understand how the improved Web site definition structure affects the layout of your application content, and how the associated configuration is described in the IIS 7.0 configuration files.

Web Sites, Applications, Virtual Directories, and Application Pools

As in the previous version of IIS, IIS 7.0 enables the server administrator to deploy application content to the server by creating Web sites, Web applications, application pools, and virtual directories. IIS 7.0 defines clearer relationships between these objects, relationships that more precisely express the objects' purpose and run-time behavior. For example, in IIS 6.0, a Web site may contain a number of virtual directories, each of which may be labeled as an application when you set certain configuration properties. In IIS 7.0, the Web site is a container of applications, which in turn contain virtual directories. In this structure, the application becomes a top-level container of run-time functionality and serves as an isolated logical object unit being associated with a specific application pool. The virtual directory simply becomes a mechanism to map specific parts of the application's Uniform Resource Locator (URL) namespace to a specific physical directory that contains the application content.

IIS 7.0 continues to leverage the application pool as a mechanism for isolating the execution of applications. Let's look at more details of Web application, application pool, virtual directory and site objects.

Web Sites

A Web site is a top-level container of IIS content and functionality. It contains a set of applications that segregate parts of the Web site, from a run-time execution perspective, and that may be placed into different application pools for isolation purposes. The applications, in turn, define virtual directories that partition the application's URL namespace and map parts of it to physical directories that contain application content (more about applications and virtual directories in a moment).

The Web site also specifies one or more bindings, which are sets of information that describe a connection endpoint that clients use to access the Web site. Each binding specifies the binding protocol (for example, HTTP and HTTPS) and the protocol-specific binding configuration (for example, the HTTP binding configuration of IP addresses, Port, and Host Header detail).

Multiple bindings are allowed, enabling the Web site to be accessible from several different endpoints for the same protocol or even multiple protocols. For example, in terms of protocol, you can configure HTTPS for secure communication in addition to standard HTTP access. Alternatively, you can configure multiple Web sites by using a single IP with different Host Header configurations. In addition, with the introduction of Windows Process Activation Services (WAS) in IIS 7.0, you can deliver hosted Web services by using Windows Communication Foundation and Named Pipes, TCP, Message Queuing (also known as MSMQ), or custom protocols in addition to HTTP and HTTPS.

You'll find more information about configuring Web site bindings in the section titled "Configuring a Web Site's Bindings" later in this chapter.

Direct from the Source: A True Application Server

In IIS 6.0, IIS provides a worker process architecture for processing requests to Web applications in a reliable and secure manner. The IIS World Wide Web Publishing Service's (W3SVC) architecture decouples the monitoring for incoming HTTP requests, performed by the HTTP.sys kernel mode driver, from their processing by the IIS Web server engine loaded in the IIS worker processes. The W3SVC service is likewise responsible for managing the IIS worker processes, creating them on demand to process incoming requests from HTTP.sys and managing their health and lifetime to ensure the Web server's stability and availability. With IIS 6.0, this architecture has proven to dramatically increase the reliability of Web applications by isolating the application code from the long-lived system components responsible for maintaining high availability of the server in the face of errors, memory leaks, and crashes that are common in application code.

In IIS 7.0, the new Worker Process Activation Service continues to leverage this architecture to provide a reliable framework for hosting Web applications. However, it takes it one step further by recognizing that this architecture can be used to activate and host any message-oriented applications regardless of protocol. Thus, the former Web Activation Service is now Windows Process Activation Service, which supports the extensible listener adapter architecture that enables listener adapter components to receive messages over any protocol and activate pools of worker processes that host the application components that know how to communicate with the listener adapter and process the incoming messages.

The IIS 7.0 Web server was the first product to use this architecture. The Windows Communication Foundation was the second, providing support for hosting applications using the net.tcp, net.pipe, net.msmq, and other protocols. FTP 7.0, the next generation FTP server from the IIS team, is the third, enabling IIS Web sites to also become publishing endpoints over the FTP protocol. Soon, we expect even more applications to be developed that take advantage of the WAS architecture to host reliable applications over protocols of the future.

Mike Volodarsky,

IIS Core Program Manager

Web site configuration is declared in the *<sites>* configuration section under a *<site>* element in the applicationHost.config file. For example, the following configuration shows two Web sites configured in the Web server. Site ID 1 belongs to Contoso Corp and has two bindings (an HTTP binding on port 80 with *http://www.contoso.com* as the host header as well as an HTTPS protocol accessed via port 443). On the other hand, the Fabrikam Inc. Web site is bound to all Web server IP addresses, with the unique host header value of *http://www.fabrikam.com*.

```
<sites>
    <site name="Contoso Corp" id="1">
        <application path="/">
            <virtualDirectory path="/" physicalPath="d:\contoso" />
        </application>
        ...
        <bindings>
            <binding protocol="http"
                bindingInformation="*:80:www.contoso.com" />
            <binding protocol="https"
                bindingInformation="*:443:www.contoso.com" />
        </bindings>
    ...
    </site>
    <site name="Fabrikam Inc" id="2">
        <application path="/">
            <virtualDirectory path="/" physicalPath="d:\fabrikam" />
```

```
            </application>
            <bindings>
                <binding protocol="http"
                    bindingInformation="*:80:www.fabrikam.com" />
            </bindings>
    ...
    </site>
    ...
            <siteDefaults>
                <logFile logFormat="W3C"
                    directory="%SystemDrive%\inetpub\logs\LogFiles" />
                <traceFailedRequestsLogging
                    directory="%SystemDrive%\inetpub\logs\FailedReqLogFiles" />
            </siteDefaults>
            <applicationDefaults applicationPool="DefaultAppPool" />
            <virtualDirectoryDefaults allowSubDirConfig="true" />
</sites>
```

Default settings for new Web sites are inside the *<sites>* section. In the sample configuration, site default configuration includes Web site logging settings and failed request tracing settings.

Next, we will look at the application and virtual directory configuration contained inside each Web site definition.

IPv6

By default, Windows Server 2008 and Vista have IPv6 enabled. Most servers are not yet using this protocol. However, in the next few years, IPv6 is expected to be in more widespread use as the government and military rapidly adopt the standard because of its resiliency and better security. Both Vista and Windows Server 2008 support IPv6 on many levels, from networking to various applications. IIS 6.0 had limited IPv6 support, in that you could not enter an IPv6 address into the IIS Manager. If you assigned an IPv6 address to the NIC and then used the default All Unassigned setting for your Web site, everything worked as expected. By using hosting headers or unique port numbers, you could have unique IP addresses; otherwise you were limited to one Web site. The IIS 7.0 Manager allows you to enter an IPv6 address (for example, 3ffe:ffff:101:ffff:230:6eff: fe04:d9ff) for Web sites just as you would an IPv4 address, so this IIS 6.0 limitation is gone. This is good news for those who want to take advantage of the many new features of IPv6.

See *http://technet.microsoft.com/en-us/network/bb530961.aspx* for more details.

Applications

An application is typically a set of content, scripts, and/or executable files that provides certain functionality to its user. The application concept is most meaningful to application frameworks such as ASP or ASP.NET, enabling them to create a run-time execution environment for the associated set of content and to establish a shared set of state. Previous versions of IIS enabled certain virtual directories to be marked as applications to indicate the application root to these application frameworks. Other than that, IIS provided no special support for the application.

In IIS 7.0, the application becomes a top-level container in the Web site's structure, providing a way to scope application functionality for application frameworks and isolate it from other applications by placing it in the desired application pool. A unique virtual path identifies each application, serving to partition the Web site's URL namespace into one or more applications.

The application itself contains virtual directories that map parts of the application's URL namespace to physical directories containing the application content. Each application contains at least one virtual directory, called the root virtual directory, that maps the root of the application's URL namespace to its root physical directory. You'll find more information about virtual directories in the section titled "Virtual Directories" later in this chapter.

Think about the difference between applications and virtual directories like this: An application is a group of content and services that execute together in the same execution environment (in a specific IIS worker process, and possibly in an application framework–specific application context for frameworks such as ASP or ASP.NET). A virtual directory is the physical location of the application's content, defining where that content is stored on disk and how it should be accessed.

The following *<sites>* section from the applicationHost.config file shows how the site, application, and virtual directory definitions might be declared.

```
<sites>
        <site name="Contoso Corp" id="1">
            <application path="/">
                <virtualDirectory path="/" physicalPath="d:\contoso" />
                <virtualDirectory path="/images" physicalPath="g:\images" />
            </application>
            <application path="/payment" applicationPool="MyAppPool">
                <virtualDirectory path="/" physicalPath="d:\KDbank" />
            </application>
            ...
        </site>
        ...
</sites>
```

Each application has a starting point, more commonly known as an application root. By default, when you create a new Web site with IIS Manager, it creates a root application whose virtual path is "/". The application boundary applies to every file and directory underneath the root directory until you specified another application starting point within the Web site. At the same time, IIS Manager also creates a root virtual directory for the application, whose virtual path is "/". The physical path is the Web site's root directory.

In the previous example, the application path root is <application path="/">. Two applications are defined in the sample configuration. First, the root directory of the Web site is the virtual directory entry defined as <virtualDirectory path="/" physicalPath="d:\contoso" />. Second is the "/payment" application, defined as <virtualDirectory path="/" physicalPath="d:\KDbank" />. Note that the "MyAppPool" application pool hosts the "payment" application, whereas the root application uses "DefaultAppPool", which is defined in the default application pool settings in the <sites> configuration section. You will learn more about application pools in the next section.

Virtual Directories

A virtual directory is a mapping between a part of an application's URL namespace and a physical location for the corresponding content, which may be a directory on a local file system or Universal Naming Convention (UNC) path to a network share. Typically, each application contains a root virtual directory that maps all of its URL namespace to the corresponding root physical location. However, you can create additional virtual directories to map parts of your application to a folder that resides at a different path or volume on the local computer, or even on a remote network share. In addition, each virtual directory can specify the credentials that should be used to access its content.

For example, if you are developing an intranet Web site for the finance department, instead of copying all standard corporate image files from the corporate Web site, you can create a new virtual directory in the finance Web site and map it to the physical image file folder on the corporate Web site's server.

In IIS 7.0, each Web site must contain a root application, and each application must contain a root virtual directory. That means that each Web site has a root virtual directory that points to the physical directory root for the Web site. You can add additional virtual directories or additional applications that contain virtual directories. The virtual directories are specified as children of each application in the <site> configuration collection in the applicationHost.config configuration file.

> **Note** Unlike IIS 6.0, virtual directories are always contained inside applications. Additionally, virtual directories cannot be associated with application pools; only applications can. This more clearly expresses the application as being the run-time container for the Web site functionality, and the virtual directory being the physical location of the application's content.

Continuing with the previous example, two applications are in the Contoso Corp. Web site. Each application contains a set of virtual directories that maps parts of the application to the physical locations for the content to be delivered within the scope of the application. Note the "/images" virtual directory in the Web site's root application. It is configured for the Web site to conveniently refer to for files outside of the Web application's root.

The section titled "Managing Virtual Directories" later in this chapter discusses virtual directories in more detail.

Application Pools

The application pool concept was first introduced in IIS 6.0. An application pool uses a separate IIS worker process (W3WP.exe) to process requests for one or more Web applications associated with the application pool. Application pools serve as the boundary between IIS 7.0 applications, whereby all IIS features and application run times are hosted in a separate IIS worker process, in which the worker process takes care of application requests processing. Each IIS worker process is independent from other worker processes, meaning each has its own process ID, memory space, and lifetime.

Applications running in different worker processes are isolated from one other so that a crash of one worker process typically will not affect the operation of another. This increases the robustness and availability of applications, because faulty applications will not affect other applications running on the same IIS server.

Additionally, the application pool can serve as a security sandbox, enabling different applications to run in IIS worker processes started under different application pool identities. Because of this, you can isolate applications by controlling the access to corresponding application content and server resources granted to each application pool identity. This way, applications in each application pool are isolated in separate process memory spaces at run time, and their corresponding resources on the server are isolated from each other as well via Windows access control lists (ACLs).

> **Note**   Application pool isolation combined with proper resource access control is the only reliable mechanism to isolate multiple applications running on the server. For more information about configuring application pool isolation, see Chapter 14, "Implementing Security Strategies."

When you create a Web site in IIS Manager, a new application pool is automatically created for you, and the site's root application is assigned to run in the pool. If you create a site programmatically, you must explicitly assign the application pool to each application in the site (otherwise, they will use the application pool configured to be the default). You can also create an application pool manually if you would like to assign specific applications to execute in this application pool.

In addition, you can also use application pool to specify a number of run-time settings that affect request execution for applications hosted therein. These settings include:

- The .NET Framework version, indicating what version of the Common Language Runtime (CLR) is loaded in the IIS worker process and therefore the version of ASP.NET that is used for the ASP.NET applications in the application pool.

- The ASP.NET integration mode, Integrated (default) versus Classic. This affects how ASP.NET applications work in this application pool.

- The bitness of the application pool when on 64-bit operating systems, affecting whether this application pool loads native 64-bit components or loads 32-bit components by using the SYSWOW64 emulation mode.

Therefore, the selection of a properly configured application pool becomes very important in IIS 7.0 to define the correct run-time behavior for Web applications.

You will find application pools discussed in more detail in Chapter 10, "Managing Applications and Application Pools."

Administrative Tasks

When IIS is installed, a Web site named Default Web Site is created, and it contains a single root application with the root virtual directory mapped to the %systemdrive%\inetpub\wwwroot folder. You can configure this default Web site to serve your Web application, or you can create a new Web site to publish the application.

> **Note**   It is a best practice to place your Web content on a nonsystem drive.

For typical administrative tasks in IIS 6.0, you use wizards provided by the IIS 6.0 Management Console. In IIS 7.0, you can use the IIS Manager console to create and administer Web sites.

In addition, you can use the Appcmd.exe command line tool to manage the Web site and associated configuration from the command line. You can also leverage one of several programmatic APIs such as Microsoft Web Administration and Windows Management Instrumentation (WMI) for managing IIS configuration, or edit server configuration files such as applicationHost.config or web.config directly. Note that manipulating configuration files directly is not recommended.

> **Note**   IIS 7.0 continues to support the legacy configuration scripts that IIS 6.0 provides, including ADSUTIL.VBS, IISWEB.VBS, IISVDIR.VBS, and others. These scripts are provided for compatibility only and require the IIS 6.0 Compatibility components to be installed. It is highly recommended that you use the new Appcmd.exe command line tool or programmatic APIs to manage IIS configuration, because the legacy tools may produce unintended configuration in certain cases because they are not optimized for the new configuration system.

In this section of the chapter, you'll see some common administrative tasks for managing IIS Web sites using both IIS Manager and Appcmd and review the relevant configuration file changes.

Adding a New Web Site

With IIS 7.0, you can create one or more Web sites to publish your Web applications and services. Before you create a new Web site, consider how you want it to be accessible by determining the IP addresses, ports, and (optionally) host headers that will be used to receive requests for the site. You will use this information to configure one or more protocol bindings for the Web site.

In IIS 7.0, each Web site serves as a logical container for Web applications and virtual directories. When you add a new Web site in IIS 7.0, IIS creates four different objects:

- A Web site that defines the site name, ID, bindings, and (optionally) more settings

- A root application

- A root virtual directory for the root application, mapping its "/" URL namespace to the Web site's physical root directory

- If using IIS Manager, an application pool to host the Web site's root application (unless you select one of the existing application pools)

> **Important**   As a security best practice, log on to your computer by using an account that does not have administrator privileges. Then use the *Runas* command to run IIS Manager as an administrator. For example, at the command prompt, type the following: **runas /user:<*admin_acct*> "%windir%\system32\inetsrv\inetmgr.exe"**

To use IIS Manager to create a Web site, in the Connections pane, expand the IIS computer node, right-click the Sites node in the tree, and then choose Add Web Site. The result is as shown in Figure 9-1.

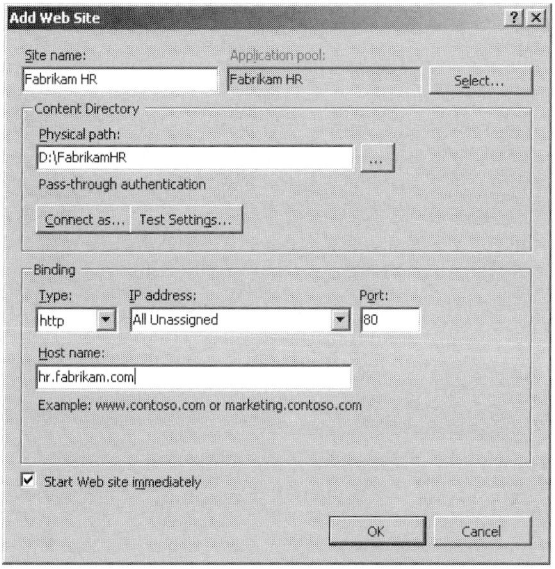

Figure 9-1   Adding a Web site via IIS Manager.

The Add Web Site dialog box enables you to create the new Web site by specifying all of the basic information necessary to create the Web site: a single binding, the root application, the root virtual directory, and by default, a new application pool to host the application. You can also define specific credentials to use when accessing the content in the site's root virtual directory. More about creating and managing virtual directories is found in the section titled "Managing Virtual Directories" later in this chapter.

If you would like to make additional modifications to the Web site's settings, you can also choose to not start the new Web site immediately, leaving it in a stopped state so that you can set additional configuration before manually starting it later. You can find out more about starting and stopping Web sites in the section titled "Starting and Stopping Web Sites" later in this chapter.

You can also use the following Appcmd command to add new Web site.

```
appcmd add site /name:string /id:uint /bindings:string /physicalPath:string
```

Table 9-1 describes the parameters for this command.

Table 9-1 Syntax for Appcmd to Add a Web Site

Parameter	Description
name	Minimum required field. The string represents the friendly name of the Web site.
	When IIS detects a duplication error in the element attribute value of either /name or /id, the command will fail and the Web site will not be created.
id	An unsigned integer indicating the Web site ID. If this value is omitted, IIS 7.0 increments the highest existing Web site ID by 1 to be the new Web site ID.
	When IIS detects a duplication error in the element attribute value of either /name or /id, the command will fail and the Web site will not be created.
bindings	A colon-separated list of the binding strings, including the protocol, and associated binding information. HTTP and HTTPS binding information includes the IP address, port, and host header value. Each binding string is in the form of [protocol]/[bindingInformation], where the [binding-Information] for the HTTP and HTTPS protocols is in the form of [ip|*]:[port]:[host header]. For example, *http/*:80:www.contoso.com* indicates that the Web site host header name is *http://www.contoso.com*, and it is bound to all IP addresses on port 80.
physicalPath	Represents the root application path for the Web site. The path can be located in the local computer, for example, d:\fabrikamhr, or a remote server, for example, \\remoteserver\share. For a shared remote server, you can specify a custom connectivity user account, which has access permissions on remote share.
	If physicalPath is not specified, the root application and root virtual directory are not automatically created and must be added later.

Note   If you specify the full path *%windir%\system32\inetsrv\appcmd.exe,* you can run the examples from any path without having to change directories.

The following example creates a new Web site with site ID 9, a site name of Fabrikam HR (for the Fabrikam human resources department), hr.fabrikam.com as the host header value, and the access port specified as a standard HTTP port. The root path of the Web site is mapped to d:\fabrikamHR physical folder.

```
appcmd add site /name:"Fabrikam HR" /id:9
    /bindings:http/*:80:hr.fabrikam.com /physicalPath:"d:\fabrikamHR"
```

Note   Long commands are sometimes shown formatted on multiple lines to fit on the printed page.

Take note of the command output, which shows that three different objects are created (site, application, and virtual directory). While in the IIS Manager UI, four different objects are created, because by default, the IIS Manager creates a new application for the new Web site. This is because a *physicalPath* is specified, and IIS creates the root application along with defining the virtual root directory of the Web site.

```
SITE object "Fabrikam HR/" added
APP object "Fabrikam HR/" added
VDIR object "Fabrikam HR/" added
```

If you don't specify *physicalPath*, as in the following example, only the site object is created, because IIS does not have enough information to create the associated application and virtual directory. As a result, the Web site is created, but cannot be started until you configure *physicalPath*.

```
appcmd add site /name:"Fabrikam Finance"
    /bindings:http/*:80/finance.fabrikam.com
```

Caution   When you create a new Web site via Appcmd without specifying bindings or *physicalPath* information, the new Web site is created, but you cannot start the Web site.

The following shows the *<site>* element for the Fabrikam HR Web site that has been created using Appcmd as in the first example in this section.

```
<sites>
...
    <site name="Fabrikam HR" id="9">
        <application path="/">
            <virtualDirectory path="/" physicalPath="d:\fabrikamHR" />
```

```
        </application>
        <bindings>
            <binding protocol="http"
                bindingInformation="*:80:hr.fabrikam.com" />
        </bindings>
    </site>
...
</sites>
```

Configuring a Web Site's Bindings

Web site bindings specify protocol-specific endpoints on which requests to the Web site are received. Each binding defines the protocol and the protocol-specific binding information.

> **Note**   Servers that have support for additional protocols, such as "net.tcp" provided by the Windows Communication Foundation and "ftp" provided by FTP 7.0, can specify bindings by using these protocols. Consult the documentation for each of these products to determine the binding information format each protocol uses.

IIS Web sites will typically contain bindings that use the HTTP or HTTPS protocols. These bindings specify endpoint information that designates the IP address, Port number, and Host Header (if any) to which the Web site will bind when it starts. This enables IIS Web sites to be hosted using some of the following setups:

- A Web site listening on a specific port on all available interfaces.

- A Web site listening on a specific port on a specific interface/specific IP address. This may be useful to limit the accessibility of a Web site to clients on a specific network, such as an internal network or localhost.

- A Web site listening on a specific port for a specific host header.

In addition, it is possible to host multiple Web sites on the same server by using bindings that use distinct ports, interface addresses, or host headers to differentiate multiple Web sites. The following outlines different ways for multiple Web sites bindings:

- Multiple Web sites listening on different ports.

- Multiple Web sites listening on the same port, on different interfaces/IP addresses. This may be done to expose different Web sites on internal versus external IP addresses of the server. You can also use it as a technique for hosting multiple Web sites if each Web site has separate IP addresses bound to the server's interfaces.

- Multiple Web sites listening on the same port and interface/IP address with different host headers. This technique is most commonly used to host multiple public Web sites. In addition, shared Web hosting servers use this technique.

Note   Be careful when using "All Unassigned" or "*" for the list of interfaces in an HTTP or HTTPS site binding. This configures the binding to listen on all interfaces that have not yet been taken by other bindings, and therefore the interfaces that the binding listens on will be dependent on what other currently active sites have bindings that use the same port on some or all of the server's interfaces. For deterministic results, consider specifying the list of addresses that you would like the binding to be active on.

Finally, to use a combination of these setups to achieve the desired accessibility, you can use multiple bindings on each site.

Note   You cannot host multiple Web sites using host headers on the same port/interface if each Web site requires a separate secure socket layer (SSL) certificate. For more information, see Chapter 14.

In IIS 7.0, you can use IIS Manager to configure binding information via the Bindings link in the Actions pane. IIS 7.0 lets you specify protocol bindings other than HTTP and HTTPS for the Web site. You can no longer specify an underscore character (_) as part of the host header.

To use IIS Manager to change existing bindings or configure new bindings for a Web site, expand the IIS computer node in the Connections pane. Then navigate to the Sites node and expand the tree view. In the Site tree listing, select the Web site that you want to change and then click the Bindings link in the Actions pane. The result is shown in Figure 9-2. Select the desired binding configuration and click Edit. Alternatively, click Remove to delete the binding.

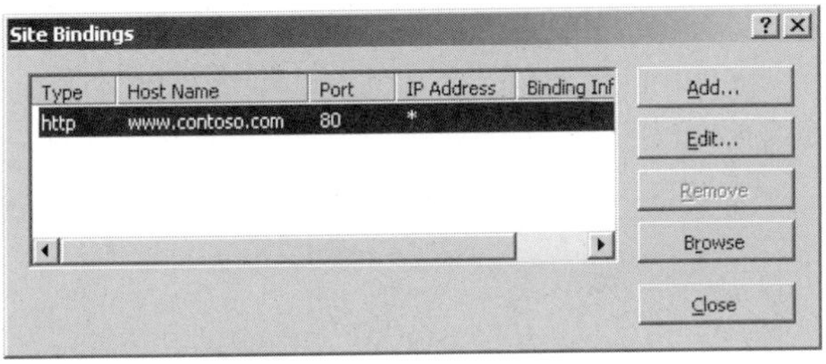

Type	Host Name	Port	IP Address	Binding Inf
http	www.contoso.com	80	*	

Buttons: Add... Edit... Remove Browse Close

Figure 9-2   Configuring Web site bindings by using IIS Manager.

Note   If you are configuring an HTTPS binding, you will need to select the SSL certificate for binding, and SSL certificates must already be installed. You can view certificate information by clicking the View button at the Add Site Binding dialog box when editing the Web site's binding information. For more information on how to configure SSL in IIS 7.0, see Chapter 14.

Use the following Appcmd syntax to show the bindings for a specific Web site.

```
appcmd list site SiteName
```

To configure a Web site's bindings, use the following command.

```
appcmd set site SiteName /bindings:string
```

Table 9-2 describes the parameters for this command.

Table 9-2 Syntax for Appcmd to Set Bindings

Parameter	Description
SiteName	The string represents the friendly name of the Web site.
bindings	A colon-separated list of the binding strings, including the protocol, and associated binding information. HTTP and HTTPS binding information includes the IP address, port, and host header value. Each binding string is in the form of [protocol]/[bindingInformation], where the [binding-information] for the HTTP and HTTPS protocols is in the form of [ip|*]:[port]:[host header]. The host header value can be blank if a specific host header is not specified.
	The list of bindings will replace the current bindings set for the site.

> **Note** For more information on using Appcmd to set bindings and the binding format, see Chapter 7, "Using Command Line Tools."

The following syntax lists Fabrikam HR Web site details, including the site's binding information.

```
appcmd list site "Fabrikam HR"
```

As shown in the following code, the output indicates that the Fabrikam HR Web site is bound to the HTTP protocol on port 80 for all IP addresses (*) with the host header value of hr.fabrikam.com.

```
SITE "Fabrikam HR" (id:9,bindings:http/*:80:hr.fabrikam.com,state:started)
```

To configure myhr.fabrikam.com as a new host header in addition to hr.fabrikam.com, use the following syntax.

```
appcmd set site "Fabrikam HR"
    /+bindings.[protocol='http',bindingInformation='*:80:myhr.fabrikam.com']
```

The preceding syntax adds another binding at the end of Fabrikam's existing binding information, specifying a new host header, the HTTP protocol, and all IP addresses with port 80. Using the previous example, if you want to change existing binding information from myhr.fabrikam.com to askhr.fabrikam.com, you would use the following syntax.

```
appcmd set site "Fabrikam HR"
    /bindings.[bindingInformation='*:80:myhr.fabrikam.com'].bindingInformation:*:80:askhr.
fabrikam.com
```

The bindings for a Web site are stored in the Web site's *<site>* element. The following shows the *<site>* element in the applicationHost.config file after running the preceding Appcmd examples.

```
<sites>
...
    <site name="Fabrikam HR" id="9">
        <application path="/">
            <virtualDirectory path="/" physicalPath="d:\fabrikamHR" />
        </application>
        <bindings>
            <binding protocol="http"
                bindingInformation="*:80:hr.fabrikam.com" />
            <binding protocol="http"
                bindingInformation="*:80:askhr.fabrikam.com" />
        </bindings>
    </site>
...
</sites>
```

Limiting Web Site Usage

As in earlier versions of IIS, you can configure Web site limits such as the maximum bandwidth usage, the concurrent connection limit, and the connection time-out. You can use these limits to constrain the usage of each Web site or to enable some Web sites to handle more concurrent connections and/or use more bandwidth than others. You can set three limits:

- Bandwidth usage (maxBandwidth)

- Connection (maxConnections)

- Connection time-out (connectionTimeout)

The bandwidth limit controls the network bandwidth usage to the Web site at any given time. The HTTP.sys kernel driver dynamically performs bandwidth throttling. In IIS 6.0, the throttling value is in kilobytes per second (Kbps) format. In IIS 7.0, it's in bytes per second format with a minimum value of 1024 bytes per second. When throttling is enabled, HTTP.sys sticks to the configured limit and will insure that the site's bandwidth usage will not exceed the specified bandwidth limit at any given time.

> **Important**   IIS does not guarantee precise bandwidth allocation between connections or specific requests to the Web site, only that the total bandwidth usage does not exceed the configured limit.

The connection limit specifies the maximum number of permitted connections for a particular Web site. By limiting connections to Web sites, you can effectively allocate system resources. For example, you might limit the connections for a low-priority Web site so that the system has more connections or resources available for high-priority or busy Web sites. When IIS hits the connection limits configured for a Web site, it sends back the HTTP 503 Service Unavailable error message to the client browser and writes a *ConnLimit* entry to the HTTP error log (httperr*.log at %windir%\system32\logfiles\httperr\).

The connection time-out specifies the connection idle time after which IIS disconnects an inactive user's connection. By closing free, idle, or invalid connections, IIS makes more connections and ports available to valid user connections. By default, the connection time-out is set at 120 seconds.

You can set all three limits from a single dialog box in IIS Manager. To use IIS Manager to limit the number of connections and bandwidth for a particular Web site, expand the IIS computer node in the Connections pane, navigate to the Sites node, and expand the tree view. In the Sites tree listing, select the Web site that you want to change and then click on the Limits link in the Actions pane. The result is shown in Figure 9-3.

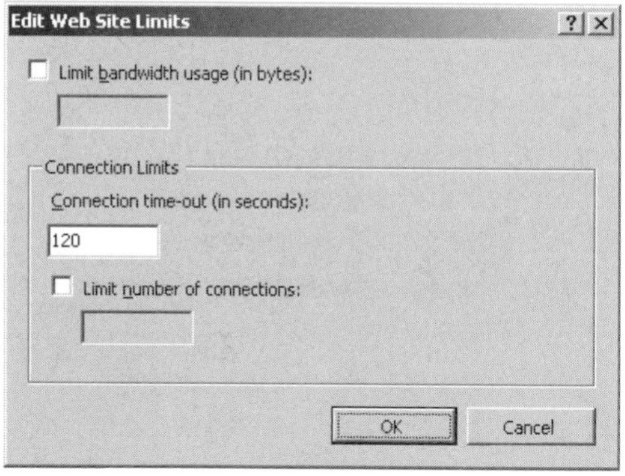

Figure 9-3   Limiting Web site usage through IIS Manager.

Use the following Appcmd command to show or configure a Web site's connection limits and bandwidth throttling.

```
appcmd set site SiteName /limits.connectionTimeout:integer
    /limits.maxBandwidth:integer /limits.maxConnections:integer
```

Table 9-3 describes the parameters for this command.

Table 9-3   Syntax for Appcmd to Set Connection Limits and Bandwidth Throttling

Parameter	Description
SiteName	The string represents the Web site's friendly name.
limits.connectionTimeout	The string specifies the HTTP connection time-out value in time span format (hh:mm:ss). For example, 00:02:00 is the default value of two minutes.
limits.maxBandwidth	The string specifies the throttle Web site's bandwidth in number of bytes. The value must be an integer between 1024 and 214783647.
limits.maxConnections	The string specifies the maximum number of connections to the Web site. The value must be an integer between 0 and 4294967295.

Because a Web site's limit settings belong to a *<site>* element, you cannot use Appcmd to list specific element values. Rather, you must list the Web site's *<site>* element in detail and examine the value using the /config switch. The following command queries the Fabrikam HR Web site details.

```
appcmd list site /site.name:"Fabrikam HR" /config
```

In the output, notice that the Web site connection limits and bandwidth throttling are defined in the *<limits>* element within the *<site>* element. The following syntax limits the Fabrikam HR Web site to support a maximum connection of 500 and throttles the Web site bandwidth at 10 MB.

```
appcmd set site "Fabrikam HR" /limits.maxBandwidth:10485760
    /limits.maxConnections:500
```

The following shows the *<limits>* element with the *maxBandwidth* and *maxConnections* attributes configured using the previous syntax.

```
<sites>
...
    <site name="Fabrikam HR" id="9">
        <application path="/">
            <virtualDirectory path="/" physicalPath="d:\fabrikamHR" />
        </application>
        <bindings>
            <binding protocol="http"
                bindingInformation="*:80:hr.fabrikam.com" />
            <binding protocol="http"
                bindingInformation="*:80:askhr.fabrikam.com" />
        </bindings>
        <limits maxBandwidth="10485760" maxConnections="500" />
    </site>
...
</sites>
```

Configuring Web Site Logging and Failed Request Tracing

After the Web site is created, you can also configure how requests to this Web site are logged, including selecting the log format, the location of the log files, and the schedule for creating log files. You can access the logging setting by selecting the Web site in the tree view and selecting the Logging feature icon in the main feature panel. You can learn more about configuring and using request logs in Chapter 15, "Logging."

In addition, to assist with troubleshooting activities, you can enable Failed Request Tracing so that detailed request execution logs will be generated for failed requests. You can access the Failed Request Tracing (FRT) settings from the IIS Manager by selecting the Web site in the tree view and clicking Failed Request Tracing. In the resulting dialog box, you can enable Failed Request Tracing and set the location and maximum number of trace files that can be generated for the Web site.

To learn more about using Failed Request Tracing to quickly diagnose and troubleshoot errors, see Chapter 16, "Tracing and Troubleshooting."

Starting and Stopping Web Sites

By default, when a Web site is created, it is configured to automatically begin listening to requests whenever the IIS World Wide Web Publishing Service (W3SVC) is started. When a Web site is actively listening to requests, it is considered to be started.

You can stop the Web site to temporarily prevent it from accepting new requests. Stopping a Web site does not terminate any currently executing requests or affect any currently active IIS worker processes and applications belonging to the site. To learn more about unloading currently active applications and IIS worker processes, see Chapter 10.

Stopping a Web site is a temporary action, which is undone whenever the W3SVC service restarts. If you want to prevent the Web site from starting automatically, you can configure it to not start automatically.

You can see the current state of each Web site when you view the Web site list in IIS Manager. You can start and stop any Web site in the list by right-clicking the Web site (in the tree view or on the Web sites list), expanding the Manage Web Site menu, and choosing Start or Stop.

> **Note**   When using IIS Manager to start a Web site, IIS Manager will also mark the Web site to start automatically when IIS is starting up. The Appcmd.exe command line tool will not do this, so you have the flexibility of setting the automatic start state yourself.

You can also start and stop Web sites by using the Appcmd.exe command line tool. To list the state of the Web sites on the server, you can use the following syntax.

```
appcmd list sites
```

The resulting list of sites indicates the state of each Web site as started or stopped.

```
SITE "Default Web Site" (id:1,bindings:http/*:80:,state:Started)
```

You can optionally use the /state parameter with values of "*started*" or "*stopped*" to display only the started or stopped Web sites.

To start a stopped Web site, you can use the following syntax.

```
appcmd start site SiteName
```

To stop a started Web site, you can use the following command.

```
appcmd stop site SiteName
```

In both cases, *SiteName* is the name of the site to start or stop.

As noted earlier, starting or stopping the Web site with AppCmd will not automatically change whether it will automatically start when the IIS core service is starting up or shutting down. To change this, you can set the serverAutoStart configuration property on the Web site. For example, you can mark the "Default Web Site" to not start automatically as follows.

```
appcmd set site "Default Web Site" /serverAutoStart:false
```

You can use both the *Start Site* and *Stop Site* commands and the *Set Site* command to effectively stop and start the Web site in a way that persists across W3SVC restarts.

Managing Virtual Directories

You can use virtual directories to publish application content that does not reside under an application's root virtual directory. Using virtual directories is an effective way to decouple the client-facing URL structure of your application from the physical structure of its content. You'll also need virtual directories if your application content is located in a disparate set of physical locations.

Adding a New Virtual Directory

You can create a virtual directory to provide a virtual path mapping for resources outside the Web site root directory. As discussed earlier in this chapter, virtual directories and Web applications are two distinct types of objects in IIS 7.0, but they are closely related. This poses the following considerations when creating virtual directories:

- Each Web application must have a root virtual directory (having the "/" path) that is mapped to a physical path that becomes the physical root of the application. When you create an application, you will also create its root virtual directory.

- All virtual directories must belong to an existing application. Therefore, when you create a virtual directory, you must add it to an existing application or create a new application that has the desired virtual path.

- If the virtual directory must serve as an application root for an application framework, configure enabled IIS modules, or be associated with a specific application pool, you must create an application instead.

To use IIS Manager to create a virtual directory, expand the IIS computer node in the Connections pane, navigate to the Sites node, and select the Web site in which you want to create a virtual directory. You can also expand the selected Web site node and select a child application or folder node into which you'd like to add the virtual directory. Right-click the desired node and select Add Virtual Directory.

In the resulting dialog box, you can specify the alias of the virtual directory, which will combine with the current path at which it is being added to determine the virtual path for the virtual directory. You also specify the physical path to which the virtual directory's URL namespace will map.

Configuring Access Credentials for the Virtual Directory

By default, the Web server will access the content in the physical path of the virtual directory using the IIS worker process identity as the process identity, and additionally insure that the authenticated user associated with the request as request identity has access to the requested resource. This means that the following identities need access to the content located on the share:

- The application pool identity (Network Service by default)

- The anonymous user (IUSR by default) if anonymous authentication is allowed

- The authenticated user identity for all users that are allowed to access the content in the virtual directory, if Windows-based authentication methods including Windows Authentication or Basic Authentication are used

Note The default virtual directory behavior is identical to the pass-through authentication mechanism used for virtual directories mapped to UNC paths in IIS 6.0.

If you would like to have the Web server use a single set of credentials that have access to the resources in the virtual directory, you can configure those credentials in the Connect As dialog box. If you specify these credentials, the Web server will always impersonate these credentials to access all content and configuration located in this virtual directory, instead of the IIS worker process identity. It will also no longer check whether the authenticated user associated with the request has access to the physical resources.

Note If specified, IIS always uses the credentials for a virtual directory to access the content and configuration files in that virtual directory, regardless of whether the physical location of the virtual directory is local or on a remote network share. This is unlike IIS 6.0, which only uses the provided credentials if the physical location resides on a network share indicated by a UNC path.

This provides a convenient mechanism for granting access to content located on remote network shares. Considerations for using virtual directories that point to physical content located on remote network shares are described in detail in the section titled "Managing Remote Content" later in this chapter.

Creating Virtual Directory with AppCmd

You can also create virtual directories by using the AppCmd command line tool with the following command.

```
appcmd add vdir /app.name:string /path:string /physicalPath:string /userName:string
/password:string /logonMethod:enum /allowSubDirConfig:bool
```

The parameters for this command are listed in Table 9-4.

Table 9-4   Syntax for AppCmd to Add a Virtual Directory

Parameter	Description
app.name	The path of the parent application to which the virtual directory is added. This parameter is required.
path	The virtual path for the virtual directory. This is relative to the parent application's virtual path. This parameter is required.
physicalPath	The physical path of the virtual directory. This parameter is required.
userName	The user name for virtual directory content access. If you do not specify this during virtual directory creation, it defaults to using pass-through authentication.
password	The password to use with the user name to access the virtual directory content.
logonMethod	The logon method used to create the logon token for the virtual directory credentials. Can be "Interactive", "Batch", "Network", or "ClearText". The default is "ClearText". For more information on these types, see "LogonUser Function" at *http://msdn2.microsoft.com/en-us/library/aa378184.aspx*.
allowSubDirConfig	Boolean that specifies whether or not the Web server will look for configuration files located in the subdirectories of this virtual directory. Setting this to false can improve performance on servers with very large numbers of web.config files, but doing so prevents IIS configuration from being read in subdirectories. Defaults to true.

The following example adds a new virtual directory named images within the Contoso Corp. Web site.

```
appcmd add vdir /app.name:"Contoso Corp/" /path:/images
    /physicalPath:g:\images
```

The command output shows that IIS creates a *VDIR* object that belongs to the Contoso Corp. root application. The virtual directory mapping forms the URL http://www.contoso.com/images, which links to image files residing in the physical folder g:\images.

```
VDIR object "Contoso Corp/images" added
```

Configuring Virtual Directories

When you are adding or changing a virtual directory, it is important to understand its underlying relationship with the Web application. For example, if you want to just enable references to an image folder on a remote share, the virtual directory does not need to be an application by itself. Instead, it can reside as part of the Web site's root application.

To make changes to an existing virtual directory, select the virtual directory you want to edit and then click Basic Settings in the Actions pane. The result is shown in Figure 9-4. To delete a virtual directory, select the virtual directory and then click Remove in the Actions pane.

> **Warning**   Removing a virtual directory does not delete the contents of the physical file system's mapped path. It removes only the mapping relationship between the URL alias and physical folder.
>
> Also note that it is not possible to remove a Web site's root virtual directory or an application's root virtual directory.

Edit Site

Site name:
www.contoso.com

Application pool:
DefaultAppPool   Select...

Physical path:
D:\contoso   ...

Pass-through authentication

Connect as...   Test Settings...

OK   Cancel

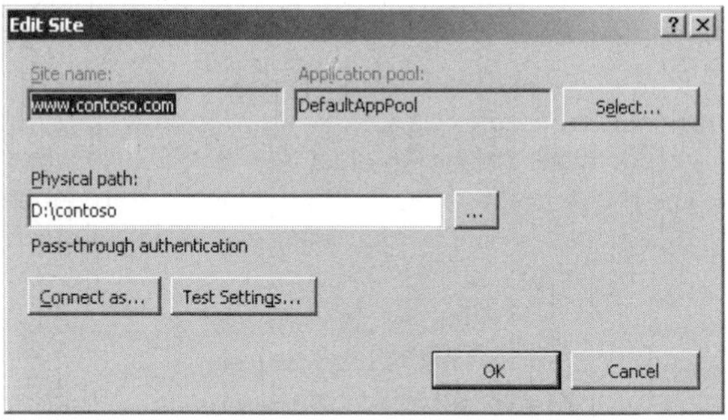

Figure 9-4   Configuring a virtual directory by using IIS Manager.

To set configuration settings on an existing virtual directory, use the following command.

```
appcmd set vdir VirtualDirectoryName /physicalPath:string
    /userName:string /password:string /logonMethod:enum /allowSubDirConfig:bool
```

To delete an existing virtual directory, use the following syntax.

```
appcmd delete vdir VirtualDirectoryName
```

The parameters for this command are listed in Table 9-5.

Table 9-5 Syntax for AppCmd to Configure a Virtual Directory

Parameter	Description
VirtualDirectoryName	The full virtual path of the virtual directory that uniquely identifies it. This is required to edit or delete an existing virtual directory.
physicalPath	The physical path of the virtual mapping.
userName	The user name for virtual directory content access. If this is not specified during virtual directory creation, it defaults to using pass-through authentication.
password	The password to use with the user name to access the virtual directory content.
logonMethod	The logon method used to create the logon token for the virtual directory credentials. Can be "Interactive", "Batch", "Network", or "ClearText". The default is "ClearText". For more information on these types, see "LogonUser Function" at *http://msdn2.microsoft.com/en-us/library/aa378184.aspx*.
allowSubDirConfig	Boolean that specifies whether or not the Web server will look for configuration files located in the subdirectories of this virtual directory. Setting this to false can improve performance on servers with very large numbers of web.config files, but doing so prevents IIS configuration from being read in subdirectories. Defaults to true.

To delete an existing virtual directory, you must specify the full virtual path of the virtual directory, as in this example.

```
appcmd delete vdir "Contoso Corp/oldimages"
```

Imagine that Contoso Corp.'s legal department has published a new set of corporate images on its file share server. To change the virtual directory mapping and specify a custom user account named "Webuser" to access the remote share, use the following command.

```
appcmd set vdir "Contoso Corp/images"
    /physicalPath:\\ContosoLegal\pub\images\ /userName:"Webuser"
    /password:"passw@rd1"
```

Along with site information, virtual directory configuration is defined in a *<virtualDirectory>* element within a *<site>* element in the applicationHost.config file. The following shows the configuration that results from executing the previous command.

```
    <site name="Contoso Corp" id="1">
        <application path="/">
```

```
            <virtualDirectory path="/" physicalPath="d:\contoso" />
            <virtualDirectory path="/images"
                    physicalPath="\\ContosoLegal\pub\images" userName:"Webuser"
                    password=
"[enc:AesProvider:oGSyoej3RKswi3gsrYarpbMQrxOrVIY6nFHkPmjQAhE=:enc]"/>
            </application>
            <application path="/payment" applicationPool="MyAppPool">
                <virtualDirectory path="/" physicalPath="d:\KDbank" />
            </application>
            ...
        </site>
```

Note that, by default, the user credential for a virtual directory is stored inside the application-Host.config file and is encrypted using the Microsoft Advanced Encryption Standard (AES) cryptographic provider. The application path "/" indicates the root application of the Web site and that the virtual directory "/images" belongs to the root application.

Searching Virtual Directories

When managing many Web sites with hundreds of virtual directories and applications, you sometimes need to locate or find a specific virtual directory or a group of virtual directories belonging to an application or Web site. IIS 6.0 provides limited tools and UI features to locate specific virtual directories. But in IIS 7.0, IIS Manager enables you to quickly find and display a list of virtual directories defined in the Web server.

To use IIS Manager to find and list virtual directories, expand the IIS computer node in the Connections pane, navigate to the Sites node, and select the Web site for which you want to list virtual directories. In the Actions pane, click View Virtual Directories. The result is shown in Figure 9-5.

If the virtual directory itself is not an application and belongs to the Web site root application, it is displayed as a root application in the Application Path column. The Identity column shows the request user account will be used as a request identity when accessing the virtual directory's content.

Note   If the identity field is not populated, pass-through authentication is being used for content access. For example, in anonymous authentication, the default IUSR account is the request identity.

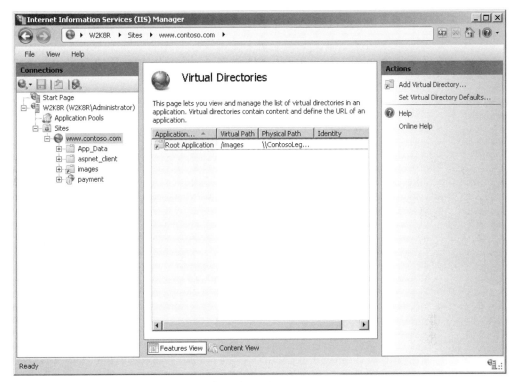

Figure 9-5   Viewing virtual directories by using IIS Manager.

Use the following AppCmd command to display mapping details of virtual directories.

```
appcmd list vdir VirtualDirectoryPath /app.name:string
```

The parameters for this command are listed in Table 9-6.

Table 9-6   Syntax for AppCmd to Search a Virtual Directory

Parameter	Description
VirtualDirectoryPath	The string represents the full virtual path of the virtual directory. If a value is omitted, the query displays all virtual directories of the Web server.
	This string can also be a URL, which will make the URL be resolved to the closest parent virtual directory.
app.name	The application virtual path. If specified, all of the virtual directories belonging to the application will be returned.

The following command queries the "/images" virtual directory configuration detail.

```
appcmd list vdir "Contoso Corp/images"
```

As shown in the resulting output, the virtual directory is mapped to a UNC share.

```
VDIR "Contoso Corp/images" (physicalPath:\\ContosoLegal\pub\images)
```

To list all of the Web server's virtual directories, enter the following command.

```
appcmd list vdir
```

The resulting output lists all virtual directories, as shown in the following example.

```
VDIR "Contoso Corp/" (physicalPath:d:\contoso)
VDIR "Contoso Corp/images" (physicalPath:\\ContosoLegal\pub\images)
VDIR "Contoso Corp/payment" (physicalPath:d:\KDbank)
VDIR "Fabrikam HR/" (physicalPath:d:\FabrikamHR)
```

You can also specify filtering expressions based on any virtual directory configuration property, such as path or user name, to list all of the virtual directories that satisfy these filter expressions. Additionally, you can search for virtual directories that belong to a specific site. To learn more about using AppCmd to search for objects, see Chapter 7.

Managing Remote Content

Typically, the files that comprise a Web application are stored on the IIS server's local file system. Though this certainly makes sense when you are running a small set of Web applications, in a large or complex environment—such as a hosting company running Web farms with thousands of Web sites across many servers or a complex application consisting of many small applications that sit on different servers managed by various parties—it is almost impossible to host the application contents locally.

In some scenarios, you might need more than a single Web server to deliver a high-volume traffic Web application. Though it is definitely possible to copy the same set of contents to many Web servers serving the same application, this creates additional administrative overhead because you need to make sure that contents are synchronized on all servers, and potential replication issues could impact the application availability and content integrity. On top of that, managing content across different servers requires additional maintenance for user access accounts as well as access permissions for the content files. All of this increases the complexity of the overall deployment. Storing content locally might grant you a performance advantage, but it creates many drawbacks when scaling your application.

To work around these issues, IIS 7.0 enables you to host Web applications that have content located on a network share, which enables multiple Web servers to connect a single set of content from a file server. Though this will often increase the overhead of accessing this content, you may find significant benefits to setting up a centralized remote content store. The benefits include:

- **Lower administrative overhead**   Instead of setting up file system security on many Web servers, you manage the file system access only at the centralized content store. This reduces account and content management tasks to the centralized content store rather than a number of servers when content is hosted locally.

- **Better fault tolerance**   To increases content availability, the content can be hosted in Microsoft Cluster, Distributed File System (DFS), or even Storage Area Network (SAN) or Network Attached Storage (NAS) devices.

- **More cost-effective**   When compared with fault-tolerance setup at each Web server, for example, installing a set of Redundant Array of Inexpensive Disks (RAID) at every single Web server. Implementing fault-tolerance just to the centralized content store is more cost-effective and requires less hardware maintenance to have a pair of file share clusters compared to deploying a set of RAID to each sever inside a Web farm.

This section outlines the key concepts of remote content access, steps for setting up remote content, security consideration for remote content access, and a few notes on remote content configuration. These concepts generally apply to remote content management in various environments such as file share clusters and NAS devices.

Configuring the Application to Use Remote Content

Using virtual directories to map to remote content makes the content as part of an application's URL namespace or the entire application to the remote network path at which the content is located.

To configure an application to use remote content, you need to do the following:

1. Set the physical path of the root virtual directory for the Web site or Web application to the network path where the content is located. If you would like to map only a part of the application to use remote content, you can simply create a virtual directory with the desired path in an existing application. Virtual directory creation is described in detail in the section titled "Adding a New Virtual Directory" earlier in the chapter.

2. Determine the desired security model for accessing network content, either using current credential via pass-through or custom fixed user for access credential.

3. Create the file share hosting the remote content on the network server and then grant required permissions to the file share.

Selecting the Security Model for Accessing Remote Content

To select the proper security model, it is important to consider how the Web server accesses the remote content. The following access is required:

- The web.config files located inside the remote content directory structure—to correctly apply delegated configuration for the remote content, IIS 7.0 will attempt to locate and read the web.config configuration files for all remote content directories. IIS accesses the configuration file before any content and the authenticated user is known. Because of this, either fixed virtual directory credentials must be set, or the IIS worker process identity must have read access to the remote content share.

- The content—IIS features such as the static file handler and application frameworks will access content files located in the remote content share. If the fixed credentials are set for the virtual directory, they will be used. Otherwise, the currently authenticated user identity will be used to access these files. If anonymous authentication is used, then the anonymous user identity will be used for this access.

> **Note** To access content, most IIS 7.0 modules and application frameworks will use the fixed credentials for the virtual directory or the authenticated user identity. However, in certain cases, they may fall back to the IIS worker process identity, in which case the IIS worker process identity must have access to the content. ASP.NET will do this by default. You may need to configure each application framework to use the correct identity. See Chapter 11, "Hosting Application Development Frameworks," for details about the execution identity for common application frameworks.

Generally, you can use two different security models for configuring access to the remote content share:

- **Pass-through authentication** In this model, the Web server will access the remote content by using the IIS worker process identity and the identity of the authenticated user associated with the request. This is the default model.

- **Fixed credentials** In this model, to access the remote content, the Web server will always use the fixed credentials configured on the virtual directory.

These options are similar to those provided by IIS 6.0. However, the need to access web.config files makes it more difficult to configure remote content access using pass-through authentication, because the authenticated user is not available when the Web server must read web.config files. This in turn requires the IIS worker process identity to have access to the remote content share. Alternatively, the fixed credential model has to be used.

> **Note** It is possible to disable the use of web.config files in the virtual directory by setting the *allowSubDirConfig* attribute on the virtual directory definition to "false". This disables the ability to use distributed configuration in web.config files inside this virtual directory, but it enables the use of pass-through authentication. For more information, please see Chapter 14.

Additionally, different application frameworks will behave differently when using the pass-through authentication model. Some application frameworks, including ASP.NET, will revert to the IIS worker process identity. Others, such as ASP, will always use the authenticated user identity. This makes it more difficult to manage access to the remote content when using the pass-through authentication model. Because of these reasons, the fixed credential model is recommended in most cases for setting up access to remote content on IIS 7.0.

The fixed credential model is simpler because it is not dependent on the Web server authentication mechanism, and it does not require all Web server users to have access to the remote content share. It also does not require delegation and protocol transition to be configured, which is required for many IIS 7.0 authentication mechanisms to use the authenticated identity to access the remote network share. This makes the fixed credential model significantly easier to configure and maintain in a networked environment.

However, because it does not use the authenticated user's identity to access the remote content, it does not enable ACLs on the remote content to be used for authorization and auditing.

> **Note**   The fixed credentials model does not enable NTFS file system (NTFS) ACLs to be used for auditing and authorization of authenticated users. IIS 7.0 does provide the URL authorization feature that can be used to create declarative authorization rules in configuration, which apply to the authenticated user. In addition, it is now possibly to quickly implement custom authorization solutions via IIS 7.0 modules. Likewise, auditing can be accomplished by inspecting request logs or developing a custom IIS 7.0 auditing module. For more information on using custom IIS 7.0 modules, please see Chapter 12, "Managing Web Server Modules."

You may be able to use the pass-through model instead of the fixed credential model if:

- You need to access the remote content with the identity of the authenticated user for authorization or auditing purposes, and you cannot use the IIS URL authorization feature, custom authorization through an IIS 7.0 module, and log-based or custom auditing through an IIS 7.0 module.

- Your Web server and file server are in a domain environment.

- You are using an authentication mechanism that enables delegation of authenticated user identities (Basic authentication, Kerberos-based Windows authentication) to the remote network share, or if you have configured constrained delegation and protocol transition to enable delegation for other authentication mechanisms.

- You do not use anonymous authentication or have configured anonymous authentication to use a custom identity that has access to the network share.

- You have disabled distributed web.config configuration files in the virtual directory, or the application pool identity uses a domain account that has access to the network share to read web.config configuration files.

To learn more about configuring access to server resources, including using the pass-through authentication model to configure access to remote content, see Chapter 14.

Configuring Fixed Credentials for Accessing Remote Content

To use the fixed credential model to configure access to the remote content, you need to set the user name and password on the virtual directory that points to the remote share. This user name and password must correspond to a valid local account on the file server or to a domain account that has read access to the network share specified by the virtual directory.

You can do this in IIS Manager when creating a new Web site or application, or by creating a new or editing an existing virtual directory. You can also do this by creating a new virtual directory or editing an existing virtual directory by using the AppCmd command line tool.

> **Note**   Unlike the IIS 6.0 *UNCUserName* and *UNCPassword* metabase properties, IIS always uses the virtual directory credentials (if specified) to access the content and configuration files in that virtual directory, regardless of whether the physical location of the virtual directory is local or on a remote network share. This means that you can specify fixed access credentials for any virtual directory whether it refers to a local path or a remote UNC path.

To learn more about setting up fixed credentials for virtual directories, see the section titled "Managing Virtual Directories" earlier in this chapter.

Granting Access to the Remote Content

After selecting the security model for accessing the remote content and configuring the Web server to use the desired model, you need to grant the required access to the network share containing the remote content. To do this, you will need to create the network share on the file server and set the required access permissions for both the network share and the underlying files in the file system.

To do this, you will generally need to do the following:

1. Create the physical directory that will contain the remote content for the virtual directory being set up for remote content.

2. Share this directory with the desired share name via Windows Explorer.

3. Configure the share permissions to allow the identity used by IIS to connect to the share. The identity must have at least Read permission, and possibly Write/Full Access permissions if you are using IIS as a publishing mechanism. When you are using the fixed credentials for the virtual directory, this is the identity whose credentials are set on the virtual directory. This identity must be either a local account on the server or a domain account.

> **Note**   See Chapter 14 for more information on configuring permissions for pass-through authentication scenarios.

4. Configure the NTFS permissions on the remote content directory used by the share, in the same manner as for the network share. Retain the existing NTFS permissions on the directory to make sure that Administrators and Local System continue to have full access.

Caution   It is not recommended to grant IIS permissions beyond Read access. If the Web server is compromised, doing so can allow the attacker to gain control of the remote share. Only do this if you are using IIS to publish content, such as when using Web-based Distributed Authoring and Versioning (WebDAV). In all other cases, create a separate account for publishing content to the remote content directory.

Caution   If the account IIS uses for accessing the remote content has administrative privileges on the remote network server, an attacker can gain complete control of the file server if the Web server is compromised. Never use identities with Administrative privileges on the file server to access remote content.

When setting permissions, consider using a group to which the allowed identities belong instead of granting access to individual users for both the share and the NTFS permissions. Doing so makes it significantly easier to manage access to the remote content. It is especially valuable when using pass-through authentication to grant access to a large number of authenticated users.

Summary

In this chapter, you learned about the fundamentals of IIS 7.0 Web sites. You also reviewed the basic tasks for using the IIS Manager tool and the AppCmd command line tool to create and manage Web sites. You can learn more about using each tool to perform key administrative tasks in Chapter 6, "Using IIS Manager," and Chapter 7.

You also learned how to use virtual directories to control the physical structure of a Web site's content and enable a Web site to use content from a remote share. For more information about securing Web site content as well as enabling advanced content access scenarios with pass-through authentication and constrained delegation, see Chapter 14.

In the next chapter, Chapter 10, you will learn how to manage applications and application pools to ensure reliable and secure operation of Web sites. You can also consult Chapter 11 for more information about using IIS 7.0 as an application server, including hosting applications with the use of specific application frameworks such as ASP, ASP.NET, and PHP.

Additional Resources

These resources contain additional information and tools related to this chapter:

- Chapter 4, "Understanding the Configuration System," contains information about the new XML-based configuration system and important configuration files in IIS 7.0.

- Chapter 6, "Using IIS Manager," provides information about using IIS Manager in IIS 7.0.

- Chapter 7, "Using Command Line Tools," covers information about using the AppCmd command line tool in IIS 7.0.

- Chapter 10, "Managing Applications and Application Pools," includes information on managing Web applications and application pools in IIS 7.0.

- Chapter 11, "Hosting Application Development Frameworks," provides information about enabling application frameworks in IIS 7.0.

- Chapter 12, "Managing Web Server Modules," contains information about configuring and managing both native and managed modules in IIS 7.0.

- Chapter 14, "Implementing Security Strategies," includes information about deploying SSL certificates to Web sites as well as various security configurations in IIS 7.0.

- Chapter 15, "Logging," provides information about various logging methods supported in IIS 7.0.

- Chapter 16, "Tracing and Troubleshooting," contains information about enabling request tracing as well as troubleshooting techniques in IIS 7.0.

- Mike Volodarsky's blog post titled "Creating IIS 7 Sites, Applications, and Virtual Directories" discusses new objects' definition in IIS 7.0 and can be found at *http://mvolo.com/blogs/serverside/archive/2007/07/12/Creating-IIS7-sites_2C00_ -applications_2C00_-and-virtual-directories.aspx.*

Chapter 10
Managing Applications and Application Pools

 On the Disc Browse the CD for additional tools and resources.

In Chapter 9, "Managing Web Sites," you learned about the basic Web site structure and the relationship between key Internet Information Services (IIS) objects such as the application, virtual directory, and application pool.

In this chapter, you will look further at managing IIS applications and creating and managing application pools to isolate IIS applications for reliability and security purposes. In addition, you will review the new capabilities for monitoring the operation of applications and application pools.

Managing Web Applications

A Web application is a container that provides a way to segregate part of your Web site's uniform resource locator (URL) namespace from a run-time execution perspective, potentially isolating the execution of its contents from other applications and/or enabling run-time state to be shared between different URLs of the application (depending on the application framework technology), for example, assigning an application pool to a specific application, thereby isolating it from other applications via a process boundary. In addition, the application is the level at which ASP.NET application domains and ASP applications are created.

Each Web site in IIS 7.0 must contain a root application, thereby making contents below the root path belong to the same application, until another application is found underneath the root path. In IIS 7.0, the Web application object has clearer definitions to distinguish it from a virtual directory, as it formed a unique virtual path for each application as part of the

Web site's URL namespace into one or more applications. Each application contains at least one virtual directory, called the root virtual directory, that maps the root of the application's URL namespace to its root physical directory. On the other hand, not all virtual directories are defined as application root, simply because it is not an application starting point. Rather, it belongs to another application.

Creating Web Applications

Before adding a new application to the Web server, consider whether the functionality can be hosted within an existing application or whether it requires a separate application of its own. You will typically want to create an application if any of the following apply:

- You need to host your content or functionality in a separate application pool to isolate it from the rest of the Web site for reliability or security purposes.

- You need to host your content or functionality in a separate application pool to configure .NET Integrated mode. You will also want to create an application if the .NET Framework version or bitness is different from that of the parent application.

- You need to have a separate ASP or ASP.NET application.

- You need to add, remove, or otherwise modify the set of IIS modules enabled for your content or functionality.

For example, imagine that you are adding new content (such as image files) that does not require its own ASP.NET application domain and does not need to be in a separate application pool. The "images" virtual directory should not be configured as a Web application but rather as a normal virtual directory that maps the URL to the directory containing the image files. On the other hand, if you are trying to provide a new payment method (such as for credit cards) on your shopping cart Web portal system, and you are using third-party or legacy components that require custom settings from the application pool, then you might want to create a new application and host it under a separate application pool. Application isolation helps you achieve better availability, because an application hosted in a different application pool is served by different worker processes. That way, if the new payment application is having problems, it will not affect the main shopping Web portal application.

You can create applications at any URL in your Web site. In IIS 7.0, when you add a new Web site via IIS Manager, the tool automatically creates a root application. IIS Manager also, by default, creates a new application pool and associates it with the Web site's root application. Using IIS Manager, you can create a new Web application, either by adding a new application directly or by converting an existing virtual directory to an application. (You can also create a new application later for an existing Web site even if there is no existing virtual directory.) Either way, it is important to understand how the application will interact with other applications as well as in which application pool the Web application resides.

> **Important**   As a security best practice, log on to your computer by using an account that does not have administrator privileges, then use the *Runas* command to run IIS Manager as an administrator. For example, at the command prompt, type the following:
>
> **runas /user:<*admin_acct*> "%windir%\system32\inetsrv\inetmgr.exe"**

To create a new Web application by using IIS Manager, expand the IIS computer node in the Connections pane and then expand the Sites node in the tree listing. Right-click the Web site from which you want to create an application and then click Add Application. The result is as shown in Figure 10-1.

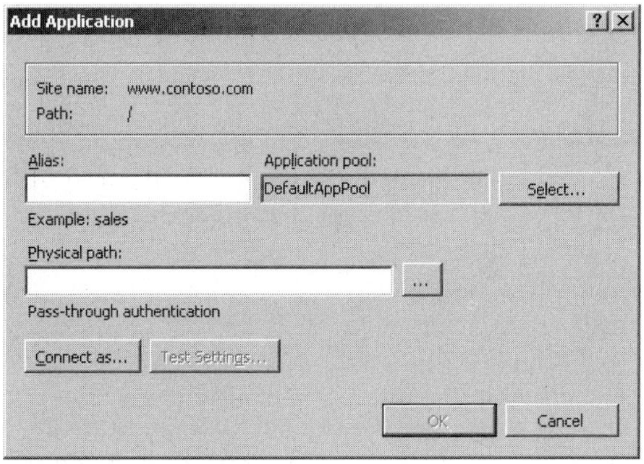

![Add Application dialog box showing Site name: www.contoso.com, Path: /, Alias field, Application pool: DefaultAppPool with Select button, Physical path field, Pass-through authentication with Connect as and Test Settings buttons, and OK/Cancel buttons.]

Figure 10-1   Creating a new Web application by using IIS Manager.

IIS Manager automatically creates a root virtual directory for the application by using the physical path you specify during application creation. You can also configure the credentials that should be used for accessing the content in the application root by using the Connect As option shown in Figure 10-1. You can learn more about creating virtual directories and setting the access credentials in Chapter 9.

To convert an existing physical or virtual directory to an application, expand the IIS computer node in the Connections pane and then expand the Sites node in the tree listing. Right-click the directory or virtual directory for the Web site and then click Convert To Application, as shown in Figure 10-2.

This automatically creates an application at this virtual path and sets the corresponding physical path to be the root virtual directory of the application. The existing virtual directory, if present, is removed, and its settings are copied to the new root virtual directory for the application.

You can use the following Appcmd syntax to add a new Web application.

```
appcmd add app /site.name:string
/path:string /physicalPath:string /applicationPool:string
/enabledProtocols:string
```

Figure 10-2   Converting an existing physical or virtual directory to a new application root by using IIS Manager.

Table 10-1 describes the parameters for this syntax.

Table 10-1   Syntax for Appcmd to Add a Web Application

Parameter	Description
site.name	The name of the Web site to which this application will be added. This parameter is required.
path	The virtual path of the application. Path information must begin with "/", for example, "/Stock". This parameter is required.
physicalPath	The physical path for the root virtual directory of this application. If specified, a root virtual directory is created.
applicationPool	The application pool for hosting the application. If not specified, the application will use the application pool from the application pool defaults (by default, DefaultAppPool).
enabledProtocols	Comma-separated list of protocol names that are enabled in this application. The default is HTTP.

This command cannot be used to specify additional settings for the root virtual directory created when the physicalPath parameter is specified. To set additional settings, such as the user name and password for the virtual directory, you will need to use the Appcmd SET VDIR command to edit the root virtual directory of the application. You can find more information on doing this in Chapter 9.

You can use the following Appcmd syntax with the parameters listed in Table 10-2 to change an existing Web application.

```
appcmd set app AppName /path:string
/applicationPool:string /enabledProtocols:string
```

Table 10-2   Syntax for Appcmd to Change a Web Application

Parameter	Description
AppName	The string represents the virtual path of the Web application.
path	The virtual path of the application. Path information must begin with "/", for example, "/Stock".
applicationPool	The application pool for hosting the application.
enabledProtocols	Comma-separated list of protocol names that are enabled in this application. The default is HTTP.

The following example creates a new Web application named Stock for Fabrikam human resources (HR). The application content path is mapped to the physical folder d:\fabrikamStock.

```
appcmd add app /site.name:"Fabrikam HR"
/path:/Stock /physicalPath:"d:\fabrikamStock"
```

Take note of the command output, because two objects are created: the application and virtual directory objects. Because the example specifies the */physicalPath* parameter, the Web application must contain a root virtual directory. Therefore, when the new application is created, a root virtual directory mapping is automatically created as well.

```
APP object "Fabrikam HR/Stock" added
VDIR object "Fabrikam HR/Stock" added
```

When the */physicalPath* parameter is not specified, only the *APP* object is created, because Appcmd does not have enough information to create the associated virtual directory. Here's an example of such a command.

```
appcmd add app /site.name:"Fabrikam HR" /path:/Benefit
```

Appcmd enables this usage for scenarios where you might be required to create the virtual directory in a second step, or where you need to specify additional virtual directory settings not supported by the *ADD APP* command. As a result, when you manage the Web site via IIS Manager, you will get an error message indicating that the virtual directory does not exist for the application. To fix this error, use Appcmd to add a virtual directory to the application.

Note   It is not possible to create a root virtual directory for an application by using the Appcmd *SET APP* command with the physicalPath parameter.

To change an existing application alias name (which is not possible in IIS Manager), you can specify the new application name in the */path* parameter. For example, the following syntax changes the application path /myImages to /images.

```
appcmd set app /app.name:"Fabrikam
HR/myImages" /path:/images
```

To convert an existing directory to an application, first you need to delete the existing virtual directory. Then to create the new application, you must use the ADD verb, along with the */physicalPath* parameter to automatically create the new application's root virtual directory that points to the right physical path. (Or you can manually create the root virtual directory later.) For example, the following Appcmd command removes the "Payment" virtual directory from the Web site root and then re-creates it as an application in a separate application pool.

```
appcmd delete vdir "Fabrikam HR/Payment"

appcmd add app /site.name:"Fabrikam HR"
/path:/payment /physicalPath:"d:\HRPayment"
/applicationPool: "HR Payment"
```

Note that the first command removes the virtual directory from the Web site root application. Because this is just a virtual directory that resides in the root application, you cannot use the DELETE APP syntax because it is not an application by itself. When deleting an application, IIS does not delete physical file system content of the mapped path. It removes only the mapping relationship between the application URL alias and physical folder.

Caution   Do not remove a Web site's root application. Removing the root application via Appcmd will bring down the Web site.

When you create a new Web application or convert an existing directory to an application, a new *<application>* element is added by IIS Web core to the *<site>* element in the applicationHost.config file. At the same time, a *<virtualDirectory>* element under the *<application>* element defines the application root path. The following shows the *<site>* configuration of the newly created Stock application of the Fabrikam human resources' Web site.

```
<sites>
...
    <site name="Fabrikam HR" id="9">
        <application path="/">
            <virtualDirectory path="/" physicalPath="d:\fabrikamHR" />
            <virtualDirectory path="/images" physicalPath="g:\images" />
        </application>
        <application path="/Stock">
            <virtualDirectory path="/" physicalPath="d:\fabrikamStock" />
        </application>
```

```
        <application path="/payment" applicationPool="HR Payment">
            <virtualDirectory path="/" physicalPath="d:\HRPayment" />
        </application>
        ...
    </site>
...
</sites>
```

Listing Web Applications

IIS 6.0 offers no way to display or find a particular Web application. In IIS 7.0, both IIS Manager and Appcmd provide a convenient way to locate and query Web applications.

To view a list of Web applications in IIS Manager, expand the IIS computer node in the Connections pane, navigate to the Sites node, and select the Web site for which you want to view a list of Web applications. In the Actions pane, click View Applications to see a list of Web applications that you can sort, filter, and group, as shown in Figure 10-3.

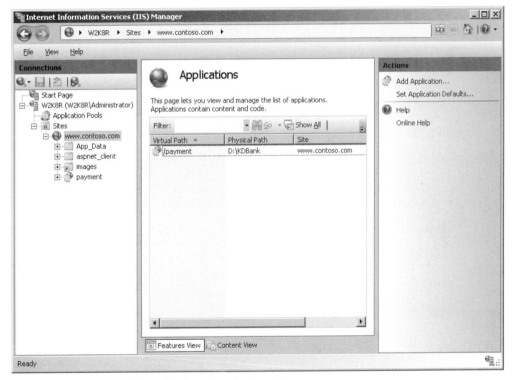

Figure 10-3   Listing Web applications by using IIS Manager.

Use the following Appcmd syntax to query a list of Web applications.

```
appcmd list app AppPath /site.name:string /apppool.name:string
```

Table 10-3 describes the parameters for this syntax.

Table 10-3   Syntax for Appcmd to Query a List of Web Applications

Parameter	Description
AppPath	The string represents the name of the Web application. The name of the application is the Web site name combined with the application's virtual path. If omitted, the query displays all the Web server's Web applications.
	It can also specify a URL, in which case Appcmd displays the application that contains this URL.
site.name	The name of the parent Web site. If specified, lists all of the applications in the specified Web site.
apppool.name	The name of the application pool. If specified, lists all of the applications that belong to the application pool.

The following example queries the "Stock" Web application configuration detail.

```
appcmd list app "Fabrikam HR/Stock"
```

As shown in the following output, the Stock application is running under the Fabrikam Stock application pool.

```
APP ""Fabrikam HR/Stock" (applicationPool:Fabrikam Stock)
```

To list all the Web server's Web applications, use the following command.

```
appcmd list app
```

The resulting output lists all Web applications, as shown here.

```
APP "Contoso Corp/"" (applicationPool:DefaultAppPool)
APP "Contoso Corp/payment" (applicationPool:MyAppPool)
APP "Fabrikam HR/" (applicationPool:DefaultAppPool)
APP "Fabrikam HR/Stock" (applicationPool:Fabrikam Stock)
```

To find applications associated with Fabrikam HR, use the following command.

```
appcmd list app /site.name:"Fabrikam HR"
```

This example queries the configuration system and displays application objects that belong to the Fabrikam HR Web site. The resulting output will look like the following.

```
APP "Fabrikam HR/" (applicationPool:DefaultAppPool)
APP "Fabrikam HR/Stock" (applicationPool:Fabrikam Stock)
```

To search for an application hosted by a certain application pool, you can use the
/*apppool.name* parameter. For example, to list all applications belonging to the DefaultAppPool application pool, use the following command.

```
appcmd list app /apppool.name:"DefaultAppPool"
```

This would yield output as follows.

```
APP "Contoso Corp/" (applicationPool:DefaultAppPool)
APP "Fabrikam HR/" (applicationPool:DefaultAppPool)
```

To find all root applications related to all Web sites, use this command.

```
appcmd list app /path:"/"
```

Specifying */path:"/"* in the command instructs IIS to look for all applications that have a path attribute of "/", or all applications on the server that are root applications for their respective Web sites. You can use any other parameter on the application object to filter by. For more information about searching for objects, see Chapter 7, "Using Command Line Tools."

Managing Application Pools

Application pools facilitate hosting a group of Web applications inside a separate set of IIS worker processes that share the same configuration. Application pools enable you to isolate applications for better security, reliability, and availability. The worker process serves as the process boundary that separates each application pool so that when one worker process or application is having an issue, other applications or worker processes are not affected. For example, imagine you plan to install an old ASP application that uses legacy component objects. To protect other applications in the Web site, you can create a new application pool and host the legacy application inside the new application pool. In this example, if the legacy application fails, other applications will not be affected, because the legacy application is served by a different application pool.

Each application pool can have one or more worker processes serving the application pool. However, each worker process belongs to only one application pool.

Web Gardens

An application pool with more than one worker processes is known as a Web garden. Many worker processes serving the same application can sometimes provide better throughput performance and application response time. Take note that in a Web garden, each worker process has its own process threads and memory space. If the application uses in-process session variables, the application will not function correctly, because the same user requests are picked up by different worker processes that do not share the same session details. ASP.NET applications can overcome this issue by using out-of-process session management options, such as the session state service or SQL Server–based session state.

Web gardens are not recommended most of the time because they hurt performance except in very specific cases, such as the following:

■   Your application makes long-running synchronous requests that significantly reduce concurrency.

- Your application is very unstable and crashes a lot, so having multiple processes helps maintain availability. (In this case, of course, the best approach is to fix the application.)

- Your application has process-wide resources that run low or uses process-wide locks that significantly reduce concurrency.

In most of these cases, redesigning your application to perform long-running tasks asynchronously, eliminating process-wide locking, and reducing crashes is a better long-term approach than relying on Web gardens.

Application Pool Considerations

By default, there are two predefined application pools when IIS 7.0 is installed. As shown in Table 10-4, there are two application pools with different worker process models. The Web Server (IIS) role setup creates the *DefaultAppPool* application pool and is the default application pool for new applications. The ASP.NET role service setup creates the *Classic .NET AppPool* to enable ASP.NET applications to run with the Classic ASP.NET Integration mode. You can configure applications to run in these default application pools, or you can create a new application pool.

Table 10-4   Predefined Application Pools

Application Pool	.NET Framework	Managed Pipeline	Identity
Classic .NET AppPool	Version 2.0	Classic	NetworkService
DefaultAppPool	Version 2.0	Integrated	NetworkService

Note   The Classic .NET AppPool application pool is created during ASP.NET 2.0 setup. The installation of the .NET Framework 1.1 calls the aspnet_regiis.exe tool to install ASP.NET 1.1, which creates the ASP.NET 1.1 application pool.

Neither application pool is created by default when IIS 7.0 is installed. For more information on using these application pools to manage the ASP.NET version for ASP.NET applications, see Chapter 11, "Hosting Application Development Frameworks."

Before you create a new application pool, you need to consider—from many perspectives—if such an application pool is needed. Because a dedicated worker process fulfills each application pool, the more application pools, the more worker processes may be running on the system to handle requests to the applications on the server. This could impact overall system performance, because each worker process consumes system resources such as processor time and memory. Even so, for most administrators, maintaining separate application pools for different applications will never cause any problems.

> **Note**   For reliability reasons, you should by default use separate application pools try to host each application (and Web site). Doing so can also allow you to take advantage of least privilege by granting the minimal set of permissions to each application pool identity, helping isolate the application from each other. See Chapter 14, "Implementing Security Strategies," for application pool isolation techniques.

If you have thousands of pools or have clear performance data showing that multiple pool configuration hurts your performance, then consider the information provided in the sidebar titled "Capacity Analysis for Large Numbers of Application Pools." Even for shared hosting servers, Microsoft recommends site-per-pool isolation, because IIS 7.0 supports much better site density in this configuration.

Capacity Analysis for Large Numbers of Application Pools

No fixed formula exists to determine the maximum number of worker processes that can run on a server. Similar to figuring out the maximum number of Web sites that can be hosted in IIS 7.0, you must perform capacity analysis to evaluate the overall system performance when a large number of worker processes will be run on the system. The analysis should look at the memory footprint of the application under heavy loading, the impact of recycling, the number of concurrent requests per application, and so on. Performance load testing will help with this analysis. You can use Microsoft Visual Studio Team Edition as well as the Web Capacity Analysis Tool (WCAT) to assist with these evaluations. As a Web administrator, you must evaluate the importance of having dedicated application pools and then find an appropriate balance between application isolation and performance throughput for your Web server. For more information on WCAT, see *http://www.iis.net/downloads/default.aspx?tabid=34&g=6&i=1466*.

Consider the following factors before creating new application pools:

- **Security**   You can create a new application pool and configure a custom application pool identity with access rights when the application requires custom access to certain resources. A custom application that updates system configuration is an example of such a situation. As another example, consider applications that belong to two different customers and for which content access must be absolutely restricted to each respective customer. Chapter 14 covers these issues in depth.

- **Reliability**   You can create a new application pool to isolate unstable or new applications. For example, you can isolate a legacy component application that crashes from time to time, or separate the new integration applications that are still in testing phase. Isolating these applications increases the reliability of other applications as failures in the legacy or testing applications will not affect other applications.

■ **Customization**   You can create a new application pool when an application requires different application pool settings. Such a situation arises if you have an old application that must run in the Classic process model, and others must run in Integrated mode. (Integrated mode is discussed in Chapter 11.) In IIS 7.0, the ASP.NET Integration mode and .NET Framework version are configurable at the application pool level. In addition, creating a new application pool allows you to configure a unique set of worker process settings (such as the application pool recycling interval or queue size) that are different from the common application pool. You might also want to isolate an application based on application types. For example, you might want different application pools for ASP and ASP.NET.

Note   Although IIS 7.0 supports side-by-side execution of applications using different versions of the .NET Framework, you should understand that different .NET Framework applications require different application pools because each application pool is assigned to only one .NET Framework run-time version.

Adding a New Application Pool

To use IIS Manager to create a new application pool, expand the IIS computer node in the Connections pane and navigate to the Application Pools node. Right-click the Application Pools node and select Add Application Pool. Alternatively, click Add Application Pool in the Actions pane. The result is shown in Figure 10-4.

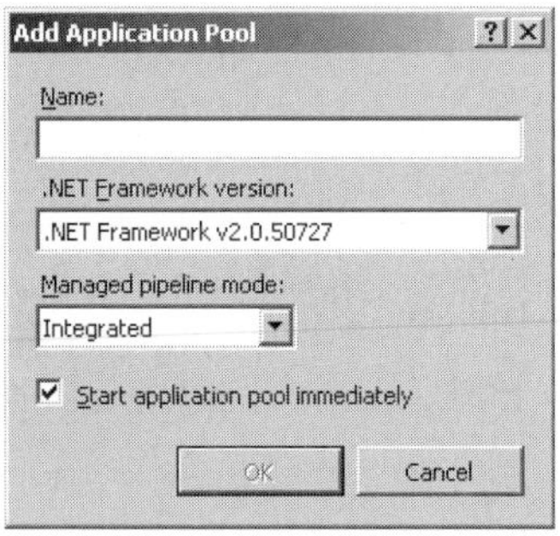

Figure 10-4   Adding a new application pool by using IIS Manager.

Note   When using IIS Manager to add an application pool, select the Start Application Pool Immediately check box if you want to start the application pool right after creating it.

When an application picks up a request from an application pool which is not running, IIS 7.0 returns a 503 HTTP "The service is unavailable" error to the client browser.

After you have created an application pool, you can either create a new application to run in the new application pool or assign the new application pool to an existing application. To assign an application pool to an existing application by using IIS Manager, expand the IIS computer node in the Connections pane and then expand the Site node in the tree listing. Navigate to the desired application and then click Basic Settings in the Actions pane. Click the Select button to choose the new application pool from the list of available application pools, as shown in Figure 10-5.

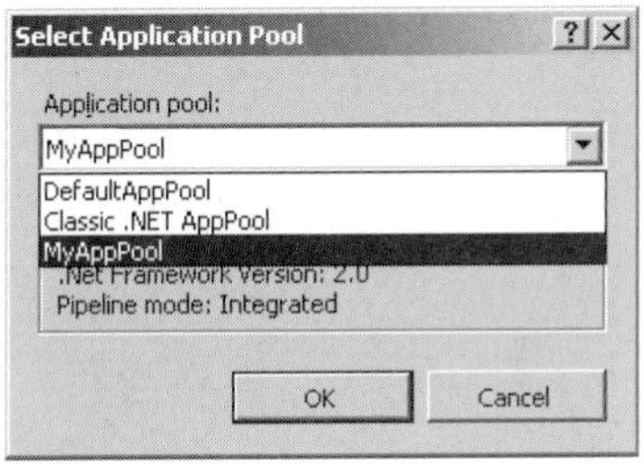

Figure 10-5   Assigning an application pool to an existing application by using IIS Manager.

Caution   Assigning a new application pool to or changing the application pool for an application that is running may end up loading the application in the new worker processes for the newly assigned application pool, but application details or variables in the old worker process are not visible to the new worker process. The application will continue processing existing requests in the old worker process but will not receive any additional requests after the changes are applied and are detected by the original worker process.

Use the following Appcmd syntax to create a new application pool.

```
appcmd add apppool /name:string /managedPipelineMode:enum /managedRuntimeVersion:string
```

To set the properties on an existing application pool, use this syntax.

```
appcmd set apppool ApppoolName /managedPipelineMode:enum /managedRuntimeVersion:string
```

Table 10-5 describes the parameters for *ADD APPPOOL* or *SET APPPOOL* syntaxes.

Table 10-5   Syntax for Appcmd to Configure Application Pool Properties

Parameter	Description
name	The name of the new application pool. Required to add an application pool.
AppPoolName	The application pool name. Required when editing an existing application pool.
managedRuntimeVersion	Specifies the .NET run-time version for the application pool. Can be "v1.1", "v2.0", or "" for no Common Language Runtime (CLR). Future versions of the .NET Framework will support new versions strings. The default is "v2.0".
managedPipelineMode	The ASP.NET integration mode for the application pool. Values are "Classic" or "Integrated". Default is "Integrated".

The following command creates a new application pool with the name "Fabrikam Stock".

```
appcmd add apppool /name:"Fabrikam Stock"
```

The output, shown in the following syntax, indicates a new application pool object has been added to the configuration store.

```
APPPOOL object "Fabrikam Stock" added
```

To change the new application pool's basic settings, such as the process model and the .NET run-time version, use the *SET* command. The following command reconfigures the newly created "Fabrikam Stock" application pool to run on .NET run-time version 1.1 and changes the process model to Classic ISAPI mode.

```
appcmd set apppool /apppool.name:"FabrikamStock"
/managedRuntimeVersion:"v1.1" /managedPipelineMode:"Classic"
```

> **Note**   To enable support for .NET Framework version 1.1, you need to install the .NET Framework 1.1. By design, when it is installed, a new application pool named as ASP.NET 1.1 is created. This new application pool is configured to run in the Classic worker process model with the .NET Framework 1.1 run time. You can learn more about ASP.NET versioning in Chapter 11.

Finally, when the new application pool is ready, you can either create a new application to run on the application pool or assign the application pool to any existing application. For example, the following syntax configures the existing "Stock" application to run in the "Fabrikam Stock" application pool.

```
appcmd set app "Fabrikam HR/Stock"
/applicationPool:"Fabrikam Stock"
```

> **Caution**   When using Appcmd to set the application pool for an application, the command line tool does not verify if the specified application pool exists in the configuration system. If the application pool does not exist, the application will fail to load at run time.

When adding a new application pool, the configuration system creates a new application pool element under the *<applicationPools>* section in the applicationHost.config file. The element includes the name of the application pool, the worker process model, and the process identity if it is different from the default settings. The following shows the *<applicationPools>* configuration of the newly created Fabrikam Stock application pool in .NET Framework version 1.1 run time.

```
<applicationPools>
    <add name="DefaultAppPool" />
<add name="Classic .NET AppPool" managedPipelineMode="Classic" />
<add name="ASP.NET 1.1" managedRuntimeVersion="v1.1"
```

```
    managedPipelineMode="Classic" />
    <add name="Fabrikam Stock" managedRuntimeVersion="V1.1"
        managedPipelineMode="Classic" />
    <applicationPoolDefaults>
        <processModel identityType="NetworkService" />
    </applicationPoolDefaults>
</applicationPools>
```

When you assign a new application pool to an existing application, the *<application>* element inside *<site>* element is updated by IIS Web core. For more information, see the section titled "Managing Web Applications" earlier in this chapter.

Managing Application Pool Identities

You can configure the identity under which worker processes in the application pool will run by assigning an account to the application pool. Application pool identity configuration is an important aspect of security in IIS 7.0, because it determines the identity of the worker process when the process is accessing resources. In IIS 5.0, the process runs under the LocalSystem account. That has significant security implications, because the user account has high access privileges. This changed in IIS 6.0 with the introduction of an application pool for which NetworkService is the default application pool identity. In IIS 7.0, the predefined worker process identities are the same as for IIS 6.0. Table 10-6 illustrates the built-in application identities in IIS 7.0.

Table 10-6   Built-In Application Pool Identities

Identity	Description
LocalSystem	LocalSystem is a built-in account that has administrative privileges on the server. It can access both local and remote resources. The account technically has access privileges similar to the system administrator account with unrestricted access to local resources. Application pools should *never* be assigned this identity. (If an application requires this identity, it indicates that the application is poorly designed, and you should strongly consider changing the application so that it does not require administrative privileges.)
LocalService	The LocalService account is a special built-in account that has reduced privileges similar to an authenticated local user account. It does not have network access privileges.
NetworkService	NetworkService is a built-in account that has reduced privileges similar to an authenticated local user account. It can access remote resources as the machine account. This is the default account that IIS application pools use, and it has limited access to resources on local and remote computers.

On top of built-in accounts, you can create a custom user account to run the worker process in the context of the custom user account. Chapter 14 covers this in detail. You will learn more about configuring a custom account as the application pool identity in the section titled "Configuring Application Pool Identity" later in this chapter.

Security Account Changes in IIS 7.0

In IIS 7.0, both the anonymous user account (IUSR_*computername*) and IIS_WPG user groups have been removed and replaced by system built-in accounts rather than normal user and group accounts. Using a built-in predefined user Security Identifier (SID) ensures that the same common accounts exist in the remote IIS 7.0 computer. The built-in account initiative also eliminates the need to manage issues with user credentials, such as password expiration. The following built-in accounts are created during IIS 7.0 installation:

- **IUSR**   The default user account for anonymous identity; replaces IUSR_*computername* account

- **IIS_IUSRS**   New built-in user group; replaces the IIS_WPG user group

> **Note**   IUSR_*computername* is created if the FTP Publishing Service (the legacy IIS 6.0 FTP) role service is installed in Windows Server 2008.

On top of the security user and user group account changes, IIS 7.0 introduces two additional enhancements related to application pool identity:

- **Application Pool Identity as Anonymous Account**   Designate the application pool identity as the anonymous user account. (Simply set the *userName* in the *anonymous-Authentication* configuration section to be blank. To learn about this new feature, see Chapter 14.) The main advantage of configuring application pool identity as the anonymous user is that you do not have to manage security for a separate account.

- **Automatic IIS_IUSRS Membership**   In IIS 6.0, when you configure custom application pool identity, the custom account must be a member of IIS_WPG, because this user group has preconfigured access permissions and rights to start the worker process. Similar access permissions and rights have been granted to the IIS_IUSRS user group in IIS 7.0. However, the custom account does not need to be explicitly added to the IIS_IUSRS group, because this is done implicitly by IIS 7.0. (The application pool identity is not actually added to the IIS_IUSRS group. The group SID is injected into the worker process token at run time, so it acts as a member of IIS_IUSRS. No changes to the local user database or Microsoft Active Directory directory service domain group membership are made.)

    To revert to IIS 6.0 behavior, you can configure manual IIS_IUSRS group membership. This setting is per application pool, meaning that for the application pool with manual group membership, you will need to explicitly add the custom account to the IIS_IUSRS group. The following Appcmd syntax configures DefaultAppPool for manual IIS_IUSRS group membership.

```
appcmd set apppool "DefaultAppPool" /processModel.manualGroupMembership:True
```

Direct from the Source: Using Application Pools to Sandbox Applications

The application pool is the fundamental unit of isolation for IIS applications, because it sandboxes the application code in a separate IIS worker process and allows sandboxing external access from resources within the process by applying access control lists (ACLs) to the application pool identity as well as granting or denying access to the application pool identity. Using application pools makes it possible to achieve a more thorough level of isolation between applications on the same server than is possible with any other technique, including impersonation or ASP.NET partial trust sandboxing.

IIS 7.0 goes further, enabling the application pool to be effectively used for isolation scenarios. It does this by automatically providing a unique account security identifier (SID) for each application pool so that the SID can be used in securing the resources with ACLs for that application pool. Windows Process Activation Service (also known as WAS) automatically creates this SID and therefore does not require you to create and use custom application pool identities. Moreover, IIS 7.0 also automatically isolates the global server configuration, by generating filtered copy of applicationHost.config configuration file for each application pool that contains only the configuration applicable to the application pool and does not retain configuration for other application pools such as their application pool definitions and identity information.

Combined with the increased worker process density, these improvements make it easier than before to create truly sandboxed application environments through the use of application pools.

Mike Volodarsky

IIS Core Program Manager

Configuring Application Pool Identity

Although NetworkService is an account with reduced access privileges, you might change the worker process identity due to your business needs. For example, a security application might require access to system resources for which NetworkService does not have the necessary permissions. In this case, you can run the worker process from a custom account with necessary access rights. Chapter 14 discusses managing application pool identity with respect to security.

To use IIS Manager to configure application pool identity, expand the IIS computer node in the Connections pane and navigate to the Application Pools node. In the Application Pools display pane, select the application pool for which you want to change the identity account. Then click Advanced Settings in the Actions pane. In the Process Model section of the Advanced Settings dialog box, select the Identity property and then click the browse button (...) to display the Application Pool Identity dialog box, shown in Figure 10-6.

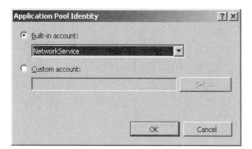

Figure 10-6 Configuring application pool identity by using IIS Manager.

Caution When changing the application pool identity, IIS 7.0 shuts down the current worker process if it is running and initiates a new worker process with the selected user identity. This impacts the availability of the application, and session details are lost during the application pool changes.

Use the following Appcmd syntax and the parameters shown in Table 10-7 to configure application pool identity.

```
appcmd set apppool ApppoolName /processModel.identityType:enum
/processModel.userName:string /processModel.password:string
```

Table 10-7 Syntax for Appcmd to Configure Application Pool Identity

Parameter	Description
ApppoolName	This string represents the application pool name.
processModel.identityType	The identity type represents either built-in accounts such as LocalService, LocalSystem, NetworkService, or customer account as SpecificUser for the application pool.
processModel.userName	The user account name for the custom application pool identity.
processModel.password	The user account password for the custom application pool identity.

The following example changes the default worker process identity from NetworkService to LocalService for the "Fabrikam Stock" application pool.

```
appcmd set apppool "Fabrikam Stock"
/processModel.identityType:LocalService
```

The *identityType* enumeration is case sensitive inside the configuration store. If you enter the correct value, Appcmd executes the command successfully and returns output like this.

```
APPPOOL object "Fabrikam Stock" changed
```

If you enter an incorrect value, you will see the following error messages.

```
ERROR ( message:Unknown attribute "identityType".. Reason: Enum must
be one of LocalSystem, LocalService, NetworkService, SpecificUser. )
```

To configure a custom application worker process identity, enter *SpecificUser* as the *identityType* attribute value. Then specify the user credentials by using the *userName* and *password* properties.

```
appcmd set apppool /apppool.name:"Fabrikam Stock"
/processModel.identityType:SpecificUser
/processModel.userName:"MyAppUsr"
/processModel.password:"passw@rd1"
```

The preceding example configures the MyAppUsr user account as the Fabrikam Stock application pool identity and specifies the account password as passw@rd1.

IIS updates changes in application pool identity in the *<applicationPools>* section in the applicationHost.config file. The element value includes the name of the application pool, the worker process model, and the process identity, if it is different from the default settings. The following shows the *<applicationPools>* configuration of the custom worker process identity configured for Fabrikam Stock application pool.

```
<applicationPools>
...
    <add name="Fabrikam Stock" managedRuntimeVersion="V1.1"
        managedPipelineMode="Classic">
        <processModel identityType="SpecificUser" userName="MyAppUsr"
password="[enc:AesProvider:oGSyoej3RKswi3gsrYarpbMQrxOrVIY6nFHkPmjQAhE=
:enc]/>
    </add>
    ...
</applicationPools>
```

Advanced Application Pool Configuration

Though IIS 7.0 application pool configuration is similar to IIS 6.0, the configuration UI has been reorganized together with the new IIS Manager. All settings are now visible and configurable in the UI. Most configuration settings are the same as in IIS 6.0, such as application recycle options and rapid failed protection. This section discusses some key configurations that are new to IIS 7.0.

Enabling User Profile Loading

A typical Web application includes both reading and writing data in the application logic, and typically Web applications require read and write access to the Windows temporary directory, *%Temp%*. Consider, for example, an ASP application uses a Microsoft Access database. In IIS 6.0, by design, the operating system grants read and write access to the temporary directory to all users, including the worker processes account, regardless of the process identity. Although this default behavior in IIS 6.0 enables Web applications to run perfectly without any issues, it has security implications, because all worker processes are sharing the same temporary directory.

To better address the security risk, IIS 7.0 grants you the ability to load the user account profile during worker process startup. This provides a separate environment with different temporary folders for each process identity. However, by default, the temporary directory of the process identity is only accessible by the process account. For a Web application that requires access to a temporary directory, you need to grant access to those related user accounts. By default, user profile loading is disabled in IIS 7.0, so it behaves like IIS 6.0. When user profile is enabled, it may break some applications such as those that use the Microsoft Access databases. This is because the default application pool identity, NetworkService, does not have access to the Temp directory that the Access database engine requires.

Note By design, user profile loading is enabled in Windows Vista, but the setting is disabled in Windows Server 2008 and Windows Vista Service Pack 1 (SP1). It is also important to remember that user profile loading is configurable per application pool.

After installing Windows Vista SP1 and reinstalling IIS 7.0, the *loadUserProfile* setting is disabled by default.

To use IIS Manager to enable user profiles in IIS 7.0, expand the IIS computer node in the Connections pane and navigate to the Application Pools node. In the Application Pools display pane, select the application pool for which you want to change user profile loading and then click Advanced Settings in the Actions pane. In the Process Model section of the Advanced Settings dialog box, click the Load User Profile property and select True in the drop-down list, as shown in Figure 10-7.

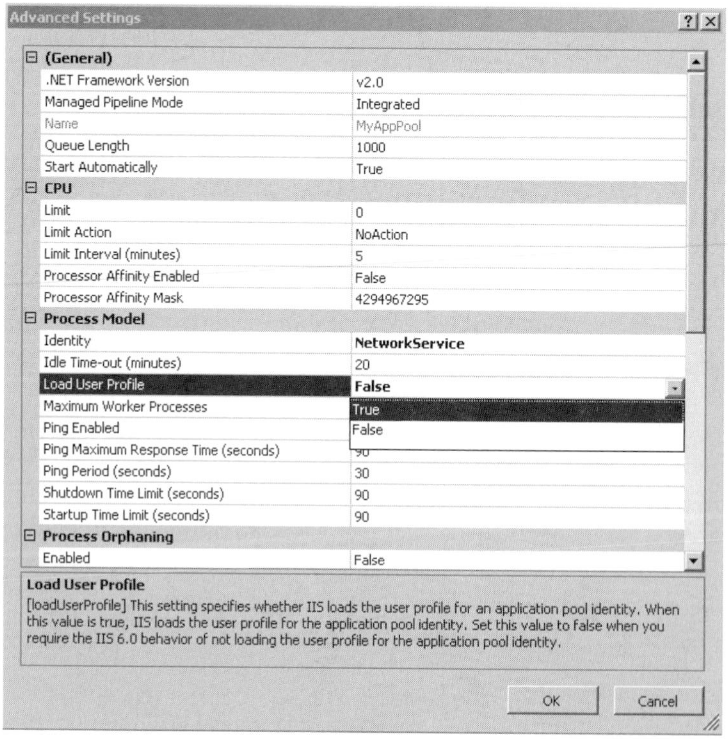

Advanced Settings	? X
(General)	
.NET Framework Version	v2.0
Managed Pipeline Mode	Integrated
Name	MyAppPool
Queue Length	1000
Start Automatically	True
CPU	
Limit	0
Limit Action	NoAction
Limit Interval (minutes)	5
Processor Affinity Enabled	False
Processor Affinity Mask	4294967295
Process Model	
Identity	NetworkService
Idle Time-out (minutes)	20
Load User Profile	False
Maximum Worker Processes	True
Ping Enabled	False
Ping Maximum Response Time (seconds)	90
Ping Period (seconds)	30
Shutdown Time Limit (seconds)	90
Startup Time Limit (seconds)	90
Process Orphaning	
Enabled	False

Load User Profile
[loadUserProfile] This setting specifies whether IIS loads the user profile for an application pool identity. When this value is true, IIS loads the user profile for the application pool identity. Set this value to false when you require the IIS 6.0 behavior of not loading the user profile for the application pool identity.

OK   Cancel

Figure 10-7 Enabling user profiles by using IIS Manager.

After you have enabled the load user profile setting, you need to grant relevant user accounts access to the account profile's temporary directory, because by default, only the process identity has access to its profile directories. By default, the built-in accounts profile folder is stored in the *%systemRoot%*\ServiceProfiles\ directory. For the default worker process identity (NetworkService), the folder is located under *%systemRoot%*\ServiceProfiles\NetworkService\ AppData\Local\Temp. For more information on granting access permissions for the temporary directory, see the Microsoft Knowledge Base article at *http://support.microsoft.com/kb/ 926939/*.

Use the following Appcmd syntax and the parameters listed in Table 10-8 to enable user profile loading for an application pool.

```
appcmd set apppool "apppool name"
/processModel.loadUserProfile:Boolean
```

Table 10-8   Syntax for Appcmd to Enable User Profile Loading

Parameter	Description
apppool name	The string represents the application pool name.
processModel.loadUserProfile	Specifies if the worker process should load the user profile during startup.

The following code turns on user profile loading for the DefaulAppPool application pool.

```
appcmd set apppool /apppool.name:"DefaultAppPool"
/processModel.loadUserProfile:true
```

Upon successfully executing the command syntax, you will see the output shown in the following code. After enabling the user profile, do not forget to grant relevant account access, as discussed previously.

```
APPPOOL object "DefaultAppPool" changed
```

Like the other changes to an application pool, the user profile setting is defined together with the application pool definition in the *<applicationPools>* section of the applicationHost.config file. The attribute value *loadUserProfile* is declared with the *processModel* element. The following shows the *<applicationPools>* configuration for the DefaultAppPool user profile loading setting.

```
<applicationPools>
<add name="DefaultAppPool">
        <processModel loadUserProfile="true" />
    </add>
    <add name="Classic .NET AppPool" managedPipelineMode="Classic" />
    ...
    <applicationPoolDefaults>
        <processModel identityType="NetworkService" />
    </applicationPoolDefaults>
</applicationPools>
```

Monitoring Application Pool Recycling Events

Effective monitoring of application pool recycling events allows you to have a good understanding of the application pool's health status. It also gives you a detailed description of the event and further helps you when troubleshooting application availability. In IIS 6.0, similar event loggings are configurable via a command line tool only, and not all application pool events are captured. For example, the application pool idle shutdown event is not captured. For more information about IIS 6.0 application pool recycling events, see the Microsoft Knowledge Base article at *http://support.microsoft.com/kb/332088/*. In IIS 7.0, recycling event monitoring is now configurable using IIS Manager, including all recycling events for application pools. Table 10-9 shows the event log ID and details of each recycling event.

Table 10-9   Application Pool Recycling Events

Event/Attribute Value	Description	Event ID
Application Pool Configuration Changed (ConfigChange)	The worker processes serving application pool '%1' are being recycled due to one or more configuration changes in the application pool properties. These changes necessitate a restart of the processes.	System 5080
ISAPI Reported Unhealthy (IsapiUnhealthy)	ISAPI '%1' reported itself as unhealthy for the following reason: '%2'.	Application 2262
	ISAPI '%1' reported itself as unhealthy. No reason was given by the ISAPI.	Application 2263
Module Reported Unhealthy (ReportUnhealthy)	An application has reported being unhealthy. The worker process will now request a recycle. Reason given: %1. The data is the error.	Application 2299
Manual Recycle (OnDemand)	An administrator has requested a recycle of all worker processes in application pool '%1'.	System 5079
Private Memory Limit Exceeded (PrivateMemory)	A worker process with process ID of '%1' serving application pool '%2' has requested a recycle because it reached its private bytes memory limit.	System 5117
Regular Time Interval (Time)	A worker process with process ID of '%1' serving application pool '%2' has requested a recycle because it reached its allowed processing time limit.	System 5074
Request Limit Exceeded (Requests)	A worker process with process ID of '%1' serving application pool '%2' has requested a recycle because it reached its allowed request limit.	System 5075
Specific Time (Schedule)	A worker process with process ID of '%1' serving application pool '%2' has requested a recycle because it reached its scheduled recycle time.	System 5076
Virtual Memory Limit Exceeded (Memory)	A worker process with process ID of '%1' serving application pool '%2' has requested a recycle because it reached its virtual memory limit.	System 5077

In the case of worker process idle shutdown (default is 20 minutes), WAS writes the following event log.

```
Event ID: 5186
Detail: A worker process with process id of '%1' serving application
pool '%2' was shutdown due to inactivity. Application Pool
timeout configuration was set to %3 minutes. A new worker process will be
started when needed.
```

By default, the following recycling events are turned on:

- Private Memory Limit Exceeded (default value 0 [kb], no limit)

- Regular Time Interval (default value 1740 [minutes], 29 hours)

- Virtual Memory Limit Exceeded (default value 0 [kb], no limit)

To enable more application pool recycling events by using IIS Manager, expand the IIS computer node in the Connections pane and then navigate to the Application Pools node. In the Application Pools display pane, select the application pool for which you want to enable recycling events. Then click Advanced Settings in the Actions pane. In the Advanced Settings dialog box, scroll down to the Recycling section, expand the Generate Recycle Event Log Entry node, click the appropriate event log entry option, and select True in the drop-down list to enable logging for that event (see Figure 10-8).

Note   You need to configure all relevant properties to capture the recycling event log. For example, if you enable the Request Limit Exceeded option, you must specify a limit for the Request Limit property. Otherwise, the default value of 0 indicates there is no request limit configured for the application pool, and an event log will not be generated, because there is no limit to check against.

Use the following Appcmd syntax and the parameters in Table 10-10 to configure logging for various application pool recycling events.

```
appcmd set apppool "ApppoolName"
/recycling.logEventOnRecycle: flags
```

Table 10-10   Syntax for Appcmd to Configure Logging for Recycling Events

Parameter	Description
ApppoolName	The string represents the application pool name.
recycling.logEventOnRecyle	Specifies the recycling event options. The flags include Time, Requests, Schedule, Memory, IsapiUnhealthy, OnDemand, ConfigChange, and PrivateMemory.

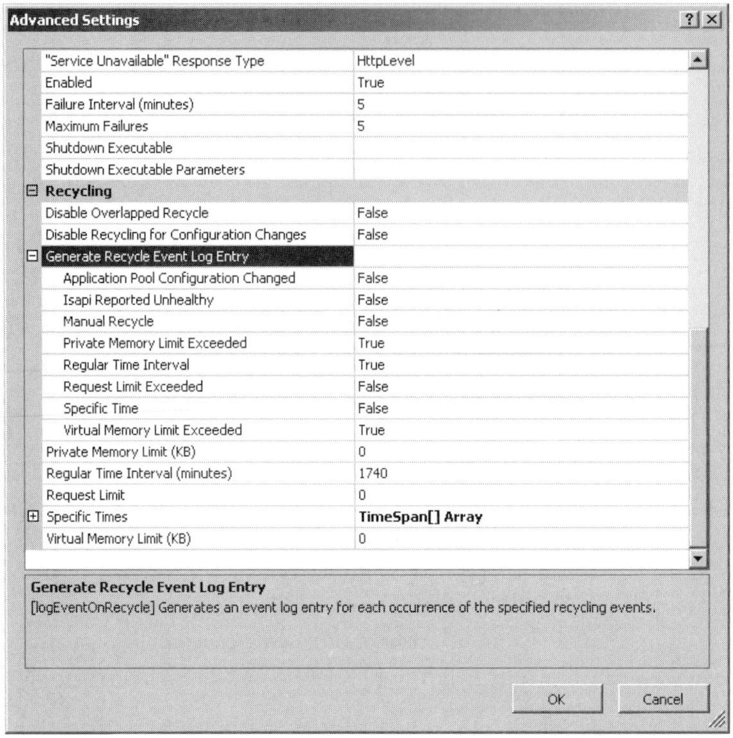

Figure 10-8 Enabling application recycling events by using IIS Manager.

The following syntax enables all recycling event logs for the DefaulAppPool application pool.

```
appcmd set apppool "DefaultAppPool"
/recycling.logEventOnRecycle:"Time, Requests, Schedule, Memory,
IsapiUnhealthy, OnDemand, ConfigChange, PrivateMemory"
```

To disable all event logging, simply remove all attribute flag values. For example, the following command disables all recycling events for the Test application pool.

```
appcmd set apppool "Test" /recycling.logEventOnRecycle:""
```

As noted previously, it is important that you configure relevant settings when you are enabling application pool recycling event logging. For example, you must limit the number of requests for a particular application pool so that you can generate an event log when worker processes for the application pool recycle after hitting the request limit. The following syntax sets the request limit to 500 and enables Request Limit Exceeded event logging for the Test application pool.

```
appcmd set apppool "Test"
/recycling.periodicRestart.requests:500
/recycling.logEventOnRecycle:"Requests"
```

Notice the */recycling.periodicRestart* parameter. All application pool recycling options are configured under this element. It includes the following nodes for setting the application pool recycling options: *.memory* for virtual memory limits, *.privateMemory* for private memory limits, *.schedule* for regular time intervals, and *.time* for specific time intervals.

Similar to the other changes in an application pool, application pool recycling event loggings are defined with the application pool definition in the *<applicationPools>* section in the applicationHost.config file. The event log entry type is declared in the *<recycling>* element, and limits or restrictions for each setting are defined in the *<periodicRestart>* subelement. The following shows the *<applicationPools>* configuration that results from the previous example.

```
<applicationPools>
<add name="DefaultAppPool">
        <recycling logEventOnRecycle="Requests">
            <periodicRestart request="500" />
        </recycling>
    </add>
    <add name="Classic .NET AppPool" managedPipelineMode="Classic" />
    <applicationPoolDefaults>
        <processModel identityType="NetworkService" />
    </applicationPoolDefaults>
</applicationPools>
```

Managing Worker Processes and Requests

The worker process is the heart and soul of Web applications in IIS 7.0. The worker process runs in W3WP.exe and is responsible for processing application requests. In IIS 6.0, worker processes are managed by the World Wide Web Publishing Service service, but in the revamped core engine of IIS 7.0, the WAS owns worker processes.

In IIS 6.0, querying worker process information such as the Process ID (PID) of currently running worker processes and its associated application pool can be done only via the command line script Iisapp.vbs. It is also not possible in IIS 6.0 to peek inside a worker process to look at current request status. Nevertheless, if you are familiar with Event Tracing for Windows (ETW), you can use IIS components as providers to send trace data and events to ETW so that you can look at the request processing details inside a worker process. Although ETW is a powerful tool for request-based tracing, it is not easy to implement, it has no user interface, and it is not really part of the IIS core architecture.

In IIS 7.0, managing worker processes has never been easier and can be done through both IIS Manager and through Appcmd. Thanks to the new core architecture, a request-based tracing feature is now built into IIS 7.0. You can now easily query current requests inside a particular worker process with a few mouse clicks in IIS Manager. Alternatively, you can simply use Appcmd to query the run-time status. Available details include the HTTP verb of the particular request, requested resource name, the processing state of the request, and the module that is currently processing the request.

Monitoring Worker Processes and Requests

Monitoring worker processes gives you a good picture about overall Web server resource usage. You can also use the information to stop a bad worker process that constantly uses all CPU resources or to shut down a bad application pool in which worker processes have long-running requests. To use IIS Manager to query current worker processes and request status, click the IIS computer node in the Connections pane and then double-click Worker Processes in the Features View pane. The Worker Processes page is shown in Figure 10-9.

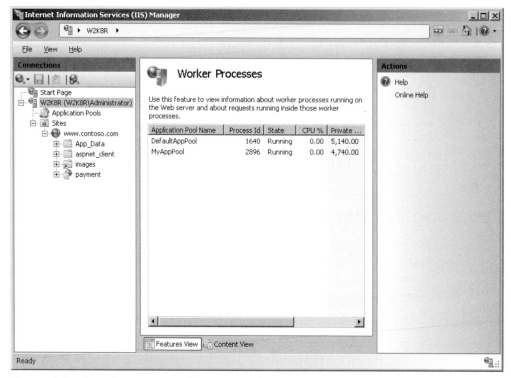

Figure 10-9   Querying current worker processes by using IIS Manager.

To see a list of currently running worker processes, select a worker process in the grid view and click View Current Requests in the Actions pane. Alternatively, right-click a worker process and select View Current Requests. The Requests page is shown in Figure 10-10.

Use the following Appcmd syntax to display a list of worker processes.

```
appcmd list wp PID /apppool.name:string
```

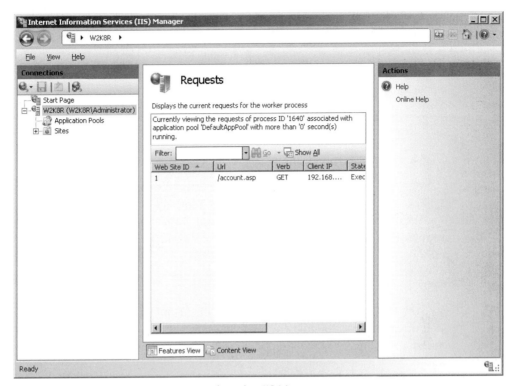

Figure 10-10   Viewing current requests by using IIS Manager.

The commonly used parameters are listed in Table 10-11.

Table 10-11   Syntax for Appcmd to List Worker Processes

Parameter	Description
PID	The process ID for the worker process to list. If omitted, lists all worker processes.
apppool.name	The application pool name for which to show the worker processes.

You can then use the following Appcmd syntax to display a list of currently executing requests.

```
appcmd list request RequestId /apppool.name:string
/elapsed:integer /site.name:string /wp.name:integer
```

The commonly used parameters are listed in Table 10-12.

Table 10-12   Syntax for Appcmd to List Executing Requests

Parameter	Description
RequestId	The unique identifier of the request, if known. If omitted, lists all requests.
apppool.name	The application pool name to filter by.
elapsed	The amount of processing time in milliseconds to filter by.
site.name	The name of the Web site to filter by. Alternatively, specify a Web site ID via /site.id.
wp.name	The integer represents the process ID of a particular worker process to filter by.

When using Appcmd to query worker process information, the output is not as comprehensive as the list of worker processes in IIS Manager. Appcmd displays only the process ID and the application pool name that the worker process is serving. To list all worker processes in an IIS 7.0 server, use the following command.

```
appcmd list wp
```

If any Web applications are running, the preceding command will list the currently running worker processes. For example, the following shows three worker processes are running, each serving a different application pool.

```
WP "1120" (applicationPool:DefaultAppPool)
WP "3918" (applicationPool:MyAppPool)
WP "3320" (applicationPool:Fabrikam Stock)
```

> **Note**   The Runtime Status and Control Data and Objects (RSCA) inside the IIS Web server core engine provide run-time data for worker processes.

To query the worker process details for a particular application pool, use the following command.

```
appcmd list wp /apppool.name:"DefaultAppPool"
```

In a Web garden setup where more than one worker process is serving the same application pool, you might see the following output, because three different worker processes are serving the DefaultAppPool application pool.

```
WP "1951" (applicationPool:DefaultAppPool)
WP "3593" (applicationPool:DefaultAppPool)
WP "3039" (applicationPool:DefaultAppPool)
```

To list all worker processes belonging to a Web site, you would first list all applications belonging to the Web site and then redirect the results to another query. For example, the following command lists worker processes belonging to Contoso Corp.

```
appcmd list app /site.name:"Contoso Corp" /xml |
appcmd list wp /in
```

Assuming two running application pools (DefaultAppPool and MyAppPool) are currently assigned to Contoso Corp.'s applications, the output lists two worker processes together with their details.

```
WP "1120" (applicationPool:DefaultAppPool)
WP "3918" (applicationPool:MyAppPool)
```

To find out the Web applications or application pools in which a particular worker process is serving, use the following command.

```
appcmd list wp "1120" /xml | appcmd list app /in
```

As shown in the preceding code, the first part of the command lists, in XML format, the worker process details including the application pool name. Sample output for this intermediate step is shown here.

```
<?xml version="1.0" encoding="UTF-8"?>
<appcmd>
    <WP WP.NAME="1120" APPPOOL.NAME="DefaultAppPool" />
</appcmd>
```

The XML output is then piped as input to the second part of the command, which lists all applications belonging to the application pool. The following shows the final output of the previous full command when root applications of both Contoso Corp. and Fabrikam HR are running in the DefaultAppPool application pool.

```
APP "Contoso Corp/" (applicationPool:DefaultAppPool)
APP "Fabrikam HR/" (applicationPool:DefaultAppPool)
```

To peek inside a worker process and look at currently executing requests, you can use the *LIST* verb and query against a *REQUEST* object via Appcmd. For example, the using the following syntax displays all currently executing requests on an IIS 7.0 Web server.

```
appcmd list request
```

The resulting output, shown in the following syntax, indicates that IIS is currently processing three ASP requests.

```
REQUEST "f80000008000000e" (url:GET /profile.asp, time:330 msec,
client:10.10.29.12, stage:ExecuteRequestHandler, module:IsapiModule)
REQUEST "f80000008000000f" (url:POST /loginform.asp, time:123 msec,
client:10.11.3.99, stage:ExecuteRequestHandler, module:IsapiModule)
REQUEST "f800000080000010" (url:GET /account.asp, time:200 msec,
client:10.10.29.88, stage:ExecuteRequestHandler, module:IsapiModule)
```

You can use the */text:** parameter to display all of the returned requests' attributes, which will contain more useful information than is displayed in the friendly view shown previously.

To list current requests for a particular application pool, use the following.

```
appcmd list request /apppool.name:"DefaultAppPool"
```

Alternatively, to display current requests in terms of processing time for the Contoso Corp. Web site with processing time longer than 60 seconds, use the following.

```
appcmd list request /elapsed:"$>60000" /site.name:"Contoso Corp"
```

Querying a *REQUEST* object gives you real-time information about current processing requests, and it can help to identify long-running queries to assist in application troubleshooting. For example, the following command lists the relevant worker processes of all application pools with long-running requests (requests for which processing took more than 60 seconds) and recycles the application pools.

```
appcmd list request /time:"$>60000"
/xml | appcmd list apppool /in /xml | appcmd recycle apppool /in
```

Take note of the previous syntax. Although it increases the application availability by recycling the application pool, existing requests and session details are lost during the recycling event. To avoid session variable loss, we recommend that you use out-of-process session management for your Web application. Although this request-based tracing via the *REQUEST* object gives you real-time information, it does not give you complete event information inside the request processing. To further troubleshoot the bad request, enable the Failed Request Tracing Rules feature so that you can capture detailed event notification inside the processing pipeline. For more information about the Failed Request Tracing Rules feature, see Chapter 16, "Tracing and Troubleshooting."

Summary

The Web application is a first-class concept in IIS 7.0, defining a container of functionality for IIS 7.0 Web sites. You can create and manage applications to control the execution parameters for your Web site's functionality. You can also isolate applications by associating them with an application pool. For reliability and security purposes, the application pool continues to be the mechanism for isolating application execution.

In this chapter, you reviewed the basic tasks for creating and managing IIS applications and application pools, as well as for using tools to monitor their operation.

Be sure to read Chapter 14 to learn more about using application pools to properly sandbox and reduce the privilege of Web applications. For more information on configuring application frameworks for your applications, see Chapter 11.

Additional Resources

These resources contain additional information and tools related to this chapter:

■ Chapter 4, "Understanding the Configuration System," provides information about the new XML-based configuration system and important configuration files in IIS 7.0.

■ Chapter 9, "Managing Web Sites," includes information about managing Web sites and virtual directories in IIS 7.0.

■ Chapter 11, "Hosting Application Development Frameworks," has information about configuring various application framework support such as ASP, ASP.NET, and CGI application in IIS 7.0.

■ Chapter 14, "Implementing Security Strategies," provides information about customizing application pools from a security perspective, as well as other security considerations in securing IIS 7.0.

■ Chapter 16, "Tracing and Troubleshooting," gives information about enabling Failed Request Event Tracing in IIS 7.0 and understanding the tracing log file.

■ Web Capacity Analysis Tool (WCAT) is a free tool from Microsoft to perform capacity analysis on an IIS Web server. To download this tool, visit *http://www.iis.net/ downloads/default.aspx?tabid=34&g=6&i=1466*.

■ Article 332088, "How to Modify Application Pool Recycling Events in IIS 6.0" in the Microsoft Knowledge Base provides information about configuring IIS 6.0 application pool recycling event monitoring. To view this article, see *http://support.microsoft.com/ kb/332088*.

■ Article 926939, "Error Message when You Request an ASP Page That Connects to an Access Database in IIS 7.0" in the Microsoft Knowledge Base has information about Access database issues that relate to *loadUserProfile* settings in IIS 7.0. To find this article, go to *http://support.microsoft.com/kb/926939*.

Chapter 11
Hosting Application Development Frameworks

On the Disc   Browse the CD for additional tools and resources.

IIS as an Application Development Platform

Internet Information Services (IIS), like many other Web server technologies, originally began as a way to serve static files, such as HTML documents and images, to browser clients using the HTTP protocol. As the needs of Web site applications evolved to include dynamic content, IIS added support for a simplistic Common Gateway Interface (CGI), which supported dynamic generation of Web content by executing programs. These programs, which were usually built with C or C++, had little or no framework support for building Web applications.

The Web of today is much different, with a multitude of development frameworks and applications environments for building dynamic Web applications, including Active Server Pages (ASP), PHP HyperText Processor (PHP), Perl, Python, Flash Server, Java Servlets, and ASP.NET. These frameworks absorb most of the complexity of developing Web applications, and they also offer rich libraries and controls to build immersive user experiences and implement key functions such as managing session state, accessing databases, personalizing content, and more.

IIS has also evolved with the Web into a platform for hosting a multitude of application development framework technologies. IIS 3.0 introduced the ASP scripting environment, which has been very popular for building Windows-based dynamic server applications (the latest version of ASP was 3.0, released with IIS 5.0). Starting with IIS 5.0 in Windows 2000, the .NET Framework 1.0 release introduced support for ASP.NET, which has since become the premier Web application development framework for Windows. Meanwhile, the IIS Internet Server Application Programming Interface (ISAPI) extension model has enabled other application frameworks, including PHP and Perl, to find their way to the IIS environment.

Besides hosting Web application frameworks on the Windows platform, the IIS environment provides significant added value. It provides a fault-tolerant model for hosting these applications in the context of IIS Web sites and application pools, ensuring their reliable execution and availability. This model also enables large numbers of applications to be hosted on the same server and forms the foundation for isolating those applications from each other so that they cannot affect each other's execution or access each other's content. Because this is done at the IIS level, the model provides a unified mechanism for administrators to deploy application content and manage associated configuration, all using a single set of tools and technologies.

In addition to this, IIS implements a wide array of request processing functionality, including authentication, secure communication with Secure Sockets Layer (SSL), response compression, request logging, and many others. When hosted in IIS, Web applications get the majority of this functionality for free regardless of the application framework technology.

> **Note**   For an overview of Web server improvements that benefit applications on IIS 7.0, be sure to read Chapter 1, "Introducing IIS 7.0."

IIS 7.0 takes the concept of an application server to a new level. First, it adds a powerful modular extensibility model that enables the server itself to be extended by replacing any part of its built-in feature set or adding new functionality. It also offers the ability to extend the server with the .NET Framework, through the use of the Integrated ASP.NET platform. This enables powerful new interoperation scenarios, including the ability to protect your entire Web site with ASP.NET Forms–based authentication even if your site uses other application framework technologies. These improvements make IIS 7.0 a much more compelling development platform and enable developers to easily enhance the functionality of any Web application regardless of the application framework technology. Second, the extensibility improvements also make it significantly easier for developers to interface new application frameworks to IIS 7.0 by leveraging its core extensibility platform.

Taking this further, IIS 7.0 expands built-in support for new Web application frameworks by enabling the FastCGI protocol. Many third-party application frameworks use the FastCGI protocol, including PHP and Ruby on Rails. FastCGI provides a more reliable and higher-performance way to host these applications than when using CGI programs or ISAPI extensions. In fact, during the Windows Server 2008 development cycle, the IIS team has worked directly with Zend and the PHP community to bring reliable PHP hosting to the IIS platform by using the FastCGI protocol. Following the success of the PHP initiative, the near future should no doubt show even more third-party application frameworks providing premier support for the IIS platform.

Adding Support for Application Frameworks

The IIS 7.0 default install enables the bare minimum of functionality required for a static file Web server. Following a default install, the Web server is capable of serving static files, such as HTML or images, directly to the client without performing any dynamic processing. This functionality is supported by the IIS 7.0 Static File module, which is configured to serve a set of known static files whose extensions are listed in the IIS MIME Type configuration.

After the default installation, if you attempt to deploy additional application content to the Web server, one of the following situations may happen when this content is requested:

■ The requested resource has an extension recognized as a static file based on the Web server's static content configuration. This resource will be served as-is to the client.

■ The requested resource is not recognized as a static file. The Static File module will reject the request with the 404.3 Not Found error, shown in Figure 11-1 (when you request the file remotely, you'll see a generic 404 error by default due to custom error security).

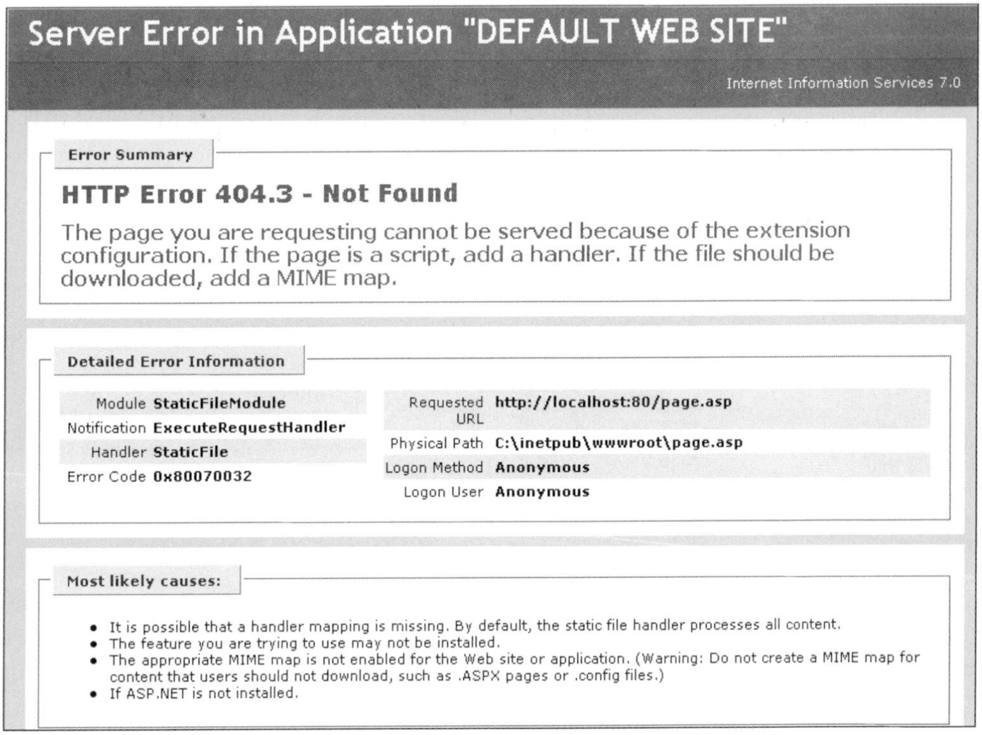

Figure 11-1   A 404.3 error indicating that the extension is not recognized as a static file.

The error shown in Figure 11-1 is what you can expect to receive whenever content that is not recognized by the Web server is requested. This is done to prevent resources unknown to the Web server from being served out as static files. If the resources unknown to the Web server *were* served out, it could result in undesired disclosure of application source code or other unservable resources. To address this error, you will need to do one of the following:

- If the resource is a static file, register its extension and corresponding MIME type to enable it to be served.

- If the resource is a script or another application resource that requires it to be dynamically processed by an application framework, you will need to install this application framework and configure a handler mapping to map the application framework to the desired content.

The rest of this chapter describes how to install and configure common application frameworks—including ASP, ASP.NET, and PHP—and also the general techniques you can use to configure other application frameworks.

To learn more about enabling new content types to be served as static files, see the section titled "Enabling New Static File Extensions to Be Served" later in this chapter.

Supported Application Frameworks

By retaining support for legacy ISAPI extensions as well as CGI programs, IIS 7.0 continues to support all of the application framework technologies that work with previous versions of IIS. In addition, IIS 7.0 provides the FastCGI protocol, which enables frameworks such as PHP, Python, and others to be hosted in the IIS environment. Table 11-1 lists some of the application frameworks that are officially supported in IIS 7.0 today (that is, those that the IIS team has tested).

Table 11-1   Supported Application Frameworks

Framework	Supported Versions	Integration Model
ASP.NET	ASP.NET 1.1, ASP.NET 2.0, and future versions	Classic (ISAPI extension): ASP.NET 1.1, ASP.NET 2.0
		Integrated: ASP.NET 2.0+
ASP	ASP 3.0	ISAPI extension
PHP	PHP 4.4.6+, PHP 5.2.1+ for FastCGI, PHP 3.0+ for ISAPI and CGI modes	FastCGI (recommended)
		ISAPI extension (not recommended for production environments)

ASP.NET has a special place among these application frameworks, because it features the new integration mode that enables you to use ASP.NET to extend the IIS Web server in managed code. This effectively makes ASP.NET the .NET extensibility model for developing IIS features and enables existing ASP.NET features to be used in framework-neutral fashion to benefit any

IIS application framework. You can read more about the changes in ASP.NET support that enable this, and how to leverage them, later in this chapter.

In addition to the frameworks listed in Table 11-1, many third-party application frameworks provide support for IIS by using the legacy ISAPI extension mechanism. This includes Cold Fusion, Perl, Python, and Tcl. The FastCGI protocol support enables many open source frameworks that work on Apache and other Web servers to also work on IIS, including Ruby on Rails and several others. They are not listed in Table 11-1 because at the time of writing, the IIS team had not officially tested them. Many of these application frameworks do work successfully on IIS 7.0, and others may have specific issues that will be addressed in upcoming versions so that they will work correctly. The IIS team is planning to engage many of the vendors and communities that build these application technologies to ensure that they work in the IIS environment and are able to effectively leverage the features of the IIS platform.

In this chapter, we will focus on deploying the ASP.NET, ASP, and PHP applications in IIS 7.0 and discuss specific considerations pertaining to hosting these frameworks. At the end of the chapter, we also discuss techniques for hosting additional frameworks on IIS 7.0 that can be used to plan deployment of existing and future application frameworks on IIS 7.0.

Hosting ASP.NET Applications

ASP.NET has been the application framework platform of choice for developing rich Web applications for an IIS environment. IIS 7.0 takes this further by integrating ASP.NET 2.0 with its request processing pipeline. This elevates ASP.NET from being an application framework that sits on top of the Web server to being a full-fidelity .NET API for extending the Web server at its core.

This design brings multiple benefits to the IIS 7.0 platform. First, it enables the modular Web server features to be developed with the power of the .NET Framework and the rich features of ASP.NET. Second, it enables many of the existing ASP.NET application services to be used on the Web server in a framework-neutral way, for both ASP.NET and other application frameworks. Thus, server administrators can, for example, apply a single set of authentication, session state, and other ASP.NET features uniformly across an entire Web site that may is using any application framework.

> ### Direct from the Source: Maintaining Backwards Compatibility With ASP.NET Applications
>
> To enable ASP.NET integration, we had to rebuild the ASP.NET 2.0 engine from scratch. The new architecture necessitated many design changes regarding how ASP.NET works on IIS 7.0 underneath the covers, and how ASP.NET applications are configured. These changes promised to significantly impact the compatibility with existing ASP.NET applications.

However, we also wanted to make sure that existing ASP.NET applications continued to work correctly using the new ASP.NET integration mode. Maintaining backwards compatibility was a key design and implementation goal for the ASP.NET integrated pipeline, and it proved to be a major challenge during the development of the project.

In the end, this goal was largely achieved in IIS 7.0. However, certain deployment and development considerations impact the behavior of ASP.NET applications on IIS 7.0. When faced with these changes, keep in mind that they were necessary in order to support the new levels of functionality for ASP.NET applications and the Web server in general. For the majority of these changes, simple workarounds exist that can allow your application to leverage the benefits of Integrated mode. In a few cases, you may opt to configure your application to run in Classic mode, in order to avoid these breaking changes—however, in doing so, you will lose the ability to leverage the many improvements granted by the Integrated mode.

Mike Volodarsky

IIS Core Program Manager

In the remainder of this section, we will discuss the key conceptual changes in how ASP.NET works on IIS 7.0 to facilitate the twofold goal of enabling the new level of Web server extensibility and maintaining compatibility with existing ASP.NET applications.

Understanding the Integrated and Classic ASP.NET Modes

IIS 7.0 offers two modes for hosting ASP.NET applications: Integrated and Classic. The Integrated mode is the new mode, providing tight integration with the IIS Web server and enabling ASP.NET services to be used as application framework–neutral Web server features. This mode is the default mode on IIS 7.0 and maintains backward compatibility with existing ASP.NET applications in the majority of cases. Existing ASP.NET applications may require some configuration changes to work correctly with Integrated mode, and the server automatically detects most of these and provides migration support to prepare the application for Integrated mode in a single step. We will discuss migration in detail later in this chapter.

The Classic mode provides an option to run ASP.NET applications in the same way as they have been in previous versions of IIS. The Classic mode does not offer any of the additional benefits provided by Integrated mode. It is intended as a fallback option for those ASP.NET applications that are impacted by specific breaking changes in Integrated mode.

Note   Do not confuse the ASP.NET Integration modes (Integrated and Classic) with the IIS worker process isolation mode. They are two completely different concepts. IIS 7.0 supports only the IIS 6.0 Worker Process Isolation Mode and no longer supports the IIS 5.0 Isolation Mode. ASP.NET always runs in-process regardless of the ASP.NET integration mode.

The differences between the two ASP.NET Integration modes are illustrated in Figure 11-2. In Classic mode, ASP.NET integrates with IIS as an ISAPI extension that processes those requests mapped only to itself. As such, it provides a duplicate request processing pipeline for ASP.NET requests. In Integrated mode, the ASP.NET features provided by ASP.NET modules and handlers plug into the main IIS request processing pipeline, eliminating duplication and executing for all requests to the server.

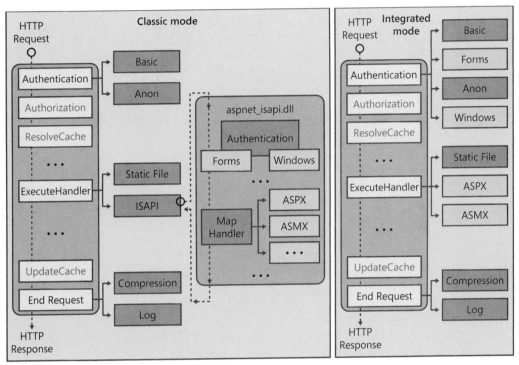

Figure 11-2   ASP.NET integration in IIS 7.0.

Integrated mode offers several key advantages—for both the existing ASP.NET applications and for new ASP.NET applications—that make Integrated mode the preferred mode of operation on IIS 7.0 and beyond:

- ASP.NET application services can be used uniformly across the entire Web site, instead of being limited to ASP.NET content only. This includes such ASP.NET features as Forms authentication, Roles, Output Caching, and any custom ASP.NET services provided by modules that are part of the application. This feature also reduces management complexity because a single set of functionality can be managed for the entire Web site.
- It makes it possible to develop modules that provide core Web server features in managed code by using ASP.NET instead of using low-level C++ interfaces. This dramatically reduces the amount of time needed to develop and deploy new server functionality.
- Key ASP.NET and IIS configurations are unified, making it easier to manage the application.
- For shared server environments, such as shared hosting servers or departmental servers, the administrator can allow applications to provide key Web server functionality by using managed modules without requiring administrative privileges or by having to install Web server features globally on the server.

> **Note**   Integrated mode is not required to store IIS and ASP.NET configuration settings in the same web.config files. It is also not required to leverage new IIS 7.0 features such as URL Authorization and Output Caching. These capabilities are part of the Web server platform and do not depend on the ASP.NET integration mode.

IIS 7.0 supports running ASP.NET applications that use both Integrated and Classic mode on the same server, enabling the ASP.NET integration mode to be selected for each application pool. This makes it easy to run most ASP.NET applications by using the default Integrated mode and to place the applications that experience difficulties into Classic mode. We will discuss selecting the integration mode for applications in detail later in the chapter.

Even if your application does not immediately take advantage of Integrated mode, it is highly recommended to run it using Integrated mode—even in cases in which it may require specific code changes. This is because using Integrated mode ensures that the application is prepared for using Integrated mode-specific Web server features that are available today and/or will be available in the future. In addition, future releases of IIS may remove support for Classic mode. Therefore, any steps you can take today toward removing Classic mode dependencies will make it easier to migrate to new versions of IIS in the future. Classic mode is intended more as a temporary mechanism to enable applications to move to IIS 7.0, rather then as a long-term option.

Running Multiple Versions of ASP.NET Side by Side

Historically, IIS has always supported using multiple versions of ASP.NET side by side to host ASP.NET applications that target different versions of the .NET Framework. This has been supported through mapping the Aspnet_isapi.dll ISAPI extension from the correct .NET Framework version directory to ASP.NET content types for each application. For example, the following script map would result in ASP.NET 2.0 being used to process requests to .aspx pages.

```
.aspx,E:\WINDOWS\Microsoft.NET\Framework\v2.0.50727\
aspnet_isapi.dll,1,GET,HEAD,POST,DEBUG
```

Administrators often used the Aspnet_regiis.exe tool located in the *%systemRoot%*Microsoft.NET\Framework*version* directory to install ASP.NET on previous versions of IIS by creating handler mappings for the corresponding version, either on the entire server or for a specific application. By using this tool, administrators could create script maps for different versions of ASP.NET for each ASP.NET application, and thereby run different ASP.NET versions side by side.

However, this approach was prone to common misconfigurations that resulted in some of the most common problems reported to the ASP.NET Product Support Team. The most infamous one occurred when two applications using different versions of ASP.NET were placed in a single application pool. Because only one version of the common language run time (CLR) is supported per process, the application that happened to be requested second would fail to load. This would result in unexpected and nondeterministic failures.

IIS 7.0 changes the ASP.NET versioning mechanism to be more deterministic by officially recognizing that only one version of ASP.NET can be used in each IIS worker process. Therefore, in IIS 7.0, the version of ASP.NET that is used is explicitly configured for each IIS application pool by using the *managedRuntimeVersion* configuration attribute. The ASP.NET handler mappings are not used to select the version. Instead, ASP.NET setup registers them globally on the server and configures them to use the version preconditions so that they are automatically selected in each application pool based on its configured CLR version. Following is an excerpt from the *system.webServer/handlers* configuration section when both ASP.NET v1.1 and v2.0 are installed.

```
<add name="ASPNET-ISAPI-1.1-PageHandlerFactory" path="*.aspx"
verb="GET,HEAD,POST,DEBUG" modules="IsapiModule"
scriptProcessor="C:\Windows\Microsoft.Net\Framework\v1.1.4322\aspnet_isapi
dll" preCondition="classicMode,runtimeVersionv1.1,bitness32" />
<add name="PageHandlerFactory-Integrated" path="*.aspx"
verb="GET,HEAD,POST,DEBUG" type="System.Web.UI.PageHandlerFactory"
preCondition="integratedMode" />
<add name="PageHandlerFactory-ISAPI-2.0" path="*.aspx"
verb="GET,HEAD,POST,DEBUG" modules="IsapiModule"
scriptProcessor="%systemroot%\Microsoft.NET\Framework\v2.0.50727\
aspnet_isapi.dll" preCondition="classicMode,runtimeVersionv2.0,bitness32"/>
```

The *runtimeVersion* precondition is used to precondition the *.aspx handler mapping for a particular ASP.NET version, enabling it to be selected automatically in application pools that use the corresponding managed run-time version. Because these handler mappings are installed globally, you do not need to ever use Aspnet_regiis.exe to manually select the version of ASP.NET for an application or to manually create ASP.NET handler mappings for the right version.

By setting the *managedRuntimeVersion* configuration attribute for each IIS application pool to the desired version, you ensure that all applications in this application pool will use the correct ASP.NET version. Therefore, the application pool becomes the unit of versioning for ASP.NET applications.

Note   Do not use the Aspnet_regiis.exe tool to install and manage ASP.NET versions for your applications. Instead, use IIS application pools to select the desired version.

The *managedRuntimeVersion* configuration attribute can have the following values: *v1.1*, *v2.0*, and "" (empty). If set to (empty), no CLR version is loaded in the application pool, and ASP.NET applications in that application pool will not work.

To ensure that your application uses a particular version of ASP.NET, you can either create a new IIS application pool that is set to use the correct ASP.NET version, or you can use one of the existing IIS application pools configured with the desired version. You will find more details about selecting a preinstalled application pool to use the correct ASP.NET version in the section titled "Selecting the Right Application Pool for the Required ASP.NET Version and Integration Mode" later in this chapter.

Installing ASP.NET

Before you can host ASP.NET applications on IIS 7.0, you need to install ASP.NET. IIS 7.0 supports the following versions of the ASP.NET framework:

- **ASP.NET 2.0**   This is the default version of ASP.NET available in Windows Vista and Windows Server 2008 as part of the .NET Framework 3.0, and it can be installed using Programs And Features in Windows Vista or as a role service by using Server Manager in Windows Server 2008. ASP.NET 2.0 supports both Integrated and Classic modes.

- **ASP.NET 1.1**   Though not included in the operating system, you can download and install the .NET Framework 1.1 redistributable together with the .NET Framework 1.1 Service Pack 1 (SP1) upgrade to install ASP.NET 1.1. ASP.NET 1.1 supports only Classic mode of operation.

ASP.NET 1.0 and .NET Framework 1.0 are no longer supported. If you need to run applications that use ASP.NET 1.0, you will need to upgrade them to run using ASP.NET 1.1.

After installing ASP.NET, you will need to create an IIS 7.0 application to host your ASP.NET application. You may then also need to create a separate application pool so that you can select the Integrated or Classic ASP.NET integration mode, and you may possibly be required to migrate your application configuration so that it will run correctly in Integrated mode. We will look at these procedures in detail in the section titled "Deploying ASP.NET Applications" later in this chapter.

Installing ASP.NET 2.0

ASP.NET 2.0 can be installed using Programs And Features in Windows Vista or as a role service by using Server Manager in Windows Server 2008. The installation will perform all necessary steps to install and create required IIS configuration to run ASP.NET 2.0 in both Classic and Integrated modes. This removes the need to run the Aspnet_regiis.exe tool to register ASP.NET with IIS. In fact, you should *not* use this tool to install ASP.NET on IIS 7.0.

 Caution   *Do not use* Aspnet_regiis.exe to install ASP.NET 2.0 on IIS 7.0.

Another option is also available to you. If you do not need the full ASP.NET functionality, such as support for ASPX pages and the built-in ASP.NET handlers and modules, you do not need to install full ASP.NET support. You can install the .NET Extensibility component, which enables custom ASP.NET modules and handlers to be used on the server in Integrated mode applications. This is a good option if you are leveraging ASP.NET Integrated mode to extend other application frameworks with custom ASP.NET modules and do not use the ASP.NET application framework itself.

> **Note**   Installing the .NET Extensibility component instead of the ASP.NET component enables the use of ASP.NET handlers and modules in Integrated mode applications. It does not install the ASP.NET application framework (ASPX pages and more), and it does *not* enable Classic mode ASP.NET applications.

For more details on using Windows Setup to install IIS 7.0 components, see Chapter 5, "Installing IIS 7.0."

Installing ASP.NET 1.1

Unlike ASP.NET 2.0, ASP.NET 1.1 is not available in the operating system by default. To install it, you need to download and install the .NET Framework v1.1 redistributable and apply the .NET Framework v1.1 SP1 update. This update is required to run ASP.NET 1.1 applications.

To install ASP.NET v1.1, you need to perform the following steps:

1. Install the IIS 6 Metabase Compatibility component. This component installs the metabase compatibility APIs that ASP.NET 1.1 uses to both install itself *and* read IIS configuration at run time. You can install IIS 6 Metabase Compatibility by using Programs And Features in Windows Vista or as a role service by using Server Manager in Windows Server 2008.

2. Download and install .NET Framework v1.1 redistributable.

3. Download and install .NET Framework v1.1 SP1 update.

4. Enable the ASP.NET v1.1.4322 entry in the ISAPI and CGI restrictions. You can do this from IIS Manager, with Appcmd.exe, or as follows.

    ```
    %systemroot%\Microsoft.NET\Framework\v1.1.4322\aspnet_regiis -enable
    ```

5. Add the IgnoreSection handler for the *system.webServer* section to the Framework v1.1 machine.config file. This is necessary because ASP.NET 1.1 is not aware of the IIS 7.0 configuration that may be placed in web.config files. Add the following inside the *<configSections>* element.

    ```
    </configSections>
      ...
      <section name="system.webServer"
    type="System.Configuration.IgnoreSection" />
    </configSections>
    ```

The installation of the .NET Framework will automatically invoke Aspnet_regiis.exe −i to install ASP.NET 1.1. Windows Server 2008 and Windows Vista SP1 use an application compatibility shim to intercept the invocation of this tool and correctly generate the required configuration for IIS 7.0 to register ASP.NET v1.1. This configuration includes the following:

- ASP.NET v1.1 handler mappings, created at the server level, that are preconditioned to take effect only in application pools configured for .NET Framework v1.1.

- The "ASP.NET 1.1" application pool, which can be used by ASP.NET v1.1 applications by default. This application pool is configured to run in 32-bit mode always (even on 64-bit operating systems) and use the Classic ASP.NET integration mode.

Caution   *Do not* use the Aspnet_regiis.exe tool to install ASP.NET v1.1 on IIS 7.0 or to set any specific application to use ASP.NET v1.1. Instead, place any application that needs to use this version of ASP.NET in the provided ASP.NET 1.1 application pool or create a new application pool that uses .NET Framework v1.1. For more information, see the section titled "Running Multiple Versions of ASP.NET Side by Side" earlier in this chapter.

If creating new application pools to host ASP.NET v1.1 applications, each application pool must:

- Set the *managedRuntimeVersion* configuration attribute to v1.1.

- Set the *managedPipelineMode* configuration attribute to Classic. ASP.NET v1.1 does not support running in Integrated mode.

- Set the *enable32BitAppOnWin64* configuration attribute to true on 64-bit operating systems. ASP.NET v1.1 does not support running in native 64-bit mode.

Deploying ASP.NET Applications

After you have installed the correct version of ASP.NET, you can deploy ASP.NET applications to the server. To do this, perform the following steps:

1. Create an IIS application.

2. Place the application in the correct application pool by using the correct ASP.NET version and integration mode.

3. Deploy ASP.NET application contents.

4. Migrate ASP.NET application configuration to allow it to run in Integrated mode (this is optional, and only for ASP.NET 2.0 applications that are running in Integrated mode and that require migration).

Creating an IIS Application

Though you can deploy ASP.NET pages to any application, virtual directory, or a subdirectory thereof, you will typically want to deploy an ASP.NET application and all of its contents to a separate IIS application. This is because many associated parts of an ASP.NET application—including the Global.asax, the /BIN directory, the /App_Code directory, and other /App_ directories—require being placed in the root of an IIS application. Likewise, many ASP.NET configuration settings must be located in the application root's web.config to take effect. In addition, you will often want to isolate the contents of one ASP.NET application from another's contents because they require a different application-level configuration or use incompatible application-level state.

This requirement isn't new in IIS 7.0, though IIS 7.0 does provide a much firmer definition of an application than previous versions of IIS do. Therefore, you need to make sure that the ASP.NET application is deployed into the root virtual directory of an IIS application, and sometimes you may be required to create a new application for this purpose. You can do this from IIS Manager, or by using Appcmd as follows.

```
%systemroot%\system32\inetsrv\appcmd.exe add app "/site.name:SiteName"
"/path:VirtualPathOfApplication"
"/physicalPath:PhysicalRootDirectoryOfApplication"
```

You may also need to create a separate IIS application so that it can be placed in the appropriate application pool that uses the correct .NET Framework version and ASP.NET integration mode. We will discuss this next.

You can learn more about creating and managing applications in Chapter 10, "Managing Applications and Application Pools."

Selecting the Right Application Pool for the Required ASP.NET Version and Integration Mode

After you create the application, you will need to configure it to use an application pool that uses the correct ASP.NET version and integration mode. Unlike IIS 6.0, the version of ASP.NET that the application uses is now set at the application pool level, via the *managedRuntimeVersion* configuration attribute. This ensures a deterministic mapping between IIS worker processes and the CLR version that they load. Likewise, the ASP.NET integration mode is also set per application pool, using the *managedPipelineMode* configuration attribute. Therefore, you will need to use the desired settings to ensure that your application is placed in an application pool. Table 11-2 lists these settings.

Table 11-2   Default Application Pools for Different Versions of ASP.NET

Desired Environment	Application Pool Settings
ASP.NET 1.1	managedRuntimeVersion: v1.1
	managedPipelineMode: Classic
	Can use the "ASP.NET 1.1" application pool
ASP.NET 2.0 Integrated mode	managedRuntimeVersion: v2.0
	managedPipelineMode: Integrated
	Can use the default application pool named "DefaultAppPool"
ASP.NET 2.0 Classic mode	managedRuntimeVersion: v2.0
	managedPipelineMode: Classic
	Can use the "Classic .NET AppPool" application pool

Because all new applications are by default set to use the "DefaultAppPool" application pool, which by default is configured for ASP.NET 2.0 Integrated mode, all new applications by default use this mode. If you want to run an ASP.NET 2.0 application in Classic mode, you can use the pre-installed "Classic .NET AppPool" application pool.

```
%systemroot%\system32\inetsrv\appcmd.exe set app "ApplicationPath"
"/applicationPool:Classic .NET AppPool"
```

If you want to run an ASP.NET 1.1 application, you can place it in the precreated "ASP.NET 1.1" application pool (created by .NET Framework 1.1 setup when ASP.NET 1.1 is installed).

```
%systemroot%\system32\inetsrv\appcmd.exe set app "ApplicationPath"
"/applicationPool:ASP.NET 1.1"
```

You can also create new application pools and set their *managedPipelineMode* and *managedRuntimeVersion* configuration attributes appropriately to host your new application. For more information about creating and managing application pools, see Chapter 10.

Migrating ASP.NET 2.0 Applications to Use Integrated Mode

After you have created an IIS application and have placed it in the appropriate application pool, you can deploy your application contents to the IIS application's root directory. Your application should then be ready to run.

As mentioned earlier, most existing ASP.NET 2.0 applications will work transparently in Integrated mode. However, in some cases, configuration changes are necessary to enable the application to function correctly. These changes are required because IIS 7.0 takes over certain ASP.NET configurations in Integrated mode to enable the integration to occur. If your ASP.NET application defines any of the configuration sections listed in Table 11-3, you will get an error message when you request content in that application, as shown in Figure 11-3.

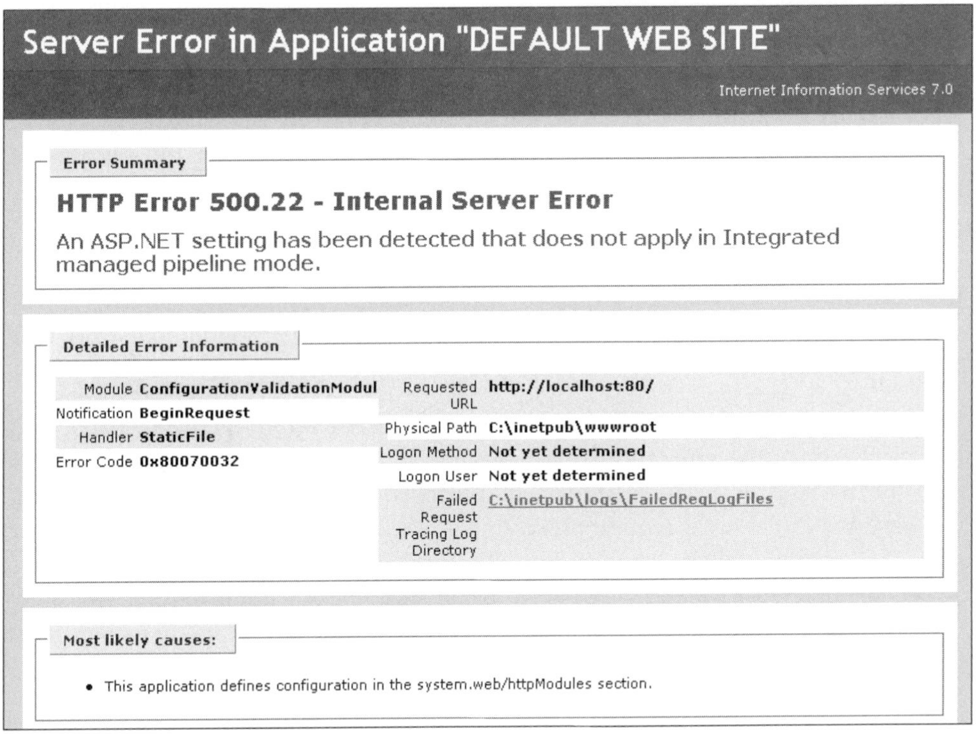

Server Error in Application "DEFAULT WEB SITE"

Internet Information Services 7.0

Error Summary

HTTP Error 500.22 - Internal Server Error

An ASP.NET setting has been detected that does not apply in Integrated managed pipeline mode.

Detailed Error Information

Module	**ConfigurationValidationModul**	Requested URL	**http://localhost:80/**
Notification	**BeginRequest**	Physical Path	**C:\inetpub\wwwroot**
Handler	**StaticFile**	Logon Method	**Not yet determined**
Error Code	**0x80070032**	Logon User	**Not yet determined**
		Failed Request Tracing Log Directory	**C:\inetpub\logs\FailedReqLogFiles**

Most likely causes:

- This application defines configuration in the system.web/httpModules section.

Figure 11-3   Server error indicating that migration is required to operate application in Integrated mode.

The error indicates that the application contains an unsupported ASP.NET configuration and indicates that it specifically contains the *system.web/httpModules* configuration section in the Most Likely Causes area. The error also suggests steps to address this issue (not shown in Figure 11-3), which include migrating the application's configuration by using the Appcmd.exe command line tool (more on this in a moment).

Table 11-3 lists cases in which this error will be generated and the suggested migration action to resolve the issue.

Table 11-3   ASP.NET Configuration That Requires Migration in Integrated Mode

Situation	Suggested Action
Application defines custom modules in the *system.web/httpModules* configuration section	Move the module entries from the *system.web/httpModules* section to the IIS *system.webServer/modules* section. The migration tool can do this automatically.
Application defines custom handler mappings in the *system.web/ httpHandlers* configuration section	Move the handler entries from the *system.web/httpHandlers* section to the IIS *system.webServer/handlers* section. The migration tool can do this automatically.
Application enables request impersonation in *system.web/identity* configuration section	Move the application to Classic mode or configure the application to ignore this error.

The first two cases revolve around the integration of ASP.NET handlers and modules with the IIS handler and module configuration. In Integrated mode, ASP.NET modules and handlers execute directly in the IIS Web server pipeline and are configured in the IIS *system.webServer/ modules* and *system.webServer/handlers* configuration sections instead of the ASP.NET *system.web/httpModules* and *system.web/httpHandlers* sections. You can perform the necessary configuration migration automatically by using the Appcmd *Migrate Config* command.

```
%systemroot%\system32\inetsrv\AppCmd Migrate Config "ApplicationPath"
```

ApplicationPath is the configuration path of the application being migrated. This command will automatically migrate the configuration, enabling the application to work correctly in Integrated mode.

The last case deserves a bit more explanation. ASP.NET applications that are configured to impersonate the authenticated user for the request traditionally have been able to impersonate that user for the entire request. In Integrated mode, because ASP.NET modules can execute earlier in the request processing pipeline, impersonation is not available until after the AuthenticateRequest stage. Typically, this is not a breaking change, because it is uncommon for ASP.NET modules to rely on impersonation early in the request processing pipeline. To be safe, however, IIS recommends moving applications that use impersonation to Classic mode. If you are positive that you do not have custom ASP.NET modules that rely on being impersonated in the BeginRequest and AuthenticateRequest stages, you can ignore this warning by turning off configuration validation for your application. Doing so is described next.

After migration has taken place, Appcmd will generate a special configuration that disables further validation for the application (you can also create this configuration manually after performing the migration yourself). This enables the ASP.NET application to retain its former ASP.NET configuration used in Classic mode/previous versions of IIS. In addition, it also provides the migrated configuration so that it can be safely moved between Classic and Integrated modes, and to down-level platforms. You can also use this configuration to disable validation so that <identity impersonate="true" /> does not cause the validation error. This configuration looks like this.

```
<system.webServer>
  <validation validateIntegratedModeConfiguration="false" />
</system.webServer>
```

After this configuration is added to the application's web.config file, IIS 7.0 will no longer attempt to validate ASP.NET configuration. Because of this, after you initially migrate the application, you are responsible for making sure that new configuration changes are made to both the Classic and Integrated configuration sections.

Taking Advantage of ASP.NET Integrated Mode

Deploying your application in Integrated mode enables you to leverage benefits provided by the ASP.NET integration. The main benefit is the ability to apply services provided by ASP.NET modules for all requests in your application, whether they are ASP.NET content, static files, or any other application content including ASP and PHP. This is especially meaningful for developers, who can quickly build new modules by using familiar ASP.NET APIs to consistently provide services to the entire Web site without having to develop using the more difficult native C++-based Web server APIs such as ISAPI. These modules can take the form of serious Web server features that provide services such as authentication, or smaller application-specific modules that perform services such as redirects or server-side URL rewriting.

> **More Info**   You can learn more about developing managed modules and see example managed modules at *http://mvolo.com/blogs/serverside/archive/2007/08/15/Developing-IIS7-Web-server-features-with-the-.NET-framework.aspx.*

In addition, ASP.NET Integrated mode also enables existing applications to immediately begin leveraging their existing modules or the existing modules that are part of ASP.NET. One popular example of this is using the built-in ASP.NET Forms Authentication module to provide forms-based authentication for the entire Web site, leveraging the powerful ASP.NET Login controls and Membership functionality for user management.

> **More Info**   You can learn about using Forms Authentication to protect your entire Web site at *http://www.iis.net/articles/view.aspx/IIS7/Extending-IIS7/Getting-Started/How-to-Take-Advantage-of-the-IIS7-Integrated-Pipel.*

Table 11-4 lists the ASP.NET modules that can be used effectively in Integrated mode applications to provide services for the entire Web site.

Table 11-4   Modules Available for All Web Site Content in Integrated Mode

Module	Use To
FormsAuthentication	Protect the entire Web site with ASP.NET's Forms-based authentication, leveraging ASP.NET Login controls and Membership service.
UrlAuthorization	Protect the entire Web site with declarative access control rules for users and roles specified in configuration (you can also use the IIS Url Authorization module).
RoleManager	Provide rich role support for any authentication method using the ASP.NET Roles service, typically used in conjunction with UrlAuthorization for declarative access control or a custom authorization scheme.
OutputCache	To achieve significant performance gains, store application responses in the ASP.NET output cache for reuse. This typically requires additional code to configure the output cache.

By default, all built-in ASP.NET modules are configured to run only for ASP.NET content types. This is done to provide a backward compatible behavior for Integrated mode applications by default. To enable an ASP.NET module to run for all requests to your application, you need to remove the managedHandler precondition from the corresponding configuration element in the *system.webServer/modules* configuration section in the application. You can do this through IIS Manager by selecting your application in the tree view, double-clicking the Modules icon, double-clicking the desired module to edit it, and clearing the Invoke Only For Requests To ASP.NET Applications Or Managed Handlers check box, as shown in Figure 11-4.

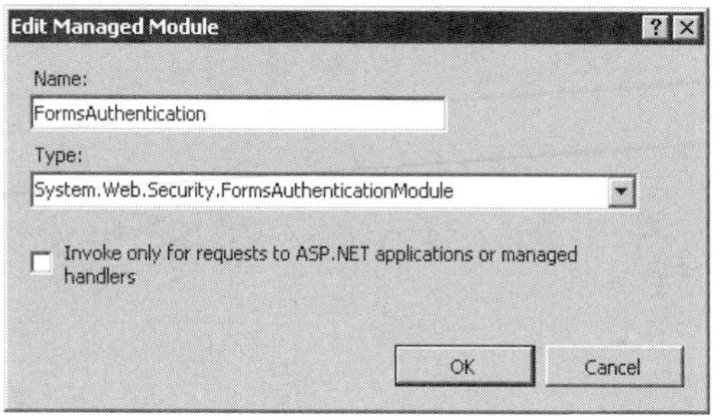

Figure 11-4   Using IIS Manager to enable the Forms Authentication module to run for all requests.

New modules added at the application level will run by default for all requests unless you explicitly chose not to allow them to. For more information about enabling ASP.NET modules to run for all requests, see the section titled "Enabling Managed Modules to Run for All Requests" in Chapter 12, "Managing Web Server Modules."

> **More Info**   You can learn more about leveraging ASP.NET modules to add value to existing applications in the MSDN article titled "Enhance Your Apps with ASP.NET Integrated Pipeline" available at *http://msdn.microsoft.com/msdnmag/issues/08/01/PHPandIIS7/default.aspx*.

Additional Deployment Considerations

This section lists some of the additional deployment considerations for ASP.NET applications running on IIS 7.0.

Breaking Changes in ASP.NET 2.0 Integrated Mode

Most ASP.NET 2.0 applications will work correctly when hosted in Integrated mode after the required configuration migration. However, some applications may experience specific breaking changes. These may require code changes in the application, or the application to be moved to Classic mode. For more information about selecting the ASP.NET integration mode for an application, see the section titled "Deploying ASP.NET Applications" earlier in this chapter.

The specific breaking changes and workarounds are available at *http://mvolo.com/blogs/ serverside/archive/2007/12/08/IIS-7.0-Breaking-Changes-ASP.NET-2.0-applications-Integrated- mode.aspx*.

Hosting ASP.NET Applications on Remote UNC Shares

By default, ASP.NET applications execute with the application pool identity. In some cases, ASP.NET applications can also be configured to impersonate the authenticated user. If they do, applications that enable anonymous access will impersonate the anonymous user, which is the built-in IUSR account by default, and will impersonate the authenticated user otherwise.

When the application is hosted on a universal naming convention (UNC) share, the default anonymous user (IUSR) and the default application pool identity (Network Service) do not have the rights to access the remote network share. Because of this, you will need to use one of the following options to configure the ASP.NET application to work correctly on a UNC share:

- Configure fixed credentials for the application's root virtual directory located on a UNC share, which *must* have access to the remote share. The Web server and the ASP.NET application will then always impersonate these credentials, instead of the process identity or the authenticated user. This option is recommended in most cases.

- Configure a custom application pool identity that has access to the share. If using anonymous authentication, configure it to use the application pool identity to access the application resources. You can use this option in cases in which you configure your application pool to use a domain account and use that domain account to isolate application and control access to network resources.

If you use a custom application pool identity, you should also use the Aspnet_regiis.exe tool to make sure the custom application pool identity has the correct permissions to run ASP.NET.

```
Aspnet_regiis.exe -ga Domain\UserName
```

Domain is the domain for the custom account, and *UserName* is the user name of the custom account. This will ensure that the custom account has all the correct permissions on the Web server for running ASP.NET applications.

In addition, you should be aware of the following limitations when hosting ASP.NET applications on a UNC:

- ASP.NET applications do not support splitting virtual directories between remote UNC and local directories. Either the root virtual directory must be on a UNC share, or no child virtual directories can be on a UNC share.

- If the ASP.NET application specifies a custom application identity in the *system.web- Server/identity* configuration section, that identity will be impersonated when on a UNC share, and therefore, it must also have access to the UNC share.

To allow .NET assemblies included with the ASP.NET application (in the /BIN or /App_Code directories) that resides on a UNC share to work properly, you also need to modify the UNC Code Access Security policy for that network share path. To do this, you can use the Caspol.exe command tool as follows (where *myshare**mydir*\ is the path to the virtual directory).

```
%systemroot%\Microsoft.NET\Framework\version\Caspol.exe -m -ag 1. -url
"file://\\myshare\mydir\*" FullTrust
```

Be aware that other application frameworks the Web site or application are using may access their content in different ways, so you have to select the access model that makes sense for all application components and that minimizes the overhead of managing permissions. This is typically the fixed virtual directory credentials model. For more information on configuring access, please see Chapter 14, "Implementing Security Strategies."

Hosting ASP Applications

IIS 7.0 continues to fully support ASP applications, but it does not introduce any significant improvements or changes to the ASP support as it does for ASP.NET. Nonetheless, ASP applications benefit from the improved configurability and new Web server features provided by IIS 7.0. In addition, the ASP.NET integrated pipeline provides the capability to use valuable ASP.NET features for ASP applications, offering a short-term functionality enhancement path that does not require a complete rewrite to ASP.NET.

> **Note**   For Web applications, ASP.NET unlocks a much richer set of Web server functionality, enables rapid development with Microsoft Visual Studio tool support, and provides greater interoperability with the features of the .NET Framework and the Windows platform.

In the next few sections of this chapter, we will discuss the steps necessary to install ASP and deploy ASP applications on IIS 7.0.

Installing ASP

Due to the modular nature of IIS 7.0, ASP support is a stand-alone component that needs to be installed before ASP applications will run on the server. ASP can be installed using Programs And Features in Windows Vista or as a role service, using Server Manager in Windows Server 2008. You can learn more about installing IIS components via the Windows Setup UI or command line in Chapter 5.

Installing ASP also installs the ISAPI extension support, because ASP is implemented as the ASP.dll ISAPI extension. It also automatically enables the ASP.dll ISAPI extension in the *system.webServer/security/isapiCgiRestriction* configuration section to allow the extension to execute on the server. After the ASP component is installed, your ASP applications should begin working.

Deploying ASP Applications

The way that ASP applications work on IIS has not changed in IIS 7.0. As a result, ASP applications should just work. You do not need to manually create handler mappings for ASP, because Windows Setup does this for you at the server level when the ASP support is installed. It also adds the ASP.dll ISAPI extension to the *system.webServer/security/isapiCgiRestriction* configuration section to enable it to run. Therefore, it is not necessary to complete this task manually as in IIS 6.0 (where you had to enable it in the Web Service Extension Restriction List). To deploy an ASP application, you simply need to perform the following steps:

1.   Create an IIS application.

2.   Deploy the contents of the ASP application.

Much like ASP.NET applications, ASP applications must be placed inside an IIS application. This requirement isn't new in IIS 7.0. However, IIS 7.0 does provide a much firmer definition of an application than previous versions of IIS do. Therefore, you need to make sure that the ASP application is deployed into the root virtual directory of an IIS application, and you may be required to create this application. You can do this from the IIS Manager, or by using Appcmd as follows.

```
%systemroot%\system32\inetsrv\appcmd.exe add app "/site.name:SiteName"
"/path:VirtualPathOfApplication"
"/physicalPath:PhysicalPathOfApplication"
```

You can learn more about creating and managing applications in Chapter 10.

You can also deploy individual ASP pages to any existing application or virtual directory on your server, in which case they will become part of the corresponding application. However, if your ASP application contains application-level functionality such as the Global.asa file, you will need to make sure that the application contents are deployed to the root of an IIS application. In some cases, you will want to create a separate application to isolate your application functionality from other applications—for example, if your ASP pages store state in the ASP *Application* object.

> **Note**   The .NET Framework version and the ASP.NET integration mode of the application pool hosting the ASP application have no effect on the ASP application. Because of this, ASP applications can work in any of the application pools regardless of those settings. However, for ASP applications to take advantage of services provided by managed modules, they must be in application pools that support ASP.NET Integrated mode.

Finally, you may want to take advantage of creating a separate application to isolate your application by placing it in a separate application pool. This can provide additional stability by creating a process boundary between your ASP application and other applications on the server, and doing so also allows you to set permissions on the application content so that only your application pool can gain access to it.

You can learn more about isolating applications in Chapter 14.

Additional Deployment Considerations

This section describes additional deployment considerations for hosting ASP applications on IIS 7.0.

Enabling Script Errors to Be Shown

IIS 7.0 disables the sending of script errors to the browser by default for security reasons. You can enable this behavior by setting the *scriptErrorSentToBrowser* configuration attribute in the *system.webServer/asp* configuration section. You can use Appcmd.exe to do this as follows.

```
%systemroot%\system32\inetsrv\Appcmd set config ConfigurationPath
/section:system.WebServer/asp /scriptErrorSentToBrowser:true
```

ConfigurationPath is the optional configuration path to set this setting for. The default is the entire server if the configuration path is omitted.

In addition, you may need to configure the IIS 7.0 custom errors feature to allow detailed errors to be sent to the browser. By default, IIS 7.0 will only send detailed error responses when the request is made from the local server, and it will send a generic error message to remote clients. For more information on configuring custom errors, please see Chapter 14.

Parent Paths Disabled by Default

Starting with IIS 6.0, the ability to use parent path ("..") segments in calls to ASP functions such as the *Server.MapPath* has been disabled to prohibit opening of files outside of the application root. This may cause issues for some applications that use parent paths with this function to calculate file paths or use them in #include directives.

If your application encounters this condition, you may receive error messages such as "The Include file 'file' cannot contain '..' to indicate the parent directory" or "The '..' characters are not allowed in the Path parameter for the MapPath method". When faced with an error such as one of these, you can modify the application to not use parent paths, or if you are sure that the use of parent paths does not create a vulnerability, you can enable parent paths by setting the *enableParentPaths* configuration attribute in the *system.webServer/asp* configuration section. You can use Appcmd.exe to do this as follows.

```
%systemroot%\system32\inetsrv\Appcmd set config ConfigurationPath
/section:system.WebServer/asp /enableParentPaths:true
```

As before, *ConfigurationPath* is the optional configuration path to set this setting for. The default is the entire server if the configuration path is omitted.

Hosting ASP Applications on Remote UNC Shares

ASP applications, like all ISAPI extensions by default, always impersonate the authenticated user when executing scripts and accessing resources. For applications that enable anonymous access, the authenticated user will be the built-in IUSR account by default. You can also configure anonymous authentication to use the application pool identity instead of a separate account.

When the application is hosted on a UNC share, the default anonymous user (IUSR) and the default application pool identity (Network Service) do not have the rights to access the remote network share. Because of this, you will need to make sure that the application pool and the authenticated user have the right to access the network share. This is typically done using one of the following options:

- Configure fixed credentials for the application's virtual directories located on a UNC share, which have access to the remote share. The ASP application will then always impersonate these credentials instead of the authenticated user.

- Configure a custom application pool identity that has access to the share. If using anonymous authentication, configure it to use the application pool identity. If using other authentication methods, make sure that all authenticated users have access to the network share.

For more information on configuring access, please see Chapter 14.

Hosting PHP Applications

IIS 7.0 provides built-in support for the FastCGI protocol, which is a more efficient and reliable mechanism for hosting PHP applications than CGI or ISAPI, the other two modes supported by PHP. The FastCGI protocol eliminates the high per-request process creation overhead associated with the CGI protocol on Windows by pooling processes and reusing them to process requests. By ensuring that only a single request is processed by each FastCGI process at a time, it maintains the required single-threaded environment needed by non–thread-safe application frameworks.

Direct from the Source: The History of PHP Support in IIS

IIS has long supported the PHP application framework. In fact, the standard PHP distributions provided two mechanisms for interfacing with IIS: a CGI-compliant executable, and an ISAPI extension. However, both of these modes have certain limitations that often preclude production-quality hosting of PHP applications on IIS 7.0.

The CGI mode often experiences very low performance, because a new PHP CGI process has to be started to handle each request. This dramatically reduces performance due to the high process creation overhead on the Windows platform. The ISAPI mode does not suffer from a performance problem, because ISAPI is a multithreaded in-process component that does not start new processes and is therefore capable of very high performance. However, historically the PHP scripting engine and most of the commonly used PHP extensions were not developed to be thread-safe, often resulting in instability and crashes when used in the multithreaded ISAPI environment. Even after the PHP scripting engine itself became thread-safe, many commonly used open source extensions remain non–thread-safe, keeping many PHP applications from being stable when hosted in ISAPI mode.

With IIS 7.0, we have taken a hard look at what it means for IIS to be an excellent application platform. We realized that this means supporting a wide variety of application frameworks and making sure that these frameworks not only work reliably on IIS but also can leverage the powerful IIS 7.0 and Integrated ASP.NET features. We saw that the PHP problems were common among other open source application frameworks, and so the FastCGI project was born. I—along with Bill Staples, IIS product unit manager—first announced this project in September 2006 as an integral part of our collaboration with Zend, the creator of PHP, to bring rock-solid PHP support to the IIS platform. You can find the first blog post on this at *http://mvolo.com/blogs/serverside/archive/2006/09/29/Making-PHP-rock-on-Windows_2F00_IIS.aspx*, and you can read more about the history of the FastCGI project at *http://mvolo.com/blogs/serverside/archive/2007/11/12/FastCGI-for-IIS-6.0-is-released-on-Download-Center.aspx*.

Since then, FastCGI support has been added to Windows Server 2008 and has been made available for IIS 6.0 as a download. This support is quickly opening doors for production hosting of PHP applications on IIS. We are also working with other application framework communities to make sure that they are able to successfully leverage the FastCGI environment, and we are hoping to see more and more application frameworks leveraging FastCGI to work better on IIS.

Mike Volodarsky

IIS Core Server Program Manager

In the remainder of this section, we will review the steps necessary to enable PHP applications to work on IIS 7.0.

Deploying PHP Applications

To enable PHP support, you will first need to install FastCGI on the server. Second, you will need to download and install the PHP framework itself.

Installing FastCGI

Before you can run PHP in FastCGI mode, you need to install FastCGI on the server.

Note   FastCGI can also be used to host other FastCGI-compliant application frameworks. You can read more about using FastCGI to host application frameworks in the section titled "Deploying Frameworks That Use FastCGI" later in this chapter.

FastCGI support is part of Windows Vista SP1 and Windows Server 2008. FastCGI can be installed as part of the CGI component using Programs And Features in Windows Vista or as a role service, or using Server Manager in Windows Server 2008.

Note   FastCGI support was not part of IIS 7.0 in Windows Vista, but it is included in SP1. You will need to install SP1 to obtain FastCGI on Windows Vista. It is included by default in Windows Server 2008.

After the CGI component is installed, FastCGI support is available on the Web server. The FastCGI module is actually a separate module from the CGI module, but both are installed as part of the CGI setup component (the reasons for this are historical). Installing FastCGI and CGI support does not automatically enable any CGI or FastCGI programs to execute on your server. You will need to manually enable the PHP FastCGI executable to allow them to run.

Installing PHP

You can download builds of the PHP framework from *http://www.php.net/downloads*. You can also download the PHP Extension Community Library (PECL) from the same site. In doing so, you will have two options:

- Download the standard Win32 binaries.
- Download the non–thread-safe Win32 binaries

Note   You also have the option to download an MSI-based installer. However, this installer has been shown to generate conflicting configurations, and therefore, it is not recommended.

The non–thread-safe binaries are optimized for the FastCGI execution environment, which does not require thread safety due to the single request per process execution model. These binaries, therefore, gain a significant performance boost due to removing the overhead of thread safety and are recommended for the IIS 7.0 FastCGI environment.

Caution   Use the standard thread-safe libraries if you are planning to use PHP in the ISAPI environment. However, doing so may still lead to instability and is not recommended, because not all PHP extensions are thread safe. Use FastCGI with the non–thread-safe PHP binaries for optimal performance and stability.

After downloading the PHP binaries, you can simply unzip them to a directory on your machine and follow the standard installation procedures for PHP, which sometimes involve renaming the php.ini-recommended configuration file in the PHP directory to Php.ini and making specific modifications to it to allow your PHP applications to run. You may at minimum need to set the PHP .INI settings listed in Table 11-5.

Table 11-5   PHP .INI Settings for IIS 7.0 FastCGI

PHP .INI Setting	Explanation
cgi.fix_pathinfo=1	This ensures the correct values for the PATH_INFO/PATH_TRANSLATED CGI server variables. PHP's previous behavior was to set PATH_TRANSLATED to SCRIPT_FILENAME and ignore PATH_INFO. Using this setting causes PHP to fix path-related variables to conform to the CGI specification.
fastcgi.impersonate = 1	This setting enables PHP to impersonate the authenticated user. You may want to set this setting. For more information, see the section titled "Configuring PHP Execution Identity" later in this chapter.

You may also need to set additional settings that are specific to the PHP application you are using, for example to load a required PHP extension library. In addition, you may want to set some FastCGI settings to tune performance to the needs of your PHP application. This is discussed later in the section titled "Ensuring Availability of PHP Applications" in this chapter.

Finally, to allow PHP to be used from IIS, you have to make sure that IIS has Read access to the directory containing the PHP framework files and the application content. By default, IIS application pools run as Network Service and therefore are members of the Users group, which does have Read access to most directories on the server. However, if Network Service does not have access, or you are using a custom application pool identity, you can grant Read and Execute access to the IIS_IUSRS group to grant IIS access to the PHP framework files.

Deploying PHP Applications

To allow PHP applications to run using FastCGI, you need to do the following:

1. Create a FastCGI application entry for each PHP version.

2. Create a FastCGI handler mapping for *.php scripts to be processed with PHP's FastCGI -compliant executable.

Because IIS Manager will automatically perform step 1 when you create the corresponding handler mapping, we will discuss creating the handler mapping in IIS Manager as a way to perform both tasks in one step.

Creating a FastCGI Handler Mapping for PHP

After the FastCGI support and the PHP framework are installed on the server, you can enable PHP scripts to be executed using FastCGI. Do this by creating an IIS handler mapping that uses the FastCGI module to process requests to PHP scripts by using the PHP FastCGI executable. This mapping can be added globally on the server to enable PHP scripts to run on all Web sites on the server, or it can be added for a specific site or URL to enable PHP scripts to run there.

The quickest way to create this handler mapping is with IIS Manager. First, select the server node or the site node in the tree view depending on the desired scope for the handler mapping. Then double-click Handler Mappings. You can learn more about creating and managing IIS handler mappings in the section titled "Adding Handler Mappings" in Chapter 12.

You can create the handler mapping for PHP by using the Add Module Mapping action, specifying the FastCGIModule in the Module drop-down list, and specifying the path to the PHP-CGI.EXE executable in your PHP installation directory, as shown in Figure 11-5.

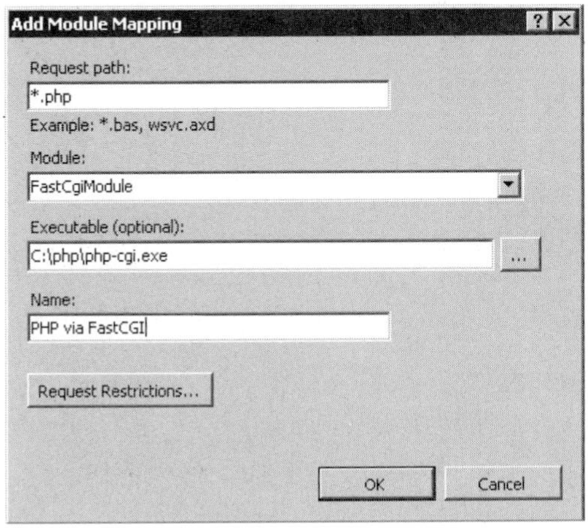

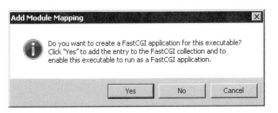

Figure 11-5   Adding a FastCGI handler mapping for PHP in IIS Manager.

When you press OK to create the mapping, you will see a dialog box asking to create the FastCGI application entry for the Php-cgi.exe executable, as shown in Figure 11-6. This is required to run Php-cgi.exe with FastCGI (this is similar to adding a CGI executable to the Web Extension Restriction List on IIS 6.0).

Figure 11-6   Add Module Mapping confirmation dialog box.

Clicking OK in this dialog box allows you to quickly create the required FastCGI application configuration without having to configure it manually. This dialog box is shown only the first time a specific path to the Php-cgi.exe executable is encountered to create a global FastCGI application entry for that executable. This means that you will see it only once for each version of PHP you use in handler mappings on the server. Because a separate FastCGI application entry is created for each unique executable, this allows you to host PHP applications on your server using more than one version of the PHP framework. To use multiple versions side by side, simply create the separate PHP handler mappings by using the appropriate version of the Php-cgi.exe executable for different sites on the server. IIS Manager will prompt you to create a FastCGI application entry once for each version.

The FastCGI application entry defines additional settings including the number of requests that a single instance of the Php-cgi.exe process will execute and how many of these processes are allowed to be created at the same time. You can learn more about configuring other FastCGI application settings and performing these tasks from the command line in the section titled "Deploying Frameworks That Use FastCGI" later in this chapter.

Additional Deployment Considerations

When PHP is running in the FastCGI environment, you may want to take into account a few additional deployment considerations. These include the following:

- Deciding on the execution identity for PHP scripts
- Ensuring availability of PHP applications by adjusting concurrency and process lifetime

These considerations are strongly related to the FastCGI process model, which impacts how PHP processes are created and used to process PHP requests when in FastCGI mode. The FastCGI process model is explained in more detail in the section titled "Deploying Frameworks That Use FastCGI" later in this chapter. If you are not very familiar with FastCGI, you may want to read this section before reading the "Configuring PHP Execution Identity" section.

Configuring PHP Execution Identity

By default, PHP scripts will be executed under the process identity of the Php-cgi.exe worker process. Unlike CGI, which starts a new process to handle each request and executes this process with the identity of the IIS authenticated user by default, FastCGI worker processes are long-lived and always execute under the same identity as the parent application pool. This means that PHP scripts will be executed with the identity of the application pool to which the IIS application that contains the scripts belongs. This aligns well with the IIS model, enabling you to manage access to resources in a uniform way across the entire site. It also enables you to securely isolate PHP applications in the same manner as the rest of the site contents by using application pool isolation. For more information about application pool isolation, please see Chapter 14.

Note Unlike CGI, FastCGI application processes, including PHP's Php-cgi.exe, always execute with the identity of the application pool to which the PHP application belongs.

However, some PHP applications rely on executing PHP scripts under the identity of the authenticated user. This is often done as a way to use the IIS authenticated user to authorize access to other resources the application uses and to isolate users from one another. In fact, PHP applications that run using the CGI or the ISAPI mode impersonate the authenticated user by default. Historically, impersonation has been especially important to lower the execution privilege of PHP scripts because the parent IIS process may have been executing as the LocalSystem account (in IIS 5.0 and previous versions). This latter requirement is no longer there in IIS 7.0 because IIS application pools are by default configured to run with the lower privilege of the Network Service account.

To enable PHP scripts to execute with the identity of the authenticated user, you can configure PHP to impersonate the authenticated user when hosted in the FastCGI environment. Though the Php-cgi.exe process will still execute under the parent application pool identity, the PHP engine will impersonate the authenticated user when executing the PHP script. This is done by setting the *fcgi.impersonate* setting in the PHP's Php.ini configuration file to 1.

```
; FastCGI under IIS (on WINNT based OS) supports the ability to impersonate
; security tokens of the calling client.  This allows IIS to define the
; security context that the request runs under.
; Set to 1 if running under IIS.  Default is zero.
fastcgi.impersonate = 1
```

Note Impersonation takes effect only when an authenticated user is available and represents a valid Windows principal. Non-Windows authentication schemes such as Forms authentication do not support impersonation.

When using impersonation and anonymous authentication, PHP scripts will execute with the IUSR identity by default (the anonymous user in IIS 7.0). You can change the anonymous user identity in the *system.webServer/security/authentication/anonymousAuthentication* configuration section as well as make the anonymous user be the identity of the worker process. See Chapter 14 for more details about IIS 7.0 anonymous authentication.

Note IIS 7.0 FastCGI provides support for impersonation of the authenticated user. However, at the time of this writing, only the PHP framework is known to support this. Other frameworks using FastCGI will execute under the identity of the parent application pool.

Hosting PHP Applications on Remote UNC Shares

When running PHP applications on remote UNC shares, you need to ensure that the Php-cgi.exe process has access to the application content on the UNC share. Due to the two mechanisms for running PHP discussed earlier in this chapter, there are two options for configuring this:

- If using impersonation, configure the fixed credentials for the virtual directory hosting the PHP application content on a remote UNC share. PHP will then impersonate these credentials when accessing the content and executing scripts. This option is recommended.

- If not using impersonation, make sure that the application pool identity has access to the UNC share.

For more information on configuring access, see Chapter 14.

Ensuring Availability of PHP Applications

The FastCGI hosting mode provides several settings that can be adjusted in order to tune the performance and availability of PHP applications. These settings are available on the FastCGI application entry for each unique version of Php-cgi.exe in use on the system, which are located in the *global system.webServer/fastCgi* configuration section.

> **More Info**   To learn about these settings and see how they can be set, see the section titled "Modifying FastCGI Application Settings" later in this chapter.

These settings may need to be used to ensure the availability of PHP applications by tuning the FastCGI pool behavior. In particular, the *instanceMaxRequests* setting for the PHP FastCGI application, which controls the number of requests processed by each Php-cgi.exe process before it is shut down, must be set to a number under the PHP request limit. This limit is 500 by default, and you can override it by specifying the PHP_FCGI_MAX_REQUESTS environment variable in the FastCGI application configuration (see the section titled "Modifying FastCGI Application Settings" for information about setting environment variables for FastCGI applications in configuration). The default *instanceMaxRequests* value is 200, which is under the PHP's default, but it is recommended to set both to 10,000 to achieve optimal performance.

Be sure to read more about the available settings in the section titled "Modifying FastCGI Application Settings" later in the chapter. Also read the section titled "Ensuring Availability of FastCGI Applications" for best practices on setting them to improve FastCGI application availability.

Techniques for Enabling Application Frameworks

IIS 7.0 provides several options for hosting third-party application frameworks, depending on how the application framework's developer chooses to interface it with IIS. The options include:

- **IIS 7.0 native module**   Application frameworks that integrate with IIS by using the IIS 7.0 native module APIs to handle requests

- **ASP.NET handler**   Application frameworks that integrate with IIS by using the ASP.NET handler APIs

- **ISAPI extension**   Application frameworks that integrate with IIS by using the legacy ISAPI extension APIs

- **FastCGI application**   Application frameworks that provide executables that support the open FastCGI protocol to integrate with IIS

- **CGI application**   Application frameworks that provide executables that support the open CGI protocol to integrate with IIS

To enable application frameworks by using any of the preceding options to work on IIS 7.0, the basic requirement is to create a handler mapping that maps requests to specific extensions to the application framework's handler component. This component may be using any one of the options listed earlier to interface with IIS. For details on creating handler mappings for each of these handler types, please see the section titled "Adding Handler Mappings" in Chapter 12.

You can create the handler mapping at the server level or for a specific Web site, application, virtual directory, or URL. Doing so will allow requests made to the level where the mapping is created to be forwarded to the application framework for processing.

> **Note**   This section reviews general techniques for integrating application frameworks with IIS 7.0. You will need to review the documentation provided with each framework for instructions that may contain framework-specific configuration steps. This chapter also contains specific information for the ASP.NET, ASP, and PHP frameworks.

For all of these options, you can use IIS modules to provide additional request processing services. This includes using any of the IIS authentication mechanisms, authorization, output caching, response compression, and logging. Furthermore, for applications running in Integrated mode, you can also leverage services provided by managed (ASP.NET) modules in the same manner for all requests regardless of the application framework. For more information about this, see the section titled "Taking Advantage of ASP.NET Integrated Mode" earlier in this chapter.

The remainder of this section will discuss the specifics of each application framework integration option in detail, including using the new FastCGI module to host FastCGI-compliant application frameworks such as PHP.

More Info   For PHP-specific deployment information, please see the section titled "Hosting PHP Applications" earlier in this chapter.

Enabling New Static File Extensions to Be Served

IIS 7.0 supports basic file server functionality in the default install, provided by StaticFileModule. This module is by default configured to handle all requests that are not otherwise handled by other handlers. This means that any request to a resource that does not match a handler mapping will be handled by the Static File module.

StaticFileModule will serve only resources whose extensions are configured to be served. This is very important, because otherwise all unknown resources in the application's servable namespace, including data files or application scripts, may end up served as static files.

The list of allowed static files is located in the *system.webServer/staticContent* configuration section. This is the equivalent of the IIS 6.0 MIME Type configuration. In IIS 7.0, the default list of allowed static files has been expanded to contain modern file types including file types used by Shockwave, Microsoft Silverlight, and Microsoft Office 2007. You can configure the list of static files at any configuration level, which allows specific applications to add or remove custom file types without affecting the entire server.

If your application contains a file type that should be served as a static file but is not currently registered in this section, you will need to add its extension and the associated MIME content type information before it can be served.

You can use IIS Manager to do this by expanding the IIS computer node in the Connections pane, navigating to the Sites node, and selecting the level at which you'd like to configure MIME types. (You can manage MIME type configuration at the site, directory, and virtual directory level.) Double-click the MIME Types feature to display the MIME Types page, as shown on Figure 11-7.

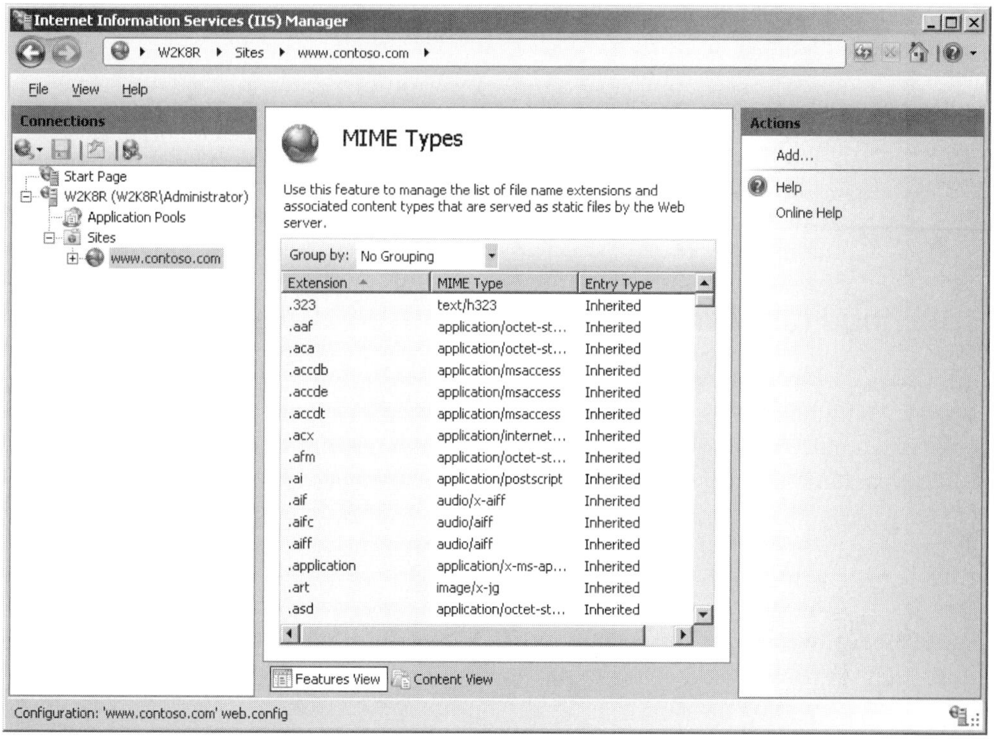

Figure 11-7   Configuring MIME types using IIS Manager.

You can also configure MIME types by using Appcmd. To add a MIME Type entry, you can use the following syntax.

```
%systemroot%\system32\inetsrv\Appcmd set config
/section:system.WebServer/staticContent "ConfigurationPath"
"/+[fileExtension='string',mimeType='string']"
```

To delete a MIME Type entry, to prevent the associated extension from being served as a static file, you can use the following syntax.

```
%systemroot%\system32\inetsrv\Appcmd set config
/section:system.WebServer/staticContent "ConfigurationPath"
"/-[fileExtension='string']"
```

The parameters to these commands are described in Table 11-6.

Table 11-6   Parameters for Adding MIME Types

Parameter	Description
ConfigurationPath	The configuration path at which to apply this configuration.
fileExtension	The file extension to add or delete.
mimeType	The MIME type of the file extension. This will be sent as the content-type header of the response when sending the contents of the associated resources to the client.

The MIME Type configuration applies only if the file extension is not already mapped to another handler in the IIS 7.0 handler mapping configuration.

> **Caution**   Do not add MIME Type entries for resources that are not meant to be served as static files, such as application script files or data files. If the frameworks that typically handle these resources are removed, the Web server may accidentally serve these files as if their MIME Types are registered in the static content configuration.

Deploying Frameworks Based on IIS 7.0 Native Modules

The IIS 7.0 native module is the preferred way to integrate application frameworks with IIS 7.0 and future versions of IIS, because it provides the maximum performance and functionality to the application framework. It is also significantly easier to develop against and more powerful than ISAPI extension API available in previous versions of IIS. However, because this is the newest API, introduced in IIS 7.0, it is also the least commonly used today (this will change as developers adopt IIS 7.0). Adding application frameworks based on IIS 7.0 native modules requires administrative privileges on the server.

To deploy an application framework that uses this mechanism, you need to do the following:

1. Install the native module on the server. This requires administrative privileges.

2. Enable the native module on the server (typically done by default when the module is installed) or for a specific application where it is used.

3. Create a module-based handler mapping entry that maps the desired URL paths to the module. Do this at the server level or for a specific site, application, or URL.

4. Optionally, install the corresponding configuration schema and UI extensions for configuring your module. Then set the module-specific configuration. You can learn about doing this in Chapter 13, "Managing Configuration and User Interface Extensions."

You can find details for performing each of these steps in Chapter 12.

Because IIS 7.0 modules are loaded In-Process by the IIS worker process, the application framework will by default execute under the identity of the parent IIS application pool (unless the framework specifically implements the ability to impersonate authenticated users or arbitrary credentials, like ASP.NET does). This means that you must set permissions on the application framework files to allow them to be read by the IIS worker process. You do this by granting Read access to the IIS_IUSRS group.

Additionally, if you need to isolate your applications for reliability or security reasons, you need to use the IIS application as a unit of isolation by placing different applications in different IIS application pools. You can learn more about isolating applications for security purposes in Chapter 14.

Deploying Frameworks Based on ASP.NET Handlers

Using ASP.NET handlers is the next best option to using native modules, offering developers most of the functionality of IIS 7.0 native modules and a significantly faster development cycle. Like IIS 7.0 modules, ASP.NET handlers are a multithreaded environment, so they are mostly appropriate for thread-safe application frameworks. Unlike other application framework options, ASP.NET handlers can be configured in the application configuration without requiring administrative privileges on the server.

The steps to deploy an application framework that uses ASP.NET handlers are as follows:

1. Deploy the ASP.NET handler assembly to the server (in the Global Assembly Cache). Alternatively, you can deploy it as part of a specific application (in the application /BIN or /App_Code directories). The latter option works well when you are deploying the application framework to servers on which you do not have administrator privileges.

2. Create a managed handler mapping entry that maps the desired URL paths to the ASP.NET handler type at the server level or for a specific site, application, or URL.

3. Optionally, install the corresponding configuration schema and UI extensions for configuring your handler. Then set the handler-specific configuration. You can learn about doing this in Chapter 13.

You can find details for performing each of these steps in Chapter 12. Note that the location for adding ASP.NET handler mappings is different depending on whether the target application uses Classic or Integrated .NET integration modes. In Integrated mode, you can add the handler mapping directly to the IIS handler mapping list in the *system.webServer/handlers* configuration section or by using IIS Manager. In Classic mode, you must add the handler mapping to ASP.NET's *system.web/httpHandlers* configuration section, and you must script-map the corresponding extension to the ASPNET_ISAPI.dll ISAPI extension in the IIS handler mappings (the latter can be done with IIS Manager).

Like IIS 7.0 native modules, ASP.NET handlers are In-Process components that the IIS worker process loads. Unlike IIS 7.0 native modules, ASP.NET handlers are loaded and executed inside the ASP.NET application. The ASP.NET application can additionally isolate the content and request execution by using partial trust.

Though by default ASP.NET handlers execute with the identity of the IIS worker process, they can also be configured to impersonate the authenticated user or an arbitrary identity through the ASP.NET *system.webServer/identity* configuration. To ensure that your application framework can access the desired files, allow them to be read by the IIS worker process by granting Read access to IIS_IUSRS group.

Additionally, if you need to isolate your applications for reliability or security reasons, you need to use the IIS application as a unit of isolation by placing different applications in different IIS application pools. You can learn more about isolating applications for security purposes in Chapter 14.

Deploying Frameworks Based on ISAPI Extensions

ISAPI extensions have traditionally been the preferred way to interface application frameworks with previous versions of IIS. As a result, a number of application frameworks that exist today use an ISAPI extension when hosted in the IIS environment. Like IIS 7.0 modules and ASP.NET handlers, ISAPI extensions are a multithreaded environment, so it is mostly appropriate for thread-safe application frameworks. Adding ISAPI extensions requires server administrator privileges.

To deploy an application framework that uses ISAPI extensions, you need to perform the following steps:

1. Create a scriptmap-based handler mapping entry that maps the desired URL paths to the ISAPI extension, at the server level or for a specific site, application, or URL.

2. Add the ISAPI extension to the *system.webServer/security/isapiCgiRestriction* configuration. This requires administrative privileges.

> **Note**   IIS Manager can automatically prompt you to create the ISAPI extension entry in the *system.webServer/security/isapiCgiRestriction* configuration section when you create the handler mapping. This requires you to be connected as a server administrator.

You can find details for performing each of these steps in Chapter 12.

ISAPI extensions, like IIS 7.0 native modules, are loaded In-Process in the IIS worker process. However, unlike IIS 7.0 native modules, they are by default made to impersonate the authenticated user if one is available. Therefore, they typically execute with the identity of the IIS anonymous user (IUSR by default) or the authenticated user if it's available and has an associated Windows principal.

However, some application frameworks may chose to revert this impersonation and instead execute with the IIS worker process identity. In IIS 7.0, it is also possible to make the anonymous user the same user as the IIS worker process identity, achieving the same behavior for anonymous requests.

As before, if you need to isolate your applications for reliability or security reasons, you need to use the IIS application as a unit of isolation by placing different applications in different IIS application pools. Learn more about isolating applications for security purposes in Chapter 14.

Deploying Frameworks That Use FastCGI

FastCGI is a new application framework option in IIS 7.0. Unlike ISAPI extensions, IIS 7.0 modules and ASP.NET handlers—which are both IIS-specific extension mechanisms—FastCGI uses the open FastCGI protocol to interface with application frameworks. This enables a variety of existing application frameworks that support FastCGI on other Web server plat-forms to work on IIS. The FastCGI protocol enables significant performance improvements over CGI, which has been supported in IIS since early versions. It does this while maintaining the single request per process requirement that many of these application frameworks have due to lack of thread safety in the framework implementation itself or the applications that use it.

The FastCGI support is implemented by the FastCGI module. This module maintains a pool of one or more FastCGI processes for each FastCGI application executable configured globally on the server. When a request that is mapped to the FastCGI module and the corresponding FastCGI application is received, it is forwarded to one of the processes in the corresponding FastCGI process pool by using the FastCGI protocol. The FastCGI application process then processes the request and returns the response to the FastCGI module, which then writes it to the response. Unlike CGI, the FastCGI application processes are long-lived and are reused on subsequent requests, which eliminates the overhead of starting and destroying application processes for each request.

To deploy an application framework that uses FastCGI, perform the following steps:

1. Create a module-based handler mapping entry that maps the desired URL paths to the FastCGIModule module, using the path of the FastCGI executable and the arguments to pass to it as the script processor. You can create this at the server level or for a specific site, application, or URL.

2. Create a FastCGI application entry for the FastCGI executable. When you add the handler mapping through IIS Manager, it will automatically prompt you to do this if you are connected as a server administrator. You must be a server administrator to create this entry.

After the FastCGI application entry for the specific FastCGI executable is created on the server (this requires administrative privileges), it can be used to create handler mappings at any configuration level. This means that after the server administrator allows a particular applica-tion framework's FastCGI executable, any application on the server can use it.

Unlike CGI, which starts a new process to handle each request and executes this process with the identity of the IIS authenticated user by default, FastCGI worker processes are long-lived and always execute under the same identity as the parent application pool. This means that FastCGI application framework executables and their scripts will be executed with the identity of the application pool to which the IIS application that contains the scripts belongs. This aligns well with the IIS model, enabling you to manage access to resources in a uniform way across the entire site. It also enables you to securely isolate FastCGI applications in the same manner as the rest of the site contents by using application pool isolation. For more information about application pool isolation, please see Chapter 14.

Modifying FastCGI Application Settings

When creating the FastCGI application entry for the FastCGI executable, you have a number of options that you can configure to modify the behavior of the corresponding FastCGI process pool. Table 11-7 illustrates these options.

Table 11-7   Parameters for Editing FastCGI Application Definitions

Setting	Description
fullPath	The full path to the FastCGI executable.
Arguments	The arguments to pass to the FastCGI executable.
maxInstances	The maximum number of processes that can be started for this application. Default is four.
idleTimeout	The time in seconds that must pass after the last request was processed by a FastCGI process before which it is shut down due to inactivity. Default is 300 seconds.
activityTimeout	The time in seconds that must pass while waiting for activity from the FastCGI process during request processing, after which the process is considered deadlocked and will be forcefully shut down. This is effectively a rolling script time-out. Default is 30 seconds.
requestTimeout	The maximum time in seconds that the FastCGI process can take to process a request. Default is 90 seconds.
instanceMaxRequests	The number of requests that each FastCGI process can process before being shut down. Default is 200.
Protocol	The FastCGI protocol to use to connect to the FastCGI process. The two allowed values are NamedPipe and Tcp. The default is NamedPipe.
queueLength	The maximum number of requests that can be queued while waiting for the next available FastCGI process before requests are rejected with a 503 error code. The default is 1000.
flushNamedPipe	Whether to flush the data sent to the FastCGI process when using named pipes. This may be necessary for some FastCGI applications that may otherwise hang while waiting for data from the FastCgi-Module, at the cost of a potential performance decrease. The default is false.
rapidFailsPerMinute	How many FastCGI process failures are allowed per minute. If the number of failures exceeds this value over a 60-second period, FastCGI will not create any more processes for the FastCGI application. The default is 10.
environmentVariables	Enables a collection of additional environment variables to be specified for the FastCGI application process. Each environmentVariable element inside the collection can specify the name of the environment variable and its value.

In Windows Server 2008, IIS Manager does not provide a way to modify these settings. Therefore, if you need to set them, you can edit the configuration directly, or use Appcmd or one of the programmatic APIs to do it. For example, to use Appcmd to create a new FastCGI application entry with the *instanceMaxRequests* attribute set to 10, you can use the following syntax.

```
%systemroot%\system32\inetsrv\AppCmd.exe Set Config
/section:system.webServer/fastCgi
"/+[fullPath='Path',arguments='Arguments'instanceMaxRequests='10']"
```

Path is the required path to the executable, and *Arguments* are the optional arguments to pass. You can also specify any of the other attributes listed in Table 11-7 to set them to a specific value, as is done for *instanceMaxRequests*.

To list the existing entries, you can use the following syntax.

```
%systemroot%\system32\inetsrv\AppCmd.exe List Config
/section:system.WebServer/fastCgi
```

You can also set specific attributes on an existing element. For example, to set the *idleTimeout* attribute to 60 seconds, you can use the following syntax.

```
%systemroot%\system32\inetsrv\AppCmd.exe Set Config
/section:system.WebServer/fastCgi
"/[fullPath='Path',arguments='Arguments'].idleTimeout:60"
```

Path and *Arguments* are keys to match a corresponding existing application entry. You can use this syntax to set any of the attributes listed in Table 11-7.

Ensuring Availability of FastCGI Applications

Depending on the behavior of your application framework, the specific application, and overall Web server configuration, you may need to adjust the FastCGI application settings to achieve optimal performance and availability of your application. You may need to do some of the following:

- Adjust the default setting for *maxInstances* upward from four processes to allow for greater request concurrency. Though this may increase CPU contention on your server by creating more processes, it can help increase your application's responsiveness, especially if it makes long-running database or network operations.

- Reduce the *idleTimeout* setting to proactively shut down unused FastCGI processes during periods of lower activity. This may be especially needed on shared hosting servers that have multiple application pools and therefore multiple FastCGI process pools for each FastCGI application.

- If your application also experiences large request volumes that lead to temporary queuing, you may need to adjust *queueLength* upward to accommodate larger queue sizes during high request activity.

- Adjust *instanceMaxRequests* to improve performance by allowing each process to handle more requests before being shut down. This may be a tradeoff with application stability if your application leaks memory or develops unstable behavior over time. In addition, it is important to keep *instanceMaxRequests* under the corresponding internal request limit of the FastCGI executable. Otherwise, the FastCGI module may fail when the FastCGI process terminates unexpectedly due to its internal request limit.

■ Adjust *activityTimeout* and *requestTimeout* to prevent errors for scripts that take a longer time to return response or complete.

> **More Info** PHP has an internal request limit of 500 requests by default, which can be overridden by setting the PHP_FCGI_MAX_REQUESTS environment variable globally on the server or specifically for the FastCGI application entry. See the section titled "Ensuring Availability of PHP Applications" earlier in this chapter for more information.

The exact values of these settings depend on the specifics of the application framework, the application, the overall Web server environment, and server hardware. As such, it is difficult to recommend specific defaults, and you'll need to do performance testing to achieve the desired settings to meet your performance and availability requirements. You can learn more about performance testing in Chapter 17, "Performance and Tuning."

Deploying Frameworks That Use CGI

IIS 7.0 continues to provide support for CGI applications that use the open CGI protocol to communicate with the Web server. The CGI protocol requires each new request to start a new CGI process to handle it, which has a very heavy performance overhead on Windows. FastCGI is a preferred alternative to CGI, because it offers much greater performance due to process reuse. However, for application frameworks that do not support FastCGI or any of the native IIS mechanisms, CGI is an option.

To deploy a CGI program, you need to perform the following steps:

1. Create a scriptmap-based handler mapping entry that maps the desired URL paths to the CGI executable path and any required arguments. You can create this mapping at the server level or for a specific site, application, or URL.

2. Add the CGI executable to the *system.webServer/security/isapiCgiRestriction* configuration. This requires administrative privileges. This is a required step to allow a unique CGI executable path and arguments combination to be executed on the Web server.

Alternatively, CGI also supports the ability to launch .exe files located within your application when the client requests the executable file directly. This requires the directory to have Execute permissions and requires the executable files themselves to enable Execute permissions for the authenticated user.

When a handler mapping is used instead, with a script processor configured to point to the CGI program, only Script permissions are required. In both cases, the exact command lines (path to the CGI program and any arguments passed to it) must be listed in the *system.webServer/security/isapiCGIRestriction* configuration section.

> **Note**   IIS Manager can automatically prompt you to create the CGI executable entry in the *system.webServer/security/isapiCgiRestriction* configuration section when you create the handler mapping. This requires you to be connected as a server administrator.

You can find details for performing each of these steps in Chapter 12.

> **Note**   It is not possible to set custom environment variables for the CGI process. CGI always passes a fixed set of server variables as environment variables for the CGI process, as defined in the CGI protocol specification. If your application framework supports the FastCGI protocol and if you are using FastCGI, you can set custom environment variables.

Because CGI starts a new process each time a request is received, it enables it to execute the CGI process under the identity of the authenticated user, if one is available. This is the default behavior. Because of this, CGI processes and the scripts the processes execute will by default run under the identity of the authenticated user, or under the IIS anonymous user (IIS_IUSR) for anonymous requests. You can disable this behavior globally on the machine by setting the *createProcessAsUser* attribute in the *system.webServer/cgi* configuration section to false.

You can set CGI configuration settings in IIS Manager, from the command line by using Appcmd, or by using configuration APIs. The *system.webServer/cgi* configuration section is global and therefore can have only a single set of settings for the entire server. You can set a configuration in this section by using the following Appcmd syntax.

```
%systemroot%\system32\inetsrv\Appcmd set config
/section:system.WebServer/cgi [/createCGIWithNewConsole:bool]
[/createProcessAsUser:bool] [/timeout:timespan]
```

The parameters for setting CGI configuration are listed in Table 11-8.

Table 11-8   Parameters for Setting CGI Configuration

Setting	Description
createCGIWithNewConsole	Whether or not to create each CGI process with a new console. The default is false.
createProcessAsUser	Whether or not to create each CGI process under the identity of the authenticated user. The default is true.
Timeout	The request time-out in seconds after which the CGI process is terminated. The default is 15 minutes.

> **Note**   If you use a custom account for the application pool, you need to grant the custom account the Adjust Memory Quotas For A Process and Replace A Process Level Token user rights. You can do this using the Local Security Policy console.

In addition, you can configure a limit of CGI processes that can be active simultaneously for any IIS worker process. If the number is exceeded, all subsequent CGI requests to the worker process will be queued until the number of CGI processes falls below the limit. This setting can be configured only in the registry by creating the *MaxConcurrentCgisExecuting DWORD* value in the registry key, HKLM\System\CurrentControlSet\Services\W3SVC\ Parameters\. By default, when this value is not set, the limit is 256 CGI processes per IIS worker process.

> **Caution**   Be aware that starting a large number of CGI processes can quickly overwhelm a Web server due to both the memory overhead of each process and the cost of starting a new process. This occurs especially if you have multiple application pools, because the limit is applied to each IIS worker process individually. Because of this, you may need to set the *MaxConcurrentCgisExecuting* limit to a much lower value. Consider using FastCGI instead of CGI to reduce this overhead.

Summary

IIS 7.0 provides a comprehensive set of options for hosting application framework technologies, expanding this set from previous versions of IIS by introducing the built-in support for the FastCGI protocol. Together with other application framework interfaces including ISAPI extensions, ASP.NET handlers, and IIS 7.0 native modules, this opens the door to many application frameworks that have not targeted IIS in the past.

Beyond simply hosting application framework technologies, IIS provides a comprehensive set of features and management capabilities that provide an enhanced experience for any application framework. With the new ASP.NET integration mode enabling IIS extensibility at the Web server level, these technologies can begin to leverage the power of the .NET Framework and ASP.NET without having to migrate to these technologies. You can learn more about extending IIS 7.0 in Chapter 12.

In this chapter, you learned how to use IIS as an application framework platform and how to install and deploy common application platforms including ASP.NET, ASP, and PHP. You also learned how to use the general application framework hosting options in IIS to add third-party application frameworks.

To learn more about securing and isolation applications on IIS 7.0, be sure to review the best practices in Chapter 14.

Additional Resources

These resources contain additional information and tools related to this chapter:

- To access the official IIS Web site, visit *http://www.iis.net.*

- To access the official ASP.NET Web site, visit *http://www.asp.net.*

- To access the official PHP Web site, visit *http://www.php.net.*

- To learn about installing and managing Web server models, see Chapter 12, "Managing Web Server Modules."

- To learn about how to improve the security of the Web server and application frameworks, see Chapter 14, "Implementing Security Strategies."

- To read a blog that frequently provides information about hosting applications on IIS, including ASP.NET and PHP, go to *http://mvolo.com.*

Chapter 12
Managing Web Server Modules

Extensibility in IIS 7.0

On the Microsoft Internet Information Services (IIS) 7.0 team, there is a running joke that every release of IIS has to be a complete rewrite of the previous version. However, when looking at the history of the product, there have been strong reasons behind each of the rewrites. IIS 6.0, which was shipped with Windows Server 2003, was a complete rewrite of Windows XP's IIS 5.1, in the wake of the infamous CodeRed and Nimbda security exploits that plagued it in the summer of 2001. The rewrite, focused on producing an extremely reliable, fast, and secure Web server, was an overwhelming success—as evidenced by the rock-solid reliability and security track record of IIS 6.0 to date.

IIS 7.0 is again a major rewrite of the Web server, but this time for a different reason—to transform the reliable and secure codebase of IIS 6.0 into a powerful next-generation Web application platform. To achieve this, the IIS 7.0 release makes a huge investment in providing complete platform extensibility. The result? The most full-featured, flexible, and extensible Web server that Microsoft has ever released.

The extensible architecture of IIS 7.0 is behind virtually all of the critical platform improvements delivered in this release. Almost all functionality of the Web server, starting with the run-time Web server features and ending with configuration and the IIS Manager features, can be removed or replaced by third parties. This enables customers to build complete end-to-end solutions that deliver the functionality needed by their applications.

What's more, IIS 7.0's very own feature set is built on top of the same extensibility model third parties can take advantage of to further customize the server. This is a key concept, because it insures that the extensibility model available to third parties is at least powerful and flexible enough to build any of the features that come in the box. It also provides a unified way to think about and manage Web server features, whether it be IIS 7.0 built-in features or those provided by third parties. This is the heart of the modularity of IIS 7.0. This modularity, together with the power of the extensibility model, enables you to turn your Web server into an efficient, specialized server that does exactly what you need and nothing more.

With IIS 7.0, you can for the first time:

- Build a low-footprint, reduced attack surface area Web server optimized for a specific workload.

- Replace any built-in feature with a custom feature developed in-house or by a third-party independent software vendor (ISV).

- Build complete end-to-end solutions that integrate seamlessly into the Web server, including request processing functionality, configuration, diagnostics, and administration.

Though traditionally topics concerning extensibility have been reserved mostly for developer audiences, with IIS 7.0, they become a critical component of deploying and operating the Web server. Thus, they necessitate a solid level of know-how from the IT staff. The ability to properly deploy, configure, tune, and lock down the feature set that comprises the Web server is critical to achieving a functional, scalable, and secure IIS production environment. Properly taking advantage of the flexibility IIS 7.0 offers can allow you to reap huge benefits in achieving small-footprint, fast, and secure Web server deployments. On the other hand, the complexity introduced by this same flexibility must be managed correctly, so that you can guarantee proper operation and reduce the total cost of ownership for your Web server farm.

This chapter takes the IT professional's perspective on the end-to-end extensibility platform provided by IIS 7.0. In this chapter, you will learn how to manage the modular feature set in IIS 7.0 to provide for an efficient, reliable, and secure IIS environment.

IIS 7.0 Extensibility Architecture at a Glance

The IIS 7.0 Web server platform is a complex system, including a number of parts necessary to operate, manage, and support Web applications running on top of it. This includes the Web server itself, the configuration system that supports the Web server and its features, the administration stack that provides an object model for managing the server, run-time state reporting application programming interfaces (APIs), and several management tools and APIs that expose the configuration and administration functionality to the user. Each of these subsystems provides a public extensibility layer and surfaces built-in functionality as modular components built on top of it. This design supports both server specialization as well as complete server customization via third-party additions or replacements to the built-in feature set. Figure 12-1 shows an overview of the extensibility architecture.

The main extensibility point lies in the Web server engine, which supports receiving HTTP requests, processing them (often with the help of application frameworks such as ASP.NET or PHP), and returning responses to the client. This is where most of the magic happens—IIS 7.0 ships with more than 40 Web server modules, which are responsible for everything from authentication, security, and response compression to performance enhancements and support for application frameworks such as ASP. These modules leverage one of the two run-time extensibility models provided by IIS 7.0—the new C++ core extensibility model or the integrated ASP.NET extensibility model—both of which provide the flexibility to replace any built-in IIS 7.0 functionality or add new functionality of their own.

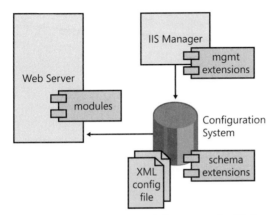

Figure 12-1   IIS 7.0 extensibility across the Web server, configuration system, and IIS Manager.

However, as you know, IIS is more than just a run time for processing requests. It also provides a brand new distributed configuration system for configuring the functionality of the Web server and its modules, with many features designed to simplify configuration, allow delegated configuration for non-administrator, and xcopy-based deployment of configuration settings with applications. In the face of increasing Web server complexity, the configuration system is more critical than ever before, and it is required to support the multitude of unique configurations and operational requirements of modern applications.

The IIS 7.0 team designed its configuration system to meet many of these challenges and to allow third-party solutions to do so by leveraging configuration extensibility. Just like the Web server features themselves, the configuration components leverage the same configuration extensibility layer that can be used to create custom configuration for third party Web server modules. This means that any custom Web server module can easily expose its own configuration settings, which can then be stored in the same configuration files and managed with the same standard APIs and tools that are used with the rest of the IIS 7.0 configuration.

In addition to static file-based configuration, IIS 7.0 provides support for administration objects, which enable dynamic configuration or management functionality to be exposed through the IIS 7.0 configuration object model. This enables new IIS management objects to be added or custom management functionality to be exposed on existing IIS objects, such as the site or application pool object, and consumed by the standard APIs and tools. Again, the administration stack is extensible, and IIS administration objects leverage that very extensibility model themselves.

Finally, IIS Manager (which replaces the old Microsoft Management Console-based InetMgr.exe) provides its own extensibility to enable graphical user interface (GUI) management pages to be added into IIS Manager, thus benefiting from the navigation, delegation, and remote management capabilities.

Together, these extensibility mechanisms provide the foundation for end-to-end solutions that can be developed on IIS 7.0, where custom Web server features can also expose custom configuration and management functionality, as well as a GUI administration experience with IIS Manager.

Direct from the Source

The IIS 7.0 release is a testament to the power of a system architecture that builds on its own extensibility foundation, rather than adding extensibility as an afterthought. Almost all components of the server, including the Web server features, their configuration, and IIS Manager management pages, are built on top of the same extensibility models that are exposed to third parties. Over the four years of working on the project, I've witnessed this power firsthand, through the unique opportunity to design and build both the core extensibility platform and the features that leverage it. In a way, IIS 7.0 has been our own best customer, helping us get the platform right before the real customers started to use it.

Mike Volodarsky

Program Manager, IIS 7.0

Managing Extensibility

The modular architecture serves as the foundation for many of the exciting new capabilities in IIS 7.0, from the ability to create specialized servers to securing and tuning server performance. However, it also exposes a fair amount of complexity to the administrator, which must be managed to harness the benefits of componentization. This moves the task of planning and managing extensibility to the IT domain, rather than being a developer-only task, as it has often been in the past. With this in mind, this chapter focuses on the key tasks around managing extensibility, rather than the information about developing extensibility components.

The first topic of interest is of course installing the extensibility components so that you can begin using them on the server. The built-in IIS 7.0 features are fully integrated with Windows Setup and can be installed using Server Manager on Windows Server 2008 and the Turn Windows Components On And Off UI on Windows Vista (you can learn more about this in Chapter 5, "Installing IIS 7.0"). Windows Setup implements all the information necessary to install and configure these components by using the IIS 7.0 configuration APIs. As such, these components typically do not require any additional work to be installed, although in some cases they may require additional configuration to control their availability to specific applications on the server.

However, this is not so for third-party components developed by ISVs or your own in-house development team. Without the support of Windows Setup, third-party components must be installed using the IIS 7.0 configuration directly. In doing so, it is often necessary to consider deployment and installation options that suit your component. In fact, because the ability to customize and tailor IIS 7.0 to the specific application solutions often relies on leveraging its modularity, the ability to properly install IIS 7.0 extensibility components and manage the enabled feature set on the server becomes critically important. Thankfully, IIS 7.0 provides a number of management tools that can be used to perform the installation tasks, and so armed with the proper know-how, you can become a pro at deploying IIS 7.0 extensibility. To that end, this chapter describes how to install and manage enabled Web server modules. You can learn how to manage configuration and IIS Manager extensions in Chapter 13, "Managing Configuration and User Interface Extensions."

After covering initial deployment, you will also review common configuration and management tasks for each extensibility type. Though not always required, these tasks are often helpful to get your component to do exactly what you want in specific situations, and they include things such as insuring the correct execution order for your modules and enabling your modules to function correctly in a mixed 32-bit/64-bit environment. These tasks vary between the different extensibility types and are largely based on the developer's experience developing and using the extensibility layers during the development of IIS 7.0.

IIS 7.0 continues the IIS 6.0 tradition of emphasizing security, providing additional lockdown by default, and introducing new security features to help you further secure your Web server assets. One of the powerful ways to improve your server's security is to take advantage of componentization and remove all unused components, which will result in the smallest attack surface area possible for your server. When adding new components, then, you need to be aware of the resulting increase in the surface area of your server, and you must understand the security implications of the new code that is now running on your server. Proper understanding of the security impact of Web server components is critical to maintaining a secure operating environment and being able to take advantage of the functionality afforded by IIS 7.0 extensibility without compromising its security.

This chapter will cover what you need to know to securely deploy Web server modules and will review key security tactics you can use to lock down your server. You will also review the specific points to watch out for when configuring a shared hosting server or departmental server, which allows extensibility components to be published by nonadministrators. You can learn about securing configuration and IIS Manager extensions in Chapter 13.

Runtime Web Server Extensibility

The Web server extensibility model provides a foundation for IIS 7.0's modular architecture, enabling the low-footprint, low attack surface area, as well as highly specialized Web server deployments. All of this is possible because built-in IIS 7.0 features are implemented as pluggable modules on top of the same extensibility APIs that are exposed to third-party modules and are configured and managed with the same configuration and management tools.

What Is a Module?

Logically, a *module* is a Web server component that takes part in the processing of some or all requests and typically provides a service that can involve anything from supporting specific authentication methods (such as the Windows Authentication module) to recording and reporting requests that are currently executing (such as the Request Monitor module). The modules operate by executing during different stages of the request processing pipeline and influencing the request processing by using the APIs exposed by the Web server extensibility model. The majority of modules provide independent services to add functionality to the Web application or otherwise enhance the Web server.

The application developer or IT administrator can then essentially put together the Web server with the precise functionality that is required by controlling which modules are enabled for the application, much like building a structure from a set of LEGO blocks. IIS 7.0 provides a fine degree of control over which modules are enabled, giving administrators control of functionality on both the server as a whole and of specific applications, which we'll cover in depth later in this chapter.

Physically, IIS 7.0 modules are implemented as either native dynamic-link libraries (DLLs) developed on top of the new IIS 7.0 native C++ extensibility model, or as managed .NET Framework classes that leverage the new ASP.NET integration model available in IIS 7.0. Both of these APIs enable modules to participate in the IIS 7.0 request processing pipeline, and manipulate the request and response processing as needed. Though these two extensibility models use two different APIs and have a number of different characteristics from both the developer and IT administrator perspective, they both implement the logical module concept. This enables IIS 7.0 to provide a consistent development abstraction to both C++ and .NET Framework developers for extending the Web server. The logical module concept also enables IIS 7.0 to expose the administrator to a largely unified view of managing the Web server feature set. For information on the differences between native and managed Web server modules and how they affect the installation and management of modules, see the section titled "Differences Between Managed (.NET) and Native (C++) Modules" later in this chapter.

The Request Processing Pipeline

The IIS 7.0 request processing pipeline is the foundation of the modular architecture, enabling multiple independent modules to provide valuable services for the same request.

> **Note** In IIS 7.0, the amount of processing the Web server engine itself performs is minimal, with the modules providing most of the request processing.

The pipeline itself is essentially a deterministic state machine that enables modules to interact with the request during a fixed set of processing stages, also known as *events*. As shown in

Figure 12-2, when the request is received, the state machine proceeds from the initial stage toward the final stage, raising the events and giving each module an opportunity to do its work during the stages it is interested in.

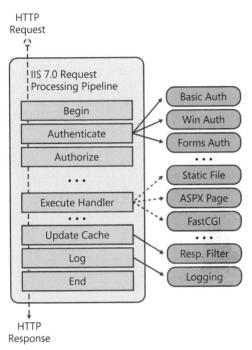

Figure 12-2   The request processing pipeline.

The majority of events in the request processing pipeline are intended for a specific type of task, such as authentication, authorization, caching, or logging. Modules that subscribe to these events can provide a specific service appropriate for the particular stage. For example, the authenticate event is home to a number of IIS 7.0 modules, including the Windows Authentication module (NTLM and Kerberos authentication), the Basic Authentication module, the ASP.NET Forms Authentication module, and so on. These events enable multiple modules to execute during the request processing and perform typical Web server processing tasks in the correct order. For example, determining the user associated with the request during the authentication stage needs to happen before determining whether that user has access to the requested resource during the authorization stage.

Other events are present for additional flexibility, enabling modules to perform tasks at a specific time during request processing (typically between the events that have specific intended roles such as authentication and authorization). Table 12-1 lists all the events, along with some IIS 7.0 modules that subscribe to them.

Table 12-1   Request Processing Events

Event	Description	Modules
BeginRequest	The request processing is starting.	Request Filtering module, IP Restrictions module
AuthenticateRequest	The authenticated user for the request is determined.	Authentication modules, including Windows Authentication module, Basic Authentication module, ASP.NET Forms Authentication module
AuthorizeRequest	Access to the requested resource is checked for the authenticated user, and the request is rejected if access is denied.	URL Authorization module
ResolveRequestCache	The server checks if the response to this request can be retrieved from a cache.	IIS Output Cache module, ASP.NET Output Cache module
MapRequestHandler	The handler for this request is determined.	
AcquireRequestState	The required state for this request is retrieved.	ASP.NET Session State module
PreExecuteRequestHandler	The server is about to execute the handler.	
ExecuteRequestHandler	The handler for the request executes and produces the response.	All modules that provide request handling, including Static File module, Directory Listing module, Default Document module, ISAPI extension module, ASP.NET PageHandler
ReleaseRequestState	The state is released.	ASP.NET Session State module
UpdateRequestCache	The cache is updated.	IIS 7.0 Output Cache module, ASP.NET Output Cache module
LogRequest	The request is logged.	Custom Logging module
EndRequest*	The request processing is about to finish.	Request Monitor module

* All of the events in this table except the *EndRequest* event also have a corresponding Post event, such as *PostBeginRequest* for *BeginRequest*. Post events exist primarily to provide additional flexibility to modules so that they can perform tasks that need to happen between specific events.

It is important to understand that though the majority of modules are self-contained and provide independent services during request processing, they do operate on a common set of request and response state and can affect the other's operation. In some cases, these relationships are part of formal patterns (such as the authentication and authorization pattern), and in others they may be unintentional. In the latter case, some modules may not be compatible with each other, or they may require a specific ordering to function correctly. Module ordering is discussed in the section titled "Controlling Module Ordering" later in this chapter.

Differences Between Managed (.NET) and Native (C++) Modules

As we mentioned earlier, IIS 7.0 supports modules developed with the native IIS 7.0 C++ API as well as modules developed using the ASP.NET module API, sometimes referred to as *managed* modules.

The IIS 7.0 C++ module API replaces the legacy ISAPI filter and extension API as the new native extensibility model for IIS 7.0 and future versions of IIS. Existing ISAPI filters and extensions are still supported, but developers are encouraged to take advantage of the module extensibility model to build new server components. In fact, the support for ISAPI filters and extensions in IIS 7.0 is implemented as a native module, developed with the new native API, which hosts and executes ISAPI DLLs. Modules developed using the new native API are similar to the ISAPI filters in that they are Win32 DLLs loaded in-process by each IIS worker process, and they can affect the processing of every request. Because they execute under the rights and privileges of the IIS worker process, they have the same security impact and therefore have to be trusted by the server administrator.

However, this is where many of the similarities end, because IIS 7.0 modules use a much more refined and significantly more powerful C++ API, have access to many more extensibility points by subscribing to one or more of the events in the request processing pipeline, and can accomplish much richer tasks. The new C++ API also significantly improves the server development experience and reduces the potential for reliability issues that plagued the overly complex ISAPI interface. This makes IIS 7.0 native modules the most powerful—and yet simpler and more reliable—way to extend IIS.

Also, for the first time in the history of IIS, IIS 7.0 provides a full-fidelity .NET extensibility model based on ASP.NET. This makes server development significantly more accessible to developers and enables them to rapidly build server features while taking advantage of powerful features of ASP.NET and the .NET Framework. This is made possible by the new ASP.NET integration engine, which elevates ASP.NET from being an application framework to being a first-class extensibility mechanism for IIS 7.0.

As a server administrator, extending IIS with the .NET Framework enables you to delegate IIS extensibility to application owners who do not have administrator privileges on the server. This is possible because of the Code Access Security (CAS)–based ASP.NET hosting model, which constrains the execution of code in ASP.NET applications when configured to run with partial trust. Unlike native modules that execute with full privileges of the IIS worker process, managed ASP.NET modules can execute with limited privileges that can prevent them from negatively affecting the server itself or other applications on the server. This enables IIS 7.0 applications to deploy IIS features to the server without requiring administrative action (such as installing COM objects or ISAPI filters), without compromising server security.

Table 12-2 is a summary of the differences between native and managed modules.

Table 12-2   Comparing Native and Managed Modules

	Native Modules	Managed Modules
Developed with	IIS 7.0 C++ module API	ASP.NET module API, any .NET language
Represented by	Win32 DLL	.NET class in a .NET assembly DLL
Scope of execution	IIS worker process	ASP.NET application domain
Execution privilege	IIS worker process identity	IIS Worker process identity, plus constrained by the ASP.NET Trust Level
Deployment model	Globally for the entire server	Globally for the entire server by using the .NET Global Assembly Cache, or xcopy-deploy inside a specific application
Deployment privilege	Administrators only	Application owners can deploy with application

IIS 7.0 configuration is aware of the differences between native and managed modules. It also enables administrators to take full advantage of the constrained execution nature of managed modules by enabling managed modules to be added on a per-application basis by packaging them together with the application content. Application-based deployment of managed modules allows for simple xcopy deployment of IIS applications because they can specify their own IIS configuration and modules.

How It Works: ASP.NET Integrated Pipeline

With the unified pipeline model that IIS 7.0 provides, both native modules developed using the IIS 7.0 native extensibility model and managed modules developed using the ASP.NET module model can participate in the Web server's request processing (when using the ASP.NET Integrated mode). Both native and managed modules can participate in all request processing stages and operate on a shared set of request and response intrinsic objects.

In practice, however, ASP.NET and IIS are two separate software products. Moreover, ASP.NET Integrated mode uses the standard ASP.NET interfaces that are used to provide request processing services to the ASP.NET application framework on previous versions of IIS. How, then, is such a tight integration possible?

The answer lies in the special native module, ManagedEngine, that is installed on IIS 7.0 when the ".NET Extensibility" Windows Setup component (Windows Vista) or Role Service (Windows Server 2008) is installed. This module implements the ASP.NET Integrated mode engine that enables the ASP.NET request processing pipeline to be overlaid on the IIS request processing pipeline, proxying the event notifications and propagating the required request state to support the pipeline integration. This module is responsible for reading the managed modules and handler entries in the IIS module and handler configuration and working together with the new ASP.NET engine

> implementation in *System.Web.dll* to set up the integrated pipeline. As a result, it enables ASP.NET modules and handlers to act as IIS modules and handlers.
>
> So, when you see the ManagedEngine module in the IIS modules list, pay it some respect—it is arguably the most complex and powerful module ever written for IIS 7.0. Also keep in mind that this module must be present for the integrated pipeline and ASP.NET applications in general to work in IIS 7.0 Integrated mode application pools.
>
> *Mike Volodarsky*
>
> *IIS Core Program Manager*

However, IIS 7.0 also provides a consistent view of managing modules, whether they are native or managed, so that administrators can control the server feature set in a standard manner regardless of the module type. You will review the differences in the installation of native and managed modules, as well as standard management tasks, later in this section.

Installing Modules

The modules that comprise the IIS 7.0 feature set in Windows Vista or Windows Server 2008 can be installed via Windows Setup. Thanks to the modular architecture, Windows Setup enables very fine-grained installation of IIS 7.0 features—you can install most of the IIS 7.0 modules separately (along with all of their supporting configuration and administration features). You can also install the *.NET Extensibility* role service, which enables ASP.NET managed modules to run on IIS 7.0, or the *ASP.NET* role service, which also installs all of the of the ASP.NET managed modules and handlers to support fully functional ASP.NET applications. You can learn more about installing IIS 7.0 features in Chapter 5.

Windows Setup actually uses the same IIS 7.0 configuration APIs that you can use to manually install a third-party module on the server. In fact, Windows Setup uses Appcmd.exe, the IIS 7.0 command line tool, to perform module installation, which is just one of the ways that you can install modules on IIS 7.0. Later in this chapter, you will look at the most common ways to perform the installation, which are IIS Manager and Appcmd.exe, as well as editing server configuration directly. Of course you also have the option of using any of the programmatic APIs, including the .NET *Microsoft.Web.Administration* API, the IIS 7.0 configuration COM objects from C++ programs or script, or WMI. The choice is yours.

Installing Native Modules

To install a native module, it must be registered with the system.webServer/globalModules configuration section at the server level, in the ApplicationHost.config configuration file. Because only server administrators have access to this file, the installation of native modules requires Administrative privileges on the server. This is by design—allowing native code to execute in the IIS worker process is a potential security risk, and so Administrators must be sure to trust the source of the module.

The globalModules section contains an entry for each native module installed on the server, specifying the module *name* and the module *image*, which is the physical path to the module DLL.

```
<globalModules>
    <add name="UriCacheModule"
image="%windir%\System32\inetsrv\cachuri.dll" />
    <add name="FileCacheModule"
image="%windir%\System32\inetsrv\cachfile.dll" />
    <add name="TokenCacheModule"
image="%windir%\System32\inetsrv\cachtokn.dll" />
    <add name="HttpCacheModule"
image="%windir%\System32\inetsrv\cachhttp.dll" />
    <add name="StaticCompressionModule"
image="%windir%\System32\inetsrv\compstat.dll" />
    <add name="DefaultDocumentModule"
image="%windir%\System32\inetsrv\defdoc.dll" />
    ...
</globalModules>
```

The *image* attribute is an expanded string, which means that it can contain environment variables (as it does for modules installed by Windows Setup). This is a good practice to make sure that the ApplicationHost.config file remains portable and can be copied between servers and works on servers with different system drives.

> **Note**   Native module DLLs should be located on the server's local file system and not on remote network shares. This is because the server attempts to load them under the application pool identity and not the identity of the authenticated user or the configured virtual path (UNC) identity. This identity will not typically have access to network shares.

The act of registering a native module instructs IIS worker processes in all application pools to load the module DLL. The globalModules configuration section is also one of the few sections that cause IIS worker processes to recycle whenever changes are made. This means that you can install new modules, or uninstall existing modules, and IIS will automatically pick up those changes without needing to manually recycle application pools, restart IIS services, or run IISRESET.

> **Note**   By adding the module to globalModules, you are instructing IIS worker processes to load the module DLL. This alone does not enable the module to run. To do that, you also need to enable the module on the server or for a particular application.

After the module is installed, it will be loaded by all IIS worker processes on the server. Unfortunately, IIS 7.0 does not enable native modules to be installed for a particular application pool, so there is no easy way to load a native module only into certain application pools and not into others.

> **Note** IIS 7.0 does provide a way to load native modules selectively into a specific application pool, by using the application pool name preconditions. See the section titled "Understanding Module Preconditions" later in this chapter for more information on this. Though loading native modules in this way is possible, you should not use this mechanism in most situations because of its management complexity.

However, loading the module alone is *not* sufficient to enable the module to execute. It also needs to be enabled by listing its name in the system.webServer/modules configuration section. This is an important distinction that serves to provide more flexible control over the enabled module set. Unlike the globalModules section, which can only be specified at the server level, the modules configuration section can be specified at the application level, such as in the application's root Web.config. This enables each application to control the set of enabled modules that process requests to itself.

Typically, a native module is also enabled at the server level (in ApplicationHost.config) during its installation, which enables it for all applications on the server by default (except for applications that specifically remove it in their configuration). This is the case for most of the built-in native modules.

```
<modules>
    <add name="HttpCacheModule" />
    <add name="StaticCompressionModule" />
    <add name="DefaultDocumentModule" />
    ...
<modules>
```

Each native module is enabled simply by listing its name in the modules collection.

Inside Global Web Server Events

If you read the globalModules section carefully, you will notice that some modules, such as the TokenCacheModule, are listed there but yet are not listed in the modules list by default. Does this mean that this module is disabled by default? No, not entirely.

Native modules loaded inside the IIS worker process can participate in global server events, which are events that are not associated with request processing. These events enable native modules to extend certain server functionality at the worker process level, such as by providing the ability to cache logon tokens for improved performance.

Native modules that offer this kind of global functionality do not need to be listed in the modules list and are able to offer it by simply being loaded in the worker process. However, only modules listed in the modules list can provide request processing functionality.

> **Note**   When the modules section changes, the IIS worker process does not need to recycle. Instead, it picks up the changes automatically and applies the resulting module set to subsequent requests. However, ASP.NET applications whose modules configuration changes will restart.

Uninstalling Native Modules

> **Caution**   Before removing modules, you should consider the security and performance implications that the module removal will have on your server. The section titled "Securing Web Server Modules" later in this chapter covers these implications in more detail.

To uninstall a native module, you need to remove the corresponding module entry from the globalModules list. This prevents the module from being loaded in IIS worker processes on the entire server. Removing the module from globalModules causes all IIS worker processes to gracefully recycle.

In addition, when the native module is removed from the globalModules list, references to it in the modules list also must be removed. Otherwise, all requests to the server or an application that enables the missing module will generate an "HTTP 500 – Internal Server Error" error until the module entry is removed. Typically, you should remove both the global-Modules and modules entry for the module at the same time. However, if you do it in two separate steps, changing the modules section will not cause a worker process recycle–IIS will automatically pick up this change by recycling any affected applications. Be sure to make a configuration backup in case you need to restore the original configuration later.

When uninstalling a native module that is part of the IIS 7.0 feature set, you should instead uninstall the corresponding IIS Windows Setup component (Windows Vista) or Role Service (Windows Server 2008). Doing so has the benefit of removing the module binaries and related configuration components, as well as indicating that the corresponding feature is not installed to the Windows Setup infrastructure. The binaries remain stored in the OS installation cache, where they are inaccessible to anyone other than the OS TrustedInstaller subsystem. This ensures that you can re-install these modules later, and that any required patches are applied to these binaries even when the patches are not installed on your server.

> **Caution**   You should *not* remove built-in IIS 7.0 modules manually. Use Windows Setup instead to uninstall the corresponding feature or role service.

When a custom module is uninstalled and all IIS worker processes have recycled, you can remove the module binary from the machine if necessary.

Look in the sections titled "Using IIS Manager to Install and Manage Modules" and "Using Appcmd to Install and Manage Modules" later in this chapter to find steps detailing how you can use IIS Manager or the Appcmd command line tool to uninstall a native module.

Installing Managed Modules

Managed modules developed using the ASP.NET APIs are not required to be installed globally on the server. Instead, they simply need to be enabled in configuration for the application where they are to be used, similar to classic ASP.NET applications in previous versions of IIS. This enables simple xcopy deployment of applications containing managed modules, since unlike native modules they do not require Administrative privileges to be deployed.

Needless to say, this makes managed modules very appealing in scenarios in which the application administrator does not have administrative privileges on the server, such as on shared hosting servers or departmental servers. Such applications can now deploy Web server features without contacting the server administrator to install a global and trusted component, which is often not possible. In these environments, the server administrator can constrain the execution of managed modules by limiting the trust of the ASP.NET applications. The section titled "Securing Web Server Modules" later in this chapter covers constraining the execution of managed modules in more detail and discusses locking down module extensibility.

> **Note**   Running managed modules requires installation of the ".NET Extensibility" Windows Setup component (Windows Vista) or Role Service (Windows Server 2008). This installs the ManagedEngine module that enables managed modules to run inside Integrated mode applications pools.
>
> Installing the "ASP.NET" setup component/role service automatically installs the ".NET Extensibility" component and also adds the modules and handler mappings used by the ASP.NET framework. It also installs the classic ASP.NET handler mappings that enable application pools that use Classic integration mode to run ASP.NET using the legacy ASPNET_ISAPI.dll integration mechanism.

To install a managed module, the module simply needs to be added to the modules configuration section. This is the same section that enables installed native modules, except managed modules do not have to be listed in the globalModules configuration section. The modules section, therefore, provides a unified view of enabled modules, whether they are native or managed. Because this configuration section can be delegated down to the application level, each application can specify the complete set of enabled modules (managed or native) by using its modules configuration. Here is a more complete example of the modules configuration section at the server level after the ASP.NET feature is installed.

```
<modules>
    <add name="HttpCacheModule" />
    <add name="StaticCompressionModule" />
    <add name="DefaultDocumentModule" />
    <add name="DirectoryListingModule" />
```

```
             . . .
                <add name="FormsAuthentication"
type="System.Web.Security.FormsAuthenticationModule"
preCondition="managedHandler" />
                <add name="DefaultAuthentication"
type="System.Web.Security.DefaultAuthenticationModule"
preCondition="managedHandler" />
                <add name="RoleManager"
type="System.Web.Security.RoleManagerModule" preCondition="managedHandler"
/>
             . . .
        </modules>
```

As you can see, this section contains both native modules that are simply identified by the *name* attribute, and managed modules that also specify a *type* attribute. For each application, the server resolves the enabled modules by looking up the native modules' names in the globalModules section and directly loading the specified .NET type for managed modules. The type is the fully qualified .NET type name that refers to the class that implements this module and resolves to an assembly that is packaged with the application or an assembly installed in the machine's Global Assembly Cache (GAC).

Important   ASP.NET applications that define modules in the system.web/httpModules configuration section and ASP.NET handler mappings in the system.web/httpHandlers configuration section need to have their configurations migrated to the IIS system.webServer/modules and system.webServer/handlers configuration sections to operate correctly in Integrated mode. The server will generate a HTTP 500 error notifying you of this requirement if you attempt to run such an application in Integrated mode. You can migrate the application easily by using the *Appcmd Migrate Config ApplicationPath* command. To learn more about why this is necessary and the options you have for running legacy ASP.NET applications, see Chapter 11, "Hosting Application Development Frameworks."

Deploying Assemblies Containing Managed Modules

Managed modules are classes implemented inside .NET assemblies. To support delegated deployment of managed modules, the server provides several options, as shown in Table 12-3, for deploying the module assemblies so that they can be added both globally on the server and for a specific application only.

Table 12-3   Managed Modules and Deployment Options

Deployment Option	Assembly Location	Module Registration Location
Server	Global Assembly Cache (GAC)	Server level modules section in ApplicationHost.config
Application	Assembly in application's /BIN directory	Application's modules section in application root's Web.config
	OR	
	Source code in application's /App_Code directory	

Deploying the Module Assembly at the Server Level   If the module is to be installed globally for all applications on the server, it needs to be registered with the machine's Global Assembly Cache (GAC). Before the managed assembly can be deployed to the GAC, it needs to be strongly signed by the developer (for more information on strongly signing .NET assemblies, see *http://msdn2.microsoft.com/en-us/library/xc31ft41.aspx*). In particular, Microsoft Visual Studio makes the signing process simple. Then, the managed assembly can be added to the GAC by running the following command.

```
gacutil.exe /if AssemblyPath
```

> **Note**   The gacutil.exe command line tool is *not* available in the .NET Framework run-time installation that comes with the operating system, so you have to download the .NET Framework SDK to obtain it. After you obtain it, though, you can copy the tool to use on other machines.

After your assembly is added to the Global Assembly Cache, you can add any of the modules it contains to the server level modules section by specifying their type. This type name must be fully qualified; that is, it must contain the full namespace path to the class (for example, *System.Web.Security.FormsAuthenticationModule*). Because when it creates your module, ASP.NET needs to locate an assembly that contains this type, the assembly must either be listed in the system.web/compilation/assemblies configuration collection or included in the type name by using the strong name notation. Here is an example of a strong name for the built-in FormsAuthentication module.

```
System.Web.Security.FormsAuthenticationModule, System.Web, Version=2.0.0.0,
Culture=neutral, PublicKeyToken=b03f5f7f11d50a3a, processorArchitecture=x86
```

> **Note**   You can get the assembly part of the strong name by using the gacutil.exe tool you used earlier when you installed the assembly to the Global Assembly Cache. Run "gacutil.exe /l *AssemblyName*" to display the assembly's strong name signature. You can omit all parts of the assembly's strong name signature except for the assembly name, and ASP.NET will attempt to find the first matching assembly based on the attributes you do include.

You may wonder why the default module entries for ASP.NET modules do not specify the strong names and simply specify the fully qualified type names. This is because their parent assembly, *System.Web.dll*, is configured to be automatically preloaded by the ASP.NET applications (by being listed in the system.web/compilation/assemblies configuration collection in .NET Framework's root Web.config). Thus, ASP.NET can locate the types of built-in ASP.NET modules by searching the preloaded assemblies, without having to specify the assembly signature in the module type string.

Deploying the Module Assembly with the Application   If the module is to be available in a specific application only, it can be xcopy-deployed with that application without registering anything globally on the server. In this case, the application owner can provide the module in two ways: as a compiled .NET assembly DLL in the /BIN subdirectory of the application root or as a source code file in the /App_Code subdirectory of the application root.

> **Note**   It is not necessary to sign the assembly in the application's /BIN subdirectory.

The /App_Code deployment model is more appropriate for development and test environments, because it enables editing of the module source code on the live server without recompiling the module DLL. The /BIN deployment model is recommended for production servers, because it does not require run-time compilation of the assembly and provides a more compact way to deploy large codebases than source code does.

Because the module type deployed inside the application is available only in the application, it can be used only in that application (unlike assemblies placed in the Global Assembly Cache, which are available to all applications on the server). To add the module, you simply need to add the fully qualified type into the modules configuration section in the application's root Web.config file. For modules whose assemblies are in the /BIN directory, you can optionally specify the assembly name, although it is not necessary—ASP.NET by default preloads all /BIN assemblies. This is also true for modules that are deployed as source code to the /App_Code directory, because ASP.NET automatically compiles and loads it.

Packaging IIS 7.0 managed modules in the application is a powerful way to create self-contained applications that can be xcopy-deployed to a server and immediately function without globally installing any functionality on the server.

Be sure to also read the section titled "Locking Down Extensibility" later in this chapter to understand the security impact of allowing managed module delegation and how to properly control it.

Uninstalling Managed Modules

> **Caution**   Before removing modules, you should consider the security and performance implications that this action will have on your server. You can find more detail in the section titled "Securing Web Server Modules" later in this chapter.

Unlike native modules, you can install managed modules simply by adding them to the modules list. Therefore, uninstalling managed modules is identical to disabling them and requires a single step.

Managed modules installed as part of ASP.NET installation cannot be individually uninstalled using Windows Setup (Windows Vista) or Server Manager (Windows Server 2008). So, if you need to remove any one of them, you have to do so by manually removing their entries from the modules section. Be sure to make a configuration backup in case you need to restore the original configuration later.

The section titled "Controlling What Modules Are Enabled" later in this chapter discusses removing managed modules. Look in the sections titled "Using IIS Manager to Install and Manage Modules" and "Using Appcmd to Install and Manage Modules" later in this chapter to find steps detailing how you can use IIS Manager or the Appcmd command line tool to remove managed modules.

Understanding Module Preconditions

The modular architecture of IIS 7.0 relies heavily on controlling which modules are installed and enabled on the server and at the application level. Sometimes, making this determination based on static configuration is not sufficient, and the decision to use the module in a specific scenario must be made based on factors known only at run time. To support this functionality, IIS 7.0 introduces the concept of preconditions, which are configured conditions that the server evaluates at run time to determine whether a particular module should be used.

The following types of preconditions are supported:

- **Module load preconditions**   These preconditions may be associated with each installed native module in the globalModules configuration section, and they determine whether a particular module is loaded by each worker process when it starts. If any of the preconditions do not evaluate to true, the module is not loaded in the worker process. These preconditions can also be used in the isapiFilters configuration section to control the loading of ISAPI filters.

- **Module enablement preconditions**   These preconditions may be associated with each enabled module in the modules configuration section, and they determine whether the module is enabled for a particular application (or request). If any of the preconditions do not evaluate to true, the module does not run.

- **Handler mapping preconditions**   These preconditions may be associated with each handler mapping in the handlers configuration section, and they determine whether this handler mapping is considered when mapping a request to handlers. If any of the preconditions do not evaluate to true, the handler mapping is ignored.

In each case, one or more precondition strings may be specified to allow the configuration entry to be selectively used in cases where all of the specified preconditions evaluate to true. If any of the preconditions fail, the module is not loaded or enabled, or the handler mapping is not considered, depending on the scenario in which the precondition is being used. Here is an example of ASP.NET setup using preconditions to load the "ManagedEngine" native module only in application pools that use Integrated mode, run Framework version 2.0, and are configured to execute in a 32-bit mode.

```
<globalModules>
   ...
   <add name="ManagedEngine"
```

```
image="%windir%\Microsoft.NET\Framework\v2.0.50727\webengine.dll"
preCondition="integratedMode,runtimeVersionv2.0,bitness32" />
</globalModules>
```

Table 12-4 lists the supported precondition strings and scenarios in which they can be used.

Table 12-4   Precondition Strings

Precondition	Applicable To
bitness32, bitness64 Matches the "bitness" of the application pool	globalModules, isapiFilters, modules, handlers
classicMode, integratedMode Matches the configured managed pipeline mode of the application pool	globalModules, isapiFilters, modules, handlers
runtimeVersionv1.1, runtimeVersionv2.0 Matches the configured .NET run-time version of the application pool	globalModules, isapiFilters, modules, handlers
appPoolName=*Name*, appPoolName!=*Name* Matches the application pool name; this precondition can be used to selectively load a native module into a specific application pool	globalModules, isapiFilters, modules, handlers
managedHandler Matches requests to handler mappings with managed handlers	modules only

The bitness32 and bitness64 preconditions match the bitness of the worker process and can be used to selectively load modules in 32-bit or 64-bit application pools. In mixed 32-bit and 64-bit IIS environments, it may be necessary to load 32-bit native modules only in 32-bit application pools, because IIS will fail to load the 32-bit native DLLs into the 64-bit worker process. To help with this, the 32-bit native modules should configure the bitness32 precondition, which selectively loads them in 32-bit application pools only. For more information about running IIS in mixed 32-bit and 64-bit, please refer to the section titled "Installing Modules for x64 Environments" later in this chapter.

The classicMode and integratedMode preconditions match the configured *managedPipelineMode* attribute of each application pool. Together with the runtimeVersion preconditions, they provide a foundation for the ASP.NET versioning in IIS 7.0 and also allow for selecting the right set of ASP.NET handler mappings based on the integration mode of the application pool. In application pools that either use the Classic ASP.NET integration mode or use a .NET version that does not support direct integration, IIS 7.0 uses legacy ISAPI-based handler mappings for ASP.NET. Both of these sets of handler mappings are configured at the server level, and they use the classicMode/integratedMode and runtimeVersion preconditions to automatically select the right set of handler mappings based on the application pool's managed pipeline mode and Framework version.

You can use the applicationPoolName precondition to selectively load/enable modules and handler mappings in a particular application pool. An IIS 7.0 mechanism is provided to enable specific customer scenarios primarily on shared Web hosting servers. IIS 7.0 does not use it by default.

Finally, the managedHandler precondition enables modules to be enabled only for requests to ASP.NET handlers. For ASP.NET Integrated mode applications, IIS 7.0 enables managed modules to execute for all requests, whether or not they are mapped to ASP.NET handlers. However, by default, all ASP.NET modules use the managedHandler precondition to run only for requests to managed handlers. This also enables the ASP.NET appdomain creation to be delayed until the first request to an ASP.NET handler is made. This precondition can be removed from each module to allow it to run for all content types, regardless of whether they are managed or native. For example, to allow ASP.NET Forms-based authentication to occur for all content on the site, you need to remove the managedHandler precondition from the "FormsAuthentication" module. You can learn more about this in the "Enabling Managed Modules to Run for All Requests" section further in this chapter.

Preconditions solve a number of key problems in IIS 7.0. However, they can also add management complexity, and if configured incorrectly, they can result in unintended behavior. The largest cause of precondition-related problems is due to preconditions preventing modules from being loaded/enabled or handler mappings from being used, resulting in missing functionality. Though the module or handler mapping may appear present, its precondition can be preventing it from being active. These types of problems may be hard to diagnose because missing functionality does not always manifest in errors.

Another common problem is precondition inconsistency, where related configuration is not preconditioned correctly and results in configuration errors. For example, if a native module has a bitness32 load precondition, but the corresponding enablement entry in the modules list does not, requests to 64-bit application pools will produce a "bad module" error because the module being enabled is not loaded. Likewise, if a handler mapping refers to a module whose enablement precondition in the modules list prevents it from being enabled, requests that are mapped to this handler mapping will encounter an error.

To avoid these problems, remember that preconditions primarily serve to prevent a module/ handler mapping from being used in scenarios where it cannot function. Make sure that the preconditions do not restrict the module from being available in scenarios where it's needed.

Also keep in mind the precondition relationships between the different configuration sections where they exist. Preconditions must get more restrictive as they go from module load preconditions, to module enablement preconditions, and finally to the handler mapping precondition for the module. For example, if the module load precondition in globalModules is "bitness32", the module enablement precondition for the corresponding entry in the modules section must at least contain that precondition. If the module is referenced in a handler mapping in the handlers configuration, the precondition of that entry must contain at least the precondition strings from the modules entry (which in turn contains at least the preconditions from globalModules entry).

Installing Modules for x64 Environments

When IIS 7.0 is installed on 64-bit versions of the operating system, it functions in native 64-bit mode by default. This means that all application pools create native 64-bit worker processes and load 64-bit IIS core engine components and modules. However, by allowing any of its application pools to use the 32-bit emulation mode called wow64, IIS 7.0 supports hosting both native 64-bit and 32-bit applications. Unlike IIS 6.0, which also provided the ability to use wow64, IIS 7.0 allows each application pool to configure this individually, enabling side by side hosting of native 64-bit and 32-bit applications on the same server.

Each application pool that has the *enable32BitAppOnWin64* property set to true will create 32-bit worker processes and load the 32-bit version of the IIS core and modules. This is possible because IIS setup on 64-bit operating systems installs both 64-bit and 32-bit versions of all IIS components and modules—the native 64-bit versions go into the standard *%windir%*\System32\Inetsrv directory, and the 32-bit versions go into the *%windir%*\ Syswow64\Inetsrv directory. At run time, when IIS tries to load modules located in the *%windir%*\System32\Inetsrv directory in a 32-bit wow64 worker process, the wow64 file system redirection feature automatically redirects the file access to the \Syswow64 directory where the 32-bit versions of the DLLs are located.

This mechanism enables IIS or third-party modules installed under the system32 directory to provide 32-bit versions under the \Syswow64 directory and then automatically load the correct version based on the "bitness" of the worker process.

However, the entire reason mixed 64-bit and 32-bit environments exist is that some functionality may not be available in native 64-bit flavors, requiring the worker process to operate in 32-bit mode. This is often needed for ASP applications that invoke in-process 32-bit COM components, 32-bit only ISAPI filters, or 32-bit only native modules. Likewise, some components may be available only in 64-bit flavors, and therefore they are not supported in 32-bit worker processes. To support such a scenario, you must be able to install native modules, ISAPI filters, and ISAPI extensions so that IIS never attempts to load a 32-bit component in a 64-bit worker process, and vice versa. IIS 7.0 provides this support via the bitness preconditions (see the section titled "Understanding Module Preconditions" earlier in this chapter), which enable native modules, ISAPI filters, and handler mappings to indicate whether they are available only in 32-bit or 64-bit application pools.

For example, handler mappings that map requests to the 32-bit version of the ASP.NET ISAPI use the bitness32 precondition to insure that they are used only inside 32-bit worker processes.

```
<handlers accessPolicy="Read, Script">

  <add name="PageHandlerFactory-ISAPI-2.0" path="*.aspx"
```

```
verb="GET,HEAD,POST,DEBUG" modules="IsapiModule"
scriptProcessor="%windir%\Microsoft.NET\Framework\v2.0.50727\aspnet_isapi
dll" preCondition="classicMode,runtimeVersionv2.0,bitness32"
responseBufferLimit="0" />
  …
</handlers>
```

By default, the 64-bit version of the .NET Framework also registers an identical mapping to the 64-bit version of the aspnet_isapi.dll, which uses the bitness64 precondition so that it is selected only in 64-bit worker processes.

Using the bitness32 and bitness64 preconditions can therefore allow native modules, ISAPI filters, and ISAPI extensions specified in the handler mapping configuration to directly target 64-bit or 32-bit application pools, without using the file system redirection mechanism to provide both 32-bit and 64-bit flavors.

Common Module Management Tasks

Besides enabling you to choose which modules are installed on the server, IIS 7.0 enables you to further fine-tune its functionality by selecting which modules are enabled on the server or even for a particular application. Furthermore, you will sometimes want to tweak other aspects of module operation, such as their relative order, or the specific scenarios in which modules should execute. This section will illustrate some of these common module management tasks.

Controlling What Modules Are Enabled

Despite the differences between installation procedures for native and managed modules, the modules configuration section provides a unified view of the enabled modules. By manipulating the module entries in the modules section, you can control which modules will be allowed to function on the server by default or for a specific application:

- Adding a module at the server level allows it to execute by default in all applications on the server, except for applications that specifically remove it.

- Removing a module at the server level prevents it from executing in all applications on the server, except for applications that specifically add it back.

- Adding a module at the application level allows it to execute in that specific application.

- Removing a server-level defined module at the application level removes this module from the specific application, while allowing other applications to use it.

In a nutshell, modules that are enabled on the server level provide a default feature set for all applications on the server. Each application can then tweak this feature set by removing unneeded modules and then adding additional modules in its modules section. It is important to remember that though you can add new managed modules at the application level, new native modules must be installed at the server level to be enabled at the application level. This means that applications cannot introduce new native modules—they can only remove existing ones that are enabled, or add back native modules that are installed but not enabled by default at the server level.

> **Note**   You can manage the enabled modules for your application by using the IIS Manager. After selecting your application in the tree view and opening the Modules feature, use the Add Managed Module action to add a new managed module, the Configure Native Modules action to enable or disable existing native modules, or the Edit or Remove actions to edit or remove existing module entries in the list. See the section titled "Using IIS Manager to Install and Manage Modules" later in this chapter for more information.

> **Note**   You can also use the Appcmd command line tool to manage the enabled modules. See the section titled "Using Appcmd to Install and Manage Modules" later in this chapter for more information.

Enabling Managed Modules to Run for All Requests

The ability to extend IIS with managed modules that execute for all content types is one of the central breakthroughs of IIS 7.0. However, for backward compatibility reasons, all of the built-in ASP.NET modules are configured to execute only for requests to managed (ASP.NET) handlers. Because of this, useful ASP.NET services such as Forms Authentication are by default available only for requests to ASP.NET content types, and they are not applied to requests to static content or ASP pages. The ASP.NET setup does this, adding the "managedHandler" precondition to each ASP.NET module element when it is added to the modules configuration section. See the section titled "Understanding Module Preconditions" earlier in this chapter for more information.

Because of this, it is necessary to remove this precondition from each ASP.NET module whose service is desired for all application content. This can be done by using Appcmd or IIS Manager to edit the specified modules element, or by manually removing the precondition from the module element. When this is desired at the application level for a module element inherited from the server level configuration, it is necessary to remove and redefine the module element without the precondition.

```
<modules>
  <remove name="FormsAuthentication" />
  <add name="FormsAuthentication"
type="System.Web.Security.FormsAuthenticationModule" />
</modules>
```

This clears the default "managedHandler" value of the *preCondition* attribute and enables the FormsAuthentication module to run for all requests.

When you use IIS Manager or Appcmd to edit the module element, this configuration is automatically generated whenever you make changes at the application level.

> **Note** New managed modules you add will not have the managedHandler precondition by default and will run for all requests. If you want to restrict the managed module to run only for requests to managed handlers, you need to manually add the managedHandler precondition.

Alternatively, you can configure your application to ignore all managedHandler preconditions and effectively always execute all managed modules for all requests without needing to remove the precondition for each one. This is done by setting the runAllManagedModules-ForAllRequests configuration option in the modules configuration section.

```
<modules runAllManagedModulesForAllRequests="true" />
```

Controlling Module Ordering

Due to the pipeline model of module execution, module ordering is often important to ensure that the server "behaves" as it should. For example, modules that attempt to determine the authenticated user must execute before modules that verify access to the requested resource, because the latter needs to know what the authenticated user is. This ordering is almost always enforced by the stages of the request processing pipeline. By doing their work during the right stage, modules automatically avoid ordering problems. However, in some cases, two or more modules that perform a similar task—and therefore execute in the same stage—may have ordering dependencies. One prominent example is built-in authentication modules. They are run during the AuthenticateRequest stage, and to authenticate the request with the strongest credentials available, they should be in the strongest to weakest order. To resolve such relative ordering dependencies, the administrator can control the relative ordering of modules by changing the order in which they are listed in the modules section.

This works because the server uses the order in the modules configuration section to order module execution within each request processing stage. By placing module A before module B in the list, you can allow module A to execute before module B.

This also means that when an application enables a new module (by adding a new managed module, or enabling a native module that was not previously enabled), that module is listed after the modules enabled by higher configuration levels due to the configuration collection inheritance. This can sometimes be a problem if the new module should run before an existing module defined at the higher level, because the configuration system does not provide a way to reorder inherited elements. In this case, the only solution is to clear the modules collection and re-add all of the elements in the correct order at the application level.

```
<modules>
    <clear/>
    <add name="HttpCacheModule" />
```

```
...
<add name="MyNewModule" type="Modules.MyNewModule" />
...
<modules>
```

Note   You can also use IIS Manager to perform the ordering task. After selecting your application in the tree view and opening the Modules feature, choose the View Ordered List action and use the Move Up and Move Down actions to adjust the sequence. If you use this feature, the tool will use the <clear/> approach that we discussed earlier to reorder the modules for your application.

Caution   By using the <clear/> approach, you are effectively disconnecting the application's module configuration from the configuration at the server level. Therefore, any changes made at the server level (removing or adding modules) will no longer affect the application and will need to be manually propagated if necessary.

Adding Handler Mappings

Though modules typically execute for all requests so that the modules can provide a content-independent service, some modules may opt to act as handlers. Handlers are responsible for producing a response for a specific content type and are mapped in the IIS 7.0 handler mapping configuration to a specific verb/extension combination. For handlers, the server is responsible for mapping the correct handler based on the handler mapping configuration, and they are also responsible for invoking that handler during the ExecuteRequest request processing stage to produce the response for this request. Examples of handlers include StaticFileModule, which serves static files; DirectoryListingModule, which displays directory listings; and the ASP.NET PageHandler, which compiles and executes ASP.NET pages.

The main conceptual difference between modules and handlers is that the server picks the handler to produce the response for requests to a specific resource, whereas modules typically process all requests in a resource-independent way and typically do not produce responses. Because of this, only the one handler mapped by the server is executed per request. If you are familiar with IIS 6.0, this is similar to the distinction between the ISAPI extensions, which provide processing for a specific extension, and ISAPI filters, which intercept all requests.

Traditionally, most application frameworks including ASP.NET, ASP, PHP, and ColdFusion are implemented as handlers that process URLs with specific extensions.

You register a handler on the server by creating a handler mapping entry in the collection located in the system.webServer/handlers configuration section. This concept is similar to the script maps configuration in previous releases of IIS, but in IIS 7.0 it is extended to allow for more flexibility and to accommodate more handler types. For applications using the Integrated mode, this section also supports managed handlers that in previous IIS versions are registered in the ASP.NET httpHandlers configuration section.

After it receives the request, the server examines the collection of handler mappings configured for the request URL and selects the first handler mapping whose path mask and verb match the request. Later, during the ExecuteRequestHandler stage, the handler mapping will be used to invoke a module to handle the request.

Each handler mapping collection entry can specify the attributes shown in Table 12-5.

Table 12-5   Attributes Specified by Handler Mappings

Attribute	Description
name (required)	The name for the handler mapping.
path (required)	The path mask that must match the request URL so that this handler mapping can be selected.
verb (required)	The verb list that must match the request verb so that this handler mapping can be selected.
resourceType	Whether the physical resource mapped to the request URL must be an existing file, directory, either, or unspecified (if the physical resource does not have to exist).
requireAccess	The accessFlag level that is required for this handler to execute.
precondition	The precondition that determines if this handler mapping is considered.
allowPathInfo	Whether or not the PATH_INFO / PATH_TRANSLATED server variables contain the path info segment; may cause security vulnerabilities in some CGI programs or ISAPI extensions that handle path info incorrectly.
responseBufferLimit	The maximum number of bytes of the response to buffer for this handler mapping. Response buffering is new in IIS 7.0 and enables modules to manipulate response data before it is sent to the client. The default is 4 MB, although ISAPI extensions installed with legacy APIs will have it automatically set to 0 for backward compatibility reasons.
Modules	List of modules that attempt to handle the request when this mapping is selected.
scriptProcessor	Additional information that is passed to the module to specify how the handler mapping should behave. Used by ISAPI extension module, CGI module, and FastCGI module.
type	The managed handler type that handles the request when this mapping is selected.

The information in the handler mapping is used as follows.

1. The *precondition* is first used to determine if the handler mapping is to be used in a particular application pool. If any of the preconditions fail, the mapping is ignored.

2. The *path* and *verb* are matched against the request URL and verb. The first mapping that matches is chosen. If no mappings matched, a "404.4 Not Found" error is generated.

3. If the accessPolicy configuration does not meet the *requireAccess* requirement for the handler mapping, a "403 Access Denied" error is generated.

4. If the *resourceType* is set to File, Directory, or Either, the server makes sure that the physical resource exists and is of the specified type. If not, a "404 Not Found" error is generated. Also, check that the authenticated user is allowed to access the mapped file system resource. If resourceType is set to Unspecified, these checks are not performed.

> **Note**   The path attribute in IIS 7.0 enables you to specify more complex path masks to match the request URL than previous versions of IIS, which enable only * or *.ext* where ext is the URL extension. IIS 7.0 enables you to use a path mask that may contain multiple URL segments separated by / and to use wildcard characters such as * or ?.

Even though the majority of IIS 7.0 handlers are added at the server level and inherited by all applications on the server, you can specify additional handlers at any level. Handler mappings added at a lower level are processed first when matching handler mappings, so new handlers may override handlers previously declared at a higher configuration level. Because of this, if you want to remap that path/verb pair to another handler for your application, it is not necessary to remove a handler added at a server level—simply adding that handler mapping in your application's configuration does the job.

> **Note**   IIS 7.0 continues to support wildcard mappings, which enable a handler to act like a filter, processing all requests and possibly delegating request processing to another handler by making a child request. Though the majority of such scenarios can now be implemented with normal modules, quite a few legacy ISAPI extensions take advantage of this model (including ASP.NET in some configurations). To create a wildcard mapping, you need to set the path and verb attributes to *, set the *requireAccess* attribute to *None*, and set the *resourceType* attribute to *Either*.

Types of Handler Mappings

Though it provides a standard way to map handlers to requests, the handlers configuration also supports a number of different types of handlers, as shown in Table 12-6.

Table 12-6   Handler Types

Handler Type	Configuration	IIS 7.0 Examples
Native module(s) The module must support the *ExecuteRequestHandler* event	*modules* specifies the list of native modules that will handle this request (typically just specifies one module)	TraceVerbHandler, OptionsVerbHandler, StaticFileModule, DefaultDocumentModule, DirectoryBrowsingModule
ASP.NET handler The application must be using the Integrated ASP.NET mode	*type* specifies fully qualified .NET type that implements ASP.NET handler interfaces	ASP.NET PageHandlerFactory (aspx pages), ASP.NET WebResourceHandler

Table 12-6   Handler Types

Handler Type	Configuration	IIS 7.0 Examples
ISAPI extension	*modules* specifies the ISAPIModule; *scriptProcessor* specifies the path to the ISAPI extension DLL to load	ASP.dll (asp pages)
CGI program	*modules* specifies the CGIModule; *scriptProcessor* specifies the path to the CGI executable	Any CGI executable
FastCGI program	*modules* specifies the *FastCGIModule*; *scriptProcessor* specifies the path and arguments for a FastCGI executable registered in the FastCGI configuration section	Any FastCGI executable (such as PHP-CGI.EXE)

Unlike script maps in previous versions of IIS, which provide hardcoded support for ISAPI extensions and CGI programs, IIS 7.0 hardcodes nothing—all types of handlers are implemented on top of the standard native or managed module API. IIS 7.0 supports ISAPI extensions by hosting them with the ISAPIModule, supports CGI programs with the CGI module, and features new support for FastCGI programs with FastCgiModule. The IsapiModule, CgiModule, and FastCgiModule modules are all native modules, much like StaticFileModule, except they support interfacing with external handler frameworks to handle the request, using the ISAPI, CGI, and FastCGI protocols respectively.

If you look at the handler mappings created by default by a full IIS 7.0 install, you will see some of the following.

```
<handlers accessPolicy="Read, Script">
        <add name="ASPClassic" path="*.asp" verb="GET,HEAD,POST"
modules="IsapiModule" scriptProcessor="%windir%\system32\inetsrv\asp.dll"
esourceType="File" />
        <add name="ISAPI-dll" path="*.dll" verb="*"
modules="IsapiModule" resourceType="File" requireAccess="Execute"
allowPathInfo="true" />
        ...
        <add name="PageHandlerFactory-Integrated" path="*.aspx"
verb="GET,HEAD,POST,DEBUG" type="System.Web.UI.PageHandlerFactory"
preCondition="integratedMode" />
        ...
        <add name="PageHandlerFactory-ISAPI-2.0" path="*.aspx"
verb="GET,HEAD,POST,DEBUG" modules="IsapiModule"
scriptProcessor="%windir%\Microsoft.NET\Framework\v2.0.50727\aspnet_isapi
dll" preCondition="classicMode,runtimeVersionv2.0,bitness32"
responseBufferLimit="0" />
        ...
        <add name="StaticFile" path="*" verb="*"
modules="StaticFileModule,DefaultDocumentModule,DirectoryListingModule"
resourceType="Either" requireAccess="Read" />
        </handlers>
```

This configuration fragment shows a good cross-section of the kinds of handler mappings that you can create. First is IsapiModule handler mapping, which enables ASP pages to be executed with the ASP.dll ISAPI extension. Second is the IsapiModule mapping, which supports direct requests to ISAPI extensions located in the application directories, which require the Execute permission.

Then, you see two mappings for the ASP.NET PageHandlerFactory, which supports the processing of ASPX pages. The first mapping uses the aspnet_isapi.dll ISAPI extension to process the request, and the second uses the Integrated mode for executing ASP.NET handlers directly. Each of these mappings uses a precondition to make sure that only one of the mappings is active in each application pool based on the ASP.NET integration mode. Classic mode application pools use the ISAPI mapping, and Integrated mode application pools use the integrated mapping. You can read more about ASP.NET integration and ASP.NET handler mappings in Chapter 11. Finally, you see the static file handler mapping, designed to be a catch-all mapping that is mapped to all requests that do not match any of the other handler mappings by specifying "*" for both path and verb. This is similar to previous versions of IIS where any requests not mapped to an ISAPI extension scriptmap are handled by the static file handler in IIS. This mapping also illustrates letting multiple modules attempt to handle the request as part of a single handler mapping. First, StaticFileModule attempts to serve a physical file if one is present, then DefaultDocumentModule performs the default document redirect, and finally DirectoryBrowsingModule attempts to serve a directory listing.

> **Security Alert**   The fact that the catch-all mapping uses StaticFileModule means that requests to resources that have not yet had a handler configured *but* are not listed in the server's MIME type configuration will result in a "404.3 Not Found" error. This error typically indicates that either you need to add a MIME map entry for the file's extension to the server's staticContent configuration section to allow the file to be downloaded, or you need to add a handler mapping to appropriately process the file. This is an important security measure that prevents scripts from being downloaded as source code on servers that do not yet have the right handler mappings installed. For more information on adding MIME type entries, see Chapter 11.

You will find out more about using IIS Manager and Appcmd to create handler mappings in the sections titled "Using IIS Manager to Install and Manage Modules" below and "Using Appcmd to Install and Manage Modules" later in this chapter.

Using IIS Manager to Install and Manage Modules

IIS Manager provides a powerful UI for managing modules on the server. This UI can be used to install both native and managed modules, as well as manage enabled modules on the server and for specific applications.

The Modules feature provides this functionality, and it can be accessed at two separate levels for slightly different functionality:

■ By server administrators at the server level, to install native modules on the server, add new managed modules, and configure modules that are enabled on the server by default.

■ By server or site administrators at the application level, to add new managed modules and configure enabled modules for the application.

At the server level, you can select the machine node in the tree view and then double-click the modules to access the Modules feature, as shown in Figure 12-3.

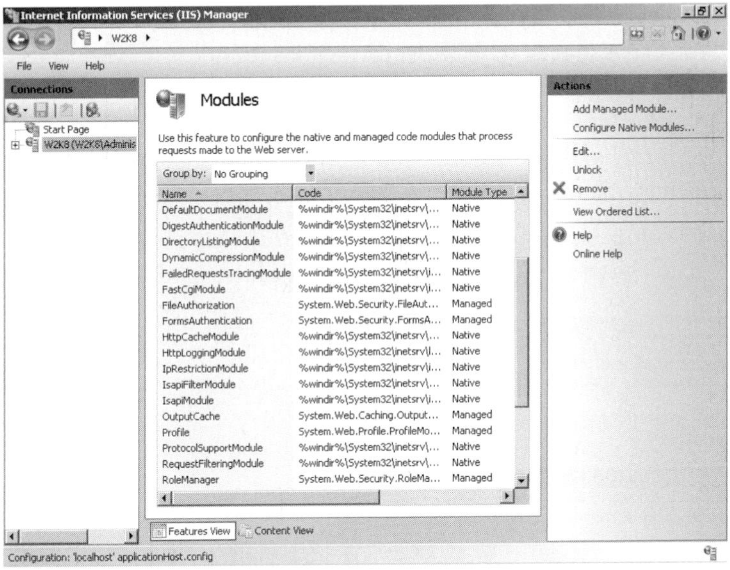

Figure 12-3   The Modules feature in IIS Manager.

You will see the list of modules enabled at the server level, which corresponds to the list of modules in the modules configuration section at the server level in ApplicationHost.config. For each module, you will see its name. For native modules, you'll also see the path to the image DLL. For managed modules, you'll also see the module type name. You will also see three actions available on this page:

■ **Add Managed Module**   Enables you to add a new managed module to the list of enabled modules. In the resulting dialog box, you can specify the name of your new module, as well as the module's type.

You can select a module type from the Type drop-down list, which contains all module types available from the assemblies located in the machine's Global Assembly Cache listed in the system.web/compilation/assemblies section of the .NET Framework's root Web.config. You can also type in your own type if it's not yet listed. Select the Invoke Only For Requests To ASP.NET Applications Or Managed Handlers check box if you want your module to use the managedHandler precondition and only execute for requests to ASP.NET handlers (see the section titled "Understanding Module Preconditions" for more information about this).

- **Configure Native Modules**   Enables you to enable an already installed native module, install a new native module, or uninstall an existing native module.

Here, you can enable native modules that are installed but not currently enabled by selecting one or more of them. You can also use the Register button to install a new native module, the Edit button to edit the name or the path for an installed module, or the Remove button to uninstall the selected native module.

- **View Ordered List**   Enables you to display the list of modules in an ordered list so that you can adjust their sequence by using the Move Up and Move Down actions. When this is done at the server level, you can reorder the modules without resorting to clearing the modules collection (see the section titled "Controlling Module Ordering" earlier in this chapter for more information).

Also, when you select a module entry in the list, three additional actions become available:

1. **Edit.** This action enables you to edit the modules entry. For native modules, you can directly change the native module installation information including its name and path to native image DLL. For managed modules, you can edit the module name and the module type.

2. **Lock/Unlock.** These actions enable you to lock the specific module item at the server level, such that it cannot be removed or modified at the application level. See the section titled "Locking Down Extensibility" later in this chapter for more information about locking modules.

3. **Remove.** This action enables you to remove the module entry. For native modules, this disables the module by default. For managed modules, this removes the module entry, requiring you to later re-add this entry at the application level to enable it there.

To access the Modules feature at the application level, go to the tree view and select the application you would like to administer. Then double-click the Modules feature icon. You will be presented with the same view as before, except for the following differences:

■ You will no longer be able to add new native modules from the Configure Native Modules dialog box. Remember, this is because native modules are installed for the entire server, and you must have Administrative privileges to do that. Instead, you will only be able to enable already installed native modules that are not currently enabled for your application.

■ You will no longer be able to edit native module information or edit managed module information for managed modules that are enabled at the server level (you can still edit module information for managed modules added in your application).

■ You will not be able to lock/unlock modules.

■ When adding managed modules, the tool will also inspect all assemblies in the /BIN and /App_Code source files for possible modules to add.

■ You can use the Revert To Inherited action to discard whatever changes were made to the modules configuration section at the application level and then revert to the default module configuration at the server level.

Despite these limitations, site administrators can still use IIS Manager to install new managed modules or manage their applications' module feature set without requiring Administrative privileges on the machine. This is especially valuable given the ability of IIS Manager to enable remote delegated administration for application owners. Of course, server administrators can also benefit from IIS Manager for unrestricted module management.

Using IIS Manager to Create and Manage Handler Mappings

IIS Manager also provides a convenient interface to manage handler mappings, thus removing some of the complexity involved with editing the handler mappings manually. This functionality is provided by the Handler Mappings feature, which both server administrators and site administrators can access.

After selecting the node at which you'd like to manage handler mappings, you can select the feature by double-clicking the Handler Mappings icon. This presents the Handler Mappings view, as shown in Figure 12-4.

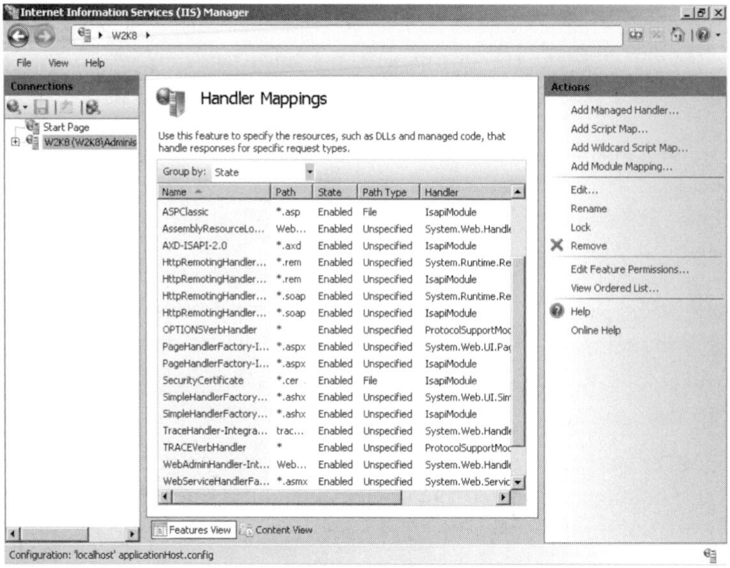

Figure 12-4   The Handler Mappings feature in IIS Manager.

Here, you will see a list of handler mappings including the handler mapping name, path, and other useful information. The Handler column provides a summary of how the handler is implemented, showing either the modules list for native handlers or the type for managed handlers. The Path Type indicates the resourceType of the handler mapping. The State column indicates if this handler is enabled (this applies only to handler mappings using IsapiModule or CgiModule) and indicates whether the ISAPI extension or CGI program specified by the mapping is enabled in the system.webServer/security/isapiCgiRestrictions configuration (analogous to the Web Service Restriction List in IIS 6.0).

The tool provides a number of ways to add new handler mappings, breaking them out by type to simplify handler mapping creation:

■ **Add Managed Handler**   This action enables you to create handler mapping to an ASP.NET handler. This mapping is available only in application pools that are using Integrated mode. It is shown in Figure 12-5.

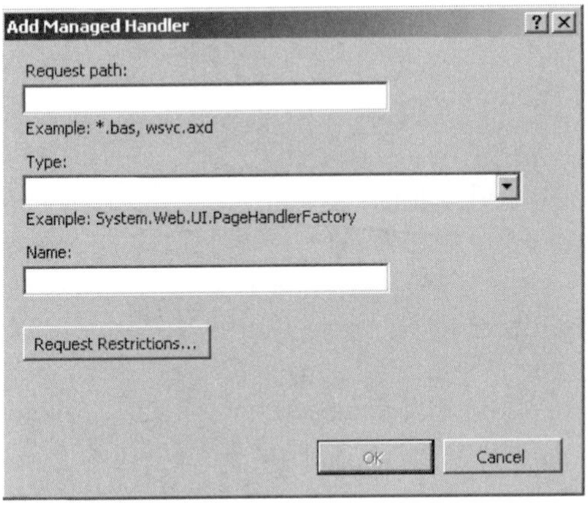

Figure 12-5   Add Managed Handler dialog box.

In this dialog box, you specify the path mask for the handler mapping, as well as the ASP.NET handler type that should provide processing for it. Much like when adding managed modules, the tool searches for usable types in the assemblies from the Global Assembly Cache (GAC) that are referenced in the ASP.NET compilation/assemblies collection. It also searches for application assemblies when you're adding the handler at the application level. You can use the Request Restrictions dialog box to also specify the verb list for the handler mapping (otherwise, it defaults to "*"), restrict the mapping to physical resources such as a file or directory (the default is unspecified), and set access level as required to execute the mapping (defaults to Script). You should indeed set these to the strictest possible levels for added security instead of leaving them at default values.

■ **Add Script Map**   This action enables you to create an ISAPI extension or CGI program handler mapping, similar to the IIS 6.0 scriptmap. This is shown in Figure 12-6.

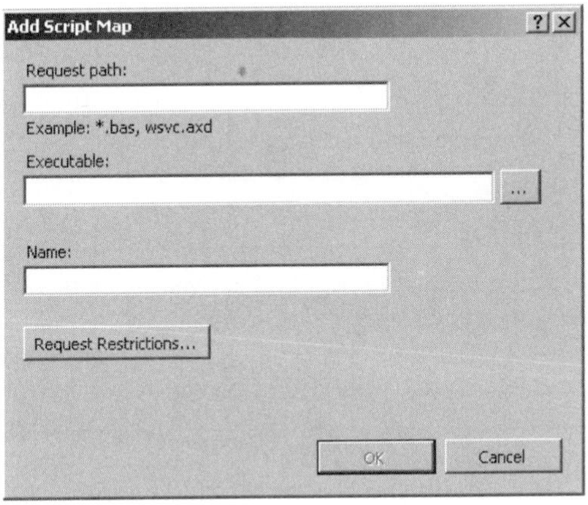

Figure 12-6   Add Script Map dialog box.

This is similar to the previous dialog box, except instead of the .NET handler type, you select the ISAPI extension, DLL, or CGI program executable on the server's local file system. This dialog box also prompts you to automatically create the isapiCgiRestriction entry to allow the ISAPI extension or CGI program to execute on the server.

- **Add Wildcard Script Map**   This is identical to the Add Script Map dialog box, except that it enables you to create a wildcard script map that intercepts all requests.

- **Add Module Mapping**   This is the most interesting action, because it enables you to create a general handler mapping that specifies one or more native modules and option-ally a script processor. You can use this dialog box to create ISAPI extension, CGI, and FastCGI handler mappings in addition to simple handler mappings for native modules, as shown in Figure 12-7.

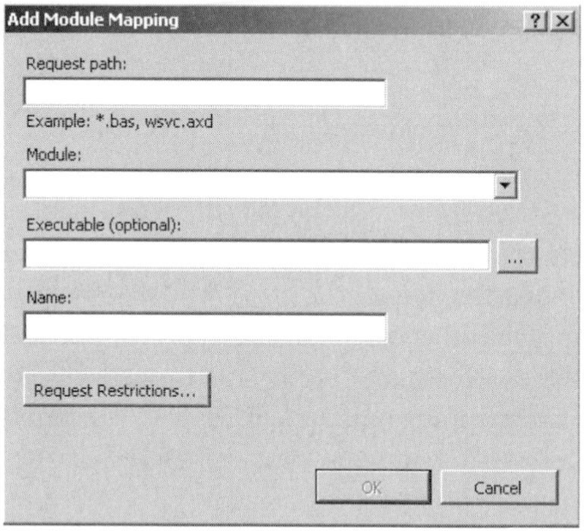

Add Module Mapping

Request path:

Example: *.bas, wsvc.axd

Module:

Executable (optional):

Name:

Request Restrictions...

OK   Cancel

Figure 12-7   Add Module Mapping dialog box.

The dialog box enables you to specify the Module (and it displays a list of available native modules, although not all of them can function as handlers) and the Executable (the script processor). It also provides special handling for IsapiModule, CgiModule, and FastCgiModule handler mappings by prompting you to automatically create the corresponding isapiCgiRestrictions or FastCGI configuration needed for the mapping to work correctly.

> **Note**   It is not possible to edit preconditions via the Handler Mappings feature. Instead, the tool automatically generates the correct preconditions for handler mappings to make it function correctly by default. If you would like to change the preconditions, you need to edit configuration directly by hand, with Appcmd, or with other configuration APIs.

In addition to adding new handler mappings, you can also edit or delete existing handler mappings by clicking the item in the list and using the Edit or Delete commands that become available. At the server level, you can also lock handler mappings to prevent them from being removed at the lower level, although this has less effect than locking modules because handler mappings can be overridden by adding new handler mappings for the same path/verb.

You can also use the "View Ordered List" action to order handler mappings. Keep in mind that just as it is for modules, ordering inherited elements requires the tool to use <clear/> to clear the handlers collection and add again all parent items into the configuration level being edited, essentially orphaning the configuration from the parent handler mappings configuration.

If you edit handler mappings as a site administrator, you have virtually the same functionality available to you for managing the handler mappings for your site, application, or any URL inside your site. However, the tool will not prompt you to enable ISAPI extensions, CGI programs, and FastCGI programs that the administrator has not already enabled at the server level.

Using Appcmd to Install and Manage Modules

The Appcmd command line tool also provides top-level support for managing modules. To begin with, you can always edit the IIS configuration via the Appcmd Config object to perform all the tasks necessary to install and manage modules. However, the tool also provides a module object, which directly supports common module management tasks. This is why Windows Setup calls into Appcmd to install modules and is the reason Appcmd is often the quickest way to install and manage modules. Appcmd is also the only tool available for managing modules on Windows Server 2008 Server Core installations, which do not support IIS Manager.

Appcmd is located in the *%windir%*\System32\Inetsrv directory, which is not present in the PATH variable by default, so you need to use the full path to the tool to run it.

```
%windir%\system32\inetsrv\AppCmd
```

You must be logged in as an administrator when using Appcmd. Also, be sure to execute Appcmd commands from an elevated command line prompt (click Start, right-click Command Prompt, and choose Run As Administrator). You can refer to Chapter 7, "Using Command Line Tools," for more information about the tool. If you get lost while learning Appcmd, be sure to check out the built-in command line help, which provides parameters and examples.

```
AppCmd module /?          - See all commands on the module object
AppCmd install module /?  - See the usage help for the install module command
```

In the help output for the MODULE object, you can see that the tool supports the following commands:

- **List** Enables you to examine enabled modules at the server level or for a specific application.

- **Install** Enables you to install new native modules on the server.

- **Uninstall**   Enables you to uninstall currently installed native modules on the server.

- **Add**   Enables you to add a new module. You can also opt to enable an installed native module for a specific application.

- **Delete**   Enables you to disable a managed module You can also opt to disable a native module, optionally for a specific application.

- **Set**   Enables you to edit specific entries in the modules configuration section for the purposes of changing the name or preconditions of a module or editing type information for managed modules.

In the next section, we'll provide some examples of using these commands to manage modules with Appcmd.

Installing and Uninstalling Modules

The Install and Uninstall module commands provide support for—you guessed it—installing and uninstalling native modules on the server.

To install native modules, you can use the following syntax.

```
AppCmd Install Module /name:string /image:string [/precondition:string]
[/add:bool] [/lock:bool]
```

This command accepts the parameters shown in Table 12-7.

Table 12-7   Appcmd Install Module Parameters

Parameter	Description
name (required)	Module name.
image (required)	The path to the module DLL.
preCondition	Optionally specifies the list of valid load preconditions for the module. If specified, controls whether the module is loaded by the IIS worker processes in particular application pools. The default is empty.
add	Optionally specifies whether to also enable the module at the server level. The default is TRUE.
lock	Optionally specifies whether to also lock the module entry so that it cannot be disabled by applications. This only applies if the module is being enabled. The default is FALSE.

The simplest case is installing a module by simply specifying its name and image path.

```
AppCmd install module /name:MyNativeModule /image:c:\modules\mymodule.dll
```

This installs and automatically enables the new module at the server level so that it's loaded by all IIS worker processes and enabled for all applications by default. If you wanted to install the module but enable it selectively for specific applications only, you would include the /add:false parameter. Then, you could use the Appcmd *Add Module* command later to enable it for a specific application by using the /app.name parameter. If, on the other hand, you wanted to install and enable this module and prevent applications from disabling it, you would include the /lock:true parameter for the install command. You could also set the precondition parameter to one of the supported values (see the section titled "Understanding Module Preconditions" earlier in this chapter) to control which application pools the module is loaded and available in.

To uninstall a module, you can use the following syntax.

```
AppCmd Uninstall Module ModuleName
```

This command accepts the module's name as the identifier.

> **Tip**   The uninstall command uses the standard Appcmd identifier pattern for specifying the module name, as opposed to using the /name parameter that the Install command uses. This is done so that all commands that work on specific existing instances of objects can use the identifier format instead of using different parameter names to identify objects.

Here is an example of how you can uninstall the module you installed earlier.

```
AppCmd uninstall module MyNativeModule
```

> **Note**   This also automatically disables the module at the server level, which makes sense because allowing this module to be enabled would result in an incorrect configuration after the module is uninstalled. However, if for some reason you wanted to uninstall a module but leave it enabled (this would cause request errors on the entire server if left unchanged), you can specify the **/**remove:false parameter.

Enabling and Disabling Modules

You can use the *Add Module* and *Delete Module* commands to manage the modules enabled on the server or for a particular application. You can also use the *Add Module* command to add new managed modules. These commands manipulate the modules configuration section, which contains the entries for enabled native modules and defines managed modules. Therefore, you can perform a number of different tasks around module management.

One of the most common uses for the *Add Module* command is to add new managed modules. Because native modules have to be installed on the server first before they are enabled, the *Install Module* command is more appropriate for installing and automatically enabling them. You can add a new managed module at the server level or for any particular application using the following syntax.

```
AppCmd Add Module /name:string [/type:string]  [/precondition:string]
[/app.name:string] [/lockItem:bool]
```

This command supports the parameters shown in Table 12-8.

Table 12-8 Appcmd Add Module Parameters

name (required)	Module name.
type (required)	The fully qualified .NET type of the module. If the module is being added at the server level, the type must be in an assembly registered with the machine's Global Assembly Cache. If it's being added for a specific application, then it can also be deployed with the application. Refer to the section titled "Deploying Assemblies Containing Managed Modules" for more information.
preCondition	Optionally specifies the list of valid enablement preconditions for the module. If specified, controls whether the module is enabled in specific application pools and for specific requests. The default is empty.
app.name	Optionally specifies the application path for the modules to be added to. The default is empty, meaning the server level.
lockItem	Optionally specifies whether or not to lock the module entry against removal at lower configuration levels.

For example, to add a new managed module at the server level, you can do the following.

```
AppCmd add module /name:MyManagedModule /type:MyModules.MyModule
```

This makes this module enabled by default for all applications on the server. If you wanted to add it only to the root application in the default Web site, you would also add the /app.name:"Default Web Site/" parameter. You could also set the preCondition parameter to one of the supported values (see the section titled "Understanding Module Preconditions" earlier in this chapter) to control for which application pools and requests the module is enabled.

You can also use the lockItem parameter just like you can when creating new configuration collection entries to lock the module entry, which prevents lower configuration levels from removing the module configuration entry. You can leverage this when adding new managed modules at the server level to prevent them from being disabled at the application level. This is discussed more in the section titled "Locking Down Extensibility" later in this chapter.

Another common use of the *Add Module* command is to enable a native module that is not currently enabled. For example, if you installed a native module with the /add:false parameter, resulting in it being installed but not enabled by default, you can directly enable it.

```
AppCmd add module /name:MyNativeModule
```

You can use the /app.name parameter here to specify the application where the module should be enabled. This only works for native modules; that is, when re-enabling managed modules for a specific application, you always have to specify the type because this information is not available elsewhere like it is for native modules.

You can use the *Delete Module* command to do the opposite—to disable a module that is currently enabled. You can also use this command to disable native module or managed modules at the server level, or for a specific application, using the following syntax.

```
AppCmd Delete Module ModuleName [/app.name:string]
```

> **Tip**   The delete command uses the standard Appcmd identifier pattern for specifying the module name, as opposed to using the /name parameter that the add command uses. This syntax exists so that all commands that work on specific existing instances of objects can use the identifier format instead of using different parameter names to identify objects.

For example, to disable a module that is enabled at the server level, you can do the following.

```
AppCmd delete module MyModule
```

This works for both managed and native modules, with a slight caveat: if you disable a native module, you can re-enable it simply by using the *Add Module /name:ModuleName* command. However, if you disable a managed module, you will need to specify its full type to re-enable it. If you delete a managed module at the level where it's defined for the first time, you may lose the type information in case you need to re-add it later.

Examining Enabled Modules

In addition to installing/uninstalling and enabling/disabling modules, Appcmd supports examining the enabled modules with the LIST command. This can prove valuable when diagnosing module-related issues by enabling you to quickly determine which modules are enabled for a specific application, or if a specific module is enabled.

The *List Module* command, much like the LIST commands for other Appcmd objects, enables you to display all modules as well as query for modules that satisfy a specific query. In the simplest use, it enables you to quickly list the modules that are enabled at the server level.

```
AppCmd list modules
```

To see which modules are enabled for a specific application, use the /app.name:*AppPath* parameter to specify the application path for which the enabled modules should be displayed.

> **Note**   Because applications can remove certain modules or add new ones, their module set can often be different from that of the server itself. Be sure to check the module list for the application you're interested in when you're investigating problems with that application.

You can also specify queries for one or more of the module attributes, including *precondition* and *type*, to find modules that have that attribute. For example, to find all managed modules that have the managedHandler precondition set, you can use the following code.

```
AppCmd list modules "/type:$<>" "/precondition:$=*managedHandler*"
```

You can also look for specific modules by using the module name as the identifier.

```
AppCmd list module DefaultDocumentModule
```

Creating and Managing Handler Mappings

Though Appcmd provides a top-level Module object for managing modules, it does not provide a top-level view of the handler mappings configuration. However, you can always use the *CONFIG* object to directly manage the system.webServer/handlers configuration section to accomplish any needed handler mapping management task.

Discussing the full collection editing syntax of the CONFIG object is out of scope for this section (see Chapter 7), but here are some examples for using it to do basic handler mapping management tasks.

Adding a Handler Mapping

To add a handler mapping to a native module, run the following command on one line.

```
AppCmd set config /section:handlers "/+[name='TestHandler',path='*test',
verb='GET,POST,HEAD',modules='TestModule']"
```

> **Note**   Long commands are sometimes shown formatted on multiple lines to fit on the printed page.

This adds a server-level handler mapping that maps GET, POST, and HEAD requests to *.test URLs to the "TestModule" native module. Though only the name, path, and verb attributes are required (and the modules attribute should be set for the native module handler mapping), you can also specify any of the other attributes that apply. You can also specify the configuration path at which this mapping should be added instead of adding it at the server level, as shown in the next example.

To add a handler mapping to a managed handler type, run the following command on one line.

```
AppCmd set config "Default Web Site/" /section:handlers
"/+[name='ASPNHandler',path='*.aspn',verb='*',
type='MyHandlers.ASPNHandler',precondition='integratedMode']"
```

This adds a handler mapping for the root of the "Default Web Site" Web site, which maps all requests to *.aspn URLs to the .NET MyHandlers.ASPNHandler handler type. Notice that the handler mapping is also preconditioned to be used only in application pools running in Integrated mode. This is required for handler mappings to managed types, because only Integrated mode supports adding managed handler types directly into IIS handler mappings.

Editing a Handler Mapping

To edit a handler mapping, use the following code.

```
AppCmd set config /section:handlers /[name='TestHandler'].verb:GET
```

This sets the verb attribute of the handler mapping identified by the name TestHandler to the new value of GET. Note that the name attribute serves as the unique collection key for the handlers configuration section.

You can use this syntax to edit any of the handler mapping attributes. You can also edit the handler mapping you created at the Default Web Site/ level by specifying that path after the *SET CONFIG* command.

Deleting a Handler Mapping

To delete a handler mapping, you can use the /- prefix for deleting configuration collection elements.

```
AppCmd set config /section:handlers /-[name='TestHandler']
```

This deletes the handler mapping you created earlier, identified by the name *TestHandler*. You can also delete the handler mapping you created at the "Default Web Site/" level by specifying that path after the *SET CONFIG* command.

Adding Entries to the ISAPI CGI Restriction List (Formerly Web Service Restriction List)

When creating handler mappings that use CgiModule or IsapiModule to support CGI programs or ISAPI extensions respectively, you also need to allow the specific CGI program or ISAPI extension by adding it to the ISAPI CGI Restriction List. In IIS 6.0, this is known as the Web Service Restriction List and is a key security measure to control the execution of third-party code on the server.

For example, to add an ISAPI extension DLL to the system.webServer/security/isapiCgi-Restriction list, use the following command.

```
appcmd set config /section:isapiCgiRestriction /+[path='c:\myisapi.dll',
allowed='true']
```

To allow (or disallow) an existing entry in the list, use the following command.

```
appcmd set config /section:isapiCgiRestriction
/[path='c:\myisapi.dll'].allowed:true
```

To delete an entry in the list, use the following command.

```
appcmd set config /section:isapiCgiRestriction /-[path='c:\myisapi.dll']
```

You can specify both CGI programs (executables) and ISAPI extensions (DLLs) in this list.

> **Note**   FastCGI program executables are not added to the isapiCgiRestriction list. Instead,
> they must be registered in the system.webServer/fastCGI configuration section to allow
> FastCGI application pools to be created for this executable.

Securing Web Server Modules

The extensibility architecture in IIS 7.0 is in many ways the recognition of the fact that it's not really the server but rather the application that runs on it that makes all the difference. Unfortunately, history shows that it is also the application that is most commonly the cause of security vulnerabilities. The lockdown approach to security that IIS 6.0 provides—restricting the ability to run new code on the server and reducing the privilege of that code—has been immensely successful in reducing Web server exploits. Now, with IIS 7.0, server administrators must strike a balance between the functionality afforded by the new extensibility model and server security. Therefore, it is now more important than ever to understand the security impact of hosting server extensibility and to know how to properly lock it down to avoid weakening the security of your server.

When it comes to securing the server, one of the biggest problems administrators face today is dealing with system complexity and being able to properly apply key security best practices rather than being bogged down in the details. This approach, though not a replacement for proper security threat modeling and penetration testing at the application level, enables you to significantly reduce the general security risk to the server. Basically, you need to be able to answer the following question: Assuming you cannot trust the code running on your server to be completely foolproof, how can you control what it can and cannot do, and at the same time prevent your server from being compromised if this code is exploited?

The best answer to this question is to approach it in the following stages. First, you need to know how to reduce the server's surface area to a minimum, removing all functionality that is not essential to its operation. Second, you need to understand the privilege of code that executes on the server and then reduce it as much as possible. Finally, you need to maintain control over the extensibility that is allowed on the server, preventing undesired functionality from being added or desired functionality from being removed. You should also apply the best practices listed in Chapter 14, "Implementing Security Strategies," to secure individual features.

Taking Advantage of Componentization to Reduce the Security Surface Area of the Server

To completely secure a Web server, you would need to disconnect it from the network, unplug it, and bury it in a thick slab of concrete. This would guarantee its security by removing the possibility of any malicious interactions with the system. However, because this will also make the Web server useless, you have to find other ways to apply the security principle of reducing the attack surface area.

Direct from the Source: The Most Secure Web Server in the World

My first demo for the IIS 7.0 breakout session at the conference TechEd 2005 was to showcase the componentization capabilities of IIS 7.0 by showing off the "most secure Web server in the world."

As part of the demo, I showed editing the configuration in the ApplicationHost.config file, removing all of the modules, and removing handler mappings. After saving the file, the IIS worker process automatically picked up the changes and restarted, loading absolutely no modules. After making a request to the default Web site, I got back a swift empty 200 response (this configuration currently returns a "401 Unauthorized" error because no authentication modules are present). The server performed virtually no processing of the request and returned no content, thus becoming the "most secure Web server in the world." After a pause, I commented that though secure, the server was also fairly useless. Then I segued into adding back the functionality that we needed for our specific application.

I have done this demo before for internal audiences to much acclaim, but I will always remember the audience reaction during the TechEd presentation. The people in the audience went wild, some breaking out into a standing ovation. This was a resounding confirmation of our efforts to give administrators the ability to start from nothing, building up the server with an absolutely minimal set of features to produce the most simple-to-manage, low-surface-area Web server possible.

Mike Volodarsky

Program Manager, IIS 7.0

The ability of IIS 7.0 to remove virtually all features of the Web server is fundamental here, enabling us to eliminate the threat of any known or unknown attack vectors that may exist in those features. In addition, removing extra functionality reduces management complexity and reduces the chance of your server being forced offline if a patch affects the removed features. You can leverage this ability by doing the following:

1. Determine the set of features that you need for your server/application.

2. Install *only* the required IIS 7.0 features by using Windows Setup.

3. Manually remove any modules that your application does not need.

At the end of step 2, you should have the minimum required set of functionality installed globally for your server. You can then further reduce the surface area by disabling the modules you do not need in each of your applications, in the case where each application requires slightly different server functionality.

In some other cases, you may need to disable modules for the entire server if the setup packaging is not granular enough. This is often the case with ASP.NET, which installs all of the ASP.NET modules and handlers whether or not they are all necessary in your application.

Sounds simple, right? Unfortunately, the biggest challenge lies in step 1, determining the set of features your application needs. Doing this requires knowing which functionality can be safely removed without negatively affecting your application's functionality or compromising its security. That's right—you can actually end up making your server *a lot* less secure if you remove a security-sensitive feature. For example, if you remove an authorization module that is responsible for validating access to an administration page in your application, you may end up allowing anonymous users to take administrative action on your server! Likewise, removing certain features may contribute to decreased performance or reduced stability. Or removing these features may simply break your application.

> **Caution**   It is possible to have IIS configuration that configures an IIS feature to perform a certain function and yet to not have this function be performed by the server if the module that is responsible for this function is not enabled. This can happen if someone disables the module or configures its preconditions to prevent it from running in a specific application pool. Because of this, you need to make sure that the required modules are present and are correctly preconditioned to insure the correct operation of your application.

Therefore, it is important to understand what features your application requires, and which it does not. To help with this, you can consult Table 12-9, which illustrates the function played by each built-in IIS 7.0 module whose removal may have a security impact on the server.

Table 12-9   Function of Built-In Modules with Security Implications

Module	Purpose and Removal Effect
Anonymous Authentication Module	**Purpose:** Authenticates the request with an anonymous user if no other authentication mechanism is present.
	If removed: Access to resources will be denied for anonymous requests.
Basic Authentication Module	**Purpose:** Supports basic authentication.
	If removed: Clients will not be able to authenticate with basic authentication.
Certificate Mapping Authentication Module	**Purpose:** Supports client certificate authentication.
	If removed: Clients will not be able to authenticate with client certificates.
Configuration Validation Module	**Purpose:** Validates ASP.NET configuration in integrated mode
	If removed: Strong warning—ASP.NET applications that define modules and handlers using legacy configuration will silently run in integrated mode, but the modules will not be loaded. This may result in unexpected application behavior and security vulnerabilities for unmigrated ASP.NET applications.

Table 12-9   Function of Built-In Modules with Security Implications

Module	Purpose and Removal Effect
CustomError Module	**Purpose:** Detailed error messages will not be generated for IIS errors. **If removed: Strong warning**—Sensitive application error information may be sent to remote clients.
Default Authentication	**Purpose:** Supports the ASP.NET DefaultAuthentication_OnAuthenticate event. When ASP.NET is configured to use the Forms Authentication mode, removing this module may lead to errors in other ASP.NET modules during anonymous requests. **If removed: Warning**—The DefaultAuthentication_OnAuthenticate event will not be raised, so any custom authentication code depending on this event will not run. This is not common.
Digest Authentication Module	**Purpose:** Supports digest authentication. **If removed:** Clients will not be able to use digest authentication to authenticate.
File Authorization	**Purpose:** Verifies that the authenticated client has access to physical resources. **If removed: Strong warning**—Access may be granted to resources that deny access to the authenticated user.
Forms Authentication	**Purpose:** Supports forms-based authentication. **If removed:** Clients will not be able to use forms authentication to authenticate.
HttpCache Module	**Purpose:** Supports IIS output caching and kernel caching of responses. **If removed: Warning**—Response output caching will not occur, possibly resulting in increased load on the server and in the worst case Denial of Service (DoS) conditions.
HttpLogging Module	**Purpose:** Supports request logging. **If removed: Warning**—Requests may not be logged.
IISCertificate Mapping Authentication Module	**Purpose:** Supports IIS configuration–based client certificate authentication. **If removed:** Clients may not be able to authenticate with client certificates against IIS configuration.
HttpRedirection Module	**Purpose:** Supports configuration-based redirection rules. **If removed: Warning**—If the application depends on redirection rules for restricting access to content, removing this module may make otherwise protected resources available.
IsapiFilter Module	**Purpose:** Supports ISAPI filters. **If removed: Strong warning**—ISAPI filters that enforce access or have other security functionality will not run.
OutputCache	**Purpose:** Supports ASP.NET response output caching. **If removed: Warning**—ASP.NET response output caching will not occur, possibly resulting in increased load on the server and in the worst case Denial of Service (DoS) conditions.

Table 12-9   Function of Built-In Modules with Security Implications

Module	Purpose and Removal Effect
RequestFiltering Module	**Purpose:** Enforces various request restrictions and protects hidden content.
	If removed: Strong warning—Removing this module may result in protected content being served. It may also lead to nonspecific security vulnerabilities resulting from allowing unrestricted request input into the application.
RoleManager	**Purpose:** Supports the ASP.NET roles functionality.
	If removed: Strong warning—Roles for the authenticated user may not be available, which may cause authorization decisions to be affected. Typically, this will only restrict access, but in some cases where access is denied based on roles, this may grant access to otherwise unauthorized users.
Static Compression Module	**Purpose:** Supports compression of static resources.
	If removed: Warning—Removing this module may result in significantly higher bandwidth for the site, because compression of static resources will be disabled.
Url Authorization	**Purpose:** Supports declarative access rules.
	If removed: Strong warning—URL authorization access rules will be ignored, and access may be granted to unauthorized users.
Url Authorization Module	**Purpose:** Supports declarative ASP.NET access rules.
	If removed: Strong warning—ASP.NET url authorization access rules will be ignored, and access may be granted to unauthorized users.
Windows Authentication	**Purpose:** Supports NTLM and Kerberos authentication.
	If removed: Clients will be unable to authenticate with NTLM or Kerberos Windows authentication.
Windows Authentication Module	**Purpose:** Supports raising the ASP.NET WindowsAuthentication_OnAuthentication event.
	If removed: Warning—WindowsAuthentication_OnAuthentication event will not be raised, so any custom ASP.NET authentication code dependent on this event will not run. Note that this module is not required for Windows authentication.

You should always verify that the application does indeed have all of the required modules enabled after deployment. In addition, you should always test the application whenever the module configuration changes to insure its correct operation with the new module set. Armed with the knowledge of which modules can be safely removed, you can take advantage of IIS 7.0's modularity to significantly reduce the surface area of your server, without accidentally reducing its security.

Understanding and Reducing the Privilege of Code that Runs on Your Server

Now that you have reduced the surface area of your server to the acceptable minimum, you need to secure the remaining functionality. This is typically done in two ways: by restricting the inputs to the application as much as possible by using security features such as authorization and request filtering (IIS 7.0's version of UrlScan) and by reducing the privilege with which the code in the application executes so that even if it is compromised, it is limited in the amount of harm it can do. You can learn more about both of these approaches in Chapter 14.

The former approach is an extension of reducing the surface area approach you took earlier, attempting to block as many of the attack vectors as possible by constraining the input to the server. The latter approach uses the principle of least privilege and focuses on what happens if the functionality on the server is compromised. With an understanding of how the extensibility code executes in the context of IIS, you can do much to reduce its privilege, which often makes compromising the server a lot harder or impossible. Also, this knowledge helps you understand the trust requirements for adding features or application components to the server.

Table 12-10 illustrates the privilege with which IIS Web server modules execute on the server.

Table 12-10   Module Privileges

Feature	Execution Scope	Privilege Level	Who Can Add
Native modules	IIS worker process	Application pool identity	Administrator
Managed modules and handlers	ASP.NET appdomain	Application pool identity (default) OR Authenticated user AND Limited by ASP.NET trust level	Application owner
ISAPI filters	IIS worker process	Application pool identity	Administrator
ISAPI extensions	IIS worker process	Authenticated user (default) OR Application pool identity	Administrator
CGI programs	CGI program process (single-request)	Authenticated user (default) OR Application pool identity	Administrator
FastCGI programs	FastCGI program process	Application pool identity	Administrator

The majority of IIS extensibility is hosted within a long-running IIS worker process (everything except CGI and FastCGI programs that execute out of process), which executes under the configured application pool identity (Network Service by default). This includes native modules as well as ISAPI extensions and filters (managed modules and handlers are also included, but they provide an additional constrained execution model that is discussed later in this chapter). This code, therefore, can do everything that the application pool identity is allowed to do, based on the privileges granted to the identity by the system and rights granted by ACLs on Windows resources. Reducing the privilege of this identity from Local System in

IIS 5.1 to Network Service in IIS 6.0 was one of the fundamental security improvements that enabled IIS 6.0 to achieve its stellar security record. You can learn how to take advantage of reducing the privilege of the IIS application pools in Chapter 14.

Remember that despite all other constraining measures that may be in place, including ASP.NET Code Access Security, the privileges and rights granted to worker process that contains the code define what code in the process may or may not do (when impersonating, you also need to consider the rights and privileges assigned to the impersonated identity). In other words, when you add code to the server, even if it is application code, assume that it can do everything that your worker process is allowed to do. By maintaining least privilege application pools, you can significantly reduce the damage to the server in the case of an application compromise.

The story is slightly different when it comes to managed (ASP.NET) module and handler components. These components are hosted within the ASP.NET application, and in addition to being limited by the IIS worker process, they are also limited by the .NET Code Access Security (CAS) policy configured for the ASP.NET appdomain. This means that managed modules and handlers can execute with a lower privilege than the one granted by the IIS worker process identity.

By default, ASP.NET applications are configured to execute with Full trust, which means that they are not additionally constrained. By configuring the application to execute with lower trust levels via the system.web/trust configuration section, you can create an additional limitation on the execution of .NET code that precludes managed modules from performing certain actions and accessing resources outside of those located in their subdirectories. You can learn more about the built-in trust levels in Chapter 14.

> **Note**   You can also use IIS Manager to configure the default trust level for ASP.NET applications or the trust level for a particular application on your server.

The recommended trust level is Medium. At this trust level, the application cannot access resources that do not belong to it, though it can still use most ASP.NET features and execute code that affects its own operation. At this trust level, multiple applications running within a single application pool are largely isolated from each other, making this level the correct one to use for shared hosting (although it is preferable to host each customer in a separate fully isolated application pool), where hosted applications are allowed to upload code to the server.

You should take advantage of the Medium trust level where possible to further reduce the privilege of the managed components of your application. Be aware that some ASP.NET applications or modules may not function in Medium trust, due to the use of .NET APIs that required a higher trust level. The number of these applications is getting smaller, due to both API improvements in .NET Framework 2.0+ and application improvements to facilitate operation in partial trust environments. Also, the ASP.NET run time may experience reduced performance in a partial trust. This needs to be evaluated in each specific case to determine whether it is a significant enough factor to warrant using higher trust levels.

> **Note**   Though ASP.NET trust levels provide an additional way to constrained the execution of managed code on your server, they should not be used as a substitute for reducing the privilege of the hosting IIS worker process.

CGI and FastCGI programs are not hosted inside the IIS worker process, but instead execute inside their own processes that are spawned by the IIS worker process. CGI programs by default execute under the identity of the authenticated user, although you can configure them to execute with the identity of the worker process. Therefore, when using CGI programs, be aware that the code has the privilege of the invoking user. If that user is an administrator on the server, the code can perform administrative tasks that can lead to complete server compromise if the code is successfully exploited.

> **Note**   When using anonymous authentication while impersonating, the new IIS_IUSR account will be used to execute the CGI, FastCGI, and ISAPI extension–based applications (unless the server is configured to use the process identity instead). Unless you are using the IIS_IUSR account to use lower privilege for the executing code than the one provided by the worker process identity, you should consider using the worker process identity instead to manage one less account. You can do this by setting the *userName* attribute of the anonymousAuthentication section to "".

FastCGI programs always execute with the identity of the IIS worker process, so they have the same privilege as code in the IIS worker process. FastCGI does provide a way for the FastCGI program to impersonate the authenticated user, which can be done by PHP in FastCGI mode. In this case, the same warning applies to code running in the worker process as when running CGI programs.

> **Important**   In a number of cases, server code impersonates the authenticated user. This is done by default for all ISAPI extensions, ASP pages, PHP pages running in CGI, ISAPI or FastCGI mode, and ASP.NET applications that enable impersonation. If impersonation is used, be aware that the code will execute with very high privileges when the request is made by a user who has administrative privileges on this machine. You should strongly consider disallowing administrative users from using your application except when necessary.

All that said, the bottom line is that you must trust the source of the code running on your server as far as the privilege level under which this code executes. If you do not trust the code, you must insure that it runs with a low privilege level by constraining it with a very low privilege application pool identity. If the code is native, that is the best you can do. If the code is managed, you can use ASP.NET's partial trust levels to further constrain it, which provides a foundation for allowing third-party application code to run on your server.

If you do trust the code, you can harden it against unforeseen exploits by reducing its privilege as much as possible using the techniques described earlier in this chapter. Though you can never be completely sure that a piece of code is foolproof against attacks, using the least privilege principle can significantly limit or eliminate damages.

Locking Down Extensibility

Now that you have built a minimal surface area Web server that runs with least privilege, you need to make sure it stays that way. If you are running a dedicated server, this is less of an issue because you are the one who controls the configuration that defines which components are enabled and how they execute. However, if you delegate application management to someone else, as is the case with shared hosting servers and sometimes departmental servers, things are different.

To understand this, let's first look at the difference in extensibility delegation between IIS 6.0 and IIS 7.0. In IIS 6.0, the administrator in the metabase controls the server functionality. If a user wants to serve .php3 pages with the PHP scripting engine, they need to contact the administrator to create a handler mapping for their application. The same is the case for adding or removing an ISAPI filter. In IIS 7.0, the delegated configuration system enables applications to remove or add new functionality in some cases, without requiring administrator level changes. This is nice for allowing xcopy deployment of applications that define their own configuration and functionality, and reducing total cost of ownership. However, in some cases, this may be undesired from a security perspective, and so the administrator has a fine degree of control over what changes are allowed at the application level. This is done by controlling configuration delegation for the system.webServer/handlers and system.webServer/modules configuration sections via configuration locking.

In the default IIS 7.0 installation, both of these sections are locked at the server level. This means that application A cannot add new modules or create new handler mappings, and application B cannot remove or change existing modules or handler mappings.

This is a very restrictive state that prevents many ASP.NET applications from working correctly, because ASP.NET applications often need to declare new modules and create new handler mappings. In general, it prevents IIS applications from defining their handler mappings and modules in their configuration. Because of this, when the ".NET Extensibility" or the "ASP.NET" role service is installed on the server, these sections are unlocked. This allows applications to specify a configuration that does the following:

1. Enable/add new managed modules.

2. Disable/remove existing modules.

3. Add new handler mappings.

4. Override/remove existing handler mappings.

Because adding new native modules requires installing them at the server level, and adding new ISAPI filters/extensions and CGI/FastCGI programs also requires configuration changes at the server level (the isapiCgiRestrictions and fastCgi sections), applications cannot introduce new native code. However, they *can* introduce new managed modules and handlers. Because of this, in shared environments where the application is not trusted by the administrator, server administrators must do one of the following:

■ Prevent new managed modules/handlers from being added by locking the modules and handlers sections. This will break many applications (especially ASP.NET applications running in Integrated mode).

■ Reduce the trust level of the application to Medium trust to constrain the execution of managed code.

■ Use a low-privilege application pool to host the application.

The application can also by default disable any of the modules defined at the server level. This can be a problem if the server administrator wants to mandate the presence of a particular module, such as a bandwidth monitor module or logging module that tracks the operation of the application. To counteract that, the server administrator can lock each module that should not be removable at the server level, preventing it from being removed by the application. This can be done by adding a *lockItem* = *"true"* attribute to each module element in the modules configuration section at the server level. In fact, when the modules section is unlocked, ASP.NET setup automatically locks each native module that is installed against removal (in some cases, you may want to unlock some of these modules if you do not mind them being disabled by the application).

Because the application can also create new handler mappings, the application can override mappings defined at the server level. The locking approach does not work here because new mappings take precedence over earlier mappings, so it is not necessary to remove existing mappings to redirect them to other handler types. However, the ability to remap requests in the application to another handler is not a security concern outside of the ability to execute the code, which is already controlled by the application trust level and/or the application pool identity. The handlers section does expose the *accessPolicy* attribute, which controls what access levels are granted to the handlers. This attribute is by default locked at the server level, so the application cannot modify it.

The trust level configuration for the application is also something that should be locked at the server level. By default, it isn't—so the application can elevate its own trust level to Full to remove the constraint on the execution of the .NET code. Server administrators should always lock this configuration in the framework's root Web.config file to prevent it from being overridden when they are relying on the partial trust security model for applications. For convenience, you can do this using the following Appcmd command.

```
AppCmd lock config /section:trust /commit:MACHINE/WEBROOT
```

This prevents applications from overriding the trust level setting in the framework root Web.config.

 On the Disc Browse the CD for additional tools and resources.

Summary

The modular architecture of IIS 7.0 Web server provides the foundation for many key production scenarios, enabling you to build low-footprint specialized servers and leverage rich add-on functionality provided by end-to-end extensibility. Though traditionally the domain of developers, managing Web server extensibility becomes a central IT theme in IIS 7.0, providing both opportunities and challenges for the administrator. Armed with the right know-how, you can effectively leverage the modularity of the server to achieve your business goals today with built-in IIS 7.0 features and when you take advantage of Microsoft or third-party modules to enhance your server in the future.

In the next two chapters, we will cover the extensibility model exposed by the configuration system, the administration stack, and IIS Manager, which complete the end-to-end extensibility picture for the server.

Additional Resources

These resources contain additional information and tools related to this chapter:

- Chapter 11, "Hosting Application Development Frameworks," for information on enabling and hosting common application framework technologies on IIS 7.0.

- Chapter 14, "Implementing Security Strategies," for information on locking down the server.

- The blog at *http://www.mvolo.com* for in-depth coverage of many IIS 7.0 extensibility and module management topics.

- The Web site *http://www.iis.net* for articles on extending IIS 7.0.

- The IIS 7.0 Operations Guide, available at *http://technet2.microsoft.com/ windowsserver2008/en/library/d0de9475-0439-4ec1-8337-2bcedacd15c71033.mspx.*

Chapter 13
Managing Configuration and User Interface Extensions

Taking a look at the history of Internet Information Services (IIS) really underscores the importance of a flexible and manageable configuration system. What started as a few registry settings grew to the metabase with IIS 5.0, a binary store for maintaining URL-based configuration, which was replaced with an XML-based metabase in IIS 6.0. IIS 7.0 once again makes a leap toward better manageability, investing in a distributed XML file–based configuration system to enable delegated management and xcopy application deployment. But, IIS 7.0 goes one step further—it recognizes that a great manageability story cannot stop at the Web server itself, and it needs to stretch to the application to allow for a cohesive end-to-end management experience. This is the key reason that, similar to the Web server itself, the IIS 7.0 configuration system and the entire administration tool stack is also completely extensible, enabling third-party modules and application components to expose and manage their configuration the same way as is done for the server.

Administration Stack Overview

In addition to providing an extensible platform for building Web server features, IIS 7.0 focuses strongly on improving its manageability and simplifying application deployment. The cornerstone of this effort is the new administration stack that is built around the new configuration system to provide a full array of application programming interfaces (APIs) and tools for working with IIS configuration and performing management tasks.

The IIS 7.0 configuration system attempts to solve a number of critical limitations of its predecessor, the IIS 6.0 Metabase. First, it is no longer limited to a centralized Administrator-only configuration store, but instead supports a hierarchy of XML configuration files including those that can travel alongside application content. This forms the basis for simplified xcopy-based deployment of IIS applications and delegated configuration management.

The file-based approach to configuration enables simplified deployment of applications and facilitates tasks such as backing up and restoring configuration. The format of the configuration is compatible with the ASP.NET configuration system, which enables both IIS and ASP.NET configuration to exist side-by-side in the same configuration files. The configuration itself is expressed in simple and structured XML that can be edited by hand or with development tools.

Note   You can learn more about the IIS 7.0 configuration system in Chapter 4, "Understanding the Configuration System."

Though Notepad is all that is necessary to work with IIS 7.0 configuration, the IIS 7.0 administration stack (see Figure 13-1) offers a full spectrum of tools to enable key deployment and management scenarios. It surfaces a Component Object Model (COM) for managing configuration programmatically from C++ programs, a new Microsoft Windows Management Instrumentation (WMI) provider for scripting, and the *Microsoft.Web.Administration* namespace for .NET Framework applications. In addition to this, it offers the redesigned IIS Manager for graphical user interface (GUI)–based Web server management and Appcmd.exe, a single tool for Web server command line administration.

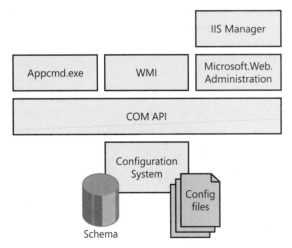

Figure 13-1   The administration stack in IIS 7.0.

It should not come as a surprise that, much like the Web server itself, the entire IIS 7.0 administration stack is designed to be completely extensible. At the base level, all configuration for built-in IIS 7.0 features is described using a publicly extensible schema mechanism, the same mechanism that is used to add custom configuration sections. This enables new Web server modules to expose custom configuration in the same way that IIS 7.0 features do, placing it in the same configuration files side by side with the existing IIS configuration data and automatically exposing it through all of the standard configuration tools and APIs.

In addition to adding new configuration, the configuration system supports adding administration extensions or extending existing configuration sections to expose new administration functionality that goes beyond file-based configuration. This functionality is exposed via public configuration system APIs to management clients, including several IIS 7.0 management tools and APIs. This facilitates reuse of administration functionality, enabling it to be installed on the system once and then automatically exposed through all of the standard management tools and APIs.

Finally, IIS Manager provides its own extensibility architecture, enabling third parties to plug in custom management services and corresponding UI elements to surface that functionality to end users.

In the remainder of this chapter, you will drill into the extensible architecture of the IIS 7.0 administration stack, showing how extensions can be added to expose new management functionality and how to properly manage and secure these extensions in a production environment.

Managing Configuration Extensions

Configuration extensions are extensions to the configuration system. The configuration system is at the core of the IIS 7.0 administration stack. Its primary purpose is to provide an interface to reading and writing IIS configuration, which is consumed by Web server run time and modules, and which is managed through the tools and APIs in the administration stack. The configuration data itself is stored in a hierarchy of XML files and is broken up into units called configuration sections. In Chapter 4, you can learn more about the configuration file hierarchy and the structure of the configuration sections.

Each configuration section is an XML element that can contain attributes, subelements, and collections of child elements that describe the configuration data for the section. This data can be specified at multiple locations in the configuration file hierarchy to specify configuration settings for a particular configuration path. For example, the following configuration for the <defaultDocument> section placed in an application's Web.config file adds Index.php as an eligible default document and enables the default document feature for that application:

```
<configuration>
    <system.webServer>
        <defaultDocument enabled="true">
            <files>
                <add value="index.php" />
            </files>
        </defaultDocument>
    </system.webServer>
</configuration>
```

Typically, each Web server module has its own section, and the Web server core itself defines a number of sections such the <sites>, <applicationPools>, and <serverRuntime> sections. The configuration section is the basic unit of extensibility for the configuration system, giving custom Web server features the ability to provide their own configuration sections in the same way that IIS 7.0 features do.

Unlike the ASP.NET configuration system, which relies on .NET classes implementing the System.Configuration.Section base class to understand the contents of each configuration section, the IIS configuration system is declarative. Each configuration section is defined by registering its schema on the server, which enables the configuration system to process the configuration data for this section. By manipulating the schema, you can add new configuration sections to the system, remove existing ones, or extend existing configuration sections to contain more functionality.

Direct from the Source: The Tale of Two Teams and Two Configuration Systems

Since its inception, the ASP.NET team has had an intertwined history with the IIS team, both in terms of people and the technology. After the release of IIS 5.1, a number of IIS team members went on to be involved with a project that aimed to rebuild the Web server entirely using .NET Framework (before they came back to work on IIS 6.0). Scott Guthrie was one of the developer interns on that project, and he later left to found ASP.NET.

In early 2004, as the ASP.NET team was in the midst of the ASP.NET 2.0 development cycle, things seemed to have come full circle. The IIS team rejoined the ASP.NET team to form the Web Platform and Tools group. One of the key reasons for this reorganization was to take advantage of the ASP.NET configuration system, which promised to unify the configuration between IIS and ASP.NET, and to provide the foundation for delegated management of IIS configuration.

Over the next year, the IIS team invested in leveraging the ASP.NET configuration system for the next generation Web server, IIS 7.0. Unfortunately, the ASP.NET configuration system proved to be too heavy a weight to be used at the IIS level, which demanded an extreme level of scalability and performance that was not expected from ASP.NET applications. However, the ability to use the same configuration files, and to specify ASP.NET and IIS configuration side by side, was too huge of a customer win to pass up. Therefore, the new IIS 7.0 configuration system was born. The team designed it from the ground up to meet the scalability demands of the IIS worker process and yet be syntactically compatible with the ASP.NET configuration system.

In addition to the configuration unification, the merging of the two teams was a great opportunity for me to drive both the core ASP.NET 2.0 infrastructure and the design of the IIS 7.0 Web server. Over the next several years, I continued to drive the design and development of both projects, which helped tremendously to deliver the ASP.NET integration in IIS 7.0 as well as key IIS 7.0 features such as URL Authorization and the Output Cache.

Mike Volodarsky

IIS Core Server Program Manager

Next, we will look at the configuration schema mechanism in detail and see how it can be used to add custom configuration sections.

Configuration Section Schema

The configuration section schema definitions are stored in XML files located in the *%windir%*\System32\Inetsrv\Config\Schema directory. After installation, IIS 7.0 contains the following schema files:

- **IIS_schema.xml**   Defines all of the IIS configuration sections

- **ASPNET_schema.xml**   Defines all of the ASP.NET configuration sections declared in Framework Root.config

- **FX_schema.xml**   Defines all of the .NET Framework configuration sections declared in Machine.config

- **rscaext.xml**   Defines administration extensions to the IIS <sites> and <application-Pools> configuration sections to expose run-time state information and control APIs. (We cover administration extensions in the section titled "Administration Extensions" later in this chapter.)

Caution   Never attempt to modify any of the built-in IIS schema files. You can add new schema to define new configuration sections and even add dynamic functionality to existing configuration sections by publishing new schema files, as described in the section titled "Administration Extensions" later in this chapter.

These files define the schema for the configuration sections used by IIS and its features, which expect these configuration sections to be in a specific format. These files are not intended to be modified except by Windows Setup, and therefore they are protected to be writable by TrustedInstaller only. This also means that it is not necessary to back up these schema files, because they are protected and can be restored from Setup (although you should back up custom schema files).

The IIS 7.0 configuration system is not used by ASP.NET or other .NET Framework programs to read the contents of .NET Framework and ASP.NET configuration sections specified in the Framework Machine.config and root Web.config files. The .NET and ASP.NET programs use the .NET configuration system (developed by the ASP.NET team) to read that configuration. So, you may wonder why the IIS configuration system provides schema information for those configuration sections. It is to allow the rich IIS 7.0 administration stack to manage ASP.NET configuration so that Administrators can manage the entirety of server configuration with a single set of tools and APIs. Although ASP.NET provides its own API for managing .NET configuration (*System.Configuration.dll*), it does not support IIS configuration and does not provide the same level of tool and automation support provided by the IIS 7.0 administration stack.

However, the IIS schema files are provided for .NET Framework 2.0 only and, because of configuration changes, may not work correctly when used for other versions of .NET Framework. The IIS team may provide a versioning solution for .NET configuration schema in the future, but it is not there in IIS 7.0. Moreover, some tools in the IIS administration stack (including the Appcmd command-line tool) hardcode v2.0.50727 of the .NET Framework when working with configuration in Machine.config and root Web.config files, so they cannot be used to edit machine-level configuration for other .NET Framework versions.

Here is an example of how the <defaultDocument> configuration section for the Default Document feature is defined inside *IIS_schema.xml*:

```
<sectionSchema name="system.webServer/defaultDocument">
  <attribute name="enabled" type="bool" defaultValue="true"/>
  <element name="files">
    <collection addElement="add" clearElement="clear" removeElement="remove" mergeAppend="
false">
      <attribute name="value" type="string" isUniqueKey="true"/>
    </collection>
  </element>
</sectionSchema>
```

The schema definition specifies each attribute and defines what child elements and element collections can be contained within the section. In addition to defining the XML structure, the schema definition also provides various metadata for attributes, child elements, and collections that control the behavior of the configuration system with respect to the section. For example, it specifies that the type of the *enabled* attribute is Boolean, that its default value is *true*, and that the *value* attribute of the collection element is the collection key.

The *IIS_schema.xml* file, arguably the main schema file, contains the description of the schema information that can be specified for each section. For each section, this information can contain the items listed in Table 13-1.

Table 13-1 Schema Elements

Schema Element	Description
<sectionSchema> element	Contains all of the schema information for a configuration section, as well as the fully qualified name (containing the section group path and the section name) for the section.
<attribute> element	Defines an attribute that can be used in the configuration section or its child elements. It specifies the name, data type, and other applicable information including default value, whether it is required, whether it should be encrypted, and validation information.
<element> element	Defines a child element, which can specify additional attributes, as well as other child elements and collections.
<collection> element	Defines a configuration collection, which can contain a list of elements that can be indexed via attributes marked as collection keys. Also supports various collection semantics such as ordered lists and hierarchical merging of elements.

Each of these elements supports a number of schema properties that control the specific behavior of the configuration system with respect to the configuration section being defined. For more details on using these properties to specify the behavior of your configuration section, refer to the comments in the IIS_Schema.xml configuration file.

Note   The schema files are local to the server. If you are using a shared configuration to host ApplicationHost.config on a network share, you must make sure that the required schema files are installed on each server that references the configuration file. Servers that do not have the required schema files will not be able to read the custom configuration sections for which they are missing the schema information. This is only needed for schema files that are not part of IIS 7.0 by default, because the latter are always installed when IIS is installed.

By including additional XML files containing section schema, you can add new configuration sections or extend existing ones to contain more configuration information or expose additional administration functionality. Before new configuration sections can be used in the configuration files, they must also be declared. We'll look at this next.

Caution   Never attempt to delete or modify the schema files that are included with IIS 7.0 installation. Unlike the modules, most of these schema components are installed with the base IIS 7.0 installation, and their removal may break core pieces of the system that expect the configuration sections defined therein to be available. Likewise, you should not modify the schema of built-in IIS 7.0 configuration sections, because core components rely on their specific structure. This is one of the reasons these schema files have a TrustedInstaller-only access control list (ACL) that prevents modification. You can, however, add new administration extensions to existing IIS sections by adding new schema files. This topic is covered in the section titled "Administration Extensions" later in this chapter.

Declaring Configuration Sections

After the configuration section schema is in place, the configuration system becomes capable of processing the section's configuration data. However, before the section can be used in the configuration file, it must also be declared somewhere in the file's configuration file hierarchy. This is necessary to provide the Administrator with control over certain behaviors of the configuration section that cannot be easily managed if they are specified in the schema.

The declaration is performed by adding a *<section>* element to the built-in <configSections> configuration section. Each declaration may be nested within one or more section groups, which are essentially grouping constructs for configuration sections (however, sections cannot be nested inside one another). For example, the code that follows is the declaration of the <defaultDocument> configuration section, part of the *system.webServer* section group, located in *ApplicationHost.config* alongside the declarations of other IIS configuration sections.

> **Note** You can tell a bit about configuration sections by looking at the section group to which they belong. For example, IIS configuration sections that define global server configuration used by Windows Activation Service (WAS), including the <sites> and <applicationPools> configuration sections, reside in the *system.applicationHost* configuration section group. Web server configuration sections reside in the *system.webServer* section group. ASP.NET configuration sections are in the *system.Web* section group. When you define your own section, you can create your own section group (simply by declaring it in the configuration file) and place it in one of the existing section groups, or you can just declare your section in the top-level scope.

```
<configSections>
    ...
    <sectionGroup name="system.webServer">
        ...
        <section name="defaultDocument" overrideModeDefault="Allow" />
    <sectionGroup name="system.webServer">
<configSections>
```

This declaration indicates that the "defaultDocument" section can be used in the Application-Host.config file and any configuration files further down in the hierarchy. It also indicates that by default, lower configuration levels can later override the section, effectively enabling control over this section to be delegated to the application.

> **Important** Before editing configuration files, always back them up so that you can restore configuration if necessary. By default, the Application Host Helper Service automatically saves snapshots of server-level configuration files every two minutes, which may or may not be a sufficient level of protection for you.

To manually back up configuration before making a change, use the *%windir%*\System32\ Inetsrv\Appcmd Add Backup <BackupName> command. To restore a backup made earlier, you can use the *%windir%*\System32\Inetsrv\Appcmd Restore Backup <BackupName> command. To list the backups available for restore that you made and ones made by Configuration History Service, use the *%windir%*\System32\Inetsrv\Appcmd List Backups command. For more information about backing up and restoring configuration, see Chapter 4.

Each declaration can specify the information shown in Table 13-2.

Table 13-2   Specifying Declarations

Declaration	Description
Name	The name of the configuration section. Combined with the section group path, this name must match the name of the section's schema definition. This is required.
allowDefinition	The level at which configuration for this section is allowed, including MachineOnly, MachineToApplication, AppHostOnly, and Everywhere. This corresponds to parts of the configuration hierarchy where the configuration section can be used. Default is Everywhere.
overrideModeDefault	Whether the configuration for this section can be defined at levels below the current file where it is declared. Sections that set this to Deny effectively lock the configuration at this level, preventing its delegation. Default is Allow.
allowLocation	Whether this section can be specified for a particular path using location tags. Default is true.
type	The .NET section handler type that is responsible for processing this section. This is required for configuration sections that are read by the .NET configuration system, and therefore it is not needed for IIS configuration sections (unless you plan to access them by using the .NET configuration system). None of the IIS configuration sections define this attribute. If you declare the configuration section in the .NET Framework's Machine.config, root Web.config, or distributed Web.config files inside your Web site directory tree, you can set this attribute to the special *System.Configuration.IgnoreSection* type to avoid errors from the ASP.NET configuration system.
requirePermission	Specifies whether partial trust .NET applications can read the contents of this section by using the .NET *System.Configuration* (ASP.NET configuration system) or *Microsoft.Web.Administration* (IIS configuration system) APIs. If set to false, these sections will not be readable by applications running in partial trust. Default value is true.

Though the schema definitions for configuration sections are globally defined in the *%windir%*\System32\Inetsrv\Config\Schema directory, the section declarations can be located at different levels of the configuration hierarchy, thereby making the section available only at that level or below. By default, IIS 7.0 configuration hierarchy declares configuration sections as follows:

- **Framework Machine.config**   Declares .NET configuration sections available for all .NET programs, not just ASP.NET. All .NET programs receive configuration from this file.

- **Framework root Web.config**   Declares ASP.NET-specific sections that are only available in Web applications. When reading configuration, ASP.NET programs receive merged configuration from Machine.config and this file.

- **ApplicationHost.config**   Declares IIS configuration sections. When reading configuration, IIS configuration consumers receive configuration from the Framework Machine.config, root Web.config, and this file.

- **Distributed Web.config**   Contains configuration settings for the site/application, and it sometimes declares application-specific configuration sections (typically ASP.NET configuration sections consumed via *System.Configuration* APIs).

Two other configuration files also declare configuration sections: Redirection.config and Administration.config. These files are not typically part of the configuration hierarchy for Web applications, though they are used in specific scenarios. The configuration system uses Redirection.config to redirect the ApplicationHost.config accesses to a network location, in order to enable shared configuration on a Web farm. IIS Manager uses Administration.config to specify console-specific configuration, including a list of IIS Manager extensions that the console loads (for more information, see the section titled "How IIS Manager Extensions Work" later in the chapter).

> **Note**   For more information about the configuration file hierarchy, see Chapter 4.

Developers often use the section declarations to control the default delegation state of configuration sections, as well as to restrict the scope of where the configuration can be specified. The former is done to prevent non-Administrators from overriding certain configuration sections in Web.config files that they have access to. The latter is done to restrict the usage of the configuration section to the levels where it is actually read by the corresponding Web server feature. For example, WAS and IIS worker processes read the <sites> configuration section at the server level only, and therefore this section is declared with *allowDefinition = AppHostOnly*. We will discuss the delegation of configuration sections later in the chapter when we talk about locking down configuration.

Installing New Configuration Sections

Armed with an understanding of schema definitions and declarations, adding a new configuration section becomes a two-step process:

1. Register the section schema.

2. Declare the section in the desired configuration file.

To register the section schema, use the format described in *IIS_schema.xml* to create an XML file that contains the definition of the section. Then copy it to the *%windir%*\System32\ Inetsrv\Config\Schema directory. Because the IIS 7.0 configuration system is an In-Process component, you will need to restart each process that needs to read the new configuration section in order to force the process to load the new schema file. This usually means recycling the target application pool or restarting IIS services from a command prompt with Iisreset.exe, which restarts worker processes in all application pools.

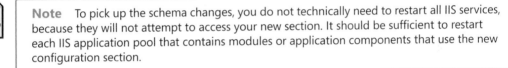

> **Note**   To pick up the schema changes, you do not technically need to restart all IIS services, because they will not attempt to access your new section. It should be sufficient to restart each IIS application pool that contains modules or application components that use the new configuration section.

To declare the configuration section, you need to add the section declaration element to the <configSections> section at the level where you want the section to become available. Most IIS configuration sections should be declared in ApplicationHost.config, which enables them to be used at the server level as well as in delegated application Web.config files.

If the section needs to be different for different versions of the .NET Framework, you should declare it in the .NET Framework Machine.config or root Web.config files. This is where the rest of the .NET Framework and ASP.NET sections respectively are declared. Web server features that access configuration inside the IIS worker process automatically receive the configuration from the Framework configuration files of the version specified by the application pool's *managedRuntimeVersion* attribute.

If you were planning to use the section only for a particular Web site or application, you could declare it a Web.config file inside the application. However, then you will not be able to read this configuration for other applications nor will you be able to specify the base configuration at the server level for configuration reuse between applications.

That's it. Once your section definition is registered and the section is declared at the right configuration level, you can now use it in the configuration files side-by-side with IIS configuration.

The Iisschema.exe Tool

Unlike registering section schema, which can be done simply by copying the schema file to %windir%\System32\Inetsrv\Config\Schema, declaring the section requires writing code to manipulate the section declarations for a particular configuration file. In Windows Server 2008 and Windows Vista Service Pack 1 (SP1), you can do this from a .NET application by using the *Microsoft.Web.Administration* API, as well as from script using WMI or the IIS 7.0 configuration COM objects. To make this easier, you can use the Iisschema.exe command line tool, which dramatically simplifies installing and managing configuration sections. You can also use the tool to quickly check which sections are installed and declared on the server or a specific configuration level.

For example, you can quickly install the schema file and automatically declare all of the sections defined therein in ApplicationHost.config by using the following command:

```
IisSchema.exe /install <schemafile.xml>
```

Alternatively, you can declare specific configuration sections at a specific configuration path and then set specific section declaration attributes by using the *"Iisschema.exe /reg <SectionName> /path:<ConfigPath>"* command. You can also modify any of the existing declarations or list all of the configuration sections declared at a specific configuration path.

To get help for all of the parameters supported by the tool, run it without parameters as follows:

```
IisSchema.exe
```

The Iisschema.exe tool is available on this book's companion media. You can learn more about the tool and download it from *http://mvolo.com/blogs/serverside/archive/2007/08/04/IISSCHEMA.EXE-_2D00_-A-tool-to-register-IIS7-configuration-sections.aspx*.

Securing Configuration Sections

Unlike Web server modules, configuration sections do not contain any code and therefore pose significantly less risk to the system. At the time of this writing, we are not aware of ways that you can reduce the security of your server by installing new configuration sections. You can, however, introduce risk by installing administration extensions that do contain code, which we will discuss in the section titled "Administration Extensions" later in this chapter.

The topic of securing configuration is rather extensive and is covered in detail in Chapter 14, "Implementing Security Strategies." In this section, we will focus on a few specific aspects of configuration security that you should consider when adding a new configuration section. Be sure to also follow the general guidelines presented in Chapter 14 for securing configuration on your server.

When adding a new configuration section, you must consider a few concerns. First, because configuration is intended to alter the behavior of the server, it is important to maintain control over who can modify it and how to avoid compromising the server's operation.

By default, IIS 7.0 already restricts the ability to change configuration in server-level configuration files to Administrators. However, on servers where control over the application content is delegated to non-Administrators, those users can specify configuration in delegated Web.config files and thereby override the configuration set at the server level for those sites/ applications. Even in cases where the server administrator controls the application content, application components from third parties can end up making undesired configuration settings. Because of this, Administrators need to determine which configuration sections should be used only at the server level, where the server administrator maintains control, and which can be overridden at the application level. The next section discusses controlling configuration delegation.

Second, the configuration data itself may contain sensitive information, such as account passwords or connection strings, and therefore you may want to take additional precautions to prevent unintended disclosure of this information. You can do this by requesting that certain parts of the new configuration section be automatically encrypted when the configuration is written so that the data is not persisted in clear-text form. This supplements the protection afforded by access restrictions on the configuration files and also protects the information from disclosure when the files are transported off of the physical server. In this section, we'll take a closer look at doing this.

Controlling Configuration Delegation

If you are running a shared server on which the server administrator is not the same person as the site or application administrator, you should consider which configuration sections can be overridden at the site or application level. You should not allow delegation for any configuration section that can enable the application to compromise the security of the server, dramatically affect its performance, or gain access to other applications' configuration or data.

The basic mechanism for controlling the delegation of a new section is to prevent it from being overridden at a lower level, unless it is explicitly unlocked by the Administrator. This is done by specifying *allowOverrideDefault = False* in the section declaration. Most IIS configuration sections declared in ApplicationHost.config use this technique.

> **Note**   You can also use the *allowDefinition* attribute in the section declaration to limit the use of this section to Machine or ApphostOnly scopes. However, it should never be used as a mechanism for controlling delegation for the section because it cannot be "unlocked" by the Administrator, unlike *allowOverrideDefault*. The *allowDefinition* attribute is meant to restrict the use of the section to configuration levels where the section is applicable based on how this section is interpreted by the corresponding run-time consumer.

Once you specify *allowOverrideDefault* = *False* in the section declaration, by default, lower configuration levels cannot override this section. However, Administrators can always unlock this section later to allow it to be specified at lower levels. To do this, they wrap the configuration section by using a location tag that can specify the *overrideMode* attribute to indicate that the section is locked or unlocked. The following example shows a configuration section with *allowOverrideDefault="Deny"* being unlocked:

```
<location path="" overrideMode="Allow">
    <system.webServer>
        <tracing>
            <traceFailedRequests />
        </tracing>
    </system.webServer>
</location>
```

Setting *overrideMode* to "Deny" would lock the section. The *path* attribute indicates which configuration path the location section is used for, and it therefore determines the scope of the locking or unlocking decision. The """ value in this case means unlock for all configuration levels, whereas a value of *"Default Web Site/"* would mean unlock for the site called "Default Web Site" only.

Instead of modifying configuration directly, you can do it easily with the Appcmd command line tool. For example, to unlock the <asp> section so that it can be defined anywhere in the configuration hierarchy, use this code.

```
%windir%\system32\inetsrv\AppCmd unlock config /section:asp
```

In addition, the Administrator can unlock this section for a specific site or application and then leave it locked for others. For example, to unlock the <asp> section only for the "Default Web Site/MyApp" application, use this code:

```
%windir%\system32\inetsrv\AppCmd unlock config "Default Web Site/MyApp"
    /section:<SectionName>
```

By using the *Appcmd Lock Config* command, the Administrator can also lock sections that are currently unlocked. They can also manage the delegation state of configuration sections by using IIS Manager.

> **Caution**   Configuration delegation is intended to control write access to configuration on shared servers, and it is less applicable on dedicated servers where the server administrator controls both the server and site configuration. However, it is good practice to always restrict the delegation of configuration sections, even on dedicated servers, and to unlock each configuration section specifically whenever it needs to be used at the application level. This reduces the risk of the application code accidentally specifying undesired configuration settings in the future without the knowledge of the Administrator. This is especially useful when installing applications that come from third parties and that may end up including undesired configuration in Web.config files.

In some cases, section-level delegation control is not flexible enough, and you'll need to allow some parts of the configuration section to be overridden while at the same time locking others. The configuration system provides a number of mechanisms to accomplish this via attribute, element, and collection locking. Chapter 4 provides more information about these types of locking.

Protecting Sensitive Configuration Data

The IIS 7.0 configuration system provides an encryption mechanism that can protect sensitive information from being accessed by an attacker if access is gained to the physical configuration file. This is primarily intended to protect the configuration data when it is transported off the machine and is not properly protected by ACLs. While on the server, the ACLs on configuration files are the main mechanism for securing access to configuration.

You can use configuration encryption to manually encrypt the value of any attribute in any IIS 7.0 configuration section. However, if you know your configuration section contains sensitive data, you should take advantage of automatic encryption by marking the sensitive attributes in your configuration section schema to always be encrypted. This is similar to the encrypted properties support in the metabase in previous versions of IIS, except you can easily take advantage of it to encrypt any part of your own configuration section.

Note   The IIS 7.0 configuration system provides attribute-level encryption support, unlike the ASP.NET configuration system that uses section-level encryption. Though this is a more flexible and sometimes more efficient mechanism (it enables you to encrypt only the sensitive data in the section and leave the rest unencrypted), it does have a few unfortunate side effects. The first is that you cannot use Aspnet_regiis.exe or ASP.NET encryption to encrypt IIS configuration sections.

The second, and arguably the most painful, side effect is that you cannot use the IIS administration stack to access ASP.NET configuration that has been encrypted with section-level encryption. You can, however, use the *Microsoft.Web.Administration* APIs to access the IIS configuration sections from ASP.NET modules and .NET applications, instead of using *System.Configuration*. Finally, you cannot use IIS attribute-level encryption to encrypt .NET Framework or ASP.NET configuration sections.

This is done by including the *encrypted* property to true on any of the attribute definitions in your configuration section schema. Several built-in IIS 7.0 configuration sections use this mechanism to insure that their sensitive content remains encrypted. For example, the anonymousAuthentication section marks the anonymous user password attribute as encrypted.

```
  <sectionSchema
name="system.webServer/security/authentication/anonymousAuthentication">
    ...
```

```
    <attribute name="password" type="string" caseSensitive="true"
encrypted="true" defaultValue="[enc:AesProvider::enc]" />
    ...
  </sectionSchema>
```

By specifying the *encrypted* property on the attribute schema definition, you insure that whenever any configuration API or tool writes data to this attribute, it is persisted in the encrypted form. You specify the default encryption provider that the configuration system uses for this property by referencing it through the default value, as in the previous example.

The encryption is transparent to the writer. In addition, whenever this attribute is read by a caller that has access to the configuration encryption key, the decryption is also transparent so that the caller obtains the plain text value of this attribute.

> **Caution**   Although encryption protects your configuration data from being accessed if someone gains physical access to the file, it does not protect your configuration from code within the IIS worker process. The configuration system inside the worker process automatically decrypts any encrypted configuration (assuming the worker process has access to the key container). Therefore, any code inside the worker process can access the information. In fact, aside from using application pool isolation to prevent access to configuration intended for other application pools, there is no way to restrict configuration access to a particular component within the worker process and not make it available to other components in the process. You can read more about application pool isolation in Chapter 9, "Managing Web Sites," and in Chapter 14.

Be sure to read more about the options you have for using encryption to protect access to configuration in Chapter 14.

Managing Administration Extensions

The IIS 7.0 configuration system provides a structured mechanism for controlling the behavior of IIS and its features. In a way, the configuration system exposes an object model for IIS, enabling you to inspect and control IIS objects such as sites, application pools, applications, and virtual directories. The configuration system is also extensible through the configuration section schema, which enables additional Web server functionality to expose configuration through its object model.

Though the ability to manage Web server configuration is its primary purpose, the IIS 7.0 configuration system takes the concept of a management object model to the next logical level. It enables configuration sections to also expose dynamic properties and methods that are backed by code instead of static configuration data.

This is done through the use of administration extensions to the configuration system. A great example of the value that administration extensions bring to IIS 7.0 administration is IIS 7.0's own <applicationPools> configuration section, which contains a collection of application pool definitions and associated configuration. IIS 7.0 also ships a schema extension to this section, adding dynamic attributes and methods backed by the Runtime State and Control API (RSCA). This enables the reader of the <applicationPools> configuration section to also retrieve run-time information for each application pool element, including:

- Its state (started/stopped)
- The list of currently running worker processes in the application pool
- The list of currently executing requests in each worker process
- The list of currently loaded ASP.NET appdomains in each worker process

In addition, it exposes methods that enable the caller to recycle each application pool or unload an ASP.NET appdomain in a particular worker process. All of this functionality is exposed through the same APIs that are used to navigate the configuration object model, blurring the line between static configuration and run-time behavior exposed by IIS objects.

For example, here is a C# script that uses the IIS 7.0 configuration objects to list all application pools on the system, including some of their configuration information and the list of currently executing worker processes (provided by the RSCA administration extension):

```
var adminManager = new ActiveXObject("Microsoft.ApplicationHost.AdminManager");

var appPoolsSection = adminManager.GetAdminSection(
    "system.applicationHost/applicationPools",
     "MACHINE/WEBROOT/APPHOST");

//
//  Enumerate the application pools collection
//
var appPoolsCollection = appPoolsSection.Collection;
for(var i = 0; i < appPoolsCollection.Count; i++)
{
    var appPoolElement = appPoolsCollection.Item(i);

    var name = appPoolElement.GetPropertyByName("name").Value;
var appPoolStateProperty = appPoolElement.GetPropertyByName("state");
    var state =
            appPoolStateProperty.Schema.PossibleValues.Item
                    (
                      appPoolStateProperty.Value
                    ).Name;
    WScript.Echo("Application Pool *" + name + "* (" + state + ")");

    //
    //  Enumerate the worker processes collection
    //
    var workerProcessesElement =
appPoolElement.ChildElements.Item("workerProcesses");
    var workerProcessCollection = workerProcessesElement.Collection;
```

```
            for(var wp = 0; wp < workerProcessCollection.Count; wp++)
            {
                var workerProcess = workerProcessCollection.Item(wp);
                WScript.Echo("  Worker process - " +
workerProcess.GetPropertyByName("processId").Value);
            }
    }
```

A sample output of this script (which follows) shows the application pools configured on the machine, their state, and the list of active worker processes in each pool. The latter two pieces of information come from the RSCA administration extension, yet the programming experience to access them is indistinguishable from accessing attributes coming from configuration. The sample output looks like this:

```
Application Pool *DefaultAppPool* (Started)
  Worker process - 2900
Application Pool *Classic .NET AppPool* (Started)
```

In addition to exposing run-time information through the configuration object model, administration extensions also provide a convenient way to package administration or deployment tasks and expose them as methods on the related configuration sections. Next, you will look at how administration extensions work.

How Administration Extensions Work

An administration extension is a COM object that implements one or more interfaces published by the IIS 7.0 configuration system to provide values of dynamic attributes and/or execute dynamic methods on configuration sections.

It is linked to the section via the section's schema definition. For dynamic attributes, the attribute definition can simply specify the COM ProgId of the administration extension's COM object via the *extension* schema property. The schema can also contain method definitions for dynamic methods that can accept arguments and return information. For an example of both, we can turn to the RSCA extension schema, contained in Rscaext.xml, that adds the dynamic functionality to the base <sites> and <applicationPools> configuration sections.

```
  <sectionSchema name="system.applicationHost/sites">
    <collection addElement="site">
      <attribute name="state" type="enum"
extension="Microsoft.ApplicationHost.RscaExtension">
        <enum name="Starting" value="0" />
        <enum name="Started" value="1" />
        <enum name="Stopping" value="2" />
        <enum name="Stopped" value="3" />
        <enum name="Unknown" value="4" />
      </attribute>
      <method name="Start"
extension="Microsoft.ApplicationHost.RscaExtension" />
      <method name="Stop"
extension="Microsoft.ApplicationHost.RscaExtension" />
    </collection>
  </sectionSchema>
```

The schema adds a *state* attribute to each *<site>* element, which is backed by the *Microsoft.ApplicationHost.RscaExtension* COM object. It also defines the *Start* and *Stop* methods that are also backed by that extension.

> **Note**   You may notice that the Rscaext.xml file contains schema definitions for dynamic attributes and methods for already defined <sites> and <applicationPools> configuration sections. This takes advantage of the configuration schema merging support in the configuration system, which enables new schema files to extend existing configuration sections and not just add new ones.

When the configuration script accesses the dynamic properties or invokes the dynamic methods in the configuration section, the administration extension is invoked to provide the attribute value and execute the method. If the caller does not ask for dynamic attributes or invoke methods, then the Administration extension is never created and invoked, and the user continues to work with static configuration only.

Installing Administration Extensions

To install administration extensions, register them with the section schema, either as part of new configuration section definitions or by adding new dynamic attributes and method definitions for existing configuration sections. From the schema perspective, the installation of new Administration extensions is the same as installing new configuration sections (see the section titled "Installing New Configuration Sections" earlier in this chapter).

Because Administration extensions are backed by COM objects, the COM object that implements the required interfaces must be registered on the system (this is typically done with Regsvr32.exe or with Regasm.exe for .NET COM objects). The COM registration information must include the friendly ProgId name that is referenced in the configuration section schema.

Securing Administration Extensions

Unlike configuration sections, Administration extensions contain code and therefore pose a risk to your server. What's more, Administration extensions are invoked by management tools and scripts that are typically run by Administrators, which enables their code to execute with administrative privileges. In fact, many administration extensions require administrative privileges to operate, including the RSCA extension that is included with IIS 7.0.

This is in contrast with Web server modules that by default execute in IIS worker processes that run under lower privilege identities and can be further sandboxed by ASP.NET's Code Access Security (for managed modules). Therefore, Administration extensions can pose a significantly higher risk to the server then Web server modules.

The ability to publish configuration section schema is restricted to Administrators (as is the ability to register COM objects on the machine). This eliminates the possibility of untrusted users on the machine being able to register Administration extensions. However, Administrators themselves must exercise caution when installing administrative extensions and be sure to trust the source of each extension.

Table 13-3 shows some of the configuration system's typical users that have the ability to load and invoke administration extensions.

Table 13-3   Users and Privileges for Administration Extensions

User	Execution Privilege
WAS	Does not use extensions
IIS Worker Processes	Does not use extensions
Metabase Compatibility (Inetinfo.exe)	Does not use extensions
WMI Service	Local System
Appcmd	Does not use extensions
IIS Manager (Inetmgr.exe)	Caller (typically Administrator)
Configuration scripts, Microsoft.Web. Administration programs	Caller (typically Administrator)

WAS, IIS worker processes, Metabase Compatibility, and Appcmd.exe all disable the use of administration extensions (for different reasons). However, the WMI service, scripts that use the configuration system COM objects, and .NET programs that use the *Microsoft.Web.Administration* APIs all have access to running administration extensions and often run (and have to run) with administrative privileges (this happens whenever the caller has administrative privileges). As such, there is no easy way to sandbox administration extensions. Therefore, extreme caution must be taken in installing those extensions on the server.

Managing IIS Manager Extensions

In addition to the programmatic and command line options, the IIS 7.0 administration stack also provides a GUI management tool. IIS Manager, which replaces the legacy MMC snap-in from previous IIS versions, has been completely redesigned to provide end users with an intuitive task-based GUI experience for managing the server. The tool, shown in Figure 13-2, also serves as a foundation for remote IIS 7.0 management, providing secure HTTPS-based remote connectivity and delegated site management. You can learn more about using IIS Manager in Chapter 6, "Using IIS Manager."

In the spirit of IIS 7.0, IIS Manager provides its own extensibility platform, which enables you to add new UI management features and extensively customize the appearance and functionality of the interface. This completes the extensibility picture of the IIS 7.0 administration stack, enabling new configuration sections and administration extensions added at the configuration system layer to also have corresponding UI management experiences for the end user. These UI extensions also benefit from the remote management and delegation capacities that the tool provides. The tool handles all of the network connectivity, authentication against Windows or non-Windows credential stores, and delegated management, enabling your UI extension to focus on the actual management task without taking into account whether it's being used for local or remote management.

Figure 13-2   IIS Manager.

How IIS Manager Extensions Work

A UI extension's primary job is to provide the UI experience for managing the particular configuration section or performing any management task. You can learn more about IIS Manager and the default features it provides in Chapter 6. Each UI extension typically consists of the following:

■ **The client-side UI module**   This is the client-side component that provides the UI experience, including new UI pages and other customizations of the tool's interface. It invokes the corresponding module service to carry out the required management tasks.

■ **The server-side module service**   This is the server-side component that provides the underlying management functionality, typically invoking *Microsoft.Web.Administration* APIs to access the IIS 7.0 administration stack.

The separation between the client UI functionality and the server management functionality is necessary to enable support for remote management. The client-side component is always instantiated on the client, which may be running on the same physical machine as the server being managed or on a remote machine that is connecting to the server through IIS Manager's management service. The module service is the server-side component, which carries out the underlying management tasks and is always instantiated on the server. This way, the management functionality in the UI extension does not need to concern itself with remote management, because it is always local to the server.

Both the client-side and server-side components are implemented as strongly named .NET assemblies, both of which must be installed into the server's Global Assembly Cache (GAC) and registered in the server's configuration. Because of this, both assemblies must be signed by the developer before they can be installed.

IIS Manager uses its own server-level configuration file, Administration.config, which is different from the server-level configuration file used by the Web server (ApplicationHost.config). It is also located in the *%windows%*\System32\Inetsrv\Config directory. IIS Manager substitutes this file for the root Framework Web.config file when reading its own configuration. This configuration contains the registration information for all of the IIS Manager extensions.

```
<moduleProviders>
    <!-- Server Modules-->
    <add name="Modules"
type="Microsoft.Web.Management.Iis.Modules.ModulesModuleProvider,
Microsoft.Web.Management.Iis, Version=7.0.0.0, Culture=neutral,
PublicKeyToken=31bf3856ad364e35" />
    <add name="Handlers"
type="Microsoft.Web.Management.Iis.Handlers.HandlersModuleProvider,
Microsoft.Web.Management.Iis, Version=7.0.0.0, Culture=neutral,
PublicKeyToken=31bf3856ad364e35" />
    …
</moduleProviders>
<!-- For all Sites -->
<location path=".">
    <modules>
        <add name="Modules" />
        <add name="Handlers" />
        …
    </modules>
</location>
```

In the excerpt shown here, two UI features that manage IIS 7.0 Web server modules (the "Modules" feature) and Web server handler mappings ("Handlers") are registered and are enabled by default for delegated management of all Web sites.

The <moduleProviders> section defines all of the IIS Manager extensions that are registered on the system and specifies the associated fully qualified type names of the corresponding module provider. Each module provider is responsible for providing the type information for the client-side UI modules and the corresponding server-side module service components at run time. This information is then used by IIS Manager and the management service to initialize the right components.

The <modules> section provides a mechanism to selectively enable the UI modules for a particular site. By default, all of the UI modules are enabled for all sites by being added at the "." level.

> **Note**   In remote management scenarios, the client machine does not need to have the UI extension registered on the server. When IIS Manager makes a remote connection to the server, it can automatically download the client components of the UI extensions registered on the server and display their UI features on the client.

Installing IIS Manager Extensions

Installing IIS Manager extensions is fairly simple. To do so, follow these steps:

1. Install the client and server .NET assemblies in the server's GAC.

2. Register the module provider type in the Administration.config configuration file and optionally enable it for delegated site management.

Remember that the client and server assemblies that comprise the IIS Manager extension must be strongly named, that is, signed by the developer.

To register the module provider type, you have to add its fully qualified type to the <moduleProviders> collection and list the selected name of the module in the <modules> collection inside the Administration.config configuration file. To do this, you need to know the fully qualified type name of the module provider class, which is typically provided by the extension's developer.

> **Caution**   You must trust the source of the code before installing the extensions on your server because the extensions may execute with administrative privileges when you launch IIS Manager on your computer.

Securing IIS Manager Extensions

Just like administration extensions to the configuration system, IIS Manager extensions pose a relatively high risk because they contain code that may run with administrative privileges on the server. As such, if they are malicious or are compromised, they are not restricted in the damage that they can do.

Table 13-4 lists the programs that load IIS Manager extensions and the privilege under which they are executed.

Table 13-4   Programs That Load IIS Manager Extensions

Program	Execution Privilege
IIS Manager GUI (Inetmgr.exe)	Caller (typically Administrator for local server administration)
Web Management Service (Wmsvc.exe)	Local Service (NT Service\wmsvc)
	Authenticated user (if using Windows Authentication)

When you use IIS Manager locally to manage the server, it runs with the identity of the user that launched the tool. Because local administrators typically do this—it is required for much of the server-level administration such as creating sites and changing server-level configuration—the extensions in the tool run with administrative privileges.

When you use the Web Management Service to administer the server remotely, it runs with the Local Service account (mapped to NT Service\wmsvc by service isolation) or under the impersonated identity of the authenticated user if Windows Authentication was used for the remote connection. As such, administration extensions run with administrative privileges only if the remote user is an Administrator on the machine and Windows Authentication was used to authenticate. When non-Windows authentication is used, the extension will still have access to a number of server resources that the NT Service\wmsvc SID has access to. This affords more protection in case the administration extension is somehow compromised by a remote attack. Of course, the remote management service is locked down and requires authentication to access its functionality, so only users that are specifically granted the right to administer the server remotely and are allowed to use the specific extensions can execute them.

Because IIS Manager supports delegated management of Web sites, users that do not have administrative privileges on the server can be allowed to remotely (or locally) manage their Web site configuration. This management is controlled to a large extent by the configuration delegation, but IIS Manager provides an additional mechanism for controlling what UI features are available to site administrators. This is important when you consider that new administration extensions can expose UI features that go beyond configuration and in some cases do not implement their own delegation control.

In these scenarios, the server administrator needs to prevent site administrators from having access to those UI features. This can be done from the Feature Delegation feature available when connected to the server as a server administrator, as shown in Figure 13-3. You can completely hide the feature from nonadministrative users by setting its delegation state to "Not Delegated". Or, configure it so that its contents can be viewed but no changes to the underlying state can be made by setting the state to "Read Only". However, keep in mind that the administration extension has the responsibility of properly implementing delegation support. So if in doubt, use the "Not Delegated" option.

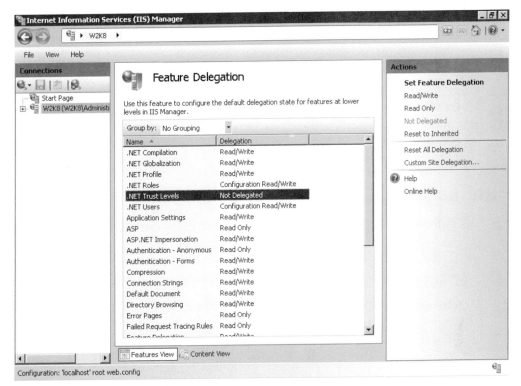

Figure 13-3   Feature Delegation.

When a remote client uses IIS Manager to connect to the server, IIS Manager compares the module providers available on the server with what is available on the client. If a new extension is available on the server, IIS Manager prompts the client to download and install that extension. If the client accepts, IIS Manager installs the extension in the user's profile (it is not installed to the GAC) and loaded inside IIS Manager, which may be running as an Administrator on the client machine (even though the client may be using nonadministrative credentials to connect remotely to the server). Because of this, it is critical for the server administrator to trust the source of the extension and for the client to trust the server. Otherwise, a malicious extension can be used to compromise the security of the client machines that are using IIS Manager to connect to the server.

You can take advantage of the publisher certificate–based trust model provided by IIS Manager to insure that all extensions you install on your server are signed by a publisher that you trust. You can also configure the clients to trust this specific publisher, thereby ensuring that the code downloaded to their machines is safe. In other words, do not install extensions coming from unknown or untrusted publishers or from unknown or untrusted Web servers!

Caution   Do not install administration extensions that come from untrusted publishers, especially when you are connected to a server you do not trust.

Even if you do not accept the download of the extension, your remote administration session will continue working properly, and you will be able to use all of the existing management functionality except for the extension you choose not to download. Next time you connect, you will have an opportunity to download it again.

 Note   If for whatever reason the extensions you downloaded have become corrupted or are no longer wanted on your client, you can purge the extension download cache by using the Inetmgr.exe /reset command.

Summary

Much like the Web server itself, the IIS 7.0 administration stack provides end-to-end extensibility to facilitate third-party configuration and management solutions. This extensibility is also the core platform of the administration stack itself, with all of the built-in feature configuration and management functionality built on top of that very same extensibility platform.

You can take advantage of this to deploy custom configuration for your custom Web server features and administer this configuration with the power of IIS 7.0 configuration tools and APIs in the exact same way that you administer built-in server configuration. Going further, you can enhance the functionality of the administration stack by adding new administration extensions that provide rich run-time data about IIS 7.0 or expose useful administration functionality. Finally, you can provide an integrated GUI management experience for this configuration and administration functionality through IIS Manager extensions, as well as leverage the tool's built-in secure remote administration and delegation support.

This chapter rounds out the extensibility story for IIS 7.0 and gives you the knowledge you need to properly deploy and secure extensions to the IIS 7.0 administration stack. For more on how to manage the Web server's run-time modules, see Chapter 12, "Managing Web Server Modules."

Additional Resources

These resources contain additional information and tools related to this chapter:

- See Chapter 14, "Implementing Security Strategies," for information on securing configuration.

- See Chapter 4, "Understanding the Configuration System," for information about using the configuration system.

- See IIS.NET for articles and information about IIS7.

- For information on using IISSchema.exe to install IIS 7.0 configuration section schema, see *http://mvolo.com/blogs/serverside/archive/2007/08/04/IISSCHEMA.EXE-_2D00_ -A-tool-to-register-IIS7-configuration-sections.aspx*.

Chapter 14

Implementing Security Strategies

On the Disc   Browse the CD for additional tools and resources.

The predecessor of Internet Information Services (IIS) 7.0–IIS 6.0–established a high bar for providing a secure Web server platform. IIS 7.0 builds on much of the IIS 6.0 feature codebase and secure practices formulated during the IIS 6.0 development life cycle. It also builds on many of the design principles that contributed to the excellent security track record of IIS 6.0, taking them further to improve the security of the Web server and applications that run on it. This includes the secure by default design and an emphasis on reducing the surface area and using least privilege to minimize the risk of exposed application vulnerabilities being successfully exploited by an attacker. IIS 7.0 makes it easier than ever before to apply these crucial security principles by offering modularity that enables you to build minimal surface area Web servers and running your applications in an isolated environment.

Many of the security features in IIS 6.0 remain applicable in IIS 7.0. In this chapter, we will start by reviewing the changes to the security features as well as the new features that IIS 7.0 introduces to help improve the Web server and application security. Then, we will look at applying the general security principles of reducing the surface area and using least privilege to further strengthen the security of the Web server. Finally, we will take a detailed look at using the security features in IIS 7.0, including the authentication and authorization features, securing network communications with Transport Layer Security (TLS), and safeguarding the configuration.

Security Changes in IIS 7.0

IIS 7.0 builds on the security focus established in its predecessor, IIS 6.0. As a result, the overwhelming majority of the core security principles and features established in IIS 6.0 are still in use today. However, IIS 7.0 does introduce improvements to help enhance the security of the Web server:

- **The anonymous user configured by default for anonymous authentication is the new built-in IUSR account.**   This account is built in and does not require a password that needs to be renewed and synchronized between servers. Additionally, permissions set for IUSR accounts are effective when copied to another IIS 7.0 server because the IUSR account has a well-known Security Identifier (SID) that is the same on every computer. For more information, see the section titled "Anonymous Authentication" later in this chapter.

- **The IIS_WPG group has been replaced with the built-in IIS_IUSRS group.**   This group is built in and enables permissions set for IIS_IUSRS to remain effective when copied to another IIS 7.0 server because it has a well-known Security Identifier (SID). In addition, this SID is automatically injected into the worker process token for each IIS worker process, eliminating the need for manual group membership for any custom application pool identities. For more information, see the section titled "Set NTFS Permissions to Grant Minimal Access" later in this chapter.

- **Anonymous authentication can be configured to use the application pool identity.**   This enables the content to require permissions only for the application pool identity when using anonymous authentication, simplifying permission management. For more information, see the section titled "Set NTFS Permissions to Grant Minimal Access" later in this chapter.

- **IIS worker processes automatically receive a unique application pool Security Identifier (SID) that you can use to grant access to the specific application pool to enable application isolation.**   For more information, see the section titled "Isolating Applications" later in this chapter.

- **Configuration isolation automatically isolates server-level configuration for each application pool.**   The global server-level configuration contained in applicationHost.config is automatically isolated by creating filtered copies of this configuration for each application pool and preventing other applications pools from being able to read this configuration. For more information, see the section titled "Understanding Configuration Isolation" later in this chapter.

- **Virtual directories can specify fixed credentials regardless of whether they point to Universal Naming Convention (UNC) shares or a local file system.**   Unlike IIS 6.0, which supports fixed credentials for specifying access to UNC shares only, IIS 7.0 enables fixed credentials to be used for any virtual directory.

- **Windows Authentication is performed in the kernel by default.**   This improves the configurability of the Kerberos protocol on the server. It also improves the performance of Windows Authentication. However, it may affect some applications that have custom clients that presend authentication credentials on the first request. This behavior can be turned off in the configuration. For more information, see the section titled "Windows Authentication" later in this chapter.

■ **The new Request Filtering feature provides extended URL Scan functionality.** You can use the new Request Filtering feature to protect your Web server against nonstandard or malicious request patterns and additionally protect specific resources and directories from being accessed. For more information, see the section titled "Request Filtering" later in this chapter.

■ **The new URL Authorization feature enables applications to control access to resources through configuration-based rules.** The new URL Authorization feature provides flexible configuration-based rules to control access to application resources in terms of users and roles, and it supports the use of the ASP.NET Roles service. For more information, see the section titled "URL Authorization" later in this chapter.

Additionally, IIS 7.0 introduces several changes to existing security features and removes several deprecated security features that could impact your application. These changes to security-related features are listed here:

■ **IIS 6.0 Digest Authentication is no longer supported.** It is being replaced by Advanced Digest Authentication (now simply referred to as Digest Authentication), which does not require the application pool to run with LocalSystem privileges. See the section titled "Digest Authentication" later in this chapter for more information.

■ **.NET Passport Authentication is no longer supported.** The .NET Passport Authentication support is not included in Windows Vista and Windows Server 2008, and therefore IIS 7.0 does not support it.

■ **IIS 6.0 URL Authorization is no longer supported.** The IIS 6.0 URL Authorization was overly complex and not often used. It has been replaced by the new configuration-based URL Authorization feature. See the section titled "URL Authorization" later in this chapter for more information.

■ **IIS 6.0 Sub-Authentication is no longer supported.** The Sub-Authentication feature enabled IIS 6.0 Digest Authentication (which has been removed) and synchronized anonymous account passwords (the anonymous account now uses the new built-in IUSR account that does not have a password). It is no longer needed in IIS 7.0 and therefore has been retired.

■ **IIS Manager no longer provides support for configuring IIS Client Certificate Mapping Authentication.** You can edit the configuration directly, use Appcmd from the command line, or use another configuration application programming interface (API) to configure this feature. For more information, see the section titled "IIS Client Certificate Mapping Authentication" later in this chapter.

- **Several authentication and impersonation differences exist in ASP.NET applications when running in the default Integrated mode.** This includes an inability to use both Forms authentication and an IIS authentication method simultaneously, and an inability to impersonate the authenticated user in certain stages of request processing. For more information on security changes impacting ASP.NET applications, see the list of breaking changes at *http://mvolo.com/blogs/serverside/archive/2007/12/08/IIS-7.0-Breaking-Changes-ASP.NET-2.0-applications-Integrated-mode.aspx.*

- **Metabase access control lists (ACLs) are no longer supported.** With the new configuration system, you cannot set permissions on individual configuration settings. IIS 7.0 provides built-in support for delegating configuration settings to Web site and application owners, replacing metabase ACLs as a mechanism for configuration delegation. For more information, see the section titled "Controlling Configuration Delegation" later in this chapter.

- **Metabase auditing is no longer supported.** The ability to audit changes to specific configuration settings is not supported out of the box. This is a consequence of IIS 7.0 not supporting metabase ACLs.

Reducing Attack Surface Area

Reducing the attack surface area of the Web server is a key strategy in reducing the risk of a security vulnerability being successfully exploited by an attacker. The principle of attack surface area reduction is not exclusive to Web servers—it is generally accepted as one of the most direct ways to improve the security of any software system. When applied to IIS 7.0, it provides the following benefits:

- It directly reduces the number of features and services exposed by the Web server to outside clients, minimizing the amount of code available for an attacker to exploit.

- It reduces complexity, which makes it easier to configure the Web server in a secure manner.

- If a vulnerability is exposed, the uptime of the Web server is not affected as much, because if the component affected by the vulnerability is not installed, it is not necessary to take the Web server offline or patch it immediately.

IIS 7.0 gives you an unparalleled ability to reduce the attack surface area of the Web server through its modular architecture by enabling you to remove all functionality other than what is absolutely necessary to host your application. By leveraging this ability, you can deploy low-footprint Web servers with minimal possible surface area.

After installing the minimal set of features, you can further reduce the surface area of the Web server by configuring your application to operate with the minimal functionality, for example, configuring which application resources should be served.

In the rest of this section, we will review the cumulative process for reducing the surface area of the Web server and your application. This process includes the following steps:

1.   Reduce the surface area of the Web server.

   a.   Install the minimal required set of Web server features.

   b.   Enable only the required Internet Server Application Programming Interface (ISAPI) filters.

   c.   Enable only the required ISAPI extensions.

   d.   Enable only the required Common Gateway Interface (CGI) applications.

   e.   Enable only the required FastCGI applications.

2.   Reduce the surface area of the application.

   a.   Enable only the required modules.

   b.   Configure the minimal set of application handler mappings.

   c.   Set Web site permissions.

   d.   Configure a minimal set of MIME types.

The modular architecture of IIS 7.0 gives you the ability to install only the Web server features required for the correct operation of your Web server. This forms the foundation of the surface area reduction strategy.

In addition, you can continue to control what extensions that do not use the IIS 7.0 modular extensibility model can execute on the server. This includes ISAPI extensions and filters and CGI and FastCGI programs.

Installing the Minimal Required Set of Web Server Features

The IIS 7.0 modular feature set comprises more than 40 individual Web server modules that provide various request processing and application services. The Web server core engine retains only the minimal set of functionality needed to receive the request and dispatch its processing to modules. You can leverage this architecture to deploy minimal surface area Web servers by installing only the modules that are required for the Web server's operation.

The modular feature set provided in IIS 7.0 is fully integrated with Windows Setup. This means that you can install or uninstall most of the IIS 7.0 modules by installing IIS 7.0 features directly from the Turn Windows Features On Or Off page in Windows Vista, or the Web Server (IIS) role in Server Manager on Windows Server 2008 as shown in Figure 14-1. Each feature typically corresponds to one module (or in some cases several modules) and installs any corresponding configuration information as well as feature dependencies.

The default installation of IIS 7.0 includes only the features necessary for IIS 7.0 to function as a static file Web server. In many cases, this may not be sufficient to properly host your application, so you will need to install additional features, including support for hosting dynamic application technologies. When you do this, you will be prompted to install any dependencies of the feature you are installing and configure the proper default configuration for that feature.

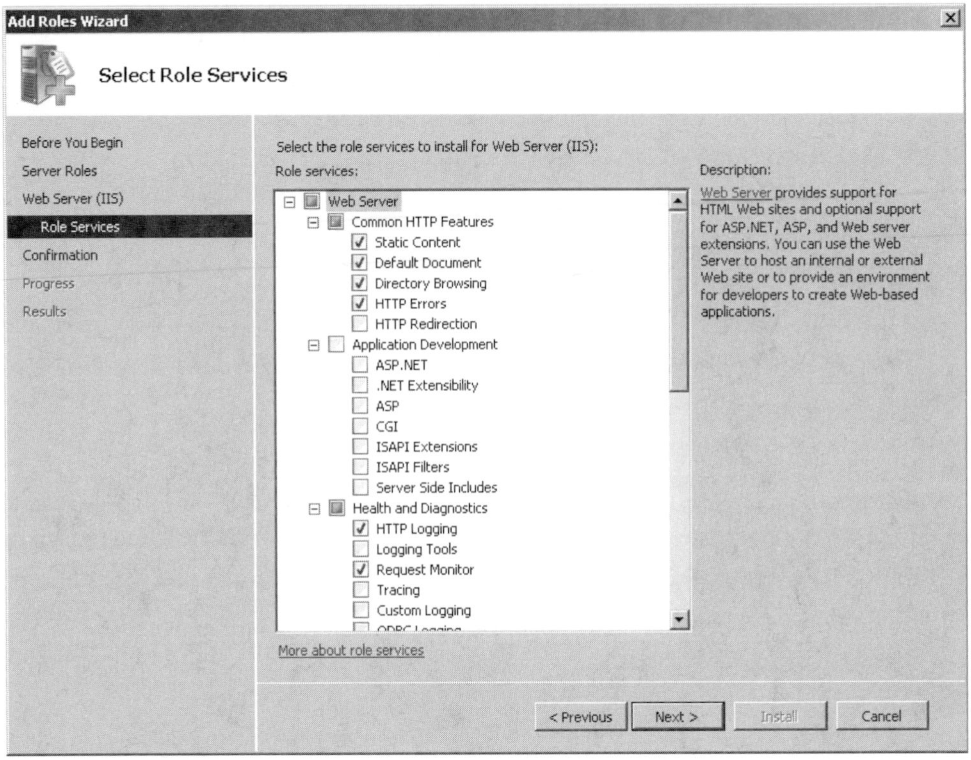

Figure 14-1   Installing IIS 7.0 using the Add Roles Wizard.

Caution   Do not install all the IIS 7.0 features if you are unsure of what you need. Doing so can unnecessarily increase the surface area of the Web server.

By ensuring that only the required modules are installed, you can significantly reduce the surface area of the Web server. This provides the following benefits:

■ Removes the potential for an attacker to exploit known or future threats in features that are not installed.

■ Reduces management complexity, making it easier to configure the server in a secure manner.

■ Reduces the downtime and costs associated with reacting to a vulnerability or applying patches. If the patched component is not installed, you do not need to take the server offline to perform the patch. You can also perform patching on your own schedule instead of being forced to perform it immediately if a vulnerability is found.

Note When you apply a patch to a component of a Web server feature that is not installed, it is stored in the operating system installation cache. This way, when you install the feature in the future, it will use the patched version automatically. Therefore, be sure to continue installing all operating system updates, even if the corresponding features are not currently being used on the server.

To reduce the surface area of the Web server, you should take the following steps:

1. **Determine the set of features your applications need.** In the majority of cases, you should be able to tell what features are required by your application by reviewing the list of setup components and comparing it with your application's requirements. As a guide, you can often use the recommended set of modules for specific application workloads. You can find more information on recommended installation workloads at *http://www.iis.net/articles/view.aspx/IIS7/Deploy-an-IIS7-Server/Installing-IIS7/Install-Typical-IIS-Workloads?Page=2*. You should exercise caution when removing Web server features that are security sensitive, because doing so may have a negative impact on your server's security. To review the list of modules that have a security impact, see the section titled "Taking Advantage of Componentization to Reduce the Security Surface Area of the Server" in Chapter 12, "Managing Web Server Modules."

2. **Install only the required features.** After you have determined the required features, you should install them using the roles or features wizards. For more information on the options for installing IIS 7.0 features, see Chapter 5, "Installing IIS 7.0." When in doubt, do not install all features, because doing so will result in an unnecessary surface area increase.

3. **Install only the required third-party modules.** IIS 7.0 applications may require third-party modules to be installed to add additional functionality or replace a built-in IIS 7.0 feature. You should exercise caution when installing any module on the Web server and make sure that you trust its source. Installing untrusted or buggy modules can compromise the security of the Web server or negatively affect its reliability and performance. For information about installing third-party modules, see Chapter 12.

4. **Test your application.** You should always test your application to ensure that it operates correctly given the installed feature set. Your application may experience errors if a required module is not installed. The symptoms of this error will depend on the service provided by the missing module. If your testing shows an error and you believe that it is due to a missing feature, make sure that the error is removed or changed by installing that specific feature. If the error remains, uninstall the feature and try again. Never blindly install multiple or all features to get the application to work.

When you run multiple applications on the same Web server, you will need to install the superset of the modules required by each application. You can then further reduce the surface area of each application by controlling which modules are enabled at the application level. We will review how to do this in the section titled "Enabling Only the Required Modules" later in this chapter.

For more information on using the roles or features wizards to install IIS 7.0 features and other available features, see Chapter 5. For more information on installing and enabling modules, including third-party modules, see Chapter 12.

Enabling Only the Required ISAPI Filters

IIS 6.0 provides support for ISAPI filters, to allow third parties to extend IIS request processing. IIS 7.0 replaces ISAPI filters with IIS 7.0 modules as the preferred mechanism for extending the Web server. However, IIS 7.0 continues to support ISAPI filters for backward compatibility reasons.

> **Note**   To enable ISAPI filters to work on IIS 7.0, the ISAPI Filters role service must be installed. This role service installs the IsapiFilterModule module, which provides support for hosting ISAPI filters. If this module is removed, ISAPI filters will not be loaded. This role service is not enabled by default; it is however enabled when the ASP.NET role service is installed.

If your Web server uses ISAPI filters, to minimize the Web server surface area you should ensure that only the required ISAPI filters are enabled.

> **Note**   You must be a server administrator to enable ISAPI filters.

To properly configure ISAPI filters, you should take the following steps:

1. **If your Web server uses ISAPI filters, install the ISAPI Filters role service.** Without this role service, the ISAPI filters will not be loaded and therefore may create a security risk if they are responsible for security-sensitive functionality.

2. **If your Web server does not use ISAPI filters, *do not* install the ISAPI Filters role service.** This eliminates the possibility of unwanted ISAPI filters being configured on your server.

3. **Determine the ISAPI filters that your application requires.** In the majority of cases, your Web server should not require any ISAPI filters (with the exception of the ASP.NET ISAPI filter; see the note later in this section). Therefore, you will typically need to configure ISAPI filters only if you are migrating an existing application from previous versions of IIS that require specific ISAPI filters, or if you are installing a new third-party ISAPI filter.

4. **Enable the required ISAPI filters.** You can control which ISAPI filters are enabled on your server, and for a specific Web site, by using IIS Manager.

To use IIS Manager to configure the ISAPI filters, click the Web server node or Web site node in the tree view and then double-click ISAPI Filters, as shown in Figure 14-2. Exercise extreme caution when installing third-party ISAPI filters and be sure you trust their source. Installing untrusted or buggy ISAPI filters can compromise the security of the Web server or negatively affect its reliability.

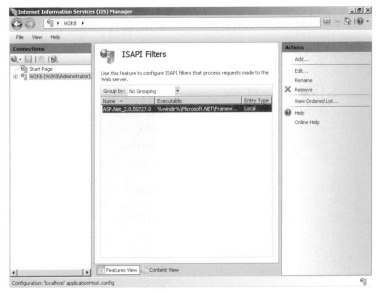

Figure 14-2   Using IIS Manager to configure ISAPI filters.

Note   IIS 7.0 does not install any ISAPI filters by default. However, ASP.NET 1.1 and ASP.NET 2.0 will install an ISAPI filter named ASP.NET_2.0.50727.0. This filter is required for cookie-less ASP.NET features to work properly. You should not remove this filter.

You can also control which filters are enabled for the Web server or for a specific Web site by editing the *system.webServer/isapiFilters* configuration section directly, with the Appcmd command line tool, or with another configuration API.

Enabling Only the Required ISAPI Extensions

IIS 6.0 provides support for ISAPI extensions, which allows third parties to extend IIS request processing by returning responses for specific content types. IIS 7.0 replaces ISAPI extensions with IIS 7.0 modules as a preferred mechanism for extending IIS. However, IIS 7.0 continues to support ISAPI extensions for backward compatibility reasons.

> **Note**   To enable ISAPI extensions to work on IIS 7.0, the ISAPI Extensions role service must be installed. This role service installs the IsapiModule module, which provides support for hosting ISAPI extensions. If this module is removed, ISAPI extensions will not be loaded. This role service is not enabled by default, but it is enabled when ASP.NET is installed.

Today, dynamic application framework technologies frequently use ISAPI extensions to interface with IIS. Therefore, it is likely that if you are using dynamic application technologies, you will need to use ISAPI extensions. For example, both ASP.NET (for Classic mode applications) and ASP are implemented as ISAPI extensions.

If your Web server uses ISAPI extensions, to minimize the Web server surface area you should ensure that only the required ISAPI extensions are enabled.

> **Note**   You must be a server administrator to enable ISAPI extensions.

To properly configure ISAPI extensions, you should take the following steps:

1.   **If your Web server uses ISAPI extensions, install the ISAPI Extensions role service.** Without this role service, the ISAPI extensions will not be loaded, and requests to resources mapped to ISAPI extensions will return errors.

2.   **If your Web server does not use ISAPI extensions, *do not* install the ISAPI Extensions role service.** This eliminates the possibility of unwanted ISAPI extensions being configured on your server.

3.   **Configure the allowed ISAPI extensions.** Each ISAPI extension must be allowed to execute on the server before it can be used. You can use IIS Manager to configure all ISAPI extensions that are allowed to execute on the server. Doing so is explained in more detail later in this section. Exercise extreme caution when allowing third-party ISAPI extensions and be sure you trust their source. Installing untrusted or buggy ISAPI extensions can compromise the security of the Web server or negatively affect its reliability.

4.   **Configure the desired handler mappings.** To use ISAPI extensions, you need to create handler mappings that map allowed ISAPI extensions to specific content types in your application. For more information on creating handler mappings for ISAPI extensions, see Chapter 12. We will discuss securing handler mappings in the section titled "Configuring the Minimal Set of Handler Mappings" later in this chapter.

You must explicitly allow any ISAPI extension that has to execute on your server. When you allow a specific ISAPI extension path, any application on the server can load this extension, if the server configures a handler mapping to this extension. Table 14-1 specifies the common ISAPI extensions and when they are installed.

Table 14-1   **Common ISAPI Extensions**

ISAPI Extension	Default State	When Installed
Active Server Pages	Allowed	ASP role service is installed
ASP.NET v1.1.4322	Not Allowed	.NET Framework v1.1 SP1 is installed
ASP.NET v2.0.50727	Allowed	ASP.NET role service is installed

On IIS 6.0, you have to explicitly allow the ISAPI extensions corresponding to ASP and ASP.NET 2.0. On IIS 7.0, these ISAPI extensions are automatically allowed when you install the corresponding role services. In addition, only ASP.NET applications running in Classic mode use the ASP.NET 2.0 ISAPI extension. It is a more reliable practice to use the roles or features wizards to control the availability of these features, instead of allowing or not allowing them in the ISAPI and CGI Restrictions. However, you still need to manually enable the ISAPI extension for ASP.NET v1.1.

On IIS 6.0, you can allow an ISAPI extension in the Web Service Extension Restriction List. On IIS 7.0, you can use IIS Manager to do this by clicking the Web server node in the tree view and then double-clicking ISAPI And CGI Restrictions to open the feature shown in Figure 14-3. To add a new ISAPI extension, click Add in the Actions pane and then enter the exact path of the ISAPI extension. If you would like to allow the ISAPI extension to execute, check the Allow Extension Path To Execute check box. You can also allow or deny existing extensions.

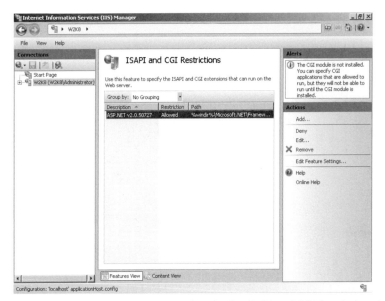

Figure 14-3   Allowing ISAPI extensions in the ISAPI and CGI Restrictions by using IIS Manager.

In addition to using IIS Manager, you can also edit the *system.webServer/security/isapiCgi-Restriction* configuration section directly by using the Appcmd command line tool or with another configuration API. For more information about configuring enabled ISAPI extensions, see the section titled "Adding Entries to the ISAPI CGI Restriction List (Formerly Web Service Restriction List)" in Chapter 12.

Enabling Only the Required CGI Programs

IIS 7.0 continues to support CGI programs as one of the ways to extend the functionality of the Web server.

> **Note**   To enable CGI programs to work on IIS 7.0, the CGI role service must be installed. This role service installs the CgiModule module, which provides support for launching CGI programs. If this module is removed, CGI programs will not be usable. This role service is not enabled by default.

By default, IIS 7.0 does not provide any CGI programs, so they should be used only if your application uses third-party CGI programs. If it does, you should ensure that only the required CGI programs are allowed to minimize the Web server surface area.

> **Note**   You must be a server administrator to allow CGI programs.

To properly configure CGI programs, you should take the following steps:

1. **If your Web server uses CGI programs, install the CGI role service.** Without this role service, the CGI programs will not be created, and requests to resources mapped to CGI programs will return errors.

2. **If your Web server does not use CGI programs, *do not* install the CGI role service.** This eliminates the possibility of unwanted CGI programs being configured on your server.

3. **Configure the allowed CGI programs.** Each CGI program must be allowed to execute on the server before it can be used. You can use IIS Manager to configure all CGI programs that are allowed to execute on the server. This is explained in more detail later in this section. Exercise extreme caution when allowing third-party CGI programs and be sure you trust their source. Installing untrusted or buggy CGI programs can compromise the security of the Web server or negatively affect its reliability.

4. **Configure the desired handler mappings.** To use CGI programs, you need to create handler mappings that map allowed CGI programs to specific content types in your application. For more information on creating handler mappings for CGI programs, see Chapter 12. We will discuss securing handler mappings in the section titled "Configuring the Minimal Set of Handler Mappings" later in this chapter.

Similar to ISAPI extensions, you must explicitly allow any CGI program that has to execute on your server. When you allow a specific CGI program path, this CGI program can now be launched by any application on the server that configures a handler mapping to this CGI program. To be allowed, each allowed CGI program entry must specify the full path and arguments exactly the same way they are specified in each handler mapping. CGI programs are allowed in the ISAPI and CGI Restrictions feature, similar to the process described in the section titled "Enabling Only the Required ISAPI Extensions" earlier in this chapter.

Enabling Only the Required FastCGI Programs

IIS 7.0 supports hosting FastCGI programs by using the FastCGI feature, which provides a more reliable way to host many application frameworks than CGI does.

> **Note**   To enable FastCGI programs to work on IIS 7.0, the CGI role service must be installed. This role service installs the FastCgiModule module, which provides support for launching FastCGI programs. If this module is removed, FastCGI programs will not be usable. This role service is not enabled by default.

By default, IIS 7.0 does not provide any FastCGI programs, so they should be used only if your application uses third-party FastCGI programs. If so, to minimize the Web server surface area, you should ensure that only the required FastCGI programs are allowed.

> **Note**   You must be a server administrator to allow FastCGI programs.

To properly configure FastCGI programs, you should take the following steps:

1. **If your Web server uses FastCGI programs, install the CGI role service.** Without this role service, the FastCGI programs will not be usable, and requests to resources mapped to FastCGI programs will return errors.

2. **If your Web server does not use FastCGI programs, *do not* install the CGI role service.** This eliminates the possibility of unwanted FastCGI programs being configured on your server.

3. **Configure the allowed FastCGI programs.** Each FastCGI program must be allowed to execute on the server before it can be used. Though there is no IIS Manager support for configuring FastCGI programs that are allowed to execute on the server, you can do this by editing the *system.webServer/fastCgi* configuration section. For more information on configuring FastCGI programs, see Chapter 11, "Hosting Application Development Frameworks." Exercise extreme caution when allowing third-party FastCGI programs and be sure you trust their source. Installing untrusted or buggy FastCGI programs can compromise the security of the Web server or negatively affect its reliability.

4. **Configure the desired handler mappings.** To use FastCGI programs, you need to create handler mappings that map allowed FastCGI programs to specific content types in your application. For more information on creating handler mappings for FastCGI programs, see Chapter 12. We will discuss securing handler mappings in the section titled "Configuring the Minimal Set of Handler Mappings" later in this chapter.

Unlike ISAPI extensions and CGI programs, FastCGI programs are not allowed through the ISAPI and CGI Restriction feature. Instead, in the *system.webServer/fastCgi* configuration section, you need to create an entry for each allowed FastCGI program. For more information on configuring FastCGI programs, see Chapter 11.

Reducing the Application's Surface Area

Installing only the required Web server features and locking down the enabled ISAPI extensions, ISAPI filters, and CGI and FastCGI programs is a great way to reduce the surface area of the Web server as a whole. You can take it a step further by reducing the set of functionality available at the application level, by limiting the modules enabled in each application, and by constraining the set of resources that the application is configured to serve.

Enabling Only the Required Modules

When your Web server is configured to run a single dedicated application, you should install only the modules necessary to host this application. However, if your Web server hosts multiple applications, you may need to install a superset of all IIS features and third-party modules that each application requires. In this case, you can further reduce the surface area of each application by disabling at the application level any modules that the application does not need.

To do this, you can configure the set of enabled IIS modules (managed or native) for each application. You can do this by using IIS Manager: select your application node in the tree view, double-click Modules, and remove any modules that are not needed in the application. You can learn more about the process for removing modules in Chapter 12.

> **Caution**   Exercise caution when removing modules because removing security-sensitive modules that perform tasks—for example, those that perform authorization—can result in weakening application security. See the section titled "Securing Web Server Modules" in Chapter 12 for information about removing modules and which built-in IIS modules may be security-sensitive.

If you are operating a Web server on which third parties are able to publish application content, be aware that they can by default enable new managed modules that are included with their application to process requests to their application. Likewise, they can disable any module that is installed and enabled at the server level, as long as it is not locked by default.

If this is not what you want, you should consider locking the *system.webServer/modules* configuration section or using fine-grain configuration locking to lock specific modules against being removed. For more information on locking down modules, see the section titled "Locking Down Extensibility" in Chapter 12.

> **Note**   It is not possible to add new native modules at the application level. Similarly, it is not possible to remove native modules associated with IIS features at the application level by default because IIS setup locks them at the server level.

Configuring the Minimal Set of Handler Mappings

Handler mappings directly determine what resource types the Web server is configured to serve. They do this by mapping extensions or URL paths to modules or ASP.NET handlers that provide processing for the corresponding resource type. Similar to modules, handler mappings are typically installed at the server level when IIS features or third-party application frameworks are installed. This is done to enable all applications on the server to serve the associated content.

If your application does not serve specific content types or does not use specific application framework technologies installed on the Web server, you should remove the associated handler mapping entries in the *system.webServer/handlers* configuration section at the application level to prevent the Web server from attempting to use them to satisfy requests to your application. This reduces the risk of unintended script functionality executing in your application, or an application framework specific vulnerability being exploited. Note that the latter may occur even if your application does not contain any resources or scripts for a particular application framework, if the application framework contains a vulnerability that manifests before it attempts to locate the requested script.

Use the following techniques to configure the minimal set of handler mappings for your application:

- **Review the handler mappings to understand what resource types can be processed in your application.**   Keep in mind that the Web server will attempt to satisfy each incoming request with the first handler mapping that matches the URL *path* and *verb* of the incoming request. Typically, the *StaticFileModule* will process all requests that have not matched other handler mappings, thus serving the requested resource as a static file if its extension is listed in the application's MIME type configuration. For more information on how handler mappings are selected, see the section titled "Adding Handler Mappings" in Chapter 12.

- **Remove any unused handler mappings in your application.**   You can do this by removing the specific handler mappings. If possible, remove all handler mappings by clearing the *system.webServer/handlers* configuration section and re-adding only the handler mappings that your application uses.

- **Be aware of preconditions.**   Because preconditions can be set on handler mappings to disable the use of these mappings in some application pools, some handler mappings may be ignored, resulting in the request being served using another matching handler mapping. To avoid security problems, do not create multiple handler mappings that rely on order to match similar requests.

- **Add applicable restrictions to handler mappings.**   When adding new handler mappings, make use of the resource type restrictions to restrict the handler mappings only to requests that map to existing physical files or directories in your application. This can help stop malicious requests to resources that do not exist in your application. Additionally, make use of the access restrictions as described in the section titled "Setting Web Site Permissions" later in this chapter.

See Chapter 12 to learn more about creating handler mappings, how preconditions affect them, and using the resource type and access restrictions.

If you are operating a Web server on which third parties can publish application content, be aware that they can modify the handler mappings in any way to control how requests to their applications are processed. They can add new handler mappings to any enabled module, remove any of the existing handler mappings, or map requests to other handlers. If you do not want this to happen, you should consider locking the *system.webServer/handlers* configuration section. For more information on locking down the handler mappings, see the section titled "Locking Down Extensibility" in Chapter 12.

> **Note**   Handler mappings that map requests to ISAPI extensions (IsapiModule), CGI programs (CgiModule), and FastCGI programs (FastCgiModule) are further limited by the ISAPI and CGI Restrictions and FastCGI program configuration at the Web server level, which can be set only by the administrator.

Setting Web Site Permissions

Web site permissions are an additional restriction that can be placed on a Web site, application, or URL in configuration to control what requests IIS is allowed to serve. These permissions are implemented at two levels. First, each handler mapping specifies the required permission level by using the *requireAccess* attribute. If the request that matches this handler mapping is made and the required permission is not granted for the requested URL, IIS will reject the request with a 403.X response status code. Second, some IIS components have hard-coded requirements for certain permissions, and they will reject the request if they are processing a request to a URL that does not have this permission.

> **Note**   Web site permissions control what functionality is enabled to be used at a particular URL. They do not consider the identity of the requesting user and therefore cannot be used to replace IIS authorization schemes when implementing access control.

Table 14-2 indicates the permission types that can be granted for a particular URL.

Table 14-2 Permission Types Granted for URLs

Permission	Description
None	No permissions are granted.
Read	Read access to files and directories is enabled.
	In particular, this enables the following: static file handler serving static files, directory listings, and default documents.
Script	Script processing is enabled.
	In particular, this enables the following: ISAPI extensions, CGI programs, FastCGI programs, and ASP.NET handlers. ISAPI extensions and CGI programs must specify a fixed script processor.
Execute	Running executables is enabled.
	In particular, this enables the following: ISAPI extensions and CGI programs with no script processor set (that execute the file provided in the request path). If granted, this permission will by default lead to IIS trying to execute EXE files as CGI applications and load DLL files as ISAPI extensions instead of downloading them.
Source	In previous versions of IIS, this permission enables WebDav requests to access the source of script files. No special handling of this permission is present in IIS 7.0.
Write	In previous versions of IIS, this permission enables WebDav requests to write files. No special handling of this permission is present in IIS 7.0.
NoRemoteRead	Prevents remote requests from using the Read permission.
NoRemoteScript	Prevents remote requests from using the Script permission.
NoRemoteExecute	Prevents remote requests from using the Execute permission.
NoRemoteWrite	Prevents remote requests from using the Write permission.

In IIS Manager, you can set the permission granted for a particular Web site, application, or URL by selecting the appropriate node in the tree view and then clicking Handler Mappings. There, you can set the Read, Script, and Execute permissions by clicking Edit Permissions in the Actions pane. Doing this also automatically shows the handlers that require a permission that is not granted as disabled, to let you know that requests to these handlers will be rejected.

You can set the permissions directly in configuration by editing the *accessPolicy* attribute of the *system.web/handlers* configuration section or by using Appcmd or other configuration APIs to do it. For example, to grant only the Read permission to the /files subfolder of the Default Web Site, you can use the following Appcmd syntax.

```
%systemroot%\system32\inetsrv\Appcmd set config "Default Web Site/files"
/section:handlers /accessPolicy:Read
```

Note When you specify a configuration path to apply configuration to a specific Web site or URL, you may get an error indicating that the configuration is locked. This is because most security configuration sections, including all authentication sections, are locked at the Web server level to prevent delegated configuration. You can unlock these sections to allow delegated configuration, or you can persist the configuration to applicationHost.config by using the */commit:apphost* parameter with your Appcmd commands.

Use the following guidelines when setting Web site permissions:

- **Remove unnecessary permissions for URLs that do not require them.** By default, Read and Script permissions are granted. For URLs that do not require the ability to execute dynamic application technologies, remove the Script permission. Do not grant additional permissions such as Execute unless necessary.

- **Keep in mind that applications can configure handler mappings that do not require permissions.** By default, applications can change existing handler mappings or create new handler mappings to not require permissions. Because of this, do not rely on Web site permissions for controlling which handler mappings can or cannot be created by applications that use delegated configuration. The permissions are only guaranteed for built-in IIS features including the static file handler, IsapiModule, CgiModule, and ASP.NET handlers, which hardcode the permission requirements. In other cases, the permissions are guaranteed only if the *system.webServer/handlers* configuration section is locked and prevents changes to the handler mappings set by the Web server administrator. For more information about locking down the handlers configuration section, see the section titled "Locking Down Extensibility" in Chapter 12.

Note Unlike in IIS 6.0, wildcard handler mappings no longer ignore Web site permissions. In IIS 7.0, they require the same level of permissions as they would when mapped with nonwildcard handler mappings. Because of this, configurations in which a wildcard-mapped ISAPI extension is used for URLs that do not allow the Script permission will now be broken and require the Script permission to be granted.

Configuring Minimal Sets of MIME Types

By default, to serve the corresponding physical file to the client, IIS handler mappings are preconfigured to direct all requests not mapped to other modules to the *StaticFileModule* (if the file does not exist, a 404 error response code is returned).

Note In IIS 7.0, the MIME types configured by default have been upgraded to contain many of the new common file extensions.

For security reasons, the *StaticFileModule* will serve only files whose extensions are listed in the MIME type configuration. This behavior is extremely important, because otherwise applications that contain scripts and other content that is processed by application framework technologies may end up serving these resources directly if the appropriate application framework handler mappings are not installed or become removed. In this situation, the MIME type configuration protects these resources from being served to the client and results in a 404.3 error returned to the client.

Note   You can learn about configuring MIME types in the section titled "Enabling New Static File Extensions to Be Served" in Chapter 11.

The default list of MIME types in IIS 7.0 should be safe for most applications. You can further configure the MIME types at the server level—or for a Web site, application, or URL—to mandate which file extensions are servable by the StaticFileModule. By reducing this list to only the extensions of the files known to be safe to serve, you can avoid accidentally serving files that are part of an application and are not meant to be downloaded.

Caution   MIME type configuration prevents only unlisted files from being downloaded directly through the StaticFileModule. It does not protect the resources from being accessed through the application, nor does it protect them from being downloaded if they are mapped to custom handlers. To protect application resources that are not meant to be accessed, you should forbid their extensions or use Request Filtering to place the content in a directory that is configured as a hidden segment. For more information, see the section titled "Request Filtering" later in this chapter.

You should use the following guidelines to securely configure the MIME types list:

- **Do not add file extensions to the MIME types configuration that are not meant to be downloaded directly.**   This refers to any of the file types that are used by the application, such as ASP, ASPX, or MDB.

- **Configure a minimal set of MIME types for each application.**   If possible, configure the MIME types for each application to contain only the minimal set of extensions. This can help prevent accidental serving of new files when they are added to the application. For example, if your application uses XML files to store internal data, you should make sure that your application does not include *xml* in its MIME type configuration even though the .xml extension is listed there by default when IIS is installed.

Configuring Applications for Least Privilege

Next to reducing its surface area, the most effective strategy to reduce the risk of a successful attack on your Web server is to configure your applications to run with the least privilege possible. Doing this minimizes the amount of damage that results if an attacker successfully exploits any known or future vulnerability. Similar to reducing the surface area, this technique is not limited to blocking specific threats—it works well for any threat that may be present in your application today or that may be found in the future.

The key to reducing the privilege of the application code in the IIS environment is to understand the identity under which the code executes, select the identity with the minimal number of privileges required, and limit the rights of the identity to access server resources. To help achieve least privilege, we will review these techniques:

- Use a low privilege application pool identity
- Set NTFS file system (NTFS) permissions to grant minimal access
- Reduce trust of ASP.NET applications
- Isolate applications

These techniques are discussed next in this section.

Use a Low Privilege Application Pool Identity

The majority of code executed as part of a Web application is executed in the context of the IIS worker process and typically runs under the identity configured for the application pool. Therefore, using a least privilege application pool identity is the primary way to constrain the privileges and rights granted to the application code.

By default, IIS application pools are configured to run using the built-in Network Service account, which has limited rights on the Web server. When each IIS worker process is started, it also automatically receives membership in the IIS_IUSRS group. This group replaces the IIS_WPG group used in IIS 6.0 as the required group identifying all IIS worker processes on the computer. IIS setup may still create the IIS_WPG group for backward-compatibility reasons, in which case IIS_IUSRS will be made a member of this group.

In addition, certain code in your application may execute with the identity of the authenticated user associated with each request. Table 14-3 summarizes the identities that may be used in your application.

Table 14-3   Application Identities

Identity Type	Used When...	Identities
Application pool identity	■ Accessing all files necessary for the execution of the IIS worker process	■ *Network Service* by default; otherwise configured application pool identity
	■ Accessing web.config files	■ *IIS_IUSRS* group
	■ Running FastCGI applications (by default)	■ Application Pool SID (*IIS APPPOOL\ <ApppoolName>*)
	■ Running ASP.NET applications (by default)	

Table 14-3 **Application Identities**

Identity Type	Used When...	Identities
Authenticated user	■ Accessing static files ■ Running ISAPI extensions ■ Running CGI programs (by default) ■ Running FastCGI applications (if impersonation is enabled) ■ Running ASP.NET applications (if impersonation is enabled)	■ *IUSR* by default when using anonymous authentication; otherwise configured anonymous user or application pool identity ■ Authenticated user if Windows token authentication methods are used
Virtual directory fixed credentials (when configured)	■ Accessing all application content	■ The configured virtual directory credentials

When using authentication schemes that produce Windows tokens, such as Windows Authentication or Basic Authentication, be aware that when highly privileged users access your application, it will execute with higher privileges than intended. Therefore, it is recommended that you do not allow users that have administrative privileges on the server to access your application. For more information on what identity each application framework executes under, see Chapter 11.

Caution   When using authentication schemes that produce Windows identities, your applications may execute with the identity of the authenticated user.

Also, when using anonymous authentication, you may opt for configuring the anonymous user to be the application pool identity, to ensure that all code always executes under the application pool identity. This makes it significantly easier to manage the access rights of the worker process. You can learn about configuring this in the section titled "Anonymous Authentication" later in this chapter.

Note   To simplify access management, configure the anonymous authentication user to be the application pool identity.

When selecting the application pool identity for your applications, use the following guidelines to maintain or improve the security of your Web server:

■ **Ensure that the application pool identity is not granted sensitive privileges or unnecessary rights to access resources.**   Often, in the face of "access denied" errors, administrators tend to grant the application pool identity full or otherwise unnecessary access to resources. This increases the privilege of the worker process and increases the risk of a serious compromise if the code in the worker process is compromised. Only grant the worker process the minimal access needed for the application to work. If this minimal access involves privileges or rights typically associated with administrative users, you need to re-evaluate your application's design.

■ **Do not use highly privileged or administrative identities for IIS application pools.**   Never use LocalSystem, Administrator, or any other highly privileged account as an application pool identity. Just say no!

■ **Consider using a lower privilege identity.**   If your application allows it, consider using a custom low privilege account for the IIS worker process. Unlike IIS 6.0, IIS 7.0 automatically injects the new IIS_IUSRS group into the worker process, eliminating the need for you to make the new identity a member of any group.

■ **Separate code with different privilege requirements into different application pools.**   If your server has multiple applications that require different levels of privilege (for example, one requires the privilege to write to the Web application, and the other one doesn't), separate them into two different application pools.

■ **When using anonymous authentication, configure the anonymous user to be the application pool identity.**   This significantly simplifies configuring access rights for your application by making the application code always execute with the application pool identity.

■ **Grant minimal access.**   When granting access to the application pool identity, grant the minimal access necessary. You can use this in conjunction with separating applications into different application pools to maintain least privilege for your applications. To grant access to a resource for all IIS application pools, grant it to the IIS_IUSRS group. To grant access to a resource for a specific application pool, use the unique application pool identity. Alternatively, use the automatic Application Pool SID that is named IIS APP-POOL\<*ApppoolName*> (the latter does not work for UNC content, only local content). Do not grant access rights to Network Service because it grants access to all services running on the server under the Network Service identity.

Set NTFS Permissions to Grant Minimal Access

By default, all files required for IIS worker processes to function grant access to the IIS_IUSRS group, which ensures that IIS worker processes can function regardless of the selected application pool identity. However, it is up to you to grant access to the application content so that the Web server and the application can successfully access its resources. Additionally, it is up to you to grant access to the additional resources the IIS worker process uses, such as ISAPI extensions, CGI programs, or custom directories configured for logging or failed request tracing.

Table 14-4 indicates the level of access the Web server typically requires for different kinds of resources.

Table 14-4   **Access Levels for Web Server Resources**

Resource Type	Identity	Required Access
Content (virtual directory physical path and below)	■ Fixed credentials set on the virtual directory (if set) OR ■ Authenticated users ■ IIS worker process identity (application pool identity)	■ Read ■ Write, if your application requires being able to write files in the virtual directory (granting Write is not recommended)
Additional resources IIS features use: CGI programs, ISAPI extensions, native module dynamic-link libraries (DLLs), compression directory, failed request tracing directory, logging directory, and more	■ IIS worker process identity (application pool identity)	■ Read ■ Execute, for CGI programs ■ Write, for compression or logging directories, or whenever the Web server needs to write data

When granting access to content directories, you can use one of the following techniques:

- **Grant access to IIS_IUSRS.**   This enables all IIS worker processes to access the content when using the application pool identity, or when using anonymous authentication. However, this does not enable you to isolate multiple application pools. If using a Windows-based authentication scheme, you also will need to grant access to all of the authenticated users that use your application.

- **Grant access to the identity of the application's application pool.**   This will enable only the IIS worker processes running in the application pool with the configured identity to access the content. If using anonymous authentication, you additionally need to set the anonymous user to be the application pool identity. If using a Windows-based authentication scheme, you also will need to grant access to all of the authenticated users that use your application. This approach is the basis for application pool isolation. For more information, see the section titled "Isolating Applications" later in this chapter.

- **Configure fixed credentials for the application's virtual directory and grant access to these credentials.**   This will prompt the IIS worker process to access the content by using the fixed credentials, regardless of the authenticated user identity. This option is often used when granting access to remote UNC shares to avoid the difficulties of ensuring that authenticated user identities can be delegated to access the remote network share. It can also be an efficient way to manage access to the content for a single identity regardless of the authenticated user (which can be set to the application pool identity when using custom application pool identities). Finally, it can be used to control access to the application when you host multiple applications inside the same application pool.

> **Note**   If you are using IIS Manager to administer the application remotely, you will also need to grant Read access to the NT Service\WMSvc account. For more information, see Chapter 8, "Remote Administration."

If you are using an authentication scheme (other than anonymous authentication) that produces Windows identities for authentication users, such as most of the IIS authentication schemes, you will also need to make sure that all authenticated users that require the use of your application have access to its content. This is because the Web server will use the authenticated user identity to access application content. Also, many application frameworks will by default impersonate the authenticated user when executing application code and accessing application resources.

When you need to allow multiple Windows users to use the application, you should add all of these users to a specific group and grant this group access to the application content. Alternatively, when using the fixed credentials model, you do not have to grant access to the authenticated users. Instead, IIS and application code will always impersonate the fixed virtual directory credentials. For more information on setting up the fixed credentials model, see the section titled "Managing Remote Content" in Chapter 9, "Managing Web Sites."

When your content is on a UNC share, you will likely need to use the fixed credentials model because most IIS authentication schemes do not produce Windows tokens that can be used for remote network shares (with the exception of basic authentication and IIS client certificate mapping authentication). Alternatively, you can configure your Web server for Constrained Delegation and Protocol Transition to allow the authenticated user tokens to be used against the remote share. However, using the fixed credentials for virtual directories on UNC shares is significantly easier to configure, so it is recommended over setting up delegation. For more information, see the section titled "UNC Authentication" later in this chapter.

> **Note**   Unlike in IIS 6.0, in which the authenticated user having access to the content directory is typically sufficient (except for ASP.NET applications), IIS 7.0 also requires the IIS worker process identity to have access to the content directories before they can read the web.config configuration files. This happens before IIS determines the authenticated user.

Reduce Trust of ASP.NET Applications

In addition to constraining the execution rights of the application by using a low privilege application pool identity, you can further sandbox the .NET parts of your application by using the ASP.NET trust levels. The ASP.NET parts of the application include the ASP.NET applications themselves, as well as managed modules that provide services for any application in ASP.NET Integrated mode applications.

ASP.NET trust levels use the Code Access Security (CAS) infrastructure in the .NET Framework to limit the execution of the application code, by defining a set of code permissions that control what application code can and cannot do. By default, ASP.NET applications and managed modules execute using the Full trust level, which does not limit their execution. In this trust level, the application can perform any action that is allowed by the Windows privileges and resource access rights.

You can reduce the trust level of ASP.NET applications to limit their execution further. This can be an effective way to achieve lower privilege for your application. By default, you have options described in Table 14-5, which are defined by the ASP.NET trust policy files.

Table 14-5   Default Trust Level Options

.NET Trust Level	Execution Limits	Rights
Full (internal)	None	All
High (web_hightrust.config)	None/.NET	Can do anything except call native code
Medium (web_mediumtrust.config)	Application is trusted within its own scope, but should not be able to affect other applications or the rest of the machine	■ Access files in the application root ■ Connect to SQL and OLEDB databases ■ Connect to Web services on the local machine ■ Manipulate threads and execution for its own requests
Low (web_lowtrust.config)	Application is not highly trusted; meant for applications that can use built-in ASP.NET features but do not run custom code	Only read access within application root
Minimal (web_minimaltrust.config)	Application is untrusted; ability to use built-in ASP.NET features is extremely restricted	Minimal permissions for executing code

It is recommended that you run ASP.NET applications by using the Medium trust level. In this trust level, the application is not able to access resources outside of itself and cannot perform operations that can compromise the security of the Web server overall. However, if you do this, you should test the application to make sure that it does not experience any security exceptions due to the lack of required permissions. You may also want to performance test the application to make sure that using the reduced trust level does not negatively impact your application's performance.

Note   The Medium trust level is the recommended trust level to constrain the execution of ASP.NET applications and managed modules, and to host multiple applications on a shared Web server.

You can use IIS Manager to configure the trust level used for ASP.NET applications and managed modules by double-clicking .NET Trust Levels. You can do this for the entire Web server—or for a specific application—by selecting that application node prior to using the .NET Trust Levels feature. You can also set the trust level directly by changing the *level* attribute in the *system.web/trust* configuration section.

> **Caution**   The *system.web/trust* configuration section is not locked by default, which means that any application can configure its own trust level. If you don't want this, lock the configuration section at the server level.

Isolating Applications

Application pools provide a great way to isolate multiple applications running on the same machine, both in terms of availability and security. This provides the following benefits:

■ Failures, instability, and performance degradation experienced in one application do not affect the applications in a different application pool.

■ Applications running in a different application pool can restrict access to their resources to that application pool only, preventing other applications from being able to access their resources.

The recommended way to configure applications for isolation is to place each application into a separate application pool. When you do this, IIS 7.0 makes it easy to isolate applications by automatically injecting a unique application pool security identifier, called the application pool SID, into the IIS worker process of each application pool. Each application pool SID is generated based on the application pool name and has the name *IIS APPPOOL\ <Apppool-Name>*. The application pool SID makes it possible to quickly isolate applications by placing NTFS permissions on their content to grant access only to the application pool SID of the application's application pool.

> **Note**   You can quickly isolate applications by setting permissions on their content to allow only the Application Pool SID of the corresponding application pool.

To make Application Pool SID–based isolation effective, you need to do the following:

1. Configure anonymous authentication to use the application pool identity.

2. Grant access to the application content for the *IIS APPPOOL\ <ApppoolName>* SID.

3. Do not grant access to the application content to IIS_IUSRS, IIS_WPG or any other application pool identity that may be used by another application pool.

4. Configure separate locations for all temporary and utility directories that IIS and the application use for each application or application pool, and set permissions on them to allow access only for the *IIS APPPOOL\ <ApppoolName>* SID.

Table 14-6 shows some of the common directories that IIS and ASP.NET applications use. The directories must be configured for isolation for each Web site or application and receive the appropriate permissions to enable access only by the associated application pool.

Table 14-6   Common Directories Used by IIS and ASP.NET Applications

Directory	Configured In...
Content directories	Virtual directory physical path
Windows TEMP directory (*%TEMP%* or *%TMP%*): used by Windows components	Set the *loadUserProfile* attribute to *true* in the *processModel* element of each application pool. This causes the TEMP directory to point to *%SystemDrive%\Users\%UserName%\AppData\Local\Temp*.
Web site log file directory	*directory* attribute of the *logFile* element for each site. The default is *%SystemDrive%\Inetpub\Logs\LogFiles*.
Web site Failed Requests Logs directory	*directory* attribute of the *traceFailedRequestsLogging* element of each site. The default is *%System-Drive%\Inetpub\Logs\FailedReqLogFiles*.
IIS Static Compression directory	Isolated automatically by creating a subdirectory for each application pool and applying ACLs to each directory for the Application Pool SID.
ASP.NET Temp directory: used by ASP.NET compilation system	*tempDirectory* attribute in *system.web/compilation* section for each application. The default is *%SystemRoot%\Microsoft.NET\Framework\<version>\Temporary ASP.NET Files*.
ASP Template Disk Cache directory	Isolated automatically by applying ACLs to each file for the Application Pool SID.

Note   The Application Pool SIDs can be used only for isolating local content. If you are using content located on a UNC share, you need to either use a custom application pool identity or configure fixed credentials for each virtual directory. Then you should use that identity to grant access to the network share.

IIS 7.0 provides automatic isolation of the server-level configuration by using configuration isolation. No action is necessary to enable this, because it is done by default. For more information about configuration isolation, see the section titled "Understanding Configuration Isolation" later in this chapter.

> **Note** The server-level configuration in applicationHost.config is isolated automatically using configuration isolation.

However, .NET Framework configuration in the machine.config and root web.config files—as well as the configuration in the distributed web.config files that are part of the Web site's directory structure—are not isolated. To properly isolate the distributed web.config files, set the appropriate permissions on the content directories, as described earlier in this section.

Implementing Access Control

Web applications require the ability to restrict access to their content, to protect sensitive resources, or to authorize access to resources to specific users. IIS 7.0 provides an extensive set of features that you can use to control the access to application content. These features are logically divided into two categories, based on the role they play in the process of determining access to the request resource:

- **Authentication** Authentication features serve to determine the identity of the client making the request, which can be used in determining whether this client should be granted access.

- **Authorization** Authorization features use the authenticated identity on the request or other applicable information to determine whether or not the client should be granted access to the requested resource. Authorization features typically depend on the presence of authentication features to determine the authenticated identity. However, some authorization features determine access based on other aspects of the request or the resource being requested, such as Request Filtering.

IIS 7.0 supports most of the authentication and authorization features available in IIS 6.0, and it introduces several additional features. These features (role services) are listed here in the order in which they apply during the processing of the request:

1. **IP and Domain Restrictions.** Used to restrict access to requests clients make from specific IP address ranges or domain names. The default install does not use this feature.

2. **Request Filtering.** Similar to UrlScan in previous versions of IIS, request filtering is used to restrict access to requests that meet established limits and do not contain known malicious patterns. In addition, Request Filtering is used to restrict access to known application content that is not meant to be served to remote clients. Request filtering is part of the default IIS 7.0 install and is configured to filter requests by default.

3. **Authentication features.** IIS 7.0 offers multiple authentication features that you can use to determine the identity of the client making the request. These include Basic Authentication, Digest Authentication, Windows Authentication (NTLM and Kerberos), and

many others. The Anonymous Authentication feature is part of the default IIS install and is enabled by default.

4. **Authorization features.** IIS 7.0 provides a new URL Authorization feature that you can use to create declarative access control rules in configuration to grant access to specific users or roles. In addition, it continues to support NTFS ACL-based authorization for authentication schemes that yield Windows user identities. IIS uses NTFS ACL-based authorization by default.

> **Note**   In IIS 7.0, all of these role services are available as Web server modules that can be individually installed and uninstalled and optionally disabled and enabled for each application. Be careful when removing authentication, authorization, and other access control modules, because you may unintentionally open access to unauthorized users or make your application vulnerable to malicious requests. To review the list of security-sensitive modules that ship with IIS 7.0, and considerations when removing them, see the section titled "Securing Web Server Modules" in Chapter 12.

You should leverage access control features to ensure that only users with the right to access those resources can access them. To do this, you need to configure the right authentication and authorization features for your application.

In addition, you should take advantage of Request Filtering to limit usage of the application as much as is possible, by creating restrictions on content types, URLs, and other request parameters. Doing so enables you to preemptively protect the application from unexpected usage and unknown exploits in the future.

IP and Domain Restrictions

The IP and Domain Restrictions role service enables you to restrict access to your application to clients making requests from a specific IP address range or to clients associated with a specific domain name. This feature is largely unchanged from IIS 6.0.

> **Note**   The IP and Domain Restrictions role service is not part of the default IIS install. You can manually install it from the IIS \ Security feature category in Windows Setup on Windows Vista, or from the Security category of the Web Server (IIS) role in Server Manager on Windows Server 2008. See Chapter 12 for more information about installing and enabling modules.

You can use this feature to allow or deny access to a specific range of IP addresses, or to a specific domain name. The IP and Domain Restrictions role service will attempt to match the source IP address of each incoming request to the configured rules, in the order in which rules are specified in configuration. If a matching rule is found, and the rule is denied access to the request, the request will be rejected with a 403.6 HTTP error code. If the rule allows access, the request will continue processing (all additional rules will be ignored).

You can specify any number of allow or deny rules and indicate whether access should be granted or denied if no rules match. The common strategies for using IP Address and Domain Restrictions rules include:

- Denying access by default and creating an Allow rule to grant access only to a specific IPv4 address range, such as the local subnet. You can do this to grant access only to clients on the local network or to a specific remote IP address.

- Allowing access by default and creating a Deny rule to deny access to a specific IP address or IPv4 address range. You can do this to deny access to a specific IP address that you know is malicious.

Caution   Allowing access by default and denying access for specific IP address ranges is not a secure technique, because attackers can and often will use different IP addresses to access your application. Also, clients that use IPv6 addresses instead of the IP addresses will not match a Deny rule that uses an IPv4 address range.

If you are looking to restrict access to your application to clients on the local network, you may be able to implement an additional defense measure by specifying that your site binding should listen only on the IP address associated with the private network. For servers that have both private and public IP addresses, this can restrict requests to your site to the private network only. You should use this in conjunction with IP and Domain Restrictions where possible. For more information on creating Web site bindings, see Chapter 9.

Though you can create rules that use a domain name instead of specifying an IP address, we don't recommend that you do so. This is because domain name-based restrictions require a reverse Domain Name System (DNS) lookup of the client IP address for each request, which can have a significant negative performance impact on your server. By default, the feature does not enable the use of domain name–based rules.

To configure the IP and Domain Restrictions rules, you will need to perform the following steps:

1. Use IIS Manager to configure the rules by selecting the Server node, a Site node, or any node under the site in the tree view. Then double-click the IP Address And Domain Restrictions feature, which is shown in Figure 14-4.

2. Use the Add Allow Entry or the Add Deny Entry command in the Actions pane to create allow or deny rules.

3. You can also use the Edit Feature Settings command to configure the default access (allow or deny) and whether or not domain name–based rules are allowed.

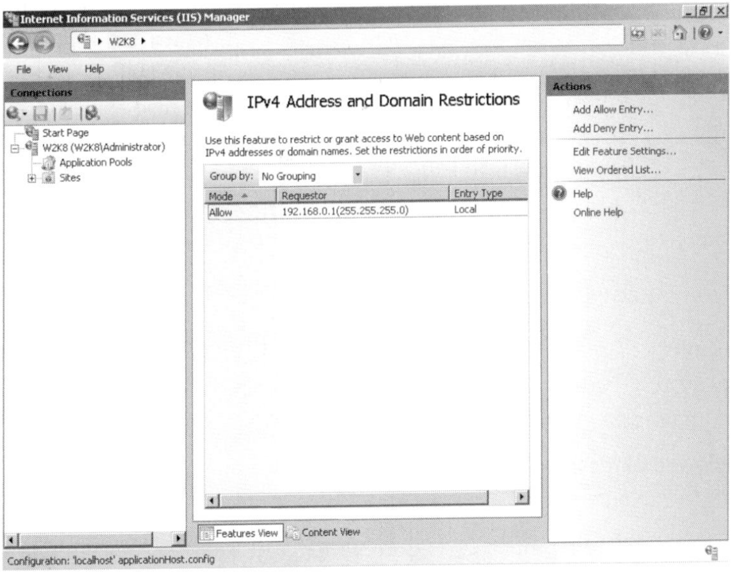

Figure 14-4   Configuring IP and Domain Restrictions using IIS Manager.

> **Note**   Although the IP and Domain Restrictions feature enables you to use IPv6 addresses, you cannot configure addresses that use IPv6 rules using IIS Manager. Also, requests that are made over IPv6 connections do not match rules using IPv4 addresses. Likewise, requests made over IPv4 connections do not match rules that specify IPv6 addresses.

> **Note**   By default, the *ipSecurity* configuration section is locked at the server level. You can unlock this section by using the *Appcmd Unlock Config* command to specify IP and Domain Restriction rules in web.config files at the site, application, or URL level.

You can also configure the IP and Domain Restrictions configuration by using Appcmd or configuration APIs to edit the *system.webServer/security/ipSecurity* configuration section.

Request Filtering

The Request Filtering feature is an improved version of the UrlScan tool available for previous versions of IIS. The Request Filtering feature enforces limitations on the format of the request URL and its contents to protect the application from possible exploits that may arise from exceeding these limits. With IIS 6.0 and previous versions of IIS, these limits have thwarted the majority of known Web application exploits, such as application-specific buffer overruns resulting from long malicious URLs and query strings. Though the Web server itself, starting with IIS 6.0, has been engineered to not be vulnerable to these attacks, these limits remain valuable in preventing both known and unknown future exploits for the Web server and applications running on it.

In addition to enforcing request limits, the Request Filtering feature also serves to deny access to certain application resources that are not meant to be served to Web clients, but are located in the servable namespace for an application. These files include the web.config configuration files for IIS and ASP.NET, as well as contents of the /BIN and /App_Code directories for ASP.NET applications.

You can use Request Filtering to do the following:

- **Set request limits**   Configure limits on the length and encoding of the URL, the length of the query string, the length of the request POST entity body, allowed request verbs, and maximum lengths of individual request headers.

- **Configure allowed extensions**   Configure which file extensions are allowed or rejected, regardless of the selected handler mapping.

- **Configure hidden URL segments**   Configure which URL segments are not served, to hide parts of your URL hierarchy.

- **Configure denied URL sequences**   Configure which URL patterns are not allowed, possibly to prevent known exploits that use specific URL patterns.

IIS 7.0 depends on request filtering by default to reject requests that may contain malicious payloads and to protect certain content from being served by the Web server. You can also use it to further restrict the input to your application, or to protect additional URLs, directories, and files or file extensions from being served by the Web server.

Caution   Request filtering is a critical security component and should not be removed unless it is absolutely clear that it is not needed. Always prefer to relax request filtering limits by setting the configuration rather than uninstalling or removing the Request Filtering module.

The request filtering configuration does not have an associated IIS Manager page, so these settings cannot be set through IIS Manager. To set them, you can configure the *system.web-Server/security/requestFiltering* configuration section directly at the command line by using Appcmd.exe or other configuration APIs. The *requestFiltering* section is unlocked by default, so you can set request filtering configuration in web.config files at the site, application, or URL level.

The remainder of this section will illustrate how to modify common request filtering configuration tasks.

Setting Request Limits

You can use Request Filtering to configure even tighter request limits if allowable in your application's usage to further reduce attackers' ability to exploit your application with malicious input. At other times, you may need to relax the default request limits to allow your application to function correctly, for example, if your application uses long query strings that may exceed the default limit of 2048 characters.

You may need to modify request limits applied by request filtering if any of the default limits interfere with your application usage.

You can use Appcmd to set request filtering limits as follows.

```
%systemroot%\system32\inetsrv\Appcmd set config [ConfigurationPath]
/section:system.webServer/security/requestFiltering
[/allowDoubleEscaping:bool] [/allowHighBitCharacters:bool]
[/requestLimits.maxAllowedContentLength:uint] [/requestLimits.maxUrl:uint]
[/requestLimits.maxQueryString:uint]
```

This command uses the parameters in Table 14-7.

Table 14-7   Parameters for Requesting Filtering Limits

Parameter	Description
ConfigurationPath	The configuration path at which to set this configuration.
allowDoubleEscaping	Whether or not request URLs that contain double-encoded characters are allowed. Attackers sometimes use double-encoded URLs to exploit canonicalization vulnerabilities in authorization code. After two normalization attempts, if the URL is not the same as it was after one, the request is rejected with the 404.11 response status code. The default is *false*.
allowHighBitCharacters	Whether or not non-ASCII characters are allowed in the URL. If a high bit character is encountered in the URL, the request is rejected with the 404.12 response status code. The default is *true*.
requestLimits.maxAllowed-ContentLength	The maximum length of the request entity body (in bytes). If this limit is exceeded, the request is rejected with the 404.13 response status code. The default is *30000000* bytes (approximately 28 megabytes).
requestLimits.maxUrl	The maximum length of the request URL's absolute path (in characters). If this limit is exceeded, the request is rejected with the 404.14 response status code. The default is *4096* characters.
requestLimits.maxQueryString	The maximum length of the query string (in characters). If this limit is exceeded, the request is rejected with the 404.15 response status code. The default is *2048* characters.

Note   You can also configure the request header length limits for each header by adding header limits in the *headerLimits* collection in the *system.webServer/security/requestFiltering* section. If the request exceeds a configured header limit, it will be rejected with a 404.10 response status code. Additionally, you can configure which verbs are allowed by adding those verbs to the *verbs* collection. If the request specifies a verb that is not allowed, it is rejected with a 404.6 response status code.

Configuring Allowed Extensions

By default, the Web server will process only extensions for which a handler mapping exists. By default, StaticFileModule processes all unmapped extensions. StaticFileModule serves only extensions listed in the *system.webServer/staticContent* configuration section (known as Mimemaps in IIS 6.0 and previous versions of IIS). Therefore, the handler mapping configuration and the static content configuration serves as the two-level mechanism for controlling which extensions can be served for a particular URL.

However, as a defense in depth measure, you may still want to use Request Filtering to deny requests to a particular extension, after making sure that it is not configured in the IIS handler mappings and the static content list. This makes sure that requests to this extension are rejected very early in the request processing pipeline, much before they otherwise would be rejected by the configuration mentioned earlier.

To add a prohibited or explicitly allowed extension by using Appcmd, use the following syntax.

```
%systemroot%\system32\inetsrv\Appcmd set config [ConfigurationPath]
/section:system.webServer/security/requestFiltering
/+fileExtensions.[fileExtension='string',allowed='bool']
```

The fileExtension string is in the format of .extension.

To delete a prohibited extension by using Appcmd, use the following syntax.

```
%systemroot%\system32\inetsrv\Appcmd set config [ConfigurationPath]
/section:system.webServer/security/requestFiltering
/-fileExtensions.[fileExtension='string']
```

These commands use the parameters in Table 14-8.

Table 14-8 Parameters for Deleting Prohibited Extension

Parameter	Description
ConfigurationPath	The configuration path at which to set this configuration.
fileExtension	The extension, in the format of .*extension*, that should be allowed or denied.
allowed	Whether or not the extension is allowed or denied.

You can set this configuration for a particular site, application, or URL by specifying the configuration path with commands shown earlier in this section.

> **Note** Alternatively, you can configure the *fileExtensions* collection to deny all unlisted extensions, explicitly enabling the extensions that are allowed. This may be a more effective practice for reducing surface area than prohibiting specific extensions. However, it requires you to know and maintain the exhaustive list of all allowed extensions necessary for your application. To do this, set the *allowUnlisted* attribute on the *fileExtensions* collection at the desired configuration path to *false*.

Configuring Hidden URL Segments

You may also want to prohibit a URL segment from being servable. ASP.NET uses this technique to prohibit requests to the /BIN, /App_Code, and other special /App_xxx directories that contain ASP.NET application resources that the application is not to serve. You can create your own special directories that contain nonservable content and protect them with URL segments. For example, to prevent content from being served from all directories named data, you can create a hidden segment named data.

Direct from the Source: Protecting ASP.NET Special Directories

The debate on how to protect special directories containing application content not meant to be served directly, such as the ASP.NET /BIN directory, dates back to IIS 5.0 days. The ASP.NET team has gone through multiple attempts at achieving this, starting with the explicit removal of Read permissions from the /BIN directory on IIS 5.0 during ASP.NET application startup, to adding the code that prohibited requests containing the /BIN segment to the ASP.NET ISAPI filter.

During the development of ASP.NET 2.0, I had the opportunity to guide the solution to this problem for the several new directories introduced by ASP.NET 2.0, such as the new App_Code directory. Unfortunately, removing the Read permissions from these directories was no longer an option, because on IIS 6.0, ASP.NET no longer had Write access to the IIS metabase. In the absence of a general Web server feature to protect special directories, we had no better option than to add blocking support for all new directories to the ISAPI filter. Arguably, the most painful part of the project was the decision to ask the community for the preferred naming of these special directories, which resulted in much debate and the changing of the directory names from Application_Code, to App$_Code, and finally to App_Code. At the end, we were so fed up with changing the names that the development manager ordered hats for all of us that were printed with "App$."

IIS 7.0 finally provides a general solution for protecting special directories, a solution that ASP.NET leverages to protect its special directories when installed. Therefore, it no longer relies on the ISAPI filter for this support. Additionally, hidden URL segments provide a general mechanism for anyone to configure protected directories as appropriate for their applications, without writing special code to perform the blocking.

Mike Volodarsky

IIS Core Program Manager, Microsoft

To add a hidden URL segment by using Appcmd, use the following syntax.

```
%systemroot%\system32\inetsrv\Appcmd set config [ConfigurationPath]
/section:system.webServer/security/requestFiltering
/+hiddenSegments.[segment='string']
```

The segment string is the segment to protect.

To delete a hidden URL segment by using Appcmd, use the following syntax.

```
%systemroot%\system32\inetsrv\Appcmd set config [ConfigurationPath]
/section:system.webServer/security/requestFiltering
/-hiddenSegments.[segment='string']
```

> **Note**   Unlike file extensions, there is no way to prohibit all segments other than the ones configured. You can only deny specific segments by adding them using the preceding command.

You can target configuration for a particular site, application, or URL by specifying the configuration path with the preceding commands.

Configuring Denied URL Sequences

In some cases, you may want to reject requests that contain specific sequences in the URL, whether or not they are a complete segment. If it is not possible to fix the application itself, this may be an effective way to protect an application from certain URL patterns that are known to cause issues.

To add a denied URL sequence by using Appcmd, use the following syntax.

```
%systemroot%\system32\inetsrv\Appcmd set config [ConfigurationPath]
/section:system.webServer/security/requestFiltering
/+denyURLSequences.[sequence='string']
```

The sequence string is the sequence to reject.

To delete a denied URL sequence by using Appcmd, use the following syntax.

```
%systemroot%\system32\inetsrv\Appcmd set config [ConfigurationPath]
/section:system.webServer/security/requestFiltering
/-denyURLSequences.[sequence='string']
```

> **Note**   Unlike file extensions, there is no way to prohibit all URL sequences other than the ones configured. You can only deny specific sequences by adding them using the preceding command.

You can set this configuration for a particular site, application, or URL by specifying the configuration path with the preceding commands.

Authorization

As mentioned earlier, authorization is the second phase in the process of determining whether or not a client has the right to issue a particular request. Authorization refers to determining if the user identity determined during the authentication phase is allowed to access the requested resource.

IIS 7.0 provides several authorization mechanisms that can be leveraged to control access to resources:

- **NTFS ACL-based authorization**   By default, IIS 7.0 verifies that the authenticated user identity has the right to access the physical file or folder corresponding to the requested URL. This check is performed only for requests that map to physical files or directories and use authentication methods that produce Windows tokens. This authorization mechanism has multiple usage limitations that are discussed in detail later in this section.

- **URL Authorization**   The new IIS 7.0 URL Authorization role service enables applications to create declarative configuration-based rules to determine which authenticated users and/or roles have the right to access the Web site or specific URLs therein. This feature replaces the IIS 6.0 URL Authorization feature, which is no longer supported.

- **ASP.NET URL Authorization**   The ASP.NET URL Authorization feature, available since ASP.NET 1.0, is similar to IIS URL Authorization, with a slightly different configuration syntax and rule processing behavior. ASP.NET applications that use this feature today can configure it to control access to all Web site content when they run using ASP.NET integrated mode.

In addition, developers can provide custom authorization features by developing modules by using the IIS 7.0 native module APIs or the ASP.NET APIs for applications using ASP.NET Integrated mode. In fact, you can use most existing ASP.NET authorization modules immediately in applications that are using ASP.NET Integrated mode. This makes it significantly easier to develop custom authorization features that implement business authorization rules and can leverage the powerful ASP.NET membership and role infrastructures. For more information on installing and leveraging custom modules, see Chapter 12.

> **Caution**   Exercise extreme caution when configuring or removing authorization modules. If you remove an authorization module that is used to restrict access to the application, parts of the application may become exposed to unauthorized users. See the section titled "Securing Web Server Modules" in Chapter 12 for more information about removing security-sensitive modules.

In the remainder of this section, we will review the authorization features in detail.

NTFS ACL-based Authorization

The IIS 7.0 server engine (rather than a module) automatically performs NTFS ACL-based authorization. During this authorization, the Web server checks that the authenticated user identity has the rights to access the physical file or folder being requested.

> **Note**   NTFS ACL-based Authorization is part of the IIS Web server core and therefore is always installed when the Web server is installed. Though it cannot be uninstalled or disabled, you can remove one of the requirements in the following list to configure your application to not use it.

This authorization occurs automatically when all of the following conditions are met:

- The authenticated user identity must have a Windows token. If the request is authenticated using an authentication method that does not provide Windows tokens, for example Forms Authentication, this authorization is not performed.

- The selected handler mapping for the request specifies a resource type of File, Directory, or Either. Some mappings use the resource type of Unspecified to enable requests to virtual URLs that do not have a corresponding physical resource on disk. For these handler mappings, this authorization is not performed.

> **Note**   Most ASP.NET handler mappings are marked as Unspecified by default. However, ASP.NET includes additional functionality that ensures that if the URL maps to a physical file or folder, the access check is performed (with the exception of content located in a virtual directory that stores its files on a UNC path).

- The request URL maps to a physical file or folder that exists on disk. If the file or directory does not exist, IIS does not perform the check.

- The virtual directory corresponding to the request being made does not specify fixed access credentials. If the virtual directory specifies fixed credentials, they will be used to access all content for the virtual directory, and therefore IIS does not use the authenticated user to check access.

In addition, for you to successfully use NTFS ACL-based authorization, the following conditions must also be true:

- The physical resources have ACLs configured to properly grant or deny access to each authenticated user. This is typically done by placing all of the allowed users in a group, and granting this group access to the content.

- If the virtual directory corresponding to the request refers to a remote UNC share and does not specify fixed UNC credentials, the authenticated user identity must be able to delegate to the remote server. This requires basic authentication, or requires Constrained Delegation or Protocol Transition to be configured. For more information, see the section titled "UNC Authentication" later in this chapter.

Because of the aforementioned limitations and the overhead of managing NTFS ACL permissions for multiple users, NTFS ACL-based authorization is not recommended as a generic mechanism for restricting access to IIS resources. Use it only if your application meets the preceding requirements and you would like to use ACLs as an authorization mechanism (for example, if you are sharing static resources for users with domain or local machine accounts, and the resources already have the right permissions configured).

Because this authorization happens automatically for physical resources, you *must* configure all required resources to grant access to the authenticated identities that need to use your application. See the section titled "Set NTFS Permissions to Grant Minimal Access" in this chapter for more information on properly configuring NTFS ACLs for use with NTFS ACL authorization.

URL Authorization

The IIS 7.0 URL Authorization feature is new in IIS 7.0. It provides a way to configure declarative access control rules that grant or deny access to resources based on the authenticated user and its role membership.

> **Note**   URL Authentication is not part of the default IIS install. You can manually install it from the Windows Features IIS feature category through Windows Features on Windows Vista or from the Security role service category of the Web Server (IIS) role in Server Manager on Windows Server 2008. See Chapter 12 for more information about installing and enabling modules.

Unlike NTFS ACL-based authorization, URL Authorization has the following advantages:

- It is not tied to authentication schemes that produce Windows identities. It can be used with any authentication schemes, including Forms Authentication, which produces custom authenticated user identities.

- It enables rules to be configured for specific URLs, not underlying files or directories. Therefore, it is not tied to specific resource types and does not require files or directories to exist.

- It stores authorization rules in the configuration, instead of NTFS ACLs. These rules are easier to create and manage, and they can be specified in distributed web.config files that travel with the application when it is deployed or copied between servers.

- It integrates with the ASP.NET Membership and Roles services, which enables custom authentication and role management modules to provide the authenticated users and their roles. You can use ASP.NET Forms Authentication with Membership and Roles to quickly deploy a data-driven user and roles credential store for your application.

> **Note**   The IIS 7.0 URL Authorization feature is new. It is not related to the similarly named IIS 6.0 URL Authorization feature, which is overly complex, difficult to configure, and not widely used. The IIS 6.0 URL Authorization feature is not included with IIS 7.0.

The ASP.NET URL Authorization feature inspired the new URL Authorization feature, which implements similar functionality. However, some key differences exist in how rules are configured and processed. We'll discuss these differences later in this section.

Using URL Authorization to Restrict Access

To use URL Authorization to restrict access to your application, you need to configure one or more URL Authorization rules. These rules can be configured at the Web server level. Alternatively, you can configure them for a specific Web site, application, or URL. This makes it very easy to use URL Authorization to quickly restrict access to any part of your Web site to a specific set of users or roles.

These rules can be one of the following types:

- **Allow**   An allow rule grants access to the resource being requested and allows request processing to proceed.

- **Deny**   A deny rule denies access to the resource being requested, rejecting the request.

Both types of rules can specify a set of users, roles, and/or verbs that URL Authorization uses to match each rule to the request. As soon as a rule matches, the corresponding action (Allow or Deny) is taken. If the request is denied, URL Authorization will abort request processing with a 401 unauthorized response status code. If no rules matched, the request will also be denied.

Unlike ASP.NET URL Authorization, the deny rules are always processed before allow rules. This means that the relative order between deny and allow rules does not matter. In addition, the order between rules defined by parent configuration levels and the current configuration level does not matter, because all deny rules from all levels are always processed first, followed by all allow rules. Finally, the default behavior when no rules match is to deny the request.

By default, URL Authorization has a single rule configured at the Web server level that provides access to all users. You can restrict access to your Web site or a part of it by creating authorization rules by using the following techniques:

- Remove the default allow rule for all users and create explicit allow rules only for users and roles that should have access to the current URL level. This way, by default, all requests will be denied unless the authenticated user or role matches the configured allow rule. This is the recommended practice, because it ensures that only the configured users and roles have access to the resource, and it denies access to everyone else.

■ Create explicit deny rules for users and roles that should *not* have access to the current URL level. This may be appropriate to prevent access for only the specific users and roles. However, it is not generally a secure practice, because the set of users and roles is typically unbounded. The exception to this rule is the technique of creating a deny all anonymous users rule to restrict access only to authenticated users.

> **Note**   When designing the access control rules for your application, prefer to grant access to roles instead of specific users. This makes it easier to manage authorization rules as more users are added.

See the following section titled "Creating URL Authorization Rules" for information on configuring URL Authorization rules.

Creating URL Authorization Rules

You can use IIS Manager to configure URL Authorization rules by selecting the desired node in the tree view and double-clicking Authorization Rules. In the resulting window shown in Figure 14-5, you can see the list of rules currently in effect at the level you selected, which will include both the rules configured at higher configuration levels and the rules configured at the current configuration level.

Figure 14-5   Configuring URL authorization rules.

You can remove existing authorization rules (including parent authorization rules that are not locked) by selecting them in the list and clicking Remove in the Actions pane. You can add an allow or deny rule by clicking Add Allow Rule or Add Deny Rule in the Actions pane. Figure 14-6 shows an allow rule that can be used to allow access to all users or specific users or roles.

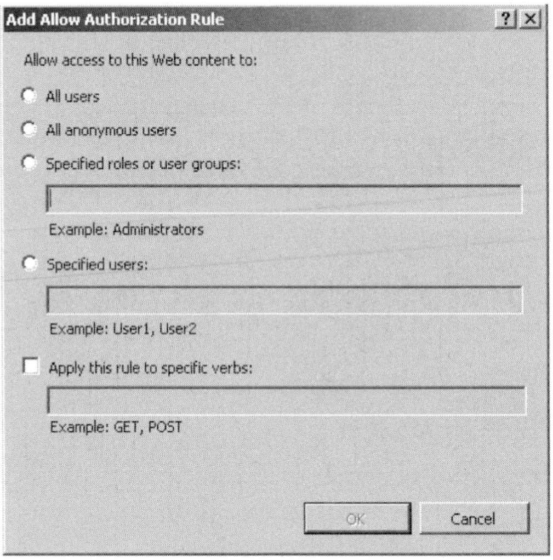

Figure 14-6   Adding an Allow URL authorization rule.

You can also edit URL Authorization rules by configuring them directly in the *system.web-Server/security/authorization* configuration section, by using Appcmd from the command line, or by using configuration APIs. This configuration section is unlocked by default to facilitate storing URL authorization rules in your application's web.config files, which enables them to travel with the corresponding application content when deploying the application to another Web server.

To add a URL authorization rule with Appcmd, you can use the following syntax.

```
%systemroot%\system32\inetsrv\Appcmd.exe set config [ConfigurationPath]
/section:system.webServer/security/authorization
"/+[users='string',roles='string',verbs='string',accessType='enum']"
```

To delete a URL authorization rule with Appcmd, you can use the following syntax.

```
%systemroot%\system32\inetsrv\Appcmd.exe set config [ConfigurationPath]
/section:system.webServer/security/authorization
"/-[users='string',roles='string',verbs='string']"
```

The parameters to these commands are shown in Table 14-9.

Table 14-9   Parameters for Adding URL Authorization Rule

Parameter	Description
ConfigurationPath	The configuration path at which this configuration is set.
users	The comma-separated list of user names that this rule allows or denies. Each user name is matched with the user name of the authenticated user set for the request, and the rule matches as soon as a single user matches (or a role matches). For Windows identities that represent domain accounts, use the domain qualified user name format of "domain\user" rather than the fully qualified domain name format of "user@domain.com". Use "*" to refer to all users and "?" to refer to anonymous users. The default is "".
roles	The comma-separated list of roles that this rule allows or denies. Role membership for each role is tested for the authenticated user set for the request, and the rule matches as soon as a single role matches (or user matches). The default is "".
verbs	The comma-separated list of verbs (case-sensitive) that matches the request verb. If specified, one of the verbs must match the request verb for the rule to apply. The default is "".
accessType	Whether the rule should allow or deny access. Accepted values are Allow and Deny. This parameter must be specified to add a rule.

Using ASP.NET Roles with URL Authorization

In applications using the ASP.NET Integrated mode, it is possible to configure the ASP.NET Roles feature to provide application-specific roles for each authenticated user. IIS 7.0 URL Authorization rules can specify access rules that use roles provided by the .NET Roles feature or another ASP.NET module to implement application-specific authorization schemes, much like the original ASP.NET URL Authorization feature. You can learn about setting up the ASP.NET Roles feature at *http://msdn2.microsoft.com/en-us/library/9ab2fxh0.aspx*.

When the .NET Roles feature is enabled, and a role provider is configured for your application, you can begin configuring URL Authorization rules that rely on these roles in your application. To make sure that the roles are available for requests to non-ASP.NET content types, be sure to remove the managedHandler precondition from the RoleManager module. For information about enabling managed modules to run for all requests by removing the managedHandler precondition, see the section titled "Enabling Managed Modules to Run for All Requests" in Chapter 12.

You can also create roles directly using IIS Manager by selecting the application node in the tree view and then clicking.NET Roles. In the resulting page, you can manage existing roles, create new roles using the configured Role provider for the application, and associate application users with roles.

Authentication

Authentication is the process of determining the identity of the user making the request to the Web server. Authorization features can then use this identity to allow or reject the request to specific resources or parts of the application. In some cases, the Web server or the application can impersonate it to access resources. Finally, the application can use the identity to personalize the application experience for the requesting user.

IIS 7.0 includes the following authentication features:

- **Anonymous Authentication**   This authentication method provides a configured Windows identity for all anonymous users of the application without the need to provide any client credentials. It is used to allow anonymous (unauthenticated) access.

- **Basic Authentication**   This authentication method enables the client to provide the user name and password to the Web server in clear text. Basic Authentication is defined in RFC 2617, and virtually all browsers support it.

- **Digest Authentication**   This authentication method is a more secure version of Basic Authentication, and it enables the client to provide user credentials via a hash of the user name and password. Digest Authentication is defined in RFC 2617, and most browsers support it. The implementation used in IIS 7.0 was known as the Advanced Digest Authentication method in IIS 6.0.

- **Windows Authentication**   This authentication method supports the NT LAN Manager (NTLM) or Kerberos Windows authentication protocols.

- **Client Certificate Mapping Authentication**   This authentication method enables client SSL certificates to be mapped to Windows accounts by using Active Directory directory services.

- **IIS Client Certificate Mapping Authentication**   This authentication method enables client SSL certificates to be mapped to Windows accounts via one-to-one or many-to-one mappings stored in IIS configuration.

- **UNC Authentication**   Though this is not a true authentication method in the sense that it does not help to establish the identity of the requesting client, IIS 7.0 uses UNC Authentication to establish an identity to access remote content located on a UNC share.

In addition, IIS 7.0 applications using ASP.NET Integrated mode use a unified authentication model between IIS and ASP.NET. This enables existing ASP.NET authentication modules or new managed authentication modules developed with ASP.NET APIs to be used for all content in the application. When ASP.NET is installed, the following authentication methods are also available:

- **Forms Authentication**   This ASP.NET authentication method supports forms-based authentication against pluggable credentials stores via the ASP.NET Membership service. For more information on using ASP.NET Forms Authentication to protect all

Web site content, see *http://www.iis.net/articles/view.aspx/IIS7/Extending-IIS7/ Getting-Started/How-to-Take-Advantage-of-the-IIS7-Integrated-Pipel.*

The following IIS 6.0 authentication methods are no longer supported:

- **IIS 6.0 Digest Authentication**   IIS 7.0 Advanced Digest Authentication method is now provided as the only digest authentication method.

- **.NET Passport Authentication**   The Passport support is not included in Windows Server 2008, and therefore this method is also no longer supported.

Developers can also provide custom authentication features developed with the new IIS 7.0 native module API or with ASP.NET APIs for applications using the Integrated mode. In fact, applications running in Integrated mode can use most existing custom ASP.NET authentication modules immediately to provide site-wide authentication. For more information on installing and leveraging custom modules, see Chapter 12.

You can configure one or more authentication methods for your Web site, application, or part thereof to protect it with user-based authorization, enable impersonation for resource access, or allow for application personalization.

> **Note**   IIS 7.0 requires that each request is authenticated. Because of this, at least one authentication method must be enabled and be able to provide an authenticated user for each request.

In the remainder of this section, we will review each of the authentication methods.

Anonymous Authentication

Anonymous authentication enables clients to access public areas of your Web site without requiring the client to provide any credentials. Anonymous authentication is the default authentication method enabled in IIS 7.0.

> **Note**   Anonymous authentication is part of the default IIS install and is enabled by default. You can manually install or uninstall it by installing or uninstalling the Anonymous-AuthnenticationModule module. See Chapter 12 for more information about installing and enabling modules.

Anonymous authentication applies for all requests that do not have an authenticated user identity determined by other authentication methods. It works by setting the authenticated user identity for such requests to be a Windows identity corresponding to the configured anonymous user account.

> **Caution**   Be sure to disable anonymous authentication for parts of your Web site that you *do not* want to be accessed by anonymous users. You *must* do this even if you have other authentication methods enabled.

By default, anonymous authentication is configured to use the new built-in IUSR account. It no longer uses the custom IUSR_*ComputerName* account that is used by default with anonymous authentication in IIS 6.0. Because IUSR is a built-in account, it does not have a password that must be periodically changed or synchronized between multiple servers. In addition, because it is built in, the IUSR account has the same SID on all machines. Therefore, ACLs that reference it remain valid when copied from one IIS 7.0 server to another.

When using anonymous authentication, you have the following options:

- **Use the built-in IUSR account.**   This is the default.

- **Use a custom account.**   You can configure a custom account that should be used for anonymous requests instead of the IUSR account.

- **Use the application pool identity.**   You can configure anonymous authentication to use the identity of the IIS worker process (application pool identity) instead of a separate anonymous account.

You can use the application pool identity option to simplify resource access management. This ensures that that resource access is always made under the application pool identity, both when the Web server accesses application resources using the application pool identity and when the Web server or application access resources while impersonating the authenticated user. This way, you only need to manage access rights for a single identity. See the section titled "Set NTFS Permissions to Grant Minimal Access" earlier in this chapter for more information about setting permissions.

You can use IIS Manager to enable or disable anonymous authentication and set the anonymous user options. Select the desired node in the tree view and double-click Authentication. Then, select Anonymous Authentication in the list and use the *Enable, Disable,* and *Edit* commands in the Actions pane to configure it.

You can also set anonymous authentication configuration directly; use Appcmd.exe from the command line, or use configuration APIs to configure the *system.webServer/security/ anonymousAuthentication* section. You do this with Appcmd by using the following syntax.

```
%systemroot%\system32\inetsrv\Appcmd set config [ConfigurationPath]
/section:system.webServer/security/anonymousAuthentication [/enabled:bool]
[/username:string] [/password:string] [/logonMethod:enum]
```

The parameters of this command are shown in Table 14-10.

Table 14-10   Parameters to Set Anonymous Authentication and Anonymous User Options

Parameter	Description
ConfigurationPath	The configuration path at which to set the specified configuration. If you specify this parameter, you may also need to specify the */commit:apphost* parameter to avoid locking errors when applying configuration to Web site or URL levels.
enabled	Whether to enable or disable anonymous authentication.
username	The user name to use for anonymous authentication. Set to "" to use the application pool identity. Default is IUSR.
password	The password to use when specifying a custom account for anonymous authentication.
logonMethod	The logon method to use for the anonymous user. Allowed values are *Interactive, Batch, Network, ClearText*. Default is *ClearText*. See *http://msdn2.microsoft.com/en-us/library/aa378184.aspx* for more information about logon types.

Basic Authentication

Basic authentication implements the Basic Authentication protocol, a standard HTTP authentication scheme defined in RFC 2617 and supported by most HTTP client software. It enables the client to pass both the user name and the password in clear text, and it uses these credentials to log on locally at the Web server or the Web server's domain. The credentials, therefore, must correspond to a valid local or domain account, and they result in the request being authenticated with a Windows token corresponding to this account.

Note   Basic authentication is not part of the default IIS install. You can manually install it from the Security feature category through Windows Features On And Off on Windows Vista. You can also install it from the Security role service category of the Web Server (IIS) role in Server Manager on Windows Server 2008. See Chapter 12 for more information about installing and enabling modules.

Basic authentication is a challenge-based authentication scheme. When a client makes the initial request to a resource that requires authentication, and basic authentication is enabled, the request will be rejected with a 401 unauthorized status that will include a "WWW-Authenticate: basic" response header. If the client supports basic authentication, it will usually prompt the user for credentials and then reissue the request with the credentials included. The basic authentication module will see that credentials are present on the subsequent request and attempt to authenticate the request by logging on with those credentials. The client will typically send these credentials again on every request to the same URL or any URL that is below the URL included in the initial authenticated request.

Caution   Just enabling basic authentication does not mean that authentication is required for your application. You must either disable anonymous authentication and/or configure URL authorization rules or NTFS permissions that deny access to the anonymous user.

Basic authentication is not secure because it passes the credentials in clear text, and therefore may enable an attacker to steal them by eavesdropping on the request packets at the network level. This can be mitigated by using SSL to secure the communication channel between the client and the server. If SSL is used to protect all requests that include the credentials, basic authentication may be a secure option. For more information on configuring secure communication with SSL, see the section titled "Securing Communications with Secure Socket Layer (SSL)" later in this chapter.

Caution   Basic authentication may enable user credentials to be leaked because it sends them to the Web server in an unencrypted form. When using basic authentication, use SSL to secure the Web site.

Because basic authentication performs the logon locally at the Web server, the resulting Windows token can be used to access resources on a remote server without configuring delegation or Protocol Transition. See the section titled "Understanding Authentication Delegation" later in this chapter for more information.

By default, basic authentication caches the logon token for the corresponding user name and password in the token cache. During this time, the token may be available inside that process. If the worker process is compromised, malicious code can use this token to elevate privileges if the token represents a user with high privileges. If you do not trust the code in the process, you can either disable token caching by uninstalling the token cache module or reduce the amount of time the tokens are cached by setting the *HKLM\SYSTEM\CurrentControlSet\ Services\InetInfo\Parameters\UserTokenTTL* value to the number of seconds to cache tokens for.

You can use IIS Manager to enable or disable basic authentication and set the logon method options. Select the desired node in the tree view and double-click Authentication. Then, select Basic Authentication from the list and use the *Enable*, *Disable*, and *Edit* commands in the Actions pane to configure it.

You can also set basic authentication configuration directly; use Appcmd.exe from the command line, or use configuration APIs to configure the *system.webServer/security/basic-Authentication* section. You do this with Appcmd by using the following syntax.

```
%systemroot%\system32\inetsrv\Appcmd set config [ConfigurationPath]
/section:system.webServer/security/basicAuthentication [/enabled:bool]
[/realm:string] [/defaultLogonDomain:string] [/logonMethod:enum]
```

The parameters of this command are shown in Table 14-11.

Table 14-11   Parameters for Setting Basic Authentication Configuration Directly

Parameter	Description
ConfigurationPath	The configuration path at which to set the specified configuration. If you specify this parameter, you may also need to specify the *"/commit:apphost"* parameter to avoid locking errors when applying configuration to Web site or URL levels.
enabled	Whether to enable or disable basic authentication.
realm	The basic authentication realm that will be indicated to the client for informational purposes. The Web server does not use the realm during the logon process.
defaultLogonDomain	The domain that will be used by the server to log on using the credentials provided by the client. If the client user name specifies the domain, it will be used instead. If empty, the computer domain is used. The default value is "".
logonMethod	The logon method to use for the logon. Allowed values are *Interactive*, *Batch*, *Network*, and *ClearText*. Default is *ClearText*. See *http://msdn2. microsoft.com/en-us/library/aa378184.aspx* for more information about logon types.

Digest Authentication

The Digest Authentication feature implements the Digest Authentication protocol, a standard HTTP authentication scheme defined in RFC 2617 and supported by some HTTP client software. Unlike basic authentication, the client sends an MD5 hash of the user name and the password to the server so that the real credentials are not sent over the network. The Digest Authentication scheme in IIS 7.0 was known as the Advanced Digest Authentication in IIS 6.0 (IIS 7.0 no longer supports the IIS 6.0 Digest Authentication). If successful, Digest Authentication authenticates the request with a Windows token corresponding to the user's Active Directory account.

> **Note**   Digest authentication is not part of the default IIS install. You can manually install it from the Security feature category through Windows Features On And Off on Windows Vista. You can also install it through the Security role service category of the Web Server (IIS) role in Server Manager on Windows Server 2008. See Chapter 12 for more information about installing and enabling modules.

Like basic authentication, digest authentication is a challenge-based authentication scheme. When a client makes the initial request to a resource that requires authentication, and digest authentication is enabled, the request will be rejected with a 401 unauthorized status that includes a "WWW-Authenticate: digest" response header containing additional information required by the Digest Authentication scheme. If the client supports digest authentication, it will usually prompt the user for the credentials and then reissue the request with the hash of the credentials and the nonce information in the challenge. The Digest Authentication module will see that the hash is present on the subsequent request and attempt to authenticate the hash by comparing it with the hash stored in Active Directory. The client will typically send the hash information again on every request to the same URL or any URL below the URL used in the initial authenticated request.

The Web server and the clients accessing it must meet the following requirements to use IIS 7.0 Digest Authentication:

- Both the Web server and the clients using your application must be members of the same domain, or the client must be a member of a domain trusted by the Web server.

- The clients must use Microsoft Internet Explorer 5 or later.

- The user must have a valid Windows user account stored in Active Directory on the domain controller.

- The domain controller must be using Windows Server 2003 or Windows Server 2008.

Unlike the IIS 6.0 Digest Authentication, the IIS 7.0 Digest Authentication does not require the application pool identity to be LocalSystem. In fact, you should not ever use LocalSystem or any other identity with Administrative privileges on the server as an application pool identity. For more information on configuring least privilege identities for application pools, see the section titled "Configuring Applications for Least Privilege" earlier in this chapter.

> **Caution**   Just enabling digest authentication does not mean that authentication is required for your application. You must either disable anonymous authentication and/or configure URL authorization rules or NTFS permissions that deny access to the anonymous user.

Unlike basic authentication, the authenticated token is not suitable for accessing remote resources, and it requires Constrained Delegation or Protocol Transition to be configured to do so. For more information, see the section titled "Understanding Authentication Delegation" later in this chapter.

You can enable or disable digest authentication by using IIS Manager. Select the desired node in the tree view and double-click Authentication. Then, select Digest Authentication from the list and use the *Enable*, *Disable*, and *Edit* commands in the Actions pane to configure it.

You can also set digest authentication configuration directly; use Appcmd.exe from the command line, or use configuration APIs to configure the *system.webServer/security/digestAuthentication* section. You do this with Appcmd by using the following syntax.

```
%systemroot%\system32\inetsrv\Appcmd set config [ConfigurationPath]
/section:system.webServer/security/digestAuthentication [/enabled:bool]
[/realm:string]
```

The parameters of this command are shown in the Table 14-12.

Table 14-12   **Parameters for Setting Digest Authentication**

Parameter	Description
ConfigurationPath	The configuration path at which to set the specified configuration. If specifying this, you may also need to specify the */commit:apphost* parameter to avoid locking errors when applying configuration to Web site or URL levels.
enabled	Whether to enable or disable digest authentication.
realm	The digest authentication realm that will be used as specified in the RFC 2617.

Windows Authentication

The Windows Authentication scheme enables Windows clients to authenticate with two Windows authentication protocols, NTLM (NT LAN Manager) and Kerberos. Both of these schemes involve a cryptographic exchange between the client and the server to authenticate the client.

> **Note**   Unlike Windows Server 2003, Windows Authentication is not part of the default IIS install and is not enabled by default. You can manually install it from the Security feature category through Turn Windows Features On And Off on Windows Vista. You can also install it via the Security role service category of the Web Server (IIS) role in Server Manager on Windows Server 2008. See Chapter 12 for more information about installing and enabling modules. After the module is installed, you have to explicitly enable Windows Authentication for it to be available.

Windows Authentication, similar to other IIS authentication methods, is challenge-based. When a request is rejected with a 401 unauthorized response status code, Windows Authentication will issue a WWW-Authenticate challenge header including one or both of the following authentication scheme names:

- **NTLM**   Indicates to the client that it can use the NTLM authentication protocol to authenticate. This is included for older clients that do not support the negotiate wrapper.

- **Negotiate**   Indicates to the client that it can use Kerberos *or* NTLM protocols to authenticate. Negotiate is used to allow either Kerberos or NTLM authentication, depending on what is available on the client.

> **Note**   Both Kerberos and NTLM authentication methods involve the client making several (typically two to three) requests to the server as part of the authentication handshake. This means that your modules may see multiple requests as part of the authentication process. By default, authentication occurs once per connection, so it does not occur again for subsequent requests using the same connection.

The client then makes the decision to use either Kerberos (if available) or NTLM and initiates a sequence of requests to authenticate using the selected protocol. The choice of protocol is based on whether or not the client is configured to be able to use Kerberos to authenticate with the server, which requires a direct connection to the Key Distribution Center (KDC) on the domain controller as well as direct access to Active Directory. NTLM can be used in a non-domain scenario against local Windows accounts on the server or when the connection to domain services required for Kerberos is unavailable.

> **Note**   Windows Authentication is best suited for intranet environments.

Windows Authentication is a reasonable choice for Windows-based intranet environments, but for other environments, keep in mind the following limitations:

- It does not work over HTTP proxies. This is because Kerberos and NTLM are connection-based, and proxies may not keep connections open or may share connections between requests from multiple clients.

- The Kerberos protocol requires both the client and the server to be members of the same domain or two domains with a trust relationship and have a direct connection to Active Directory and the KDC services located on the domain controller.

- The Kerberos protocol requires correct Service Principal Name (SPN) registration in Active Directory for all application pools performing Kerberos authentication.

Configuring Windows Authentication

You can enable or disable Windows Authentication by using IIS Manager. Select the desired node in the tree view and double-click Authentication. Then, select Windows Authentication in the list and use the *Enable*, *Disable*, and *Edit* commands in the Actions pane to configure it.

You can also set digest authentication configuration directly; use Appcmd.exe from the command line, or use configuration APIs to configure the *system.webServer/security/windowsAuthentication* section. You do this with Appcmd by using the following syntax.

```
%systemroot%\system32\inetsrv\Appcmd set config [ConfigurationPath]
/section:system.webServer/security/windowsAuthentication [/enabled:bool]
[/authPersistSingleRequest:bool] [/authPersistNonNTLM:bool]
[/useKernelMode:bool] [/useAppPoolCredentials:bool]
```

The parameters of this command are shown in Table 14-13.

Table 14-13   Parameters for Configure Authentication

Parameter	Description
ConfigurationPath	The configuration path at which to set the specified configuration. If you specify this, you may also need to specify the /commit:apphost parameter to avoid locking errors when applying configuration to Web site or URL levels.
enabled	Whether to enable or disable Windows Authentication.
authPersistSingleRequest	Whether or not to require each new request to reauthenticate. If set to false, the client will perform the authentication handshake only once per connection, and the server will cache the authenticated identity for all subsequent requests. Otherwise, each request will require the authentication handshake. Default is false.
authPersistNonNTLM	Whether to require each new request to reauthenticate when using Kerberos. If set to false, the client will perform the authentication handshake only once per connection, and the server will cache the authenticated identity for all subsequent requests. Otherwise, each request will require the authentication handshake. Default is false.
useKernelMode	Whether to perform Windows Authentication in the kernel. The default is true.
useAppPoolCredentials	Whether to use the application pool identity instead of LocalSystem when performing kernel Windows Authentication. This is needed when you are using a domain account as the application pool identity to enable Kerberos authentication on a Web farm. The default is false.

In addition, you can also control whether the server uses NTLM or Negotiate protocols. To do this, you can edit the *providers* collection in the *system.webServer/security/windowsAuthentication* configuration section. By default, this collection contains both NTLM and Negotiate protocol providers. You can force the server to use only NTLM by removing the Negotiate protocol provider. However, you cannot force the server to use only Kerberos in this configuration, because the negotiate wrapper enables the client to use either NTLM or Kerberos. There is no way to tell the client that only Kerberos is supported.

You can, however, configure the NTLM authentication level by using the Local Security Policy console and modifying the Security Settings\Local Policies\Security Options\Network Security: LAN Manager Authentication Level option, as shown in Figure 14-7. The default setting is *Send NTLMv2 Response Only*, which enables the server to accept all levels. You can set this setting to *Send NTLMv2 Response Only. Refuse LM & NTLM* for maximum security while allowing clients that do not have the ability to use Kerberos to use the NTLMv2 scheme.

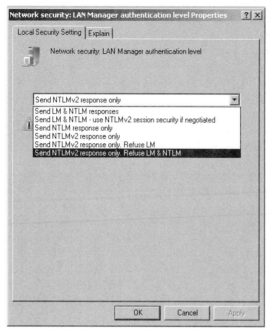

Figure 14-7   Configure NTLM Authentication Level.

In IIS 6.0, to use the Kerberos authentication protocol, you have to use the Setspn.exe command line tool to register Service Principal Names (SPNs) in Active Directory for the NetBIOS and the Fully Qualified Domain Name (FDQN) names for each application pool account. Additionally, you could have only one application pool account registered for each SPN, preventing multiple application pools with different identities from using Kerberos authentication.

In IIS 7.0, kernel-based Windows Authentication (enabled by default) offers improved functionality. Because HTTP.sys performs the authentication process in the kernel, it is done under the LocalSystem account regardless of the application pool identity. This results in the following improvements:

- It should no longer be necessary to configure separate SPNs, because Kerberos will use the default NetBIOS SPN entry created automatically when the Web server computer is joined to the domain.

- Application pool identity can be changed without the need to reregister the SPN with the new account. The application pool account no longer needs to be a domain account.

- Multiple application pools can use Kerberos authentication.

These changes make it significantly easier to deploy and use the Kerberos protocol with IIS.

Note   You need to use the application pool identity and register SPNs for Kerberos authentication when you are using it on a Web farm.

However, if you are using IIS on a Web farm and require the Kerberos protocol, you will need to disable the use of the LocalSystem identity for Kerberos authentication by setting the *useAppPoolCredentials* attribute in the *system.webServer/security/authentication/windows-Authentication* configuration section to *true*. In addition, you will need to use a domain account as an identity for the application pool. You will also be required to use Setspn.exe to register the Web site host name using this domain account under which the application pools are configured to run in Active Directory. For more information about registering SPNs for Kerberos with Setspn.exe, see *http://www.microsoft.com/technet/prodtechnol/WindowsServer2003/Library/IIS/523ae943-5e6a-4200-9103-9808baa00157.mspx?mfr=true.*

Client Certificate Mapping Authentication

Client Certificate Mapping Authentication enables clients to authenticate with the Web server by presenting client certificates over Secure Socket Layer (SSL) connections.

> **Note** Certificate-based authentication enables clients to use client certificates to authenticate with the Web server. It is not required to enable secure communication between the client and the server.

The Client Certificate Mapping Authentication uses the Directory Services Mapper (DS Mapper) service in Active Directory to map client certificates provided by the user to domain accounts. IIS also provides a custom certificate mapping feature, the IIS Client Certificate Mapping Authentication, which allows for more flexible mapping of client certificates to Windows accounts. See the section titled "IIS Client Certificate Mapping Authentication" later in this chapter for more information.

> **Note** Client Certificate Mapping Authentication is not part of the default IIS install and is not enabled by default. You can manually install it from the Security feature category through Turn Windows Features On And Off on Windows Vista. You can also install it via the Security role service category of the Web Server (IIS) role in Server Manager on Windows Server 2008. See Chapter 12 for more information about installing and enabling modules. After the module is installed, you have to explicitly enable Client Certificate Mapping Authentication for it to be available.

To use Client Certificate Mapping Authentication, you need to meet the following requirements:

- The Web server must be a member of a Windows domain.
- You must issue client certificates to your users by using a Certificate Authority (CA) trusted by the Web server.
- You must map each client certificate to a valid domain account in Active Directory.

> **Note**   You do not need to use Client Certificate Mapping Authentication to require clients to present client certificates. You can configure the server to always require client certificates to access the server, but use another authentication scheme to authenticate the client. To do this, see the section titled "Client Certificates" later in this chapter.

To enable Client Certificate Mapping Authentication on the Web server, you need to perform the following steps (after installing the Certificate Mapping Authentication module).

1. **Enable Client Certificate Mapping Authentication.** You can do this in IIS Manager by clicking the server node, double-clicking Authentication, selecting Active Directory Client Certificate Authentication, and clicking Enable in the Actions pane. Note that this can only be done at the server level when using IIS Manager, although you can enable Client Certificate Mapping Authentication for a specific URL through configuration.

2. **Configure SSL on each Web site using this authentication method.** Certificate authentication is possible only if the Web site is being accessed over an SSL connection and therefore requires an SSL binding to be configured for the Web site. See the section titled "Configuring SSL" later in this chapter for more details.

3. **Enable DS Mapper for each Web site SSL binding.** IIS Manager does this automatically for each Web site when the Client Certificate Mapping Authentication is enabled and you add an SSL binding for the Web site. To do this manually, use the *Netsh.exe* command with the following syntax: **netsh http add sslcert IP Address:Port dsmapperusage=enable**, where *IP Address* and *Port* are the IP address and port of the corresponding binding.

4. **Configure each Web site using this authentication method to accept client certificates** (and possibly require them). This ensures that the server accepts client certificates when provided by the client and can also configure the server to require the client to present a certificate to proceed with the request. See the section titled "Client Certificates" later in this chapter for more details.

You can also enable Client Certificate Mapping Authentication by editing the *system.webServer/security/authentication/clientCertificateMappingAuthentication* configuration section directly or by using Appcmd or other configuration APIs. You can enable this authentication method by using the following Appcmd syntax.

```
%systemroot%\system32\inetsrv\Appcmd set config /section:
system.webServer/security/authentication/
clientCertificateMappingAuthentication /enabled:true
```

The *enabled* attribute specifies whether or not the Client Certificate Mapping Authentication is enabled. You can enable this method for a specific URL. However, do note that the decision to use the Directory Services Mapper to map certificates to Windows domain accounts is dependent on each Web site binding having been configured to use the HTTP.sys DS Mapper setting.

You can read more about configuring SSL and configuring the server to accept client certificates in the section titled "Client Certificates" later in this chapter.

IIS Client Certificate Mapping Authentication

IIS Client Certificate Mapping Authentication enables clients to authenticate with the Web server by presenting client certificates over Secure Socket Layer (SSL) connections.

> **Note**   Certificate-based authentication enables clients to use client certificates to authenti-cate with the Web server. It is not required to enable secure communication between the client and the server using SSL.

The IIS Client Certificate Mapping Authentication provides a more flexible mechanism for authenticating clients based on client certificates than does the Active Directory–based Client Certificate Mapping Authentication. Instead of relying on the Directory Services Mapper (DS Mapper) service to map client certificates to Windows accounts, it uses the configuration to perform the mapping. As such, it also does not require the user accounts to be domain accounts and does not require Active Directory to operate.

> **Note**   IIS Client Certificate Mapping Authentication is not part of the default IIS install and is not enabled by default. You can manually install it from the Security feature category through Turn Windows Features On And Off on Windows Vista. You can also install it via the Security role service category of the Web Server (IIS) role in Server Manager on Windows Server 2008. See Chapter 12 for more information about installing and enabling modules. After the module is installed, you have to explicitly enable IIS Client Certificate Mapping Authentication for it to be available.

The IIS Client Certificate Mapping Authentication feature supports the following mapping types:

- **One-to-one mapping**   Map a single client certificate to a specific Windows account. The server will use an exact copy of the client certificate to perform the match and therefore must possess a copy of each client certificate.

- **Many-to-one mapping**   Map client certificates to a Windows account by matching wildcard expressions involving specific certificate fields, such as *issuer* or *subject*. This does not require a copy of the client certificate.

To use IIS Client Certificate Mapping Authentication, you need to meet the following requirements:

- You cannot use Active Directory–based Client Certificate Mapping Authentication on any of the sites for which you enable IIS Client Certificate Mapping Authentication.

- You must have the passwords for all Windows accounts used to map certificates. Unlike Client Certificate Mapping Authentication, which relies on Active Directory to generate the Windows token for the account, you will need to specify both the user name and password for each account being mapped so that IIS can generate the token.

■ To use one-to-one mappings, you must have an exact copy of each client certificate being mapped. If you provide the certificates to users, you will have this copy. Otherwise, you will need each user to provide you with an exported copy of the certificate. When using many-to-one mappings, you do not need copies of the certificates.

> **Note**   You do not need to use IIS Client Certificate Mapping Authentication to require clients to present client certificates. You can configure the server to always require client certificates to access the server and then use another authentication scheme to authenticate the client. For more about how to do this, see the section titled "Client Certificates" later in this chapter.

To enable IIS Client Certificate Mapping Authentication for a specific Web site or URL, you need to perform the following steps (after installing the IIS Certificate Mapping Authentication module):

1. **Enable IIS Client Certificate Mapping Authentication.** This option is not available in IIS Manager. To do this, you will need to edit the *system.webServer/security/authentication/iisClientCertificateMappingAuthentication* section directly. Alternatively, you can use Appcmd or another configuration API. You can enable IIS Client Certificate Mapping Authentication with Appcmd by using the following syntax (see details on configuring this configuration section later in this section).

    ```
    %systemroot%\system32\inetsrv\Appcmd set config [ConfigurationPath]
    /section:system.webServer/security/authentication/
    iisClientCertificateMappingAuthentication /enabled:true /commit:apphost
    ```

2. **Configure SSL on each Web site using this authentication method.** Certificate authentication is possible only if the Web site is being accessed over an SSL connection. Therefore, it requires an SSL binding to be configured for the Web site. See the section titled "Configuring SSL" for more details.

3. **Configure each Web site using this authentication method to accept client certificates** (and possibly require them). Doing so ensures that the server accepts client certificates when the clients provide them. Doing so can also configure the server to require the client to present a certificate to proceed with the request. See the section titled "Client Certificates" for more details.

4. **Configure the required one-to-one or many-to-one mappings.** Create the mappings to map certificates to Windows accounts.

> **Note**   Although you can enable the IIS Client Certificate Mapping Authentication feature for a specific URL, the mapping configuration can only be set at the server or Web site level, and it is ignored if it is set at a lower configuration level.

You can read more about configuring SSL and configuring the server to accept client certificates in the section titled "Client Certificates" later in this chapter. We will describe the process for configuring certificate mappings for IIS Client Certificate Mapping Authentication next in the sections titled "Creating One-to-One Certificate Mappings" and "Creating Many-to-One Certificate Mappings."

Creating One-to-One Certificate Mappings

You can use one-to-one certificate mappings as part of a strong authentication and authorization scheme to control access to application resources based on the exact identity of the client. It can be used instead of a user name and password authentication scheme that requires the user to supply credentials. To use one-to-one mappings, you need to have the exact copy of each certificate.

IIS Manager does not provide support for configuring one-to-one mappings. You can configure them by using the Appcmd command line tool. You can also do it by editing the *system.webServer/security/authentication/iisClientCertificateMappingAuthentication* configuration section directly or with other configuration APIs. You can add a one-to-one mapping by using the following Appcmd syntax.

```
%systemroot%\system32\inetsrv\Appcmd set config [SiteName]
/section:system.webServer/security/authentication/
iisClientCertificateMappingAuthentication /+oneToOneMappings
[certificate='string',enabled='bool',username='string',password='string']
```

You can remove a one-to-one mapping by using the following Appcmd syntax.

```
%systemroot%\system32\inetsrv\Appcmd set config [SiteName]
/section:system.webServer/security/authentication
/iisClientCertificateMappingAuthentication /-oneToOneMappings
[certificate='string']
```

These commands use the parameters in Table 14-14.

Table 14-14   Parameters for Creating Certificate Mappings

Parameter	Description
SiteName	The site name of the Web site for which to set these settings. If omitted, this parameter sets them for the entire Web server. If you specify these settings for a configuration path deeper than the Web site root, these settings will not take effect.
certificate	The exact text of the certificate (not the certificate hash).
enabled	Whether or not this mapping is enabled.
userName	The user name for the account to which the certificate maps.
password	The password for the account to which the certificate maps. This value is stored in the encrypted form.

You can obtain the exact text of the certificate from an exported certificate file (containing unencrypted certificate information) or by dumping the certificate from the local or domain certificate store. To do the latter, you can use the following command.

```
certutil -encode -f CertName cert.cer
```

CertName is the friendly name of the certificate. You can view the certificate store and obtain the friendly name of the installed certificates with the following command.

```
certutil -viewstore StoreName
```

StoreName is the name of the certificate store. Use *MY* for the personal certificate store.

> **Note**   You must specify the exact base64 encoded certificate contents for the one-to-one mapping, with the training line feed removed. Do not use the certificate hash. If you do not specify the certificate correctly, you will get a 401.1 status error when making requests to the Web site. This error will show the 0x8009310b HRESULT, indicating that IIS failed to load the certificate from the mapping entry.

Creating Many-to-One Certificate Mappings

Many-to-one mappings, unlike one-to-one mappings, are not typically used to authenticate specific users. Instead, you can use them to authenticate a group of users by matching fields in their certificates to a single Windows account. Therefore, authorization based on the authenticated user produced by a many-to-one mapping is similar to role- or group-based authorization, with the authenticated user representing a group to which multiple users belong. For example, you can match all certificates issued by a specific organization to that organization's account. As such, many-to-one mappings may be less appropriate for user-based personalization or access control than one-to-one mappings, depending on your authorization strategy.

> **Note**   One-to-one mappings are always processed before many-to-one mappings.

Many-to-one mappings do not require the server to have the exact certificate for each user. Instead, you simply configure wildcard rules based on one or more fields in the certificate that map all certificates with matching fields to a Windows account.

IIS Manager does not provide support for configuring many-to-one mappings. You can configure them by using the Appcmd command line, too. You can also edit the *system.web-Server/security/authentication/iisClientCertificateMappingAuthentication* configuration section directly or with other configuration APIs. You can add a one-to-one mapping by using the following Appcmd syntax.

```
%systemroot%\system32\inetsrv\Appcmd set config [SiteName]
/section:system.webServer/security/authentication/
iisClientCertificateMappingAuthentication /+manyToOneMappings
[name='string',enabled='bool',permissionMode='enum',
username='string',password='string',description='string']
```

Then, you have to add one more matching rule to the mapping by using the following Appcmd syntax, specifying the name of the mapping created in the command shown previously.

```
%systemroot%\system32\inetsrv\Appcmd set config [SiteName]
/section:system.webServer/security/authentication/
iisClientCertificateMappingAuthentication /+manyToOneMappings
[name='string'].rules.[certificateField='enum',
certificateSubField='string',matchCriteria='string',
compareCaseSensitive='bool']
```

You can delete a mapping by using the following Appcmd syntax.

```
%systemroot%\system32\inetsrv\Appcmd set config [SiteName]
/section:system.webServer/security/authentication/
iisClientCertificateMappingAuthentication /-manyToOneMappings
[name='string']
```

These commands use the parameters in Table 14-15.

Table 14-15 Parameters for Creating Certificate Mappings

Parameter	Description
SiteName	The site name of the Web site for which to set these settings. If omitted, sets them for the entire Web server. If you specify these settings for a configuration path deeper than the Web site root, these settings will not take effect.
name	The name of the mapping; can also be used to add rules to it or delete it.
enabled	Whether or not this mapping is enabled.
permissionMode	Whether to allow or deny access to the user who is given this mapping.
userName	The user name for the account to which the certificate maps.
password	The password for the account to which the certificate maps. This value is stored in the encrypted form.
description	The friendly description of the mapping.
certificateField	The certificate field to match in the current rule. Common fields are Issuer and Subject. For more information, get the details about the contents of the certificate from the CA.
certificateSubField	The certificate subfield to match in the current rule. For more information on the subfields, get the details about the contents of the certificate from the CA.
matchCriteria	The match criteria. This can include * and ? wildcard matching characters.
compareCaseSensitive	Whether or not the comparison should be case-sensitive.

UNC Authentication

The Web server core uses UNC authentication to establish an identity for accessing remote application content inside virtual directories that reside on a UNC share. It is not a true authentication method in the sense that it does not itself support an authentication scheme for establishing the identity of the client. Rather, it is a mechanism for using the authenticated user that has been established through other authentication mechanisms—and in some cases a fixed identity set in configuration—to determine which identity should be used for remote content access.

IIS uses UNC authentication whenever a request is made to a resource that resides in a virtual directory whose physical path is located on a UNC share (whether or not the UNC share is on the local computer). During UNC authentication, the Web server determines the identity to be used for accessing remote content as follows:

1. **Uses the virtual directory's fixed credentials.** In IIS 7.0, any virtual directory can specify fixed credentials that IIS uses for all accesses to that location. This replaces the *UNCUserName* and *UNCPassword* properties in IIS 6.0 that were used only when the virtual directory referred to a UNC share.

2. **Otherwise, uses the authenticated user if available.** If the virtual directory does not specify fixed credentials, use the authenticated user if it has already been determined by an authentication method. This is referred to as pass-through authentication. You cannot use this to access web.config files, because this access occurs before IIS determines the authenticated user.

3. **Otherwise, uses process identity.** If IIS has not yet determined the authenticated user, it will use the identity of the IIS worker process. The Web server uses this option to access web.config files (if virtual directory credentials are not configured), because configuration is read prior to the authentication stage.

> **Note**   IIS 7.0 cannot use pass-through authentication to access web.config files located on the remote UNC share. Because of this, the virtual directory must specify fixed credentials, or the application pool identity must have Read access to the remote UNC share.

By default, IIS cannot access remote UNC content. This is because the default anonymous user IUSR is a local built-in account that does not have network privileges. Additionally, because IIS is required to access web.config by using the IIS worker process identity, it has a similar problem because the Network Service account also does not typically have the right to access remote resources. Therefore, you typically have two options for configuring UNC authentication to allow proper access of remote content:

- **Use pass-through authentication**   Pass-through authentication requires both the application pool identity and all allowed authenticated user identities to have access to the remote UNC share. Additionally, it requires the use of an authentication scheme that is capable of delegating the user identity to a remote computer or configuring Constrained Delegation and/or Protocol Transition to enable this for other authentication schemes.

■ **Use virtual directory fixed credentials**   This is the recommended approach, because it requires you to grant access to the share for a single identity. Also, it does not have the requirement of ensuring that the authentication scheme can delegate its identities to the remote UNC share, because the fixed identity is always used to access the content. However, the fixed credential model does not enable the use of NTFS authorization and auditing for authenticated users accessing the share, because the access is always made under the specified credentials and not the authenticated user identity. For more information on setting up fixed credentials for virtual directories, see the section titled "Managing Remote Content" in Chapter 9.

> **Note**   It is highly recommended that you use the fixed credential model to configure access to remote UNC shares. Use this in all cases when you do not rely on NTFS ACL-based access control or auditing of remote content for your authenticated users.

If you do choose to use pass-through authentication, you will need to take the following steps:

1. Use a custom application pool identity that has access to the UNC share.

2. If using anonymous authentication, configure the anonymous user to be the application pool identity. Alternatively, configure a custom anonymous user that has access to the UNC share.

3. If you are using other authentication methods that produce Windows identities, ensure that these methods can delegate identities to the UNC share. Then, ensure that all authenticated users have access to the UNC share.

For more information about ensuring that your authentication scheme supports delegating authenticated user identities to remote resources, see the following section titled "Understanding Authentication Delegation."

Understanding Authentication Delegation

Many IIS authentication methods produce Windows identities that can be impersonated for the purpose of accessing resources. When the resources being accessed reside on a remote machine, the authenticated user identity needs to be transmitted to the remote machine for authentication with the remote service. This process is referred to as delegation. It occurs when IIS attempts to access files located on remote UNC shares, or when the application impersonates the authenticated user identity to connect to a remote server such as SQL Server.

Most IIS authentication methods do not produce authenticated identities that are suitable for delegation. This means that when IIS is configured to use these authentication methods, IIS and the application may fail to access resources located on remote machines when impersonating the authenticated identity.

> **Note**   In general, the rule for remembering which authentication methods can be delegated is to remember which authentication methods perform their logon locally on the Web server. For example, any authentication scheme in which the user name and password are available on the Web server—such as Basic Authentication, IIS Client Certificate Mapping Authentication, or Anonymous Authentication—use the Web server to log on and therefore can delegate authenticated identities.

To ensure that your application has access to its backed resources located on remote servers, you generally have three options:

- Use an authentication method that supports delegation (see Table 14-16).

- Use fixed virtual directory credentials to create an authentication identity that can be delegated to and can be impersonated instead of the authenticated user. For more information, see the section titled "UNC Authentication" earlier in this chapter.

- Configure Constrained Delegation and Protocol Transition to upgrade the authenticated identity to an authenticated identity you can delegate to using the Kerberos protocol.

Table 14-16 lists the built-in IIS authentication schemes and the required configuration to enable delegation of authenticated identities.

Table 14-16   Built-In IIS Schemes and Required Configuration to Enable Delegation of Authenticated Identities

Authentication	Configuration
Anonymous	Delegates when using a custom anonymous user or when using a custom application pool identity as the anonymous user (1 hop)
Basic	Delegates by default (1 hop)
Windows (Kerberos)	Requires Constrained Delegation
Windows (NTLM)	Requires Constrained Delegation and Protocol Transition
Digest	Requires Constrained Delegation and Protocol Transition
Client certificate mapping	Requires Constrained Delegation and Protocol Transition
IIS Client certificate mapping	Delegates by default (1 hop)

Most of the authentication schemes that do not perform the logon locally on the machine require Constrained Delegation and Protocol Transition to be able to delegate the authenticated identity to a remote machine. Constrained Delegation refers to the ability of a service to use a user identity obtained using the Kerberos protocol to access remote resources. Protocol Transition, used in conjunction with Constrained Delegation, enables other authentication schemes to obtain a Kerberos identity to be used with Constrained Delegation to access remote resources. To learn more about setting up Constrained Delegation and Protocol Transition, see *http://technet2.microsoft.com/WindowsServer/en/library/c312ba01-318f-46ca-990e-a597f3c294eb1033.mspx.*

Securing Communications with Secure Socket Layer (SSL)

By default, all communication between the Web server and the client occurs over a clear-text connection, which has the potential to expose the information included in the requests and responses to an attacker able to listen to the communication at the network layer. This includes packet sniffing at a local network, or compromising a router or a proxy server that is located on the path between the client and the Web server. This can result in the unintended disclosure of the response information, which may contain sensitive information, client credentials that are sent as part of some authentication methods (such as basic authentication or forms-based authentication methods), cookies, and more. The attacker can sometimes successfully use this information to misrepresent the client by providing these credentials to the Web server in a replay attack.

To prevent this from happening, you can use the Secure Socket Layer (SSL) or the newer Transport Layer Security (TLS) protocols to secure the communication between the client and server. TLS is a widely accepted standard that most browser technologies implement. In the rest of this section, we will refer to both of these protocols collectively as SSL for ease of reference.

In addition to securing the communication between the client and the Web server, SSL serves to confirm the identity of the Web server to the client. This process is widely used on the Internet today to ensure that the client is dealing with the entity that the Web site claims to represent. IIS can also use it to establish the identity of the client, if the client has an acceptable certificate. Client certificates are discussed later in the section titled "Client Certificates" later in this chapter.

Configuring SSL

To configure SSL, you must perform the following steps:

1. **Obtain a server certificate from a trusted Certificate Authority.** The Certificate Authority (CA) must be a trusted root CA for all of the clients that connect to the Web site that uses this certificate. For intranet sites, this may be a domain CA provided by the Active Directory Certificate Services. For Internet sites, this is usually a CA that is trusted by most client browsers by default. You can obtain the certificate by making a certificate request using the Server Certificates feature in IIS Manager. Alternatively, you can use a self-issued (or self-signed) certificate if you control both the Web server and the clients, and if you intend to use this certificate for testing purposes.

2. **Create a secure binding by using the HTTPS protocol and port 443 (or another port), and specify the server certificate for each Web site.** You can do this by creating a binding in IIS Manager, or by adding a binding programmatically and then using the *netsh http add sslcert ipport=IPAddress:443 certstorename=MY certhash=hash appid=GUID* command to associate the certificate with the binding. You can obtain the certificate hash from the Certificates console by viewing the certificate details and copying the value of the *Thumbprint* property.

> **Note**   Unlike IIS 6.0, where certificate association information is stored in the metabase, and the Web Publishing Service (W3SVC) is responsible for associating the site bindings with certificates when it is started, IIS 7.0 stores the certificate information directly in the HTTP.sys configuration. You can manipulate these associations by using IIS Manager or by using the *netsh http add sslcert* command.

To be accepted by the clients, the server certificate must contain Common Name (CN) entries for all of the host headers that the Web site used. This needs to be done when the certificate is requested.

> **Note**   It is possible to have multiple SSL Web sites that use unique server certificates if each Web site uses a separate IP address or port for its HTTPS binding. As in IIS 6.0, IIS 7.0 does not support having multiple Web sites with their own server certificates if the HTTPS bindings for those Web sites are on the same IP address/port and differentiate only by using host headers. This is because the host header information is not available when the SSL negotiation occurs. Because of this, the only way to have multiple Web sites on the same IP address that use host headers is to configure all of those Web sites to use the same SSL certificate with a wildcard CN. For more information, see *http://www.microsoft.com/technet/prodtechnol/ WindowsServer2003/Library/IIS/596b9108-b1a7-494d-885d-f8941b07554c.mspx?mfr=true*.

For more information on configuring site bindings, see Chapter 9. You can also read more about requesting certificates in the IIS 7.0 online documentation at *http://technet2.microsoft.com/windowsserver2008/en/library/d780d806-e8a8-4bc5-8d7a-9f045d1f3e221033.mspx?mfr=true*

Requiring SSL

To ensure that the communication between your Web server and clients is protected, you may choose to require that clients request your Web site content over secure connections. This is an effective way to protect clients' authentication credentials or sensitive cookies issued by the Web site over unsecure connections.

Caution   If your Web site enables mixed SSL usage, such as by allowing the Web site to be accessed over both SSL and unsecure connections, or by allowing portions of your Web site to be accessed over unsecure connections, be aware that requests made over these connections may leak sensitive information. For example, if your Web site uses Forms authentication to authenticate users, uses cookie-based session state, or stores sensitive information about the user in cookies, your clients may leak these cookies when making requests over unsecure connections. Therefore, always prefer to protect your entire Web site with SSL by requiring SSL for the entire Web site's URL namespace. Also, configure your cookies to include the *secure bit* to make sure the browser will not attempt to send them over unencrypted connections.

You can require SSL in IIS Manager by selecting the Web server, Web site, or another node corresponding to the URL for which you'd like to require SSL. Then double-click SSL Settings. In this feature, select the Require SSL check box to mandate SSL, as shown in Figure 14-8. You also have the option of selecting the Require 128-Bit SSL check box.

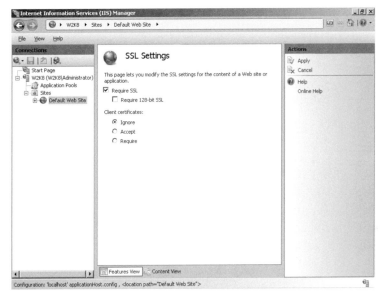

Figure 14-8   Configuring SSL settings using IIS Manager.

Alternatively, you can require SSL by editing the *system.webServer/security/access* section directly by using Appcmd or another configuration API. For example, you can set this configuration using the following Appcmd syntax.

```
%systemroot%\system32\inetsrv\Appcmd set config [ConfigurationPath]
/section:system.webServer/security/access /sslFlags:enum
```

This command has the parameters presented in Table 14-17.

Table 14-17   **Parameters for Configuring SSL Settings**

Parameter	Description
ConfigurationPath	The configuration path for which to apply this configuration. If you specify this, you may also need to specify the */commit:apphost* parameter to avoid locking errors when you apply configuration at Web site or URL levels.
sslFlags	A comma-separated list of one or more of the following values: *None, Ssl, Ssl128, SslNegotiateCert,SslRequireCert*. Set this to *Ssl* to require SSL, and *Ssl,Ssl128* to require 128-bit SSL. For a description of *SslNegotiateCert* and *SslRequireCert*, see the following section titled "Client Certificates."

Client Certificates

Though SSL is typically used to confirm the identity of the Web server to the client, it can also be used to confirm the client's identity to the Web server if the client has certificates issued by a CA that the Web server trusts. Client certificates can be used as part of a strong two-factor authentication scheme that requires both a user name/password as well as a physical authentication method to provide the client certificate, such as a Smart Card. Or, it can be used as a single authentication method with one of the client certificate mapping authentication methods that IIS supports.

To use client certificates, you must meet the following requirements:

- The Web site must be configured to use SSL and have a valid server certificate.

- The client must have a client certificate issued by a CA that the Web server trusts.

When a client makes a connection that uses SSL, the Web server negotiates the client certificates (if configured to do) by indicating the list of trusted CAs on the server, causing the client to respond with the list of certificates that are available on the client and that are issued by those CAs. The server then validates the certificates, including checking their expiration times and making sure that they are not listed on the Certificate Revocation List (CRL) on the Web server.

IIS supports multiple levels of using client certificates:

1. **Negotiate certificates.** This requests the client to provide a client certificate when the request is made, but it does not require the certificate. If the client provides it, the server validates the certificate, and the certificate is made available to the application. To do this, set the *sslFlags* attribute of the *system.webServer/security/access* configuration section to include *SslNegotiateCert,* as described in the section titled "Requiring SSL" earlier in this chapter.

2. **Require certificates.** This requires that the client provide a client certificate when the request is made. If the certificate is not provided, the request is rejected with a 403.7 – Client Certificate Required error. If the certificate is not successfully validated by the

server, the request will be rejected with a 403.16 – Client Certificate Is Untrusted Or Invalid error. It could also be rejected with a 403.17 – Client Certificate Has Expired Or Is Not Yet Valid error. To require certificates, set the *sslFlags* attribute of the *system.webServer/security/access* configuration section to include *SslNegotiateCert,Ssl-RequireCert,* as described in the section titled "Requiring SSL" earlier in this chapter. You can require certificates to implement a strong two-factor authentication scheme. Alternatively, you can require certificates in conjunction with a client certificate mapping authentication scheme as the primary authentication scheme for your Web site. For more information, see the sections titled "Client Certificate Mapping Authentication" and "IIS Client Certificate Mapping Authentication" earlier in this chapter.

3. **Authenticate users with client certificates.** IIS can also be configured to authenticate clients based on the client certificates. To learn more about using client certificate authentication, see the sections titled "Client Certificate Mapping Authentication" and "IIS Client Certificate Mapping Authentication" earlier in this chapter.

Securing Configuration

Previous versions of IIS have used a centralized configuration store known as the metabase. IIS 7.0 abandons the metabase in favor of a new configuration system based on a hierarchy of XML configuration files, in order to provide for simpler deployment and more flexible management of the Web server.

 Note You can learn more about the new IIS 7.0 configuration system in Chapter 4, "Understanding the Configuration System."

In this section, we will take a look at the files that comprise the IIS 7.0 configuration hierarchy and how they are accessed. We will also review security best practices for limiting access to these files to ensure that the configuration contained therein is secure against unauthorized information disclosure and tampering. In addition, we'll look at isolating the configuration between application pools that are using the new configuration isolation support.

Because the configuration is stored in plain text XML files, some of which may be taken off the server during deployment or otherwise exposed, it is sometimes necessary to protect the information stored therein from being discovered. The configuration system provides built-in encryption support to protect secrets stored in configuration files against disclosure even if an attacker is able to access the file. Later in this section, we'll take a look at best practices for storing secrets in configuration files and using encryption to protect them.

The configuration file hierarchy goes beyond centralized configuration and includes distributed web.config configuration files access that can be delegated to the site or application owner. This enables sites and applications to contain required configuration as part of their content for single-step deployment that does not require administrative rights on the server. It also enables site and application owners to manage their applications remotely without having administrative rights. In this section, we will review the best practices for securely configuring configuration delegation.

> **Note**   For more information about enabling and securing remote delegated management, see Chapter 8.

Restricting Access to Configuration

IIS 7.0 configuration is stored in a hierarchy of configuration files, including both server-level configuration files and distributed web.config files that may be delegated to site and application owners. Because these files store configurations by using plain text XML, anyone with the ability to access them can read and/or tamper with a server configuration without using any additional tools or APIs. Therefore, the NTFS access permissions placed on these files determine who can access server configuration and what they can do with it.

To properly secure configuration files, it is important to understand the files that comprise the hierarchy and how they are accessed. This can help define and maintain the proper access strategy in your environment.

> **Note**   You can learn about the configuration file hierarchy, the locations of each file, and their role in configuring the server in Chapter 4.

The files that constitute the IIS 7.0 configuration hierarchy, and their default access permissions, are listed in Table 14-18.

Table 14-18   Default Access Permissions for Configuration Files

File	Description	Default Permissions
Framework machine.config	Machine-level .NET Framework configuration	BUILTIN\IIS_IUSRS:(RX) BUILTIN\Users:(RX)
Framework root web.config	Machine-level configuration for ASP.NET applications	BUILTIN\IIS_IUSRS:(RX) BUILTIN\Users:(RX)
applicationHost.config	IIS machine-level configuration	NT SERVICE\WMSvc:(R) NT SERVICE\WMSvc:(R)
<AppoolName>.config	Auto-generated version of applicationHost.config for each application pool	IIS APPPOOL*<ApppoolName>*:(R)
Distributed web.config (wwwroot)	Delegated configuration files in the Web site directory structure	BUILTIN\IIS_IUSRS:(RX) BUILTIN\Users:(RX)

Table 14-18   **Default Access Permissions for Configuration Files**

File	Description	Default Permissions
administration.config	Machine-level configuration file for IIS Manager	NT SERVICE\WMSvc:(R)
redirection.config	Machine-level configuration file for configuring remote location of applicationHost.config	NT SERVICE\WMSvc:(R)

Note   The default permissions for all entries in Table 14-18 also contain permissions granting full rights to NT AUTHORITY\SYSTEM and BUILTIN\Administrators. These were removed from this table for clarity.

Looking at the default permissions lets you see that:

- The server-level configuration files, including Framework machine.config, Framework root web.config, applicationHost.config, administration.config, and redirection.config are writable only by the System and members of the Administrators group.

- All members of the Users group and the IIS_IUSRS group Framework can read machine.config and root web.config files. Unlike IIS server-level configuration files, any user on the machine—as well as any application running inside the IIS worker processes—can read the configuration in these files. This is due to the fact that these files are used to configure the behavior of .NET Framework components in any .NET application that runs on the machine.

- The IIS server-level configuration files, applicationHost.config, redirection.config, and administration.config, are only readable by the system, members of the administrators group, and the Web Management Service (NT Service\WMSvc). Unlike .NET Framework configuration files, they *cannot* be read by non-administrative users or even IIS worker processes. IIS worker processes receive a subset of configuration in the applicationHost.config file from the automatically generated *ApppoolName*.config files for each application pool.

- The Windows Process Activation Service (WAS) automatically generates the *Apppool-Name*.config files for each application pool, which are readable only by the IIS worker processes in the corresponding application pool. This is the basis of configuration isolation explained in the section titled "Understanding Configuration Isolation" later in this chapter.

- The distributed web.config files located in the site directory structure are by default readable by members of the Users group. These files typically must also grant access to the IIS_IUSRS group to allow access to the IIS worker process (IIS setup automatically grants this for the default Web site root located in *%SystemDrive%*\Inetpub\Wwwroot).

Setting Permissions on Configuration Files

The configuration files in the IIS hierarchy have restrictive permissions configured by default and should typically not be changed (with the exception of distributed web.config files that are part of your site directory structure). Changes to the permissions on these files may cause these files to become more vulnerable to unauthorized access. Keep the following in mind to maintain the security of these files:

- Never grant non-administrative identities (with the exception of NT SERVICE\WMSvc) access to applicationHost.config, redirection.config, and administration.config (either Read or Write). This includes Network Service, IIS_IUSRS, IUSR, or any custom identity used by IIS application pools. IIS worker processes are not meant to access any of these files directly. See the following section titled "Understanding Configuration Isolation" for information on how IIS worker processes get the configuration from application-Host.config.

- Never share out applicationHost.config, redirection.config, and administration.config on the network. When using Shared Configuration, prefer to export applicationHost.config to another location (see the section titled "Setting Permissions for Shared Configuration" later in this chapter).

- Keep in mind that all users can read .NET Framework machine.config and root web.config files by default. Do not store sensitive information in these files if it should be for administrator eyes only. Encrypt sensitive information that should be read by the IIS worker processes only and not by other users on the machine.

The only exception to this rule is the distributed web.config files that are part of your Web site's directory structure. It is up to you to ACL these files correctly to prevent unauthorized access to their contents. You should follow the standard guidance for setting permissions for your Web site content provided in the section titled "Setting NTFS Permissions to Grant Minimal Access" earlier in this chapter, including using application pool isolation to properly restrict access to the application pool to which the application belongs and setting required permissions to allow remote delegated administration through IIS Manager.

Understanding Configuration Isolation

As mentioned earlier, IIS worker processes do not have Read access to applicationHost.config. How, then, are they able to read any of the configuration set in this file?

The answer lies in the configuration isolation feature provided by IIS 7.0, which is always on by default. Instead of enabling IIS worker processes to read applicationHost.config directly when reading the configuration file hierarchy, IIS generates filtered copies of this file and uses these copies as a replacement of applicationHost.config when configuration is read inside the IIS worker process.

The reason for doing this is to prevent IIS worker processes from application pool A to be able to read configuration information in applicationHost.config that is intended for application pool B. Because applicationHost.config may contain sensitive information, such as the user name and password for custom application pool identities, as well as user name and password for virtual directories, allowing all application pools to access applicationHost.config would break application pool isolation.

WAS is responsible for generating the temporary application pool configuration files that each IIS worker process uses as a replacement of applicationHost.config. These files are placed by default in the *%SystemDrive%*\Inetpub\Temp\Apppools directory and are named *AppPool-Name.config*. As mentioned earlier, these files are configured to allow access only to the IIS worker processes in the corresponding application pool, by using the IIS APPPOOL*AppPool-Name* Application Pool SID.

> **Note** This process occurs automatically each time applicationHost.config is changed and therefore does not require any manual action from the administrator outside of normal configuration procedures.

Each application pool configuration file contains the configuration in applicationHost.config, with the following information removed:

- All application pool definitions in the *system.applicationHost/applicationPools* configuration section. Only WAS is required to read this configuration section.

- Any Web site definitions in the *system.applicationHost/sites* configuration section for sites that do not have applications in the current application pool.

- Any configuration in location tags for specific Web sites, applications, or URLs that do not reside inside the applications in the current application pool.

> **Caution** All application definitions (and their virtual directory definitions, possibly containing user name and password credentials) for any site that has at least one application in the current application pool will be present in the application pool configuration file. To disable this behavior and include only the application definitions for applications in the application pool, set the *IsolationWholeSiteInclude* DWORD value to 0 in the HKLM\System\CurrentControlSet\Services\WAS\Parameters key and perform an IISRESET. This may break applications in sites with applications in multiple application pools when they attempt to map physical paths for URLs in other applications.

Keep in mind that global configuration settings set in the applicationHost.config (without using location tags to apply them to specific Web sites, applications, or URLs) are not filtered. Each application pool configuration file will contain all of these settings.

Configuration isolation is a key part of the application pool isolation strategy in IIS 7.0. It is enabled by default to provide configuration isolation for server-level configuration in applicationHost.config. For strategies on achieving proper application pool isolation, see the section titled "Isolating Applications" earlier in this chapter.

> **Caution** Configuration stored in .NET Framework machine.config and root web.config files is not isolated. Only configuration stored in applicationHost.config is isolated.

Setting Permissions for Shared Configuration

IIS 7.0 supports sharing server configuration in the applicationHost.config configuration file between multiple Web servers on a Web farm. Using a shared configuration requires exporting the configuration from the source Web server, placing it on a network share, and configuring the share so that all member Web servers have access to it. The process of doing this is explained in Chapter 4.

To prevent unauthorized access to the shared configuration, follow these guidelines:

- Do not grant Write access to the identity that the Web server uses to access the shared applicationHost.config. This identity should have only Read access.

- Use a separate identity to publish applicationHost.config to the share. Do not use this identity for configuring access to the shared configuration on the Web servers.

- Use a strong password when exporting the encryption keys for use with shared configuration.

- Maintain restricted access to the share containing the shared configuration and encryption keys. If this share is compromised, an attacker will be able to read and write any IIS configuration for your Web servers, redirect traffic from your Web site to malicious sources, and in some cases gain control of all Web servers by loading arbitrary code into IIS worker processes. Consider protecting this share with firewall rules and IPsec policies to allow only the member Web servers to connect.

> **Warning** Maintain restricted access to the share containing shared configuration. Malicious access to this share can cause complete Web server compromise.

For more information on setting up shared configuration, see Chapter 4.

Securing Sensitive Configuration

The information in the configuration files in the IIS 7.0 configuration hierarchy is protected by the restricted permissions specified by the NTFS ACLs on each file. These permissions should prevent unauthorized users from being able to access these files. For more information on maintaining secure permissions on the configuration files, see the section titled "Restricting Access to Configuration" earlier in this chapter.

However, this alone may not provide a sufficient level of protection for especially sensitive information stored in configuration files, such as user names and passwords of custom application pool identities. It is essential to prevent this information from being discovered even if an attacker manages to compromise the local Web server and gain access to the configuration file containing the information. In addition, if someone copies the configuration file off the server for archival or transport reasons, an attacker should not be able to read the secrets stored in the configuration file. To ensure this, IIS 7.0 provides the ability to encrypt specific information stored in configuration.

Using Configuration Encryption to Store Configuration Secrets

IIS 7.0 configuration encryption works by encrypting the contents of configuration attributes for which encryption is enabled before storing their values in the configuration file. Therefore, even if someone obtains access to the file, they cannot read the contents of the attribute without decrypting it first.

Whether or not configuration encryption is used for each attribute is determined by the attribute's definition in the schema of the containing configuration section. You can find more information about how encryption is configured in the configuration section schema in the section titled "Protecting Sensitive Configuration Data" in Chapter 13, "Managing Configuration and User Interface Extensions." The schema also serves as a mechanism to select the encryption provider used to encrypt the data for this attribute (you can learn more about available encryption providers in the following section titled "Selecting Encryption Providers").

When any configuration tool or API writes the value of each encrypted attribute, the configuration system will automatically encrypt it using the configured encryption provider before persisting it to the configuration file on disk. If you inspect the resulting configuration file, you will see the encrypted value, as shown in the following code example for the password attribute in the application pool definition inside the *system.applicationHost/applicationPools* configuration section.

```
<applicationPools>
    <add name="MyAppPool">
        <processModel identityType="SpecificUser" userName="TestUser"
password="[enc:IISWASOnlyAesProvider:N8mr4dLU6PnMW5xlmCWg6914cKePgeU0fTbxew
ZppiwyTLmBQhOmZnFywQO78pQY:enc]" />
    </add>
</applicationPools>
```

The configuration system decrypts the attribute automatically when it is accessed, provided that the caller of the configuration system has the rights to use the encryption provider used to perform the encryption. Therefore, the decryption and encryption process is completely transparent to the administrator, while ensuring that the resulting configuration is not stored in plain text.

Selecting Encryption Providers

IIS provides several encryption providers that can be used to encrypt configuration, in addition to several encryption providers provided by the .NET Framework. One of these providers is used for each configuration attribute that is marked for encryption. The providers are listed in Table 14-19.

Table 14-19   Configuration Encryption Providers

Provider	Use	Encryption Key Access
RsaProtectedConfiguration Provider	Encrypting .NET Framework configuration sections using exportable RSA encryption	RSA machine key: SYSTEM and administrators only; grant access using Aspnet_regiis.exe -pa.
DataProtectionConfiguration Provider	Encrypting .NET Framework configuration sections using machine-local Data Protection API encryption	By default, everyone on the Web server; optionally user-based key
IISWASOnlyRsaProvider	Encrypting IIS configuration sections read by WAS using exportable RSA encryption	RSA machine key: SYSTEM and administrators only
IISWASOnlyAesProvider	Encrypting IIS configuration sections read by WAS using AES encryption	Session key encrypted with RSA machine key: SYSTEM and administrators only
AesProvider	Encrypting IIS configuration sections read by the IIS worker process using AES encryption	Session key encrypted with RSA machine key: IIS_IUSRS, NT Service\WMSvc

.NET Framework creates both the RsaProtectedConfigurationProvider and the DataProtectionConfigurationProvider providers. These providers are primarily used to encrypt .NET configuration for ASP.NET applications using the Aspnet_regiis.exe tool. For more information on using the .NET Framework configuration encryption, see *http://msdn2.microsoft.com/en-us/library/53tyfkaw.aspx.*

Note   You cannot use IIS configuration encryption to encrypt .NET configuration sections. Likewise, you cannot use .NET configuration encryption to encrypt the contents of IIS configuration sections with Aspnet_regiis.exe. If you attempt to read .NET configuration sections encrypted with .NET configuration encryption by using IIS configuration APIs, you will receive an error, because IIS does not support section-level encryption used by the .NET Framework configuration system.

You can use the IIS encryption providers—IISWASOnlyRsaProvider, IISWASOnlyAesProvider, and AesProvider—to encrypt IIS configuration sections.

IISWASOnlyRsaProvider and IISWASOnlyAesProvider are both used to encrypt configuration sections that WAS reads, such as the *system.applicationHost/applicationPools* section, and do not allow IIS worker processes to decrypt the configuration. The IISWASOnlyAesProvider provides better performance because it uses AES encryption using an RSA encrypted session key, instead of using full RSA encryption, and is used by default. The session key itself is encrypted using the RSA key container used by IISWASOnlyAesProvider, so it has the same access requirements. Configuration attributes encrypted using these providers can only be decrypted by SYSTEM and members of the Administrators group.

The *AesProvider* provider is an AES provider that uses a session key encrypted using an RSA key container that has permissions for the IIS_IUSRS group, therefore allowing IIS worker processes to encrypt and decrypt configuration encrypted with this provider. This is the provider used by default by all IIS configuration sections that are read by IIS worker processes. It is also the provider you should consider using to protect your custom configuration sections. Configuration attributes encrypted using this provider can be decrypted by any IIS application.

> **Note**   The IIS configuration system does not support pluggable encryption providers unlike the .NET configuration system. However, you can configure new instances of the IIS configuration provider types to use different key containers for encryption purposes.

You can also create additional instances of the RSA and AES providers by creating new entries in the *configProtectedData* configuration section, and configure them to use new RSA key containers. You can create new RSA key containers by using the Aspnet_regiis.exe –pc command, as described at *http://msdn2.microsoft.com/en-us/library/2w117ede.aspx*.

You can then manipulate the permissions on the RSA key to determine who can use it to encrypt and decrypt configuration by using the *Aspnet_regiis.exe –pa* and *Aspnet_regiis –pr* commands.

Keep in mind the following guidelines when using encryption:

- Configuration encrypted with IISWASOnlyAesProvider can only be decrypted by members of the Administrators group. This provider is only used to encrypt configuration read exclusively by WAS.

- Configuration encrypted using *AesProvider* can be decrypted by any IIS application. It can be used to protect configuration from being disclosed outside of the Web server, but it is not a way to protect configuration from applications running on the Web server. It also does not protect configuration used by one application pool from another application pool (although this protection may be afforded by proper NTFS permissions configured for application pool isolation).

■ If you require to encrypt configuration for each application pool as an additional isolation measure, you should create separate RSA keys for each application pool identity and ACL them for that application pool using the Application Pool SIDs or custom application pool identities. Then you can create a provider for each application pool, using the corresponding RSA keys, and encrypt the configuration for each application pool using the corresponding provider.

■ In order to share a configuration on a Web farm or deploy an application with a encrypted configuration to another server, you must share encryption keys and provider definitions between the original server on which encryption was performed and the target server. When exporting encryption key containers, be sure to use a strong password and protect these keys from being accessed by unauthorized users. You can learn more about exporting encryption keys here: *http://msdn2.microsoft.com/en-us/library/2w117ede.aspx*. In addition, you can export encryption keys by using IIS Manager when setting up shared configuration. For more information, see Chapter 4.

Caution   Changing the permissions on the RSA key containers may lead to compromise of the encryption keys and therefore may expose your encrypted configuration. Do not change the default permissions on the built-in IIS RSA key containers.

Limitations of Storing Secrets in Configuration

When you store secrets in configuration, the secret is protected by both the NTFS permissions on the configuration file (see the section titled "Restricting Access to Configuration" earlier in this chapter) and configuration encryption, if configured. However, you should be aware of the following limitations that may impact the security of your secret:

■ NTFS permissions provide the basic level of protection for secrets in configuration files. However, when configuration files are archived, copied off the machine, or sent over a network, this protection is lost. Always use encryption to provide protection for secrets in these cases.

■ Any code in the IIS worker process can decrypt any encrypted configuration data that the IIS worker process has access to. By default, any IIS worker processes can decrypt any configuration data encrypted using the default IIS encryption provider (*AesProvider*).

■ Encryption is only as secure as the key that is used to perform the encryption. Therefore, be sure that only the users authorized to perform decryption have access to the key container used to perform the encryption and make sure that this key container is not compromised if it is exported off the machine.

Limiting Access to Configuration from Managed Code in Partial Trust Environments

When accessing IIS configuration from native code, the permissions set on the configuration files are the basis for determining whether or not access to the configuration is granted. Native modules and other code running in the IIS worker process can therefore read any of the configuration in the configuration file hierarchy that is not hidden by application pool isolation or encrypted with encryption keys that the IIS worker process does not have access to.

However, when managed code modules access configuration using the *Microsoft.Web. Administration* API, their ability to read some configuration sections can be further constrained through Code Access Security (CAS) policy configured for the application. This is similar to how CAS is used to prevent managed code applications from performing other actions that the hosting process may otherwise be allowed to perform, such as accessing files or opening network connections.

You can leverage this mechanism to prevent ASP.NET applications running in partial trust from being able to access information from certain configuration sections. This is done by setting the *requirePermission* attribute on the section declaration to *true*. When this is done, only ASP.NET applications and managed modules running with Full Trust can read the contents of these configuration sections. For more information on setting the *requirePermission* attribute as part of the section declaration process, see the section titled "Declaring Configuration Sections" in Chapter 13.

> **Note** The *requirePermission* attribute only prevents the application from using the configuration APIs to read the configuration section when in partial trust. The application can still access the file directly, if the CAS policy and file permissions allow it. Because of this, *requirePermission* is only effective at preventing medium or below trust applications from reading the contents of configuration sections specified outside of the application's directory structure, such as in applicationHost.config. The application can still open the distributed web.config files in its directory structure by using file IO APIs directly.

By default, no IIS configuration sections are declared with *requirePermission* set to *true*, so the contents of IIS configuration sections can be read by partial trust applications. So, this technique is more applicable to new configuration sections being declared.

For more information on using ASP.NET trust levels to constrain the execution of managed modules and ASP.NET applications, see the section titled "Reduce Trust of ASP.NET Applications" earlier in this chapter.

Controlling Configuration Delegation

One of the key management scenarios that the IIS 7.0 configuration system has in mind is configuration delegation. Configuration delegation refers to the ability of the Web site or application owner to specify the required IIS configuration for their application without being an administrator on the Web server computer. To allow this, the IIS 7.0 configuration file hierarchy supports specifying configuration in distributed web.config files, which can be located anywhere in the Web site's directory structure to override the configuration specified at the server level. This also allows Web sites and applications to become portable by including all of the configuration files necessary alongside their content, so they can be deployed by simply being copied to the Web server.

If configuration delegation was an all or nothing approach, it likely wouldn't work, because most Web server administrators would not want to allow the Web site or application to be able to override all of the configuration set at the server level, especially for configuration sections that affect security, reliability, and performance of the Web server. Therefore, the IIS 7.0 configuration system provides an extensive set of controls that server administrators can use to determine which configuration sections, and further yet, which specific configuration attributes, can be overridden at the Web site or application level. If you manage a Web server that allows others to publish application content, you will likely need to review the configuration allowed for delegation, and in some cases lock or unlock specific configuration for delegation.

Further, IIS 7.0 also provides the infrastructure for Web site and application administrators to manage their configuration remotely through IIS Manager, without having administrative privileges on the Web server computer. Again, as a server administrator, you have fine-grained control over who can manage the Web sites and applications on your computer remotely, and what management features they can use. You can learn more about configuring remote management permissions in Chapter 8.

Controlling Which Configuration Is Delegated

The configuration section is the basic unit of configuration delegation. By default, each configuration section is marked to initially allow or deny delegation when it is first declared, by specifying the *overrideModeDefault* attribute in the section declaration (this is typically determined by the developer based on whether the section is considered sensitive and should not be modifiable by non-Administrators by default). If the section is marked as not delegated, any attempt to specify the configuration for this section at any lower level in the configuration hierarchy will lead to a configuration error when this section is accessed.

> **Note**   You can learn more about declaring configuration sections and the *overrideMode-Default* attribute in the section titled "Declaring Configuration Sections" in Chapter 13.

By default, all IIS configuration sections are declared in applicationHost.config. Each section declaration specifies whether or not this section is available for delegation, based on the Microsoft IIS team's criteria for whether or not the configuration section is sensitive. This criteria includes considerations of whether the configuration section can be used to weaken the security, reduce reliability, or significantly impact the performance of the Web server overall, or allow the Web site or application to access information outside of its boundaries.

> **Note**   You can also manage the delegation of .NET configuration sections using the IIS administration stack. Both IIS and .NET configuration use the same mechanism for controlling delegation, including section-level locking and fine-grained configuration locking. For more information, see Chapter 4.

The default delegation of IIS configuration sections is shown in Table 14-20.

Table 14-20   Default Delegation of IIS Configuration Sections

Section	Default State	Reason
system.applicationHost		
applicationPools	n/a	Section can be specified only in applicationHost.config
configHistory	n/a	Section can be specified only in applicationHost.config
customMetadata	n/a	Section can be specified only in applicationHost.config
listenerAdapters	n/a	Section can be specified only in applicationHost.config
log	n/a	Section can be specified only in applicationHost.config
sites	n/a	Section can be specified only in applicationHost.config
webLimits	n/a	Section can be specified only in applicationHost.config
system.webServer		
asp	Deny	Contains security, performance, and reliability sensitive settings for ASP applications
caching	Allow	
cgi	Deny	Security sensitive: createProcessAsUser
defaultDocument	Allow	
directoryBrowse	Allow	
fastCgi	n/a	Section can be specified only in applicationHost.config
globalModules	n/a	Section can be specified only in applicationHost.config

Table 14-20   Default Delegation of IIS Configuration Sections

Section	Default State	Reason
handlers	Deny; Allow when .NET Extensibility is installed	For compatibility with IIS 6.0; section is effectively unlocked as soon as .NET Extensibility is installed; see "Locking Down Extensibility" section in Chapter 12
httpCompression	n/a	Section can only be specified in applicationHost.config
httpErrors	Deny	Security sensitive: ability to specify error pages outside of the application
httpLogging	Deny	Security sensitive: turning off logging can create repudiation issues
httpProtocol	Allow	
httpRedirect	Allow	
httpTracing	Deny	Performance sensitive: list of ETW URLs to trace
isapiFilters	n/a	Section can be specified only in applicationHost.config
modules	Deny; Allow when .NET Extensibility is installed	For compatibility with IIS 6.0; section is effectively unlocked as soon as .NET Extensibility is installed; see "Locking Down Extensibility" section in Chapter 12
odbcLogging	Deny	Security sensitive: configuring logging to external database
serverRuntime	Deny	Security, performance, and reliability affecting settings for the core Web server engine
serverSideInclude	Deny	Security sensitive: enabling server-side include can allow the application to access content outside of its boundaries
staticContent	Allow	
urlCompression	Allow	
validation	Allow	
system.webServer/security		
access	Deny	Security sensitive: configure SSL requirements
applicationDependencies	n/a	Section can be specified only in applicationHost.config
authorization	Allow	

Table 14-20 **Default Delegation of IIS Configuration Sections**

Section	Default State	Reason
ipSecurity	Deny	Security sensitive: determine who can access the application
isapiCgiRestriction	n/a	Section can only be specified in applicationHost.config
requestFiltering	Allow	Caution: delegated, but application can end up removing basic protection configured at server level and lessen its security
system.webServer/security/ authentication		
anonymousAuthentication	Deny	Security sensitive: enable or disable authentication method
basicAuthentication	Deny	Security sensitive: enable or disable authentication method
clientCertificateMapping Authentication	Deny	Security sensitive: enable or disable authentication method
digestAuthentication	Deny	Security sensitive: enable or disable authentication method
iisClientCertificate Mapping-Authentication	Deny	Security sensitive: enable or disable authentication method
windowsAuthentication	Deny	Security sensitive: enable or disable authentication method
system.webServer/ tracing		
traceFailedRequests	Allow	
traceProviderDefinitions	n/a	Section can only be specified in applicationHost.config

The default delegation state for IIS configuration sections is just that—a default—and may not work for everyone. If you allow third parties to publish Web site or application configuration on the server, you will need to review the impacts of allowing each section to be delegated and strike a balance between application requirements for delegation and the need to protect the Web server from unintended or malicious configuration changes. Then, you can lock or unlock configuration sections to allow them for delegation or even use fine-grained configuration locking to allow section delegation but lock specific configuration attributes, elements, or collection entries.

Note For information about how to lock and unlock sections, and use fine-grained configuration locking, see the "Delegating Configuration" and "Granular Configuration Locking" sections in Chapter 4.

When determining which configuration should be delegated, keep the following guidelines in mind:

- Err on the side of leaving configuration sections locked at the server level and unlock specific sections as needed by the application. You can also unlock specific sections for specific Web sites or applications only and leave them locked for others. This is an effective method to avoid unexpected configuration changes at the application level even if you do not delegate configuration to other parties.

- When unlocking a specific section, you can still lock parts of it that contain sensitive configuration or configuration you do not want to be changed. Use fine-grained configuration locking to lock the attributes, elements, or collection elements that you don't want changed while allowing other parts of the configuration section to be delegated.

Summary

IIS 7.0, much like its predecessor, comes with secure defaults that minimize the risk of exploits against the Web server. As you deploy your applications to the Web server and change configuration, you should familiarize yourself with the configuration and features to make sure that you do not introduce any threats to the Web server. In this chapter, you have reviewed the security changes and new security features in IIS 7.0 that can help you maintain the security of the Web server.

Unfortunately, history has shown that most Web server exploits are directed at the application running on the Web server rather than at the Web server itself. Applications are often tested less rigorously then the Web server features and are often designed with less understanding of the threat vectors that exist for Web-facing applications. Because of this, it is important to perform rigorous threat modeling and security testing at the application layer to minimize application vulnerabilities.

In addition, it is important to take an approach to security that does not depend on specific application threat vectors. IIS 7.0 makes it possible to apply such an approach, by reducing the surface area of the Web server and running the application components with least privilege possible. Together, these two techniques can both minimize the risk of any known or future exploit and reduce the damage if such an exploit does occur. By using the best practices in this chapter, you can successfully apply these techniques to your application to minimize the risk of a security compromise of your Web server.

Finally, be aware that a Web server does not function in a vacuum. It depends on a variety of Windows subsystems for its security and relies on the security of the network and other services around it. Be sure to consider the security of the network overall and related services when designing a secure Web farm.

Additional Resources

- Chapter 4, "Understanding the Configuration System," for information about configuring IIS7.

- Chapter 11, "Hosting Application Development Frameworks," for information about the execution privileges of application frameworks.

- Chapter 12, "Managing Web Server Modules" for information about managing and securing web server modules.

- Improving Web Application Security: Threats and Countermeasures: *http://msdn2.microsoft.com/en-us/library/ms994921.aspx.*

- *http://www.iis.net.*

- *http://www.mvolo.com* for frequent blog coverage of IIS 7.0, including security information.

Part IV
Troubleshooting and Performance

Chapter 15

Logging

 On the Disc Browse the CD for additional tools and resources.

Though not technology's most fascinating topic, Web server log files are extraordinarily important. They are a core resource used, for example, as the basis for billing, reliability, performance, compliance, and forensics. This chapter discusses Internet Information Services logging and related features in Microsoft IIS 7.0.

What's New?

In IIS 7.0, as in IIS 6.0, log files are handled by the HTTP.sys kernel mode device driver. No user code runs in this service because HTTP.sys runs in kernel mode. In general, not a lot has changed related to logging, but a few differences as well as new opportunities are notable. You'll find that many of the enhancements to logging introduced as late as Windows Server 2003 Service Pack 1 (SP1) are included in IIS 7.0. For example, you can use World Wide Web Consortium (W3C) centralized logging and binary logging; you can use standard log formats such as W3C extended, National Center for Supercomputing Applications (NCSA), and IIS; and you can set the custom logging option.

One of the more interesting features in IIS 7.0 is its modular architecture and the Integrated Pipeline. The Integrated Pipeline is covered in depth in Chapter 2, "Understanding IIS 7.0

Architecture." Logging greatly benefits from the flexibility provided by the modularity in IIS 7.0 and the Integrated Pipeline because you can write your own logging module and inject it into the pipeline. Your custom module can capture just the information needed for your application.

IIS 7.0 incorporates several changes pertinent to logging:

- You use the IIS Manager to configure logging-related settings.

- The new configuration system is based on XML.

- There are a number of new logging configuration options and a new set of status codes.

- IIS 7.0 provides logging for a new service that enables remote administration of an IIS 7.0 server.

IIS Manager

IIS 7.0 introduces a completely new user interface, the IIS Manager. The IIS Manager makes it easier to browse and make changes to IIS settings, including log file settings. For example, if you wanted to implement the centralized logging in IIS 6.0, you had to use ADSUtil.vbs. Now, the Centralized Logging option is exposed in the IIS Manager, as shown in Figure 15-1.

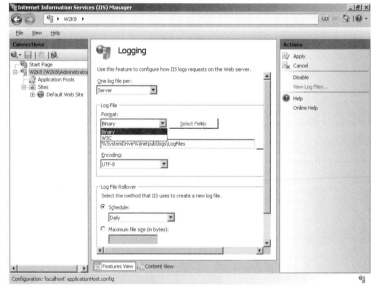

Figure 15-1   The Centralized Logging option in the IIS Manager.

Chapter 6, "Using IIS Manager," provides an in-depth look at the IIS Manager.

The XML-Based Logging Schema

IIS 7.0 uses a new configuration system that is XML-based and is very similar to the ASP.NET configuration system. Each configuration section is defined in XML schema files located in

%*SystemRoot*%\system32\inetsrv\config\schema. Details on the configuration sections are covered in Chapter 4, "Understanding the Configuration System." Because information is defined in XML files, it is easy to determine what attributes, elements, and enums are used. The schema for IIS 7.0 contains a list of all the configurable options, so looking in the schema file is a quick way to identify all the configurable settings for any feature, including logging.

The following listing is from the system.applicationHost/log section that is located in %*SystemRoot*%\system32\inetsrv\config\schema\IIS_Schema.xml. (Some long lines have been split to fit on the printed page.) As you can see, the XML clearly defines the names and data types associated with each item.

```xml
<sectionSchema name="system.applicationHost/log">
    <attribute name="logInUTF8" type="bool" defaultValue="true" />
    <attribute name="centralLogFileMode" type="enum" defaultValue="Site" >
      <enum name="Site" value="0"/>
      <enum name="CentralBinary" value="1"/>
      <enum name="CentralW3C" value="2"/>
    </attribute>
    <element name="centralBinaryLogFile">
      <attribute name="enabled" type="bool" defaultValue="false" />
      <attribute name="directory" type="string" expanded="true"
          defaultValue="%SystemDrive%\inetpub\logs\LogFiles" />
      <attribute name="period" type="enum" defaultValue="Daily">
        <enum name="Hourly" value="4"/>
        <enum name="Daily" value="1"/>
        <enum name="Weekly" value="2"/>
        <enum name="Monthly" value="3"/>
        <enum name="MaxSize" value="0"/>
      </attribute>
      <attribute name="truncateSize" type="int64" defaultValue="20971520"
          validationType="integerRange"
          validationParameter="1048576,4294967295" />
      <attribute name="localTimeRollover" type="bool"
          defaultValue="false"/>
    </element>
    <element name="centralW3CLogFile">
      <attribute name="enabled" type="bool" defaultValue="true" />
      <attribute name="directory" type="string" expanded="true"
          defaultValue="%SystemDrive%\inetpub\logs\LogFiles"
          validationType="nonEmptyString" />
      <attribute name="period" type="enum" defaultValue="Daily">
        <enum name="Hourly" value="4"/>
        <enum name="Daily" value="1"/>
        <enum name="Weekly" value="2"/>
        <enum name="Monthly" value="3"/>
        <enum name="MaxSize" value="0"/>
      </attribute>
      <attribute name="truncateSize" type="int64" defaultValue="20971520"
          validationType="integerRange"
          validationParameter="1048576,4294967295" />
      <attribute name="localTimeRollover" type="bool"
          defaultValue="false"/>
      <attribute name="logExtFileFlags" type="flags"
          defaultValue="Date, Time, ClientIP, UserName, SiteName, ServerIP,
```

```
                              Method, UriStem, UriQuery, HttpStatus, Win32Status,
                              ServerPort, UserAgent, HttpSubStatus">
            <flag name="Date" value="1"/>
            <flag name="Time" value="2"/>
            <flag name="ClientIP" value="4"/>
            <flag name="UserName" value="8"/>
            <flag name="SiteName" value="16"/>
            <flag name="ComputerName" value="32"/>
            <flag name="ServerIP" value="64"/>
            <flag name="Method" value="128"/>
            <flag name="UriStem" value="256"/>
            <flag name="UriQuery" value="512"/>
            <flag name="HttpStatus" value="1024"/>
            <flag name="Win32Status" value="2048"/>
            <flag name="BytesSent" value="4096"/>
            <flag name="BytesRecv" value="8192"/>
            <flag name="TimeTaken" value="16384"/>
            <flag name="ServerPort" value="32768"/>
            <flag name="UserAgent" value="65536"/>
            <flag name="Cookie" value="131072"/>
            <flag name="Referer" value="262144"/>
            <flag name="ProtocolVersion" value="524288"/>
            <flag name="Host" value="1048576"/>
            <flag name="HttpSubStatus" value="2097152"/>
          </attribute>
        </element>
      </sectionSchema>
```

Centralized Logging Configuration Options

Following is the logging section defined in the ApplicationHost.config file that controls Centralized Logging options. You can change this so that your files are stored on another drive or volume. You can enable options you want and disable whatever options you do not need.

```
<log>
    <centralBinaryLogFile enabled="true"
        directory="%SystemDrive%\inetpub\logs\LogFiles" />
    <centralW3CLogFile enabled="true"
        directory="%SystemDrive%\inetpub\logs\LogFiles" />
</log>
```

SiteDefaults Configuration Options

The SiteDefaults section in the ApplicationHost.config file, shown in the following code, controls the logging settings that are used when creating new sites. You can configure two options: the format of the log file and the location in which Failed Request tracing files are stored.

```
<siteDefaults>
    <logFile logFormat="W3C"
        directory="%SystemDrive%\inetpub\logs\LogFiles" />
    <traceFailedRequestsLogging
        directory="%SystemDrive%\inetpub\logs\FailedReqLogFiles" />
</siteDefaults>
```

Disable HTTP Logging Configuration Options

In some cases, an IIS administrator does not require log files. If you would like to turn off httpLogging at the server level, you can disable logging in the IIS Manager. You can also disable logging at the site level. You might wonder why these options are available. It's so that you can disable logging on your test or development machines to reduce the disk space that unnecessary files use.

You should evaluate your options before disabling httpLogging. Check with your business or legal department to be certain what your company's logging requirements and policies are. The default value for this setting, as shown here, is false.

```
<httpLogging dontLog="false" />
```

> **Note** For more information about the system.webServer/httpLogging option, see the section titled "Countermeasures" in Chapter 17, "Performance and Tuning."

Default Log File Location

One of the most significant changes in IIS 7.0 is that the folder where IIS stores WWW logs has been changed to %SystemDrive%\inetpub\logs\LogFiles. For example, the Default Web Site would log to C:\inetpub\logs\LogFiles\w3svc1. This means that by default in IIS 7.0, all log files are stored in a single folder. Note, however, that log files for the legacy built-in File Transfer Protocol (FTP) and Simple Mail Transfer Protocol (SMTP) services are still located in %windir%\System32\Logfiles. You can manage these files by using the IIS Manager 6.0, an MMC console that is installed when you install the legacy FTP service or the SMTP service.

> **Note** The new FTP Publishing Service for IIS 7.0 stores its log files in %SystemDrive%\ inetpub\logs\LogFiles by default. You need to download and install this add-on, because it does not ship with IIS 7.0. The x86 and x64 versions are available at *http://www.iis.net*. Click Download and search for "Microsoft FTP Publishing Service for IIS 7.0."

Default UTF-8 Encoding

By default, IIS 7.0 stores log files by using UTF-8 encoding. This changes the default file naming convention so that the files start with u_ (for example, u_exYYMMDD.log). Here is the portion of the IIS_Schema.xml file that sets the UTF-8 encoding option. The default setting is true.

```
<sectionSchema name="system.applicationHost/log">
  <attribute name="logInUTF8" type="bool" defaultValue="true" />
...
</sectionSchema>
```

UTF-8 encoding allows for single-byte and multi-byte characters in one string. This encoding enables you to read text-based logs (for example, logs that use W3C Extended, IIS, and NCSA

Common formats) in a language other than English. IIS does not support the UTF-8 format for the built-in FTP Publishing Service log files. UTF-8 encoding is available in IIS 6.0, but it is not enabled by default. If you do not want to have your logs use UTF-8 encoding, you can use ANSI as the format.

New Status Codes

In IIS 7.0, new status codes have been introduced for HTTP and FTP. These additional error codes provide more details about events and better descriptions of how to fix errors, with suggestions about what to look for or what procedures to run. Appendix A provides a complete list of all status codes.

Management Service

IIS 7.0 introduces Management Service, which enables computer and domain administrators to remotely manage a machine by using the IIS Manager. The Management Service also enables nonadministrators to control sites and various applications by using the IIS Manager from a workstation.

This service has its own logs that are used to track information related to the Management Service. This service is not installed by default. If you install and enable this service, the logs will be saved in %*SystemDrive*%\inetpub\logs\WMSvc.

From a logging perspective, you should make sure the Management Service logging is enabled. The logs can help you audit and troubleshoot issues when clients are connecting to your server. The Management Service is discussed in depth in Chapter 8, "Remote Administration."

Log File Formats That Have Not Changed

IIS 7.0 supports all the common logging formats that are available in prior versions of IIS. There have been no changes in IIS 7.0 to the following log file formats:

- Microsoft IIS
- NCSA
- W3Svc extended

 Note   For descriptions, further discussion, and examples of these log formats, go to *http://msdn2.microsoft.com* and search for "IIS logging formats."

Centralized Logging

Centralized logging in IIS 7.0 operates the same way as it does in IIS 6.0. However, you can now configure this option in the IIS 7.0 Manager. To access this feature, go to Administrative Tools > Internet Information Services (IIS) Manager. Click the computer name and locate the Logging option listed in the IIS section.

Using the Logging option can reduce administrative costs because only one IIS log file is being maintained. If you use binary logging, the log can be stored in a much smaller file than the equivalent text log file.

W3C Centralized Logging Format

W3C centralized logging was first introduced in Windows Server 2003 SP1. W3C centralized logging is a *server*-level setting. When you enable this feature on a server, all Web sites on that server are configured to write log data to a central log file. Data is stored in the log file using the W3C Extended log file format. You can enable this setting through the IIS 7.0 Manager or by using Appcmd. If you use W3C centralized logging, you can view the log file with a text editor such as Notepad.

> **Note**   W3C centralized logging uses the W3C Extended log format, which includes the following four fields: *HostHeader, Cookie, UserAgent*, and *Referrer*. These fields are not available in centralized binary logging.

Centralized Binary Logging Format

Centralized binary logging is essentially the same as W3C centralized logging, except that the log file uses a proprietary, binary format. Because the resulting file is binary, it is smaller than an equivalent text file so that you can conserve disk space. It cannot be read with a text editor and requires parsing to produce useful information. However, this is easier than you might think when you use the Log Parser tool, which reads the centralized binary file format natively. The Log Parser tool is discussed later in this chapter.

> **Important**   The built-in FTP and SMTP services do not support W3C centralized logging.

Remote Logging

IIS 7.0 supports writing log files to a network share. This option enables you to have your log files stored in real time to a remote computer. For example, suppose that you have a Web farm configured for logging to a central location. The remote file server could be a server running DFS (distributed file system). DFS can provide multiple benefits including a central location to collect your log files and automatic replication of your logs to multiple locations. Having such a primary collection point can make handling your reporting processes much easier.

> **Important**   When you set up your remote logging environment, make sure the host (A) and pointer (PTR) DNS records are set up so that authentication and resolution happens correctly. This can help avoid problems such as Kerberos authentication errors when HTTP.sys is trying to write log files.

You can use either the IIS 7.0 Manager or Appcmd to set up Universal Naming Convention (UNC) remote logging.

Setting Up Remote Logging by Using the IIS Manager

Following are the steps to enable remote logging by using the IIS Manager:

1. Create a directory called IISLogs on the remote server that will store the log files. This machine is typically in the same domain as the Web servers. If the remote server is not in the same domain or is a stand-alone machine, you can use the procedure outlined in the following sidebar so your files are stored on a remote machine.

Using a NULL Session for Remote Logging

If your remote server will be in a different domain, you can set up a NULL Session to support remote logging. The following procedure outlines how to set up this environment. If your remote server is not in a different domain, you can skip over the details of this outline and proceed with step 2 of the procedure for setting up remote logging by using the IIS Manager.

Before setting up your environment, make sure both machines can resolve each other using DNS, WINS, or custom entries in the local HOSTS file. This procedure assumes both servers are Windows Server 2008.

1. Identify two machines, the Web server and the file server. These roles need to be on separate physical machines.

2. Create a folder called IISLogs on your file server and then create a share and grant appropriate folder security.

    a. Open a command prompt on the file server and type **mkdir c:\IISLogs**

    b. Then type **net share IISLogs=c:\IISLogs /Grant:Everyone,FULL**

    c. Then type **cacls c:\IISLogs /G Administrators:F SYSTEM:F Everyone:C**

    d. When you see the prompt "Are you sure (Y/N)?" type **y**

    e. Processed dir: c:\IISLogs

3. Configure logging on your Web site by typing

    appcmd set sites "WebsiteName" -logFile.directory:\\FileServerName\IISLogs

4. Configure Local Security Policy on the file server.

    Programs, Administrative Tools, Local Security Policy, Local Policies, Security Options

    a. Enable:Network access:Let Everyone permissions to apply to anonymous users.

> b. Add IISLogs share to the Network access:Shares that can be accessed anonymously.
>
> 5. Browse your Web site on the Web server.
>
>   a. Open http://localhost/
>
> 6. Open a command prompt on the Web server and type the following command:
>
> **netsh http flush logbuffer**
>
> 7. Check your log files to see if your sample request is listed.

2. Share the IISLogs folder you created in the previous step. Change the share permissions to—at minimum—enable both the remote machine accounts Administrators group and the account that is writing the log files full control. Change the NTFS file system (NTFS) permissions so that the remote machine accounts Administrators have full control and the account writing the log files has modify permissions. This example assumes that you are using the NETWORK SERVICE as your application pool account and that the remote server and Web server are in the same domain.

> **Note** When the NETWORK SERVICE account accesses a remote resource, it uses the computer account stored in Active Directory Domain Service as the actual account accessing the log folder.

3. In the IIS Manager, navigate to your Web site and type in the UNC path to the server. To do so, go to Administrative Tools > Internet Information (IIS) Manager. Select the computer name in the leftmost column and then double-click the Logging icon in the IIS Section. Type the path to the share in the Directory text box by using the syntax *ServerName**ShareName*, as shown in Figure 15-2.

> **Note** You can also use the syntax \\FQDN\ShareName to specify the logging path, but you might run into issues if you try to use the syntax \\IPAddress\ShareName to specify the path. The \\IPAddress\ShareName syntax can cause an authentication issue that prevents the log files from being created. The following is an example of an error generated when trying to use an IP Address when remote logging is enabled:
>
> ```
> Microsoft-Windows-HttpService , LogFileCreateFailed ,
> 49,          0,          16,          2,          59,          9,
> 0x0000000000000800, 0x00000004, 0x000005AC,                     0,
>            ,                     ,          {00000000-0000-0000-0000-
> 000000000000},                     ,
> 128277049412643098,          220,          0, 0xC0000022,
> "ResponseLogging ", "Site ", "W3C ",
> "\dosdevices\UNC\192.168.0.125\UncLogFiles\W3SVC1\u_ex070630.log",
>        0
> ```

4. Click Apply.

5. Browse a Web page in your site.

6. Open a command prompt by using elevated credentials and type **netsh http flush logbuffer**. If this is the first time entries have been logged, HTTP.sys will create the folder and a log file. Open the log file in Notepad to confirm your example entries have been logged.

![Screenshot of Internet Information Services (IIS) Manager showing the Logging feature for the Default Web Site]

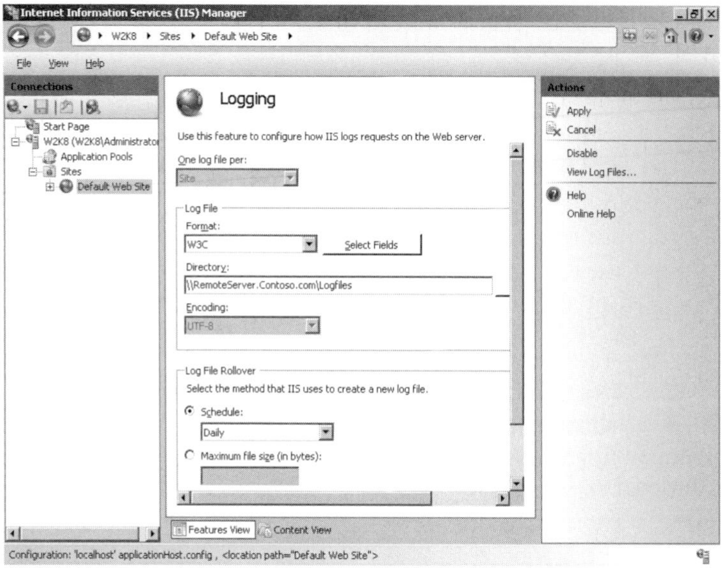

Figure 15-2 Configuring the Default Web Site to enable remote logging.

Setting Up Remote Logging by Using Appcmd

You can also use Appcmd to update the logfile directory for a specific Web site. The syntax for configuring UNC remote logging using Appcmd is shown here. (The line has been split to fit it on the printed page.)

```
//Appcmd to set the log directory path for Default Web Site
Appcmd set sites "Default Web Site"
    -logFile.directory:\\RemoteServerCMD.Contoso.com\LogFiles
```

Note To automate configuring remote logging, you could put this example into a script to which you can pass variables.

Executing this command results in the following output:

```
SITE object "Default Web Site" changed
```

Remote Logging Using the FTP 7.0 Publishing Service

The FTP 7.0 Publishing Service is an out-of-band add-on that is meant to replace the built-in FTP service. The FTP 7.0 Publishing Service supports logs stored on a remote computer, which can enhance your ability to track down security breaches. Imagine a particular machine is compromised, but you have your logs stored on a remote system. When the infiltrator tries to cover her tracks by deleting the local log files, those log files will be unavailable because they are stored on a remote share. If your remote share uses DFS, the log files can even be replicated to multiple locations. Remote logging with replication can help in your forensic efforts. To configure the FTP logs to be stored on a remote server, you just have to configure your remote server that houses your logs files the same as you would configure a Web server. Figure 15-3 shows the FTP 7.0 Publishing Service configured to log remotely.

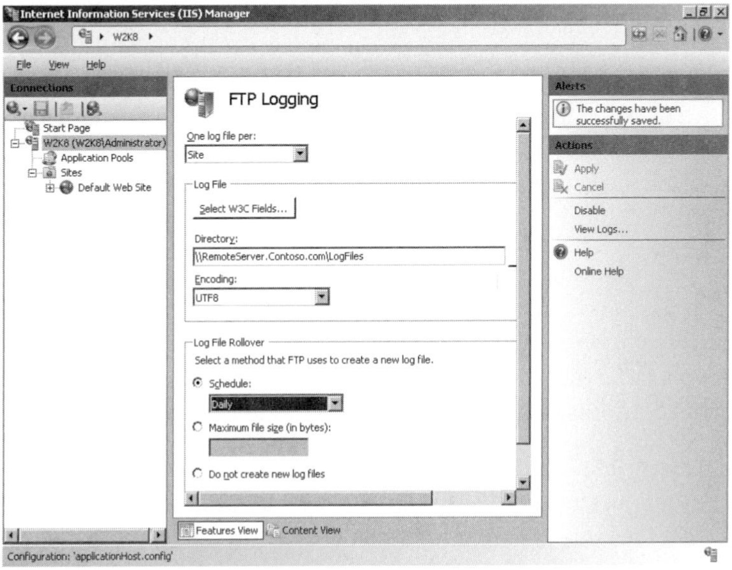

Figure 15-3   FTP 7.0 Publishing Service configured to store log files on a remote computer.

Custom Logging

The modular architecture of IIS 7.0 enables you to implement your own logging modules or extend or replace existing logging options. Your module can be implemented directly into the request pipeline. Your logging module can be either a native module or a module written using managed code. You can use any .NET language such as C# or Microsoft Visual Basic.NET.

Direct from the Source
How to Implement a SQL Logging Module

The credit for this demo goes to Carlos Aguilar Mares and Andrew Lin. It shows off something you can do only with IIS 7.0 and the Integrated Pipeline. You'll want to prepare for this demo by doing the following:

■ Download and install Visual Studio Web Developer Express.

■ Download and install SQL Server Express (as part of the previous install).

■ Download and install the SQL Server Management Studio Express.

> **Note**   Complete details for this demo are included on the companion media in the "Implement a SQL Logging module-details.doc" file and can also be found at *http://blogs.iis.net/bills/archive/2007/05/01/building-an-iis7-sql-logging-module-with-net.aspx.*

Make sure you're running Windows Vista or Windows Server 2008 with IIS 7.0 installed (including ASP.NET or at least .NET extensibility).

To start, build a simple module with a hard-coded connection string. Create the database using SQL Server Management Studio (a script named sqlLogging_CreateDB.sql is included on the companion media). When the database has been created, create a module to connect to it. Create an App_Code directory in your Web site/application and drop in your first sqlLoggingModule.cs code (also included on the companion media).

Before you can use it, you'll need to register it as a module with IIS. Go to the modules feature for this site/application and click Add Managed Module. Request a page from your site and look in the table to see the request logged. It should "just work" if all is well with the world.

Now add configuration extensibility. To do this, you'll want to create a new sqlLogging_schema.xml file (included on the companion media) and drop it in the \windows\system32\inetsrv\config\schema directory. After you've done that, you'll need to register it in the \windows\system32\inetsrv\config\ApplicationHost.config file. Add the following section under sectionGroup name=system.webServer:

```
<sectionGroup name="system.webServer">
        <section name="sqlLogging" overrideModeDefault="Allow" />
```

You'll want to make a few changes to your module. First, you need to remove that horrible hard-coded connection string and add it to your Web.config. Simply edit Web.config and add it as follows, replacing *billsiis7demo* with your machine name:

```
<sqlLogging connectionString="server=billsiis7demo\sqlexpress;database=MIX;
uid=sa;pwd=sa" />
```

Now it's time to fix your module. First, replace the hard-coded connection string with a GetConnectionString(httpContext) method. It looks like this:

```
private string GetConnectionString(HttpContext httpContext)
{
  ConfigurationSection section = WebConfigurationManager.GetSection("system.webServer/
sqlLogging");
  return (string)section["connectionString"];
}
```

Don't forget to add using Microsoft.Web.Administration in your .cs file (you might need to add a reference to \windows\system32\inetsrv\Microsoft.Web.Administration.dll first). Not only can you use Microsoft.Web.Administration to read/write to your new configuration section—just like GetConnectionString(httpContext) does above—but you also can use Appcmd.exe (our command line tool) and VB/JScript using COM.

And there you have it! A SQL logging module that was built using .NET with 66 lines of code and an IIS 7.0 configuration section that is scriptable, programmatically accessible, and usable from the command line.

Bill Staples

Microsoft Product Unit Manager

Carlos Aguilar Mares

Microsoft Senior Development Lead

Configuring IIS Logging

IIS 7.0 provides multiple ways to configure and administer your Web server, and that includes configuring your log settings. This section covers how to use the built-in graphical user interface (GUI) as well as command line tools to configure log settings. You'll learn how to use the IIS Manager, Appcmd, and Windows PowerShell.

IIS Manager

The IIS Manager is a completely rewritten tool that administrators can use to manage their Web servers. The intuitive interface enables you to quickly review and adjust all settings, including those that apply to log files. To access the Logging section of the IIS Manager, follow this procedure:

1. Go to Administrative Tools > Internet Information Services (IIS) and select the server name. Figure 15-4 shows the icon for the global Logging section when it is selected.

Figure 15-4   The icon for the global Logging section selected in the IIS Manager.

2. Double-click the Logging icon to view the interface through which you can administer logging settings for the server.

The default settings are shown in Figure 15-5. Because the server node selected is in the tree in the left pane, these settings are inherited by all Web sites configured on the server.

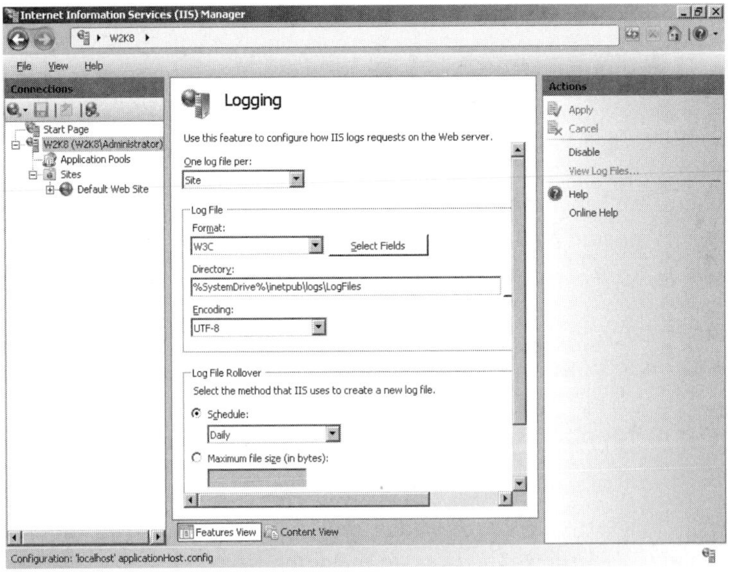

Figure 15-5   Default global settings.

3. To make changes, select the appropriate drop-down box and select the option you want. For example, to change the server from site-level logging (creating one log file per site) to server-level logging (creating one log file per server), select Server in the One Log File Per drop-down list, as shown in Figure 15-6.

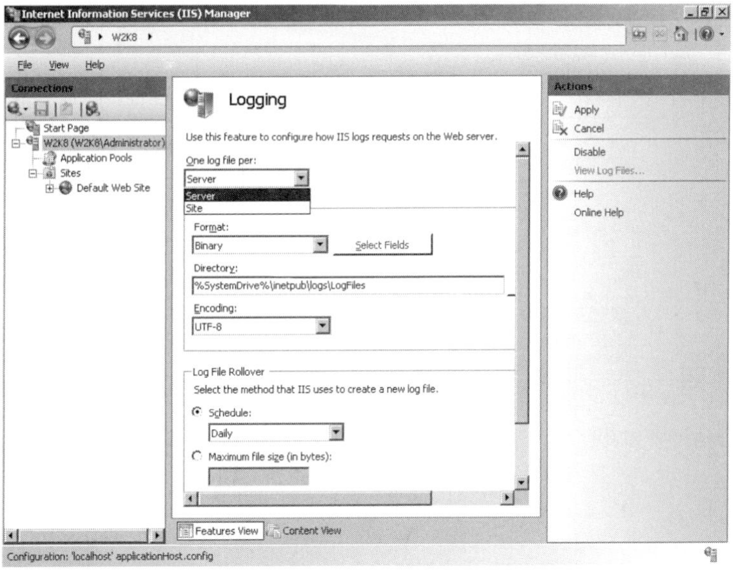

Figure 15-6   Go to the IIS Manager to change logging from site-level logging to server-level logging.

In IIS 6.0, you need to write a script to change the *CentralW3CLoggingEnabled* metabase property. This is one example of how the IIS Manager is more powerful and easier to use than it was in the previous version of IIS. (For more information about this metabase property, go to *http://technet.microsoft.com* and search for "CentralW3CLoggingEnabled.")

Note   When you configure IIS 7.0 to use server-level logging, the Binary format is selected by default. To have your server-level log use W3C extended logging, simply select W3C in the Format drop-down list.

IIS 7.0 also enables you to make changes on individual Web sites. For example, you can click the Select Fields button to adjust which options are logged for a specific Web site, as shown in Figure 15-7. In this figure, the Bytes Sent (sc-bytes), Bytes Received (cs-bytes), Time Taken (time-taken), and Referer (cs(Referer)) options have been selected. You can also adjust the log Directory setting, the Log File Rollover setting, and the Use Local Time For File Naming And Rollover setting.

Figure 15-7   Clicking the Select Fields button lets you choose which options are logged for a given Web site.

Appcmd

The IIS Manager is a great tool for managing individual settings that use a GUI. Appcmd is a tool that is intended to perform all administrative functions from a command line. Appcmd replaces a variety of scripts and tools used in previous IIS versions.

All the logging settings you might need to adjust are located in three sections of application-Host.config: system.applicationHost/log, system.applicationHost/sites, and system.web-Server/httpLogging.

The previous example uses IIS Manager to configure server-level logging. To use Appcmd to perform this same operation, follow this procedure:

1. Open a command prompt and navigate to the *%SystemRoot%*\System32\inetsrv folder where Appcmd is deployed.

> **Note**   If you add this path to your global *PATH* environment variable, you can execute Appcmd from any folder location.

2. Execute the following command from the command prompt to list the current settings:

```
Appcmd list config -section:log
```

Following are the default settings:

```
<system.applicationHost>
  <log>
    <centralBinaryLogFile enabled="true"
directory="%SystemDrive%\inetpub\logs\LogFiles" />
    <centralW3CLogFile enabled="true"
directory="%SystemDrive%\inetpub\logs\LogFiles" />
  </log>
</system.applicationHost>
```

This will display the ApplicationHost.config section where the centralLogFileMode settings are stored.

3. Next execute the following command to configure server-level logging:

```
Appcmd set config -section:log -centralLogFileMode:CentralW3C
```

4. After you have executed the command in step 3, execute the following command to list the current settings and verify the settings have been changed:

```
Appcmd list config -section:log
```

The result, showing that the centralLogFileMode has changed to CentralW3C, should look like the following. (Some lines have been split to fit on the printed page.)

```
C:\Windows\System32\inetsrv>Appcmd list config -section:log
<system.applicationHost>
  <log centralLogFileMode="CentralW3C">
    <centralBinaryLogFile enabled="true"
        directory="%SystemDrive%\inetpub\logs\LogFiles" />
    <centralW3CLogFile enabled="true"
        directory="%SystemDrive%\inetpub\logs\LogFiles" />
  </log>
</system.applicationHost>

C:\Windows\System32\inetsrv>
```

Notice the *log centralLogFileMode="CentralW3C"* setting. Before executing the *Appcmd set config* command, there was no value listed, because the Site option is the default setting as defined in the schema.

The section titled "Advanced Appcmd Details" later in this chapter explains how to find out which options can be set.

As another example, assuming you have already set the global *Server* attribute, if you want to adjust the global localTimeRollover setting, use this command:

```
Appcmd set config -section:log -centralW3CLogFile.localTimeRollover:True
```

The result should look like this:

```
Applied configuration changes to section "system.applicationHost/log" for "MACHINE/WEBROOT/
APPHOST" at configuration commit path "MACHINE/WEBROOT/APPHOST"
```

Or, for example, you might want to change the siteDefaults log format to NCSA so that all new sites will inherit this setting unless otherwise configured on a specific site. You can adjust the global Format option to NCSA with this command:

```
Appcmd set config -section:sites -siteDefaults.logFile.logFormat:NCSA
```

Here's the result:

```
Applied configuration changes to section "system.applicationHost/sites" for "MACHINE/
WEBROOT/APPHOST" at configuration commit path "MACHINE/WEBROOT/APPHOST"
```

Appcmd enables you to quickly use the command line to make changes to your IIS log settings. You can create a set of scripts that use Appcmd to replace the repetitive changes typically required when using the IIS Manager GUI. Such scripts can help streamline and automate your server configuration and deployment.

Appcmd Required for Windows Vista

By default, Windows Vista does not provide a GUI to manage your log files. You need to use Appcmd to make adjustments to your log file settings. Microsoft has provided an out-of-band add-on for IIS 7.0 on Windows Vista. To obtain the Vista logging UI add-on, go to *http://www.iis.net/go/1328*.

Advanced Appcmd Details

Appcmd enables you to perform many advanced operations. Here are some tips for using Appcmd to configure advanced properties.

When you configure the *centralLogFileMode* attribute, the only way to view which properties (also known as enums) are available is to open the IIS_Schema.xml file. It's not too much trouble to do this once in a while, but it's more efficient to use Appcmd to list the available properties. For example, the following command lists all the properties that can be set in the *system.applicationHost/log* section:

```
//List all properties available the system.applicationHost/log section
Appcmd set config -section:log -?
```

The output looks like this:

```
ERROR ( message:-logInUTF8
-centralLogFileMode
-centralBinaryLogFile.enabled
-centralBinaryLogFile.directory
-centralBinaryLogFile.period
-centralBinaryLogFile.truncateSize
-centralBinaryLogFile.localTimeRollover
-centralW3CLogFile.enabled
```

```
-centralW3CLogFile.directory
-centralW3CLogFile.period
-centralW3CLogFile.truncateSize
-centralW3CLogFile.localTimeRollover
-centralW3CLogFile.logExtFileFlags
 )
```

To adjust a property value, use the following syntax. (You can adjust multiple attributes by putting a space between each property value.)

```
Appcmd set config -section:log -property1Name:Value -property2Name:Value
```

If you are not sure which values are available to set on a particular property, you can use the following command to find out the values. This example shows how to get all values that can be set for the *centralLogFileMode* property:

```
//Find out which values can be set.
Appcmd set config -section:log -centralLogFileMode -?
```

The resulting error message lists the valid values, in this case Site, CentralBinary, and CentralW3C:

```
ERROR ( message:Unknown attribute "centralLogFileMode"..
Reason: Enum must be one of Site, CentralBinary, CentralW3C. )
```

You can change the site's log settings. To list all the properties that are available as well as their syntax, type this command:

```
//List all properties available on the Sites section
Appcmd set config -section:sites -?
```

The output shows all properties related to the Sites section. The options starting with *-siteDefaults.logFile*, shown in the next lines of code in bold, enable you to adjust the defaults inherited by new sites. (Some lines have been split to fit on the printed page.)

```
C:\Windows\System32\inetsrv>Appcmd set config -section:sites -?
ERROR ( message:-siteDefaults.name
-siteDefaults.id
-siteDefaults.serverAutoStart
-siteDefaults.bindings.
    [protocol='string',bindingInformation='string'].protocol
-siteDefaults.bindings.
    [protocol='string',bindingInformation='string'].bindingInformation
-siteDefaults.limits.maxBandwidth
-siteDefaults.limits.maxConnections
-siteDefaults.limits.connectionTimeout
-siteDefaults.logFile.logExtFileFlags
-siteDefaults.logFile.customLogPluginClsid
-siteDefaults.logFile.logFormat
-siteDefaults.logFile.directory
-siteDefaults.logFile.period
-siteDefaults.logFile.truncateSize
```

```
-siteDefaults.logFile.localTimeRollover
-siteDefaults.logFile.enabled
-siteDefaults.traceFailedRequestsLogging.enabled
-siteDefaults.traceFailedRequestsLogging.directory
-siteDefaults.traceFailedRequestsLogging.maxLogFiles
-siteDefaults.traceFailedRequestsLogging.maxLogFileSizeKB
-siteDefaults.traceFailedRequestsLogging.customActionsEnabled
-applicationDefaults.path
-applicationDefaults.applicationPool
-applicationDefaults.enabledProtocols
-virtualDirectoryDefaults.path
-virtualDirectoryDefaults.physicalPath
-virtualDirectoryDefaults.userName
-virtualDirectoryDefaults.password
-virtualDirectoryDefaults.logonMethod
-virtualDirectoryDefaults.allowSubDirConfig
-[name='string',id='unknown'].name
-[name='string',id='unknown'].id
-[name='string',id='unknown'].serverAutoStart
-[name='string',id='unknown'].bindings.
    [protocol='string',bindingInformation='string'].protocol
-[name='string',id='unknown'].bindings.
    [protocol='string',bindingInformation='string'].bindingInformation
-[name='string',id='unknown'].limits.maxBandwidth
-[name='string',id='unknown'].limits.maxConnections
-[name='string',id='unknown'].limits.connectionTimeout
-[name='string',id='unknown'].logFile.logExtFileFlags
-[name='string',id='unknown'].logFile.customLogPluginClsid
-[name='string',id='unknown'].logFile.logFormat
-[name='string',id='unknown'].logFile.directory
-[name='string',id='unknown'].logFile.period
-[name='string',id='unknown'].logFile.truncateSize
-[name='string',id='unknown'].logFile.localTimeRollover
-[name='string',id='unknown'].logFile.enabled
-[name='string',id='unknown'].traceFailedRequestsLogging.enabled
-[name='string',id='unknown'].traceFailedRequestsLogging.directory
-[name='string',id='unknown'].traceFailedRequestsLogging.maxLogFiles
-[name='string',id='unknown'].traceFailedRequestsLogging.maxLogFileSizeKB
-[name='string',id='unknown'].
    traceFailedRequestsLogging.customActionsEnabled
-[name='string',id='unknown'].applicationDefaults.path
-[name='string',id='unknown'].applicationDefaults.applicationPool
-[name='string',id='unknown'].applicationDefaults.enabledProtocols
-[name='string',id='unknown'].virtualDirectoryDefaults.path
-[name='string',id='unknown'].virtualDirectoryDefaults.physicalPath
-[name='string',id='unknown'].virtualDirectoryDefaults.userName
-[name='string',id='unknown'].virtualDirectoryDefaults.password
-[name='string',id='unknown'].virtualDirectoryDefaults.logonMethod
-[name='string',id='unknown'].virtualDirectoryDefaults.allowSubDirConfig
-[name='string',id='unknown'].[path='string'].path
-[name='string',id='unknown'].[path='string'].applicationPool
-[name='string',id='unknown'].[path='string'].enabledProtocols
-[name='string',id='unknown'].[path='string'].virtualDirectoryDefaults.path
-[name='string',id='unknown'].[path='string'].
    virtualDirectoryDefaults.physicalPath
-[name='string',id='unknown'].[path='string'].
```

```
      virtualDirectoryDefaults.userName
-[name='string',id='unknown'].[path='string'].
      virtualDirectoryDefaults.password
-[name='string',id='unknown'].[path='string'].
      virtualDirectoryDefaults.logonMethod
-[name='string',id='unknown'].[path='string'].
      virtualDirectoryDefaults.allowSubDirConfig
-[name='string',id='unknown'].[path='string'].[path='string'].path
-[name='string',id='unknown'].[path='string'].[path='string'].physicalPath
-[name='string',id='unknown'].[path='string'].[path='string'].userName
-[name='string',id='unknown'].[path='string'].[path='string'].password
-[name='string',id='unknown'].[path='string'].[path='string'].logonMethod
-[name='string',id='unknown'].[path='string'].[path='string'].
      allowSubDirConfig
)
```

You can also adjust settings for specific Web sites by using the properties starting with
-[name='string',id='unknown'].logFile. You simply need to replace the *'unknown'* value with the
Web site name. Following is an example of how to adjust settings in a specific site. Notice that
the example for the Default Web Site contains double quotation marks. This is necessary to
handle spaces in the Web site name. Remember to change the name and ID when using the
example.

```
//Example how to set the logFile.directory property with a
//Site with spaces in the name.

C:\Windows\System32\inetsrv>Appcmd set config -section:sites
/[name='"Default Web Site"',id='1'].logFile.directory:c:\wwwlogs

//Example how to setup logFile.directory property with no spaces
//in the Site name.

C:\Windows\System32\inetsrv>Appcmd set config -section:sites
/[name='Contoso.com',id='2'].logFile.directory:c:\wwwlogs
```

You can also use Windows PowerShell 1.0 to administer your IIS 7.0 server. This section
shows a few examples of setting the Logfile directory value. In the following sample script,
you first load Microsoft.Web.Administration.dll into your Windows PowerShell session. Next,
you assign an instance of the *ServerManager* object to the *$sm* variable, which allows you to
query and set Logfile values. (In the following listing, some lines have been split so that they
fit on the printed page.)

```
//Load the dll into the Powershell session
[System.Reflection.Assembly]::LoadFrom
    ( "C:\windows\system32\inetsrv\Microsoft.Web.Administration.dll" )

//Load an instance of the Server Manager object into the $sm variable
$sm = new-object Microsoft.Web.Administration.ServerManager

//List Default Web Site LogFile Directory value.
$sm.Sites["Default Web Site"].LogFile.Directory
```

```
//List SiteDefaults LogFile Directory value.
$sm.SiteDefaults.LogFile.Directory

//Set Default Website LogFile Directory
$sm.Sites["Default Web Site"].LogFile.Directory =
    "\\RemoteServer.Contoso.com\Logfiles"
$sm.CommitChanges()

//Set SiteDefaults LogFile Directory
$sm.SiteDefaults.Logfile.Directory = "\\RemoteServer.Contoso.com\Logfiles"
$sm.CommitChanges()
```

Using Windows PowerShell to administer IIS 7.0 is covered in Chapter 7, "Using Command Line Tools." For information about building a cmdlet to administer many common functions in IIS 7.0, see the following Web site: *http://www.iis.net/go/1211.*

Immediately flushing log entries to disk is introduced in Windows Server 2008. The HTTP.sys service holds requests until they are periodically flushed to disk. When you are troubleshooting an immediate issue, you can use the following *netsh* command, which can be especially useful for troubleshooting HTTP.sys-related errors.

```
//Flush log entries to disk immediately
Netsh http flush logbuffer
```

HTTP.sys Logging

In IIS 6.0, the HTTP.sys process was introduced and took over logging duties that used to be handled by Inetinfo.exe. HTTP.sys introduced another log called HTTPERR log. The HTTPERR logs for Windows Server 2008 are located in the same location as for Windows Server 2003. The path is *%SystemRoot%\System32\LogFiles\HTTPERR*. This log records all errors that are not handed off to a valid worker process, typically responses to clients, connection time-outs, and orphaned requests. This additional information can help you troubleshoot HTTP-based errors, which are logged before the request reaches IIS.

Windows Vista and Windows Server 2008 introduce enhancements to the HTTP.sys logging process. You use ETW (Event Tracing for Windows) to obtain the enhanced information. Here are steps to start, capture, and display information from an ETW tracing session:

1. Open a command prompt (click Start, select Run, and then type **cmd.exe**).

2. Start the ETW trace session for HTTP.sys by using the following command:

    ```
    logman.exe start httptrace -p Microsoft-Windows-HttpService 0xFFFF -o
        httptrace.etl –ets
    ```

3. Reproduce or perform the steps or tests that need to be traced.

4. To stop the ETW trace session for HTTP.sys, use the following command:

    ```
    logman stop httptrace –ets
    ```

5. To convert the ETL file to a comma-separated file (CSV) file, use this command:

```
tracerpt httptrace.etl -of csv -o httptrace.csv /y
```

The CSV files can then be viewed in a text editor or spreadsheet application. This complete procedure is covered in a white paper available at *http://technet.microsoft.com*; search for "HTTP.sys Manageability in Windows Vista and Longhorn Server."

> **Note** The following site discusses the new networking features in Windows Vista and Windows Server 2008: *http//technet.microsoft.com/en-us/library/bb726965.aspx.*

Application Logging

Besides the standard IIS type logs, other items can be logged. Many of these options can be set with the IIS Manager or by using Appcmd.

Process Recycling Logging

In IIS 7.0, events are logged to the Windows event log when an application pool recycles. You can control eight configuration settings with each option listed in Table 15-1.

Table 15-1   Recycling Options Under Generate Recycle Event Log Entry

Option	Description	Default Setting
Application Pool Configuration Changed	Event is logged when the application pool recycles due to a change in its configuration	No
ISAPI Report Unhealthy	Event is logged because an ISAPI extension has reported itself as unhealthy	No
Manual Recycle	Event is logged when the application pool has been manually recycled	No
Private Memory Limit Exceeded	Event is logged when the application pool recycles after exceeding its private memory limit	Yes
Regular Time Interval	Event is logged when the application pool recycles on its scheduled interval	Yes
Request Limit Exceeded	Event is logged when the application pool recycles after exceeding its request limit	No
Specific Time	Event is logged when the application pool recycles at a scheduled time	No
Virtual Memory Limit Exceeded	Event is logged when the application pool recycles after exceeding its virtual memory limits	Yes

ASP

Classic ASP (Active Server Pages) is alive and well in IIS 7.0, and you can configure options for logging ASP errors under the ASP section in the IIS Manager. Use the following options to discover issues when migrating your Classic ASP applications to IIS 7.0.

- **Enable Log Error Requests**   Controls whether the Web server writes ASP errors to the application event log

- **Log Errors To The NT Log**   Specifies that ASP errors are recorded in the Windows event log

These options are available in IIS 6.0, but you have to use ADSUtil.vbs to enable them in the metabase. Now, in IIS 7.0, you can use the IIS Manager to enable these options.

ASP.NET

All ASP.NET 2.0 unhandled exceptions are written to the Application Event log. Along with application pool recycle events or other errors in the event logs, this can be very helpful in troubleshooting application errors. You can turn off ASP.NET logging by following the instructions in the Knowledge Base article at *http://support.microsoft.com/kb/911816*.

IIS Events

Other processes related to IIS also log to the Windows Event log. This includes the HTTP, IISAdmin, FTP Publishing Service, and W3SVC services. For a complete list of events, go to *http://technet.microsoft.com* and search for "IIS events reference."

Folder Compression Option

Log files are necessary to keep track of Web site statistics and trends, and Web developers and business people use them to ensure their Web sites continue to grow. One of the biggest challenges administrators face is how to retain and manage log files. By default, IIS rolls over log files once a day. Your log files can become quite large even if you use the default log file rollover setting.

Windows Server 2008 allows for folder compression to help save space. You can enable this option by using Windows Explorer. Figure 15-8 shows a folder with compression enabled. In this example, the size of the folder is 166 megabytes (MB), but the actual space the folder uses on the disk is only 43.1 MB. If your uncompressed log files take up several gigabytes (GB), you could save yourself a lot of disk space by using folder compression.

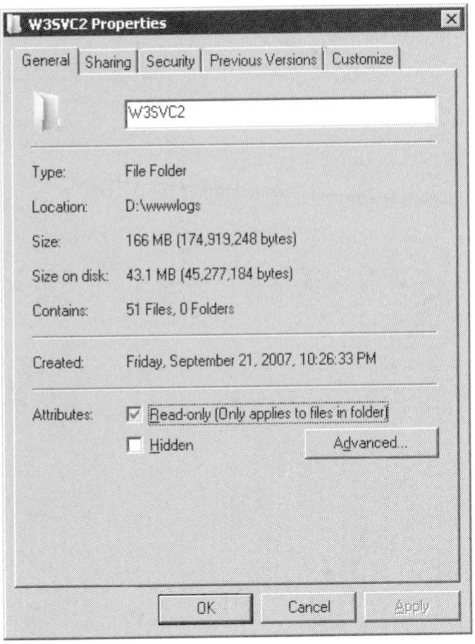

Figure 15-8 Folder compression enabled on the WWWLogs folder.

Because HTTP.sys buffers information written to the IIS log files, there will not be a perfor-mance hit if your log files are in a folder for which compression is enabled. Some people use third-party log compression products or free tools such as Gzip along with scripts to com-press their log files. Unless you have a tool that searches inside zip files, this is an acceptable method only if you rarely need to unzip and search your archived log files. If you have compression enabled, however, you can leave your files in their original, easily searchable state. At most, you'll need to implement some type of archival and deletion script by using your favorite script or third-party program.

Using the built-in compression feature provided by Windows Server 2008 can save you disk space and simplify how you retain your log files. For more information about managing log files, see Chapter 6, "Managing Log Files," in *Microsoft Log Parser Toolkit* by Gabriele Giuseppini and Mark Burnett (Syngress Publishing, Inc., 2006; *http://www.syngress.com/catalog/?pid=3110*), which discusses conversion, archival, and repudiation strategies.

Logging Analysis Using Log Parser

A chapter on logging would not be complete without mentioning Log Parser. This is one of the most useful tools for searching your logs. Teaching you Log Parser is beyond the scope of this book, but we'll give you some examples you can use in your environment. You can download Log Parser at *http://ww.iis.net/go/1287.*

> **Note**   Members of the Microsoft.com team are big fans of Log Parser. Take a look at this Web
> site for an article that discusses how they use Log Parser: *http://blogs.technet.com/mscom/*
> *archive/2005/10/19/412745.aspx.*

Here are three examples of using Log Parser to extract common information from your IIS
logs:

1. List the top 25 (most frequent) WebRequests:

    ```
    LogParser -i:iisw3c "SELECT TOP 25 cs-uri-stem,
        COUNT(*) AS HitCount INTO Results.csv FROM LOGFILENAME.LOG
        GROUP BY cs-uri-stem ORDER BY HitCount DESC" -o:csv
    ```

2. Show the 25 requests that take the longest to execute:

    ```
    //Change the date to fit your needs
    SELECT
    TOP 25
    CS-URI-STEM,
    TIME-TAKEN
    FROM LOGFILENAME.LOG
    WHERE DATE > '2007-03-26'
    ORDER BY TIME-TAKEN DESC
    ```

3. Select information between two dates and pipe results to a text file named Output.txt:

    ```
    SELECT
    DATE,
    TIME,
    CS-URI-STEM,
    SC-STATUS,
    COUNT(*) AS MaxTime
    INTO Output.txt
    FROM LOGFILENAME.LOG
    WHERE TO_TIME(time)
    BETWEEN
    TIMESTAMP('01/01 13:50:00', 'MM/dd hh:mm:ss') AND
        TIMESTAMP('01/01 18:30:00', 'MM/dd hh:mm:ss') AND SC-STATUS = 500
    GROUP BY
    CS-URI-STEM,
    DATE,
    TIME,
    SC-STATUS
    ORDER BY MaxTime DESC
    ```

If you are responsible for maintaining an IIS environment, take a look at Log Parser. You'll
want to make it one of your main tools when troubleshooting all kinds of issues. (For
more information about Log Parser, visit the community forums at *http://forums.iis.net/*
default.aspx?GroupID=51.)

Summary

IIS 7.0 takes the best features first introduced in Windows Server 2003 and builds on them. The modular architecture and Integrated Pipeline open up a lot of opportunities to enhance your application logging options. The IIS Manager exposes and simplifies how you manage your log settings. You can set your default logging settings to be on a per-site or per-server basis.

IIS 7.0 also introduces many tools for automating your log file configuration. You can use Appcmd or Windows PowerShell along with the *Microsoft.Web.Administration* namespace to configure or search for information. The new UTF-8 encoding helps standardize your logs.

IIS 7.0 exposes more data in logging than previous IIS versions. You can use the new tools provided by IIS 7.0 and Windows Server 2008 to browse the additional information as you track down and eliminate problems in your environment.

Additional Resources

These resources contain additional information and tools related to this chapter:

- IIS-related information at *http://www.iis.net.*

- Links to all tools mentioned in this chapter, including the Log Parser and FTP 7.0 Publishing Service in the Downloads section on *http://www.iis.net.*

- Notable tools by third-party vendors, some published by independent software vendors who develop IIS-related products, at *http://www.iis.net*, including IISLogs, for example, which offers two tools for managing log files and is available for download in the Administration section.

> **On the Disc**   More information about Log Parser and IISLogs is available on the companion media.

- Blogs, FORUMS, and TechCENTER at *http://www.iis.net.*

Chapter 16
Tracing and Troubleshooting

  On the Disc   Browse the CD for additional tools and resources.

Standard methods of debugging an application don't apply to most Internet client/server applications. Typically, you have little or no control over the Web browsers that visit the environments your Web server hosts. In fact, because of the nature of Internet applications, it can sometimes be difficult even to recognize when a problem exists.

Fortunately, you can apply several tools to analyze and resolve problems, and Microsoft Internet Information Services (IIS) 7.0 adds to the arsenal with Failed Request Tracing (FRT). You can use FRT along with the extensive logging capabilities of IIS 7.0 and a variety of other tools available with Microsoft Windows Server 2008 to understand and fix problems when they arise.

In the first part of this chapter, we'll explore how you can monitor your system when you suspect a problem, automatically raising flags and creating logs when failures occur. You'll find that FRT is a big improvement over debugging with Event Tracing for Windows (ETW), which can be cumbersome to install and configure, and difficult to use. An FRT log uses the XML format, so you can readily parse it with a custom tool. FRT also provides a built-in style sheet that makes the output easy to digest. FRT lets an administrator collect information on errors that occur for any and all clients—to receive the error information generated by the server, you don't have to be present at the client when the error occurs. Errors that are hard to reproduce but paradoxically occasionally recur can be caught in FRT's net.

The second part of this chapter will look at the tools and methodology for analyzing and resolving problems. Tools for troubleshooting an IIS 7.0 installation—such as ping, wfetch, and Process Monitor, range from basic command line utilities to comprehensive graphical user interface (GUI) applications. Yet each tool can provide important information as you step through the basic methodology for identifying the problem, isolating the problem, and analyzing the root cause.

The last section in this chapter will present some scenarios that administrators often find themselves troubleshooting. It will also present common problems you're likely to encounter and explain typical solutions for resolving them.

Tracing and Diagnosing Problems

FRT is a powerful diagnostic tool for examining failures in your Web server environment. How do you define a failure in an Internet application? This is more than just a rhetorical question, because FRT gives you the ability to outline your own parameters for what constitutes a failed request. You can define a failed request based on a specific HTTP error status code or range of codes, based on the time the server takes to respond to a request, based on the severity of an event, or based on any combination of these conditions. You can very precisely limit the content that you trace with a given FRT rule, and you can easily analyze the provided output at a quite granular level. The result is that you can often pinpoint the components in your application that are causing problems, tracing down into individual modules.

The first step in using FRT is to install and configure it, tasks that you can accomplish in several different ways. You can use graphical user interface (GUI) tools, command line tools, scripts, and direct modification of configuration files.

Installing the Failed Request Tracing Module

Failed Request Tracing is an optional component in the IIS 7.0 modular architecture. When installing IIS 7.0, make sure you install the Tracing role service in the Health And Diagnostics category, as shown in Figure 16-1. Refer to Chapter 5, "Installing IIS 7.0," for more information about installing IIS 7.0. To effectively troubleshoot problems, you will also want to install appropriate logging modules. See Chapter 15, "Logging," for information about Hypertext Transfer Protocol (HTTP) logging, custom logging, and other logging tools.

To check that you have the Tracing module installed, in IIS Manager, select the server in the tree control and double-click Modules. You should see a FailedRequestTracingModule entry in the resulting list.

> **Note**   You can launch IIS Manager from the Administrative Tools program group. If you prefer, from the Run text box, type **inetmgr**.

Alternatively, you can confirm the Tracing module is installed by verifying the following line is present in the *<modules>* section of the applicationHost.config file.

```
<add name="FailedRequestsTracingModule" />
```

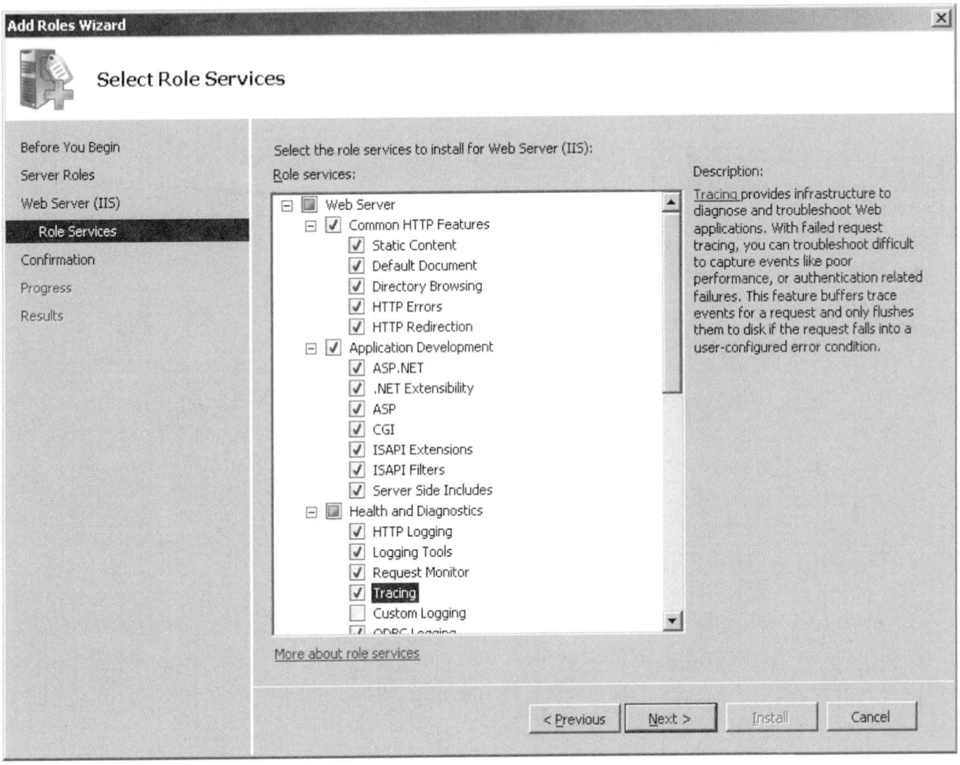

Figure 16-1   Installing the Tracing role service when adding the Web Server (IIS) role.

Enabling and Configuring FRT

To turn on tracing with FRT, you must enable FRT for each Web site you want to monitor and configure the FRT rules for the Web site or particular URL you'd like to trace. (Note that you must enable/disable FRT at the site level, but you can configure the failure definitions on *any* URL within that site. Similarly, if you don't have FRT enabled for a site, there's nothing preventing you from creating failure definitions—they just won't execute until you turn FRT on at the site level.) To enable FRT for a Web site, in IIS Manager, select the site you want to monitor in the tree. In the Actions pane on the right side of IIS Manager, click Failed Request Tracing. In the Edit Web Site Failed Request Tracing Settings dialog box, select the Enable check box, as shown in Figure 16-2. For each Web site, you can specify an alternate location for the site's FRT log files. (By default, the log files are collected in the *%SystemDrive%* Inetpub\Logs\FailedReqLogFiles folder. Whenever possible, you should specify a location other than on the system drive.) You can also configure the maximum number of log files to keep, which is important because FRT will create one log file per failure. If there are a lot of failures, the Maximum Number Of Trace Files option limits the number of failures retained on the file system.

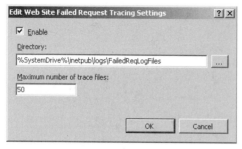

Figure 16-2   Enabling FRT for a Web site.

You can delegate FRT settings to allow application developers who are not server administrators to use FRT within their own applications. See the section titled "Troubleshooting UNC Access Errors" later in this chapter for more information about delegating FRT settings (but note that you can delegate FRT settings regardless of whether you or your content is local or remote).

Tracing a Specific Error Code

As an example, imagine you need to troubleshoot problems occurring with security access to a Web site. To configure FRT so that you can thoroughly examine all the system responses when a client receives a 401.3 Access Is Denied error code, perform the following procedure:

1.   In IIS Manager, select the Web site for which you want to configure tracing in the tree.

2.   Double-click Failed Request Tracing Rules.

> **Note**   Make sure the Features View option is selected at the bottom of the center pane.

3.   In the Actions pane, click the Add link, as shown here.

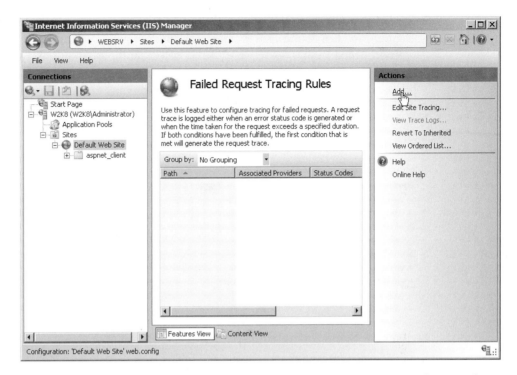

4. In the Specify Content To Trace page of the Add Failed Request Tracing Rule Wizard,
    you can specify the type of content you want to trace. For this procedure, specify
    All Content, as shown here, and click Next.

5. The Define Trace Conditions page lets you specify what you consider to be a failed request. You can define a failed request as any combination of returned status codes, response time, or event severity. If you do define multiple conditions, the first one encountered will trigger the log. (See the sidebar later in this chapter titled "Direct from the Source: The Details Behind FRT Trigger Conditions" for more information about combining failure conditions.) To define a failed request as a request that returns an Access Is Denied error code, type **401.3** in the Status Code(s) text box, as shown here, and click Next. (Note that in general, if you aren't sure of the exact error that is occurring, you typically would not specify the substatus code.)

6. In the Select Trace Providers page, you tell IIS 7.0 what you want to trace when a request fails, as well as the level of detail to include in the trace. As shown in the following image, deselect all check boxes in the Providers list except the WWW Server provider; select Verbose in the Verbosity drop-down list; in the Areas list, clear all check boxes except Authentication, Security, RequestNotifications, and Module. (You must scroll down to see the Module check box.) Refer to Table 16-1 for information about the areas you can specify for the WWW Server provider. Click Finish to add the rule for the Web site.

Table 16-1 Trace Areas for the WWW Server Provider

Area	Description
Authentication	Traces authentication-related events
Security	Traces security-related events, including authorization and access control list (ACL) checks that IIS performs on files and other resources
Filter	Traces filter events as a request goes into and comes out of various Internet Server Application Programming Interface (ISAPI) filters configured for the URL being traced
StaticFile	Traces static file events, including whether or not the file was accessed from cache
CGI	Traces events generated by the Common Gateway Interface (CGI) module, including FastCGI requests
Compression	Traces events raised as they relate to the compressing of responses and serving compressed responses
Cache	Traces cache operations for a request
RequestNotifications	Traces all request pipeline notifications to modules
Module	Traces events that are logged when each module begins and each module ends processing a request notification for an event

To test your FRT settings and generate an FRT trace for the example set up in the preceding steps, you can simply restrict security permissions for a resource on the Web site and then try to browse that resource using Microsoft Internet Explorer. The browser will report a 401.3 error, as shown in Figure 16-3, and FRT will generate a trace log.

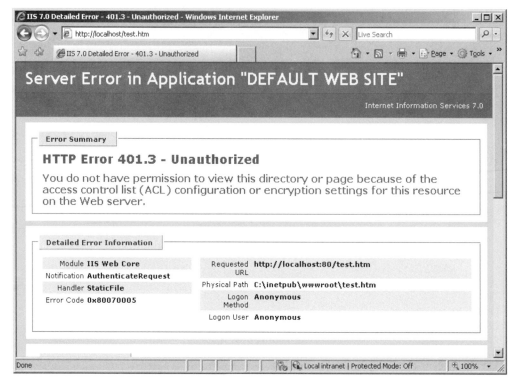

Figure 16-3   A 401.3 error in Internet Explorer.

Direct from the Source: The Details Behind FRT Trigger Conditions

Failure Request Tracing for IIS 7.0 can trigger failures on three key conditions: Status/Substatus codes, Time Taken, and Event Verbosity. One thing to remember is that the trigger overall is a logical OR of all the failure conditions defined. If you define all three conditions, say *statusCodes="400-599", timeTaken="00:00:10",* and *verbosity="Error",* the worker process will flush the trace log for the failed request upon reaching the *first* of those conditions. If your request eventually errors out with an HTTP status code of 500, but it takes 30 seconds to do that, you'll actually trigger on the *timeTaken* value. The attribute *<failedRequest failureReason="<reason>">* in the trace log will tell you exactly what failure condition triggered the flush.

The events that make it into the trace log are those that are raised *up to the point of the failure.* What this means is that only status/substatus code failure conditions *(failureReason="STATUS_CODE")* will capture the *entire* request from start to end. For *timeTaken* triggers, you'll see all the events received *up to the time limit.* In the example from the previous paragraph, a 10-second failure condition will result in IIS capturing the events up to that 10-second limit, and no more. The same thing goes for verbosity triggers—when we receive the first event whose verbosity is equal to or more severe than the trigger condition, we'll flush all events received up to that point (including the trigger event).

So let's say your trigger condition wants to flush for Foobar.aspx with verbosity level set to WARNING. Because verbosity levels that the server reports are inclusive of the lesser error levels, IIS will flush the log for Foobar.aspx when it receives the *first* trace event for a request to that URL whose verbosity level is WARNING, ERROR, or CRITICAL ERROR. Or if the failure condition's verbosity level is set to ERROR, IIS will flush upon receiving the first ERROR or CRITICAL ERROR trace event.

The goal here is to give you a flexible means of defining failure conditions and flush when a certain condition is reached. Status code and time taken are currently used most often, but verbosity is also helpful when you want to capture application failures that result in customized 200 OKs to the client that say "Sorry, cannot connect to product database." Put an ERROR trace event in your code and configure the verbosity failure condition to capture these logs to help diagnose such failures!

Eric Deily

Senior Program Manager Lead

Configuring FRT by Using Appcmd

You can also create FRT rules by using command line utilities such as Appcmd, Windows PowerShell, and Windows Management Instrumentation (WMI). The Appcmd syntax is as follows.

```
%systemroot%\system32\inetsrv\AppCmd configure trace "URL" /enable [/path:path]
[/statuscodes:code][/timeTaken:timeSpan] [/areas:areas] [/verbosity:detailLevel]
```

To delete an FRT rule, you can use the following Appcmd syntax.

```
%systemroot%\system32\inetsrv\AppCmd configure trace "URL" /disable [/path:path]
```

Don't forget that for the rules to take effect, the Web site must have FRT enabled. You can do this in IIS Manager as described earlier in this chapter, or use Appcmd as follows, where *WebSiteName* is the name of the Web site. Similarly, use /disablesite to disable FRT for a Web site.

```
%systemroot%\system32\inetsrv\AppCmd configure trace "WebSiteName" /enablesite
```

The parameters to these commands are explained in Table 16-2.

Table 16-2   Parameters for Appcmd to Configure FRT

Parameter	Description
URL	The URL that you want to trace.
path	The type of content you want to trace. Must be *, *.aspx, *.asp, or custom. If omitted, uses "*" by default.
statuscodes	The status code that you want to trace. If omitted, uses "500,400,401,403" by default.
timeTaken	A duration in seconds for response times beyond which a request is considered to have failed. If omitted, 1 minute is the default.
areas	The list of providers and subareas that you want to enable for the trace rule. This is based on the providers that are registered in the configuration—by default, it can contain the ASP, ASPNET, ISAPI, or WWW Server providers. If ASP.NET is installed, you can further specify Infrastructure, Module, Page, or AppServices. If WWW Server, you can further specify Authentication, Security, Filter, StaticFile, CGI, Compression, Cache, RequestNotifications, IISGeneral, or All. If not specified, traces all registered providers and their subareas.
verbosity	The level of detail you want IIS 7.0 to report. Must be General, Critical Errors, Errors, Warnings, Information, or Verbose. If not specified, Verbose is used as the default.

Reading the FRT Logs

To view a log generated by FRT, use Windows Explorer to browse to the FRT log file location and open the W3SVC*n* folder, where *n* is the site ID. Each event is logged in an individual XML file. The XML files use a style sheet named Freb.xsl that formats the XML log file, making it much easier to read and to navigate through. Simply double-click the Frxxxxxx.xml file you want to view. You'll see a summary page like the one shown in Figure 16-4.

> **Caution**   By default, you will not be able to view FRT log files on Windows Server 2008 because of the Internet Explorer enhanced security configuration (ESC). You might be prompted to add about:internet to the list of trusted sites. If after doing so you still are unable to view the log file on Windows Server 2008, you need to disable ESC in Server Manager. Disabling ESC weakens server security in regards to viewing Web-based content. Therefore, it's better to view the FRT log files on a client machine. Otherwise, immediately re-enable ESC when you have finished viewing the log files.

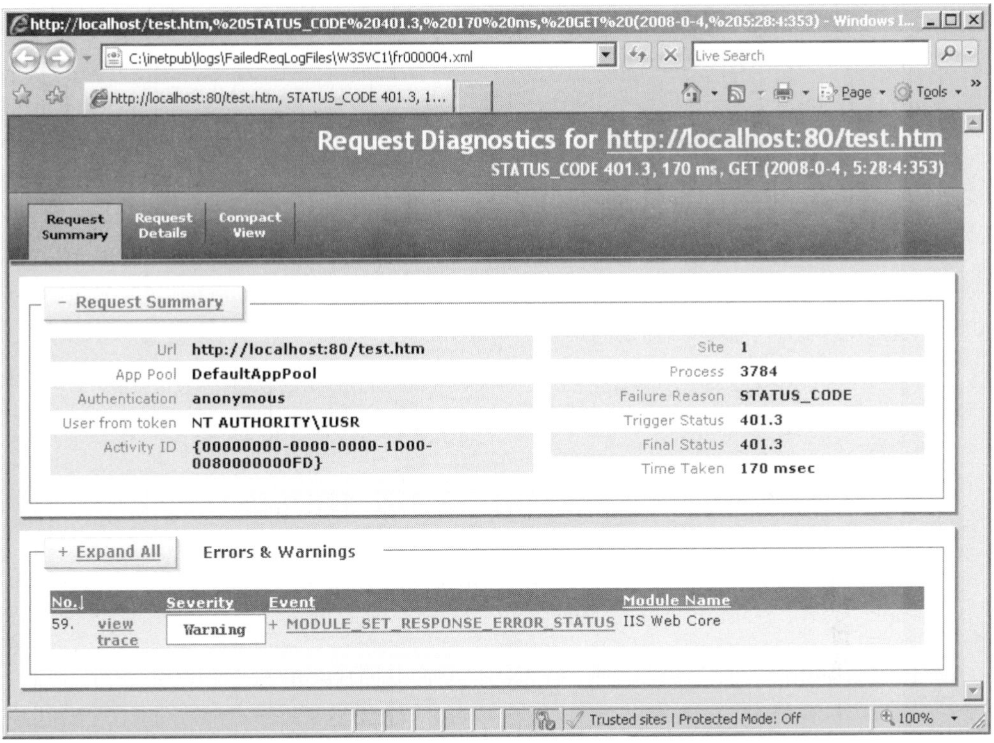

Figure 16-4   An FRT log file summary page.

Direct from the Source: Where Are My FRT Log Files?

So you've configured FRT, but you cannot find your log files. Now you've got to trouble-shoot the troubleshooting feature, eh? Let's start with the basics:

1. Make sure that you've *enabled* FRT at the site level. If you are managing a site but are not administering the IIS server, remember that although you can define failure conditions and what to trace in your web.config files, you still need to have the IIS administrator enable FRT for your site. In IIS Manager, click on the Web site in question and in the Actions pane, select Failed Request Tracing in the Configure section. This will bring up a dialog box for enabling FRT as well as for setting the directory to log to and the maximum number of files.

2. Make sure the worker process identity has FULL CONTROL access to the directory in question. This is because the worker process writes out the log files under its own identity, creates the W3SVC*n* directory (where *n* is your site ID), and deletes old files.

> **3.** Check the Event Viewer\Windows Logs\Application event log for events from the Microsoft-Windows-IIS-W3SVC-WP source. The most common errors are typically going to be permissions errors. Other possible errors can include:
>
> ❑ **Bad configuration**   The event will indicate what aspect of the configuration is incorrect, and this aspect will need to be fixed before that failure condition will be triggered.
>
> ❑ **FileSystem is full**   We're writing log files, and XML files at that. Make sure there's space on the volume for writing the log. If you hit this error on the system drive, though, problems with FRT are probably not the biggest of your worries!
>
> This should help you figure out why you're not getting FRT log files.
>
> *Eric Deily*
>
> *Senior Program Manager Lead*

If you select the Request Details tab at the top of the page, you can choose from among several formats for examining the details:

- **Complete Request Trace**   Shows each step in the trace, event by event.

- **Filter Notifications**   Shows all events generated by filters in the trace, enabling you to see each ISAPI filter that your request went through, the time it spent in the filter, and any possible changes to the request or response (such as the addition or removal of headers) that the filter made.

- **Module Notifications**   Shows each module that the request went through (in order), including the notification for which the request went through the module as well as the time it spent in the module.

- **Performance View**   Shows time spent in subactivities (such as authentication or going through ISAPI filters) and is designed to help you find where your request is spending most of its time.

- **Authentication Authorization**   Shows events related to authentication and authorization in the trace.

- **ASP.NET Page Traces**   Shows events in the trace raised through *Trace.Write()* and *Trace.Warn()* calls. When page tracing is enabled on your ASPX page, it will also capture the internally raised events for each ASP.NET page event.

- **Custom Module Traces**   Shows events generated by managed modules using the System.Diagnostics API (via *System.Diagnostics.TraceSource()* calls).

You can click the plus sign (+) next to any event to expand the event's details. Figure 16-5 shows a section of the Complete Trace view, indicating that the user was successfully authenticated before IIS set the error status. This indicates a problem with permissions, rather than authentication, which is exactly how we set up the scenario (refer back to Figure 16-3). Notice the events are nested and that the trace reports a duration in milliseconds for each step in the trace.

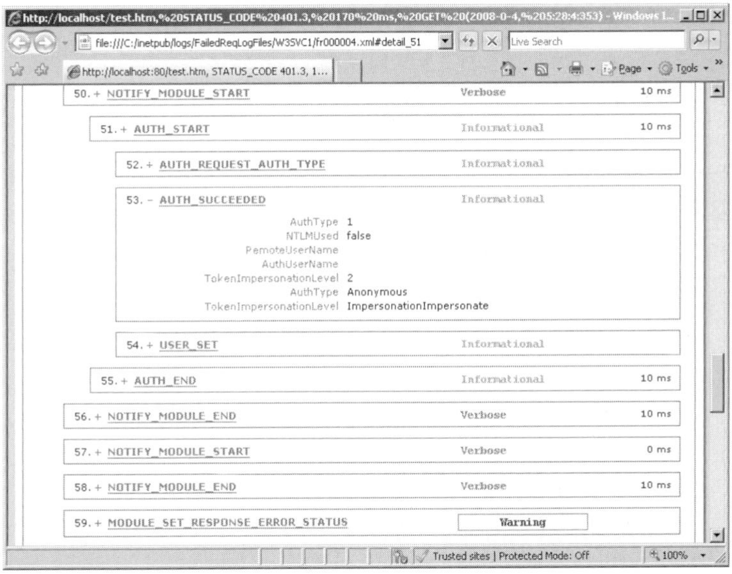

Figure 16-5   A portion of an FRT log file Request Details page.

If you select the Compact View tab at the top of the page, you can easily scroll through the full details for all events, as shown in Figure 16-6.

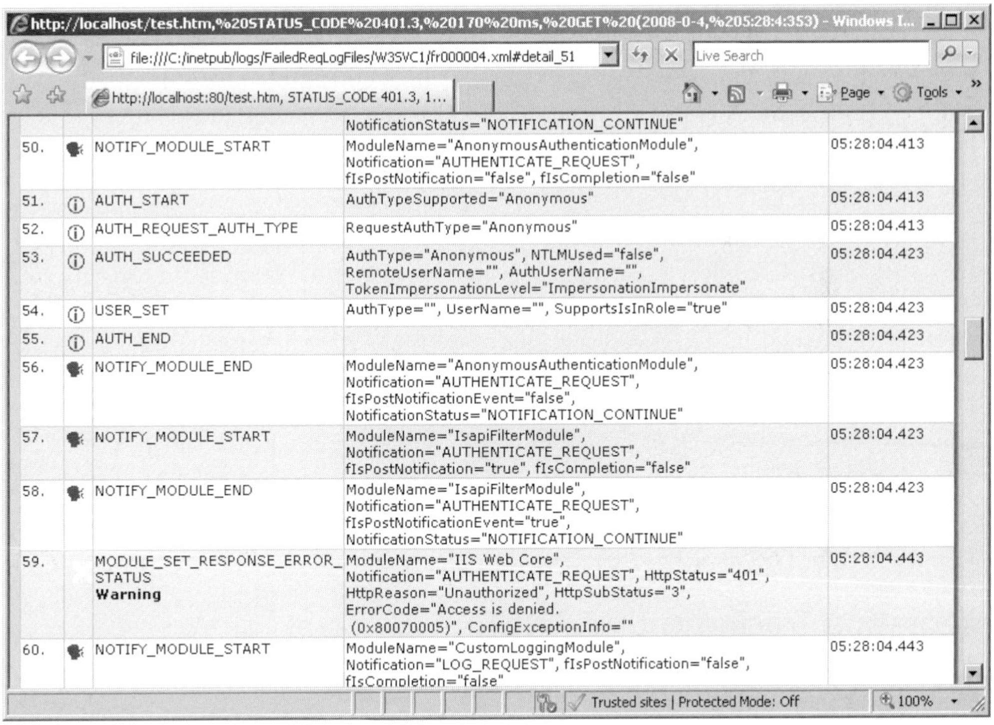

Figure 16-6   An FRT log file Compact View page.

You can use the FRT trace logs to pinpoint the source of problems. For example, if you are troubleshooting a request that has a long response time, select Performance View on the Request Details tab to quickly find which module (or modules) or ISAPI filters in the request pipeline might be responsible for the delay.

Direct from the Source: FRT Provides Context While Zeroing in on Your Target

One of my favorite features in IIS 7.0 is something we originally called FREB, which stood for Failed Request Event Buffering. It now bears the friendlier name Failed Request Tracing (FRT), but folks around here still sometimes call it FREB. FRT enables you to configure IIS to "watch for" certain error conditions and provide you detailed trace information about the request. This makes it much easier to diagnose failures than in past versions of IIS, especially those hard-to-reproduce issues that seem to only happen at 3 A.M. when you should be sleeping. IIS will not only log all of the IIS trace events we've sprinkled through our code but also ASP.NET trace events and even your own page trace events! It is one powerful feature.

Do you see requests slow down over time, or do they hang unfinished? Simply configure FRT to watch for requests that exceed a given time-out threshold, and you'll get detailed information on everything that happened during the request up to the time limit. Using that information, you should be better able to pinpoint where the hang-up is happening.

Are you seeing random 401, 404, or Server 500 errors? IIS is infamous for returning these standard error messages for lots of different reasons. With IIS 7.0, detailed errors provide much more information to you if you're on the localhost, but if you want to know which component returned the error, or what happened in sequence before the error, you have to turn to FRT.

When looking at an FRT trace log, by default you see the Request Summary tab, which shows basic information about the request, as well as all error and warning events that were found in the trace log. This is a great way to zero in on which event might have caused your error. By clicking View Trace, you can actually zoom in on the entire hierarchy of events that occurred—in order—during the request and see the event you clicked on in context.

Bill Staples

IIS Product Unit Manager

Integrating Tracing and ASP.NET

In IIS 7.0, you can use FRT to collect trace output from ASP.NET applications.

Capturing ASP.NET Trace Output with FRT

Using FRT with ASP.NET trace output provides several advantages over traditional methods of collecting and examining ASP.NET trace output. The FRT framework enables you to eliminate traces for successful requests and to view the traces in the context of trace information from other system components. Of course, FRT works in addition to traditional methods, so you can still view ASP.NET trace output when browsing the application locally on the server or by enabling Application Tracing.

Instrumenting ASP.NET Applications for Tracing

To create developer-generated trace output for debugging an ASP.NET application, simply add *Trace.Warn()* and *Trace.Write()* calls to an ASP.NET page to write out the data you want to watch. (You must also turn on page-level tracing by including a *<%@ Page Trace="true"%>* directive at the top of your page.)

To capture your ASP.NET trace output by using FRT, create—for example—an FRT rule with the settings shown in Table 16-3. These settings will capture only the ASP.NET trace output. If you want to view the ASP.NET trace output in the context of other events, add more providers or areas to the rule.

Table 16-3   Minimal FRT Rule Settings for Capturing ASP.NET Trace Output

Setting	Value
Content to trace	*ASP.NET (*.aspx)*
Status Codes	*200*
Trace Providers	*ASPNET*
Verbosity	*Verbose*
Areas	*Page*

The next time your ASP.NET page is served, provided ASP.NET page tracing is turned on for the page in question, an FRT trace log is generated and the FRT trace output will include AspNetPageTraceWriteEvent or AspNetPageTraceWarnEvent entries that you can peruse.

Taking Performance into Consideration

FRT is intended for troubleshooting known problems as well as for monitoring and periodically analyzing a system's health. It is based on the IIS tracing infrastructure, which is fairly efficient if used conservatively. You can use FRT as a constant monitor for your system, but remember that FRT does entail overhead. Although FRT generates only a log file when a request fails, it must buffer all the data required to generate a log during each request so that the data is available if the request should fail. This means that as long as you have FRT enabled for a particular kind of request, some overhead is expended (primarily involving memory) each time such a request comes through—regardless of whether the request eventually succeeds or fails.

However, FRT was designed to be run in the background on a production machine for troubleshooting errors that are hard to reproduce. Depending on the performance goals of your application, keeping FRT running in the background (using conservative settings as outlined in the next paragraph) might be acceptable and is often desirable to provide improved diagnostics of rare or hard to reproduce error conditions. If you want to use FRT in this way, implement performance tests to ensure that your FRT settings aren't interfering with your performance goals.

If you enable FRT in a production environment, you can minimize the impact on the system by narrowing the focus of the tracing rule as much as possible so that you are tracing only the content about which you are concerned. Specify a custom content-to-trace setting that includes only the URLs that you want to monitor. You can further limit the impact on your production system by setting up your tracing rules to generate the minimal set of messages you think will be required to analyze the problem. For example, if you are debugging an ASP.NET application, your FRT rule might include only the ASPNET provider and the Page area in the definition. As much as possible, narrow the rule to the individual provider, area, verbosity, URL, or request, so that you log failures only for the failure definitions you are interested in.

Tracing Extensibility

As with all other components in IIS 7.0, tracing is implemented as a module that can be extended or even replaced with custom code. Managed code modules can use the System.Diagnostics application programming interface (API) to implement code that emits traces into the IIS tracing infrastructure. This enables you to use diagnostic information from third-party components in troubleshooting both Web server problems and application problems. For more information on configuring IIS 7.0 to collect trace information emitted from managed modules and ASP.NET applications, go to *http://www.iis.net* and search for "How to Add Tracing to IIS7 Managed Modules." Follow the link to the article with the same title, then select Adding Our Module To Our Site from the Table Of Contents drop-down list.

The built-in IIS 7.0 FRT module generates trace data in XML format, which of course a custom application can easily consume. That means that if what you're after is merely an alternate way of processing trace information after the trace data has been generated, you can simply consume the existing trace logs. However, using the native Web server extensibility APIs, it is also possible to develop custom modules that consume trace information directly and apply their own determination of what trace information to consume as well as when and how to report it.

Troubleshooting

In the remainder of this chapter, we'll provide a basic overview of the typical methodology for troubleshooting an IIS 7.0 application, introduce you to some tools for troubleshooting, and explain solutions to some of the most common problems.

Applying a Methodology

Debugging an application often requires intuition and experimentation rather than rigid scientific principles. Even so, your intuition will produce better results if you work within some sort of methodological framework. In the context of IIS, your first task should be to identify the error. Identifying the error can be complicated by the levels of error reporting that come into play between the browser and the server. After you've obtained details about the error and have ruled out any obvious causes, you want to ask what is generating the unexpected response. You will use the error details and information from trace logs to pinpoint the handler or module that is generating the unexpected response that is failing or that is hogging system resources.

> **More Info**   For a detailed description of steps used to identify error details and to perform initial analysis, see *http://mvolo.com/blogs/serverside/archive/2007/07/26/Troubleshoot-IIS7-errors-like-a-pro.aspx.*

The goal in your troubleshooting efforts should be to isolate the problem from the sometimes tangled pantheon of components that service a request. This involves much more than just the IIS request processing pipeline. You might need to examine any or all of the following components, as well as others:

- Browser settings
    - How does the browser handle error reporting?
    - Is the browser correctly configured?
- Client machine settings
    - Are firewall settings correctly configured?
- Network infrastructure
    - Is the network functioning?
- Network configuration
    - Is the browser's network environment properly configured?
    - Is the server's network environment properly configured?
    - Are the browser and server able to communicate?

- Authentication/authorization
    - ❑ Is the user supplying appropriate credentials?
    - ❑ Is the user successfully being authenticated by the server?
    - ❑ Do the user's credentials permit access to the resources being requested?
- IIS functioning
    - ❑ What other requests are executing at the time of the error?
- IIS configuration and settings
    - ❑ Are the correct modules installed?
- Web site/application configuration and settings
    - ❑ Is the Web site started?
    - ❑ Are virtual directories correctly configured?
    - ❑ Is redirection working properly?
- Functioning of individual modules
    - ❑ Which modules account for the bulk of processing time?
- Functioning and response of .NET applications
    - ❑ Are custom applications running as expected?
- Current server state
    - ❑ What are the states of current application pools?
    - ❑ What are the states of current worker processes?
    - ❑ What are the states of hosted sites?
    - ❑ What is the state of the application domain?
    - ❑ What are the states of currently running requests?
- Web site content
    - ❑ What exactly is being requested?
- Server performance
    - ❑ Is the server functioning properly?

When a request fails, first gather detailed information about the problem and then systematically examine the components that service the request. This way, you'll avoid spending time guessing at solutions to an unconfirmed diagnosis.

Using Tools and Utilities

This section briefly explains a core set of troubleshooting tools and utilities. Use them to systematically examine the many components that can be at fault when a Web site or application is not responding as it should.

Become well-versed in using these utilities. When you are faced with a challenging issue, your experience will not only help you efficiently work through the problem but will also guide you in your understanding of the full range of possible causes to be explored.

> **Note**   The IIS 6 Diagnostics Toolkit (which includes AuthDiag, DebugDiag, and SSL Diag) does not work with IIS 7.0, but refer to *http://www.iis.net* for possible updates to this valuable troubleshooting tool.

Table 16-4 lists the tools and utilities covered in detail later in this chapter. The table briefly describes when and how you might apply these tools.

Table 16-4   When to Use Troubleshooting Tools

Tool or Utility	Applicability	Security or Performance Considerations for Production System
net start	Check whether or not a service is started and start it if it is stopped	None
sc query	Check whether or not a service is started	None
ping	Check for basic network connectivity	None
PortCheck	Check for connectivity through a specific port on the server	None
tasklist	Find the PID for a service; use the PID to check status with netstat	None
netstat	List all listening ports with their protocol, local and foreign address, state, and PID (look for the PID you found with tasklist)	None
WFetch 1.4	Send and receive actual headers and requests without interference from a user-friendly browser; view the raw request and response	Poses a security risk because of stored passwords and test certificates
Appcmd	List and start sites and application pools; check for correct network bindings	None
Process Monitor	Monitor file system, registry, process, thread, and dynamic-link library (DLL) activity; monitor worker processes	Turn off when not in use
IIS Manager	Examine currently running worker processes and requests	None
Event Viewer	Check for error events in Application and System logs	None

Table 16-4   When to Use Troubleshooting Tools

Tool or Utility	Applicability	Security or Performance Considerations for Production System
Failed Request Tracing (FRT)	Generate trace logs, especially for errors that are intermittent or hard to reproduce	Minimize possible performance impact by narrowly limiting the scope of monitored requests
Reliability and Performance Monitor	Check overall system performance; identify suspect processes when server appears to hang	Turn off when not in use
Network Monitor	Capture network packets and diagnose Transmission Control Protocol (TCP) session data	Turn off when not in use

Using net start and sc query

> **Note**   Explore the sections in this chapter on net start, ping, and the PortCheck tool when confronted with a 503 error code or a "Page cannot be displayed" error.

You can quickly check which services are running on a machine by using the following command at a command prompt.

```
net start
```

All active services will be listed. In particular, to accept requests, the server must be running the Windows Process Activation Service (WAS) and the World Wide Web Publishing Service (W3SVC). You can quickly check (and start if necessary) the W3SVC service, for example, as follows.

```
net start W3SVC
```

If the service was not started, it will start. Otherwise, a message will indicate that the service has already been started. W3SVC depends on WAS. If you try to stop WAS when W3SVC is running, you will be asked to confirm that you want to stop both services. Likewise, if you try to start W3SVC when WAS is stopped, the command will automatically (although silently) start WAS.

If you want to check the status of a service and not start it if it is stopped, you can alternatively use the following command, where *serviceName* is the name of the service you want to check.

```
sc query serviceName
```

For example, the output from running *sc query W3SVC* looks like this.

```
SERVICE_NAME: w3svc
        TYPE              : 20  WIN32_SHARE_PROCESS
        STATE             : 4  RUNNING
```

```
                              (STOPPABLE, NOT_PAUSABLE, ACCEPTS_SHUTDOWN)
        WIN32_EXIT_CODE    : 0  (0x0)
        SERVICE_EXIT_CODE  : 0  (0x0)
        CHECKPOINT         : 0x0
        WAIT_HINT          : 0x0
```

Using ping

> **Note**   Refer to the information in this section when you are confronted with a 503 error code or a "Page cannot be displayed" error.

You can rule out basic network issues by pinging the server from the client. First try pinging the URL host name to make sure it is being correctly resolved to an IP address. Use the ping command line tool from a command prompt, as in the following example.

```
ping www.contoso.com
```

The output should show an appropriate IP address. If it does not, make sure the client's Domain Name System (DNS) server is working properly. Also check to see if the client has a hosts file that might be interfering with proper IP address resolution. Assuming IP address resolution is not a problem, if you can't ping the server's IP address itself, there could be a problem with the network connection, either at the client or the server end. But do check to make sure firewall settings on the client aren't preventing the connection. For information about troubleshooting network connectivity issues, see the section titled "Using Network Monitor" in this chapter.

Using PortCheck

If you're unable to ping a server, it could be because the server's firewall is rejecting the connection, or the service isn't listening on the required port. The PortCheck tool can check Transmision Control Protocol (TCP) connectivity for a specific port at the IP address in question. The tool provides a detailed breakdown of the different connectivity issues you might be facing.

> **Note**   The PortCheck tool is included on the companion media, or you can download the tool from the following Web site:
>
> *http://mvolo.com/blogs/serverside/pages/Check-network-service-connectivity-with-PortChecker-tool.aspx.*

Use the PortCheck tool from the command line to check for connectivity through a specific port on a URL as follows.

```
portcheck www.contoso.com 80
```

Or you can specify the IP address, like this.

```
portcheck 192.168.1.101 80
```

Using tasklist and netstat

If you suspect problems with a service or process listening on a port, you can list all services and their process IDs (PIDs) by entering the following command at the command prompt.

```
tasklist /svc
```

The output, showing PID 564 for the W3SVC and WAS services, for example, looks like this.

```
Image Name                   PID Services
========================= ======== ============
System Idle Process            0 N/A
System                         4 N/A
smss.exe                     360 N/A
...
svchost.exe                  564 W3SVC, WAS
```

Use the output from tasklist to find the PID for the service you are troubleshooting. Next, to list all listening ports with their protocol, local and foreign address, state, and PID, enter the following command at the command prompt.

```
netstat -ano
```

Look for the PID that you located with tasklist in the netstat output and check the address and state, or look for processes that are listening on a port you are interested in. The output, showing PID 4 listening on port 80, for example, looks like this.

```
Active Connections

  Proto  Local Address        Foreign Address        State         PID
   TCP   0.0.0.0:80           0.0.0.0:0              LISTENING     4
   TCP   0.0.0.0:88           0.0.0.0:0              LISTENING     560
   TCP   0.0.0.0:135          0.0.0.0:0              LISTENING     844
   TCP   0.0.0.0:389          0.0.0.0:0              LISTENING     560
...
```

Using WFetch 1.4

> **Note**   WFetch 1.4 is included in the IIS 6 Diagnostics Toolkit. You can download WFetch 1.4 separately at the following location: *http://www.iis.net/go/1307*.

Sometimes the error reporting that the browser provides can partially obscure the symptoms of a problem. You can bypass the typical browser's user-friendly packaging by using WFetch, which is essentially a browser with no enhancements. WFetch lets you see the raw data sent between browser and server, so it's ideal for testing authentication issues or looking at custom headers in both the request and response packets.

> **Caution**   Because WFetch enables you to store passwords and manipulate test security cer-
> tificates, WFetch has the potential to expose your site to security risks. Therefore, Microsoft rec-
> ommends that this tool be used only in testing, not in a production environment.

To run WFetch 1.4 (on an x86 system for this example), execute WFetch 1.4 from the IIS Diagnostics (32bit)\WFetch 1.4 program group. Figure 16-7 shows the WFetch 1.4 user interface with log output after requesting the default Web page on localhost. You can use the interface to specify an HTTP verb (*GET, HEAD, PUT, DELETE, TRACE, POST, OPTIONS*), the host, the port, the HTTP version, and the path, as well as authentication and connection types. For complicated scenarios, you can manually add portions of a request in the Advanced Request section or have WFetch read part of the request from a file.

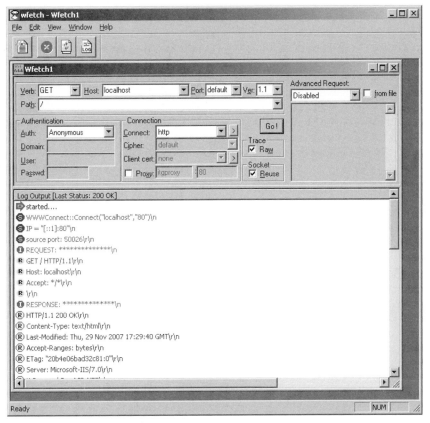

Figure 16-7   The WFetch 1.4 user interface.

> **Note**   The file format for help files included with the current release of the IIS 6 Diagnostics
> Toolkit is not supported on Microsoft Windows Vista or Windows Server 2008. Use online
> help instead or install WinHlp32.exe to use the help files. See the following Knowledge
> Base article for more information and a link to the WinHlp32.exe download location:
> *http://support.microsoft.com/kb/917607.*

Using Appcmd

If a site isn't running, or if the network bindings for the site are misconfigured because of
an error in your IIS configuration or in the site definition, the IIS server won't be able to
receive requests for that site. You can use Appcmd to quickly check that a site is running
and that its network bindings are correctly configured. Enter the following command at the
command prompt.

```
AppCmd list sites
```

If the IIS configuration is OK, the site definition's bindings are listed, along with the current
state (Started, Stopped, or Unknown). Check that the bindings make sense. If the site is not
started, a configuration error might be preventing IIS from starting the site or the application
pool. You can start a site by using Appcmd as follows.

```
AppCmd start site sitename
```

Similarly, you can check whether or not an application pool is started by using this command.

```
AppCmd list apppools
```

If necessary, start the application pool by using this command.

```
AppCmd start apppool poolname
```

> **More Info**   For more information about Appcmd, refer to Chapter 7, "Using Command Line
> Tools."

Using Process Monitor

Process Monitor lets you monitor the file system, registry, processes, threads, and DLLs. It
replaces and extends two tools used in earlier versions of IIS: Filemon and Regmon. Process
Monitor is a sophisticated tool that provides detailed system information along with searching, filters, and simultaneous file logging to help you sort through the wealth of data. You can
examine the process data in real time, or you can capture and review it later.

To start Process Monitor, run Procmon.exe from its installation location. Figure 16-8 shows the Process Monitor window displaying a small portion of the operations that take place when a user browses a site. You can toggle the display of operations related to registry activity, to file system activity, and to process/thread activity. You can filter the operations according to an extensive list of categories and values. Process Monitor also lets you search the list and jump directly to an object involved in the operation, for example, a temporary file or registry key.

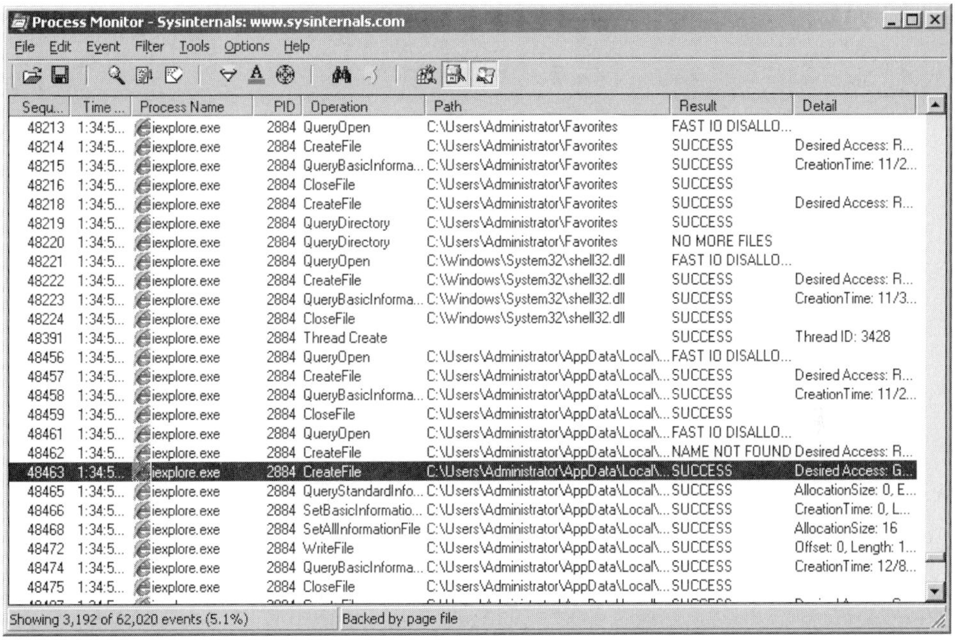

Figure 16-8   The Process Monitor window after the client has browsed a site with Internet Explorer.

Double-clicking an operation displays properties for the operation, from which you can view information about the event, the process (as shown in Figure 16-9), or the stack.

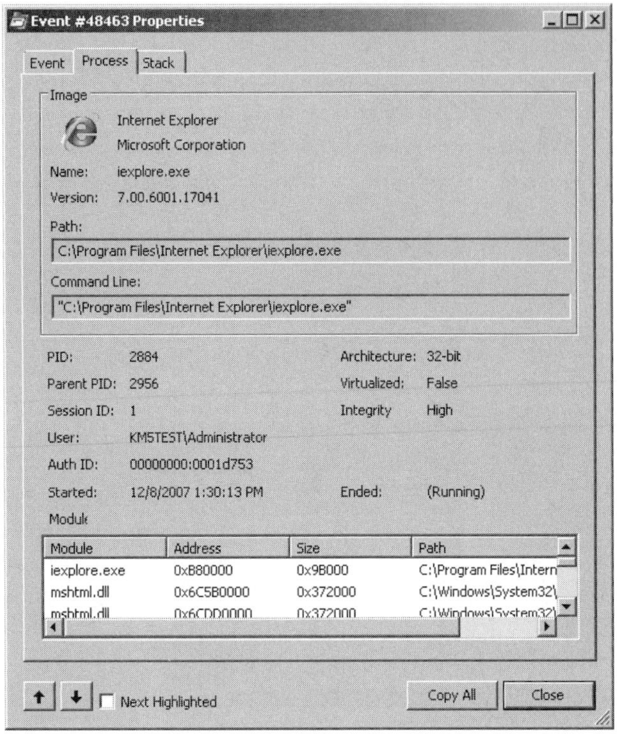

Figure 16-9 The Process tab of an operation's event properties.

You can view summary reports as well as a tree view of processes, as shown in Figure 16-10.

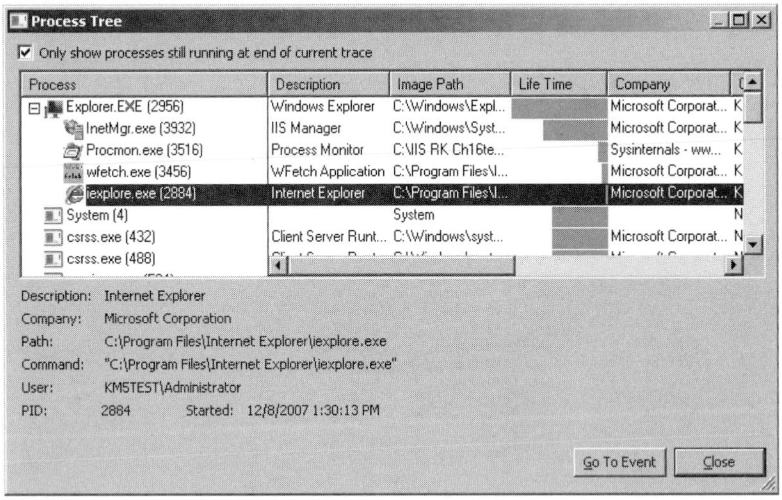

Figure 16-10 Process Monitor's Process Tree tool.

You can use Process Monitor to monitor your worker processes (filter for "Process Name is w3wp.exe"). To check which application pool the worker processes serve, use IIS Manager as explained in the next section to look at the Worker Processes list and the list of active requests. Doing so lets you peer into the worker process to see running requests and in what stage those requests are, as well as what appDomains are loaded into that process.

You can also use Process Monitor to examine system-wide details for a series of events when your troubleshooting efforts take you outside the scope of information captured by IIS-specific tools such as FRT.

> **Note**   Process Monitor is *not* part of the default install for Windows Vista or Windows Server 2008—you must select it as part of a custom installation. If necessary, you can also download Process Monitor v1.26 from the following location:
> *http://technet.microsoft.com/en-us/sysinternals/bb896645.aspx.*

Using IIS Manager

IIS Manager uses the Runtime State and Control API (RSCA) to provide a viewport onto currently running worker processes and any requests running under those processes. In IIS Manager, select the server in the tree control and then scroll down in the central pane and double-click Worker Processes in the IIS group. IIS Manager displays currently running worker processes, as shown in Figure 16-11.

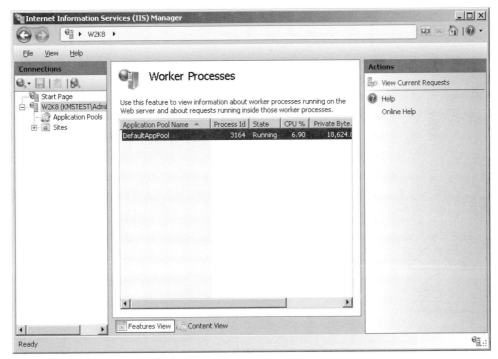

Figure 16-11   Using IIS Manager to view currently running worker processes.

Select the worker process you want to investigate and click View Current Requests in the Actions pane to display the list of current requests for that worker process, as shown in Figure 16-12.

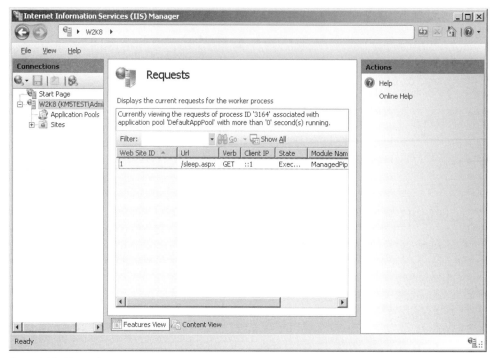

Figure 16-12   Using IIS Manager to view currently running requests.

Knowing what worker processes and requests are currently executing (the "requests in flight") can help you resolve slow request responses when the culprit is an unrelated request that's excessively consuming system resources. You might also find that an application interferes with other applications in the same application pool and decide to separate the application into its own application pool. Or you could create an FRT rule for the currently executing requests and see where they're all blocking and what happened to those requests prior to the block.

Note   You can programmatically access RSCA through the WMI provider or through managed code and the *Microsoft.Web.Administration* namespace, which exposes the following information for a request through the *WorkerProcess* class. (*GUID* is the unique request ID that is also emitted when tracing is turned on for the request.)

GUID	*Site*	*ClientIPAddress*	*CurrentModule*
ConnectionID	*LocalIPAddress*	*TimeElapsed*	*TimeInModule*
Verb	*LocalPort*	*PipelineState*	
URL	*HostName*	*TimeInState*	

> For examples of accessing RSCA via code, go to *http://www.iis.net* and search for "How to Access IIS7 RSCA Data," then click on the article with the same name.
>
> You can also access RSCA by using Appcmd, without writing any code at all! Examples of how to query worker process data by using Appcmd are given in Chapter 10, "Managing Applications and Application Pools."

Using Event Viewer

You can use Event Viewer to check why an application pool has been stopped or cannot be started. To start Event Viewer, launch Event Viewer from the Administrative Tools program group. Alternatively, from the Run text box, type **eventvwr**. In the tree, expand Windows Logs and then select Application. You can filter the list of events by event source.

Important Refer to the following online documentation, known as the IIS 7.0 "health model" (in other words, diagnostic and failure conditions experienced by software), for a list of event IDs related to IIS 7.0. Expand the documentation nodes in the left tree control or follow the links in the documentation to drill down to a list of events relating to specific managed entities or aspects of managed entities: *http://technet2.microsoft.com/windowsserver2008/en/library/b19873a2-9f72-40c8-b73d-89f39cda62781033.mspx?mfr=true*.

Errors the IIS-W3SVC-WP source generated, as shown in Figure 16-13, indicate that the worker process started but failed during initialization. This might happen, for example, if the configuration section is invalid, if a module failed to load, or if a module failed to initialize. You can double-click an event to see details about it.

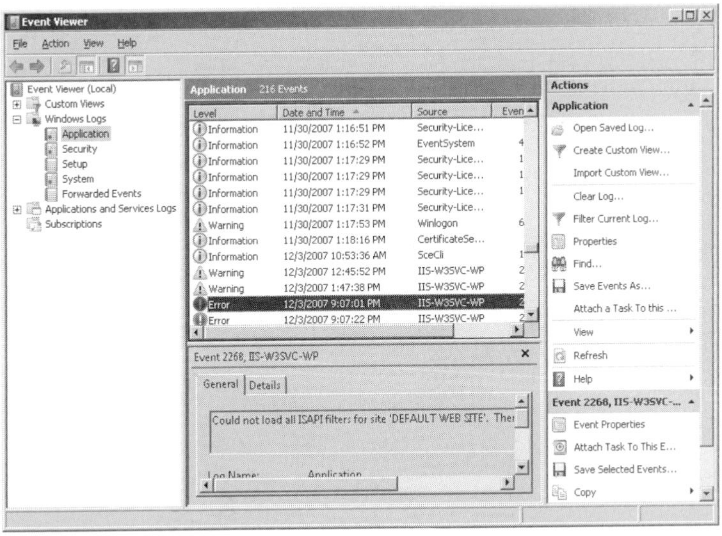

Figure 16-13 Errors in the Application log in Event Viewer indicate a problem occurred while initializing a worker process.

Also select the System node under Windows Logs. Errors generated by the IIS-W3SVC-WP or WAS source in the System log indicate that WAS could not start the worker process. This might be caused, for example, by a problem in the configuration, by a problem with the application pool identity credentials, by exceeding the number of worker processes allowed, or by running out of some other resource.

An error in the System log might also be caused by a bug in custom application code. WAS will disable an application pool if an application in the pool triggers Rapid Fail Protection (RFP). RFP is a mechanism that IIS uses to prevent repeated failures in a faulty application from bringing down the system. When IIS identifies repeated worker process crashes or hangs in a given application, RFP will shut down the entire application pool in which the application is running.

Using FRT

Use FRT to generate trace logs of IIS responses that violate conditions you set in the FRT component of IIS Manager. Refer to the section titled "Tracing and Diagnosing Problems" earlier in this chapter for details about how to use FRT. To use FRT most efficiently in your troubleshooting process, narrowly restrict the FRT rules you add so that you can examine the minimal subset of URLs that are experiencing problems.

Direct from the Source: What Conditions Will FRT *Not* Catch?

FRT is a powerful feature that will really help diagnose problems with Web applications. Unfortunately, FRT cannot help with a few conditions, which include:

- **Worker process crashes**   One thing to remember about FRT is that it buffers the trace events for the requests it's configured to track *in process memory*. So if that process suffers a failure that causes the process to terminate unexpectedly, the events buffered in that process will be lost.

- **Failures that happen before any request processing begins**   FRT reads configurations and starts accepting trace events for requests on the Begin Request notification. However, a bit of work happens *after* the request arrives in the worker process but *before* this notification. Things that happen to a request that could cause it to fail *before* the Begin Request notification include:

  - ❏ W3WP fails to load the configuration for the request
  - ❏ URL Rewriting failures

If failures happen in the aforementioned circumstances, you will *not* get an FRT log. The best alternative for you in such a case is to use ETW tracing or check the Application event log.

Eric Deily

Senior Program Manager Lead

Using Reliability and Performance Monitor

Use Reliability and Performance Monitor to examine the overall condition of your server. You can start Reliability and Performance from the Administrative Tools program group. Select the Performance Monitor node under the Monitoring Tools node in the tree. You can add and configure counters for all aspects of the server's performance, as shown in Figure 16-14.

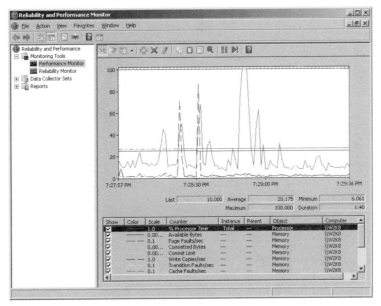

Figure 16-14   Viewing performance counters in Performance Monitor.

You will almost always want to monitor Process and Thread counters such as Processor Time and % Processor Time. When troubleshooting an ASP or ASP.NET application, also look for the Active Server Pages counters, the various .NET CLR counters, and the ASP.NET and ASP.NET Applications counters. In addition, IIS 7.0 adds many new performance counters under the groupings W3SVC_W3WP and WAS_W3WP.

Reliability and Performance Monitor is especially useful when you are investigating a server that appears to hang. You can save a performance log by creating a Data Collector Set. To do so, expand the Data Collector Sets node in the tree and then right-click the User Defined node and select New\Data Collector Set from the context menu. To isolate the problem, analyze the performance log in combination with a memory dump from the process that is running on the server. You must time the memory dump to coincide both with the hanging behavior and with a performance log that is actively collecting data.

Using Network Monitor

If you need to troubleshoot a problem that involves connectivity issues, you can use Network Monitor to capture network packets and diagnose TCP session data. You can start Network

Monitor 3.1 from the Microsoft Network Monitor 3.1 program group. After capturing a sequence of network packets, you can double-click a frame in the sequence to see complete details (including the hexadecimal contents) of the frame, as shown in Figure 16-15.

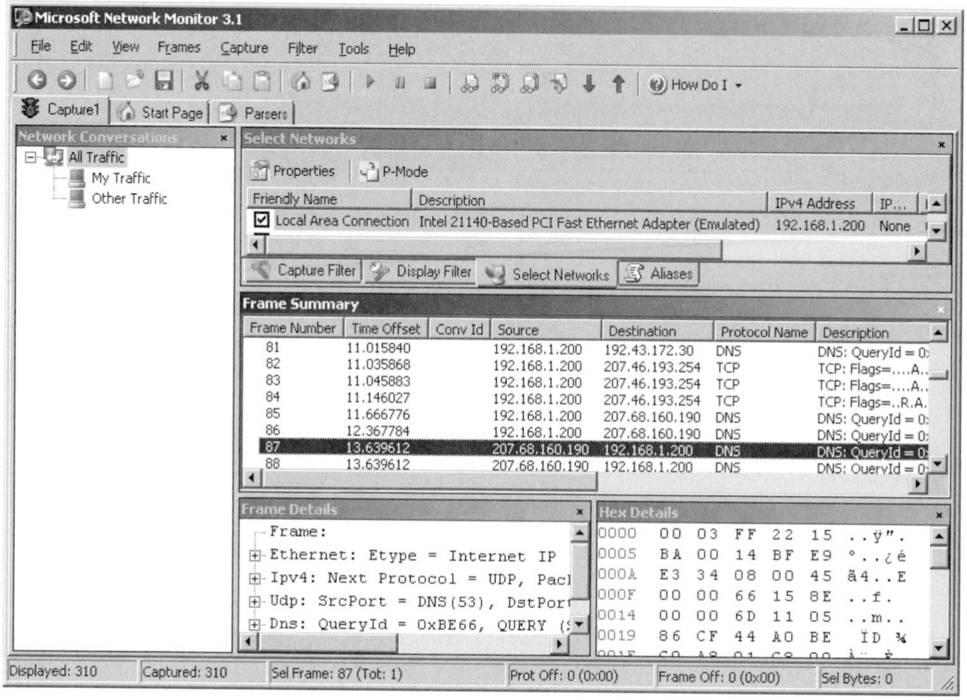

Figure 16-15   Viewing network packets in Network Monitor.

Note   Network Monitor 3.1 is *not* part of the default install for Windows Vista or Windows Server 2008. To download Network Monitor 3.1, go to *http://www.microsoft.com/downloads* and search for "Microsoft Network Monitor 3.1."

Troubleshooting HTTP

To troubleshoot HTTP problems, you should first make sure your browser is displaying accurate error information. Then check the various logs and run traces to uncover the source of any errors.

Understanding Friendly Errors, Custom Errors, and Detailed Errors

When troubleshooting HTTP issues, the first step is to make sure errors are being accurately reported in your browser. Browsers typically translate certain error responses into user-friendly text, which doesn't always accurately reflect the underlying issue. In Microsoft Internet Explorer 7.0, you can disable user-friendly error messages by selecting Internet

Options on the Tools menu. On the Advanced tab, clear the Show Friendly HTTP Error Messages check box and then close and reopen Internet Explorer.

On the server end of the process, by default, IIS 7.0 returns only general error information to the browser. IIS 7.0 has been designed this way for security reasons—you don't want to broadcast detailed error messages, because they might divulge information about your environment that would compromise your security. Furthermore, IIS can be configured to return custom error pages when a particular error code occurs. To make sure you are seeing the full and unvarnished details about an error, you need to turn off custom error responses and turn on delivery of detailed errors.

To configure IIS to send detailed error messages to the client, in IIS Manager, select the site or application you want to configure, then double-click Error Pages. Select a Status Code, click the Edit Feature Settings link in the Actions pane, and then select the Detailed Errors option. Make sure you re-enable the Detailed Errors For Local Requests And Custom Error Pages For Remote Requests option when you are finished debugging.

To configure IIS to send detailed error messages to the client by using the Appcmd command line utility, enter the following command from a command prompt.

```
%systemroot%\system32\inetsrv\appcmd set config "<site/app>" /section:httpErrors
/errorMode:Detailed
```

> **Note**   In the *httpErrors* configuration section, you must set *overrideMode* to *Allow*.

When you are finished debugging, stop the server from sending detailed errors by executing the following command.

```
%systemroot%\system32\inetsrv\appcmd set config "<site/app>" /section:httpErrors
/errorMode:DetailedLocalOnly
```

Refer to Appendix B, "IIS 7.0 Error Messages," for complete information about error message settings, including custom errors and redirection. Note that you don't want to return detailed error information in general, because such details can potentially be exploited to gain information about your system. Detailed errors list the following information:

- Status and substatus code
- Description of the error
- Module
- Notification
- Handler (static or dynamic)
- Error code

- Requested URL

- Physical path

- Logon method

- Logon user

- FRT log directory

- Most likely causes

- Things you can try (possible solutions)

- Links for more information

Pay particular attention to the module, notification, and handler information, which will at least help you narrow down which module is *reporting* the problem. This information often tells you the module that is *causing* the problem.

> **Note**   Refer to the information in this section when you are confronted with a 404 error code.

By examining the requested URL and the physical path to which it has been resolved, you can quickly identify configuration problems in a virtual directory mapping.

ASP Script Error Details

In IIS 7.0, ASP script error details are hidden by default and are replaced with a generic error. To allow the server to send the ASP script error details to a browser, go to IIS Manager and select the appropriate Web site or application in the tree. Then double-click ASP. Under the Compilation section in the resulting list, expand Debugging Properties and change the Send Errors To Browser setting to True. You can use Appcmd to update this setting by entering the following command at the command prompt.

```
%systemroot%\system32\inetsrv\appcmd set config -section:asp
-scriptErrorSentToBrowser:true
```

Don't forget to hide script error details after you've fixed the problem you are trouble-shooting.

Checking the Logs

You should check four pertinent logs when investigating HTTP issues: the event log, the firewall log, the Web site log, and the httperr log. View the event log with Event Viewer.

(See the section titled "Using Event Viewer" earlier in this chapter for more information.) You are interested in the following event sources:

- IIS-APPHOSTSVC

- IIS-W3SVC

- IIS-W3SVC-WP

- IIS-WMSVC

- WAS

- WAS-ListenerAdapter

- HttpService

The following XML query file will filter the event log, making it easy to review. This file is included on the companion CD as IIS-event-filter.xml.

```
<QueryList>
  <Query Id="0" Path="Application">
    <Select Path="Application">*[System[Provider[@Name='Microsoft-Windows-
HttpService' or @Name='Microsoft-Windows-IIS-APPHOSTSVC' or @Name='Microsoft-
Windows-IIS-W3SVC' or @Name='Microsoft-Windows-IIS-W3SVC-WP' or @Name='Microsoft-
Windows-IIS-WMSVC' or @Name='Microsoft-Windows-WAS' or @Name='Microsoft-Windows-WAS-
ListenerAdapter'] and (Level=0 or Level=1 or Level=2 or Level=3 or Level=4 or
Level=5)]]</Select>
    <Select Path="Microsoft-Windows-
HttpService/Trace">*[System[Provider[@Name='Microsoft-Windows-HttpService' or
@Name='Microsoft-Windows-IIS-APPHOSTSVC' or @Name='Microsoft-Windows-IIS-W3SVC' or
@Name='Microsoft-Windows-IIS-W3SVC-WP' or @Name='Microsoft-Windows-IIS-WMSVC' or
@Name='Microsoft-Windows-WAS' or @Name='Microsoft-Windows-WAS-ListenerAdapter'] and
(Level=0 or Level=1 or Level=2 or Level=3 or Level=4 or Level=5)]]</Select>
    <Select Path="System">*[System[Provider[@Name='Microsoft-Windows-HttpService' or
@Name='Microsoft-Windows-IIS-APPHOSTSVC' or @Name='Microsoft-Windows-IIS-W3SVC' or
@Name='Microsoft-Windows-IIS-W3SVC-WP' or @Name='Microsoft-Windows-IIS-WMSVC' or
@Name='Microsoft-Windows-WAS' or @Name='Microsoft-Windows-WAS-ListenerAdapter'] and
(Level=0 or Level=1 or Level=2 or Level=3 or Level=4 or Level=5)]]</Select>
  </Query>
</QueryList>
```

The firewall log and httperr log are stored in the *%SystemRoot%*\System32\LogFiles\Firewall and *%SystemRoot%*\System32\LogFiles\HTTPERR folders, respectively. The Web site log, by default, is stored daily in the *%SystemDrive%*\Inetpub\Logs\LogFiles\W3SVC*n* folder, where *n* is the site ID.

You can quickly scan the logs for any error conditions that appear to pertain to the problem at hand. (If the logs are saved in the default format, you can view them using Notepad, or you can use a utility such as Log Parser.) Refer to Chapter 15 for more information about log files in IIS 7.0.

> **Note** Log Parser is a tool that provides query access to text-based log files, XML files, and comma-separated value CSV files. You can download Log Parser by going to *http://www.microsoft.com/downloads* and searching for "Log Parser." Queries must be executed from within the context of the Log Parser command prompt. To open the command prompt, launch Log Parser from the Log Parser program group. For more information about Log Parser, refer to Chapter 15.

Troubleshooting Common HTTP Problem Scenarios

A few standard HTTP problem scenarios often require troubleshooting, and you can generally apply a standard approach to quickly diagnose and resolve errors. Some of the most common troubleshooting scenarios involving HTTP errors are discussed in the following sections.

Troubleshooting Static and Dynamic Content Problems

> **Note** Refer to the information in this section when you are confronted with a 404.3 error. Many 404 errors have nothing to do with MIME maps (wrong URL, wrong virtual directory structure, URL rewriting, changing URL, missing physical files, and so on).

The most frequent cause of a request returning a "Not Found" error is missing handler mappings or an application framework that is not installed. Refer to the detailed discussion of this error in Chapter 11, "Hosting Application Development Frameworks." IIS requires that known MIME types be registered to provide firm control over what types of files (as indicated by their extensions) can be served directly (as static content). MIME types can be inherited, or they can be defined or blocked at a site-specific, application-specific, or directory-specific level. If you have registered a MIME type as a static resource, IIS 7.0 simply serves the content. If a MIME type is not registered as static content, however, it can be served dynamically only if the file extension is mapped to an application framework—such as ASP or ASP.NET—by means of a mapping handler.

When you are troubleshooting a problem with a mapping handler, check that dynamic mapping handlers are configured before the *path="*" verb="*"* static file handler is declared. Refer to Chapter 11, and to Chapter 12, "Managing Web Server Modules," for more information about mapping handlers and dynamic content.

Troubleshooting UNC Access Errors

> **Note** Refer to the information in this section when you are confronted with a 500.16 error.

Content that is hosted on a distributed machine can present additional complications when you're troubleshooting. Errors involving Universal Naming Convention (UNC) content are reported as UNC Access errors. You can check a number of settings to confirm your UNC content is correctly configured. (Refer to Chapter 9, "Managing Web Sites," for more information about configuring UNC.) In addition, however, a developer or application owner often manages UNC content, and they might not have administrative privileges on the IIS server. You can delegate management of the content, including FRT settings. This typically includes setting the FRT rules to save the trace logs on the UNC share, which in turn necessitates configuring appropriate access to the log file destination for the associated worker process ID.

Before FRT can generate trace logs on a UNC share, you must give the worker process ID Full Control access for the network share and appropriate path on the distributed machine. Then on the IIS Server, you must enable FRT for the Web site and set the FRT trace log directory to the UNC location. (To make these settings in IIS Manager, select the Web site in the tree and click Failed Request Tracing in the Actions pane.)

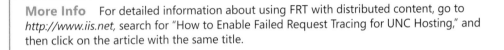

> **More Info**   For detailed information about using FRT with distributed content, go to *http://www.iis.net,* search for "How to Enable Failed Request Tracing for UNC Hosting," and then click on the article with the same title.

By default, administration of FRT settings is already set for delegation, meaning that an administrator can add FRT rules in the web.config file for an individual Web site. To confirm this setting in IIS Manager, select the server in the tree and double-click Feature Delegation in the Management group. Scroll down to find Failed Request Tracing Rules in the resulting list and check that Delegation is set to Read/Write. If necessary, update the setting by clicking Read/Write in the Actions pane.

On the distributed machine, you can add FRT rules directly to the web.config file. For example, to add the FRT rule for tracing a 401.3 error code presented in the section titled "Tracing a Specific Error Code" earlier in this chapter, the application owner would add the following *<tracing>* element to the *<system.webServer>* section of the application's web.config file.

```
<tracing>
    <traceFailedRequests>
        <clear />
        <add path="*" customActionTriggerLimit="1">
            <traceAreas>
                <add provider="WWW Server"
                    areas="Authentication,Security,RequestNotifications,Module"
                    verbosity="Verbose" />
            </traceAreas>
            <failureDefinitions timeTaken="00:00:00" statusCodes="401.3"
                    verbosity="Ignore" />
        </add>
    </traceFailedRequests>
</tracing>
```

Troubleshooting 503 Service Unavailable Errors   If the WAS service is unable to create the IIS worker process that should handle a given HTTP request, those requests will receive a 503 response indicating "Service Unavailable." Use the Appcmd list apppools command at the command prompt to check whether or not the application pool is stopped. A stopped application pool can result from the IIS 7.0 Rapid Fail Protection mechanism. Check events in the System log by using Event Viewer to see if WAS reported a 5002 event: "Application pool *xxx* is being automatically disabled due to a series of failures in the process(es) serving that application pool." Check the System log and the Application log for other events that indicate the application pool was stopped or was never started.

> **More Info**   Additional information about troubleshooting a 503 Service Unavailable error is available at *http://mvolo.com/blogs/serverside/archive/2006/10/19/Where-did-my-IIS7-server-go_3F00_-Troubleshooting-_2200_service-unavailable_2200_-errors.aspx*.

Troubleshooting Firewall Problems   You can rule out firewall problems by successfully pinging the Web site or by using the PortCheck tool to ensure the server is listening for the URL on the appropriate port.

If you suspect a firewall problem, check the firewall log for errors. Make sure that the firewall on your server's network is configured appropriately. To check settings on Windows Firewall, for example, from the Start menu, right-click Network and then click Properties. Click Windows Firewall in the lower-left corner of the window. In the Windows Firewall window, click Change Settings. On the Exceptions tab of the Windows Firewall Settings dialog box, make sure that the Web Management Service (HTTP) and World Wide Web Services (HTTP) exceptions are enabled. If appropriate for your environment, also make sure the Secure World Wide Web Services (HTTPS) exception is enabled.

Next, from the Administrative Tools program group, click Windows Firewall With Advanced Security. If you can categorize your problem as dropped traffic rather than blocked traffic, you can narrow your troubleshooting efforts. Check the following:

- There must be an active allow rule for the active profile.

- Make sure no block rules are overriding the allow rule.

- Check to see if Group Policy is preventing local rules from being applied.

- Check to see if the active allow rule permits only secure connections. If so (and if this is appropriate for your environment), check if appropriate security rules have been defined.

- Check that the outbound connection is not explicitly blocked and that connections that aren't explicitly blocked are allowed.

- Check for conflicting firewall and Internet Protocol Security (IPsec) security policies.

> **More Info**   For complete information about troubleshooting problems with Windows
> Firewall with Advanced Security, including an explanation of the firewall log files, refer to the
> help topic titled "Windows Firewall with Advanced Security: Diagnostics and Troubleshooting"
> at the following location:
>
> *http://go.microsoft.com/fwlink/?LinkId=64382*

Check that all necessary services are started (Base Filtering Engine, Group Policy Client, IKE
and AuthIP IPsec Keying Modules, IP Helper, IPsec Policy Agent, Network Location Aware-
ness, Network List Service, and Windows Firewall). You can temporarily disable the firewall
or save (export) your firewall settings and restore the default settings. If the problem goes
away, you will have a better understanding of where the problem lies. Re-enable the firewall or
restore the exported settings when you are finished troubleshooting.

Troubleshooting Parent Path Problems   To prevent a client from traversing the server's file
system, IIS 7.0 by default disallows the use of the "..\" parent path notation in ASP scripts.
To allow ASP scripts to use parent path notation, in IIS Manager, select the Web site or
application in the tree and double-click ASP. Under the Behavior section in the resulting list,
change the Enable Parent Paths setting to True. You can use Appcmd to update this setting by
entering the following command at the command prompt.

```
%systemroot%\system32\inetsrv\appcmd set config section:asp -enableParentPaths:true
```

Troubleshooting Specific Status Codes   Appendix A, "IIS 7.0 HTTP Error Codes," provides
a list of status and substatus codes. The information might help you when you know a status
code and want more information about related status/substatus codes.

> **Important**   You can refer to *http://support.microsoft.com/kb/943891* for an explanation
> of error code categories. The site lists common error codes and gives both an explanation of
> possible causes and a link to detailed instructions for resolving the error.

Solving Common Specific Issues

The most common issues that arise in an IIS 7.0 installation often have simple solutions, or at
least have a simple set of steps to identify and resolve the problems. The remainder of this
chapter looks at some frequently encountered problems and offers guidance in how to
approach fixing them.

IIS 6.0 Administration Tools Not Installed

To use IIS 6.0 administration tools (necessary, for example, if you want to use existing IIS 6.0 Active Directory Service Interfaces [ADSI] or WMI-based scripts to manage your IIS 7.0 server or if you need to remotely administer IIS 6.0 servers from your IIS 7.0 server), you must install the appropriate IIS 6 Management Compatibility role services from the Management Tools category. Refer to Chapter 5 for more information about installing IIS 7.0 modules. Note that IIS 7.0 ships a new WMI provider that is not backward-compatible with the old WMI provider (they use two different namespaces).

SSI Not Enabled

Server-Side Include (SSI) directives cause IIS to insert the specified content into the request response. A file containing an SSI directive should have a recognized SSI filename extension. By default, these are .asp (for #include directives), .stm, .shtm, and .shtml. The file should reside in a directory that has Scripts or Execute access permission. Finally, make sure your IIS installation includes the Server Side Includes role service (listed in the Application Development category).

Unexpected Recycling

When an application pool recycles, any session state information stored in the worker process is destroyed along with the worker process. If your application relies on storing its session state, update the application to store the state information outside of the worker process (use out-of-process session state with ASP.NET applications) so that application recycling doesn't interfere with the application's performance.

> **More Info**   For more information about session state and application pool recycling, refer to the following site: *http://blogs.msdn.com/david.wang/archive/2005/09/19/Why_do_I_lose_ASP_Session_State_on_IIS6.aspx.*

Crashes

If your Web site experiences an application crash, you can create a memory dump. If you want to debug the worker process (probably you'll find an unhandled exception or a memory access violation), you'll need to attach a debugger to the application's worker process.

> **More Info**   For more information, refer to the article titled "Troubleshooting IIS7 503 'Service Unavailable' Errors with Startup Debugging" at *http://mvolo.com/blogs/serverside/archive/2007/05/19/Troubleshooting-IIS7-503-_2200_Service-unavailable_2200_-errors-with-startup-debugging.aspx.*

Unable to Reach Web Site

When a client is unable to reach a Web site, first use ping and the PortCheck tool to verify that the client can connect to the server. Then use the net start command to verify that IIS is started. Finally use Appcmd and possibly the netstat command to verify that the site is started and listening for requests.

Authentication Errors

When a request is denied due to authentication, first turn on FRT tracing. In the FRT log file, go to the Request Details tab and choose the Authentication Authorization format to see authentication-related trace events. Next, use WFetch to send a request and review the headers involved in the transaction for any problems in the user credentials. Finally, check the authentication/authorization settings for the Web site in question.

Slow Responses or Server Hanging

When an application response is slow or the server appears to hang, first turn on FRT tracing. In the FRT log file, go to the Request Details tab and choose the Performance View format to see trace events sorted by duration. Doing so can help you find a module that is consuming the bulk of processing time. Next, use IIS Manager to view currently running worker processes and requests in case the slow response is caused by an unrelated request. Finally, use Reliability and Performance Monitor to examine the server's performance in general. If the server appears to be hanging, you can also create a user memory dump when hang symptoms arise.

Summary

When your IIS 7.0 environment encounters problems, or when you suspect there might be some problem, you can rely on tools that ship with IIS 7.0 to track and diagnose the symptoms. FRT is your first line of defense for identifying a problem and zeroing in on the likely culprit. However, you will need to rely on a small host of tools to troubleshoot errors that might involve such disparate issues as stopped services, network problems, server configuration errors, authentication and authorization failures, problems with firewall settings, faulty application code, or even errors in custom modules.

Using a few simple steps to diagnose the problem, you can readily resolve some of the most commonly encountered problems in an IIS 7.0 environment. Debugging has been characterized as an art form. As you become more familiar with the palette and tools of the trade, your solutions will become more efficient and more elegant.

Additional Resources

These resources contain additional information and tools related to this chapter:

- IIS 7.0 Health Model: *http://technet2.microsoft.com/windowsserver2008/en/library/b19873a2-9f72-40c8-b73d-89f39cda62781033.mspx?mfr=true.*

- List of common error codes and explanations of possible causes with links to detailed instructions for resolving them: *http://support.microsoft.com/kb/943891.*

- Latest debugging tools: *http://www.microsoft.com/whdc/devtools/debugging/default.mspx.*

- PortCheck tool: *http://mvolo.com/blogs/serverside/pages/Check-network-service-connectivity-with-PortChecker-tool.aspx.*

- Debugging tools and symbols—resources (links to training resources and support): *http://www.microsoft.com/whdc/devtools/debugging/resources.mspx.*

- Wfetch 1.4 (also included in the IIS 6 Diagnostics Toolkit): *http://www.iis.net/go/1307.*

- Details about using Wfetch: *http://support.microsoft.com/kb/284285.*

- Microsoft Windows Sysinternals (information about Process Monitor): *http://www.microsoft.com/technet/sysinternals/default.mspx.*

- Process Monitor (details and download): *http://www.microsoft.com/technet/sysinternals/SystemInformation/processmonitor.mspx.*

- Performance Monitor Wizard (simplifies creating and managing performance monitor logs): go to *http://www.microsoft.com* and search for "Performance Monitor Wizard."

- Microsoft Network Monitor 3.1: Network Protocol Analyzer (enables capturing and *protocol analysis of network* traffic): go to *http://www.microsoft.com/downloads* and search for "Microsoft Network Monitor 3.1."

- Information about attaching a debugger to an IIS 7.0 worker process or Web application using Visual Studio: go to *http://www.iis.net* and search for "Debugging IIS 7 with Visual Studio 2005 on Windows Vista," then click on the article with the same name.

- Tips for Classic ASP developers on IIS 7.0: *http://blogs.iis.net/bills/archive/2007/05/21/tips-for-classic-asp-developers-on-iis7.aspx.*

Chapter 17
Performance and Tuning

On the Disc   Browse the CD for additional tools and resources.

This chapter will discuss performance and tuning of your Microsoft Windows Server 2008 Web servers. Windows Server 2008 and Internet Information Services (IIS) 7.0 provide many options for tuning your system to balance the best possible performance with servicing the requirements of your applications. You should be able use the new features in IIS 7.0 to design a system that will maximize your resource investment to meet your business requirements.

Tuning your servers for performance is an art and a science at the same time. An example would be the tradeoff between application pool isolation and performance. Particularly in some hosting scenarios, isolating application pools can be a big problem. Though using application pools to isolate Web sites can make for a more secure server, it also requires more server resources (in particular, increased amounts of memory). URL filtering can also impact performance. Each option you decide to implement can impact both performance and security.

Striking a Balance Between Security and Performance

As physics teaches us, for each action, there is an equal and opposite reaction. And this is the balance between performance and security. Many factors can impact your server's performance. Probably the biggest resource to help your server perform is how random access memory (RAM) usage is monitored. With 64-bit operating systems being able to handle many gigabytes (GB) of RAM, you would think that keeping track of available RAM would be a thing of the past. However, it is not that simple.

One of the main features of IIS 7.0 is the ability to load just the modules you need to support a particular application. This can help keep the core server footprint to a minimum.

How to Measure Overhead

Why do you measure overhead on your server? Let's compare it with measuring overhead in any business. Each business has monthly rent, utilities, and labor costs. These types of fixed costs are overhead. This analogy helps illustrate the fact that every server has some base resources that are overhead to the system.

Security can add overhead to any application and server. Depending on your requirements, it could add a delay and affect overall application performance. Security also costs some performance gains. For example, depending on your architecture, you can expect Secure Sockets Layer (SSL) processing to affect overall performance, both at the server and application level.

Following is an example of how you can establish the baseline for your server and worker process size (w3wp.exe) before you put any applications, modules, and load on the system. The example uses a server with Windows Server 2008 Enterprise edition with the Default IIS 7.0 install workload:

1. Install the Default IIS workload, which serves static content with anonymous access.

> **Note**   See Chapter 5, "Installing IIS 7.0," for more information about how to set up an IIS 7.0 server with the Default IIS 7.0 workload. This installation simply uses the default options selected when installing IIS 7.0.

2. Open Internet Explorer and type **http://localhost**.

3. After you browse http://localhost, a w3wp.exe process should show up in Windows Task Manager. Click the Processes tab and locate the memory footprint (for this example, it's about 3.1 megabytes [MB]).

4. If you want to see which dynamic-link libraries (DLLs) are loaded into the w3wp.exe worker process, open a command prompt and type **tasklist /M /FI "Imagename eq w3wp.exe"**. Here is an example of the output you will see.

```
Image Name                       PID Modules
===================== ========  =============================================
w3wp.exe                        3572 ntdll.dll, kernel32.dll, ADVAPI32.dll,
                                     RPCRT4.dll, msvcrt.dll, USER32.dll,
                                     GDI32.dll, ole32.dll, IISUTIL.dll,
                                     CRYPT32.dll, MSASN1.dll, USERENV.dll,
                                     Secur32.dll, WS2_32.dll, NSI.dll,
                                     IMM32.DLL, MSCTF.dll, LPK.DLL,USP10.dll,
                                     NTMARTA.DLL, WLDAP32.dll, PSAPI.DLL,
                                     SAMLIB.dll, w3wphost.dll, OLEAUT32.dll,
                                     nativerd.dll, XmlLite.dll, IISRES.DLL,
                                     rsaenh.dll, mscoree.dll, SHLWAPI.dll,
                                     comctl32.dll, mscorwks.dll, MSVCR80.dll,
                                     CLBCatQ.DLL, mlang.dll, iiscore.dll,
                                     W3TP.dll, w3dt.dll, HTTPAPI.dll,slc.dll,
                                     faultrep.dll, VERSION.dll, NLAapi.dll,
                                     IPHLPAPI.DLL, dhcpcsvc.DLL, DNSAPI.dll,
                                     WINNSI.DLL, dhcpcsvc6.DLL, mswsock.dll,
                                     winrnr.dll, napinsp.dll, wshtcpip.dll,
                                     wship6.dll, rasadhlp.dll, cachuri.dll,
                                     cachfile.dll, cachtokn.dll,cachhttp.dll,
                                     compstat.dll, defdoc.dll, dirlist.dll,
                                     protsup.dll, static.dll, authanon.dll,
                                     modrqflt.dll, custerr.dll, loghttp.dll,
                                     iisreqs.dll, WSOCK32.dll, authbas.dll,
                                     authsspi.dll, NETAPI32.dll
```

> **Note**   Although this list of DLLs appears to include a lot of entries, most of the DLLs are required by the core IIS engine. Some modules such as Default Documents (defdoc.dll) are optional and could be removed. This example uses the Default install of IIS. If necessary, you could reduce the number of optional role services, which would reduce the number of DLLs loaded. The only way to really know whether or not you can reduce the number of optional role services is to bring up a server in an isolated environment and test your configuration.

Here is an example from a server running Windows Server 2008 Server Core. The w3wp.exe process is approximately 2.5 MB in this example.

```
Image Name                       PID Modules
===================== ========  =============================================
w3wp.exe                        804 ntdll.dll, kernel32.dll, ADVAPI32.dll,
                                    RPCRT4.dll, msvcrt.dll, USER32.dll,
                                    GDI32.dll, ole32.dll, IISUTIL.dll,
                                    CRYPT32.dll, MSASN1.dll, USERENV.dll,
                                    Secur32.dll, WS2_32.dll, NSI.dll,
                                    IMM32.DLL, MSCTF.dll, LPK.DLL,USP10.dll,
                                    NTMARTA.DLL, WLDAP32.dll, PSAPI.DLL,
                                    SAMLIB.dll, w3wphost.dll, OLEAUT32.dll,
                                    nativerd.dll, XmlLite.dll, IISRES.DLL,
                                    rsaenh.dll, CLBCatQ.DLL, mlang.dll,
                                    comctl32.dll, SHLWAPI.dll, iiscore.dll,
                                    W3TP.dll, w3dt.dll, HTTPAPI.dll,slc.dll,
                                    faultrep.dll, VERSION.dll, mswsock.dll,
                                    DNSAPI.dll, NLAapi.dll, IPHLPAPI.DLL,
```

```
dhcpcsvc.DLL, WINNSI.DLL, dhcpcsvc6.DLL,
wshtcpip.dll, wship6.dll, cachuri.dll,
cachfile.dll, cachtokn.dll,cachhttp.dll,
compstat.dll, defdoc.dll, dirlist.dll,
protsup.dll, static.dll, authanon.dll,
modrqflt.dll, custerr.dll, loghttp.dll,
iisreqs.dll, WSOCK32.dll, gzip.dll
```

This worker process baseline exercise shows you how to determine how big your w3wp process will be and which DLLs are loaded. If you add modules, you can run through the exercise again and see how your memory footprint has changed.

Table 17-1 lists the new WAS_W3WP Reliability And Performance Counter (perfmon) counters in IIS 7.0.

Table 17-1   WAS_W3WP Counters

Counter Name	Description
Total Health pings	Total number of health pings received by the process
Total Runtime Status Queries	Total number of Runtime Status queries received by the process
Health Ping Reply Latency	Time, in 100-nanosecond intervals, taken by worker process to reply to last health ping
Active listener channels	Number of currently active listener channels in the worker process
Active protocol handlers	Number of currently active protocol handlers in the worker process
Total WAS Messages Received	Total number of messages received by the worker process from Web Admin Service
Messages Sent to WAS	Total count of messages sent to WAS
Total Requests Served	Total number of requests served by the worker process; this counter is meaningful only when request-based recycling is enabled for the application pool
Total Messages Sent to WAS	Total number of messages sent to Web Admin Service by the worker process

The new W3SVC_W3WP Reliability and Performance Counter (perfmon) counters in IIS 7.0 are listed in Table 17-2.

Table 17-2   W3SVC_W3WP Counters in IIS 7.0

Counter Name	Description
Total HTTP Requests Served	Total number of HTTP requests served by the worker process
Requests / Sec	HTTP requests/sec being processed by the worker process
Active Requests	Current number of requests being processed by the worker process

Table 17-2   W3SVC_W3WP Counters in IIS 7.0

Counter Name	Description
Total Threads	Total number of threads available to process requests in the worker process
Active Threads Count	Number of threads actively processing requests in the worker process
Maximum Threads Count	Maximum number of threads to which the thread pool can grow as needed
Current File Cache Memory Usage	Current number of bytes used by user-mode file cache.
Maximum File Cache Memory Usage	Maximum number of bytes used by user-mode file cache.
Output Cache Current Memory Usage	Current number of bytes used by output cache
Current Files Cached	Current number of files whose contents are present in user-mode cache
Total Files Cached	Total number of files whose contents were ever added to the user-mode cache (since service startup)
File Cache Hits	Total number of successful lookups in the user-mode file cache (since service startup)
File Cache Misses	Total number of unsuccessful lookups in the user-mode file cache (since service startup)
File Cache Flushes	Total number of files removed from the user-mode cache (since service startup)
Active Flushed Entries	Number of file handles cached in user-mode that will be closed when all current transfers complete
Total Flushed Files	Total number of file handles that have been removed from the user-mode cache (since service startup)
Current URIs Cached	URI information blocks currently in the user-mode cache
Total URIs Cached	Total number of URI information blocks added to the user-mode cache (since service startup)
URI Cache Hits	Total number of successful lookups in the user-mode URI cache (since service startup)
URI Cache Misses	Total number of unsuccessful lookups in the user-mode URI cache (since service startup)
URI Cache Flushes	Total number of URI cache flushes (since service startup)
Total Flushed URIs	The number of URI information blocks that have been removed from the user-mode cache (since service startup)
Current Metadata Cached	The number of metadata information blocks currently present in user-mode cache
Total Metadata Cached	Total number of metadata information blocks added to the user-mode cache (since service startup)
Metadata Cache Hits	Total number of successful lookups in the user-mode metadata cache (since service startup)

Table 17-2 W3SVC_W3WP Counters in IIS 7.0

Counter Name	Description
Metadata Cache Misses	Total number of unsuccessful lookups in the user-mode metadata cache (since service startup)
Metadata Cache Flushes	Total number of user-mode metadata cache flushes (since service startup)
Total Flushed Metadata	Total number of metadata information blocks removed from the user-mode cache (since service startup)
Output Cache Current Items	Number of items current present in output cache
Output Cache Total Hits	Total number of successful lookups in output cache (since service startup)
Output Cache Total Misses	Total number of unsuccessful lookups in output cache (since service startup)
Output Cache Total Flushes	Total number of flushes of output cache (since service startup)
Output Cache Total Flushed Items	Total number of items flushed from output cache (since service startup)
File Cache Hits / sec	Rate of successful lookups in file cache during last sample interval
Metadata Cache Hits / sec	Rate of successful lookups in metadata cache during last sample interval
Uri Cache Hits / sec	Rate of successful lookups in URI cache during last sample interval
File Cache Misses / sec	Rate of unsuccessful lookups in file cache during last sample interval
Metadata Cache Misses / sec	Rate of unsuccessful lookups in metadata cache during last sample interval
Output Cache Misses / sec	Rate of unsuccessful lookups in output cache during last sample interval
Uri Cache Misses / sec	Rate of unsuccessful lookups in URI cache during last sample interval
Total HTTP Requests Served	Total number of HTTP requests served by the worker process
Requests / Sec	HTTP requests/sec being processed by the worker process

Authentication

IIS 7.0 Manager lists seven different authentication modules. The Anonymous module is installed by default; the others can be installed individually:

- Active Directory Client Certificate Mapping Authentication
- Anonymous Authentication
- ASP.NET Impersonation

- Basic Authentication
- Digest Authentication
- Forms Authentication
- Window Authentication

To help make your server more secure and perform better, install only the modules you need. For more information on setup, see Chapter 5.

SSL

The SSL implementation has changed in IIS 7.0. Windows Server 2003 stores all SSL configurations in the IIS metabase, and encryption and decryption happen in user mode. This requires a lot of back-and-forth communication between kernel and user mode. In Windows Server 2008, HTTP.sys handles SSL encryption and decryption in kernel mode. Secure connections should have up to 20 percent better performance than IIS 6.0. The performance gains for decrypting data are evident because the need to bounce back and forth from kernel mode to user mode has been greatly reduced.

To move SSL into kernel mode, IIS 7.0 requires SSL binding information to be stored in two locations. The binding information is stored in %windir%\system32\inetsrv\ applicationHost.config for each site. When the site starts, IIS sends the binding to HTTP.sys, and HTTP.sys starts listening for requests on the specified IP:port. The second part of SSL configuration is stored in HTTP.sys configuration. You can use Netsh to view SSL binding configuration stored in HTTP.sys.

> **Note**   Netsh is a command line scripting utility that allows you to, either locally or remotely, display or modify the network configuration of a computer that is currently running. Netsh also provides a scripting feature that allows you to run a group of commands in batch mode against a specified computer. Netsh can also save a configuration script in a text file for archival purposes or to help you configure other servers. For more information about Netsh, go to *http://technet.microsoft.com* and search for *Netsh overview*.

Here is an example showing a sample binding to 192.168.0.10. The IP address is the same that would be listed in the Web site bindings.

```
netsh http show sslcert

SSL Certificate bindings:
-------------------------

    IP:port                  : 192.168.0.10:443
    Certificate Hash         : 63ca21f32543806959aed570a081fb3f311f958a
    Application ID           : {4dc3e181-e14b-4a21-b022-59fc669b0914}
    Certificate Store Name   : MY
```

```
Verify Client Certificate Revocation     : Enabled
Verify Revocation Using Cached Client Certificate Only    : Disabled
Usage Check    : Enabled
Revocation Freshness Time : 0
URL Retrieval Timeout    : 0
Ctl Identifier          : (null)
Ctl Store Name          : (null)
DS Mapper Usage     : Disabled
Negotiate Client Certificate     : Disabled
```

When a client starts an SSL negotiation, HTTP.sys looks in its SSL configuration for the IP and port pair that the client connected to. For the SSL-based request to succeed, the HTTP.sys SSL configuration must include a certificate hash and name of the certificate's store.

SSL accelerators come in two forms: an external device and internal card. An external device is useful when you want to add capacity on demand or make sure there is room to grow. As your requirements for SSL increase, you can add devices to handle the load. An internal card, usually a PCI card, will take the load off the Web server by handling the encryption and decryption. As computers continue to get faster and add more CPU cores, there may no longer be any need for the external device.

Whatever solution you decide regarding SSL will depend on your application needs. IIS 7.0 has improved the performance of how it handles SSL, compared to IIS 6.0. After you have load-tested your application, only then will you determine if you need an external device.

No matter which way you proceed, following best practices, you should put your application in a controlled environment and load-test it. If you determine under load that your servers can handle all the operations, then this can help determine what your production environment will look like. Testing will help you clarify your decision about SSL performance.

The Impact of Constrained Resources

Every administrator has to deal with a server with constrained resources. Windows Server 2008 and IIS 7.0 offer the Reliability and Performance Monitor. This is a new and expanded performance tool in Windows Server 2008. Using it can help determine what is causing a resource issue.

Processor

The first resource performance issue usually noticed by administrators is high CPU (Central Processing Unit) usage. When users report slow performance, the first thing most administrators do is open Windows Task Manager and look at processor usage. This problem is usually a symptom of something else going on with the machine or application. It doesn't take much for an immediate CPU spike—it could be as simple as an infinite loop in code.

What Causes CPU Pressure?

If there was an easy answer to the question of what causes CPU pressure, an administrator's job would be a lot easier. Let's look at a list of common items that cause pressure:

- Poorly written applications
- Memory-intensive services
- Servers not sized to support the applications
- Too many processes on the server
- Servers not having enough RAM

As you can see by the preceding list, a variety of issues can cause CPU pressure.

Throttling

Throttling an application or process is one way of keeping server resources available and not allowing the server to become unresponsive. The term *throttling* means limiting the amount of server resources a particular process or resource can use. For example, IIS 7.0 offers various ways to throttle resources—from bandwidth to connection time-outs and limits. If your server hosts multiple Web sites, you can throttle the number of connections one Web site receives. This would help keep it from using too many connections or server resources and also prevent other Web sites hosted on the server from being affected. Figure 17-1 shows the available options in IIS 7.0 that you can throttle. This can be done a per–Web site basis.

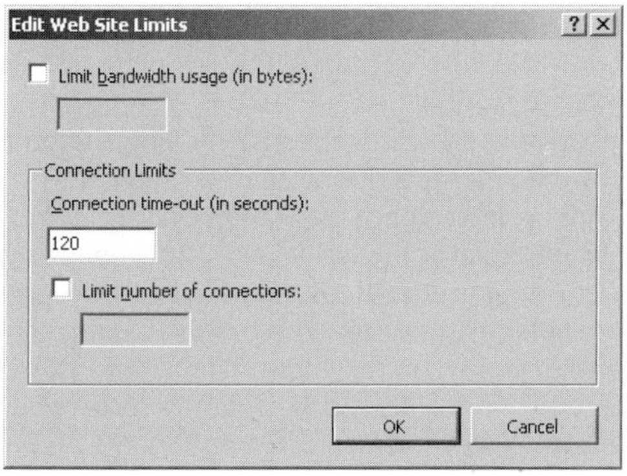

Figure 17-1   Per–Web site limits available in IIS 7.0.

IIS 7.0 offers several ways using application pool limits to throttle resources. You can set limits on worker process CPU settings, Rapid Fail Protection, Recycling, and several settings in the Process model section located in application pool settings. You can learn more about general application pool settings in Chapter 10, "Managing Applications and Application Pools."

Caching provides one of the better ways to enhance your application's performance. There are also ways to throttle how much of the server resources are used. Locking down how much RAM caching is allowed to use can impact the performance gains your application experiences.

You can use application pool options to help lower CPU usage so that your higher impact sites have resources available. This is one example of how you could control resources on your server and maximize application performance .

CPU Counters to Monitor

See Table 17-3 for a list of common counters that help identify which processes and how much of the server resources are being used when your IIS 7.0 server is experiencing high CPU conditions.

Table 17-3 CPU Counters to Measure

Counter Name	Description
Processor(_Total)\% Interrupt Time	The time the processor spends receiving and servicing hardware interrupts during sample intervals. This value is an indirect indicator of the activity of devices that generate interrupts, such as the system clock, the mouse, disk drivers, data communication lines, network interface cards, and other peripheral devices. These devices normally interrupt the processor when they have completed a task or require attention. Normal thread execution is suspended during interrupts. Most system clocks interrupt the processor every 10 milliseconds, creating a background of interrupt activity. This counter displays the average busy time as a percentage of the sample time.
Processor(_Total)\% Privileged Time	The time the processor spends receiving and servicing hardware interrupts during sample intervals. This value is an indirect indicator of the activity of devices that generate interrupts, such as the system clock, the mouse, disk drivers, data communication lines, network interface cards, and other peripheral devices. These devices normally interrupt the processor when they have completed a task or require attention. Normal thread execution is suspended during interrupts. Most system clocks interrupt the processor every 10 milliseconds, creating a background of interrupt activity. This counter displays the average busy time as a percentage of the sample time.

Table 17-3 CPU Counters to Measure

Counter Name	Description
Processor(_Total)\% Processor Time	The percentage of elapsed time that the processor spends to execute a non-idle thread. It is calculated by measuring the percentage of time that the processor spends executing the idle thread and then subtracting that value from 100%. (Each processor has an idle thread that consumes cycles when no other threads are ready to run.) This counter is the primary indicator of processor activity and displays the average percentage of busy time observed during the sample interval. It should be noted that the accounting calculation of whether or not the processor is idle is performed at an internal sampling interval of the system clock (10 ms). On today's fast processors, % Processor Time can therefore underestimate the processor utilization, as the processor may be spending a lot of time servicing threads between the system clock sampling intervals. Workload-based timer applications are one example of applications that are more likely to be measured inaccurately, as timers are signaled just after the sample is taken.
Processor(_Total)\% User Time	The percentage of elapsed time the processor spends in user mode. User mode is a restricted processing mode designed for applications, environment subsystems, and integral subsystems. The alternative, privileged (kernel) mode, is designed for operating system components, and it allows direct access to hardware and all memory. The operating system switches application threads to privileged mode to access operating system services. This counter displays the average busy time as a percentage of the sample time.
System\Context Switches/sec	The combined rate at which all processors on the computer are switched from one thread to another. Context switches occur when a running thread voluntarily relinquishes the processor, is preempted by a higher priority ready thread, or switches between user-mode and privileged (kernel) mode to use an Executive or subsystem service. It is the sum of Thread\\Context Switches/sec for all threads running on all processors in the computer and is measured in numbers of switches. There are context switch counters on the System and Thread objects. This counter displays the difference between the values observed in the last two samples, divided by the duration of the sample interval.
System\System Calls/sec	The combined rate of calls to operating system service routines by all processes running on the computer. These routines perform all of the basic scheduling and synchronization of activities on the computer and provide access to nongraphic devices, memory management, and namespace management. This counter displays the difference between the values observed in the last two samples, divided by the duration of the sample interval.

Reliability and Performance Monitor counters can help you establish a baseline for your server and can help you understand the number of resources used during normal and peak times. When an issue arises, you can use the server's baseline information and then compare the statistics collected to help identify the issue.

Using Reliability and Performance Monitor counters provides a lot of information. When used effectively, using these counters will help isolate and resolve a performance problem.

Impact of Constraints

Constraining the CPU resources on a server can impact how your application performs. This applies only when you are putting constraints on your application. When you do so, it impacts performance—one application frees up resources for another application.

Countermeasures

One example of how IIS 7.0 can help counter high CPU usage is by implementing Web gardens. Web gardens are an available feature on worker processes that help spread the workload across multiple processes. See Figure 17-2.

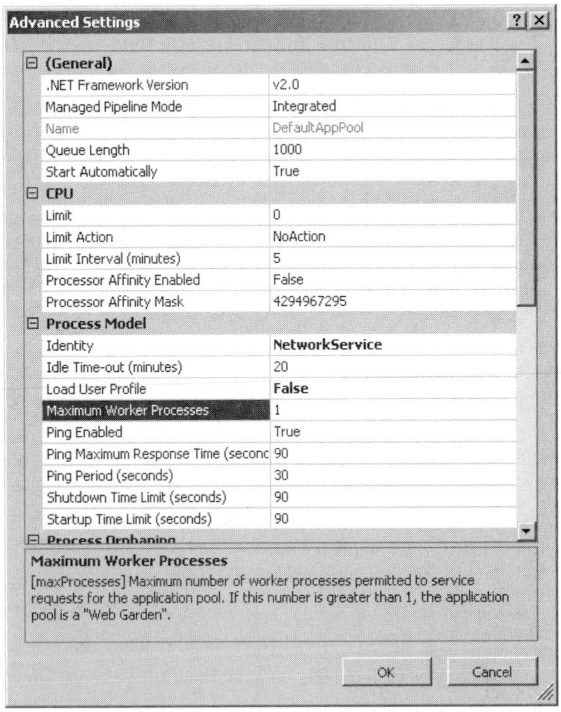

Figure 17-2   Maximum worker processes setting in IIS 7.0.

One thing to keep in mind is that Web gardens do not work on applications requiring stateful sessions. What does that mean? If you have a caching application, the variables will be cached in each application pool process and will not be shared among other processes. The reason for this is that each process has its own copy of the application state, so values are independent of other worker processes and would not match across other processes in the Web garden.

Consider this example of when to use Web gardens. Steve at Contoso Ltd. has an application that is hitting the 2 GB x86 process limit and is crashing. The application does not use session state, so it is a candidate for enabling Web gardens. After enabling Web gardens, Steve is able to spread the application load across multiple worker processes, preventing the application from crashing.

Let's take a look at another example from Steve at Contoso Ltd. He also has a database process that experiences latency. From time to time, this causes the application pool to crash. To help with performance and tuning of the application, Steve adds processes to give the application multiple processes accessing the resource (in this case, it's a database).

Memory

Memory—or the lack of it—is probably the most common bottleneck in any system, causing a slowdown that is evident to users. It's the first issue you should look at when server issues appear. With the introduction of 64-bit computing, you have the luxury of servers supporting literally terabytes of RAM. If your application requires that much RAM that users must access, you can probably find room for performance enhancements. However, 64-bit computing can help applications that have high memory requirements scale better than running the applications on a 32-bit platform.

What Causes Memory Pressure?

Normally, Web applications that consume memory by design or due to poor code implementation lead to bottlenecks. You can identify many memory bottlenecks during testing or during a pilot of your application. Following proper development processes and stress testing at the early stages can help minimize the pressure.

With the ever-growing list of features and situations an application must handle, you should—first and foremost—not push more data or information to the client. In a distributed environment, typical Web applications can try to select and cache 10,000 records. Imagine hundreds of people hitting your Web site at the same time. If your information has been cached on the server, the lack of available memory available on the server can affect your application performance.

Memory Counters to Monitor

Table 17-4 lists common memory counters that help identify which processes and how many of the server resources are being used when your IIS 7.0 server is experiencing high memory conditions.

Table 17-4   Memory Counters to Measure

Counter Name	Description
Memory\Available Mbytes	The amount of physical memory, in megabytes, immediately available for allocation to a process or for system use. It is equal to the sum of memory assigned to the standby (cached), free, and zero page lists. For a full explanation of the memory manager, refer to MSDN and/or the System Performance and Troubleshooting Guide chapter in the *Microsoft Windows Server 2003 Resource Kit* (Microsoft Press, 2005).
Memory\Cache Faults/sec	The rate at which faults occur when a page sought in the file system cache is not found and must be retrieved from elsewhere in memory (a soft fault) or from disk (a hard fault). The file system cache is an area of physical memory that stores recently used pages of data for applications. Cache activity is a reliable indicator of most application I/O operations. This counter shows the number of faults, without regard for the number of pages faulted in each operation.
Memory\Demand Zero Faults/sec	The rate at which a zeroed page is required to satisfy the fault. Zeroed pages, pages emptied of previously stored data and filled with zeros, are a security feature of Windows that prevent processes from seeing data stored by earlier processes that used the memory space. Windows maintains a list of zeroed pages to accelerate this process. This counter shows the number of faults, without regard to the number of pages retrieved to satisfy the fault. This counter displays the difference between the values observed in the last two samples, divided by the duration of the sample interval.

Table 17-4   **Memory Counters to Measure**

Counter Name	Description
Memory\Pages/sec	The rate at which pages are read from or written to disk to resolve hard page faults. This counter is a primary indicator of the kinds of faults that cause system-wide delays. It is the sum of Memory\\Pages Input/sec and Memory\\Pages Output/sec. It is counted in numbers of pages, so it can be compared to other counts of pages, such as Memory\\Page Faults/sec, without conversion. It includes pages retrieved to satisfy faults in the file system cache (usually requested by applications) and non-cached mapped memory files.
Memory\Transition Faults/sec	The rate at which page faults are resolved by recovering pages that were being used by another process sharing the page, or were on the modified page list or the standby list, or were being written to disk at the time of the page fault. The pages were recovered without additional disk activity. Transition faults are counted in numbers of faults; because only one page is faulted in each operation, it is also equal to the number of pages faulted.
Process(inetinfo)\% Processor Time	The percentage of elapsed time that all process threads used the processor to execution instructions. An instruction is the basic unit of execution in a computer, a thread is the object that executes instructions, and a process is the object created when a program is run. Code executed to handle some hardware interrupts and trap conditions are included in this count.
Process(w3wp)\% Processor Time	
Process(w3wp)\Handle Count	The total number of handles currently open by this process. This number is equal to the sum of the handles currently open by each thread in this process.
Process(w3wp)\ID Process	The unique identifier of this process. ID Process numbers are reused, so they only identify a process for the lifetime of that process.
Process(w3wp)\Private Bytes	The current size, in bytes, of memory that this process has allocated that cannot be shared with other processes.
Process(w3wp)\Thread Count	The number of threads currently active in this process. An instruction is the basic unit of execution in a processor, and a thread is the object that executes instructions. Every running process has at least one thread.

Table 17-4   **Memory Counters to Measure**

Counter Name	Description
Process(w3wp)\Virtual Bytes	The current size, in bytes, of the virtual address space the process is using. Use of virtual address space does not necessarily imply corresponding use of either disk or main memory pages. Virtual space is finite, and the process can limit its ability to load libraries.
Process(w3wp)\Working Set	The current size, in bytes, of the Working Set of this process. The Working Set is the set of memory pages touched recently by the threads in the process. If free memory in the computer is above a threshold, pages are left in the Working Set of a process even if they are not in use. When free memory falls below a threshold, pages are trimmed from Working Sets. If they are needed, they will then be soft-faulted back into the Working Set before leaving main memory.

Impact of Constraints

When a server is low on RAM, it uses the paging file, causing the worker process to have to retrieve data from disk, slowing down performance. This can be an expensive operation, because the application has introduced another potential bottleneck, Disk I/O (Input/Output). An application that is forced to use a portion of the information swapped to the paging file has added latency and causes the server to use more resources.

Generally, with 32-bit operating systems, the recommended approach is to set the paging file size to be 1.5 times the amount of RAM. In a 64-bit environment, you can set the operating system to automatically handle the paging file size.

Countermeasures

One countermeasure against memory pressure is to verify that your Web server paging file is configured properly and optimized on a separate set of disks. Spreading a paging file across separate physical disks enables you to improve paging file performance by using drives that do not contain your site's content or log files. Although these steps are basic, they can go a long way toward helping your application's performance. They can also save your company money by getting the most out of your servers.

Understanding how many resources a typical transaction uses is important. This number can be valuable when you calculate what your production environment and monitoring thresholds will be. If your database holds a lot of detail data, you can calculate how the data might grow over a period of months or years and how this might impact your application. It might perform well at first, but you might find that as the amount detail data grows, your application will be slower, and server performance will suffer.

Hard Disks

As faster and faster disks evolve, chances of the disk being the issue become less likely. Redundant Array of Inexpensive Disk (RAID) and striping technologies are not really IIS-related performance tricks, but they can help increase your server's overall performance. The real effect on hard disks depends on how much RAM your machine has.

What Causes Hard Disk Pressure?

Typically, pressure is a matter of the amount of disk reads and writes. A Web server that has a high ratio of reads to writes tends to perform better. The Reliability and Performance Monitor is a great tool for analyzing the total number of reads and writes a Web server generates. If your application requires a lot of writes, you should have faster disks and a RAID implementation to support them. Disk bottlenecks can be improved by using Kernel-mode caching, which greatly eliminates the number of direct reads from the disk.

Hard Disk Counters to Monitor

See Table 17-5 for a list of common hard disk counters that help identify which processes and how much of the server resources are being used when your IIS 7.0 server is experiencing hard disk-related issues.

Table 17-5 Disk Counters to Measure

Counter Name	Description
PhysicalDisk(_Total)\% Disk Time	The percentage of elapsed time that the selected disk drive was busy servicing read or write requests.
PhysicalDisk(_Total)\% Disk Read Time	The percentage of elapsed time that the selected disk drive was busy servicing read requests.
PhysicalDisk(_Total)\% Disk Write Time	The percentage of elapsed time that the selected disk drive was busy servicing write requests.
PhysicalDisk(_Total)\Current Disk Queue Length	The number of requests outstanding on the disk at the time the performance data is collected. It also includes requests in service at the time of the collection. This is an instantaneous snapshot, not an average over the time interval. Multispindle disk devices can have multiple requests that are active at one time, but other concurrent requests are awaiting service. This counter might reflect a transitory high or low queue length, but if there is a sustained load on the disk drive, it is likely that this will be consistently high. Requests experience delays proportional to the length of this queue minus the number of spindles on the disks. For good performance, this difference should average less than two.

Table 17-5   Disk Counters to Measure

Counter Name	Description
PhysicalDisk\Disk Reads/sec	The rate of read operations on the disk.
PhysicalDisk\Disk Writes/sec	The rate of write operations on the disk.
PhysicalDisk\Avg. Disk Bytes/Read	The average number of bytes transferred from the disk during read operations.
PhysicalDisk\Avg. Disk Bytes/Write	The average number of bytes transferred to the disk during write operations.

Impact of Constraints

Your application's performance and throughput will be affected if your IIS 7.0 server does not have enough RAM. When a server has to start writing and retrieving information from disk, there will be latency to your application's performance. Disk paging can be an expensive task, and using disk performance counters can help you measure how your server is performing.

Countermeasures

You can implement a few countermeasures to help prevent disk latency. Here are some things to keep in mind:

- Choose the correct RAID for your server(s).

- When implementing RAID, select a hardware controller over a software RAID solution. It's definitely worth the investment.

- You can spread your paging file across multiple disks.

- More spindles help with performance. Several smaller disks are faster than one large drive.

- Speed is very important. Faster disks help with performance, and in the long run they are worth the few extra dollars they cost.

- Definitely monitor performance by using the counters mentioned in this section.

- Keep your disks from becoming fragmented.

- For a Web server, have the logging and content on separate disk from the operating system. Logging can be an expensive operation, so try to move logging to a separate set of disks. Alternatively, offload it to a remote server.

Note   To help you out with logging, we'd like to point out an option called httpLogging, which enables you to control how much data is logged to your IIS log files. One attribute of httpLogging, *selectiveLogging*, enables you to control which status codes are logged to your IIS Logs. By default, the *selectiveLogging* option is set to *LogAll*, which means log all status codes. You can set the value to *LogSuccessful*, which logs all HTTP status codes from 100 to 399. The *LogError* option logs HTTP status codes from 400 to 999. The following example shows you how to adjust the *selectLogging* setting by using Appcmd. You can also set httpLogging to *dontLog*, which will prevent any logs from being generated. Logging is discussed more in Chapter 15, "Logging."

//Code sample to set the selectiveLogging attribute using Appcmd.

//LogAll is the default, LogSuccessful and LogError are the other options.

Appcmd set config -section:httpLogging -selectiveLogging:LogSuccessful

//Here is the part of the schema that controls the system.webServer/ httpLogging/selective-Logging attribute

```
<attribute name="selectiveLogging" type="enum" defaultValue="LogAll">

  <enum name="LogAll" value="0" />

  <enum name="LogSuccessful" value="1" />

  <enum name="LogError" value="2" />

</attribute>
```

Turn off unnecessary disk intensive services such as Index Server or other search type functions if the service is not in use. These types of services can continually index content and take up precious disk cycles.

Tuning your hard disk subsystem is one issue you'll probably not have to deal with when working to optimize your system. Providing your server with enough RAM can go a long way towards ensuring that your hard disk is not the cause when a problem arises.

Network

One of the best performance enhancements in Microsoft Windows Server 2008 is a complete redesign of the Transmission Control Protocol/Internet Protocol (TCP/IP) stack, also known as the Next Generation TCP/IP stack. The TCP/IP stack has been redesigned to enable high-speed multi-gigabit capabilities without consuming all of the CPU power and resources on the server. It integrates security products into the Windows platform and makes it more manageable. In addition, the TCP/IP stack has been redesigned to make it more easily serviced, to add capabilities, and to let third-party independent software vendors (ISVs) add capabilities to it (specifically in the firewall and antivirus categories).

What Causes Network Pressure?

In a perfect world, bandwidth restrictions would not be an issue. Switched networks as well as 1 GB and greater network speeds have helped, but network utilization still can be a bottleneck. How you deal with it can make your applications successful or not. The increasing availability of high-speed networks and broadband connections does not guarantee a low latency experience.

High demand for content such as video streaming or audio files can lead to pressure on the network. The Internet is one big wide area network, and it takes only one slow connection to become saturated and cause packet loss. When packet loss occurs, higher latency and slower response times for applications can occur. Low latency and slow application response are less likely in a local area network. However, the network is only as strong as the weakest link.

Network Counters to Monitor

See Table 17-6 for a list of common network counters used to identify network-related issues on your IIS 7.0 server.

Table 17-6   Network Counters to Measure

Counter Name	Description
Network Interface(NICNAME)\Bytes Total/sec	The rate at which bytes are sent and received over each network adapter, including framing characters. Network Interface\Bytes Total/sec is a sum of Network Interface\Bytes Received/sec and Network Interface\Bytes Sent/sec.
Network Interface(NICNAME)\Current Bandwidth	An estimate of the current bandwidth of the network interface in bits per second (BPS). For interfaces that do not vary in bandwidth or for those where no accurate estimation can be made, this value is the nominal bandwidth.

Impact of Constraints

Dealing with slow router points or switches that are saturated can constrain how you provide services and keep the network functional. Using QoS (Quality of Service) and scheduling network-intensive operations during off-hours can help the impact on your network.

Having tools in place to monitor your network can help you spot trends and understand if your network is operating efficiently. The Next Generation TCP/IP stack supports the IETF draft RFC 4898, "TCP Extended Statistics MIB," which defines extended performance statistics for TCP. By analyzing ESTATS on a connection, you can determine whether a connection's performance is based on the sending application, the receiving application, or the network. ESTATS is disabled by default and can be enabled per connection. With ESTATS, non-Microsoft independent software vendor (ISVs) can create powerful diagnostics and network throughput analysis applications. Tcpanalyzer.exe, which is available in the Windows Vista SDK, is a diagnostic tool based on ESTATS.

The Explicit Congestion Notification (ECN) feature also enhances performance. When a TCP segment is lost, TCP assumes that the segment was lost due to congestion at a router, and it performs congestion control, dramatically lowering the TCP sender's transmission rate. With ECN support on both TCP peers and in the routing infrastructure, a router experiencing congestion mark packets as it forwards them. TCP peers receiving marked packets lower their transmission rate to ease congestion and prevent segment losses. Detecting congestion before packet losses are incurred increases the overall throughput between TCP peers. ECN is not enabled by default. To enable ECN, run this command: **netsh interface tcp set global ecncapability=enabled**.

Countermeasures

How do you know what your network utilization is? Right-click in the Start Bar, select Task Manager, and navigate to the Networking tab. Select the network interface you would like to view and check its network utilization statistics. If your primary network card is close to 100 percent, the card is likely a bottleneck in the performance of your application. Generally, you should start to investigate if network utilization is around 50 percent. Figure 17-3 shows how Task Manager presents network utilization statistics.

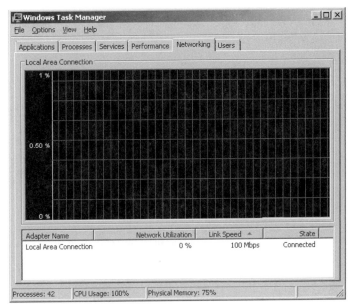

Figure 17-3   Network utilization in Windows Task Manager.

The Next Generation TCP/IP stack is a complete redesign of TCP/IP functionality for both IPv4 and IPv6 that meets the connectivity and performance needs of today's varied networking environments and technologies. The following features are new or enhanced:

- Receive Window Auto-Tuning
- Compound TCP
- Enhancements for high-loss environments
- Neighbor Unreachability Detection for IPv4
- Dead Gateway Detection

- Path Maximum Transmission Unit (PMTU) Black Hole Router Detection
- Routing Compartments
- Network Diagnostics Framework Support
- Windows Filtering Platform
- Explicit Congestion Notification

With its many new features and enhancements, Windows Server 2008 should help keep network pressure at a minimum. For more information, see the article posted on TechNet called "New Networking Features in Windows Server 2008 and Windows Vista" at *http://technet.microsoft.com/en-us/library/bb726965.aspx*.

Application-Level Counters

Microsoft provides several key application-level counters that can be useful in troubleshooting your application. Table 17-7 presents a subset of counters that can help troubleshoot ASP.NET and Web-related issues.

Table 17-7   Application Counters

Counter Name	Description
.NET CLR Exceptions(w3wp)\# of Exceps Thrown / sec	The number of exceptions thrown per second. These include both .NET exceptions and unmanaged exceptions that get converted into .NET exceptions (e.g., a null pointer reference exception in unmanaged code would get rethrown in managed code as a .NET System.NullReference-Exception). This counter includes both handled and unhandled exceptions. Exceptions should only occur in rare situations and not in the normal control flow of the program; this counter was designed as an indicator of potential performance problems due to large (>100s) rate of exceptions thrown. This counter is not an average over time; it displays the difference between the values observed in the last two samples divided by the duration of the sample interval.
.NET CLR Jit(w3wp)\% Time in Jit	The percentage of elapsed time spent in JIT compilation since the last JIT compilation phase. This counter is updated at the end of every JIT compilation phase. A JIT compilation phase is the phase when a method and its dependencies are being compiled.
.NET CLR Jit(w3wp)\IL Bytes Jitted / sec	The total IL bytes jitted since the start of the application. This counter is exactly equivalent to the "Total # of IL Bytes Jitted" counter.

Table 17-7 **Application Counters**

Counter Name	Description
.NET CLR Loading(w3wp)\% Time Loading	
.NET CLR Loading(w3wp)\Current appdomains	The current number of AppDomains loaded in this application. AppDomains (application domains) provide a secure and versatile unit of processing that the CLR can use to provide isolation between applications running in the same process.
.NET CLR Loading(w3wp)\Current Assemblies	The current number of Assemblies loaded across all AppDomains in this application. If the Assembly is loaded as domain-neutral from multiple AppDomains, then this counter is incremented once only. Assemblies can be loaded as domain-neutral when their code can be shared by all AppDomains, or they can be loaded as domain-specific when their code is private to the AppDomain.
.NET CLR LocksAndThreads(w3wp)\Queue Length / sec	The total number of times threads in the CLR have attempted to acquire a managed lock unsuccessfully. Managed locks can be acquired in many ways—by the "lock" statement in C#, or by calling System.Monitor.Enter, or by using MethodImplOptions.Synchronized custom attribute.
.NET CLR LocksAndThreads(w3wp)\Total # of Contentions	The total number of times threads in the CLR have attempted to acquire a managed lock unsuccessfully. Managed locks can be acquired in many ways—by the "lock" statement in C#, or by calling System.Monitor.Enter, or by using MethodImplOptions.Synchronized custom attribute.
.NET CLR Memory(w3wp)\% Time in GC	The percentage of elapsed time that was spent in performing a garbage collection (GC) since the last GC cycle. This counter is usually an indicator of the work done by the Garbage Collector on behalf of the application to collect and compact memory. This counter is updated only at the end of every GC, and the counter value reflects the last observed value; it is not an average.
.NET CLR Memory(w3wp)\# Total Committed Bytes	The amount of virtual memory (in bytes) currently committed by the Garbage Collector. (Committed memory is the physical memory for which space has been reserved on the disk paging file.)
.NET CLR Memory(w3wp)\# Bytes in all Heaps	The sum of four other counters—Gen 0 Heap Size, Gen 1 Heap Size, Gen 2 Heap Size, and the Large Object Heap Size. This counter indicates the current memory allocated in bytes on the GC Heaps.

Table 17-7   **Application Counters**

Counter Name	Description
.NET CLR Memory(w3wp)\# Gen 0 Collections	The number of times the generation 0 objects (youngest; most recently allocated) are garbage collected (Gen 0 GC) since the start of the application. Gen 0 GC occurs when the available memory in generation 0 is not sufficient to satisfy an allocation request. This counter is incremented at the end of a Gen 0 GC. Higher generation GCs include all lower generation GCs. This counter is explicitly incremented when a higher generation (Gen 1 or Gen 2) GC occurs. _Global_ counter value is not accurate and should be ignored. This counter displays the last observed value.
.NET CLR Memory(w3wp)\# Gen 1 Collections	The number of times the generation 1 objects are garbage collected since the start of the application. The counter is incremented at the end of a Gen 1 GC. Higher generation GCs include all lower generation GCs. This counter is explicitly incremented when a higher generation (Gen 2) GC occurs. _Global_ counter value is not accurate and should be ignored. This counter displays the last observed value.
.NET CLR Memory(w3wp)\# Gen 2 Collections	The number of times the generation 2 objects (older) are garbage collected since the start of the application. The counter is incremented at the end of a Gen 2 GC (also called full GC). _Global_ counter value is not accurate and should be ignored. This counter displays the last observed value.
.NET CLR Memory(w3wp)\# Induced GC	The peak number of times a garbage collection was performed because of an explicit call to GC.Collect. It's a good practice to let the GC tune the frequency of its collections.
.NET CLR Memory(w3wp)\Allocated Bytes/sec	The rate of bytes per second allocated on the GC Heap. This counter is updated at the end of every GC, not at each allocation. This counter is not an average over time; it displays the difference between the values observed in the last two samples divided by the duration of the sample interval.

Table 17-7 **Application Counters**

Counter Name	Description
.NET CLR Memory(w3wp)\Finalization Survivors	The number of garbage collected objects that survive a collection because they are waiting to be finalized. If these objects hold references to other objects, then those objects also survive but are not counted by this counter; the "Promoted Finalization-Memory from Gen 0" and "Promoted Finalization-Memory from Gen 1" counters represent all the memory that survived due to finalization. This counter is not a cumulative counter; it's updated at the end of every GC with count of the survivors during that particular GC only. This counter was designed to indicate the extra overhead that the application might incur because of finalization.
.NET CLR Memory(w3wp)\Gen 0 Heap Size	The maximum bytes that can be allocated in generation 0 (Gen 0); it does not indicate the current number of bytes allocated in Gen 0. A Gen 0 GC is triggered when the allocations since the last GC exceed this size. The Gen 0 size is tuned by the Garbage Collector and can change during the execution of the application. At the end of a Gen 0 collection, the size of the Gen 0 heap is in fact 0 bytes; this counter displays the size (in bytes) of allocations that would trigger the next Gen 0 GC. This counter is updated at the end of a GC; it's not updated on every allocation.
.NET CLR Memory(w3wp)\Gen 1 Heap Size	The current number of bytes in generation 1 (Gen 1); this counter does not display the maximum size of Gen 1. Objects are not directly allocated in this generation; they are promoted from previous Gen 0 GCs. This counter is updated at the end of a GC; it's not updated on every allocation.
.NET CLR Memory(w3wp)\Gen 2 Heap Size	The current number of bytes in generation 1 (Gen 1); this counter does not display the maximum size of Gen 1. Objects are not directly allocated in this generation; they are promoted from previous Gen 0 GCs. This counter is updated at the end of a GC; it's not updated on every allocation.
.NET CLR Memory(w3wp)\Large Object Heap Size	The current size of the Large Object Heap in bytes. Objects greater than 20 kilobytes (KB) are treated as large objects by the Garbage Collector and are directly allocated in a special heap; they are not promoted through the generations. This counter is updated at the end of a GC; it's not updated on every allocation.

Table 17-7   **Application Counters**

Counter Name	Description
.NET CLR Memory(w3wp)\Process ID	The process ID of the CLR process instance being monitored.
.NET CLR Security(w3wp)\% Time in RT checks	The percentage of elapsed time spent in performing run-time Code Access Security (CAS) checks since the last such check. CAS allows code to be trusted to varying degrees and enforces these varying levels of trust depending on code identity. This counter is updated at the end of a run-time security check. It represents the last observed value; it's not an average.
ASP.NET Applications(_Total_)\Cache Total Trims	Total number of entries forcibly removed from the cache due to memory pressure.
ASP.NET Applications(_Total_)\Cache Total Entries	Total number of entries within the cache (both internal and user added)
ASP.NET Applications(_Total_)\Cache Total Hit Ratio	Ratio of hits from all cache calls.
ASP.NET Applications(_Total_)\Cache Total Turnover Rate	Number of additions and removals to the total cache per second.
ASP.NET Applications(_Total_)\Output Cache Entries	Current number of entries in the output cache.
ASP.NET Applications(_Total_)\Output Cache Hits	Total number of output cacheable requests served from the output cache.
ASP.NET Applications(_Total_)\Output Cache Hit Ratio	Ratio of hits to requests for output cacheable requests.
ASP.NET Applications(_Total_)\Output Cache Turnover Rate	Number of additions and removals to the output cache per second.
ASP.NET Applications(_Total_)\Compilations Total	Number of .asax, .ascx, .ashx, .asmx, or .aspx source files dynamically compiled.
ASP.NET Applications(_Total_)\Errors Total/ Sec	Rate of errors occurred.
ASP.NET Applications(_Total_)\Pipeline Instance Count	Number of active pipeline instances.
ASP.NET Applications(_Total_)\Requests Executing	The number of requests currently executing.
ASP.NET Applications(_Total_)\Requests in Application Queue	The number of requests in the application request queue.
ASP.NET Applications(_Total_)\Requests/Sec	The number of requests executed per second.
ASP.NET\Application Restarts	Number of times the application has been restarted during the Web server's lifetime.
ASP.NET\Request Wait Time	The number of milliseconds the most recent request was waiting in the queue.

Table 17-7   **Application Counters**

Counter Name	Description
ASP.NET\Requests Current	The current number of requests, including those that are queued, currently executing, or waiting to be written to the client. Under the ASP.NET process model, when this counter exceeds the requestQueueLimit defined in the processModel configuration section, ASP.NET will begin rejecting requests.
ASP.NET\Requests Queued	The number of requests waiting to be processed.
ASP.NET\Requests Rejected	The number of requests rejected because the request queue was full.
Web Service(_Total)\Get Requests/sec	The rate at which HTTP requests using the GET method are made. GET requests are the most common HTTP request.
Web Service(_Total)\Post Requests/sec	The rate at which HTTP requests using the POST method are made.
Web Service(_Total)\Connection Attempts/sec	The rate that connections to the Web service are being attempted.
Web Service(_Total)\Current Connections	Current Connections is the current number of connections established with the Web service.
Web Service(_Total)\ISAPI Extension Requests/sec	The rate at which ISAPI Extension requests are received by the Web service.
Web Service\Service Uptime	The length of time the Web Service has been running.
Web Service\Total Method Requests	The number of all HTTP requests (since service startup).
Web Service Cache\URI Cache Hits %	The ratio of user-mode URI Cache Hits to total cache requests (since service startup).

64-Bit Mode vs. 32-Bit Mode

In general, 64-bit computing has greatly expanded resource limits over 32-bit computing. At first, the limits seem very high compared to 32-bit (x86) computing. Windows Server 2008 offers two 64-bit versions. The x64 platform provides the ability to run 32-bit and 64-bit on the same machine, and this solution is the obvious choice for most server application deployments, whether small or large.

The other type of 64-bit version is an Itanium-based system. IA64 systems are best suited for extremely large database and custom application solutions. For our purposes, the rest of this section discusses x64.

One of the major differences between IIS 6.0 and IIS 7.0 is that you could run a 32-bit application on a 64-bit machine with IIS 6.0, but the entire IIS 6.0 server is running in 32-bit mode. In IIS 7.0, you can split the .NET version on a per-application basis. You have the potential to run the application pools presented in Table 17-8 on a single x64 machine.

Table 17-8   Application Pool Version Types

Application Version	.NET Framework Version
32-bit application pool	ASP.NET 1.1
32-bit application pool	ASP.NET 2.0
64-bit application pool	ASP.NET 2.0

All handlers for various ASP.NET versions/pipeline modes are registered globally by the IIS 7.0 core server. This enables you to run an ASP.NET 2.0 application in 32-bit and 64-bit mode on the same machine. The appropriate preconditions and settings on the application pool automatically select the correct set of handlers that apply to that application pool. The preconditions apply to Internet Server Application Programming Interface (ISAPI) filters also.

Another advantage of running 32-bit applications on a 64-bit machine is that 32-bit processes running under Windows-on-Windows 64-bit (WoW64) get 4 GB of addressable virtual memory. Kernel memory is not sacrificed to squeeze out more virtual memory for user mode processes. Even with 32-bit IIS worker processes, the kernel runs 64-bit natively.

Table 17-9 presents a breakdown of the differences between Windows Server 2008 32-bit and 64-bit CPU and memory limits for each operating system version.

Table 17-9   Server CPU/Memory Limits for Windows Server 2008

Technology	Web Edition	Standard Edition	Enterprise	DataCenter	IA-Based Systems
Sockets, x86	4	4	8	32	n/a
Sockets, x64	4	4	8	64	n/a
Sockets, IA64	n/a	n/a	n/a	n/a	64
RAM, 32-bit	4 GB	4 GB	64 GB	64 GB	n/a
RAM, 64-bit	32 GB	32 GB	2 TB	2 TB	n/a
RAM, IA64	n/a	n/a	n/a	n/a	2 TB

IIS 7.0 provides a compelling reason to move your systems to Windows Server 2008 x64-bit edition. Being able to run .NET 1.1 and 2.0, as well as other frameworks on an application pool basis, enables you to experience the benefits of 64-bit computing without making any code changes.

Configuring for Performance

Configuring your environment for performance requires that you truly understand your applications and how your users will interact with the applications. How many times have you heard administrators tell the tale that an application worked great in the lab, but when it was deployed to production, it crashed? Sound familiar? I hope not! Performing adequate testing beforehand should be a requirement before you purchase production hardware.

You should consider a few scenarios when configuring your servers. First, you need to know some basic information, such as the following:

- How many users do you expect to use your application?
- At peak usage, how many concurrent users do you expect?
- Where are your users based—are they on well-connected networks such as a local area network, or are they connecting over the Internet?
- How long will a typical session last?
- Does your application require session state?
- Does your application interact with a database?
- How much RAM does a typical session take?
- Will your application be disk-intensive?

These questions are important to understand when you are configuring your environment. Your answers can influence the decision to run everything on a stand-alone or on a set of servers. A set of servers could include a Web farm front end with a separate database server.

If your current application is in production, you can use the Reliability and Performance Monitor to capture baseline numbers that will help you load-test your environment. If your application is brand new, you'll have to calculate usage numbers and estimate how much traffic you expect.

This section of the chapter is not intended to provide an in-depth discussion of application architecture. However, good development practices and methodologies can have a great impact on how you set up and scale your environment. The ultimate goal is to have well-tuned applications that provide good user experiences. A lot of planning up front can give you big wins when you decide to get in the lab and test your applications.

Server Level

You can do many things at the server level to configure your environment for performance. Before you do anything at server level, however, understanding the application you want to support will go a long way toward creating a smooth running environment. Here are a few things you can do to make sure your server will perform at acceptable levels:

- If possible, run the 64-bit version of Windows Server 2008.
- Configure your application pools to run 32-bit mode.
- Make sure your server has enough RAM.

- Make sure your server firmware and basic input/output system (BIOS) are up to date.
- If running a Web farm, try to keep your servers configured identically.
- Configure your system to use RAID.
- Install only necessary software such as monitoring agents, antivirus software, and so on.

IIS

IIS has always been pretty much a self-tuning service. There have been a few registry tweaks here and a metabase adjustment there, but overall, IIS has a good reputation for self-tuning based on a wide variety of workloads. IIS 7.0 continues this behavior. Before we say that IIS 7.0 will scale on any type of hardware, though, you need to take into account the types of applications that you will be deploying. The application types that you choose can greatly change IIS performance, but they have little to do with IIS 7.0 itself. The hardware setup, amount of RAM, and speed of the disk all contribute to the overall Web server experience.

Optimizing for the Type of Load

How you optimize your environment really depends on your needs. For example, do you need to support a large concurrent connection base of users, or is it important to provide numbers of transactions? The following sections provide a couple examples illustrating what to take into account when optimizing your environment.

Load

Load is one of the first performance requirements that should be identified in the planning stages for your application. If your application will have spikes of load, you'll need to account for that in your design. An application that has peaks and valleys can be harder to design for. Most likely, you'll need to account for spikes no matter what the load is.

Consider this example: You are the director of IT for Contoso Ltd. You are aware that every year on December 31, the Contoso.com Web site experiences a thousand times more than normal traffic. The visitors are submitting expenses for the previous year, so that they can be reimbursed. Does that mean you scale your environment to meet the volume on December 31, and the rest of the year you have excess capacity? Probably not, but realistically, you need to take into account how to plan for the additional load created by so many visitors accessing the site at one time. You may want to consider using staggered schedules or some other option to prevent all the users from being on the system at once. This might seem like an unreal example, but it provides a picture of what you should define as load and what kinds of things you need to think about when testing. In this scenario, for example, when a user finishes submitting expenses and clicks Submit, that person is going to want the transaction to work so that they don't have to enter the information again—and of course so they get paid back for their expenses sooner rather than later.

As another example, consider that you are in a situation in which you have to scale your application to meet a lot of concurrent connections. In such a case, you would want to look at having multiple servers in a Web farm to handle not only the load, but also the site availability.

Required Availability

You usually will work with your business partners to determine what an acceptable level of application availability is. As the Internet has matured, applications need to be available 24 hours a day, 7 days a week to maintain this type of availability. Performing routine mainte-nance or security patching can be tough. One recommendation is to schedule a standard maintenance window. This can be difficult, because Internet applications can be accessed from anywhere. The standard window helps provide some consistency when changes happen, however.

Performance Requirement

Having a defined SLA (service level agreement) can help you understand your performance requirements. Frequent and critical functions need to be identified and tested to ensure they perform properly. Frequently used transactions, intensive operations, and business-critical operations need to perform under load and must be available to users.

When testing your application, it is critical that you use data that is as close to real-world data and user patterns as possible to make sure your system performs optimally. Creating an application baseline in the real world is a key component to being successful.

Type of Content

The type of content in your application has a significant impact on performance and how you might design your Web server environment. You can start by looking at the amount of static content versus dynamic content used on your Web site. The server should be tuned in a way that accommodates the type of content that is more prevalent on the server. A server that contains mostly static content, for example, can take advantage of Kernel-mode caching and output caching.

IIS 7.0 output caching can handle content scenarios that are semi-dynamic, such as an ASP.NET application that pulls data from a database with content that remains relatively unchanged. One suggested technique when using output caching is that you can see a huge performance boost by caching your content for just a few seconds.

Server-Side Tools

IIS 7.0 tries to cache content in many places. Each feature covered in this section determines what type of content is cached along with how the content will be cached. Each has their own place but can help with overall server performance.

HTTP.sys Cache

Microsoft introduced Kernel-mode caching in IIS 6.0. This feature eliminates the need for accessing User-mode cache in many cases. The HTTP.sys cache helps increase server performance and reduces disk cost. The content has to be requested a few times before IIS 7.0 considers caching an URL. You can configure *frequentHitTimePeriod* and *frequentHitThreshold* thresholds in the *serverRuntime* applicationHost.config section. Here are the default *serverRuntime* settings located in the %windir%\system32\inetsrv\config\schema\IIS_schema.xml folder. These settings are inherited by default.

```
<sectionSchema name="system.webServer/serverRuntime">
  <attribute name="enabled" type="bool" defaultValue="true" />
  <attribute name="appConcurrentRequestLimit" type="uint" defaultValue="5000" />
  <attribute name="maxRequestEntityAllowed" type="uint" defaultValue="4294967295" />
  <attribute name="uploadReadAheadSize" type="uint" defaultValue="49152" validationType=
"integerRange" validationParameter="0,2147483647" />
  <attribute name="alternateHostName" type="string" />
  <attribute name="enableNagling" type="bool" defaultValue="false" />
  <attribute name="frequentHitThreshold" type="uint" defaultValue="2" validationType=
"integerRange" validationParameter="1,2147483647" />
  <attribute name="frequentHitTimePeriod" type="timeSpan" defaultValue="00:00:10" />
</sectionSchema>
```

A request is cached if more than the number of *frequentHitThreshold* requests for a cacheable URL arrive within the *frequentHitTimePeriod* setting. Following is an example of the benefits you can get by using Kernel-level cache rather than User-mode caching or no caching enabled.

The example shows how to setup Web Capacity Analysis Tool (WCAT) and run the WCAT controller, WCAT client, and setup Output Caching policies in IIS Manager. There are three tests using different Output Caching policies.

First, the following steps allow you to configure WCAT to use this example in your environment:

1. Download the IIS6 Resource Kit Tools (go to *http://www.iis.net/go/1352*), do a custom install, and install only WCAT. You'll use three files to help configure WCAT:

   ❑ A script file that tells WCAT which URLs to request. Each URL gets a unique ClassID.

   ❑ A distribution file that tells WCAT how the requests should be distributed across the URLs specified in the script file.

   ❑ A configuration file that configures the parameters of a particular performance run, for example, the duration of the tests, how many HTTP clients to simulate, and so on.

2. Create a folder named C:\LoadTest to hold the configuration files.

3. Create a file called Default.aspx in C:\LoadTest. Type <% = Datetime.Now() %> and save Default.aspx. This file will be used for load-testing.

4. Create a new file called script.cfg in C:\LoadTest and type the following text:

```
NEW TRANSACTION
    classId = 1
    NEW REQUEST HTTP
        Verb = "GET"
        URL = "http://localhost/Default.aspx"
```

5. Create a file called distribution.cfg and type the following text inside the file:

```
1 100
```

6. Create a file called config.cfg and type the following text inside the file:

```
Warmuptime 5s
Duration 30s
CooldownTime 5s
NumClientMachines 1
NumClientThreads 20
```

Next, after you have configured the LoadTest folder and supporting WCAT files, you can enable the WCAT controller. This is required to perform the tests. Open a command prompt and type the following syntax:

```
Cd \LoadTest
"%programfiles%\IIS Resources\WCAT Controller\wcctl"
    -c config.cfg -s script.cfg -d distribution.cfg -a localhost
```

After enabling the WCAT controller, you can run the WCAT client to perform your performance tests. You'll need to open another command prompt window to start the WCAT client.

```
"%programfiles%\IIS Resources\WCAT Client\wcclient.exe" localhost
```

The first test has no Output Cache policy enabled. You can set the Output caching policy in IIS Manager. Figure 17-4 shows no Output Cache policy enabled.

Per Table 17-10, running a test has results of 575 requests per second, which is an acceptable number. Let's see how caching can help improve performance.

The second test enables User-mode policy only. The test using User-mode policy assumes you are using the file notifications option displayed in Figure 17-5. Figure 17-5 also shows how to enable a User-mode cache policy.

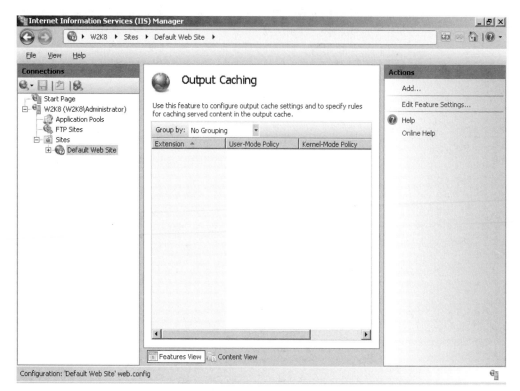

Figure 17-4   No Output Cache policy enabled.

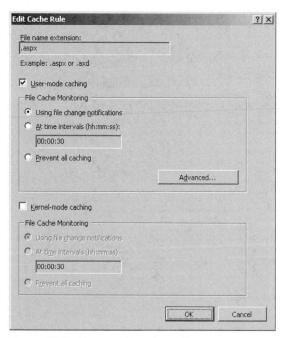

Figure 17-5   User-mode cache policy.

As you can see in Table 17-10, after running a test with User-mode caching enabled, the results are 656 requests per second, which is a 13 percent increase over no cache policy enabled.

For the third test, disable the User-mode caching policy and enable Kernel-mode caching. The Kernel-mode caching test assumes you are using the file notifications option displayed in Figure 17-6. Figure 17-6 shows how to configure a Kernel-mode caching policy.

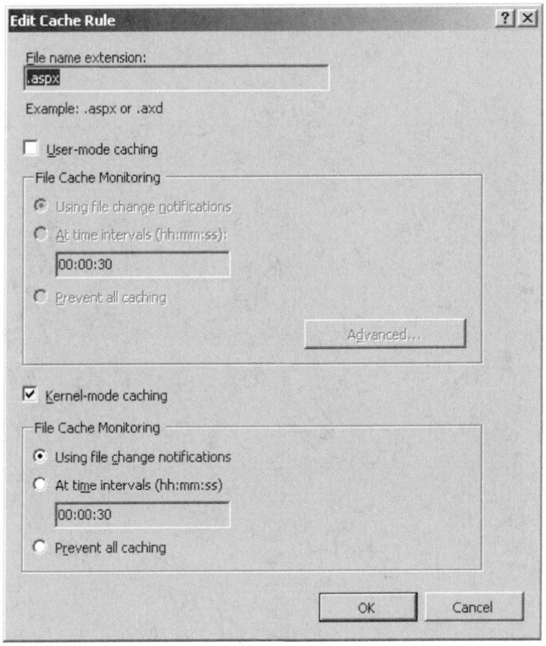

Figure 17-6   Kernel-mode caching policy.

After running the test with Kernel-mode caching enabled, the results are 946 requests per second, which is 60 percent more than if you had had no cache policy. Table 17-10 shows results from the three performance tests. The results can vary depending on what type of hardware you are using.

Table 17-10   Output Caching Results

Requests per Second	Cache Level
575	No cache enabled
656	User-mode caching only
946	Kernel-mode caching only

You should be aware of limitations when you are using Kernel-mode caching. Kernel-mode caching does not support modules and features that run in user mode, for example, if your application uses basic authentication or Windows Authentication or authorization. The content will be served, but it won't be cached. The Kernel-mode caching option supports the *varyByHeaders* attribute, but not *varyByQuerystring*. To see if a request is in the Kernel-mode cache, type **netsh http show cachestate**.

> **Note** For more information on Http.sys changes in Vista and Windows Server 2008, go to *http://technet.microsoft.com/en-us/library/bb726965.aspx* and search for HTTP.sys within the article.

User-mode Caching

One important change with User-mode caching is that any content type can be cached, not just Classic ASP or ASP.NET.

Direct from the Source: Native Output Cache Changes in IIS 7.0

Native output cache is the new user mode response cache added in IIS 7.0. This module provides functionality that is similar to that provided by the managed output cache module in ASP.NET. You can control this module's functionality by editing the *system.webServer/caching* section, located in applicationHost.config, or by using IHttpCachePolicy intrinsic. The IHttpCachePolicy intrinsic is for *getting/setting* kernel-response cache or user-mode output cache policy from code. You can set the following properties in the *system.webServer/caching* section:

- **enabled** This property tells if output caching is enabled or not for this URL. If disabled, output cache module won't do anything in *ResolveRequestCache* and *UpdateRequestCache* stages.

  Note that setting the *enabled* property to true doesn't ensure response caching. Some modules must set User-cache policy.

- **enableKernelCache** Controls if kernel caching is enabled for this URL. The output cache module calls *IHttpResponse::DisableKernelCache* if this property is set to false. The output cache module does kernel caching work in the *SendResponse* stage if no one called *DisableKernelCache* in the pipeline. Note that setting *enableKernelCache* to true doesn't ensure kernel caching of the response. Some modules must set the kernel cache policy.

- **maxCacheSize** This is the maximum size of the output cache in megabytes. A value of 0 means the maximum cache size is calculated automatically by IIS 7.0. IIS 7.0 uses half of the available physical memory or the available virtual memory—whichever is less.

- **maxResponseSize** This is the maximum size of the response in bytes that can be stored in the output cache. A value of 0 means no limit.

  Note that although you can set *maxCacheSize* and *maxResponseSize* for a URL, the output cache module uses values set at the root level only.

Per application pool properties in the future will be configurable for each application pool. If the output cache is enabled, you can control its behavior for different file types by adding profiles for different file extensions. These profiles make the output cache module populate IHttpCachePolicy intrinsic, which enables user/kernel caching of the response. Properties that you can set in a profile are similar to those available for system.web/caching/outputCacheSettings profiles. The following properties are allowed for system.webServer/caching profiles:

- *extension* For example, .asp, .htm. Use * as a wildcard entry. If the profile for a particular extension is not found, the profile for extension * will be used if it is present.

- *policy* Can be *DontCache*, *CacheUntilChange*, *CacheForTimePeriod*, or *DisableCache* (only in the server). Output cache module changes IHttpCachePolicy intrinsic, depending on the value of this property.

   Note that *DontCache* means that intrinsic is not set, but that doesn't prevent other modules from setting it and enabling caching. In the server, we have added the *DisableCache* option, which ensures that the response is not cached even if some other module sets the policy telling output cache module to cache the response.

- *kernelCachePolicy* Can be *DontCache, CacheUntilChange, CacheForTimePeriod*, or *DisableCache* (only in the server). As previously mentioned, *DontCache* doesn't prevent other modules from setting kernel cache policy. For static files, the static file handler sets kernel cache policy, which enables kernel caching of the response. In the server, the *DisableCache* option ensures that the response doesn't get cached in kernel.

- *duration* The *duration* property is used only when policy or *kernelCachePolicy* is set to *CacheForTimePeriod*.

- *location* Sets cache-control response header for client caching. The cache-control response header is set depending on value of this property, as follows:

```
Any | Downstream: public
ServerAndClient | Client: private
None | Server: no-cache
```

- *varyByHeaders* Comma-separated list of request headers. Multiple responses to requests having different values of these headers will be stored in the cache. You might be returning different responses based on Accept-Language or User-Agent or Accept-Encoding headers. All the responses will get cached in memory.

- *varyByQueryString* Comma-separated query string variables. Multiple responses get cached if query string variable values are different in different requests. In the server, you can set *varyByQueryString* to *, which makes the output cache module cache a separate response if any of the query string variable values are different.

Only user mode cache uses location headers and *varyBy*. These properties have no effect on kernel caching. So if policy is set to *DontCache*, these properties are not used. To make output cache module cache multiple responses by an ASP page for 30 minutes, which returns different responses based on value of query string variable "action" and also based on request header "User-agent," the caching section will look like the following, which is located in the applicationHost.config file:

```
<caching>
<profiles enabled="true">
<add extension=".asp" policy="CacheForTimePeriod" duration="00:30:00"
varyByQueryString="action" varyByHeaders="User-Agent"/>
</profiles>
</caching>
```

Output cache module populates the IHttpCachePolicy intrinsic in the *BeginRequest* stage if a matching profile is found. Other modules can still change cache policy for the current request, which might change User-mode or Kernel-mode caching behavior. The output cache caches 200 responses to GET requests only. If some module already flushed the response by the time the request reaches the *UpdateRequestCache* stage, or if headers are suppressed, the response is not cached in the output cache module.

The output cache module caches the response only if some other module hasn't already cached it, as indicated by *IHttpCachePolicy::SetIsCached*. In addition, caching happens only for frequently hit content. The definition of frequently hit content is controlled by the *frequentHitThreshold* and *frequentHitTimePeriod* properties, which are defined in the *system.webServer/serverRuntime* section located in applicationHost.config. Default values define frequently hit content as content that is requested twice in any 10-second period.

Kanwaljeet Singla

IIS Team Microsoft

Compression

IIS 7.0 provides static and dynamic compression capabilities. Most of the properties are managed under system.webServer\httpCompression, which is located in applicationHost.config.

Direct from the Source: Changes Made to Compression Modules in IIS 7.0

Static compression is on by default in IIS 7.0. Dynamic compression is still off by default, and you can turn it on for all content by using the following syntax.

```
Appcmd set config -section:urlCompression /doDynamicCompression:true
```

In IIS 6.0, static compression happens on a separate thread. So, upon receiving a request, the first response is uncompressed, and IIS 6.0 starts a separate thread to compress the file and keep it in compressed files cache. Requests for compressed content reaching IIS 6.0 after the compression is complete receive a compressed response.

In IIS 7.0, compression happens on the main thread. But to avoid the cost of compression for all requests, compression happens only for frequently requested content. The definition of frequently requested content is controlled by the properties *frequentHitThreshold* and *frequentHitTimePeriod* under the section *system.webServer/serverRuntime*. If IIS 7.0 receives more than the threshold number of requests in *frequentlyHitTimePeriod* for the same URL, IIS 7.0 will go ahead and compress the file to serve a compressed response for the same request that made IIS reach threshold.

This compressed response is saved in the compressed files cache, as in IIS 6.0. If the compressed response was already present in compression cache, *frequentHitThreshhold* logic is not applied, because compressed content will be picked from cache and there will be no additional cost for compressing the content. Hit count is maintained per URL. So sending the first request with Accept-Encoding: gzip and the second with deflate will still qualify as frequently hit content, and IIS will go ahead and compress the response. This will require cachuri.dll to present in the *globalModules* section, because it is the module that keeps URL hit count.

The temporary compressed files folder has a nested directory structure in IIS 7.0, whereas it is flat in IIS 6.0. IIS 7.0 creates folders for each application pool in temporary compressed files and then creates separate folders for different schemes under each application pool. Under these scheme folders, IIS 7.0 creates a folder structure similar to the folder from which the content was picked. So, if iisstart.htm from D:\inetpub\wwwroot was compressed using gzip, a cache entry will be created in the D:\inetpub\temp\IIS Temporary Compressed Files\DefaultAppPool\$^_gzip_D^\INETPUB\WWWROOT folder.

IIS 7.0 will ACL (access control list) the application pool folder with worker process identity to protect the content from worker processes serving other application pools. You can still configure the directory from config, but the default is moved from %windir%\iis temporary compressed files to %SystemDrive%\inetpub\temp\iis temporary compressed files.

Also with this change, the *maxDiskSpaceUsage* limit is applied per application pool. So, if you have a value of 100 MB for *HcMaxDiskSpaceUsage* in IIS 6.0, then that limit is applied to all the compressed content in the compressed files cache. In IIS 7.0, this limit applies to compressed files per application pool. If you have 10 application pools and have *maxDiskSpaceUsage* set to 100 MB, total space allocated to compressed files cache is actually 1 GB.

Because static compression is enabled by default, and compression is happening on the main thread, on-the-fly compression shuts off or resumes, depending on CPU load. Four properties are added to the *system.webServer/httpCompression* section to control this behavior. These are as follow:

- **staticCompressionDisableCpuUsage**   Compression is disabled when average CPU usage over a specified period of time is above this number.

- **staticCompressionEnableCpuUsage**   Compression is enabled if average CPU usage over a specified period of time falls below this number.

- **dynamicCompressionDisableCpuUsage and dynamicCompressionEnableCpuUsage**
  Enable or disable dynamic compression depending on the CPU load. IIS 7.0 will calculate average CPU utilization every 30 seconds.

In IIS 7.0, you can enable/disable compression depending on the content type of the response. In IIS 6.0, this is possible on an extension basis. In IIS 7.0, you can have just one entry in the configuration to enable static or dynamic compression for text/HTML responses. You no longer need to pick up all extensions that return text/HTML responses. When configuring these MIME types under the *httpCompression* section, you can use * as a wildcard. If the response type is text/HTML, look for an entry for text/HTML. If you find it, use the corresponding enabled value. If text/HTML is not found, look for text/* or */html. If both are present, pick the one that comes first and use that enabled property value. If you don't find them, look for */* and use the corresponding enabled value. For enabling compression for all content types, add an entry under the *httpCompression* section in applicationHost.config as shown here.

```
<staticTypes>
  <add mimeType="*/*" enabled="true" />
</staticTypes>
```

The maxDiskSpaceUsage entry in IIS 7.0 is configured in megabytes rather than bytes. We realized that people don't really want to configure the limit to the byte level, but the main reason we made this decision was because the limit is UINT, and we didn't want users to set it to a value that cannot be stored in UINT. With large disks today, having a large value won't be uncommon.

With static compression enabled by default, IIS 7.0 has only cache-compressed responses in the kernel (HTTP.sys). So if compression is enabled for a file, but the current request doesn't contain an Accept-Encoding header (or compression didn't happen because it was the first request), IIS 7.0 won't tell the HTTP.sys to cache it. Only the compressed response is cached in the kernel for which compression is enabled. Dynamically compressed responses are not cached in any of the caches (even in compressed files, as happens in IIS 6.0).

Deflate is removed in the default configuration, but the functionality is still present in gzip.dll. To add the deflate scheme, add the following in the *httpCompression* section.

```
<scheme name="deflate" dll="%windir%\system32\inetsrv\gzip.dll" />
```

You can use following Appcmd command.

```
Appcmd set config
/section:httpCompression /+[name='deflate',dll='%Windir%\system32\inetsrv\gzip.dll']
```

Because static compression is enabled by default, the default value of *staticCompression-Level* is changed from 10 in IIS 6.0 to 7 in IIS 7.0.

Kanwaljeet Singla

IIS Team Microsoft

Application Pools

IIS 7.0 offers a new behavior to allow you to create an application pool for each Web site. This is a significant change from IIS 6.0, which required you to have a pre-existing application pool. This new change can have a significant impact on, for example, Web hosters, because many of them configured sites in shared application pools.

Microsoft recommends you have each site isolated in their own application pool. If there is an issue, you can set the application pool to recycle based on a number of options.

NLB

Network Load Balancing (NLB) refers to having two or more servers handling your Web site. Spreading the load across two or more machines requires load balancing. You can use the built-in Network Load Balancing application provided by Windows Server 2008, or you can use a third-party hardware device. Using NLB can be a great way to help your application and Web site achieve good performance. We will discuss NLB more in the section titled "Performance Monitoring" later in this chapter.

Application

Configuring your application for performance starts literally the moment you start discussing application needs. Certain architecture and design considerations have the most impact on how your application will perform in the long term. How will you design your database? How much data will you store? Where will you get your data from? Will the data have to be accessed in real time, or can it be cached? How much data will you cache? Will your application use session state, or will it be stateless? How will you authenticate your visitors? What kind of security model will your application use?

The type of data you have will have an impact on your application and is something else to consider when configuring your application. Things like controlling memory usage and how many database calls will be made have an impact on performance.

Identifying and Isolating Bottlenecks

IIS 7.0 has a great story when it comes to helping isolate and identify bottlenecks in your Web applications. IIS 7.0 offers instrumentation completely through the request pipeline. IIS Manager puts Web request data at administrators' fingertips. This data was first exposed in Windows Server 2003 SP1, but it is *much* more user-friendly in IIS 7.0. Imagine, for example, that you are experiencing a problem with one of your application pools. With IIS 7.0, you can quickly identify which Web pages are executing at run time.

Failed Request Tracing (FRT) can be implemented on all content types, not just ASP or ASP.NET. You can use the data available to help make your application perform better. Following is one example: Your application makes an LDAP (Lightweight Directory Application Protocol) call to a directory service such as Microsoft Active Directory directory service to look up some group membership information. This process happens on the very first step when the application starts. This step is going to make or break the application, because it's the first thing the user will see. Using the new tracing tools, IIS 7.0 enables you to trace completely through the entire request pipeline to identify how long a step like this could take. If it takes milliseconds, that is pretty good (when compared to it taking five to seven seconds).

Before IIS 7.0, developers and administrators would have to troubleshoot where the bottleneck was occurring. The developer would point to the administrator and say, "My application performs well after it gets the group information back." The administrator would say the opposite: "My Active Directory is redundant, is running on fast servers, and has fast network connectivity. What are you trying to do inside your application?"

The administrator's point is valid if the application is round-tripping back and forth a few times. If you have the user credentials ahead of time, make one call to the directory for your group information. Doing so can cut down on latency and improve the user experience. This is one example of working together with both administrators and developers to achieve good application performance.

Best Practices

One of the key concepts to keep in mind when tuning your applications is TTFB (time to first byte) and TTLB (time to last byte). How many seconds does it take to get TTFB and how many seconds are there between TTFB and TTLB? What is the latency? Is there a quick load of the page, but then the application has to retrieve a lot of data from Web services and other data sources?

Your hardware can make or break an application. However, how an application is architected, designed, and tested will go a long way toward determining if it is successful in production.

Performance Monitoring

Monitoring is a critical component for any application or system. Architecting, designing, and testing an application or system usually get the most attention. When all the planning, testing, and tweaking have been completed, however, what is the most important and critical part of the system? The answer is rollout—yes, rollout is the most important step in this process, and it can be the most scary and exciting part of any project.

Monitoring goes along with rollout. Any application or system that can't be monitored most likely won't make it in production very long or is not a critical piece. Time and resources (both system and people) are scarce.

Microsoft has made enhancements in performance monitoring. This section is not intended to completely instruct you on all the tools and features but rather to provide you with an introduction to each of them, as well as to give pointers on how and when to use them.

The monitoring of a system is only as good as the tools available. Various tools can help you along the way to monitor, stress test, and tweak your application or system. The following tools are available for monitoring, and we will look at each one of them in turn in this section:

- Web Capacity Analysis Tool (WCAT)
- Reliability and Performance Monitor
- Failed Request Tracing (FRT), also known as FREB
- Event Viewer
- System Center Operations Manager

WCAT

The Web Capacity Analysis Tool (WCAT) is a critical tool for testing your applications and systems. It has been designed to simulate workload scenarios. WCAT enables you to determine the best configuration for your application and system. The IIS team and NT Performance team use this tool to conduct internal performance and scalability testing of IIS and ASP.NET. You can download WCAT from *http://iis.net/downloads*.

Reliability And Performance Monitor

Windows Server 2008 introduces an expanded performance monitor named Reliability and Performance Monitor. It's the utility knife for administrators when measuring performance for most anything. Windows Server 2008 and IIS 7.0 take advantage of this new tool. Figure 17-7 shows a picture of the Reliability and Performance Monitor. The four major perfmon counter categories are displayed: CPU, Disk, Memory, and Network.

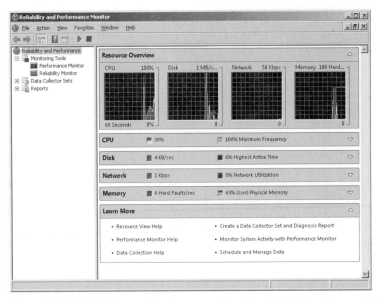

Figure 17-7   Reliability and Performance Monitor in Windows Server 2008.

FRT

One of the core features of IIS 7.0 is the diagnostics. Known as FREB in the early beta days, Failed Request Tracing (FRT) is new to IIS 7.0. It will be your primary tool for tracking down and diagnosing issues. Failed Request Tracing is discussed in more detail in Chapter 16, "Tracing and Troubleshooting."

Event Viewer

You may wonder why Event Viewer is mentioned, but Event Viewer contains good information, including information about any errors that may occur. Depending on your audit settings, the amount of information provided by Event Viewer can vary, but it is a great place to start when you are troubleshooting.

System Center Operations Manager 2007

System Center Operations Manager 2007 is usually deployed in enterprise environments. It is part of an overall monitoring and systems management suite of tools. Microsoft has management packs that plug into Operations Manager 2007. For more information about this tool, go to *http://www.microsoft.com/systemcenter/opsmgr/default.mspx.*

Scalability

Scalability depends on many factors, including the hardware used, the types of content and applications deployed, and the amount of available RAM. This section discusses ways Windows Server 2008 and IIS 7.0 greatly improve your applications.

IIS 7.0 offers many features to help with scalability. Kernel-level caching, Dynamic Compression, and Integrated Pipeline are some of the features that can help you out.

During Design

Probably nothing has more impact on scalability than the design phase of an application. You can deploy a sample and test it under load in a controlled environment during the design phase.

Understanding the Application's Nature

Understanding your application well can help with scalability. Is most of the data dynamic or static? If the application has portions that are static, you can look at caching portions of it. Are the higher volume pages static or semi-static information? Determining this can allow you to take advantage of IIS 7.0 caching features.

Other factors that can help with scalability are such things as whether your application stores information in text or XML files, and whether or not most of the information is database-driven.

User Base

Another critical requirement you should take into account is your user base. Sometimes we overlook who will be accessing our applications. Are most or all of your users local to your company, or are most of your users Internet-based?

Knowing your user base during all phases of application development, testing, and rollout provides a more realistic set of expectations concerning the time when real users will start using your application. When you're testing your application with your expected user base in mind, do try different scenarios under different loads.

Understanding how your user base will use your application and how the application acts under different situations is key to a more predictable, scalable application.

Scale Up or Out

The age-old IT question: Should you scale up or out? The answer is: it depends.

Web Farms

A Web farm is a group of two or more servers used to host a Web site. Web farms help increase the capacity of a Web site and improve availability by having redundant servers. Web farms are commonly used for high-traffic and mission critical Web sites. Here are factors to consider when attempting to run a single Web site on several servers:

- Content placement
- Session management
- Network Load Balancing

Content placement can be a key architecture and scalability question. You can either keep the files locally on the Web servers or place them on a remote file server. For single server deployments, keeping the content local to the server will have performance benefits and will be simpler to support. For Web farms, you can keep the content local on the server. However, you'll need to implement some type of file replication to keep files in sync across all machines. If your Web site has several changes or thousands of files, keeping them in sync can be challenging.

The other option regarding content placement is to store content on a remote file server. Your IIS servers would be the front end to the remote content. Keeping the content on a remote file server has many benefits, including a single source of content; greater efficiency when making updates; easier rollback changes than if your content was stored on each web farm node; and a remote file server that could be a SAN (storage area network), which has faster disks than local server disks.

You'll need to consider a few registry tweaks when you implement Universal Naming Convention (UNC)–based content. The Web server has one registry added, and two registry entries are added to the remote file server. See the following procedures for instructions to implement the changes.

To configure the registry key on the *file* server, follow these steps:

1. From the command prompt, type **regedt32** to open the registry.
2. Navigate to HKEY_LOCAL_MACHINE\SYSTEM\CurrentControlSet\Services\ lanmanserver\parameters.
3. If it doesn't exist, create a DWORD "MaxMpxCt" registry entry and set the value to 800 hexidecimal. This will specify a value of 2048 decimal.
4. If it doesn't exist, create a DWORD "MaxWorkItems" registry entry and set the value to 2000 hexidecimal. This will specify a value of 8192 decimal, or four times the "MaxMptCt" value.

To configure the registry key on the *Web* server, follow these steps:

1. From the command prompt, type **regedt32** to open the registry.

2. Navigate to HKEY_LOCAL_MACHINE\SYSTEM\CurrentControlSet\Services\ lanmanworkstation\parameters.

3. If it doesn't exist, create a DWORD "MaxCmds" registry entry and set the value to 800 hexidecimal. This will specify a value of 2048 decimal.

> **More Info**   For more information, go to the article titled "IIS Runs Out of Work Items and Causes RPC Failures When Connecting to a Remote UNC Path" at *http://support.microsoft.com/kb/221790/*.

Session management can be tricky in a Web farm. Depending on the application, you can support session state in a Web farm scenario in a variety of ways. For Classic ASP–based applications, you normally have some type of *sticky state* implemented on your load-balancer, which redirects the client to the original server that handled the initial session. All requests are redirected to that particular server for the entire session. That type of behavior can impact load on other servers, depending on traffic.

If you are using the built-in NLB feature in Windows Server 2008, the term for redirecting the session to the same server is called *affinity*. ASP.NET applications support various modes of session state. In a Web farm deployment, you need to either use a remote ASP.NET session state server or use a SQL Server session state server. The SQL Server solution could be a clustered set of machines that provides failover. The ASP.NET state server and SQL Server session options are the two available options provided by Microsoft. They scale well for applications requiring state management functionality. Third-party solutions are available to support InProc and replication of session and cache objects to other machines. The best option is to architect your applications to be stateless and not require session management. A stateless application provides for a more flexible application that should scale better in a Web farm deployment.

Web farms can be important when scaling your application. Before you proceed with scaling up or out, consider that a Web farm is probably the most cost-effective choice and is a great return on investment.

Web Gardens

Earlier in the chapter, we discussed Web gardens and how to help with scalability. Using Web gardens can help scale up and scale out on the same hardware. Systems that are multiple processor cores will automatically support Web gardens. In your efforts to increase scalability, Web gardens can be an option when your systems have multiple CPU cores.

Hardware Upgrade

Upgrading your existing hardware is sometimes overlooked when an application issue occurs. Usually, an administrator will consider bigger and faster hardware versus looking at the existing machines. Before you go to the expense of and asking for approval to purchase new hardware, first understand what is happening. If you determine the machine is CPU-constrained, consider adding more processors. A typical CPU costs less than a new machine. If you find that RAM is the bottleneck, consider adding more to the existing machine. RAM can greatly help with server performance. If disks are your bottleneck, consider looking at moving the content to a SAN, if you have one deployed in your environment. This will extend the life of the server and help with application performance.

Consider the following example. You could have a Web farm that has two nodes. The server's CPU usage averages 30 percent to 40 percent, with spikes to 60 percent and higher. Traffic has increased to a point at which performance has become an issue. After using the Reliability and Performance Monitor, you determine there are spikes due to CPU usage. The servers have single processor (two processors with hyperthreading) installed. Adding processors to the server, which is dual processor–capable, lowers the average CPU usage from 30–40 percent down to 10–15 percent. The processor costs $300 per machine. The total cost is $600 ($300 per machine times two machines in the Web farm) versus adding another machine, which could cost several thousand dollars. This is one example of extending the life of your current hardware instead of adding more to a Web farm or replacing servers that meet your needs.

NLB

NLB, or Network Load Balancing, directs requests to multiple servers to support your Web site. There are a few options when directing traffic to your Web farm. Round-robin is an option that enables you to direct requests evenly across all machines. Least-active supports sending requests to Web servers that are using the least amount of resources. Sticky-state, or affinity-based requests, sends the request back to the original server that started the session. Fastest reply sends requests to the server that's responding the quickest. Windows Server 2008 offers a built-in NLB option that supports multiple dedicated IP addresses. Many major vendors provide multilayer load-balancers. For higher traffic sites, evaluating Microsoft NLB and third-partyload-balancers is recommended before deciding which solution to choose. Using load-balancer technology can help provide high availability and redundancy and can help your application scale.

Summary

IIS 7.0 builds on enhancements first introduced in Windows Server 2003 SP1 and IIS 6.0. Caching has been expanded to help all kinds of applications perform better. Output caching can be used for Microsoft technologies such as ASP and ASP.NET, as well as for non-Microsoft languages such as PHP. There are other improvements such as SSL processing being moved into kernel mode that make SSL processing faster.

Windows Server 2008 x64 bit editions offer the ability to run 32-bit and 64-bit application pools on the same server. IIS 7.0 offers a compelling reason to upgrade to x64-bit version—no code changes are required and you get the benefits of 64-bit computing.

Improved diagnostics help identify problems quickly and have a faster resolution time. Windows Server 2008 introduces an enhanced Reliability and Performance Monitor. You can use the many counters that expose information to quickly isolate and troubleshoot your applications. Although the TCP/IP stack is more of an operating system enhancement, the performance gains will be noticeable in your Web applications. There is new information that can be exposed to help keep track and monitor your applications as well.

In conclusion, IIS 7.0 offers many enhancements that offer many ways to improve the performance of your Web application environment.

Additional Resources

The IIS team at Microsoft has done an exceptional job of publishing all kinds of targeted articles at *http://www.iis.net*, the central IIS community site. For further information on performance and tuning, check out the TechCENTER located at *http://www.iis.net*. The following resources also contain additional information and tools related to performance and tuning:

- 64-bit information is available at *http://www.microsoft.com/servers/64bit/overview.mspx*.
- An article titled "IIS7 Output Caching for Dynamic Content: Speed Up Your ASP and PHP Applications" is at *http://blogs.iis.net/bills/archive/2007/5/2/1690364.aspx*.
- For more information about output caching in IIS 7.0, see the article titled "IIS 7.0 Output Caching" at *http://www.iis.net/articles/view.aspx/IIS7/Managing-IIS7/Optimizing-Performance/Using-Output-Cache/IIS7-Output-Caching*.
- An article titled "IIS 7 C++ Module API Sample: Controlling HTTP.sys Caching" is available at *http://blogs.iis.net/rickjames/archive/2007/11/20/iis-7-c-module-api-sample-controlling-http-sys-caching.aspx*.
- For more about Secure Sockets Layer processing and IIS 7.0, see "How to Setup SSL on IIS7" at *http://www.iis.net/articles/view.aspx/IIS7/Managing-IIS7/Configuring-Security/Using-SSL/How-to-Setup-SSL-on-IIS7*.
- An article titled "Web and Application Server Infrastructure: Performance and Scalability" is available at *http://www.microsoft.com/technet/prodtechnol/windowsserver2003/technologies/webapp/iis/iis6perf.mspx#ESXAE*.
- For guidelines on ASP.NET performance monitoring, see "ASP.NET Performance Monitoring and When to Alert Administrators" at *http://msdn2.microsoft.com/en-us/library/ms972959.aspx#monitor_perf_topic12*.
- A white paper titled "Shared Hosting on IIS 7.0" is at *http://www.iis.net/articles/view.aspx/IIS7/Deploy-an-IIS7-Server/Deployment-for-Web-Hosters/Shared-Hosting-on-IIS7*.

Part V
Appendices

Appendix A
IIS 7.0 HTTP Status Codes

Table A-1 offers a list of custom HTTP codes that Internet Information Services (IIS) 7.0 uses when displaying an error. Custom error files are stored in %SystemDrive%\inetpub\ custerr\Locale (that is, %SystemDrive%\inetpub\custerr\en-us). Not all status codes have custom error pages on disk. When the custom error module detects an error, one of six actions is chosen:

1. Response is left alone

2. One-line error message is printed

3. Static file served off disk (c:\inetpub\custerr\en-us\404.htm)

4. URL is executed

5. Redirect

6. Detailed error is generated (default most common localhost behavior)

Following is a list of articles that provide more information on HTTP status codes and common causes to errors with links to troubleshooting articles.

- "Troubleshooting Failed Requests using Tracing in IIS7," available at *http:// support.microsoft.com/kb/943891*

- The following link is displayed on the "more information" link at the bottom of detailed errors: *http://go.microsoft.com/fwlink/?LinkID=66439*. When the link is displayed, the following will be included in the link: (status, substatus, hresult, buildnumber); for example, *http://go.microsoft.com/fwlink/?LinkID=62293&IIS70Error=404,0,0x80070002,6001*.

- "The HTTP Status Codes in IIS 7.0," available at *http://go.microsoft.com/fwlink/ ?LinkID=62293*.

- For more information about RFC error codes, go to *http://www.ietf.org/rfc/rfc2616.txt*.

Any third-party module can set any status, substatus, or hresult they choose, including invalid ones.

Table A-1   Custom HTTP Error Codes Used by IIS

Status Code	Substatus Code	Hresult	Description
100			Continue
101			Switching protocols

Table A-1   Custom HTTP Error Codes Used by IIS

Status Code	Substatus Code	Hresult	Description
200			OK. The client request has succeeded.
201			Created
202			Accepted
203			Nonauthoritative information
204			No content
205			Reset content
206			Partial content
301			Moved permanently
302			Object moved
304			Not modified
307			Temporary redirect
400	0		Bad request
401	0		You do not have permission to view this directory or page.
401	1		You do not have permission to view this directory or page using the credentials that you supplied.
401	2		You are not authorized to view this page due to invalid authentication headers.
401	3		You do not have permission to view this directory or page because of the access control list (ACL) configuration or encryption settings for this resource on the Web server.
401	4		You might not have permission to view this directory or page using the credentials that you supplied. The Web server has a filter installed to verify users connecting to the server and it failed to authenticate your credentials.
401	5		The URL you tried to reach has an ISAPI or CGI application installed that verifies user credentials before proceeding. This application cannot verify your credentials.
403	0		You do not have permission to view this directory or page.

Table A-1   Custom HTTP Error Codes Used by IIS

Status Code	Substatus Code	Hresult	Description
403	1		You have attempted to run a CGI, ISAPI, or other executable program from a directory that does not allow executables to run.
403	2		You have attempted to view a resource that does not have Read access.
403	3		You have attempted to write to a folder that does not have Write access.
403	4		The page you are trying to access is secured with Secure Sockets Layer (SSL).
403	5		The resource you are trying to access is secured with a 128-bit version of Secure Sockets Layer (SSL). To view this resource, you need a Web browser that supports this version of SSL.
403	6		The IP address from which you are browsing is not permitted to access the requested Web site.
403	7		The page you are attempting to access requires your browser to have a Secure Sockets Layer (SSL) client certificate that the Web server recognizes.
403	8		The DNS name of the computer from which you are browsing is not permitted to access the Web site you requested.
403	10		You have attempted to run a CGI, ISAPI, or other executable program from a directory that does not allow programs to be run.
403	12		The account to which your client certificate is mapped on the Web server has been denied access to this Web site.
403	13		Your client certificate was revoked, or the revocation status could not be determined.
403	14		The Web server is configured to not list the contents of this directory.
403	16		Your client certificate is either not trusted or is invalid.
403	17		Your client certificate has expired or is not yet valid.
403	18		The specified request cannot be processed in the application pool that is configured for this resource on the Web server.
403	19		The configured user for this application pool does not have sufficient privileges to run CGI applications.
404	0		The resource you are looking for has been removed, had its name changed, or is temporarily unavailable.

Table A-1   Custom HTTP Error Codes Used by IIS

Status Code	Substatus Code	Hresult	Description
404	2		The page you are requesting cannot be served because of the ISAPI and CGI Restriction list settings on the Web server.
404	3		The page you are requesting cannot be served because of the extension configuration. If the page is a script, add a handler. If the file should be downloaded, add a MIME map.
404	4		The resource you are looking for does not have a handler associated with it.
404	5		The request filtering module is configured to deny the URL sequence.
404	6		The request filtering module is configured to deny the HTTP verb.
404	7		The request filtering module is configured to deny the file extension.
404	8		The request filtering module is configured to deny a path in the URL that contains a *hiddenSegment* section.
404	9		This error occurs when the requested file is marked as hidden on the file system.
404	10		The request filtering module is configured to deny a request header that is too large.
404	11		The request filtering module is configured to deny a request that contains a double escape sequence.
404	12		The request filtering module is configured to deny a request URL that contains high-bit characters.
404	13		The request filtering module is configured to deny a request that exceeds the request content length.
404	14		The request filtering module is configured to deny a URL that is too long.
404	15		The request filtering module is configured to deny a request where the query string is too long.
404	16		A DAV request went to the static file handler.
404	17		The requested content appears to be script and will not be served by the static file handler.
405	0		The page you are looking for cannot be displayed because an invalid method (HTTP verb) is being used.

Table A-1   Custom HTTP Error Codes Used by IIS

Status Code	Substatus Code	Hresult	Description
406	0		The resource cannot be displayed because the file extension is not being accepted by your browser.
407	0		You must be authenticated by a proxy before the Web server can process your request.
408	0		The page cannot be displayed because the client took too long to complete its request and the server closed the connection.
409	0		The page was not displayed because there was a conflict.
410	0		The page you requested was removed.
411	0		The page cannot be displayed because the server requires a Content-Length header in the request.
412	0		The request was not completed due to preconditions that are set in the request header.
413	0		The page was not displayed because the request entity is too large.
414	0		The page was not displayed because the Request URI is too long.
415	0		The server cannot service the request because the media type is unsupported.
416	0		The page cannot be displayed because the request range was not satisfiable.
417	0		The page cannot be displayed because the expectation failed.
500	0		The page cannot be displayed because an internal server error has occurred.
500	0	0x8007000d	There is a problem with the resource you are looking for, so it cannot be displayed.
500	0	0x8007007e	There is a problem with the resource you are looking for, so it cannot be displayed.
500	0	0x8007007f	There is a problem with the resource you are looking for, so it cannot be displayed.
500	0	0x80070002	There is a problem with the resource you are looking for, so it cannot be displayed.
500	11		The request was not processed because the Web site is shutting down.
500	12		The request cannot process while the Web site is restarting.

Table A-1   Custom HTTP Error Codes Used by IIS

Status Code	Substatus Code	Hresult	Description
500	13		The request cannot be processed because the amount of traffic exceeds the Web site's configured capacity.
500	15		The global.asax is a special file that you cannot access directly from your browser.
500	16		You cannot access the page you are requesting because the UNC authorization settings are configured incorrectly on the Web server.
500	19		The requested page cannot be accessed because the related configuration data for the page is invalid.
500	21		An invalid module is in the <handlers> section.
500	22		An ASP.NET setting has been detected that does not apply in Integrated managed pipeline mode.
500	23		An ASP.NET setting has been detected that does not apply in Integrated managed pipeline mode.
500	24		An ASP.NET setting has been detected that does not apply in Integrated managed pipeline mode.
500	100		The page cannot be displayed due to an error with ASP.
501	0		The page you are looking for cannot be displayed because a header value in the request does not match configuration settings.
502	0		The specified CGI application encountered an error and the server terminated the process.
502	1		The CGI application exceeded the time allowed for processing and the process was shut down.
502	2		The specified CGI application did not return a complete set of HTTP headers.
503	0		The service is unavailable.
503	2		The serverRuntime@appConcurrentRequestLimit setting is being exceeded.
503	3		ASP.NET rejected this request because the queue limit was exceeded.
503	4		The FastCGI queue has been exceeded.
504	0		The page cannot be displayed due to a gateway time-out.
505	0		The page cannot be displayed because the HTTP version is not supported.

IIS 7.0 Error Messages

Every Web site administrator and Web developer has seen "404 – File not found," "401 – Unauthorized," or "500 – Server Error" messages in his or her browser. There is more to these errors than meets the eye. Error messages are a touchy topic, because every error reveals more about your Web site than you might want. And the more information somebody can gather about your site, the likelier it is that you'll get hacked. Just search for *google hacking* or *cross-site scripting*, and you will find a wealth of information on this topic.

But error messages are also a valuable tool for troubleshooting problems. Developers and Web site administrators want as much detail as possible when an error occurs. Ideally the error message would give recommendations on how to fix the problem. Here is how Microsoft Internet Information Services (IIS) 7.0 addresses these fundamentally opposed goals.

Note This appendix discusses HTTP errors as specified in RFC 2616. An HTTP error is always expressed by sending a response with a status code greater than 400 back to the requesting client.

Status codes between 400 and 500 specify an error made by the client, for example, bad syntax or a request to a resource that doesn't exist. You can see for yourself by requesting a fake URL from the Web site of your choice, for example, *http://\<IIS7Server\>/ this_resource_does_not_exist*. You get a "404 – File not found" error.

Status codes starting with 500 are errors caused by the server. The most common causes for 500 errors on IIS systems include the following:

- An ASP or ASPX page contains a syntax error.

- The Web server configuration or the application configuration cannot be read or is invalid.

- The site is stopped.

It is important to notice that browsers such as Microsoft Internet Explorer often replace errors returned from a Web server with their own. This sometimes makes troubleshooting harder. In Internet Explorer, you can turn this option off by clicking Tools, selecting Internet Options, selecting the Advanced tab, and clearing the Show Friendly HTTP Error Messages check box. If you want to see the raw response, you have to use HTTP tools such as Wfetch.

HTTP Errors in IIS 7.0

Two things can happen when the httpError module (custerr.dll) encounters an error:

- A custom error is generated.
- A detailed error is generated.

Custom errors are error pages that the regular users of your Web site will see. They contain a brief error description of why the error happened, but nothing else. Detailed errors are intended for local administrators and developers. They are supposed to give a wealth of information that can help to fix the problem immediately. Providing a detailed error is dangerous, of course, because detailed errors contain information about the inner workings of your Web site. Only trusted personnel should see detailed errors. The only way to ensure this is to generate a detailed error only if the request comes from the local machine. If a request is not made locally, a custom error should be generated. Examine the following flow diagram.

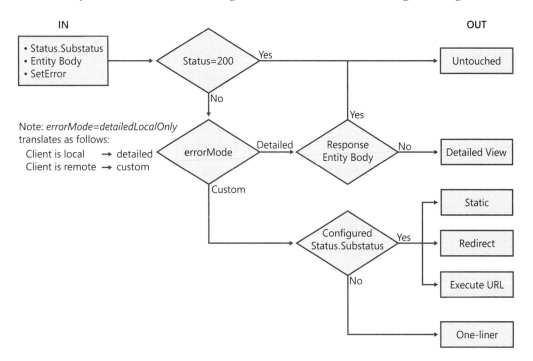

There are several steps in the process. First, the httpError module receives a notification if a response is about to be sent (RQ_SEND_RESPONSE notification). The httpError module checks the status code of this response and immediately returns if the status code is not greater than 200.

The next check is determined by the request origin (is the request a local request, or is it remote) and the setting of the *errorMode* property. If the *errorMode* property is set to *detailedLocalOnly*, then custom errors are generated for every remote request (this is what you want). If *errorMode* is set to *custom*, then all error responses will be custom errors. If *errorMode* is set to *detailed*, all error responses will be detailed errors. Table B-1 clarifies this behavior.

Table B-1   Interaction of *errorMode* Setting and Request Origin

errorMode Setting	Request Origin	Action
detailedLocalOnly (default)	Local	Detailed error
detailedLocalOnly (default)	Remote	Custom error
custom	Local	Custom error
custom	Remote	Custom error
detailed	Local	Detailed error
detailed	Remote	Detailed error

Note   In the IIS 7.0 beta, *errorMode* was named *overrideMode*, and *detailedLocalOnly* was named *RemoteOnly*. The custom and detailed settings were named *On* and *Off* respectively.

If the httpError module determines that a custom error should be generated, IIS 7.0 looks into its configuration to see if a matching error can be found. If a match is found, IIS 7.0 sends the static file, redirects the request, or executes the specified URL. If no match can be found, IIS 7.0 sends a basic one-line message containing the status code. The next section explains the custom error configuration in detail.

If custerr.dll determines that a detailed error should be generated, another check is needed. IIS 7.0 doesn't touch the response if a module overrode the entity of the response with its own error description. It might contain valuable information. ASP.NET is a good example. The entity of an ASP.NET error response might contain the exception stack and its own error description. A detailed error is generated only if the entity body of the response is empty.

<httpErrors> Configuration

Following is the IIS 7.0 custom error section that you get on a clean install.

```
<httpErrors>
  <error statusCode="401"
    prefixLanguageFilePath="c:\inetpub\custerr" path="401.htm" />
  <error statusCode="403"
```

```
      prefixLanguageFilePath="c:\inetpub\custerr" path="403.htm" />
    <error statusCode="404"
      prefixLanguageFilePath="c:\inetpub\custerr" path="404.htm" />
    <error statusCode="405"
      prefixLanguageFilePath="c:\inetpub\custerr" path="405.htm" />
    <error statusCode="406"
      prefixLanguageFilePath="c:\inetpub\custerr" path="406.htm" />
    <error statusCode="412"
      prefixLanguageFilePath="c:\inetpub\custerr" path="412.htm" />
    <error statusCode="500"
      prefixLanguageFilePath="c:\inetpub\custerr" path="500.htm" />
    <error statusCode="501"
      prefixLanguageFilePath="c:\inetpub\custerr" path="501.htm" />
    <error statusCode="502"
      prefixLanguageFilePath="c:\inetpub\custerr" path="502.htm" />
</httpErrors>
```

You can see that if the status code of a response is 401, IIS will return a file named 401.htm, for example.

Substatus Codes

Many HTTP errors have a substatus. The IIS 7.0 default Custom Errors configuration doesn't differentiate based on substatus codes. It sends you the same custom error page regardless of whether you enter the wrong credentials (401.1) or whether access is denied based on insufficient rights to access a file (401.3). You can see the different substatus codes in your log files or via a detailed error. Table B-2 lists the different 404 substatus codes that IIS 7.0 produces.

Table B-2   404 Substatus Codes

Status	Description
404.1	Site couldn't be found.
404.2	Denied by Policy. The requested Internet Server Application Programming Interface (ISAPI) or Common Gateway Interface (CGI) program is not allowed in the Restriction List.
404.3	The static file handler didn't have the file in its MIME map and therefore IIS rejected the request.
404.4	No handler was found to serve the request.
404.5	The Request Filtering Module rejected a URL sequence in the request.
404.6	The Request Filtering Module denied the HTTP verb of the request.
404.7	The Request Filtering module rejected the file extension of the request.
404.8	The Request Filtering module rejected a particular URL segment (characters between two slashes).
404.9	IIS rejected a request to serve a hidden file.
404.10	The Request Filtering module rejected a header that was too long.
404.11	The Request Filtering module rejected a request that was double escaped.
404.12	The Request Filtering module rejected a request that contained high bit characters.

Table B-2   404 Substatus Codes

Status	Description
404.13	The Request Filtering module rejected a request that was too long (request + entity body).
404.14	The Request Filtering module rejected a request with URL that was too long.
404.15	The Request Filtering module rejected a request with a query string that was too long.

A Substatus Code Example

You can configure the *<httpErrors>* section to show a custom error for particular substatus codes. For example, if you add the following line to your *<httpErrors>* configuration section, IIS 7.0 will return 404_3.htm if a file with a file extension is requested that isn't included in the IIS 7.0 MIME map (the *<staticContent>* configuration section).

```
<error statusCode="404" subStatusCode="3"
  prefixLanguageFilePath="c:\inetpub\custerr" path="404_3.htm" />
```

To make the example work, add the preceding entry to your *<httpErrors>* configuration section, create a file named 404_3.htm in your C:\inetpub\custerr\en-us directory, create a file named test.yyy in your C:\inetpub\wwwroot directory, and then request http://localhost/test.yyy. The file extension .yyy is not part of the IIS 7.0 MIME map, and the static file handler will not serve it.

Language-Specific Custom Errors

Every newer browser includes the language of the client as a request header. Here is an example of how this header might look.

```
Accept-Language: en-us
```

> **Note**   The syntax and registry of accepted languages is specified in RFC 1766.

When generating an error, IIS 7.0 takes this header into account when it looks for the custom error file it will return. It generates the path for the custom error by using the following logic:

- *prefixLanguageFilePath* configuration setting (for example, C:\inetpub\custerr) followed by:
- Accept-Language header sent by the client (for example, en-us) followed by:
- Path configuration setting (for example, 404.htm)

For example, if the browser sends a request for a nonexistent resource, and the Accept-Language header has the value of *en-us,* the file that gets returned will be C:\inetpub\custerr\en-us\404.htm.

If you are from Germany, you want your error messages in German. To do this in Windows Vista, for example, you have to install the Windows Vista Language Pack for German. This will create the C:\inetpub\custerr\de-DE directory with custom error files in it. Now if the browser sends the Accept-Language header with the value of *de-DE,* the file that gets returned will be C:\inetpub\custerr\de-DE\404.htm.

IIS 7.0 will always fall back to the system language if the de-DE subfolder doesn't exist.

> **Note**   Internet Explorer enables you to configure the Accept-Language header. Go to Tools, Internet Option. Select the General tab and click Languages.

Custom Error Options

In the preceding examples, IIS 7.0 sends the contents of the file as the custom error response. IIS 7.0 has two other ways to respond to an error: by executing a URL and by redirecting the request.

Execute a URL

If you want to do a bit more in your custom error, such as sending an e-mail or logging the error to a database, you can execute a URL. Doing so allows you to execute dynamic content such as an ASP.NET page. The following example replaces the 404 custom error. Then IIS 7.0 will execute /404.aspx whenever a 404 error occurs.

```
<httpErrors>
  <!-- default custom error for 401 errors -->
  <!-- <error statusCode="404"
    prefixLanguageFilePath="c:\inetpub\custerr" path="404.htm" />-->

  <!-- ExecuteURL replaces default file response mode -->
  <error statusCode="404" path=/404.aspx"
    responseMode="ExecuteURL"/>
  <error statusCode="403"
    prefixLanguageFilePath="c:\inetpub\custerr" path="403.htm" />
  <error statusCode="404"
    prefixLanguageFilePath="c:\inetpub\custerr" path="404.htm" />
  <error statusCode="405"
    prefixLanguageFilePath="c:\inetpub\custerr" path="405.htm" />
  <error statusCode="406"
    prefixLanguageFilePath="c:\inetpub\custerr" path="406.htm" />
  <error statusCode="412"
    prefixLanguageFilePath="c:\inetpub\custerr" path="412.htm" />
```

```
   <error statusCode="500"
      prefixLanguageFilePath="c:\inetpub\custerr" path="500.htm" />
   <error statusCode="501"
      prefixLanguageFilePath="c:\inetpub\custerr" path="501.htm" />
   <error statusCode="502"
      prefixLanguageFilePath="c:\inetpub\custerr" path="502.htm" />
</httpErrors>
```

> **Caution**   For architectural reasons, IIS 7.0 can execute the URL only if it is located in the same application pool as the request. Use the redirect feature if you need to execute a custom error in a different application pool.

Redirect the Request

IIS 7.0 can also return a 302 Redirect to the browser when a particular error occurs. Redirection is great if you have a Web farm, for example, where you can redirect all your errors to a central location that you closely monitor. Here is an example.

```
<section name="httpErrors"
    type="System.WebServer.Configuration.HttpErrorsSection,
    System.ApplicationHost, Version=7.0.0.0, Culture=neutral,
    PublicKeyToken=31bf3856ad364e35"
    overrideModeDefault="Deny" />
```

Redirecting all your errors is not without risk, however. Setting *responseMode="File"* (which is the default) allows you to specify every file on the disk. This might not work for you if you are very security conscious.

A workable scenario might be to allow the delegation of only the *errorMode* setting. This enables a developer to receive detailed errors for his or her application even if the developer is remote. All the developer has to do is to set *errorMode="detailed"*.

Here is how to configure this scenario. First, allow the delegation of the *<httpErrors>* section.

```
<section name="httpErrors"
    type="System.WebServer.Configuration.HttpErrorsSection,
    System.ApplicationHost, Version=7.0.0.0, Culture=neutral,
    PublicKeyToken=31bf3856ad364e35"
    overrideModeDefault="Allow" />
```

Second, go to the *<httpErrors>* section in your applicationHost.config file and change it so that only *errorMode* is delegated, as shown in bold type here.

```
<httpErrors lockAllAttributesExcept="errorMode" lockElements="error">
  <error statusCode="404"
    prefixLanguageFilePath="E:\inetpub\custerr" path="404.htm" />
  <error statusCode="401"
    prefixLanguageFilePath="E:\inetpub\custerr" path="401.htm" />
  <error statusCode="403"
```

```
      prefixLanguageFilePath="E:\inetpub\custerr" path="403.htm" />
    <error statusCode="405"
      prefixLanguageFilePath="E:\inetpub\custerr" path="405.htm" />
    <error statusCode="406"
      prefixLanguageFilePath="E:\inetpub\custerr" path="406.htm" />
    <error statusCode="412"
      prefixLanguageFilePath="E:\inetpub\custerr" path="412.htm" />
    <error statusCode="500"
      prefixLanguageFilePath="E:\inetpub\custerr" path="500.htm" />
    <error statusCode="501"
      prefixLanguageFilePath="E:\inetpub\custerr" path="501.htm" />
    <error statusCode="502"
      prefixLanguageFilePath="E:\inetpub\custerr" path="502.htm" />
</httpErrors>
```

IIS 7.0 Modules Listing

In this appendix:

Native Modules

Table C-1 outlines the native modules in Internet Information Services (IIS) 7.0.

Table C-1   Native Modules in IIS 7.0

Module Name: AnonymousAuthenticationModule	
Description	Provides anonymous authentication support. For example, this module generates the *HttpUser* object if a URL is configured to enable anonymous authentication.
Configuration Section	system.webServer/security/authentication/anonymous Authentication
Resource	*%SystemRoot%*\System32\Inetsrv\Authanon.dll
Dependencies	None
Potential Issues When Removing This Module	Unable to perform anonymous authentication because at least one authentication module has to be configured. After the authentication phase, the IIS server core checks if the *HttpUser* object is populated. The *HttpUser* object is an IIS data structure. A 401.2 error is generated without an authentication populating the *HttpUser* object.
Module Name: BasicAuthenticationModule	
Description	Provides standard HTTP Basic authentication as described in RFC 2617.
Configuration Section	system.webServer/security/authentication/basicAuthentication
Resource	*%SystemRoot%*\System32\Inetsrv\Authbas.dll
Dependencies	None
Potential Issues When Removing This Module	Unable to perform basic authentication because at least one authentication module has to be configured. After the authentication phase, the IIS server core checks if the *HttpUser* object is populated. The *HttpUser* object is an IIS data structure. A 401.2 error is generated without an authentication populating the *HttpUser* object.

Table C-1   Native Modules in IIS 7.0

Module Name: CertificateMappingAuthenticationModule	
Description	Maps Secure Sockets Layer (SSL) client certificates to a Microsoft Active Directory directory service account (Active Directory Certificate Mapping).
Configuration Section	system.webServer/security/authentication/clientCertificateMapping-Authentication
Resource	*%SystemRoot%*\System32\Inetsrv\Authcert.dll
Dependencies	SSL has to be configured for this module to work. The IIS machine also must be a member of an Active Directory domain.
Potential Issues When Removing This Module	Requests are allowed if Active Directory Certificate Mapping is used to protect a directory but the module is removed.
Module Name: CgiModule	
Description	Provides support for Common Gateway Interface (CGI) programs.
Configuration Section	system.webServer/cgi system.webServer/isapiCgiRestriction
Resource	*%SystemRoot%*\System32\Inetsrv\Cgi.dll
Dependencies	None
Potential Issues When Removing This Module	Unable to execute CGI programs.
Module Name: ConfigurationValidationModule	
Description	Responsible for verifying IIS 7.0 configuration systems, such as when an application is running in Integrated mode but has handlers or modules declared in the *<system.web>* section.
Configuration Section	system.webServer/Validation
Resource	*%SystemRoot%*\System32\Inetsrv\Validcfg.dll
Dependencies	None
Potential Issues When Removing This Module	No validation of configuration files during configuration
Module Name: CustomErrorModule	
Description	Responsible for the implementation of custom errors as well as the IIS 7.0 detailed error feature.
Configuration Section	system.webServer/httpErrors
Resource	*%SystemRoot%*\System32\Inetsrv\Custerr.dll
Dependencies	None
Potential Issues When Removing This Module	IIS 7.0 returns a blank page with minimal information when errors occur within the core server.
Module Name: CustomLoggingModule	
Description	Provides the ILogPlugin interface on top of IIS 7.0. ILogPlugin is a COM implementation that allows customers to extend IIS logging.

Table C-1   Native Modules in IIS 7.0

Configuration Section	system.webServer/httpLogging system.applicationhost/sites/site/logFile/customLogPluginClsid
Resource	*%SystemRoot%*\System32\Inetsrv\Logcust.dll
Dependencies	None
Potential Issues When Removing This Module	Related logging that depends on ILogPlugin will not work. For example, ODBC Logging is implemented as ILogPlugin.

Module Name: DefaultDocumentModule

Description	Implements default document functionality. For example, requests that include a trailing / will be rerouted to a document in the default document list.
Configuration Section	system.webServer/defaultDocument
Resource	*%SystemRoot%*\System32\Inetsrv\Defdoc.dll
Dependencies	None
Potential Issues When Removing This Module	Requests to the URL—for example, http://localhost/—will return a 403.14 error indicating directory listing denied. A directory listing will be generated if directory browsing is enabled.

Module Name: DigestAuthenticationModule

Description	Supports the implementation of Digest authentication as described in RFC 2617.
Configuration Section	system.webServer/security/authentication/digestAuthentication
Resource	*%SystemRoot%*\System32\Inetsrv\Authmd5.dll
Dependencies	IIS server needs to be part of an Active Directory domain.
Potential Issues When Removing This Module	Unable to perform Digest authentication, at least one authentication module has to be configured. After the authentication phase, the IIS server core checks if the *HttpUser* object is populated. The *HttpUser* object is an IIS data structure. A 401.2 error is generated without an authentication populating the *HttpUser* object.

Module Name: DirectoryListingModule

Description	Enables directory browsing functionality.
Configuration Section	system.webServer/directoryBrowse
Resource	*%SystemRoot%*\System32\Inetsrv\Dirlist.dll
Dependencies	None
Potential Issues When Removing This Module	If neither the default document module nor the directory listing module handles a request for query followed by "/", an empty response is returned.

Module Name: DynamicCompressionModule

Description	Provides in-memory compression of dynamic content.
Configuration Section	system.webServer/httpCompression system.webServer/urlCompression
Resource	*%SystemRoot%*\System32\Inetsrv\Compdyn.dll
Dependencies	None

Table C-1 Native Modules in IIS 7.0

Potential Issues When Removing This Module	No dynamic content will be compressed.

Module Name: FailedRequestsTracingModule

Description	More commonly known as Failed Request Event Buffering (FREB), this module supports tracing of failed requests. The definition and rules of what a failed request is can be specified via configuration.
Configuration Section	system.webServer/tracing system.webServer/httpTracing
Resource	*%SystemRoot%*\System32\Inetsrv\Iisfreb.dll
Dependencies	None
Potential Issues When Removing This Module	Unable to perform HTTP request tracing.

Module Name: FastCgiModule

Description	Supports FastCGI, which provides a high-performance alternative to CGI.
Configuration Section	system.webServer/fastCgi
Resource	*%SystemRoot%*\System32\Inetsrv\Iisfcgi.dll
Dependencies	None
Potential Issues When Removing This Module	Unable to support FastCGI implementation.

Module Name: FileCacheModule

Description	Enables caching file handles for files opened by the server engine and modules.
Configuration Section	None
Resource	*%SystemRoot%*\System32\Inetsrv\Cachfile.dll
Dependencies	None
Potential Issues When Removing This Module	Performance loss. If file handles are not cached, the files have to be opened for every request.

Module Name: HttpCacheModule

Description	The HttpCacheModule implements the IIS 7.0 output cache and also the logic for caching items in the HTTP.sys cache. Setting the cache size, output cache profiles, and so on can be done via configuration.
Configuration Section	system.webServer/caching
Resource	*%SystemRoot%*\System32\Inetsrv\Cachhttp.dll
Dependencies	None
Potential Issues When Removing This Module	Content won't be cached in kernel mode any longer. Cache profiles will be ignored. Removing the HttpCacheModule will probably have adverse effects on performance and resource usage.

Module Name: HttpLoggingModule

Description	Implements the HTTP.sys kernel mode driver for standard IIS logging.

Table C-1   Native Modules in IIS 7.0

Configuration Section	system.applicationHost/log
	system.webServer/httpLogging
Resource	*%SystemRoot%*\System32\Inetsrv\Loghttp.dll
Dependencies	None
Potential Issues When Removing This Module	IIS unable to perform standard IIS logging.
Module Name: HttpRedirectionModule	
Description	Provides URL redirection functionality.
Configuration Section	system.webServer/httpRedirect
Resource	*%SystemRoot%*\System32\Inetsrv\Redirect.dll
Dependencies	None
Potential Issues When Removing This Module	Potential security issue if resources were protected by redirection. When the Redirection module is removed, the content becomes accessible again.
Module Name: IISCertificateMappingAuthenticationModule	
Description	Facilitates IIS certificate mapping. Maps SSL client certificates to a Windows account. User credentials and mapping rules are stored within the IIS configuration store contrary to Active Directory Certificate mapping.
Configuration Section	system.webServer/iisClientCertificateMappingAuthentication
Resource	*%SystemRoot%*\System32\Inetsrv\Authmap.dll
Dependencies	SSL with the requirement to receive client certificates has to be configured for this module to work.
Potential Issues When Removing This Module	Unable to perform certificate mapping; at least one authentication module has to be configured. The IIS server core checks after the authentication phase if the *HttpUser* object is populated. The *HttpUser* object is an IIS data structure. A 401.2 error is generated without an authentication populating the *HttpUser* object.
Module Name: IpRestrictionModule	
Description	Implements an authorization scheme in the IP restriction feature, which is based on the IPv4 address of the client request.
Configuration Section	system.webServer/security/ipSecurity
Resource	*%SystemRoot%*\System32\Inetsrv\Iprestr.dll
Dependencies	IPv4 stack is required.
Potential Issues When Removing This Module	Clients with IP addresses that are on the ipSecurity list will be allowed access.
Module Name: IsapiFilterModule	
Description	Provides Internet Server Application Programming Interface (ISAPI) filter functionality.
Configuration Section	system.webServer/isapiFilters
Resource	*%SystemRoot%*\System32\Inetsrv\Filter.dll

Table C-1   Native Modules in IIS 7.0

Dependencies	None
Potential Issues When Removing This Module	Removing this module prevents IIS from loading ISAPI filters, and applications might stop working or might expose sensitive content. For example, the ASP.NET application needs the aspnet_filter.dll to protect sensitive content and to rewrite URLs.
Module Name: IsapiModule	
Description	Provides ISAPI extension functionality.
Configuration Section	system.webServer/isapiCgiRestriction
Resource	*%SystemRoot%*\System32\Inetsrv\Isapi.dll
Dependencies	None
Potential Issues When Removing This Module	ISAPI Extensions mapped in the *<handlers>* section (modules="Isapi-Module") or explicitly called ISAPI Extensions won't work.
Module Name: ManagedEngine / ManagedEngine64	
Description	ManagedEngine has a special place within all the other modules. It is responsible for providing the IIS integration hook-up of the ASP.NET run time.
Configuration Section	None
Resource	*%SystemRoot%*\Microsoft.NET\Framework\<version>\ webengine.dll
	%SystemRoot%\Microsoft.NET\Framework64\<version>\ webengine.dll
Dependencies	None
Potential Issues When Removing This Module	ASP.NET integration will be disabled. None of the managed modules declared in the *<modules>* or ASP.NET handlers declared in the *<handlers>* sections will be called when the application pool runs in Integrated mode.
Module Name: ProtocolSupportModule	
Description	Implements custom and redirect response headers that handle HTTP TRACE and OPTIONS verbs, and it supports keep-alive configuration.
Configuration Section	system.webServer/httpProtocol
Resource	*%SystemRoot%*\System32\Inetsrv\Protsup.dll
Dependencies	None
Potential Issues When Removing This Module	TRACE or OPTIONS requests will return a 405 Method Not Allowed error message.
Module Name: RequestFilteringModule	
Description	Provides URLSCAN's functionality in IIS 7.0 by implementing a powerful set of security rules to reject a suspicious request at a very early stage.
Configuration Section	system.webServer/security/requestFiltering
Resource	*%SystemRoot%*\System32\Inetsrv\Modrqflt.dll
Dependencies	None

Table C-1   Native Modules in IIS 7.0

Potential Issues When Removing This Module	Potential security issues. None of the rules will be applied.

Module Name: RequestMonitorModule	
Description	Implements the Runtime State and Control API (RSCA). RSCA enables its consumers to query for run-time information such as currently executing requests, the start or stop state of a Web site, or currently executing application domains.
Configuration Section	None.
Resource	*%SystemRoot%*\System32\Inetsrv\Iisreqs.dll
Dependencies	None
Potential Issues When Removing This Module	Unable to perform run-time queries.

Module Name: ServerSideIncludeModule	
Description	Supports the implementation of server-side includes (SSIs). This module is mapped as a handler. This means it is executed only for requests ending in .stm, .shtm, and .shtml.
Configuration Section	system.webServer/serverSideInclude
Resource	*%SystemRoot%*\System32\Inetsrv\Iis_ssi.dll
Dependencies	None
Potential Issues When Removing This Module	The static file module will handle .stm, .shtm, and .shtml files. If this module has MIME type mappings for these extensions, the files get served as text.

Module Name: StaticCompressionModule	
Description	Provides content compression for static content.
Configuration Section	system.webServer/httpCompression
	system.webServer/urlCompression
Resource	*%SystemRoot%*\System32\Inetsrv\Compstat.dll
Dependencies	None
Potential Issues When Removing This Module	Unable to compress static content, which will lead to potential bandwidth saturation due to uncompressed content being sent back to the client.

Module Name: StaticFileModule	
Description	Fulfills static content requests with file extensions such as .html and .txt and image files such as .gif, .jpg, and .png. The *staticContent/ mimeMap* configuration collection determines the list of file extensions.
Configuration Section	system.webServer/staticContent
Resource	*%SystemRoot%*\System32\Inetsrv\Static.dll
Dependencies	None
Potential Issues When Removing This Module	Unable to process static content requests. Empty responses will be sent to the client.

Table C-1 Native Modules in IIS 7.0

Module Name: TokenCacheModule	
Description	Caches Windows security tokens for password-based authentication schemes (anonymous authentication, basic authentication, and IIS client certificate authentication).
Configuration Section	None
Resource	*%SystemRoot%*\System32\Inetsrv\Cachtokn.dll
Dependencies	None
Potential Issues When Removing This Module	Performance loss. The user must be logged on for every request if the token is not cached. This might result in a major performance impact. For example, if a password-protected HTML page references 50 images that are also protected, the result is 51 logonUser calls to the local account database or to an off-box domain controller.
Module Name: TracingModule	
Description	Supports Event Tracing for Windows (ETW) in IIS.
Configuration Section	system.webServer/httpTracing
Resource	*%SystemRoot%*\System32\Inetsrv\lisetw.dll
Dependencies	None
Potential Issues When Removing This Module	Unable to perform Event Tracing for Windows.
Module Name: UriCacheModule	
Description	Implements a generic cache for URL-specific server state, such as configuration. With this module, the server will read the configuration only for the first request for a particular URL and then will reuse it on subsequent requests until it changes.
Configuration Section	None
Resource	*%SystemRoot%*\System32\Inetsrv\Cachuri.dll
Dependencies	None.
Potential Issues When Removing This Module	Performance loss due to state cached for each URL being retrieved for every request.
Module Name: UrlAuthorizationModule	
Description	Supports rules-based configurations for content authorization.
Configuration Section	system.webServer/security/authorization
Resource	*%SystemRoot%*\System32\Inetsrv\Urlauthz.dll
Dependencies	None
Potential Issues When Removing This Module	Authorization rules that protected content are not evaluated anymore. Content that was supposed to be protected might be served.
Module Name: WindowsAuthenticationModule	
Description	Provides Windows authentication including NTLM or Negotiate (Kerberos) schemes.
Configuration Section	system.webServer/security/authentication/windowsAuthentication
Resource	*%SystemRoot%*\System32\Inetsrv\Authsspi.dll

Table C-1   Native Modules in IIS 7.0

Dependencies	None
Potential Issues When Removing This Module	Unable to perform Windows authentication; at least one authentication module has to be configured. After the authentication phase, the IIS server core checks if the *HttpUser* object is populated. The *HttpUser* object is an IIS data structure. A 401.2 error is generated without an authentication populating the *HttpUser* object.

Managed Modules

Table C-2 outlines the managed modules in IIS 7.0.

> **Note**   The ManagedEngine module is required to support managed modules. It facilitates the integration between IIS and ASP.NET to create the integrated worker processing pipeline.

Table C-2   Managed Modules in IIS 7.0

Module Name: AnonymousIdentification	
Description	Manages anonymous identifiers, which are used by features that support anonymous identification such as .NET Profile. This module is independent of any type of ASP.NET authentications.
Configuration Section	system.web/anonymousIdentification
Resource	System.Web.Security.AnonymousIdentificationModule
Dependencies	ManagedEngine
Potential Issues When Removing This Module	Unable to support anonymous authentication via ASP.NET services.
Module Name: DefaultAuthentication	
Description	Ensures that an authentication object is present in the context.
Configuration Section	system.web/authentication
Resource	System.Web.Security.DefaultAuthenticationModule
Dependencies	ManagedEngine
Potential Issues When Removing This Module	Potential authentication failure when no authentication modules are enabled.
Module Name: FileAuthorization	
Description	Responsible for determining if a user is allowed to access a requested file against Windows access control lists (ACLs).
Configuration Section	system.web/authorization
Resource	System.Web.Security.FileAuthorizationModule
Dependencies	ManagedEngine
Potential Issues When Removing This Module	Unable to support file-based authorization checking against Windows user account via ACLs.

Table C-2   Managed Modules in IIS 7.0

Module Name: FormsAuthentication	
Description	Implements ASP.NET Forms authentication against requested resources.
Configuration Section	system.web/authentication
Resource	System.Web.Security.FormsAuthenticationModule
Dependencies	ManagedEngine
Potential Issues When Removing This Module	Unable to implement ASP.NET forms authentication.
Module Name: OutputCache	
Description	Defines the output caching policies of an ASP.NET page or a user control contained in a page.
Configuration Section	system.web/caching/outputCache
Resource	System.Web.Caching.OutputCacheModule
Dependencies	ManagedEngine
Potential Issues When Removing This Module	Unable to cache all types of managed content.
Module Name: Profile	
Description	Manages user profiles by using ASP.NET profile, which stores and retrieves user settings in a data source such as a database.
Configuration Section	system.web/profile
Resource	System.Web.Profile.ProfileModule
Dependencies	ManagedEngine
Potential Issues When Removing This Module	Unable to implement .NET Profile for application.
Module Name: RoleManager	
Description	Role management services use the provider models such as SQL Server and Windows to separate the functionality of role management—the application programming interface (API)—from the data store that contains role information.
Configuration Section	system.web/roleManager
Resource	System.Web.Security.RoleManagerModule
Dependencies	ManagedEngine
Potential Issues When Removing This Module	Unable to implement role-based access for application.
Module Name: Session	
Description	Provides session state management, which enables storage of data specific to a single client within an application on the server.
Configuration Section	system.web/sessionState
Resource	System.Web.SessionState.SessionStateModule
Dependencies	ManagedEngine

Table C-2   Managed Modules in IIS 7.0

Potential Issues When Removing This Module	Unable to support managed session state.
Module Name: UrlAuthorization	
Description	Responsible for determining if a user is allowed to access a requested URL based on user name or role membership.
Configuration Section	system.web/authorization
Resource	System.Web.Security.UrlAuthorizationModule
Dependencies	ManagedEngine
Potential Issues When Removing This Module	Unable to provide URL-based authorization.
Module Name: UrlMappingsModule	
Description	Enables mapping a real URL to a more user-friendly URL.
Configuration Section	system.web/urlMappings
Resource	System.Web.UrlMappingsModule
Dependencies	ManagedEngine
Potential Issues When Removing This Module	Unable to provide URL mapping features.
Module Name: WindowsAuthentication	
Description	Configure the user identity for an ASP.NET application when Windows authentication is enabled.
Configuration Section	system.web/authentication
Resource	System.Web.Security.WindowsAuthenticationModule
Dependencies	ManagedEngine
Potential Issues When Removing This Module	Unable to assign Windows user accounts as an ASP.NET request user identity.

Appendix D
Modules Sequence

This appendix shows the ordering of built-in IIS 7.0 modules that are loaded by IIS 7.0 worker processes by default. For each module, Table D-1 lists the module name, the code location (DLL name and location for a native module; namespace for a managed module), and a brief description.

Table D-1 Modules Sequence

Module Name	Code Location	Brief Description
UriCacheModule	%SystemRoot%\System32\Inetsrv\Cachuri.dll	Implements a generic cache for URI-specific server state, including URI configuration settings
FileCacheModule	%SystemRoot%\System32\Inetsrv\Cachfile.dll	Implements caching file handles for files that the server engine and modules open
TokenCache-Module	%SystemRoot%\System32\Inetsrv\Cachtokn.dll	Implements cache for Windows security tokens for password-based authentication schemes (anonymous authentication, basic authentication, IIS client certificate authentication)
HttpCacheModule	%SystemRoot%\System32\Inetsrv\Cachhttp.dll	Implements the output cache and also the logic for caching items in the HTTP.SYS cache
StaticCompression-Module	%SystemRoot%\System32\Inetsrv\Compstat.dll	Implements content compression for static content
DefaultDocument-Module	%SystemRoot%\System32\Inetsrv\Defdoc.dll	Implements default document functionality
DirectoryListing-Module	%SystemRoot%\System32\Inetsrv\Dirlist.dll	Implements directory browsing functionality
IsapiFilterModule	%SystemRoot%\System32\Inetsrv\Filter.dll	Enables Internet Server Application Programming Interface (ISAPI) filter functionality

Table D-1   **Modules Sequence**

Module Name	Code Location	Brief Description
ProtocolSupport-Module	*%SystemRoot%*\System32\Inetsrv\Protsup.dll	Provides additional HTTP support (custom and redirect response headers, keep-alive, and HTTP *TRACE* and *OPTIONS* verbs)
HttpRedirection-Module	*%SystemRoot%*\System32\Inetsrv\Redirect.dll	Implements the URL redirection feature
StaticFileModule	*%SystemRoot%*\System32\Inetsrv\Static.dll	Fulfills static content requests
Anonymous-Authentication-Module	*%SystemRoot%*\System32\Inetsrv\Authanon.dll	Provides anonymous authentication support
CertificateMapping Authentication-Module	*%SystemRoot%*\System32\Inetsrv\Authcert.dll	Provides Active Directory Certificate Mapping
Basic-Authentication-Module	*%SystemRoot%*\System32\Inetsrv\Authbas.dll	Provides standard HTTP authentication (RFC 2617)
Windows-Authentication-Module	*%SystemRoot%*\System32\Inetsrv\Authsspi.dll	Provides Windows authentication (NTLM or Kerberos)
RequestFiltering-Module	*%SystemRoot%*\System32\Inetsrv\Modrqflt.dll	Scans requests and rejects them according to preset security rules
CustomError-Module	*%SystemRoot%*\System32\Inetsrv\Custerr.dll	Implements custom errors and detailed error features
IsapiModule	*%SystemRoot%*\System32\Inetsrv\Isapi.dll	Enables ISAPI extension support
HttpLogging-Module	*%SystemRoot%*\System32\Inetsrv\Loghttp.dll	Provides support for HTTP.SYS kernel mode driver for standard IIS logging
TracingModule	*%SystemRoot%*\System32\Inetsrv\Iisetw.dll	Provides support for Event Tracing for Windows (ETW) in IIS
FailedRequests-TracingModule	*%SystemRoot%*\System32\Inetsrv\Iisfreb.dll	Provides tracing of failed requests
RequestMonitor-Module	*%SystemRoot%*\System32\Inetsrv\Iisreqs.dll	Implements Runtime State and Control API (RSCA)

Table D-1   Modules Sequence

Module Name	Code Location	Brief Description
Configuration-ValidationModule	*%SystemRoot%*\System32\Inetsrv\Validcfg.dll	Provides validation of configuration files
ManagedEngine	*%SystemRoot%*\Microsoft.NET\Framework\ <version>\Webengine.dll	Implements IIS integration with ASP.NET runtime
OutputCache	System.Web.Caching.OutputCacheModule	Implements output caching for ASP.NET pages and user controls
Session	System.Web.SessionState.SessionStateModule	Provides session state management
Windows-Authentication	System.Web.Security.WindowsAuthentication-Module	Provides user identity for an ASP.NET application when Windows authentication is enabled
Forms-Authentication	System.Web.Security.FormsAuthenticationModule	Implements ASP.NET Forms authentication
Default-Authentication	System.Web.Security.DefaultAuthenticationModule	Ensures that an authentication object is present in the context
RoleManager	System.Web.Security.RoleManagerModule	Implements role management application programming interface (API)
UrlAuthorization	System.Web.Security.UrlAuthorizationModule	Determines if a user is allowed access to the requested URL based on user name or role membership
FileAuthorization	System.Web.Security.FileAuthorizationModule	Validates user credentials for the requested file against Windows Access Control Lists (ACLs)
Anonymous-Identification	System.Web.Security.AnonymousIdentification-Module	Manages anonymous identifiers
Profile	System.Web.Profile.ProfileModule	Implements ASP.NET profile
UrlMappings-Module	System.Web.UrlMappingsModule	Provides mapping of a real URL to a user-friendly URL

IIS 7.0 Default Settings and Time-Outs/Thresholds

This appendix includes the default settings and time-outs for all items in Internet Information Services (IIS) 7.0. The IIS Manager categories are grouped under three major subcategories: ASP.NET, IIS, and Management. The following sections provide tables that define each of these IIS Manager categories. Categories without default values are also listed in this appendix, outside of the table format.

The fourth section contains all default Application Pool settings.

ASP.NET

The ASP.NET section in IIS Manager has the following 13 categories. Three of the settings are site-level only:

- .NET Compilation

- .NET Globalization

- .NET Profile (site-level option only; No Values by default; data can be added as necessary)

- .NET Roles (site-level option only; No Values by default; data can be added as necessary)

- .NET Trust Levels

- .NET Users (site-level option only; No Values by default; data can be added as necessary)

- Application Settings (No Values by default; data can be added as necessary)

- Connection Strings

- Machine Key

- Pages and Controls

- Providers
- Session State
- SMTP E-mail

Tables E-1 through E-9 describe each of these categories and all default values as well as minimum and maximum values, if applicable.

Table E-1   .NET Compilation

Category	Description	Subcategory	Default Value	Min	Max
Batch	Batch Compilations		True		
	Maximum File Size		1000		
	Maximum Size Of Batch		1000		
	Time-out (hh:mm:ss)		00:15:00		
Behavior	Debug		False		
	Number Of Recompiles		15		
	Url Line Pragmas		False		
	Visual Basic .NET	Explicit Compile Option	True		
		Strict Compile Option	False		
General	Assemblies	[0]	Mscorlib		
		[1]	System, Version=2.0.0.0, Culture=neutral, PublicKey-Token=b77a5c561934e089		
		[2]	System.Configuration, Version=2.0.0.0, Culture=neutral, PublicKey-Token=b03f5f7f11d50a3a		
		[3]	System.Web, Version=2.0.0.0, Culture=neutral, PublicKey-Token=b03f5f7f11d50a3a		
		[4]	System.Data, Version=2.0.0.0, Culture=neutral, PublicKey-Token=b77a5c561934e089		

Table E-1 .NET Compilation

Category	Description	Subcategory	Default Value	Min	Max
		[5]	System.Web. Services, Version=2.0.0.0, Culture=neutral, PublicKey- Token=b03f5f7f11d5 0a3a		
		[6]	System.Xml, Version=2.0.0.0, Culture=neutral, PublicKey- Token=b77a5c56193 4e089		
		[7]	System.Drawing, Version=2.0.0.0, Culture=neutral, PublicKey- Token=b03f5f7f11d5 0a3a		
		[8]	System.Enterprise- Services, Version=2.0.0.0, Culture=neutral, PublicKey- Token=b03f5f7f11d5 0a3a		
		[9]	System.Web.Mobile, Version=2.0.0.0, Culture=neutral, PublicKey- Token=b03f5f7f11d5 0a3a		
		[10]	*		
		[11]	System.Runtime. Serialization, Version=3.0.0.0, Culture=neutral, PublicKey- Token=b77a5c56193 4e089, processor- Architecture=MSIL		

Table E-1   .NET Compilation

Category	Description	Subcategory	Default Value	Min	Max
		[12]	System.Identity-Model, Version=3.0.0.0, Culture=neutral, PublicKey-Token=b77a5c56193 4e089, processor-Architecture=MSIL		
		[13]	System.ServiceModel, Version=3.0.0.0, Culture=neutral, PublicKey-Token=b77a5c56193 4e089		
	Default Language		vb		
	Temporary Directory				

Table E-2   .NET Globalization

Category	Description	Subcategory	Default Value	Min	Max
Culture	Culture		Invariant Language (Invariant Country)		
	Enable Client Based Culture		False		
	UI Culture		Invariant Language (Invariant Country)		
Encoding	File		Windows-1252		
	Requests		utf-8		
	Response Headers		utf-8		
	Responses		utf-8		

Table E-3   .NET Trust Levels

Category	Description	Subcategory	Default Value	Min	Max
Trust Level			Full (internal)		

Table E-4   Connection Strings

Name	Connection String	Entry Type
LocalSqlServer	data source=.\SQLEXPRESS;Integrated Security=SSPI; AttachDBFilename=|DataDirectory|aspnetdb.mdf; User Instance=true	Inherited

Table E-5   **Machine Key**

Category	Description	Subcategory	Default Value	Min	Max
Encryption Method			Sha1		
Decryption Method			Auto		
Validation Key	Automatically generate at run time		Checked		
	Generate a unique key for each application		Checked and AutoGenerate, IsolateApps		
Decryption Key	Automatically generate at run time		Checked		
	Generate a unique key for each application		Checked and AutoGenerate, IsolateApps		

Table E-6   **Pages and Controls**

Category	Description	Subcategory	Default Value	Min	Max
Behavior	Buffer		True		
	User Interface	Master Page File			
		Style Sheet Theme			
		Theme			
	View State	Enable Authenticated View State	True		
		Enable View State	True		
		Maximum Page State Field Length	−1		
Compilation	Base Type For Pages		System.Web.UI.Page		
	Base Type For User Controls		System.Web.UI.UserControl		
	Compilation Mode		Always		
General	Namespaces	[0]	System		
		[1]	System.Collections		
		[2]	System.Collections.Specialized		

Table E-6 **Pages and Controls**

Category	Description	Subcategory	Default Value	Min	Max
		[3]	System. Configuration		
		[4]	System.Text		
		[5]	System.Text. Regular- Expressions		
		[6]	System.Web		
		[7]	System.Web. Caching		
		[8]	System.Web. SessionState		
		[9]	System.Web. Security		
		[10]	System.Web. Profile		
		[11]	System.Web.UI		
		[12]	System.Web.UI. WebControls		
		[13]	System.Web.UI. WebControls. WebParts		
		[14]	System.Web.UI. HtmlControls		
Services	Enable Session State		True		
	Validate Request		True		

Table E-7 **Providers**

Name	Type	Entry Type
AspNetSqlRoleProvider	SqlRoleProvider (System.Web.Security.SqlRoleProvider)	Inherited
AspNetWindowsTokenRoleProvider	WindowsTokenRoleProvider (System.Web.Security. Windows- TokenRoleProvider)	Inherited
AspNetSqlMembershipProvider (.NET Users)	SqlMembershipProvider (System.Web.Security. SqlMembershipProvider)	Inherited
AspNetSqlProfileProvider (.NET Profile)	SqlProfileProvider (System.Web.Security. SqlProfile.Provider)	Inherited

Table E-8   Session State

Category	Description	Subcategory	Default Value	Min	Max
Session State Mode Settings	Not enabled				
	In process		Selected		
	Custom				
	State Server				
	Connection string		tcpip=loopback:42424		
	Time-out (in seconds)		10		
	SQL Server				
	Connection string		Data source=localhost; Integrated Security=SSPI		
	Time-out (in seconds)		30		
	Enable custom database				
Cookie Settings	Mode		Use Cookies		
	Name		ASP.NET_SessionID		
	Time-out (in minutes)		20		
	Regenerate expired session ID				
User hosting identity for impersonation			Checked		

Table E-9   SMTP E-Mail

Category	Description	Subcategory	Default Value	Min	Max
E-mail address					
Deliver e-mail to SMTP server	SMTP Server				
	Use localhost				
	Port:		25		
Authentication Settings	Not Required		Selected		
	Windows				
	Specify credentials				
Store e-mail in pickup directory					

IIS

The IIS section in IIS Manager has 21 categories total, and 2 of the settings are server-level only:

- ASP
- Authentication
- Authorization Rules
- CGI
- Compression
- Default Document
- Directory Browsing
- Error Pages
- Failed Request Tracing Rules
- Handler Mappings
- HTTP Redirect
- HTTP Response Headers
- IPv4 Address and Domain Restrictions
- ISAPI and CGI Restrictions
- ISAPI Filters
- Logging
- MIME Types
- Modules
- Output Caching
- Server Certificates (server-level only option)
- Worker Processes (server-level only option)

Tables E-10 through E-26 describe each of these categories and all default values, as well as maximum and minimum values, if applicable.

Table E-10   ASP

Category	Description	Subcategory	Default Value	Min	Max
Behavior	Code Page		0		
	Enable Buffering		True		
	Enable Chunked Encoding		True		
	Enable HTML Fallback		True		
	Enable Parent Paths		False		
	Limit Properties	Client Connection Test Interval	00:00:03		
		Maximum Requesting Entity Test Interval	200000	0	2,147,748,3647
		Queue Length	3000	0	2,147,748,3647
		Request Queue Time-out	00:00:00		
		Response Buffering Limit	4194304	0	2,147,748,3647
		Script Time-out	00:01:30		
		Threads Per Processor Limit	25	0	2,147,748,3647
	Locale ID		0		
	Restart On Config Change		True		
Compilation	Debugging Properties	Calculate Line Numbers	True		
		Catch COM Component Exceptions	True		
		Enable Client-side Debugging	False		
		Enable Log Error Requests	True		
		Enable Server-side Debugging	False		

Table E-10   **ASP**

Category	Description	Subcategory	Default Value	Min	Max
		Log Errors to NT Log	False		
		Run On End Functions Anonymously	True		
		Script Error Message	An error occurred on the server when processing the URL. Please contact the system administrator. <p/> If you are the system administrator please click <a href="http://go.microsoft.com/fwlink/?LinkID=82731"> here</a> to find out more about this error.		
		Send Errors To Browser	False		
	Script Language		VBScript		
Services	Caching Properties	Cache Directory Path	%SystemDrive%\inetpub\temp\ASP Compiled Templates		
		Enable Type Library Caching	True		
		Maximum Disk Cached Files	2000	0	2,147,748,3647
		Maximum Memory Cached Files	500	0	2,147,748,3647
		Maximum Script Engines Cached	250	0	2,147,748,3647
	Com Plus Properties	Enable Side by Side Component	False		
		Enable Tracker	False		
		Execute In MTA	False		
		Honor Component Threading Module	False		

Table E-10   **ASP**

Category	Description	Subcategory	Default Value	Min	Max
		Partition ID	00000000-0000-0000-0000-000000000000		
		Side By Side Component			
		Use Partition	False		
	Session Properties	Enable Session State	True		
		Maximum Sessions	4294967295		
		New ID On Secure Connection	True		
		Time-out	00:20:00		

Table E-11   **Authentication**

Name	Status	Response Type
Active Directory Client Certificate Authentication	Disabled	HTTP 401 Challenge
Anonymous Authentication	Enabled	
ASP.NET Impersonation	Disabled	
Basic Authentication	Disabled	HTTP 401 Challenge
Digest Authentication	Disabled	HTTP 401 Challenge
Forms Authentication	Disabled	HTTP 302 Login/Redirect
Windows Authentication	Disabled	HTTP 401 Challenge

Table E-12   **Authorization Rules**

Mode	Users	Roles	Verbs	Entry Type
Allow	All Users			Local

Table E-13   **CGI**

Category	Description	Subcategory	Default Value	Min	Max
Behavior	Time-out (hh:mm:ss)		00:15:00		
	Use New Console For Each Invocation		False		
Security	Impersonate User		True		

Table E-14 Compression

Category	Description	Subcategory	Default Value	Min	Max
Enable dynamic content compression					
Enable static content compression			Checked		
Static compression	Only compress files larger than (in bytes):		Checked; 256		
Cache directory:			%SystemDrive%\inetpub\temp\IIS Temporary Compressed Files		
Per application pool disk space limit (in MB):			100		

Table E-15 Default Document

Name	Entry Type
Default.htm	Local
Default.asp	Local
index.htm	Local
index.html	Local
iisstart.htm	Local
default.aspx	Local

Table E-16 Directory Browsing

Name	Subcategory	Default Value
Time		Checked
Size		Checked
Extension		Checked
Date		Checked
	Long date	

Table E-17 Error Pages

Status Code	Path	Type	Entry Type
401	%SystemDrive%\inetpub\custerr\<LANGUAGE-TAG>\401.htm	File	Local
403	%SystemDrive%\inetpub\custerr\<LANGUAGE-TAG>\403.htm	File	Local
404	%SystemDrive%\inetpub\custerr\<LANGUAGE-TAG>\404.htm	File	Local

Table E-17   Error Pages

Status Code	Path	Type	Entry Type
405	%SystemDrive%\inetpub\custerr\<LANGUAGE-TAG>\405.htm	File	Local
406	%SystemDrive%\inetpub\custerr\<LANGUAGE-TAG>\401.htm	File	Local
412	%SystemDrive%\inetpub\custerr\<LANGUAGE-TAG>\412.htm	File	Local
500	%SystemDrive%\inetpub\custerr\<LANGUAGE-TAG>\500.htm	File	Local
501	%SystemDrive%\inetpub\custerr\<LANGUAGE-TAG>\501.htm	File	Local
502	%SystemDrive%\inetpub\custerr\<LANGUAGE-TAG>\502.htm	File	Local

Failed Request Tracing Rules

No Values by default. Data can be added as necessary.

Table E-18   Handler Mappings: Group by State

Name	Path	State	Path Type	Handler	Entry Type
CGI-exe	*.exe	Disabled	File	CgiModule	Local
ISAPI-dll	*.dll	Disabled	File	IsapiModule	Local
ASPClassic	*.asp	Enabled	File	IsapiModule	Local
Assembly-ResourceLoader-Integrated	WebResource.axd	Enabled	Unspecified	System.Web.Handlers.Assembly-ResourceLoader	Local
AXD-ISAPI-2.0	*.axd	Enabled	Unspecified	IsapiModule	Local
HttpRemoting-HandlerFactory-rem-Integrated	*.rem	Enabled	Unspecified	System.Runtime.Remoting.Channels.Http.HttpRemotingHandlerFactory, System.Runtime.Remoting, Version=2.0.0.0, Culture=neutral, PublicKeyToken=b77a5c561934e089	Local
HttpRemoting-HandlerFactory-rem-ISAPI-2.0	*.rem	Enabled	Unspecified	IsapiModule	Local

Table E-18   Handler Mappings: Group by State

Name	Path	State	Path Type	Handler	Entry Type
HttpRemoting-HandlerFactory-soap-Integrated	*.soap	Enabled	Unspecified	System.Run-time.Remoting.Channels.Http.Http-Remoting-HandlerFactory, System.Runtime.Remoting, Version=2.0.0.0, Culture=neutral, PublicKey-Token=b77a5c561934e089	
HttpRemoting-HandlerFactory-soap-ISAPI-2.0	*.soap	Enabled	Unspecified	IsapiModule	Local
OPTIONSVerb-Handler	*	Enabled	Unspecified	Protocol-SupportModule	Local
PageHandler-Factory-Integrated	*.aspx	Enabled	Unspecified	System.Web.UI.PageHandler-Factory	Local
PageHandler-Factory-ISAPI-2.0	*.aspx	Enabled	Unspecified	IsapiModule	Local
Security-Certificate	*.cer	Enabled	File	IsapiModule	Local
SimpleHandler-Factory-Integrated	*.ashx	Enabled	Unspecified	System.Web.UI.Simple-HandlerFactory	Local
SimpleHandler-Factory-ISAPI-2.0	*.ashx	Enabled	Unspecified	IsapiModule	Local
SSINC-shtm	*.shtm	Enabled	File	ServerSide-IncludeModule	Local
SSINC-shtml	*.shtml	Enabled	File	ServerSide-IncludeModule	Local
SSINC-stm	*.stm	Enabled	File	ServerSide-IncludeModule	Local

Table E-18   Handler Mappings: Group by State

Name	Path	State	Path Type	Handler	Entry Type
svc-Integrated	*.svc	Enabled	Unspecified	System.Service Model. Activation. HttpHandler, System.Service Model, Version=3.0.0.0, Culture=neutral, PublicKey-Token=b77a5c 561934e089	
svc-ISAPI-2.0	*.svc	Enabled	Unspecified	%System-Root%\Microsoft.NET\ Framework\ v2.0.50727\asp net_isapi.dll	
TraceHandler-Integrated	trace.axd	Enabled	Unspecified	System.Web. Handlers. TraceHandler	Local
TRACEVerb-Handler	*	Enabled	Unspecified	Protocol-SupportModule	Local
WebAdmin-Handler-Integrated	WebAdmin.axd	Enabled	Unspecified	System.Web. Handlers. WebAdmin-Handler	Local
WebService-HandlerFactory-Integrated	*.asmx	Enabled	Unspecified	System.Web. Services. Protocols. WebService-HandlerFactory, System.Web. Services, Version=2.0.0.0, Culture=neutral, PublicKey-Token=b03f5f7 f11d50a3a	Local
WebService-HandlerFactory-ISAPI-2.0	*.asmx	Enabled	Unspecified	IsapiModule	Local
StaticFile	*	Enabled	File or Folder	StaticFile-Module,Default Document-Module,DirectoryListModule	Local

Table E-19   HTTP Redirect

Category	Subcategory	Value
Redirect requests to this destination		
Redirect Behavior	Redirect all requests to exact destination (instead of relative to destination)	
	Only redirect requests to content in this directory (no subdirectories)	
Status Code	Found (302)	Not enabled

Table E-20   HTTP Response Headers

Name	Value	Entry Type
X-Powered-By	ASP.NET	Local

IPv4 Address and Domain Restrictions

No Values by default. Data can be added as necessary.

Table E-21   ISAPI and CGI Restrictions

Description	Restriction	Path
Active Server Pages	Allowed	%windir%\system32\inetsrv\asp.dll
ASP.NET v2.0.50727	Allowed	%windir%\Microsoft.NET\Framework\v2.0.50727\aspnet_isapi.dll

Table E-22   ISAPI Filters

Description	Executable	Entry Type
ASP.NET v2.0.50727	%windir%\Microsoft.NET\Framework\v2.0.50727\aspnet_filter.dll	Local

Table E-23   Logging

Category	Subcategory	Value
One log file per		Site
Log File	Format	W3C
	Directory	%SystemDrive%\inetpub\logs\LogFiles
	Encoding	UTF-8
Log File Rollover	Select the method that IIS uses to create a new log file	Schedule:Daily
	Maximum file size (in bytes)	

Table E-23   Logging

Category	Subcategory	Value
	Do not create new log files	
	Use local time for file naming and rollover	

Table E-24   MIME Types

Extension	MIME Type	Entry Type
.323	text/h323	Local
.aaf	application/octet-stream	Local
.aca	application/octet-stream	Local
.accdb	application/msaccess	Local
.accde	application/msaccess	Local
.accdt	application/msaccess	Local
.acx	application/internet-property-stream	Local
.afm	application/octet-stream	Local
.ai	application/postscript	Local
.aif	audio/x-aiff	Local
.aifc	audio/aiff	Local
.aiff	audio/aiff	Local
.application	application/x-ms-application	Local
.art	image/x-jg	Local
.asd	application/octet-stream	Local
.asf	video/x-ms-asf	Local
.asi	application/octet-stream	Local
.asm	text/plain	Local
.asr	video/x-ms-asf	Local
.asx	video/x-ms-asf	Local
.atom	application/atom+xml	Local
.au	audio/basic	Local
.avi	video/x-msvideo	Local
.axs	application/olescript	Local
.bas	text/plain	Local
.bcpio	application/x-bcpio	Local
.bin	application/octet-stream	Local
.bmp	image/bmp	Local
.c	text/plain	Local
.cab	application/octet-stream	Local
.calx	application/vnd.ms-office.calx	Local

Table E-24   MIME Types

Extension	MIME Type	Entry Type
.cat	application/vnd.ms-pki.seccat	Local
.cdf	application/x-cdf	Local
.chm	application/octet-stream	Local
.class	application/x-java-applet	Local
.clp	application/x-msclip	Local
.cmx	image/x-cmx	Local
.cnf	text/plain	Local
.cod	image/cis-cod	Local
.cpio	application/x-cpio	Local
.cpp	text/plain	Local
.crd	application/x-mscardfile	Local
.crl	application/pkix-crl	Local
.crt	application/x-x509-ca-cert	Local
.csh	application/x-csh	Local
.css	text/css	Local
.csv	application/octet-stream	Local
.cur	application/octet-stream	Local
.dcr	application/x-director	Local
.deploy	application/octet-stream	Local
.der	application/x-x509-ca-cert	Local
.dib	image/bmp	Local
.dir	application/x-director	Local
.disco	text/xml	Local
.dll	application/x-msdownload	Local
.dll.config	text/xml	Local
.dlm	text/dlm	Local
.doc	application/msword	Local
.docm	application/vnd.ms-word.document.macroEnabled.12	Local
.docx	application/vnd.openxmlformats-officedocument.word-processingml.document	Local
.dot	application/msword	Local
.dotm	application/vnd.ms-word.template.macroEnabled.12	Local
.dotx	application/vnd.openxmlformats-officedocument.word-processingml.template	Local
.dsp	application/octet-stream	Local
.dtd	text/xml	Local
.dvi	application/x-dvi	Local
.dwf	drawing/x-dwf	Local

Table E-24   MIME Types

Extension	MIME Type	Entry Type
.dwp	application/octet-stream	Local
.dxr	application/x-director	Local
.eml	message/rfc822	Local
.emz	application/octet-stream	Local
.eot	application/octet-stream	Local
.eps	application/postscript	Local
.etx	text/x-setext	Local
.evy	application/envoy	Local
.exe	application/octet-stream	Local
.exe.config	text/xml	Local
.fdf	application/vnd.fdf	Local
.fif	application/fractals	Local
.fla	application/octet-stream	Local
.flr	x-world/x-vrml	Local
.flv	video/x-flv	Local
.gif	image/gif	Local
.gtar	application/x-gtar	Local
.gz	application/x-gzip	Local
.h	text/plain	Local
.hdf	application/x-hdf	Local
.hdml	text/x-hdml	Local
.hhc	application/x-oleobject	Local
.hhk	application/octet-stream	Local
.hhp	application/octet-stream	Local
.hlp	application/winhlp	Local
.hqx	application/mac-binhex40	Local
.hta	application/hta	Local
.htc	text/x-component	Local
.htm	text/html	Local
.html	text/html	Local
.htt	text/webviewhtml	Local
.hxt	text/html	Local
.ico	image/x-icon	Local
.ics	application/octet-stream	Local
.ief	image/ief	Local
.iii	application/x-iphone	Local
.inf	application/octet-stream	Local

Table E-24 MIME Types

Extension	MIME Type	Entry Type
.ins	application/x-internet-signup	Local
.isp	application/x-internet-signup	Local
.IVF	video/x-ivf	Local
.jar	application/java-archive	Local
.java	application/octet-stream	Local
.jck	application/liquidmotion	Local
.jcz	application/liquidmotion	Local
.jfif	image/pjpeg	Local
.jpb	application/octet-stream	Local
.jpe	image/jpeg	Local
.jpeg	image/jpeg	Local
.jpg	image/jpeg	Local
.js	application/x-javascript	Local
.jsx	text/jscript	Local
.latex	application/x-latex	Local
.lit	application/x-ms-reader	Local
.lpk	application/octet-stream	Local
.lsf	video/x-la-asf	Local
.lsx	video/x-la-asf	Local
.lzh	application/octet-stream	Local
.m13	application/x-msmediaview	Local
.m14	application/x-msmediaview	Local
.m1v	video/mpeg	Local
.m3u	audio/x-mpegurl	Local
.man	application/x-troff-man	Local
.manifest	application/x-ms-manifest	Local
.map	text/plain	Local
.mdb	application/x-msaccess	Local
.mdp	application/octet-stream	Local
.me	application/x-troff-me	Local
.mht	message/rfc822	Local
.mhtml	message/rfc822	Local
.mid	audio/mid	Local
.midi	audio/mid	Local
.mix	application/octet-stream	Local
.mmf	application/x-smaf	Local
.mno	text/xml	Local
.mny	application/x-msmoney	Local

Table E-24   MIME Types

Extension	MIME Type	Entry Type
.mov	video/quicktime	Local
.movie	video/x-sgi-movie	Local
.mp2	video/mpeg	Local
.mp3	audio/mpeg	Local
.mpa	video/mpeg	Local
.mpe	video/mpeg	Local
.mpeg	video/mpeg	Local
.mpg	video/mpeg	Local
.mpp	application/vnd.ms-project	Local
.mpv2	video/mpeg	Local
.ms	application/x-troff-ms	Local
.msi	application/octet-stream	Local
.mso	application/octet-stream	Local
.mvb	application/x-msmediaview	Local
.mvc	application/x-miva-compiled	Local
.nc	application/x-netcdf	Local
.nsc	video/x-ms-asf	Local
.nws	message/rfc822	Local
.ocx	application/octet-stream	Local
.oda	application/oda	Local
.odc	text/x-ms-odc	Local
.ods	application/oleobject	Local
.one	application/onenote	Local
.onea	application/onenote	Local
.onetoc	application/onenote	Local
.onetoc2	application/onenote	Local
.onetmp	application/onenote	Local
.onepkg	application/onenote	Local
.p10	application/pkcs10	Local
.p12	application/x-pkcs12	Local
.p7b	application/x-pkcs7-certificates	Local
.p7c	application/pkcs7-mime	Local
.p7m	application/pkcs7-mime	Local
.p7r	application/x-pkcs7-certreqresp	Local
.p7s	application/pkcs7-signature	Local
.pbm	image/x-portable-bitmap	Local
.pcx	application/octet-stream	Local

Table E-24   MIME Types

Extension	MIME Type	Entry Type
.pcz	application/octet-stream	Local
.pdf	application/pdf	Local
.pfb	application/octet-stream	Local
.pfm	application/octet-stream	Local
.pfx	application/x-pkcs12	Local
.pgm	image/x-portable-graymap	Local
.pko	application/vnd.ms-pki.pko	Local
.pma	application/x-perfmon	Local
.pmc	application/x-perfmon	Local
.pml	application/x-perfmon	Local
.pmr	application/x-perfmon	Local
.pmw	application/x-perfmon	Local
.png	image/png	Local
.pnm	image/x-portable-anymap	Local
.pnz	image/png	Local
.pot	application/vnd.ms-powerpoint	Local
.potm	application/vnd.ms-powerpoint.template.macroEnabled.12	Local
.potx	application/vnd.openxmlformats-officedocument.presentationml.template	Local
.ppam	application/vnd.ms-powerpoint.addin.macroEnabled.12	Local
.ppm	image/x-portable-pixmap	Local
.pps	application/vnd.ms-powerpoint	Local
.ppsm	application/vnd.ms-powerpoint.slideshow.macroEnabled.12	Local
.ppsx	application/vnd.openxmlformats-officedocument.presentationml.slideshow	Local
.ppt	application/vnd.ms-powerpoint	Local
.pptm	application/vnd.ms-powerpoint.presentation.macroEnabled.12	Local
.pptx	application/vnd.openxmlformats-officedocument.presentationml.presentation	Local
.prf	application/pics-rules	Local
.prm	application/octet-stream	Local
.prx	application/octet-stream	Local
.ps	application/postscript	Local
.psd	application/octet-stream	Local
.psm	application/octet-stream	Local
.psp	application/octet-stream	Local
.pub	application/x-mspublisher	Local

Table E-24   MIME Types

Extension	MIME Type	Entry Type
.qt	video/quicktime	Local
.qtl	application/x-quicktimeplayer	Local
.qxd	application/octet-stream	Local
.ra	audio/x-pn-realaudio	Local
.ram	audio/x-pn-realaudio	Local
.rar	application/octet-stream	Local
.ras	image/x-cmu-raster	Local
.rf	image/vnd.rn-realflash	Local
.rgb	image/x-rgb	Local
.rm	application/vnd.rn-realmedia	Local
.rmi	audio/mid	Local
.roff	application/x-troff	Local
.rpm	audio/x-pn-realaudio-plugin	Local
.rtf	application/rtf	Local
.rtx	text/richtext	Local
.scd	application/x-msschedule	Local
.sct	text/scriptlet	Local
.sea	application/octet-stream	Local
.setpay	application/set-payment-initiation	Local
.setreg	application/set-registration-initiation	Local
.sgml	text/sgml	Local
.sh	application/x-sh	Local
.shar	application/x-shar	Local
.sit	application/x-stuffit	Local
.sldm	application/vnd.ms-powerpoint.slide.macroEnabled.12	Local
.sldx	application/vnd.openxmlformats-officedocument.presentationml.slide	Local
.smd	audio/x-smd	Local
.smi	application/octet-stream	Local
.smx	audio/x-smd	Local
.smz	audio/x-smd	Local
.snd	audio/basic	Local
.snp	application/octet-stream	Local
.spc	application/x-pkcs7-certificates	Local
.spl	application/futuresplash	Local
.src	application/x-wais-source	Local
.ssm	application/streamingmedia	Local
.sst	application/vnd.ms-pki.certstore	Local

Table E-24   MIME Types

Extension	MIME Type	Entry Type
.stl	application/vnd.ms-pki.stl	Local
.sv4cpio	application/x-sv4cpio	Local
.sv4crc	application/x-sv4crc	Local
.swf	application/x-shockwave-flash	Local
.t	application/x-troff	Local
.tar	application/x-tar	Local
.tcl	application/x-tcl	Local
.tex	application/x-tex	Local
.texi	application/x-texinfo	Local
.texinfo	application/x-texinfo	Local
.tgz	application/x-compressed	Local
.thmx	application/vnd.ms-officetheme	Local
.thn	application/octet-stream	Local
.tif	image/tiff	Local
.tiff	image/tiff	Local
.toc	application/octet-stream	Local
.tr	application/x-troff	Local
.trm	application/x-msterminal	Local
.tsv	text/tab-separated-values	Local
.ttf	application/octet-stream	Local
.txt	text/plain	Local
.u32	application/octet-stream	Local
.uls	text/iuls	Local
.ustar	application/x-ustar	Local
.vbs	text/vbscript	Local
.vcf	text/x-vcard	Local
.vcs	text/plain	Local
.vdx	application/vnd.ms-visio.viewer	Local
.vml	text/xml	Local
.vsd	application/vnd.visio	Local
.vss	application/vnd.visio	Local
.vst	application/vnd.visio	Local
.vsto	application/x-ms-vsto	Local
.vsw	application/vnd.visio	Local
.vsx	application/vnd.visio	Local
.vtx	application/vnd.visio	Local
.wav	audio/wav	Local
.wax	audio/x-ms-wax	Local

Table E-24   MIME Types

Extension	MIME Type	Entry Type
.wbmp	image/vnd.wap.wbmp	Local
.wcm	application/vnd.ms-works	Local
.wdb	application/vnd.ms-works	Local
.wks	application/vnd.ms-works	Local
.wm	video/x-ms-wm	Local
.wma	audio/x-ms-wma	Local
.wmd	application/x-ms-wmd	Local
.wmf	application/x-msmetafile	Local
.wml	text/vnd.wap.wml	Local
.wmlc	application/vnd.wap.wmlc	Local
.wmls	text/vnd.wap.wmlscript	Local
.wmlsc	application/vnd.wap.wmlscriptc	Local
.wmp	video/x-ms-wmp	Local
.wmv	video/x-ms-wmv	Local
.wmx	video/x-ms-wmx	Local
.wmz	application/x-ms-wmz	Local
.wps	application/vnd.ms-works	Local
.wri	application/x-mswrite	Local
.wrl	x-world/x-vrml	Local
.wrz	x-world/x-vrml	Local
.wsdl	text/xml	Local
.wvx	video/x-ms-wvx	Local
.x	application/direct	Local
.xaf	x-world/x-vrml	Local
.xaml	application/xaml+xml	Local
.xap	application/x-silverlight-app	Local
.xbap	application/x-ms-xbap	Local
.xbm	image/x-xbitmap	Local
.xdr	text/plain	Local
.xla	application/vnd.ms-excel	Local
.xlam	application/vnd.ms-excel.addin.macroEnabled.12	Local
.xlc	application/vnd.ms-excel	Local
.xlm	application/vnd.ms-excel	Local
.xls	application/vnd.ms-excel	Local
.xlsb	application/vnd.ms-excel.sheet.binary.macroEnabled.12	Local
.xlsm	application/vnd.ms-excel.sheet.macroEnabled.12	Local
.xlsx	application/vnd.openxmlformats-officedocument.spread-sheetml.sheet	Local

Table E-24   MIME Types

Extension	MIME Type	Entry Type
.xlt	application/vnd.ms-excel	Local
.xltm	application/vnd.ms-excel.template.macroEnabled.12	Local
.xltx	application/vnd.openxmlformats-officedocument.spread-sheetml.template	Local
.xlw	application/vnd.ms-excel	Local
.xml	text/xml	Local
.xof	x-world/x-vrml	Local
.xpm	image/x-xpixmap	Local
.xps	application/vnd.ms-xpsdocument	Local
.xsd	text/xml	Local
.xsf	text/xml	Local
.xsl	text/xml	Local
.xslt	text/xml	Local
.xsn	application/octet-stream	Local
.xtp	application/octet-stream	Local
.xwd	image/x-xwindowdump	Local
.z	application/x-compress	Local
.zip	application/x-zip-compressed	Local

Table E-25   Modules

Name	Code	Module Type	Entry Type
AnonymousAuthenticationModule	%windir%\System32\inetsrv\authanon.dll	Native	Local
AnonymousIdentification	System.Web.Security.AnonymousIdentificationModule	Managed	Local
BasicAuthenticationModule	%windir%\System32\inetsrv\authbas.dll	Native	Local
CertificateMappingAuthentication-Module	%windir%\System32\inetsrv\authcert.dll	Native	Local
CgiModule	%windir%\System32\inetsrv\cgi.dll	Native	Local
ConfigurationValidationModule	%windir%\System32\inetsrv\validcfg.dll	Native	Local
CustomErrorModule	%windir%\System32\inetsrv\custerr.dll	Native	Local
CustomLoggingModule	%windir%\System32\inetsrv\logcust.dll	Native	Local
DefaultAuthentication	System.Web.Security.Default-AuthenticationModule	Managed	Local

Table E-25 **Modules**

Name	Code	Module Type	Entry Type
DefaultDocumentModule	%windir%\System32\inetsrv\defdoc.dll	Native	Local
DigestAuthenticationModule	%windir%\System32\inetsrv\authmd5.dll	Native	Local
DirectoryListingModule	%windir%\System32\inetsrv\dirlist.dll	Native	Local
DynamicCompressionModule	%windir%\System32\inetsrv\compdyn.dll	Native	Local
FailedRequestsTracingModule	%windir%\System32\inetsrv\iisfreb.dll	Native	Local
FastCgiModule	%windir%\System32\inetsrv\iisfcgi.dll	Native	Local
FileAuthorization	System.Web.Security.FileAuthorizationModule	Managed	Local
FormsAuthentication	System.Web.Security.FormsAuthenticationModule	Managed	Local
HttpCacheModule	%windir%\System32\inetsrv\cachhttp.dll	Native	Local
HttpLoggingModule	%windir%\System32\inetsrv\loghttp.dll	Native	Local
HttpRedirectionModule	%windir%\System32\inetsrv\redirect.dll	Native	Local
IISCertificateMapping-AuthenticationModule	%windir%\System32\inetsrv\authmap.dll	Native	Local
IpRestrictionModule	%windir%\System32\inetsrv\iprestr.dll	Native	Local
IsapiFilterModule	%windir%\System32\inetsrv\filter.dll	Native	Local
IsapiModule	%windir%\System32\inetsrv\isapi.dll	Native	Local
OutputCache	System.Web.Caching.OutputCacheModule	Managed	Local
Profile	System.Web.Profile.ProfileModule	Managed	Local
ProtocolSupportModule	%windir%\System32\inetsrv\protsup.dll	Native	Local
RequestFilteringModule	%windir%\System32\inetsrv\modrqflt.dll	Native	Local
RoleManager	System.Web.Security.RoleManagerModule	Managed	Local
ServerSideIncludeModule	%windir%\System32\inetsrv\iis_ssi.dll	Native	Local

Table E-25 **Modules**

Name	Code	Module Type	Entry Type
ServiceModel	System.ServiceModel.Activation.HttpModule, System.ServiceModel, Version=3.0.0.0, Culture=neutral, PublicKeyToken=b77a5c561934e089	Managed	Inherited
Session	System.Web.SessionState.SessionStateModule	Managed	Local
StaticCompressionModule	%windir%\System32\inetsrv\compstat.dll	Native	Local
StaticFileModule	%windir%\System32\inetsrv\static.dll	Native	Local
UrlAuthorization	System.Web.Security.UrlAuthorizationModule	Managed	Local
UrlAuthorizationModule	%windir%\System32\inetsrv\urlauthz.dll	Native	Local
UrlMappingsModule	System.Web.UrlMappingsModule	Managed	Local
WindowsAuthentication	System.Web.Security.WindowsAuthenticationModule	Managed	Local
WindowsAuthenticationModule	%windir%\System32\inetsrv\authsspi.dll	Native	Local

Output Caching

No Values by default. Data can be added as necessary.

Table E-26 **Server Certificates (Server-Level Only)**

Name	Issued To	Issued By	Expiration Date	Certificate Hash
No Value	WMSvc-Machinename	WMSvc-*Machinename*	10 years after being created	Varies by machine

Worker Processes (Server Level Only)

No Values by default. Data displays only running requests.

Management

The Management section in IIS Manager has five categories total, and four of the settings are server-level only:

- Feature Management (server-level option only)
- IIS Manager Permissions
- IIS Manager Users (server-level option only)

- Management Service (server-level option only)
- Shared Configuration (server-level option only)

Tables E-27 through E-29 describe each of these categories and all default values as well as maximum and minimum values, if applicable.

Table E-27   Feature Delegation

Name	Delegation
.NET Compilation	Read/Write
.NET Globalization	Read/Write
.NET Profile	Read/Write
.NET Roles	Configuration Read/Write
.NET Trust Levels	Read/Write
.NET Users	Configuration Read/Write
Application Settings	Read/Write
ASP	Read Only
ASP.NET Impersonation	Read/Write
Authentication – Anonymous	Read Only
Authentication – Basic	Read Only
Authentication – Digest	Read Only
Authentication – Forms	Read/Write
Authentication – Windows	Read Only
Authorization Rules	Read/Write
CGI	Read Only
Compression	Read/Write
Connections Strings	Read/Write
Default Document	Read/Write
Directory Browsing	Read/Write
Error Pages	Read Only
Failed Request Tracing Rules	Read/Write
Feature Delegation	Read/Write
Handler Mappings	Read/Write
HTTP Redirect	Read/Write
HTTP Response Headers	Read/Write
IPv4 Address and Domain Restrictions	Read Only
ISAPI Filters	Read Only
Logging	Not Delegated
Machine Key	Read/Write
MIME Types	Read/Write

Table E-27   **Feature Delegation**

Name	Delegation
Modules	Read/Write
Output Caching	Read/Write
Page and Controls	Read/Write
Session State	Read/Write
SMTP E-mail	Read/Write
SSL Settings	Read Only

IIS Manager Permissions

No Values by default. Data can be added as necessary

IIS Manager Users

No Values by default. Data can be added as necessary.

Table E-28   **Management Service**

Category	Subcategory	Value
Enable Remote Connections		
Identity Credentials	Windows credentials only	Selected
	Windows credentials or IIS Manager credentials	
Connections	IP Address	All Unassigned
	Port	8172
	SSL certificate	WMSvc-*MachineName*
	Log Requests to:	Checked
	Log Requests Path Textbox	%SystemDrive%\Inetpub\logs\WMSvc
IPv4 Address Restrictions	Access for unspecified clients	Allow

Table E-29   **Shared Configuration**

Category	Subcategory	Value
Enable shared configuration		
Configuration Location	Physical path	
	User name	
	Password	
	Confirm password	

Application Pool Defaults

Two application pools are created when you install IIS 7.0. The first one is named Classic .NET AppPool. The second one is named DefaultAppPool. Table E-30 contains all default settings that new application pools use as a template.

Table E-30   **Application Pool Defaults**

Category	Description	Subcategory	Default Value	Min	Max
General	.NET Framework Version		v2.0		
	Managed Pipeline Mode		Integrated		
	Queue Length		1000	10	65,535
	Start Automatically		True		
CPU	Limit		0	0	100,000
	Limit Action		NoAction		
	Limit Interval (minutes)		5	0	86,400
	Processor Affinity Enabled		False		
	Processor Affinity Mask		4294967295		
Process Model	Identity		Network Service		
	Idle Time-out (minutes)		20	0	2,592,000
	Load User Profile		False		
	Maximum Worker Processes		1	1	2,147,483,647
	Ping Enabled		True		
	Ping Maximum Response Time (seconds)		90	1	4,294,967
	Ping Period (seconds)		30	1	4,294,967
	Shutdown Time Limit (seconds)		90	1	4,294,967
	Startup Time Limit (seconds)		90	1	4,294,967
Process Orphaning	Enable		False		
	Executable				
	Executable Parameters				

Table E-30 **Application Pool Defaults**

Category	Description	Subcategory	Default Value	Min	Max
Rapid-Fail Protection	"Service Unavailable" Response Type		HttpLevel		
	Enabled		True		
	Failure Interval (minutes)		5		
	Maximum Failures		5		
	Shutdown Executable				
	Shutdown Executable Parameters				
Recycling	Disabled Overlapped Recycle		False		
	Disable Recycling for Configuration Changes		False		
	Generate Recycle Event Log Entry	Application Pool Configuration Changed	False		
		Isapi Reported Unhealthy	False		
		Manual Recycle	False		
		Private Memory Limit Exceeded	True		
		Regular Time Interval	True		
		Request Limit Exceeded	False		
		Specific Time	False		
		Virtual Memory Limit Exceeded	True		
	Private Memory Limit (KB)		0		
	Regular Time Interval (minutes)		1740		
	Request Limit		0		
	Specific Times		TimeSpan[] Array		
	Virtual Memory Limit (KB)		0		

Appendix F
IIS 7.0 and 64-Bit Windows

> **In this appendix:**

This appendix discusses Internet Information Services (IIS) 7.0 running on a 64-bit system.

Windows Server 2008 x64

In the old 32-bit operating system environment, the total virtual memory address space is 4 gigabytes (GB) and, by default, it is divided into 2 GB each for applications and the operating system kernel. Though 2 GB of available memory to application may be sufficient for small and simple applications, it definitely does not work well for large-scale and complex applications. In the context of IIS, an application may be recycled when the worker process hits the memory limit.

On the other hand, the 64-bit operating system has much greater address space compared to 32-bit, and it is able to address up to 16 terabytes (TB). Although not many applications may need more than 4 GB of memory addresses, an x64 operating system enables you to run many different applications, which is not possible for practical reasons in 32-bit operating system due to its architecture limitation.

The Windows Server 2008 x64 operating system supports native 64-bit applications as well as 32-bit applications. Running a 32-bit application on an x64 operating system is made possible via Windows on Windows 64 (WOW64) technology, where the operating system emulates the 32-bit application and maps its instruction sets to the 64-bit environment. Although 64-bit worker processes grant you larger memory addressing space when hosting application in native 64-bit mode, it may not be as effective as running in 32-bit, especially if the application does not need to address more than 2 GB of system memory. For example, in IIS resources usage perspective, running worker processes in 64-bit consumes more system resources than in 32-bit mode, because the base footprint for 32-bit worker processes is smaller, with less overhead.

> **Note** In a hosting or large application environment, Microsoft recommends that the hosting application be in a 32-bit worker process with IIS 7.0 native core running in 64-bit mode together with the operating system. Of course, native 64-bit applications with large memory access or 64-bit components are required to run in a 64-bit worker process.

Configuring a 32-Bit Application on 64-Bit Microsoft Windows

By design, configuring 32-bit worker processes is applicable only to the x64 Windows operating system, because you can only run 32-bit worker processes in 32-bit environment. Unlike IIS 6.0, where you can configure bitness for worker processes at the server level, either in 32-bit or 64-bit mode for all worker processes, IIS 7.0 allows you to configure worker processes bitness at application pool level, giving you the flexibility to run in a mixed environment by having both 32-bit and 64-bit worker processes in the same system.

When IIS 7.0 is deployed on an x64 Windows Server 2008, IIS installs both 32-bit and 64-bit versions of all relevant components. The native 64-bit binaries are stored in the %windir%\system32\inetsrv folder, and the 32-bit binaries are kept in the %windir%\syswow64\inetsrv\ folder. These 32-bit module binaries are loaded into 32-bit worker processes in a WOW64 environment when WOW64 detects the worker processes are configured to run in 32-bit mode and redirect modules loading to the %windir%\syswow64\inetsrv\ folder.

> **Note**   For more information about module configuration in a 64-bit environment, see the section titled "Installing Modules for x64 Environments" in Chapter 12, "Managing Web Server Modules."

When configuring a 32-bit application pool in 64-bit Windows, the worker process is listed as W3WP.exe*32 in the task manager, indicating that it is a 32-bit application. By default, x64 Windows runs worker processes in 64-bit mode. To enable 32-bit application on 64-bit Windows, see the following procedures.

> **Important**   As a security best practice, log on to your computer by using an account that does not have administrator privileges and then use the Runas command to run IIS Manager as an administrator. For example, at the command prompt, type the following command: **runas /user:<*admin_acct*> "%windir%\system32\inetsrv\inetmgr.exe"**.

Using IIS Manager

To use IIS Manager to enable a 32-bit application on 64-bit Windows, do the following:

1.   Click Start, All Programs, Administrative Tools, Internet Information Services (IIS) Manager.

2.   In the Connections pane, expand the IIS computer node and then navigate to the Application Pools node.

3. In the Application Pools pane, select the application pool that you want to enable as a 32-bit worker process and then click Advanced Settings in the Actions pane.

4. In the Advanced Settings dialog box, in the General section, click the Enable 32-Bit Applications option and then select True from the drop-down list.

> **Note**   The Enable 32-Bit Applications option is visible only if you are running on Windows Server 2008 or Windows Vista x64 edition.

5. Click OK.

> **Important**   As a security best practice, log on to your computer by using an account that is not in the Administrators group and then use the Runas command to execute Appcmd.exe as an administrator. At the command prompt, type **runas /user:<*admin_acct*> "cmd.exe"**. Then, at the elevated command prompt, navigate to the Appcmd.exe directory by typing **cd %windir%\system32\inetsrv**.

Using the Command Line

If you prefer the command line to IIS Manager, use the following Appcmd.exe syntax for enabling 32-bit application on x64 Windows.

```
appcmd set apppool "ApppoolName" /enable32BitAppOnWin64:Boolean
```

Table F-1 describes the parameters for this syntax.

Table F-1   Syntax for Appcmd to Configure a 32-Bit Application on x64 Windows

Parameter	Description
ApppoolName	The string represents the application pool name.
enable32BitAppOnWin64	Specifies whether or not to enable the 32-bit worker process for the application pool.

The following syntax enables 32-bit worker process for the DefaultAppPool application pool.

```
appcmd set apppool "DefaultAppPool" /enable32BitAppOnWin64:true
```

After you successfully execute the command syntax, you will see the following output. Setting the value *enable32BitAppOnWin64* has no effect if you are running on a 32-bit version of Windows Server 2008.

```
APPPOOL object "DefaultAppPool" changed
```

Configuration Changes

Like the other changes in application pool, configuring a 32-bit worker process for the application pool is defined together with the application pool definition in the *<applicationPools>* section in the applicationHost.config file. The attribute value *enable32BitAppOnWin64* is declared with the application pool name element. The following shows the <applicationPools> configuration of 32-bit application pool setting for DefaultAppPool.

```
<applicationPools>
<add name="DefaultAppPool" enable32BitAppOnWin64="true" />
<add name="Classic .NET AppPool" managedPipelineMode="Classic" />

    ...
    <applicationPoolDefaults>
        <processModel identityType="NetworkService" />
    </applicationPoolDefaults>
</applicationPools>
```

IIS Manager Features to Configuration References

ASP.NET

Table G-1 outlines the ASP.NET feature sets and references to configuration systems.

Table G-1 IIS Manager/ASP.NET Feature Sets and References

Feature Set	Configuration File/Section	Provider (Modules/Services)
.NET Compilation	web.config system.web/compilation	ASP.NET Core
.NET Globalization	web.config system.web/globalization	ASP.NET Core
.NET Profile	web.config system.web/profile	System.Web.Security.ProfileModule
.NET Roles	web.config system.web/roleManager	System.Web.Security.RoleManager Module
.NET Trust Levels	web.config system.web/trust	ASP.NET Core
.NET Users	web.config (See the "Providers" entry later in this table.)	System.Web.Security.RoleManager Module
Application Settings	web.config appSettings	ASP.NET Core
Connection Strings	web.config connectionStrings	ASP.NET Core
Machine Key	web.config system.web/machineKey	ASP.NET Core

Table G-1 IIS Manager/ASP.NET Feature Sets and References

Feature Set	Configuration File/Section	Provider (Modules/Services)
Pages and Controls	web.config	ASP.NET Core
	system.web/pages	
Providers	web.config	ASP.NET Core
	system.web/membership	System.Web.Security.RoleManager Module
	system.web/roleManager	
	system.web/profile	System.Web.Security.ProfileModule
Session State	web.config	System.Web.SessionState.SessionState Module
	system.web/sessionState	
	system.web/sessionPageState	
SMTP E-mail	web.config	.NET Framework Core
	system.net/mailSettings/smtp	

IIS

Table G-2 outlines the IIS 7.0 feature sets and references to configuration systems.

Table G-2 IIS Manager/IIS Feature Sets and References

Feature Set	Configuration File/Section	Provider (Modules/Services)
ASP	web.config*	IsapiModule (isapi.dll)
	system.webServer/asp	
Authentication:		
Anonymous	web.config*	AnonymousAuthenticationModule (authanon.dll)
	system.webServer/security/ authentication/anonymous Authentication	
ASP.NET Impersonation	system.web/identity (Web.config)	ASP.NET Core
Basic	system.webServer/security/ authentication/basicAuthentication	BasicAuthenticationModule (authbas.dll)
Digest	system.webServer/security/ authentication/digest Authentication	DigestAuthenticationModule (authmd5.dll)
Forms	system.web/authentication (web.config)	System.Web.Security.Form AuthenticationModule
Windows	system.webServer/security/ authentication/windows Authentication	WindowsAuthenticationModule (authsspi.dll)
Authorization Rules	web.config	UrlAuthorizationModule (urlauthz.dll)
	system.webServer/security/ authorization	

Table G-2   IIS Manager/IIS Feature Sets and References

Feature Set	Configuration File/Section	Provider (Modules/Services)
CGI	web.config* system.webServer/cgi	CgiModule (cgi.dll)
Compression	web.config system.webServer/ httpCompression system.webServer/ urlCompression	DynamicCompressionModule (compdyn.dll) StaticCompressionModule (compstat.dll)
Default Document	web.config system.webServer/default Document	DefaultDocumentModule (defdoc.dll)
Directory Browsing	web.config system.webServer/ directoryBrowse	DirectoryListingModule (dirlist.dll)
Error Pages	web.config* system.webServer/httpErrors	CustomErrorModule (custerr.dll)
Failed Request Tracing Rules	web.config system.webServer/tracing system.webServer/httpTracing	FailedRequestTracingModule (iisfreb.dll)
Handler Mappings	web.config system.webServer/handlers	IIS Server Core
HTTP Redirect	web.config system.webServer/httpRedirect	HttpRedirectionModule (redirect.dll)
HTTP Response Headers	web.config system.webServer/httpProtocol system.webServer/staticContent	ProtocolSupportModule (protsup.dll) StaticFileModule (static.dll)
IPv4 Address and Domain Restrictions	web.config* system.webServer/security/ ipsecurity	IpRestrictionModule (iprestr.dll)
ISAPI and CGI Restrictions**	applicationHost.config system.webServer/security/ isapiCgiRestriction	CgiModule (cgi.dll) IsapiModule (isapi.dll)
ISAPI Filters	web.config* system.webServer/isapiFilters	IsapiFilterModule (filter.dll)
Logging	applicationHost.config system.applicationHost/log system.webServer/httpLogging system.applicationHost/sites/site/ logfile system.applicationhost/sites/site/ logFile/customLogPluginClsid	IIS Server Core HttpLoggingModule (loghttp.dll) CustomLoggingModule (logcust.dll)

Table G-2 IIS Manager/IIS Feature Sets and References

Feature Set	Configuration File/Section	Provider (Modules/Services)
MIME Types	web.config	StaticFileModule (static.dll)
	system.webServer/staticContent	
Modules	web.config	IIS Server Core
	system.webServer/globalModules	
	system.webServer/modules	
Output Caching	web.config	HttpCacheModule (cachhttp.dll)
	system.webServer/caching	
Server Certificates**	Certificate Store	Operating System Core
SSL Settings	web.config*	IIS Server Core
	system.webServer/security/access	
Worker Processes**	applicationHost.config	Windows Process Activation Service (WAS; svchost.exe)
	system.applicationHost/sites	
	system.applicationHost/webLimits	

* By default, locked feature configurations are defined at \<location path\> in the applicationHost.config file. If unlocked, configuration is stored at web.config of the configuration path.

** Features only available at server level.

Management

Table G-3 outlines the IIS Management feature sets and references to configuration systems.

Table G-3 IIS Manager/Management Feature Sets and References

Feature Set	Configuration File/Section	Provider (Modules/Services)
Feature Delegation	applicationHost.config	IIS Server Core
	\<location path="" override-Mode="Allow"\>	
IIS Manager Permissions*	Administration.config	IIS Server Core
	system.webServer/management/ authorization/authorization/ authorizationRules	
IIS Manager Users	Administration.config	IIS Server Core
	system.webServer/management/ authentication/credentials	
Management Service	Registry Key	Web Management Service (WMSvc.exe)
	HKEY_LOCAL_MACHINE\ SOFTWARE\Microsoft\ WebManagement\Server	
Shared Configuration	Redirection.config	IIS Server Core
	configurationRedirection	

* All features are available at the server level only, except IIS Manager Permissions, which is applicable only at the site and application level.

Appendix H
IIS 6.0 Metabase Mapping to IIS 7.0

Table H-1 presents the metabase properties in Microsoft Internet Information Services (IIS) 6.0 and the corresponding configuration settings for new XML configuration systems in IIS 7.0. It also provides deprecated metabase keys that do not have direction mapping or relationships in the new configuration systems. The deprecated metabase properties are related to legacy Simple Mail Transfer Protocol (SMTP) and File Transfer Protocol (FTP) services in IIS 7.0. The IIS 6.0 Management Compatibility in IIS 7.0 setup components is required to support the configuration of the deprecated metabase properties.

Table H-1   IIS 6.0 Metabase Mapping to IIS 7.0

IIS 6.0 Metabase Property	IIS 7.0 Configuration Element/Attribute
AccessFlags	<handlers accessPolicy />
AccessSSLFlags	<access sslFlags />
ADConnectionsPasswords	N/A: IIS 6.0 FTP–related
ADConnectionsUserName	N/A: IIS 6.0 FTP–related
AddNoHeaders	N/A: IIS 6.0 SMTP–related
AdminACL	N/A: deprecated
AdminACLBin	N/A: deprecated
AdminEmail	N/A: deprecated (Network News Transfer Protocol [NNTP])
AdminName	N/A: deprecated (NNTP)
AdminServer	N/A: deprecated
AllowAnonymous	N/A: IIS 6.0 FTP–related
AllowClientPosts	N/A: deprecated (NNTP)
AllowControlMsgs	N/A: deprecated (NNTP)
AllowFeedPosts	N/A: deprecated (NNTP)
AllowKeepAlive	<httpProtocol allowKeepAlive />
AllowPathInfoForScriptMappings	<handlers allowPathInfo />
AlwaysUseSsl	N/A: IIS 6.0 SMTP–related
AnonymousOnly	N/A: IIS 6.0 FTP–related
AnonymousPasswordSync	N/A: deprecated
AnonymousUserName	<anonymousAuthentication userName />
AnonymousUserPass	<anonymousAuthentication password />
AppAllowClientDebug	<asp appAllowClientDebug />

Table H-1   IIS 6.0 Metabase Mapping to IIS 7.0

IIS 6.0 Metabase Property	IIS 7.0 Configuration Element/Attribute
AppAllowDebugging	<asp appAllowDebugging />
AppFriendlyName	N/A: deprecated
AppIsolated	N/A: deprecated
ApplicationDependencies	<applicationDependencies />
AppOopRecoverLimit	N/A: deprecated
AppPackageID	N/A: deprecated
AppPackageName	N/A: deprecated
AppPoolAutoStart	<applicationPools autoStart />
AppPoolCommand	N/A: deprecated
AppPoolId	<applicationPools name />
AppPoolIdentityType	<processModel identityType />
AppPoolQueueLength	<applicationPools queueLength />
AppPoolState	N/A: deprecated
AppRoot	<virtualDirectoryDefaults path />
AppWamClsid	N/A: deprecated
ArticleTableFile	N/A: deprecated (NNTP)
ArticleTimeLimit	N/A: deprecated (NNTP)
AspAllowOutofProcComponents	N/A: deprecated
AspAllowSessionState	<session allowSessionState />
AspAppServiceFlags.* properties (ASPEnableTrackers, ASPEnableSxs, etc.)	<comPlus appServiceFlags />
AspBufferingLimit	<limits bufferingLimit />
AspBufferingOn	<asp bufferingOn />
AspCalcLineNumber	<asp calcLineNumber />
AspCodePage	<asp codePage />
AspDiskTemplateCacheDirectory	<asp diskTemplateCacheDirectory />
AspEnableApplicationRestart	<asp enableApplicationRestart />
AspEnableAspHtmlFallback	<asp enableAspHtmlFallback />
AspEnableChunkedEncoding	<asp enableChunkedEncoding />
AspEnableParentPaths	<asp enableParentPaths />
AspEnableTypelibCache	<cache enableTypelibCache />
AspErrorsToNTLog	<asp errorsToNTLog />
AspExceptionCacheEnable	<asp exceptionCacheEnable />
AspExecuteInMTA	<comPlus executeInMta />
AspKeepSessionIdSecure	<session keepSessionIdSecure />
AspLCID	<asp lcid />
AspLogErrorRequests	<asp logErrorRequests />

Table H-1   **IIS 6.0 Metabase Mapping to IIS 7.0**

IIS 6.0 Metabase Property	IIS 7.0 Configuration Element/Attribute
AspMaxDiskTemplateCacheFiles	*< cache maxDiskTemplateCacheFiles />*
AspMaxRequestEntityAllowed	*< limits maxRequestEntityAllowed />*
AspPartitionID	*< comPlus partitionId />*
AspProcessorThreadMax	*< limits processorThreadMax />*
AspQueueConnectionTestTime	*< limits queueConnectionTestTime />*
AspQueueTimeout	*< limits queueTimeout />*
AspRequestQueueMax	*< limits requestQueueMax />*
AspRunEndOnEndAnonymously	*< asp runEndOnEndAnonymously />*
AspScriptEngineCacheMax	*< cache scriptEngineCacheMax />*
AspScriptErrorMessage	*< asp scriptErrorMessage />*
AspScriptErrorSentToBrowser	*< asp scriptErrorSentToBrowser />*
AspScriptFileCacheSize	*< asp scriptFileCacheSize />*
AspScriptLanguage	*< asp scriptLanguage />*
AspScriptTimeout	*< limits scriptTimeout >*
AspSessionMax	*< session max />*
AspSessionTimeout	*< session timeout />*
AspSxsName	*< comPlus sxsName />*
AspTrackThreadingModel	*< comPlus trackThreadingModel />*
AuthChangeURL	N/A: deprecated
AuthExpiredUnsecuredURL	N/A: deprecated
AuthExpiredURL	N/A: deprecated
AuthFlags	N/A: deprecated
AuthFlags.AuthAnonymous	*< anonymousAuthentication enabled />*
AuthFlags.AuthBasic	*< basicAuthentication enabled />*
AuthFlags.AuthMD5	*< digestAuthentication enabled />*
AuthFlags.AuthNTLM	*< windowsAuthentication enabled />*
AuthFlags.AuthPassport	N/A: deprecated
AuthNotifyPwDExpUnsecureURL	N/A: deprecated
AuthNotifyPwdExpURL	N/A: deprecated
AuthPersistence	*< windowsAuthentication authPersistSingleRequest />*
AutoShutdownAppPoolExe	*< failure autoShutdownExe />*
AutoShutdownAppPoolParams	*< failure autoShutdownParams />*
AuthTurnList	N/A: IIS 6.0 SMTP–related
AzEnabled	N/A: deprecated
AzImpersonationLevel	N/A: deprecated
AzScopeName	N/A: deprecated
AzStoreName	N/A: deprecated

Table H-1   IIS 6.0 Metabase Mapping to IIS 7.0

IIS 6.0 Metabase Property	IIS 7.0 Configuration Element/Attribute
BadMailDirectory	N/A: IIS 6.0 SMTP–related
BannerMessage	N/A: IIS 6.0 SMTP–related
BINSchemaTimeStamp	N/A: deprecated
CacheControlCustom	*<clientCache cacheControlCustom />*
CacheControlMaxAge	*<clientCache cacheControlMaxAge />*
CacheControlNoCache	*<clientCache cacheControlMode />*
CacheISAPI	N/A: deprecated
CentralBinaryLoggingEnabled	*<centralBinaryLogFile enabled />*
CentralW3CLoggingEnabled	*<centralW3CLogFile enabled />*
CertCheckMode	*<clientcertificateMappingAuthentication enabled />* *<iisClientCertificateMappingAuthentication enabled />*
CGIRestrictionList	See *WebSvcExtRestrictionList*
CGITimeout	*<cgi timeout />*
ChangeNumber	N/A: deprecated
ClientPostHardLimit	N/A: deprecated (NNTP)
ClientPostSoftLimit	N/A: deprecated (NNTP)
ClusterEnabled	N/A: deprecated
CollectionComment	N/A: deprecated
ConnectResponse	N/A: IIS 6.0 SMTP–related
ConnectionTimeout	*<limits connectionTimeout />* *<webLimits connectionTimeout />*
ContentIndexed	N/A: deprecated
CPUAction	*<cpu action />*
CPULimit	*<cpu limit />*
CPUResetInterval	*<cpu resetinterval />*
CreateCGIWithNewConsole	*<cgi createCGIWithNewConsole />*
CreateProcessAsUser	*<cgi createProcessAsUser />*
CSideEtrnDomains	N/A: IIS 6.0 SMTP–related
CustomErrorDescriptions	N/A: deprecated
DefaultDoc	*<defaultDocument />*
DefaultDocFooter	*<staticContent defaultDocFooter />*
DefaultDomain	N/A: IIS 6.0 SMTP–related
DefaultLogonDomain	*<basicAuthentication defaultLogonDomain />* *<iisClientCertificateMappingAuthentication* *defaultLogonDomain />*
DefaultModeratorDomain	N/A: deprecated (NNTP)
DemandStartThreshold	*<webLimits demandStartThreshold />*

Table H-1   IIS 6.0 Metabase Mapping to IIS 7.0

IIS 6.0 Metabase Property	IIS 7.0 Configuration Element/Attribute
DirBrowseFlags.DirBrowse-Show(date,time,size,extensions)	*< directoryBrowse showFlags />*
DirBrowseFlags.EnableDefaultDoc	*< defaultDocument enabled />*
DirBrowseFlags.EnableDirBrowse	*< directoryBrowse enabled />*
DirectoryLevelsToScan	N/A: deprecated
DisableNewNews	N/A: deprecated (NNTP)
DisableSocketPooling	N/A: deprecated
DisableStaticFileCache	N/A: deprecated
DisallowOverlappingRotation	*< recycling disallowOverlappingRotation />*
DisallowRotationOnConfigChange	*< recycling disallowRotationOnConfigChange />*
DoDynamicCompression	*< httpCompression doDynamicCompression />* *< UrlCompression doDynamicCompression />*
DontLog	*< dontLog />*
DoStaticCompression	*< doStaticCompression />*
DownlevelAdminInstance	N/A: IIS 6.0 FTP–related
DropDirectory	N/A: IIS 6.0 SMTP–related
Enable32BitAppOnWin64	*< applicationPools enable32BitAppOn64 />*
EnableDocFooter	*< enableDocFooter />*
EnableEditWhileRunning	N/A: deprecated
EnableHistory	*< configHistory />*
EnableReverseDns	*< ipSecurity enabledReverseDns />*
EnableReverseDnsLookup	N/A: IIS 6.0 SMTP–related
EtrnDays	N/A: IIS 6.0 SMTP–related
EtrnSubdomains	N/A: IIS 6.0 SMTP–related
ExitMessage	N/A: IIS 6.0 FTP–related
ExMdbGuid	N/A: deprecated (NNTP)
ExpireNewsgroups	N/A: deprecated (NNTP)
ExpirePolicyName	N/A: deprecated (NNTP)
ExpireSpace	N/A: deprecated (NNTP)
ExpireTime	N/A: deprecated (NNTP)
Feed* properties (FeedAccountName, FeedAdminError, etc.)	N/A: deprecated (NNTP)
FilterDescription	N/A: deprecated
FilterEnableCache	*< isapiFilters enableCache />*
FilterEnabled	*< filter enabled />*
FilterFlags	N/A: deprecated
FilterLoadOrder	N/A: deprecated
FilterPath	*< isapiFilters path />*

Table H-1   IIS 6.0 Metabase Mapping to IIS 7.0

IIS 6.0 Metabase Property	IIS 7.0 Configuration Element/Attribute
FilterSate	N/A: deprecated
FrontPageWeb	N/A: deprecated
FsPropertyPath	N/A: deprecated (NNTP)
FtpDirBrowseShowLongDate	N/A: IIS 6.0 FTP–related
FtpLogInUtf8	N/A: IIS 6.0 FTP–related
FullyQualifiedDomainName	N/A: IIS 6.0 SMTP–related
GreetingsMessage	N/A: IIS 6.0 FTP–related
GroupHelpFile	N/A: deprecated (NNTP)
GroupListFile	N/A: deprecated (NNTP)
GroupvarListFile	N/A: deprecated (NNTP)
HcCacheControlHeader	*<httpCompression cacheControlHeader />*
HcCompressionBufferSize	N/A: deprecated
HcCompressionDirectory	*<httpCompression directory />*
HcCompressionDll	*<httpCompression dll />*
HcCreateFlags	N/A: deprecated
HcDoDiskSpaceLimiting	*<httpCompression doDiskSpaceLimiting />*
HcDoDynamicCompression	*<httpCompression doDynamicCompression />*
HcDoOnDemandCompression	N/A: deprecated
HcDoStaticCompression	*<httpCompression doStaticCompression />*
HcDynamicCompressionLevel	*<httpCompression dynamicCompressionLevel />*
HcExpiresHeader	*<httpCompression expiresHeader />*
HcFileExtensions	N/A: deprecated
HcFilesDeletedPerDiskFree	N/A: deprecated
HcIoBufferSize	N/A: deprecated
HcMaxDiskSpaceUsage	*<httpCompression maxDiskSpaceUsage />*
HcMaxQueueLength	N/A: deprecated
HcMimeType	*<httpCompression mimeType />*
HcMinFileSizeForComp	*<httpCompression minFileSizeForComp />*
HcNoCompressionForHttp10	*<httpCompression noCompressionForHttp10 />*
HcNoCompressionForProxies	*<httpCompression noCompressionForProxies />*
HcNoCompressionForRange	*<httpCompression noCompressionForRange />*
HcOnDemandCompLevel	N/A: deprecated
HcPriority	N/A: deprecated
HcScriptFileExtension	N/A: deprecated
HcSendCacheHeaders	*<httpCompression sendCacheHeaders />*
HeaderWaitTimeout	*<webLimits headerWaitTimeout />*
HistoryExpiration	N/A: deprecated (NNTP)

Table H-1 IIS 6.0 Metabase Mapping to IIS 7.0

IIS 6.0 Metabase Property	IIS 7.0 Configuration Element/Attribute
HistoryMajorVersionNumber	N/A: deprecated
HistoryTableFile	N/A: deprecated
HonorClientMsgIds	N/A: deprecated (NNTP)
HopCount	N/A: IIS 6.0 SMTP–related
HttpCustomHeaders	*<httpProtocol customHeaders />*
HttpErrors	*<httpErrors />*
HttpErrors.Path	*<error path />*
HttpErrors.StatusCodes	*<error statusCodes />*
HttpErrors.SubstatusCodes	*<error subStatusCodes />*
HttpErrors.ResponseMode	*<error responseModel />*
HttpExpires	*<clientCache staticContent httpExpires />*
HttpPics	N/A: deprecated
HttpRedirect	*<httpProtocol redirectHeader />*
IdleTimeout	*<processModel idleTimeout />*
IIS5IsolationModeEnabled	N/A: deprecated
Imap properties (ImapClearTextProvider, ImapDefaultDomain, etc.)*	N/A: deprecated (Microsoft Exchange-related)
InProcessIsapiApps	N/A: deprecated
IsapiRestrictionList	See *WebSvcExtRestrictionList*
IPSecurity	*<ipSecurity allowUnlisted />*
KeyType	N/A: deprecated
LoadBalancerCapabilities	*<failure loadBalancerCapabilities />*
LocalDomains	N/A: IIS 6.0 SMTP–related
LocalRetryAttempts	N/A: IIS 6.0 SMTP–related
LocalRetryInterval	N/A: IIS 6.0 SMTP–related
LogAnonymous	N/A: IIS 6.0 FTP–related
LogCustomProperty properties (LogCustomPropertyDataType, LogCustomPropertyHeader, etc.)*	N/A: deprecated
LogEventOnRecycle	*<recycling logEventOnRecycle />*
LogExtFileFlags	*<log logExtFileFlags />* *<centralW3CLogFile logExtFileFlags />*
LogFileDirectory	*<centralBinaryLogFile directory />* *<centralW3CLogFile directory />*
LogFileLocalTimeRollover	*<centralBinaryLogFile localTimeRollover />* *<centralW3CLogFile localTimeRollover />*
LogFilePeriod	*<centralBinaryLogFile period />* *<centralW3CLogFile period />*

Table H-1   IIS 6.0 Metabase Mapping to IIS 7.0

IIS 6.0 Metabase Property	IIS 7.0 Configuration Element/Attribute
LogFileTruncateSize	*<centralBinaryLogFile truncateSize />* *<centralW3CLogFile truncateSize />*
LoginUTF8	*<log logInUTF8 />*
LogModuleID	N/A: deprecated
LogModuleUiId	N/A: deprecated
LogModuleList	N/A: deprecated
LogonMethod	*<virtualDirectory logonMethod />* *<virtualDirectoryDefaults logonMethod />* *<anonymousAuthentication logonMethod />* *<basicAuthentication logonMethod />* *<iisClientCertificateMappingAuthentication logonMethod />*
LogNonAnonymous	N/A: IIS 6.0 FTP–related
LogOdbc* properties (LogOdbcData-Source, LogOdbcPassword, etc.)	*<odbcLogging />*
LogPluginClsid	*<logFile customLogPluginClsid />*
LogType	N/A: deprecated
MajorIisVersionNumber	N/A: deprecated
MasqueradeDomain	N/A: IIS 6.0 SMTP–related
MaxBandwidth	*<limits maxBandwidth />*
MaxBandwidthBlocked	N/A: deprecated
MaxBatchedMessages	N/A: IIS 6.0 SMTP–related
MaxClientsMessages	N/A: IIS 6.0 FTP–related
MaxConnections	*<limits maxConnections />*
MaxDirChangeIOSize	N/A: IIS 6.0 SMTP–related
MaxEndPointConnections	See *<logEventOnRecycle>*
MaxErrorFiles	N/A: deprecated
MaxGlobalBandwidth	*<webLimits maxGlobalBandwidth />*
MaxHistoryFiles	*<configHistory maxHistories />*
MaxMailObjects	N/A: IIS 6.0 SMTP–related
MaxMessageSize	N/A: IIS 6.0 SMTP–related
MaxOutConnections	N/A: IIS 6.0 SMTP–related
MaxOutConnectionsPerDomain	N/A: IIS 6.0 SMTP–related
MaxProcesses	*<processModel maxProcesses />*
MaxRecipients	N/A: IIS 6.0 SMTP–related
MaxRequestEntityAllowed	*<limits maxRequestEntityAllowed />*
MaxSearchResults	N/A: deprecated (NNTP)
MaxSessionSize	N/A: IIS 6.0 SMTP–related
MaxSmtpErrors	N/A: IIS 6.0 SMTP–related
MaxSmtpLogonErrors	N/A: IIS 6.0 SMTP–related

Table H-1 IIS 6.0 Metabase Mapping to IIS 7.0

IIS 6.0 Metabase Property	IIS 7.0 Configuration Element/Attribute
MD_*properties *(MD_APP_LAST_OUTPROC_PID,* *MD_ETAG_CHANGENUMBER, etc.)*	N/A: deprecated
MimeMap	*<staticContent MimeMap />*
MinFileBytesPerSec	*<webLimits minBytesPerSecond />*
MinorIisVersionNumber	N/A: deprecated
ModeratorFile	N/A: deprecated (NNTP)
MSDOSDirOutput	N/A: IIS 6.0 FTP–related
NameResolutionType	N/A: IIS 6.0 SMTP–related
NewPickupDirectory	N/A: deprecated (NNTP)
NewsCrawlerTime	N/A: deprecated (NNTP)
NewsDropDirectory	N/A: deprecated (NNTP)
NewsFailedPickupDirectory	N/A: deprecated (NNTP)
NntpClearTextProvider	N/A: deprecated (NNTP)
NntpCommandLogMask	N/A: deprecated (NNTP)
NntpOrganization	N/A: deprecated (NNTP)
NntpServiceVersion	N/A: deprecated (NNTP)
NntpUucpName	N/A: deprecated (NNTP)
NotDeletable	N/A: deprecated (NNTP)
NTAuthenticationProviders	*<providers />*
OrphanActionExe	*<failure orphanActionExe />*
OrphanActionParams	*<failure orphanActionParams />*
OrphanWorkerProcess	*<failure orphanWorkerProcess />*
PassivePortRange	N/A: IIS 6.0 FTP–related
PassportRequiredADMapping	N/A: deprecated
Passwordproperties	N/A: deprecated
Path	*<virtualDirectory path />*
PeriodicRestartMemory	*<recycling periodicRestart memory />*
PeriodicRestartPrivateMemory	*<recycling periodicRestart privateMemory />*
PeriodicRestartRequests	*<recycling requests />*
PeriodicRestartSchedule	*<periodicRestart schedule />*
PeriodicRestartTime	*<periodicRestart time />*
PickupDirectory	N/A: IIS 6.0 SMTP–related
PingingEnabled	*<processModel pingingEnabled />*
PingInterval	*<processModel pingInterval />*
PingResponseTime	*<processModel pingResponseTime />*
PoolIdcTimeout	N/A: deprecated

Table H-1 IIS 6.0 Metabase Mapping to IIS 7.0

IIS 6.0 Metabase Property	IIS 7.0 Configuration Element/Attribute
Pop3*properties (Pop3ClearTextProvider, Pop3DefaultDomain, etc.)	N/A: deprecated (Post Office Protocol 3 [POP3])
PostmasterEmail	N/A: IIS 6.0 SMTP–related
PostmasterName	N/A: IIS 6.0 SMTP–related
PrettyNamesFile	N/A: deprecated (NNTP)
ProcessTCRIfLoggedOn	N/A: deprecated
QueueDirectory	N/A: IIS 6.0 SMTP–related
RapidFailProtection	*<failure rapidFailProtection />*
RapidFailProtectionInterval	*<failure rapidFailProtectionInterval />*
RapidFailProtectionMaxCrashes	*<failure rapidFailProtectionMaxCrashes />*
Realm	*<basicAuthentication realm />* *<digestAuthentication realm />*
RedirectHeaders	*<httpProtocol redirectHeaders />*
RelayForAuth	N/A: IIS 6.0 SMTP–related
RelayIpList	N/A: IIS 6.0 SMTP–related
RemoteRetryAttempts	N/A: IIS 6.0 SMTP–related
RemoteRetryInterval	N/A: IIS 6.0 SMTP–related
RemoteSmtpPort	N/A: IIS 6.0 SMTP–related
RemoteSmtpSecurePort	N/A: IIS 6.0 SMTP–related
RemoteTimeout	N/A: IIS 6.0 SMTP–related
RevocationFreshnessTime	N/A: deprecated
RevocationURLRetrievalTimeout	N/A: deprecated
RouteAction	N/A: IIS 6.0 SMTP–related
RouteActionString	N/A: IIS 6.0 SMTP–related
RoutePassword	N/A: IIS 6.0 SMTP–related
RouteUserName	N/A: IIS 6.0 SMTP–related
RoutingDll	N/A: IIS 6.0 SMTP–related
RoutingSources	N/A: IIS 6.0 SMTP–related
SaslLogonDomain	N/A: IIS 6.0 SMTP–related
ScriptMaps	*<handlers />*
ScriptMaps.Extension	*<handlers path />*
ScriptMaps.Flags	*<handlers requireAccess />*
ScriptMaps.Script	See *<handlers requireAccess />*
ScriptMaps.Flags.Script	See *<handlers requireAccess />*
ScriptMaps.Check_Path_Info	*<handlers resourceType />*
ScriptMaps.ScriptProcessor	*<handlers scriptProcessor />*
ScriptMaps.Verbs	*<handlers verb />*

Table H-1   IIS 6.0 Metabase Mapping to IIS 7.0

IIS 6.0 Metabase Property	IIS 7.0 Configuration Element/Attribute
SecureBindings	*<site>* *<bindings />* *</site>*
SecuritySetupRequired	N/A: deprecated
SendBadTo	N/A: IIS 6.0 SMTP–related
SendNdrTo	N/A: IIS 6.0 SMTP–related
ServerAutostart	*<sites serverAutoStart />*
ServerBindings	*<security>* *<access sslFlags />* *</security>*
ServerCommand	N/A: deprecated
ServerComment	N/A: deprecated
ServerConfigFlags	N/A: deprecated
ServerID	N/A: deprecated
ServerListenBacklog	N/A: deprecated
ServerListenTimeout	N/A: deprecated
ServerSize	N/A: deprecated
ServerState	N/A: deprecated
SessionKey	N/A: deprecated
ShouldDeliver	N/A: IIS 6.0 SMTP–related
ShouldPickupMail	N/A: IIS 6.0 SMTP–related
ShouldPipelineIn	N/A: IIS 6.0 SMTP–related
ShouldPipelineOut	N/A: IIS 6.0 SMTP–related
ShutdownLatency	N/A: deprecated (NNTP)
ShutdownTimeLimit	*<processModel shutdownTimeLimit />*
SmartHost	N/A: IIS 6.0 SMTP–related
SmartHostType	N/A: IIS 6.0 SMTP–related
SMPAffinitized	*<cpu smpAffinitized />*
SMPProcessAffinityMask	*<cpu smpProcessorAffinityMask />*
Smtpproperties	N/A: IIS 6.0 SMTP–related
SSIExecDisable	*<serverSideInclude ssiExecDisable />*
SSLAlwaysNegoClientCert	N/A: deprecated
SSLCertHash	N/A: deprecated
SslCtlIdentifier	N/A: deprecated
SslCtlStoreName	N/A: deprecated
SSLStoreName	N/A: deprecated
SslUseDsMapper	N/A: deprecated
StartupTimeLimit	*<processModel startupTime />*

Table H-1   IIS 6.0 Metabase Mapping to IIS 7.0

IIS 6.0 Metabase Property	IIS 7.0 Configuration Element/Attribute
SuppressDefaultFtpBanner	N/A: IIS 6.0 FTP–related
TraceUriPrefix	*<httpTracing traceUrls />*
UNCPassword	*<virtualDirectory password />*
UNCUserName	*<virtualDirectory userName />*
UpdateDefaultDomain	N/A: IIS 6.0 SMTP–related
UpdateFQDN	N/A: IIS 6.0 SMTP–related
UploadReadAheadSize	*<serverRuntime uploadReadAheadSize />*
UseDigestSSP	N/A: deprecated
UserIsolationMode	N/A: IIS 6.0 FTP–related
VrDoExpire	N/A: deprecated (NNTP)
VrDriverClsid	N/A: deprecated (NNTP)
VrDriverProgid	N/A: deprecated (NNTP)
VrOwnModerator	N/A: deprecated (NNTP)
VrUseAccount	N/A: deprecated (NNTP)
WAMUserName	*<applicationPools userName />*
WAMUserPass	*<applicationPools password />*
WebDAVMaxAttributesPerElement	N/A: deprecated
WebSvcExtRestrictionList	*<isapicgiRestriction />*
WebSvcExtRestrictionList.dll	*<isapicgiRestriction path />*
WebSvcExtRestrictionList.exe	*<isapicgiRestriction path />*
WebSvcExtRestrictionList.Description	*<isapicgiRestriction description />*
WebSvcExtRestrictionList.Enabled	*<isapicgiRestriction allowed />*
WebSvcExtRestrictionList.GroupID	*<isapicgiRestriction groupId />*
WebSvcExtRestrictionList.Path	*<isapicgiRestriction path />*
Win32Error	N/A: deprecated
XMLSchemaTimeStamp	N/A: deprecated
XoverTableFile	N/A: deprecated (NNTP)

IIS 7.0 Shared Hosting

The opposite of dedicated hosting is shared hosting or high density hosting, whereby the focus is to run as many Web sites or applications on one physical system with one operating system as possible. This generally lowers the total cost of ownership (TCO) with a minimum set of hardware and software to be maintained.

Although shared hosting is the most economical option, especially for Web hosting providers to maximize revenue versus setup and maintenance cost, hosting from tens to hundreds of Web applications on a single machine is not a simple task. There are many considerations when it comes to shared hosting, such as dedicated application pools versus a single shared application pool for applications, application account identities for worker processes and request access, and many more.

With the revamped IIS core architecture, Internet Information Services (IIS) 7.0 is designed for shared hosting, especially in application isolation, which sandboxes each application by default; security account changes allow worker processes identity to be both process and request identities.

Note To learn more about basic shared hosting information, see the article titled "Shared Hosting on IIS 7.0" at *http://www.iis.net/articles/view.aspx/IIS7/Deploy-an-IIS7-Server/ Deployment-for-Web-Hosters/Shared-Hosting-on-IIS7*. The section of the article at this location highlights two special features designed for shared hosting in IIS 7.0.

Implementing Process Gating

By design, when you create a new Web site in IIS 7.0 via IIS Manager, a new application pool with the same name as the Web site name is created automatically. This sandbox initiative aims to secure and isolate the new application for both security and availability so that it has a dedicated application pool and dedicated worker processes. This simplifies administration, especially in a shared hosting environment, so that administrators do not need to manually create a new application pool for the Web site. On the other hand, as more Web sites are created, more worker processes will be running at the same time. Without careful capacity planning, Web server performance may suffer when too many worker processes are running simultaneously. To address this issue, IIS offers a process gating control, enabling you to specify the maximum number of worker processes that can be run at any one time on the Web server.

Process gating is not a new concept. It is actually a feature in IIS 6.0, though not many know about it, primarily because it is not available through IIS Manager and is more applicable to high-density Web site hosting. Similar to IIS 6.0, IIS 7.0 always performs a demand start for Web applications. Worker processes are invoked by Windows Process Activation Service (WAS) only when the application pool receives the first incoming request. Before WAS initializes the new worker process, it checks the total number of currently running worker processes. If the total number of worker processes (current + new) is more than the maximum number of worker processes allowed, the new worker process is not started, and IIS keeps the request in the queue and waits until the number of worker processes drops below the limit. Only then does IIS 7.0 start the new worker process.

By default, the process gating feature is not enabled. That is, the default total number of worker processes allowed is 2,147,483,647, which technically is equivalent to no limit. Before you decide to implement process gating, you need to analyze your current application loading and server resource usage–in a process similar to capacity planning. To determine the number of concurrent users supported for a particular Web site, you need to determine the potential maximum number of worker processes that can be running at the same time. You will evaluate the server performance loading, fine-tuning Web applications as well as IIS 7.0 configurations to help decide the maximum number of worker processes. To learn more about optimizing IIS 7.0 and performance analysis, see Chapter 17, "Performance and Tuning."

To specify the maximum number of worker processes allowed, configure the *demandStart-Threshold* attribute in the *web.Limits* section of the configuration system. Take note that this is a server-wide configuration, which applies to all application pools and which is configurable only via the command line tool. To implement process gating, see the following procedures.

Using the Command Line

Following is the Appcmd syntax for specifying the maximum number of worker processes in IIS 7.0.

```
appcmd set config /section:webLimits /demandStartThreshold: integer
```

Table I-1 describes the parameters for this syntax.

Table I-1   Syntax for Appcmd to Configure demandStartThreshold

Parameter	Description
webLimits	Specify the configuration under the webLimits section.
demandStartThreshold	The total number of worker processes running concurrently on the Web server. It is an unsigned integer with a valid range from 10 to 2,147,483,647.

The following syntax specifies 100 as the maximum number of worker processes allowed for a particular Web server.

```
appcmd set config /section:webLimits /demandStartThreshold:100
```

After you successfully execute the command syntax, you will see output similar to that shown here.

```
Applied configuration changes to section "system.applicationHost/webLimits" for
"MACHINE/WEBROOT/APPHOST" at configuration commit path "MACHINE/WEBROOT/APPHOST"
```

When WAS detects that the demandStartThreshold limit has been reached, it writes a warning entry into the System event log.

```
Event ID: 5196
Detail: A request to create a new worker process has arrived. The demandStartThreshold
setting has been reached. The Windows Process Activation Service (WAS) will not start any
worker processes until this drops.
```

Configuration Changes

Process gating configuration is defined at the *<webLimits>* section in the applicationHost.config file. The *demandStartThreshold* attribute's value holds the maximum number of worker processes that can run concurrently on a Web server. The following shows the configuration of the 100 worker processes limit, using the preceding syntax.

```
<system.applicationHost>
    <sites>
        <site name="Contoso Corp" id="1">
        ...
        </site>
    </sites>
    ...
    <webLimits demandStartThreshold="100" />
</system.applicationHost>
```

Enabling Dynamic Idle Threshold

In addition to the process gating feature, IIS 7.0 offers a brand-new feature that dynamically adjusts the application pool idle shutdown time based on system memory usage. A worker process is idle when it is not processing requests or when no pending requests are in the application pool's request queue. Idle shutdown time indicates the amount of time a worker process will remain idle before WAS decides to shut down the worker process.

Recall that the application pool idle shutdown time is set to 20 minutes by default and is configurable per application pool via the *dynamicIdleTimeout* attribute under the *<processModel>* configuration element. This new dynamic idle threshold focuses on the percentage of committed physical memory used by worker processes. WAS monitors the worker processes' memory usage and dynamically adjusts the idle shutdown time of worker processes. When memory usage approaches the threshold, WAS dynamically lowers the worker process idle shutdown time and shuts down worker processes faster for those Web sites or application pools that are not active. Doing so returns more system resources for other busy worker processes that may require more resources for request processing. This innovative feature is valuable especially in a shared hosting environment in which hundreds of Web sites or Web applications are running in the same system. By using the dynamic idle threshold feature to shut down idle worker processes faster, IIS 7.0 dynamically adjusts to improve overall system performance.

By default, this threshold monitoring is not enabled, and by default, the *dynamicIdleThreshold* attribute value is set to 0 under the *<webLimits>* configuration section. Before enabling this idle shutdown threshold for worker processes, you need to evaluate current system performance and incoming request traffic patterns. For example, if the system has limited memory, and more than half of the Web sites or applications are experiencing few visits and/or requests, you may analyze the request pattern against memory usage and then specify an acceptable threshold for WAS to dynamically adjust the idle time-out. On the other hand, if you are using dedicated hosting on a high-end, multicore system with just a few Web sites, you may simply ignore the threshold setting and stick with the default 20 minutes idle time-out value.

The threshold value unit is provided as a percentage (%) with a valid range from 0 to 10,000. No threshold monitoring is indicated by 0%. WAS monitors the worker processes' memory usage at five different levels and calculates the new idle time-out bases on divisor value. Table I-2 shows levels of threshold limits with the divisor for application pool idle time-out.

Table I-2   Idle Threshold and Divisor Value

Level	Threshold	Divisor
1	80%	2
2	85%	4
3	90%	8
4	95%	16
5	99%	32

Two different monitoring events take place before WAS decides to adjust an application pool's idle time-out value. First, WAS polls the memory usage every 30 seconds, and second, each worker process checks its idle time-out value in the application pool every 60 seconds. Worker processes' idle time-out values revert to configured values when the threshold falls below 75 percent. For example, if the threshold is hitting 88%, the new idle time-out value is 20 minutes divided by 4, which is 5 minutes. The lowest possible idle time-out value is 1 minute.

The following scenario illustrates the series of events WAS generates while governing the worker processes' memory usage. The *dynamicIdleThreshold* is set to 100%, the machine is equipped with 1000 MB of physical memory, it is using the default idle time-out value of

20 minutes, and it has two worker processes running with one of the worker processes slowly using more memory in the system.

When the busy worker process addressed 81 percent of threshold value, the following log entry is written to the System event log by WAS.

```
Event ID: 5192
Detail: The dynamic Idle load is '%1' percent of the dynamic idle threshold. The Windows
Process Activation Service (WAS) will start to reduce worker process idle timeouts. Current
number of worker processes: '%2', current total commit: '%3' MB, total physical memory: '%4'
MB, current physical memory free: '%5' MB.
```

Using the divisor number per different levels of threshold monitoring, WAS dynamically adjusts the idle time-out value as the worker process slowly occupies more memory space. The idle time-out is divided by 2 and become 10 minutes, and the following event log is written.

```
Event ID: 5193
Detail: The dynamic Idle load is '%1' percent of the dynamic idle threshold. The Windows
Process Activation Service (WAS) will start to aggressively reduce worker process idle timeouts.
Current number of worker processes: '%2', current total commit: '%3' MB, total physical
memory: '%4' MB, current physical memory free: '%5' MB.
```

Next, WAS writes another event log entry indicating that it has adjusted the idle time-out value for the less busy worker process in another application pool.

```
Event ID: 5195
Detail: A worker process with process id of '%1' serving application pool '%2' was shut down
due to inactivity. The system is under high load and has decreased the idle timeout of this
worker process to '%3' minutes from its original '%4' minutes. A new worker process will be
started when needed.
```

On the other hand, assuming that the memory usage of the busy worker processes falls back to normal levels after peak hours, WAS resets the idle time-out setting back to the default value and writes another entry in the System event log.

```
Event ID: 5194
Detail: The dynamic Idle load is '%1' percent of the dynamic idle threshold. The Windows
Process Activation Service (WAS) will return worker process idle timeouts to their configured
settings. Current number of worker processes: '%2', current total commit: '%3' MB, total
physical memory: '%4' MB, current physical memory free: '%5' MB.
```

Similar to process gating, the threshold configuration is not available in IIS Manager. To configure *dynamicIdleThreshold* via the command line tool, see the following procedures.

Using the Command Line

Following is the Appcmd syntax to configure dynamic idle shutdown time for all application pools in IIS 7.0.

```
appcmd set config /section:webLimits /dynamicIdleThreshold:integer
```

Table I-3 describes the parameters for this syntax.

Table I-3   Syntax for Appcmd to Configure dynamicIdleThreshold

Parameter	Description
webLimits	Specify the configuration as *webLimits* section
dynamicIdleThreshold	The committed memory usage (%) against the total physical memory of the system; valid range from 0 to 10,000

The following syntax specifies 100% threshold monitoring against total physical memory for a particular Web server.

```
appcmd set config /section:webLimits /dynamicIdleThreshold:100
```

After you have successfully executed the command syntax, you will see output similar to that shown here.

```
Applied configuration changes to section "system.applicationHost/webLimits" for
"MACHINE/WEBROOT/APPHOST" at configuration commit path "MACHINE/WEBROOT/APPHOST"
```

The configuration applies to run time directly. After setting the threshold percentage, WAS starts to monitor worker processes' usage immediately and constantly checks the threshold value.

Configuration Changes

Idle time-out threshold configuration is defined in the *<webLimits>* section in the applicationHost.config file. The *dynamicIdleThreshold* attribute's value holds the worker processes' memory percentage usage against total physical memory available in the system. The following shows the configuration of 100% threshold for idle time-out, using the preceding syntax.

```
<system.applicationHost>
    <sites>
        <site name="Contoso Corp" id="1">
        ...
        </site>
    </sites>
    ...
    <webLimits dynamicIdleThreshold="100" />
</system.applicationHost>
```

Appendix J

Common Administrative Tasks Using IIS Manager

The three tables provided in this appendix list the location in this book of information about using IIS Manager to accomplish common administrative tasks. The tasks are categorized as follows:

- Table J-1 lists IIS Manager object-specific tasks for connection tree objects (application, server, site, and virtual directory).

- Table J-2 lists common IIS Manager tasks for application pools.

- Table J-3 lists common administrative tasks by IIS Manager feature.

In Table J-1, the tasks are grouped by the object to which they relate and then are ordered alphabetically within each grouping.

Table J-1   Administrative Tasks by Connection Tree Object

Connection Tree Object	Task	Location in Text		
		Chapter	Section	Page
Application	Assign an application to an application pool	1	Assigning an Application to an Application Pool	21
	Connect to an application	6	Creating New Connections	160
	Convert an existing physical or virtual directory to a new application root	10	Creating Web Applications	292
	Create an application	1	Creating an Application	17
		10	Creating Web Applications	292
	List Web applications	10	Listing Web Applications	297
Server	Connect to a server	6	Creating New Connections	160
Site	Add a new Web site	9	Adding a New Web Site	267
	Configure Web site IP bindings	9	Configuring a Web Site's Bindings	270
	Connect to a site	6	Creating New Connections	160
	Create a Web site	1	Creating a Web Site	15
	Limit Web site usage	9	Limiting Web Site Usage	273

Table J-1   Administrative Tasks by Connection Tree Object

Connection Tree Object	Task	Location in Text		
		Chapter	Section	Page
Virtual directory	Configure virtual directories	9	Configuring Virtual Directories	279
	Convert an existing physical or virtual directory to a new application root	10	Creating Web Applications	292
	Create a virtual directory	1	Creating a Virtual Directory	19
		9	Adding a New Virtual Directory	277
	Search virtual directories	9	Searching Virtual Directories	282

Table J-2 lists administrative tasks for managing application pools. The tasks are listed in alphabetical order.

Table J-2   Application Pool Administrative Tasks

Task	Location in Text		
	Chapter	Section	Page
Assign an application pool to an existing application	10	Adding a New Application Pool	302
Change application pool mode	2	Request Processing in Application Pool	42
Configure application pool identity	10	Configuring Application Pool Identity	307
Create an application pool	1	Creating an Application Pool	20
Enable application pool recycling events	10	Monitoring Application Pool Recycling Events	312
Enable user profile loading	10	Enabling User Profile Loading	309

Table J-3 lists common administrative tasks by IIS Manager feature. The tasks are grouped according to the feature to which they relate and then are ordered alphabetically within each grouping.

Table J-3   Administrative Tasks by Feature

Feature	Task	Location in Text		
		Chapter	Section	Page
.NET Trust Levels	Configure the trust level used for ASP.NET applications and managed modules	14	Reduce Trust of ASP.NET Applications	470
ASP	Allow ASP scripts to use parent path notation	16	Troubleshooting Parent Path Problems	601
	Allow server to send ASP script error details to a client	16	ASP Script Error Details	596

Table J-3   Administrative Tasks by Feature

Feature	Task	Location in Text		
		Chapter	Section	Page
Authentication	Configure URL Authorization rules	14	Creating URL Authorization Rules	487
	Enable anonymous authentication and set anonymous user options	14	Anonymous Authentication	491
	Enable basic authentication and set logon method options	14	Basic Authentication	493
	Enable Client Certificate Mapping authentication	14	Client Certificate Mapping Authentication	501
	Enable digest authentication	14	Digest Authentication	495
	Enable Windows authentication	14	Configuring Windows Authentication	498
Error pages	Configure IIS to send detailed error messages to the client	16	Understanding Friendly Errors, Custom Errors, and Detailed Errors	594
	Set up error messages to be sent to the client	16	Understanding Friendly Errors, Custom Errors, and Detailed Errors	594
Failed Request Tracing Rules	Configure Failed Request Tracing (FRT) rules	16	Tracing a Specific Error Code	566
Feature Delegation	Configure delegation for Failed Request Tracing (FRT) rules	16	Troubleshooting UNC Access Errors	598
	Modify delegation settings	4	Delegation Settings in the IIS Manager	98
Handler Mappings	Create a FastCGI handler mapping for PHP	11	Creating a FastCGI Handler Mapping for PHP	348
	Create and manage handler mappings	12	Using IIS Manager to Create and Manage Handler Mappings	400
	Set handler permissions for a Web site, application, or file (URL)	14	Setting Web Site Permissions	462
IIS Manager Permissions	Set permissions for managing sites and applications	8	Managing Users and Permissions	240
IIS Manager Users	Add an IIS Manager user	8	Managing Users and Permissions	240
IPv4 Address and Domain Restrictions	Configure the IPv4 and Domain Restrictions rules	14	IP and Domain Restrictions	475
ISAPI and CGI Restrictions	Allow ISAPI Extensions in the ISAPI and CGI Restrictions	14	Enabling Only the Required ISAPI Filters	454

Table J-3 Administrative Tasks by Feature

Feature	Task	Location in Text		
		Chapter	Section	Page
ISAPI Filters	Configure ISAPI filters	14	Enabling Only the Required ISAPI Filters	454
Logging	Configure IIS centralized logging	15	IIS Manager	536
	Set up remote logging	15	Setting Up Remote Logging by Using the IIS Manager	542
Management Service	Configure Web Management Service to use a certificate	8	Enable Remote Connections, SSL Certificate, and IP Configuration	234
	Enable remote connections	6	Remote Administration	184
MIME Types	Configure MIME types	11	Enabling New Static File Extensions to Be Served	354
Modules	Configure the set of enabled IIS modules	14	Enabling Only the Required Modules	460
	Control module ordering	12	Controlling Module Ordering	391
	Enable an ASP.NET module to run for all requests	11	Taking Advantage of ASP.NET Integrated Mode	339
	Enable IIS modules	14	Enabling Only the Required Modules	460
	Install and manage modules	12	Using IIS Manager to Install and Manage Modules	396
	Manage enabled modules for your application	12	Controlling What Modules Are Enabled	389
	Verify your installation	5	Validation	143
	View and change the order of modules on the server	2	Module Ordering	51
Shared Configuration	Enable shared configuration	4	Sharing Configuration Between Servers	107
	Export configuration files	4	How Shared Configuration Works	108
SSL Settings	Require clients to request Web site content over secure connections	14	Requiring SSL	512
Worker Process	Examine Runtime Status and Control API (RSCA) data (currently executing worker processes and requests)	16	Using IIS Manager	589
	Monitor worker processes and requests	10	Monitoring Worker Processes and Requests	316

About the Authors

Michael Volodarsky

Michael Volodarsky is a Program Manager on the Microsoft Internet Information Services (IIS) team, in charge of design and development of the IIS 7.0 core Web server engine. He got his start at Microsoft on the ASP.NET team, where he has driven the development of the ASP.NET 2.0 run time. Michael's interest in low-level server software drove him to take the technical leadership role on the IIS 7.0 project, using his ASP.NET perspective to bring the modular Web server architecture and ASP.NET integration to the IIS 7.0 platform. Michael's true technical passion is writing code, which has led him to develop a number of IIS 7.0 features including the Appcmd command-line tool, IIS bitrate throttling, and other modules that you can find on his blog at *http://mvolo.com*.

He now lives in Philadelphia with his wife Rachel. In his spare time, he enjoys blogging about IIS 7.0, spending time with friends and family, and drinking Belgian beer.

Olga Londer

Olga Londer is an Infrastructure Architect at Microsoft where she works worldwide, across countries and geographies, to help IT Professionals to take the best advantage of Microsoft's products and technologies. Olga has been working with Internet technologies since the early nineties, the Jurassic era of the Internet. In 1992, she wrote one of the first training courses on Internet technologies, and in the following years she led numerous projects in this area, including teaching and writing. Olga joined Microsoft in 2004, and she now leads an international team of infrastructure experts tasked with driving the adoption of Microsoft's next generation technologies and products. She is an author of several books, a winner of the British Computer Society IT Trainer Award, a frequent conference speaker, and a technical content lead for many international Microsoft events, including TechEd and IT Forum. Olga is based in London, UK.

Brett Hill

Before joining Microsoft, Brett Hill was an IIS MVP for three years and ran IISTraining.com, where he taught advanced server administration and security classes.

He was hired in Feb 2005 by Microsoft as an IIS evangelist and currently holds a position in the Online Business Services group. Brett still writes for *Windows IT Pro* magazine, speaks at conferences on IIS, and actively posts at *http://brettblog.com*.

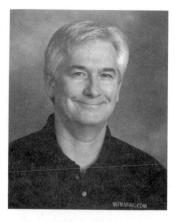

Bernard Cheah

Bernard Cheah, Microsoft IIS MVP since 2003, is currently an Enterprise Architect at Intel Corporation (Malaysia), where his primary role is an infrastructure architect for the manufacturing computing division. Previously, Bernard was a contract solution consultant with an Irish company. Bernard is active in many online IIS communities, including public and private Microsoft newsgroups and IIS.net. In addition, he has coauthored the book *CYA Securing IIS 6.0* (Syngress Publishing, Inc., 2004), contributed to the *Microsoft Log Parser Toolkit* (Syngress Publishing, Inc., 2004), and helped to write a few Microsoft Knowledge Base articles and monthly IIS Insider columns.

Steve Schofield

Steve Schofield is a Microsoft IIS MVP, speaker, and Senior Support Engineer for ORCS Web (*http://www.orcsweb.com*), a company that provides Managed Hosting Solutions for Microsoft platforms and products. He has been involved in the Microsoft community since 1999. Some of his projects include starting ASPFree.com, being an ASP / ASP.NET MVP, and writing an IIS logging utility called IISLogs (*http://www.iislogs.com*). He enjoys helping people in the IIS and related Microsoft communities. When he is not playing with technology, his family keeps him busy. He lives in Greenville, Michigan, with his wife Cindy and their three boys, Marcus, Zachary, and Tayler.

Carlos Aguilar Mares

Carlos Aguilar Mares is a Senior Development Lead on the IIS product group at Microsoft. His team focuses on building administration tools, remote administration, and the managed configuration API for IIS 7.0. Previously, Carlos worked for two years on the ASP.NET 2.0 Page and Controls team, and before that, he was a Development Consultant working in Microsoft Consulting Services Mexico, where he is originally from, and where he joined Microsoft more than eight years ago. When not at work, Carlos enjoys being with his family as well as playing tennis, guitar, and Xbox; coding games; and pretty much anything related to computers.

Kurt Meyer

Kurt Meyer has worked as a programmer as well as a technical editor, writer, and reviewer in the software industry since receiving a degree in Computer Science from the University of Washington in 1989. He has developed projects ranging from database interfaces to image processing. Kurt currently lives and works in western Massachusetts, where he enjoys spending time with his family on a small farm.

Tito Leverette

Tito Leverette is a Web Platform Architect on the Developer and Platform Evangelism team at Microsoft. Before joining Microsoft, Tito was an Infrastructure Architect in the financial sector; prior to that, he spent several years working in the hosting industry. He has a passion for helping customers become successful in deploying Windows Web platforms. When he is not working, Tito enjoys traveling and spending time with family and friends. Tito resides in Atlanta, Georgia.

Index